THE COLLECTED WORKS OF
Walter Pater

VOLUME IX

Correspondence

EDITED BY

ROBERT M. SEILER

OXFORD
UNIVERSITY PRESS

Portrait of Walter Pater, William Rothenstein, 1894. *Oxford Characters: A Set of Lithographs* (London: Bodley Head, 1893-95). Courtesy of Thomas Fisher Rare Book Library, University of Toronto.

THE COLLECTED WORKS OF WALTER PATER

VOLUME IX

Correspondence

THE COLLECTED WORKS OF
Walter Pater

GENERAL EDITORS:
Lesley Higgins and David Latham

Volume I
The Renaissance

Volume II
Marius the Epicurean

Volume III
Imaginary Portraits

Volume IV
Gaston de Latour

Volume V
Studies and Reviews, 1864–1889

Volume VI
Appreciations, and Studies and Reviews, 1890–1894

Volume VII
Plato and Platonism

Volume VIII
Classical Studies

Volume IX
Correspondence

Volume X
Manuscripts

For Tamara P. Seiler

For art comes to you promising frankly to give nothing but the highest quality to your moments as they pass, and simply for those moments' sake.

    Walter Pater, *Studies in the History of the Renaissance* (1873)

GENERAL EDITORS' PREFACE

The ten volumes of *The Collected Works of Walter Pater* are commissioned to serve scholars as the definitive edition for at least as long as the unscholarly 1910 'New Library Edition' has served. Determining a definitive copy-text for a major author remains a controversial goal for scholars in the twenty-first century. Pater is among the most consummate wordsmiths of his Victorian era, a prose stylist who fussed like a poet over every choice of phrase, rhythm, and punctuation. As Gerald Monsman observes: 'All of Pater's writing is always on the way to some further stage of perfection; one never quite arrives at Pater's final' copy (*CW* iv). This attention to the process of composition without reaching a definitive product suggests that Pater would suit a Foucauldian approach to the text as an ongoing social production, with the early editors of periodicals and the later generations of readers sharing as much as the author a responsibility for producing the text.

Pater's revisions, however, reveal none of the Sisyphean futility that would validate each iteration as being equal in merit; rather, they exemplify a patient author polishing his way towards a progressive end. From the start of his career, Pater revealed his faith in craftsmanship. As he observed approvingly of Johann Winckelmann, in his second published essay, 'He remodel[led] his writings with constant renewal of insight' (*CW* i). *The Collected Works* edition provides documentation of this process of composition. The textual apparatus enables readers to view the revisions for each different version of Pater's texts: the occasional manuscript, the periodical essay, and the successive editions of his books. The collation of these revisions dispels the myth that Pater would shy away from controversy by suppressing his boldest expressions. Too much has been made of a cautious Pater withdrawing his controversial 'Conclusion' from the second edition of *The Renaissance*, and not enough credit is given to the courageous Pater who restored it in the subsequent editions despite a threat to expose a scandal with a student that could have cost Pater his position at Oxford.

The rumours about a fresher and bolder writer in his youth would lead one to expect that the periodical iterations and first book-editions might reveal a raw, rough style which the later Pater would refine into a mannered, contrived, overly controlled prose, with a less daring argument. We find nothing of the kind. The collation of textual variants shows that

Pater's revisions are refinements in precision and rhythm, refinements that can be considered improvements in terms of being more interesting and exciting as ideas and more rhythmical and striking in style. Often, he is revising little more than a comma to a colon, and hesitating whether or not to particularize the general 'an' to 'the'. The exceptional revisions that may first trouble us, revisions that raise questions about Pater's judgement, are those we learn the most from.

In *The Renaissance*, for example, his 1893 revision of the penultimate sentence of the 'Conclusion' to the fourth edition—revising 'art for art's sake' to 'art for its own sake'—initially looks less striking than the original, suggesting a cautious retreat from the crusading efforts of Théophile Gautier and A. C. Swinburne, with whom Pater had been promoting the amorality of a decadent 'art for art's sake' aesthetics. Yet, closer study of the context of the phrase reveals that the revision typifies Pater's fastidious and altogether telescopic concern for the overall unity of his book, the penultimate sentence of his 'Conclusion' returning the reader to the similar phrasing of 'for their own sake' in the penultimate sentence of his 'Preface'. Moreover, Pater returns to embrace the 'art for art's sake' phrase in his 1893 collection *Plato and Platonism*, published the same year as that fourth edition of *The Renaissance*. Those who wish to argue that this fourth edition shows Pater cautiously cutting his ties from the decadent aesthetics of Swinburne must reconcile such a claim with Pater's return to this clarion call for an 'art for art's sake' principle twenty years later in a new, controversial context, insisting on using the phrase to draw Plato into his own camp of relativism within the context of the heated debates over Plato scholarship among his colleagues at Oxford. Pater admires Plato not for his ethics but for his aesthetics, not for a process of philosophic enquiry that leads to a central truth but for the aesthetics of Plato's style which, Pater maintains, 'anticipates the modern notion that art as such has no end but its own perfection,—"art for art's sake" ' (*CW* vii). Pater has no qualms about identifying Plato as an ally of the new, reflexive paradigm that Pater was championing for art, a bold stand to take in the 1870s amidst the 'fleshly school of poetry' controversy and an equally bold stand in the 1890s, one that risked riling his Oxford peers amid those ongoing wars waged over Plato.

Indeed, in stark contrast to the alleged image of a timid Pater suppressing and obscuring his ideas and expressions, his revisions often reveal him learning how to repeat himself in order to foreground more clearly his boldest motifs. His early review of the 'Poems by William Morris' identifies the literary grotesque as a signature characteristic of the new Pre-Raphaelite poetry: mixing the 'mystic religion' of Christianity with the 'mystic passion' of paganism, 'the two threads of sentiment are here interwoven and contrasted . . ., confronted', an incongruity epitomized in two of his most haunting examples: 'the strange suggestion of a deliberate choice between Christ and a rival lover'; and 'the continual suggestion . . . of . . . the desire of beauty quickened by the sense of death' (*CW* v). From the first edition of *The Renaissance* to its fourth edition, we can see Pater further emphasizing the centrality of the grotesque—the jarring juxtaposition of such discomforting incongruities as the sexual and the sacred—by refining and repeating words and phrases; in the fourth edition, he refers to these grotesques as 'correspondences': 'Everywhere there is an unbroken system of correspondences', with 'grotesque emblems' that overcome the boundaries of 'rigidly defined opposites' through the 'picturesque union of contrasts', the 'strange interfusion of sweetness and strength', the 'interfusion of the extremes of beauty and terror' (*CW* i). In the first edition, that first passage is expressed as 'an unbroken system of analogies', the different word ('analogies' rather than 'correspondences') thus failing to signal the continuity of his motif; 'rigidly defined opposites' does not appear in the first edition, so that Pater initially missed the opportunity to introduce the grotesque motif early in his argument.

Always polishing and hence never finishing his perfectionist process of creating art, Pater may resist an editor's effort to construct a definitive edition, but the consistent quality of his revisions gives us confidence in choosing the later Pater—his last overseen iteration—as the general rule for the project's copy-text. Painstakingly, he revised his phrases, sentences, and paragraphs at all stages in the creative and publication process, frequently working towards a meta-narrative moment in which the work of editing creatively is highlighted. In the ever-appreciative Winckelmann, Pater discerns a 'novel power of refraction, selecting, transforming, recombining the images' and ideas 'according to the choice of [an] imaginative intellect' (*CW* i). In *Marius*, the narrator salutes 'a wonderful tact of selection, exclusion, juxtaposition, begetting thereby a unique effect of freshness, a grave yet wholesome beauty' (*CW* ii). In *Plato and Platonism*, he applauds Plato for producing texts that are 'a palimpsest, a tapestry of which the actual threads have served before' (*CW* vii). For Pater, editorial agency, intellectual will, and a sensuous sensibility were conjoined, rarely leaving us in doubt about the improvement.

Pater published six books in his lifetime: *The Renaissance*, *Marius the Epicurean* (a novel in two volumes), *Imaginary Portraits*, *Appreciations*, *Plato and Platonism*, and a limited edition of *An Imaginary Portrait: The Child in the House*. His contributions to the leading periodicals of the day—essays, reviews, revised lectures, short works of fiction—were substantial. After his death, friends Edmund Gosse and Charles Shadwell arranged for four additional volumes to appear: *Miscellaneous Studies*, *Essays from 'The Guardian'*, *Greek Studies*, and chapters from the unfinished novel *Gaston de Latour*. The *Collected Works* preserves the integrity of Pater's arrangements for his writings, augments several of those volumes, and brings together, for the first time, all of his literary journalism and academic studies, his extant correspondence, and transcriptions of his manuscripts. Our collective editorial initiative has been designed, to paraphrase 'The School of Giorgione', to demonstrate that 'the sensuous material' of each Pater text 'brings with it a special phase or quality of beauty' matched only by intellectual and creative integrity.

LESLEY HIGGINS AND DAVID LATHAM
YORK UNIVERSITY

ACKNOWLEDGEMENTS

This project can be traced to the hours I spent in the Reading Room of the British Museum during the 1970s transcribing letters housed in the Macmillan Archive, now held in the British Library, Manuscript Collections. Over the years I have benefited immensely from conversations I have had with colleagues, friends, and family on aspects of this complex enterprise. I am indebted to many individuals, including the late Miriam Allott, Elisa Bizzotto, the late James Black, Laurel Brake, Joseph Bristow, Ken Carpenter, Kenneth Daley, Denis Donoghue, Georgina Edwards, the late Lawrence Evans, the late Ian Fletcher, Peter Henderson, Daichi Ishikawa, Ronald J. Kopnicki, Clyde McConnell, Peter Montieth, Gerald Monsman, Michael Holroyd, Billie Andrew Inman, Mark Samuels Lasner, Francis O'Gorman, Lene Østermark-Johansen, Amanda Paxton, the late Robin Peedell, Carol and Joel Prager, Bernard Richards, Michael Seeney, Tamara P. Seiler, the late William F. Shuter, Ian Small, Donald Smith, Nancy Townshend, Paul Tucker, Ana Parejo Vadillo, Carolyn Williams, and the late Samuel Wright.

I wish to thank the following individuals for helping me obtain copies of manuscript letters and others documents central to my project: Elaine Ardia and Michelle Belden, Archivists, Bates College, Lewiston, Maine; Christina E. Barber and Peter Nelson, Amherst College, Amherst, Massachusetts; Elizabeth Boardman (retired) and Georgina Edwards, Archivists, Brasenose College, Oxford; Titus Boeder and Sam Cotterell, Maggs Bros., London; Michael Bott, Keeper of Archives and Manuscripts, University of Reading, Reading; Guillaume Boyer, Curator, Bourget Archive, Fels Library, Paris; Patricia Burdick, Assistant Director for Special Collections, Colby College, Waterville, Maine; Jean M. Cannon, Literary Collections Research Associate, the Harry Ransom Center, the University of Texas, Austin, Texas; James Capobianco, Reference Librarian, Houghton Library, Harvard University, Cambridge, Massachusetts; Courtney E. Chartier and Tara Craig, Rare Book & Manuscript Library, Columbia University; Meghan R. Constantinou, Librarian, The Grolier Club, New York; Martha O'Hara Conway, Director, Special Collections Research Center, University of Michigan; Karen Cook, Special Collections Librarian, University of Kansas, Lawrence, Kansas; Judith Dartt, Digitization Manager, Special Collections Research Center, University of Chicago, Chicago, Illinois: Robin Darwall-Smith, Archivist, Magdalen

College, Oxford; Olivia DeClark, Mark Samuels Lasner Collection, University of Delaware; Ava Dickerson and Kristina Krasny, Lilly Library, Indiana University; Kathleen Dow, Archivist, University of Michigan, Ann Arbor, Michigan; Isaac Gewirtz, Curator, Berg Collection, the New York Public Library, New York; Sophie Glidden-Lyon, Assistant Archivist, Fales Library, New York; Colin Harris, Imaging Services, Bodleian Libraries, Oxford; Peter Henderson, Archivist, the King's School, Canterbury; Sarah Hobbs, Archivist, Archives & Local History, Manchester Central Library, Manchester; Daichi Ishikawa, Department of English, Queen Mary University, London; Andrew Isidoro, Library Assistant, John J. Burns Library, Boston College, Chestnut Hill, Massachusetts; Scott Jacobs, Reader Services, Clark Library, Los Angeles; Benn Joseph, Head of Collections Services, McCormick Library of Special Collections and University Archives, Northwestern University; Peter Kennedy, Archivist, the King's School, Canterbury; Karen V. Kukil, Associate Curator of Special Collections, William Allan Neilson Library, Smith College, Northampton, Massachusetts; Dana M. Lamparello and Janet C. Olson, Archivists, Northwestern University, Evanston, Illinois; Caitlin Lampman, Archivist, and Pat Webber, Director, Edmund S. Muskie Archives and Special Collections, Bates College; Daniel J. Linke, University Archivist and Deputy Head of Special Collections, Princeton University; Rebecca Fenning Marschall, Manuscripts & Archives Librarian, William Andrews Clark Memorial Library, UCLA; Nicholas Martin, Curator for the Arts & Humanities, NYU Special Collections; Stephen Mielke and the Reference & Research Services Team at the Harry Ransom Center, University of Texas, Austin; Gerald Monsman, Department of English, University of Arizona, Tucson, Arizona; Peter Montieth, Assistant Archivist, King's College, Cambridge; Francis O'Gorman, Department of English Literature, University of Edinburgh, Edinburgh; Joanna Parker, Librarian, Worcester College, Oxford; Robert E. Parks, Curator of Autograph Manuscripts, The Morgan Library & Museum, New York; Isabel Planton, Public Services Librarian, The Lilly Library, Indiana University, Bloomington, Indiana; Stephanie Plowman, Archivist, Foley Library, Gonzaga University, Spokane, Washington; Helen Price, Brotherton Library, and Rebecca Higgins, Special Collections & Galleries, Leeds University; Catherine Carson Ricciardi, Archivist, Rare Book and Manuscript Library, Columbia University, New York; Gayle M. Richardson, Catalog Librarian, Huntington Library, San Marino, California; Niki Russell, Public Service Manager, University of Glasgow, Glasgow; Michael Seeney, scholar and collector of Oscar Wilde items; Adrienne Leigh Sharpe, Access Services Assistant, Beinecke Rare Book and Manuscript Library, Yale University, New Haven, Connecticut; Chris Sheppard, Archivist, Brotherton Collection, Library, Leeds University, Leeds; Don C. Skemer, Curator of Manuscripts, Rare Books and Special Collections, Library, Princeton University, Princeton, New Jersey; Chantalle Smith, Librarian, Research Access, Alexander Turnbull Library, National Library of New Zealand; Zoe Stansell, Manuscripts & Maps Reference Service, the British Library, London; Helen Sumping, Archivist, Brasenose College; Natalie Trapuzzano, Reference Assistant, Rare Books and Special Collections, University of British Columbia, Vancouver; Paul Tucker, Dipartimento di Storia, Archaelogia, Geografia, Arte e Spettacolo, University of Florence, Florence; Abbie Weinberg, Reference & Outreach Specialist, Folger Shakespeare Library, Washington, DC; Alex Wong, Research Fellow, St. John's College, Cambridge; Theodore Wolf, Reference Specialist, Rare and Manuscript Collections, Cornell University, Ithaca, New York; Lewis Wyman, Reference Librarian, Library of Congress, Washington, DC; Shana McKenna, Archivist, Isabella Stewart Gardner Museum, Boston, Massachusetts; Rosella Mamoli Zorzi, Università Ca'Foscari Venezia, Isabella Stewart Gardner scholar; and Maxwell Zupke, Public Services, UCLA Library of Special Collections.

I wish to express my gratitude to the individuals and the institutions listed in Appendix C for kindly granting permission to publish the letters printed here, especially Georgina Edwards, Archivist, Brasenose College; Christopher Fletcher, the Keeper of Special Collections, the Bodleian Libraries; Anne-Marie Hansen, Head, Rights & Permissions, Oxford University Press; and Jonathan Vines, Image & Brand Licensing Manager, the British Library. A special note of thanks is due to Cecelia Jones (and Michael and Wendy Staples, her son and daughter-in-law), who is a granddaughter of Mary Ottley, the friend of Clara and Hester Pater to whom Hester left her estate, including some Pater manuscripts, when she died in 1922. If I have failed to obtain permission from the executors of any letters, I apologize with assurance that in every case I have made exhaustive efforts to trace them.

At Oxford University Press, I wish to thank Jacqueline Norton; Eleanor Collins, Senior Publishing Editor; Kathleen Fearn; Caroline Quinnell, copy editor; and the dedicated members of the production staff for their assistance. For her studious work in copy-editing, proofreading, and indexing the volume, I wish to thank Sylvia Vance. Rachelle Stinson has been a dedicated and essential research assistant.

I must acknowledge my huge debt to the general editors of *The Collected Works of Walter Pater*, Lesley Higgins and David Latham, who offered invaluable advice and support throughout this project.

Finally, I owe a special debt of gratitude to my wife, Tamara P. Seiler, and to the rest of our family, Tanya Palmer and James Maciukenas and their children, Harper and Theodore, and Mark Palmer, who provided unflagging encouragement. Tamara read the manuscript at various stages of development and offered valuable suggestions for improvement. I dedicate the volume to Tamara with love.

CONTENTS

General Editors' Preface	xi
Acknowledgements	xv
List of Illustrations	xxi
List of Abbreviations	xxiii
Chronology	xxv
Biographical Register	xxxvii
Critical Introduction	1
Textual Introduction	33
Correspondence	47
Appendix A: Further Letters by Walter Pater	385
Appendix B: Index of Correspondents	391
Appendix C: Sources of MS. Letters	395
Bibliography	399
Index	437

LIST OF ILLUSTRATIONS

Frontispiece. Portrait of Walter Pater, William Rothenstein, 1894. *Oxford Characters: A Set of Lithographs* (London: Bodley Head, 1893–95).   v

1. Walter Pater to John Pendergast, 5 June [1864]. Brasenose College Archives, Oxford.   34
2. Walter Pater to John Chapman, 27 November 1872. Yale University, New Haven, Connecticut.   36
3. Walter Pater to Charlotte Symonds Green, 10 February [1887]. Bates College, Lewiston, Maine.   38
4. Walter Pater to John Lane, 5 April 1894. Brasenose College Archives, Oxford.   40

LIST OF ABBREVIATIONS

All references to the texts of Walter Pater, published and unpublished, are to *The Collected Works of Walter Pater* published by Oxford University Press. The titles are abbreviated as follows:

CW i　　*The Renaissance*
CW ii　　*Marius the Epicurean*
CW iii　*Imaginary Portraits*
CW iv　*Gaston de Latour*
CW v　　*Studies and Reviews, 1864–1889*
CW vi　*Appreciations, and Studies and Reviews, 1890–1894*
CW vii　*Plato and Platonism*
CW viii　*Classical Studies*
CW ix　*Correspondence*
CW x　　*Manuscripts*

I have also relied on certain other short titles and abbreviations to indicate works not by Pater:

Benson　　　Benson, A. C., *Walter Pater* (London: Macmillan, 1906).
Hagiwara　　Hagiwara, Hiroko, *Walter Pater and His Circle*, intro. Tatsuhiko Arakawa (Tokyo: Yushodoh, 1984).
Hill　　　　Pater, Walter, *The Renaissance: Studies in Art and Poetry*, ed. Donald L. Hill (Berkeley, Calif.: University of California Press, 1980).
LWP　　　　Pater, Walter, *Letters of Walter Pater*, ed. Lawrence Evans (Oxford: Clarendon Press, 1970).
Letter Books　Information from the Macmillan Archive in the British Library, specifically the Macmillan Letter Books, Brit Lib MSS 55393 to 55542.
TBB　　　　Seiler, Robert, ed., *The Book Beautiful: Walter Pater and the House of Macmillan* (London: Athlone Press, 1999).
VLL　　　　Paget, Violet, *Vernon Lee's Letters*, ed. Irene Cooper Willis (London: privately printed, 1937).
Wright　　　Wright, Thomas, *The Life of Walter Pater*, 2 vols (London: Everett, 1907).

CHRONOLOGY

1835 Pater's brother William (1835–87) is born, the first child of Maria Hill (bap. 1803, d. 1854) and Richard Glode Pater (1797?–1842).

1837 Pater's sister Hester (1837–1922) is born.

1839 On 25 January, John Henry Newman, then a Fellow of Oriel College, Oxford, publishes 'Tract 90: Remarks on Certain Passages in the Thirty-Nine Articles'.
4 August: Walter Pater is born near Whitechapel, east London.

1841 Pater's sister Clara Ann (1841–1910) is born.

1842 28 January: death of Pater's father Richard. Later that year, the family moves to a house near Chase Side, Enfield, where they live with Richard's sister for ten years.

1845 Famine in Ireland (1845–52); this is a period of mass starvation and disease.
October: John Henry Newman resigns his fellowship at Oriel College on 3 October; six days later, is received into the Roman Catholic Church.

1847 Pater's family moves to Enfield, Middlesex.

1848 The 'year of revolutions' features a number of republican revolts against monarchies, beginning in Italy and spreading to France, Germany, and Austria. They end in failure. Pater's paternal grandmother Hester dies.
September: William Holman Hunt, D. G. Rossetti, John Everett Millais, F. G. Stephens, Thomas Woolner, James Collinson, and William Michael Rossetti form the Pre-Raphaelite Brotherhood; members hold their first meeting 31 December.

1849 February: Matthew Arnold publishes *The Strayed Reveller, and Other Poems*.

1851 1 May to 11 October: the Great Exhibition, Crystal Palace, Hyde Park, London.

1852 Pater attends Enfield Grammar School from 1852 to 1853.
11 November: in London, the new Houses of Parliament (Palace of Westminster) designed by Charles Barry and Augustus Pugin open.

1853 Pater's family moves to Harbledown, Kent, so that he can attend the King's School, Canterbury, as a day pupil.

1854 Henry Dombrain joins the King's School, soon to become Pater's close companion.
25 February: death of Pater's mother Maria. Aunt 'Bessie' Pater becomes the orphans' guardian.

1855 John Rainier McQueen enters the King's School and develops a close friendship with Pater.
McQueen, Dombrain, and Pater form a secret society called 'The Three Inseparables'.

1856 Pater writes the poems 'The Chant of the Celestial Sailors', 'The Legend of Saint Elizabeth of Hungary', and 'Poets Old and New'.
October: Gustave Flaubert's *Madame Bovary* is serialized in *La revue de Paris* (until 15 December).

1857 South Kensington Museum established in London (later renamed the Victoria and Albert Museum).
Pater writes the poem 'Cassandra'.
January: Flaubert is tried in Paris for obscenity, but acquitted on 7 February; the novel is released in book form in April.
June: Charles Baudelaire, *Les fleurs du mal*.
14 November: Matthew Arnold's inaugural lecture as Oxford Professor of Poetry, 'On the Modern Element in Literature'.

1858 William Morris, *The Defence of Guenevere, and Other Poems*.
Pater writes the poem 'Chant of the Celestial Sailors when they first put out to sea' and the story 'Saint Gertrude of Himmelstadt' (both lost), and the poem 'Watchman, What of the Night?'.
June: Pater matriculates at Queen's College, Oxford.
5 August: Speech Day at the King's School. Pater leaves King's having received prizes in Latin and ecclesiastical history, and a three-year Exhibition (scholarship) of £60.
October: Pater enters Queen's College, Oxford; W. W. Capes is his principal tutor.
December: Pater travels to Heidelberg (Elizabeth Pater, his aunt Bessie, had moved there, along with his sisters Hester and Clara, in October).

1859 February: John Stuart Mill, *On Liberty*.
23 September: death of Anne Pater, Pater's great-aunt, aged eighty.
October: Pater writes the poem 'The Acorn'.
November: Charles Darwin, *On the Origin of Species*.

1860 Pater and his friend Ingram Bywater begin to study with Benjamin Jowett.
Pater's friendship with McQueen ends.
Pater writes the poems 'Oxford Life' and 'The Greek Minstrel's Song, from "Iphigenia"', and completes the poem 'The Fan of Fire: A Study from Wordsworth'.

January: first issue of the *Cornhill Magazine* is published (founded by George Murray Smith; edited by W. M. Thackeray).

1862 Christina Rossetti, *Goblin Market and Other Poems*.
December: McQueen writes to the Bishop of London to prevent Pater's ordination, denouncing him as an apostate.
11 December: Pater receives his BA from Queen's College with second-class honours in *Literae Humaniores*.
28 December: Elizabeth Pater, Pater's aunt Bessie, dies in Dresden; Pater attends the funeral then returns to London (to Lonsdale Square) with his sisters.

1863 Early January: Pater moves to 9 Grove Street (now Magpie Lane, off the High Street), Oxford, and coaches students privately.
Pater joins Oxford's Old Mortality essay society.
January: Pater competes unsuccessfully for a clerical fellowship at Brasenose College.
Summer: Pater competes unsuccessfully for a clerical fellowship at Trinity College.

1864 Pater burns his poetry, believed to have been largely religious.
February: Pater reads his 'Subjective Immortality' essay to the Old Mortality.
5 February: Pater is elected to a non-clerical fellowship at Brasenose College, where he begins to tutor.
March: Pater attends Arnold's lecture on 'Pagan and Mediaeval Religious Sentiment'.
July: Pater reads 'Diaphaneitè' essay to the Old Mortality.
Summer: Pater spends the Long Vacation in Paris with his sisters.
29 October: Arnold lectures on 'The Function of Criticism at the Present Time'.

1865 Pater takes up residence at Brasenose College.
Pater receives MA degree.
Summer: Pater travels to Italy with Oxford colleague Charles L. Shadwell.
December: Pater and his sisters take rooms at 50 Jermyn Street, near Piccadilly Circus, in London, during the Christmas Vacation.

1866 January: Pater publishes 'Coleridge's Writings' in the *Westminster Review*, his first publication.
April: Pater begins 'coaching' Balliol student Gerard Manley Hopkins, until June 1867.
July: A. C. Swinburne, *Poems and Ballads*.

1867 Pater takes up lecturing at Brasenose.
January: Pater publishes 'Winckelmann' in the *Westminster Review*.
31 August: death of Charles Baudelaire.

1868 William Morris, the first volume of *The Earthly Paradise: A Poem*.

Simeon Solomon gives Pater a version of his drawing *The Bride, the Bridegroom, and the Friend of the Bridegroom*.
17 June: Pater lunches with Hopkins, then visits Solomon's studio and the Royal Academy.
October: Pater publishes 'Poems by William Morris' in the *Westminster Review*.

1869 Pater moves with his sisters to 2 Bradmore Road, Oxford.
Pater is elected to the New Club (later the Savile Club), London.
November: Pater publishes 'Notes on Leonardo da Vinci' in the *Fortnightly Review*.

1870 Dante Gabriel Rossetti, *Poems*.
Ruskin is elected first Slade Professor of Fine Art at Oxford.
August: Pater publishes 'A Fragment on Sandro Botticelli' in the *Fortnightly Review*.

1871 18 June: University Tests Act removes religious tests for higher degrees at British universities.
October: Pater publishes 'Pico della Mirandola' in the *Fortnightly Review*.
November: Pater publishes 'The Poetry of Michelangelo' in the *Fortnightly Review*.

1872 Simeon Solomon draws Pater's portrait at Brasenose.
Pater meets Edmund Gosse at William Bell Scott's studio.
July: Pater publishes review of Sidney Colvin's *Children in Italian and English Design* in the *Academy*.

1873 Victor Hugo et al., *Le tombeau de Théophile Gautier*.
February: Pater publishes *Studies in the History of the Renaissance*.
11 February: Solomon is arrested and charged with buggery.

1874 February: letters surface from Pater to Balliol student William Money Hardinge, signed 'yours lovingly'. Pater's bid for an Oxford proctorship is unsuccessful; Hardinge is suspended.
April: Pater publishes 'On Wordsworth' in the *Fortnightly Review*.
November: Pater publishes 'A Fragment on *Measure for Measure*' in the *Fortnightly Review*.

1875 John Keble, *Sermons for the Christian Year*.
July: Pater publishes a review of John Addington Symonds's *Renaissance in Italy: The Age of Despots* in the *Academy*.
Summer: Pater visits Oscar Browning at Eton College.
September: Oscar Browning is dismissed as housemaster at Eton.
26 September: Pater lunches with Henry Smith and Mountstuart Grant Duff in Oxford.

November: Pater lectures on 'Demeter and Persephone' at the Birmingham and Midland Institute.

1876 John Richard Green, *Stray Studies from England and Italy*.
January: Pater publishes 'The Myth of Demeter and Persephone' in the *Fortnightly Review*.
June–December: Pater is satirized as Mr Rose in W. H. Mallock's *The New Republic* (serialized in *Belgravia*; vol. published in 1877).
November: Pater publishes 'Romanticism' in *Macmillan's Magazine*.
December: Pater publishes 'A Study of Dionysus' in the *Fortnightly Review*.

1877 Frederick Wedmore, *Pastorals of France*; Gustave Flaubert, *Trois contes*.
February: Pater hosts Edmund Gosse and his wife, Ellen Epps, in Oxford.
March: Pater withdraws candidacy for Oxford's Professorship of Poetry.
24 May: Pater issues a second edition of *Studies*, now titled *The Renaissance: Studies in Art and Poetry*; the 'Conclusion' is omitted.
2 June: Pater hosts the Gosses in Oxford.
July: Ruskin denounces Whistler's *Nocturne in Black and Gold: The Falling Rocket*; Whistler sues for libel (he wins the November 1878 trial, but is awarded only a farthing in damages).
Summer: Pater and his sisters travel to France.
October: Pater meets Oscar Wilde, a student at Magdalen College, Oxford. Pater publishes 'The School of Giorgione' in the *Fortnightly Review*.
December: Julia Constance Fletcher (pseud. George Fleming) publishes *Mirage*, a novel that she dedicates to Pater.

1878 Spring: Pater meets art critic John Miller Gray when Gray is holidaying in Oxford.
August: Pater publishes 'Imaginary Portraits. I. The Child in the House' in *Macmillan's Magazine*.
October: Pater publishes 'The Character of the Humourist: Charles Lamb' in the *Fortnightly Review*.
30 November: Pater cancels the publication of *Dionysus and Other Studies* with Macmillan.
December: Hopkins, now a Jesuit priest, is transferred to Oxford to be curate at St Aloysius (until October 1879); renews his friendship with Pater.

1879 11 February: Pater and his sisters entertain Hopkins.
22 May: Pater dines with Hopkins.

1880 Gilbert and Sullivan, *Patience*.

Pater publishes an introduction to 'Samuel Taylor Coleridge' in T. Humphry Ward's *The English Poets*.
February: Pater publishes 'The Beginnings of Greek Sculpture I. The Heroic Age of Greek Art' in the *Fortnightly Review*.
March: Pater publishes 'The Beginnings of Greek Sculpture II. The Age of Graven Images' in the *Fortnightly Review*.
April: Pater publishes 'The Marbles of Aegina' in the *Fortnightly Review*.

1881 D. G. Rossetti, *Ballads and Sonnets*; Alfred Joshua Butler, *Amaranth and Asphodel: Songs from the Greek Anthology*; Vernon Lee, *Belcaro: Being Essays on Sundry Aesthetical Questions*.

Pater meets Violet Paget (pseud. Vernon Lee).

1882 Hall Caine, *Recollections of Dante Gabriel Rossetti*; William Sharp, *Dante Gabriel Rossetti: A Record and a Study*.
26 March: death of Thomas Hill Green.
10 April: death of D. G. Rossetti.
July: Sharp visits Pater in Oxford.
1–3 August: Violet Paget visits Pater and his sisters in Oxford.
Summer: Pater and his sisters vacation in Cornwall.
December: Pater travels to Rome for work on *Marius the Epicurean*.

1883 Pater publishes an introduction to 'Dante Gabriel Rossetti' in T. Humphry Ward's *The English Poets*, second edition.
Pater resigns from his tutorship at Brasenose.
March: Pater publishes a review of *Love in Idleness: A Volume of Poems*, by Henry Charles Beeching, in the *Oxford Magazine*.

1884 Mary Arnold Ward, *Miss Bretherton*; Sharp, *Earth's Voices, Transcripts from Nature, Sospitra, and Other Poems*; Vernon Lee, *Miss Brown: A Novel* and *Euphorion: Being Studies of the Antique and the Medieval in the Renaissance*; Eugene Lee-Hamilton, *Apollo and Marsyas, and Other Poems*.
1 February: the first volume of the *Oxford English Dictionary* is published (–1928).
18–21 June: Violet Paget stays with the Paters in Oxford.

1885 Mark Pattison, *Memoirs*; Gosse, *From Shakespeare to Pope*; Henri-Frédéric Amiel, *Amiel's Journal* (trans. Mary Ward); *Specimens of English Prose Style from Malory to Macaulay*, ed. George Saintsbury.
Pater's candidacy for the position of Slade Professor of Fine Art at Oxford is unsuccessful.
20 February: Whistler delivers 'Ten O'Clock Lecture' in London.
25 February: Pater publishes a review of *The English School of*

Painting, by Ernest Chesneau (trans. L. N. Etherington), in the *Oxford Magazine*.
4 March: Pater publishes *Marius the Epicurean*.
Summer: Sharp and his wife Elizabeth visit Pater and his sisters in Oxford. In the afternoon, the group tours Iffley Woods.
Pater meets Irish novelist George Moore.
August: Pater moves with Clara and Hester to 12 Earl's Terrace in Kensington district of London.
October: Pater publishes 'A Prince of Court Painters' in *Macmillan's Magazine*.
12 November: second edition of *Marius* appears.
December: Pater publishes 'On Love's Labours Lost' in *Macmillan's Magazine*.

1886 Frances Hodgson Burnett, *Little Lord Fauntleroy*; Marie Corelli, *A Romance of Two Worlds*; Thomas Hardy, *The Mayor of Casterbridge*; Moore, *Confessions of a Young Man*; Ruskin, vol. i of *Praeterita: Outlines of scenes and thoughts perhaps worthy of memory in my past life* (vol. ii, 1887; vol. iii, 1888–9); Stevenson, *The Strange Case of Dr Jekyll and Mr Hyde* and *Kidnapped*; Octave Feuillet, *Aliette (La morte)* (trans. J. E. Simpson); Sharp, *Sonnets of this Century*.
17 February: Pater publishes 'Four Books for Students of English Literature' in *The Guardian*.
March: Pater publishes 'Sebastian van Storck' in *Macmillan's Magazine*.
17 March: Pater publishes his review of *Amiel's Journal, The Journal Intime of Henri-Frédéric Amiel*, in *The Guardian*.
May: Pater publishes 'Sir Thomas Browne' in *Macmillan's Magazine*.
October: Pater publishes 'Denys L'Auxerrois' in *Macmillan's Magazine*.
November: Frederick William Bussell is elected as clerical Fellow at Brasenose.
27 November: Pater publishes 'English at the Universities' in *Pall Mall Gazette*.
December: Pater publishes 'M. Feuillet's *La Morte*' in *Macmillan's Magazine*.

1887 Flaubert, *Correspondance, Première Série, 1830–1850*.
24 April: Pater's brother William dies of heart disease. He is buried in Highgate Cemetery, London on 27 April.
May: Pater publishes 'Duke Carl of Rosenmold' in *Macmillan's Magazine*.
24 May: Pater publishes *Imaginary Portraits*.
21 June: Queen Victoria's Golden Jubilee (fifty years as monarch).

26 June: Pater dines with Sir Mountstuart Grant Duff.
5 August: Pater publishes review of *Juvenilia: Being a Second Series of Essays on Sundry Aesthetical Questions*, by Vernon Lee, in the *Pall Mall Gazette*.
August–September: Pater holidays in France.
November: Pater publishes 'M. Lemaître's Serenus, and Other Tales' in *Macmillan's Magazine*.
9 November: Pater publishes review of *An Introduction to the Study of Browning* (1886) by Arthur Symons, in *The Guardian*.

1888 Wilde, *The Happy Prince, and Other Tales*; *The Complete Poetical Works of William Wordsworth*, ed. John Morley; *Selections from Wordsworth*, ed. William Knight et al.; Gosse, *Life of Congreve*; *Nero & Other Plays*, ed. Herbert Horne, Havelock Ellis, Symons, and A. Wilson Verity; Sharp, *Romantic Ballads and Poems of Phantasy*.
28 March: Pater publishes a review of *Robert Elsmere*, by Mary Arnold Ward, in *The Guardian*.
April: third edition of *The Renaissance* appears, with amended 'Conclusion'.
27 June: Pater publishes a review of 'Their Majesties' Servants' in *The Guardian*.
29 June: the first known classical music recording, Handel's *Israel in Egypt*, is recorded using a wax cylinder at the Crystal Palace.
June–October: Pater publishes five chapters of *Gaston de Latour* in *Macmillan's Magazine*.
7 August: Pater meets Symons in London.
13 August: Pater departs for a trip to Switzerland.
25 August: Pater publishes 'The Life and Letters of Gustave Flaubert' in the *Pall Mall Gazette*.
14 October: Louis Le Prince films the first motion picture, *Roundhay Garden Scene*, in Roundhay, West Yorkshire, England.
December: Pater publishes 'Style' in the *Fortnightly Review*.
Pater hosts Symons in Oxford.

1889 Michael Field, *Long Ago*. John Lane and Elkin Mathews establish The Bodley Head Press.
26 January: Pater publishes a review of *The Complete Poetical Works of William Wordsworth*, *The Recluse*, and *Selections from Wordsworth* in the *Athenaeum*.
February: Pater revises his review of *The Complete Poetical Works of William Wordsworth*, *The Recluse*, and *Selections from Wordsworth* for *The Guardian*.
13 February: Symons visits Pater at Oxford.
23 March: Pater publishes 'A Poet with Something to Say', a review of

Days and Nights by Symons, in the *Pall Mall Gazette*.
April: Pater publishes a review of *Toussaint Galabru* (1887), by Ferdinand Fabre, in *The Nineteenth Century*.
5 April: Pater publishes 'Shakespeare's English Kings' in *Scribner's Magazine*.
15 April: Pater reviews *It is Thyself*, by Marc André Raffalovich, in the *Pall Mall Gazette*.
25 April: Pater lunches with Symons in Kensington.
May: Pater publishes 'The Bacchanals of Euripides' in *Macmillan's Magazine*.
8 June: death of Gerard Manley Hopkins.
12 June: Pater publishes 'An Idyll of the Cévennes', a review of *Norine* (1889), by Ferdinand Fabre, in *The Guardian*.
4 July: Symons visits Pater in London.
22 July: Katharine Harris Bradley and Edith Emma Cooper (pseud. Michael Field) visit Pater in Kensington.
August: Pater publishes 'Giordano Bruno' in the *Fortnightly Review*.
Pater publishes 'Hippolytus Veiled' in *Macmillan's Magazine*.
3 August: Pater publishes a review of *Correspondance de Gustave Flaubert, Deuxième Série (1850–4)* in the *Athenaeum*.
12 August: Pater holidays on the Continent; the trip includes visits to Bergamo and Brescia.
13 October: Pater is hosted by Grant Duff and his wife, Anna Webster, at York House in Twickenham. They are joined by Arthur Russell, Henry James, and others.
15 November: Pater publishes *Appreciations: With an Essay on Style*.
20 November: Symons visits Pater at Oxford.
December: Pater publishes a review of *A Century of Revolution*, by William Samuel Lilly, in *The Nineteenth Century*.

1890 Wilde, *The Picture of Dorian Gray* in *Lippincott's Magazine* (July 20); James Frazer, *The Golden Bough*; Field, *The Tragic Mary*; Jules Lemaître, *Dix contes*.
12 January: Pater dines with Grant Duff.
18 February: Pater visits Lionel Johnson in regard to Johnson's review of *Appreciations*.
May: second edition of *Appreciations* appears, without 'Aesthetic Poetry'.
July: Pater publishes 'Tales of a Hundred Years Since', a review of *Contes du centenaire*, by Augustin Filon, in *The Guardian*.
July 27: Pater is visited by the American playwright William Clyde Fitch.

October: Pater reviews *On Viol and Flute*, by Gosse, in *The Guardian*.
November: second edition of *Imaginary Portraits* appears.
November: Pater publishes 'Art Notes in North Italy' in *The New Review*.
17 November: Pater lectures on 'Prosper Mérimée' at Taylor Institution, Oxford.
23 November: Pater lectures on Wordsworth at Toynbee Hall in London.
24 November: Pater lectures on 'Prosper Mérimée' at the London Institute.
December: Pater is elected a member of the Oxford Dante Society.
Pater publishes 'Prosper Mérimée' in the *Fortnightly Review*.

1891 Louis Dyer, *Studies of the Gods in Greece at Certain Sanctuaries Recently Excavated*; Richard Le Gallienne, *The Book-Bills of Narcissus*.
Elementary Education Act of 1891 provides for free elementary schooling in Britain.
William Morris establishes the Kelmscott Press.
Pater is elected to the Library Committee of the Oxford Union (serves until 1892).
3–4 January: Pater visits Grant Duff.
21 January: Pater begins lecture series on 'Plato and Platonism' at Oxford.
August–September: Pater travels to Italy.
November: Pater publishes 'A Novel by Mr. Oscar Wilde', a review of *The Picture of Dorian Gray*, in *The Bookman*.

1892 Mary Arnold Ward, *The History of David Grieve*; Field, *Sight and Song*; Gosse, *The Secret of Narcisse: A Romance*.
February: Pater publishes 'The Genius of Plato' in the *Contemporary Review*.
May: Pater publishes 'A Chapter on Plato' in *Macmillan's Magazine*.
June: Pater publishes 'Lacedaemon' in the *Contemporary Review*.
June–July: Pater publishes 'Emerald Uthwart' in *The New Review*.
27 July: Pater dines with the Gosses in London.
August: third edition of *Marius* appears.
2 August: Pater lectures on Leonardo da Vinci at the meeting of the delegates for the Extension of Teaching beyond the Limits of the University in Oxford.
September: Pater publishes 'Introduction' to Shadwell's *The Purgatory of Dante Alighieri*.
October: Pater publishes 'Raphael' in the *Fortnightly Review*.
Pater meets writer Richard Le Gallienne at a dinner party hosted by

C. H. O. Daniel in Oxford.
6 October: death of Tennyson.

1893 9 February: Pater publishes *Plato and Platonism: A Series of Lectures*.
19 April: death of John Addington Symonds.
June: Pater publishes 'Apollo in Picardy' in *Harper's New Monthly Magazine*.
10 June: Pater publishes 'Mr. George Moore as an Art Critic', a review of Moore's *Modern Painting*, in the *Daily Chronicle*.
14 June: Pater hosts Gosse for dinner.
29 June: Gosse hosts a luncheon at the National Club in London attended by Pater, Thomas Hardy, A. C. Benson, and others.
3 July: Pater hosts Violet Paget, Clementine Anstruther-Thomson, and J. S. Cotton for dinner.
Summer: Pater relocates to 64 St Giles' Street, Oxford, with sisters.
Late summer: Pater travels to France.
1 October: death of Benjamin Jowett.
November: Paul Verlaine visits England for the fourth and last time; lectures in Oxford on 23 November.
December: Pater is confined to his rooms with bronchitis.
December: fourth edition of *The Renaissance* appears.

1894 Moore, *Esther Waters*.
February: Wilde's *Salome* is published in English, with Aubrey Beardsley's illustrations.
Pater publishes 'The Age of Athletic Prizemen' in the *Contemporary Review*.
28 February: Pater attends Stéphane Mallarmé's lecture on 'Music and Literature' and meets Mallarmé in the rooms of Frederick York Powell.
March: Pater publishes 'Some Great Churches of France. I. Notre-Dame d'Amiens' in *The Nineteenth Century*.
April: *The Yellow Book* commences publication.
5 April: Pater writes to John Lane to request that his portrait not appear in William Rothenstein's *Oxford Characters*.
13 April: Pater is awarded honorary LLD by University of Glasgow.
The Daniel Press issues 250 copies of *An Imaginary Portrait: The Child in the House* to be sold at the Venetian Fête in the Worcester College gardens, held on 12 and 13 June in honour of the parish of St Thomas the Martyr, Oxford.
June: Pater suffers from gout and then rheumatic fever; he is nursed by his sisters and Charlotte Symonds Green.
June: Pater publishes 'Some Great Churches of France. II. Vézelay' in *The Nineteenth Century*.

30 July: death of Pater, from a heart attack.
2 August: Pater is buried at Holywell Cemetery, Oxford.
Autumn: Pater's sisters relocate to 6 Canning Place, Kensington.
14 October: Pater's friend Frederick William Bussell delivers a memorial sermon in the Brasenose College chapel.

1895 Rothenstein's portrait of Pater appears in Part 4 of *Oxford Characters*.
January: *Greek Studies* is published, edited by Shadwell.
February: 'Pascal' is published in the *Contemporary Review*, edited by Gosse.
6 April: Oscar Wilde is arrested at the Cadogan Hotel, London, after losing a libel case against the Marquess of Queensberry. The first trial for 'gross indecency' results in a hung jury; after the second trial he is found guilty and sentenced to two years in Reading Gaol.
1 August: Clara and Hester Pater travel to St Margaret's-at-Cliffe for a month's stay at a cottage.
October: Shadwell edits and publishes *Miscellaneous Studies: A Series of Essays*, containing the first printing of 'Diaphaneitè'.

1896 October: *Gaston de Latour* appears, edited by Shadwell.
Essays from 'The Guardian' is published, edited by Gosse.

1897 19 May: Wilde is released from prison.

1900 First of the eight-volume *The Works of Walter Pater*, Edition de Luxe, is issued by Macmillan (1900–1).

30 November: death of Oscar Wilde.

1903 Thomas Bird Mosher publishes *Uncollected Essays by Walter Pater*.

1910 *New Library Edition of the Works of Walter Pater* is issued.

9 August: Pater's sister Clara dies of cancer; is buried in Holywell Cemetery.

1919 *Sketches and Reviews* is published, edited by Albert Mordell.

1922 Pater's sister Hester dies and is buried in Holywell Cemetery with her siblings.

1931 1 April: 'Imaginary Portraits 2: An English Poet' is published in the *Fortnightly Review*.

1970 *Letters of Walter Pater*, ed. Lawrence Evans, is published by Oxford.

BIOGRAPHICAL REGISTER

AINSLIE, GRANT DUFF DOUGLAS (1865–1948), Scottish poet, diplomat, translator, and critic, was born into an aristocratic family; Pater was good friends with his uncle, Sir Mountstuart Elphinstone Grant Duff,* Governor of Madras, 1881–6. In his memoir, *Adventures Social and Literary* (1922), he describes how he and his fellow students established the Oxford University Dramatic Society (OUDS) in 1885. Ainslie invited Oscar Wilde* to review OUDS's first production, *Twelfth Night*, which opened at the New Theatre on St Valentine's Day, 1886; Wilde obliged with a critique in the *Dramatic Review* (20 February 1886). Wilde introduced Ainslie to Pater, 'a pale-faced, rather sad-looking man', and the two became quite close, dining together often. Ainslie offered A. C. Benson,* Pater's biographer, some of his reminiscences. After graduation, Ainsley served as an attaché to the British Legation in Athens, The Hague, and Paris, 1891–4. In 1906 he discovered the work of philosopher Benedetto Croce (1866–1952), and spent twenty years translating into English his principal texts on aesthetics and literary criticism. From the early 1920s, Ainslie studied Hindu poetry and philosophy, especially that of Paramahansa Yogananda (1893–1952), a yogi and guru who taught meditation. Yogananda's *The Science of Religion* (1924) includes a preface by Ainslie. In 1938, he migrated to Los Angeles, then a locale for spiritual discovery.

BENSON, ARTHUR CHRISTOPHER (1862–1925), poet, essayist, biographer, short-story-writer, and diarist, was the second of six children born to the Revd Edward W. Benson and his wife, Mary Sidgwick (sister of Henry Sidgwick, philosopher). All members of the Benson family were accomplished. After attending King's College, Cambridge, 1881–4, Benson served as classics master at Eton, 1885–1903. Overwhelmed by the 'grind', he resigned and moved to Cambridge, where, as Fellow and later Master of Magdalene College, 1904–25, he wrote at leisure. In 1899 he published a biography of his father, Archbishop of Canterbury from 1882 to 1896, and co-edited the letters of Queen Victoria (1907). The essays collected in *From a College Window* (1906) and *The Upton Letters* (1905), and his biographies of D. G. Rossetti (1904), Edward FitzGerald (1905), and Walter Pater (1906), bolstered his position as a best-selling author. Benson's diaries (1897–1925), which include unpublished material on

Pater, run to 180 volumes. Benson and Pater met at a luncheon hosted by Edmund Gosse* at the National Club, London, in June 1893. In October 1904, George Macmillan* asked Benson to prepare a volume on Pater for the 'English Men of Letters' series, one that would 'answer' the biography that Thomas Wright* was preparing. Benson interviewed a number of Pater's friends and relations, including Clara* and Hester Pater,* who gave their approval for the project and permission to quote from Walter's letters. *Walter Pater* appeared on 11 May 1906.

BOURGET, PAUL CHARLES JOSEPH (1852–1935), poet, novelist, and critic, taught Greek and Latin at the École Bossuet, Paris. Disenchanted with teaching, he became a writer, publishing three volumes of verse (Claude Debussy set several of his poems to music). Bourget also wrote portraits of Charles Baudelaire, Gustave Flaubert, Ernest Renan, Hippolyte Taine, and Ivan Turgenev, collected in *Essais de psychologie contemporaine* (1883). His analysis of pessimism in Baudelaire's *Les fleurs du mal* became an early manifesto of literary decadence. His first psychological novel, *Cruelle énigme* (1885), was also a success. To investigate British people and institutions, he visited often, including Oxford in May and June 1883; it is thought that Ingram Bywater* introduced Bourget to the personalities of the day, including Mark Pattison* and Pater. Bourget recorded his 'Sensations d'Oxford' for *La Nouvelle Revue* (October 1883). He also spent May to September 1884 in London, studying D. G. Rossetti's paintings and socializing with Henry James, John Singer Sargent, and Oscar Wilde*; it is possible that he met Pater at the dinner party the Robinson family hosted at their residence in London on 20 July 1884.

BOWES, ROBERT (1835–1919), a nephew of Daniel Macmillan* and Alexander Macmillan,* travelled from Ayrshire in 1846 to join the firm of booksellers and publishers, which had recently acquired the bookselling business located at 1 Trinity Street, Cambridge. Bowes moved to London in 1858 to manage the publishing branch of the firm that the Macmillan brothers had established. When the publishing concern moved to London in 1863, Bowes returned to Cambridge to take charge of the bookselling branch, which had become an independent business, with Alexander as a partner until his death in 1896. In 1899 Bowes took on his son, George Brimley Bowes (1875–1946), as a partner, but retained the name 'Macmillan and Co.' until 1907, when the business became 'Bowes and Bowes'. A man of many activities, Bowes served as a member of the town council and treasurer of the Cambridge Antiquarian Society. His absorbing hobby centred on Cambridge books and Cambridge printers. He produced several monographs on bibliographical subjects.

BRETT, GEORGE EDWARD (1829–90), bookseller and publisher, travelled to New York City in August 1869 under the auspices of Alexander Macmillan,* with a view to creating and managing the New York branch of Macmillan and Co. Brett opened the branch office in a private house at 63 Bleecker Street. Business expanded rapidly, and in 1874 Brett's son, George Platt Brett (1858–1936), joined the staff as a travelling salesman. When Brett senior died in 1890, Brett junior took over the business. When Macmillan and Co. underwent a re-organization in 1896, the English firm became Macmillan and Co., Ltd., and the American branch was incorporated as the Macmillan Co., a separate entity with Brett as president.

BROWNING, OSCAR (1837–1923), historian, biographer, and educator, studied classics at King's College, Cambridge, 1856–9, and taught at Eton, 1860–75, where he made a name for himself as an inspiring but unorthodox teacher. During the long vacations he often travelled with a student as a companion. The headmaster at Eton dismissed Browning in 1875 for breaching regulations (colleagues suspected intimate relations with students). 'O. B.', as he was called, took up a resident fellowship at King's College, Cambridge, in 1876, planning to rehabilitate his reputation. He served as Lecturer in History from 1880 and University Reader in History from 1884. Browning promoted the study of modern history and pioneered teacher training, serving first as a member and then as Principal of the Cambridge University Day Training College for teachers, 1891–1909. A man of great industry, he produced books on many topics, including *An Introduction to the History of Educational Theories* (1881), *Historical Studies* (1882), *Life of George Eliot* (1890), *Goethe: His Life and Writings* (1892), and *A History of the Modern World: 1815–1910* (1912). Browning and Pater met in Oxford early in 1868; Browning regarded Pater as 'a soul of rare and precious quality'. Pater spoke to Browning's students at Eton and Cambridge, and the two visited each other at Oxford and Cambridge. The friendship lasted until the summer of 1880. (See Browning, 'Recollections', *Cam*, 14 February 1906, 4–5.)

BUSSELL, FREDERICK WILLIAM (1862–1944), clergyman and scholar, attended Magdalen College, Oxford, 1881–5, and served as Fellow (from 1886), Chaplain (from 1891), and Vice-Principal (1896–1913) of Brasenose College. An Oxford personality, Bussell was distinguished by his monocle and loud check suits and by his vast store of knowledge, which he rarely paraded: too erudite to be a popular teacher, he nevertheless made a profound impression on those undergraduates in whom he took an interest. Bussell taught classics, history, philosophy, and theology. His books include *The School of Plato* (1896), *The Future of Ethics* (1902), and

Augustine's City of God (1903). Bussell retired in 1913, but resided at Brasenose until 1917, when he married Mary Winnifred Dibdin (1885–1977) and accepted the college 'living' of Northolt, Middlesex, which he vacated in 1925. During the early 1890s, Bussell was one of Pater's most devoted friends; in his recollections, he stressed Pater's religious engagement, his attendance at chapel on Sundays, and his interest in the liturgy. Bussell preached the memorial sermon on Pater in the Brasenose chapel on 14 October 1894; 'In Memoriam: W. H. Pater' appeared in the *Oxford Magazine*, 17 October 1894, 7–8.

BYWATER, INGRAM (1840–1915), a classical scholar, studied at Queen's College, Oxford, 1858–62. His closest friend at Queen's was Pater (they attended the same lectures) and his principal tutors were Benjamin Jowett* and Robinson Ellis; T. H. Green was one of his private 'coaches'. Bywater won an open fellowship at Exeter College in 1863, and became close friends with Mark Pattison* and his wife Emilia (later, Lady Dilke*). With them Bywater travelled on the Continent, visiting libraries and museums. In 1877 his edition of Heraclitus demonstrated his scholarly and editorial acumen; he was also famous for his editions of Aristotle (*Aristotelis Ethica Nicomachae*, 1890). In 1884, he was appointed to a new university readership in Greek; when Jowett died, Bywater was named Regius Professor of Greek. In 1885 he married Charlotte Cornish Sotheby, an accomplished scholar specializing in ancient and modern Greek. As a delegate of Oxford University Press, Bywater contributed significantly to the Oxford Classical Texts series and to the *Oxford English Dictionary*.

CHAPMAN, JOHN (1821–94), publisher, author, and physician, apprenticed as a watch-maker before studying medicine in Paris and London. With financial assistance from his wife Susanna, he bought the London publishing firm of John Green (1844), intending to publish his own quasi-philosophical treatise on human nature. Supported by wealthy patrons, he published works that challenged orthodox views, including D. F. Straus's *The Life of Jesus, Critically Examined* (1835–6) in 1846 and Ludwig Feuerbach's *The Essence of Christianity* (1841) in 1854. In 1847 he moved the firm to a former hotel at 142 The Strand, conducting his publishing and book-selling business on the ground floor and living with his family on the upper floor. In 1851 Chapman acquired the *Westminster Review*, planning to establish a forum for 'the ablest and most liberal thinkers of the time'. He hired Marian Evans (George Eliot) as his unofficial assistant editor, and recruited an array of talent, including James Anthony Froude, T. H. Huxley, George Henry Lewes, Francis William Newman, Harriet and James Martineau, and Herbert Spencer. In due course, 142 The

Strand became a centre of enlightened radicalism. Chapman graduated in medicine at St Andrews in 1857 and later published several medical studies; he edited the *Westminster Review* until his death. He moved to Paris in 1874, serving the medical needs of the British expatriate community.

COLLINS, JOHN CHURTON (1848–1908), literary critic, extension lecturer, and polemicist, was an inspiring teacher and campaigner for the importance of literature in education. Settling in London in 1872, he determined to make his mark as a writer; he wrote for newspapers and periodicals and coached candidates for the Civil Service examinations. In 1880, he secured employment with the recently created London Society for the Extension of University Teaching; for twenty-seven years he delivered hundreds of lectures and gave classes for the Society and other branches of the movement for adult education. He urged university officials and the general public to take seriously the proposition that the study of classical and English literature was essential for a complete education. In 1885, he failed to secure the Merton Professorship of English at Oxford. In 1904, however, he became Professor of English Literature at Birmingham University, and continued 'extension' teaching into 1907. His many publications include *The Study of English Literature* (1891). Over the years, Collins acquired a reputation as a vitriolic critic who quarrelled with anyone of consequence in the literary world (including Edmund Gosse*).

COLVIN, SIDNEY (1845–1927), art critic, biographer, and administrator, grew up in east Suffolk, where friends and neighbours included the Ruskin family. After studying classics at Trinity College, Cambridge, 1863–7, he moved to London, where he served as an art critic for the *Fortnightly Review*, *Pall Mall Gazette*, *Westminster Review*, and *Cornhill Magazine*; the reviews were reprinted in *Children in Italian and English Design* (1872) and *A Selection from Occasional Writings on Fine Art* (1873). Colvin served as Slade Professor of Fine Art at Cambridge, 1873–85, and as director of the Fitzwilliam Museum, 1876–84, where he pursued his interest in archaeology and ancient Greek sculpture, creating a gallery of plaster casts. Later he served as Keeper of Paintings and Drawings at the British Museum, 1884–1912. Colvin was on friendly terms with many eminent artists and writers of the day. It is likely that he and Pater met in 1869, when they were elected to the New (later the Savile) Club, whose members included James Bryce, John Morley, and Pater's friends Ingram Bywater* and Simeon Solomon.* Pater reviewed Colvin's *Children in Italian and English Design*, in the *Academy* (July 1872) (see *CW* v), and Colvin very likely wrote the unsigned, appreciative notice of *Studies in the History of* *the Renaissance* for the *Pall Mall Gazette*, 1 March 1873. In later years, his relations with Pater cooled; there is no mention of Pater in Colvin's *Memories and Notes of Persons and Places, 1852-1912* (1921).

CRAIK, GEORGE LILLIE (1837-1905), who studied accounting at Glasgow University, joined Macmillan and Co. as a partner in 1865, the year he married Dinah Maria Mulock (1826-87), the author of *John Halifax, Gentleman* (1857) and many books for children. Craik became known as Alexander Macmillan's right-hand man, an administrator 'full of energy and character'. With a refined taste in literature, his special bent lay in poetry; he was devoted to the poetry of William Wordsworth and Alfred, Lord Tennyson. Craik joined Stopford Brooke and others in a scheme to preserve Wordsworth's house (Dove Cottage, Grasmere) as a kind of museum, filled with memorials of the poet.

DANIEL, (CHARLES) HENRY OLIVE (1836-1919), printer and college administrator, operated the Daniel Press, starting as a child at Frome, Somerset, 1845-58, and then at Oxford, 1874-1919. Daniel studied at Worcester College, Oxford, 1854-8, and served Worcester as Fellow, 1863-1903, Tutor, 1865-75, Proctor, 1873-4, Bursar, 1870-1903, and Provost, 1903-19. He was chiefly responsible for the decoration of the college chapel and hall, carried out from the designs of William Burges. In 1878 he married his cousin Emily Crabb Olive (1852-1933), bookbinder and illustrator, who helped him run the Daniel Press from Worcester. Daniel exerted considerable influence at Oxford as printer, largely because of his adoption in 1876 of the Fell type that had lain unused at the Clarendon Press for 150 years. One of the most interesting productions of the Daniel Press was *The Garland of Rachel* (1881), a celebration in verse of the first birthday of the Daniels' daughter Rachel, featuring works by Robert Bridges, Lewis Carroll, Austin Dobson, Edmund Gosse,* and Andrew Lang; Emily Daniel contributed capital letters and other ornamental designs. Some of Daniel's books were reprints of *Desiderii Erasmi colloquia duo* (1880), William Blake's *Songs* (1885) and *Songs of Innocence* (1893), and *Odes, Sonnets, and Lyrics of John Keats* (1895). Other books are by his contemporaries and friends, particularly the plays and poems of Bridges (fifteen printed between 1883 and 1903). In June 1894 the press published a special edition of Pater's *An Imaginary Portrait: The Child in the House* for a fundraising event (see Appendix, *CW* iii).

DILKE, LADY EMILIA, née EMILY FRANCIS STRONG (1840-1904), art historian, critic, and trade unionist, published anonymously and as Mrs Mark Pattison, E. F. S. Pattison, and (after 1885) Emilia Dilke. She studied

French, German, Greek, and Latin with private tutors. Beginning in 1858, she attended the South Kensington School of Art until she married, in September 1861, the Revd Mark Pattison* (1813-84), a formidable academic who had recently become the Rector of Oxford's Lincoln College. He encouraged her to study the works of cultural historian Jacob Burckhardt (1818-97) and Positivist philosopher Auguste Comte (1798-1867); and he advised her to choose a subject that captivated her and to become an 'authority' in it. She chose as her subject the arts in France and as her approach, analyses of the social, economic, and political conditions under which the arts flourished. Cutting a striking figure with her irreverence and sharp wit, she wrote reviews of art books; articles on art, archaeology, and politics; and books on *The Renaissance of Art in France* (1879), on Sir Frederic Leighton (1881), on Claude Lorrain (1884), on art in the modern state (1888), and on art in France in the eighteenth-century (in four vols, 1899-1902). From 1864, Dilke and Pater enjoyed a polite but cautious friendship. Pater attended a number of the acclaimed dinner parties hosted at Lincoln College by the Pattisons. In the *Westminster Review*, April 1873, she claimed that *Studies in the History of the Renaissance* failed to deliver an accurate account of the Renaissance because it lacked a scientific method. In the third edition of *The Renaissance* (1888), Pater referred to *The Renaissance of Art in France* as 'a work of great taste and real learning'. She favourably reviewed *Imaginary Portraits* in the *Athenaeum* (June 1887). After Mark Pattison died, she married Sir Charles Wentworth Dilke (1843-1911), a radical politician who had also studied at the South Kensington School of Art.

FIELD, MICHAEL, was the pseudonym for Katharine Harris Bradley (1846-1914) and her niece, Edith Emma Cooper (1862-1913), who lived together (from the late 1870s) and co-wrote (from 1884) more than thirty volumes of lyric poems and verse dramas published in beautifully designed limited editions. Robert Browning inadvertently revealed the joint identity of the women when he spoke publicly of Michael Field as his 'two Greek women', thereby calling attention to their commitment to the aesthetic grace of Greek lyric forms and to the ancient endorsement of same-sex relationships. Bradley and Cooper never achieved the fame they yearned for, in part because they spurned literary modernity in their choice of subjects, genres, and idioms. They admired Pater's writings immensely; on 11 June 1889 they sent him a copy of *Long Ago* (1889), hoping he would appreciate their expansion of the fragments of Sappho's poetry into complete lyrics. Pater acknowledged the gift in a letter dated 4 July [1889], praising the volume as the work of 'a true poet' who exuded 'Attic calm', and he invited

'Michael Field' to visit him. On 22 July 1889 Bradley and Cooper attended an 'at home' at 12 Earl's Terrace, and described Pater as a serious, kind man with 'constant kind [blue] eyes'. They expected that this meeting would lead to an intellectual relationship; however, Pater's enthusiasm for their work waned, and he avoided them: frequently, when they visited December 1889 through to February 1892, they found only the Pater sisters at home. A close friend, Charles Ricketts, described their relationship with Pater in these terms: 'Walter Pater till his death counted as a highly-prized acquaintance; his books not his actual personality had left their mark upon their habits in life and on their valuation of beauty in art and beauty in nature.' They declared their admiration for Pater in a poetic tribute, an 'imaginary portrait' called 'Walter Pater', which appeared in the *Academy*, 11 August 1894. Bradley and Cooper chronicled their life and work together in a journal entitled *Works and Days: From the Journal of Michael Field*, ed. T. Sturge Moore, 28 vols (1933).

GALTON, REVD ARTHUR HOWARD (1852–1921), a classicist, critic, and priest, was a cousin of the polymath Sir Francis Galton (1822–1911). After studying classics at Clare College, Cambridge, 1873–7, he converted to Roman Catholicism and was ordained a priest in 1880. He served as parish priest in Windermere, but he left the church six years later to attend New College, Oxford, 1886–90. He next settled in London, where he associated with such figures as Lionel Johnson,* Herbert Horne,* and Selwyn Image, and wrote articles on art and cultural topics for the *Academy* and the *Century Guild Hobby Horse*. From 1893 to 1898 he served as the private secretary to Sir Robert Duff, Governor of New South Wales, Australia. When he returned to Great Britain, he re-joined the Church of England, serving as the curate at Windermere, 1898–1901, Chaplain to the Bishop of Ripon, 1901–3, and curate at Edenham, Lincolnshire, 1904–21. Galton's publications include *Studies of Five Living Poets* (1884), *The Character and Times of Thomas Cromwell* (1887), *Two Essays upon Matthew Arnold, with Some of his Letters to the Author* (1897), and *Acer in Hostem* (1913). Very likely Galton, Johnson, and Pater met in 1887. Galton regarded Pater as 'a very dear friend', and Pater praised Galton in the footnote in 'Style' (*Appreciations*, *CW* vi). Galton wrote an affectionate portrait of Pater, 'the most learned' and possibly 'the most original scholar then living' in Oxford.

GOSSE, SIR EDMUND (1849–1928), poet and critic, memorialized his early life in the highly regarded biography *Father and Son* (1907). Gosse worked as an assistant in the British Museum's library, 1867–75, and later served as Librarian to the House of Lords, 1904–14. Friendship with

William Bell Scott (see letter, 30 April [1882]) and Ford Madox Brown led to the company of Pre-Raphaelite artists and such writers as Henry James, R. L. Stevenson, and Pater, whom he met in March 1872, likely in Bell Scott's studio. Gosse married the artist Ellen (Nellie) Epps (1850–1929), a former student of Ford Madox Brown who exhibited at the Grosvenor Gallery. Gosse's credentials as a critic were established with *Studies in the Literature of Northern Europe* (1879) and regular contributions to *Cornhill Magazine*, *Saturday Review*, *St James's Gazette*, *Century Magazine*, and *The Times* of London. He delivered the Lowell Lectures in Boston, Massachusetts, 1884–5 and the Clark Lectures at Trinity College, Cambridge, 1888. After his poetry and verse drama went unpraised, Gosse wrote successful biographies of his zoologist father P. H. Gosse, Coventry Patmore, and A. C. Swinburne.* His unwavering friendship with Pater lasted twenty-two years, with a steady exchange of visits, letters, and favourable reviews. Gosse wrote a memorial study of his friend for the *Contemporary Review* (December 1894) and published Pater's essay on 'Pascal' (see *CW* x). He also prepared for private circulation Pater's *Essays from 'The Guardian'* (1896), later included in the Library Edition of Pater's works. He supplied A. C. Benson,* but not Thomas Wright,* with first-hand reminiscences. Gosse took an active part in obtaining for Hester* and Clara* Pater a Civil List pension from the Crown. By 1916, however, the proceeds from the sale of Pater's books had begun to fall off so markedly that Hester, now alone and seventy-nine, found herself financially hard-pressed. Gosse secured an additional £50 for her pension.

GRANT DUFF, MOUNTSTUART ELPHINSTONE (1829–1906), politician, administrator, and author, studied at Balliol College, Oxford, 1847–50, a pupil of Benjamin Jowett* (they became close friends), and later attended the Inner Temple, 1850–4, but never practised law. Turning to politics, Grant Duff was elected to the House of Commons in 1857 as the Liberal MP for Elgin Burghs, Scotland (serving for twenty-four years). He also served as the Under-Secretary of State for India, 1868–74, Under-Secretary of State for the Colonies, 1880–1, and the Governor General of Madras, 1881–6. Upon his return to Great Britain, he retired from politics and devoted his time to the arts and sciences, serving as President of the Royal Geographical Society, 1889–93, and the Royal Historical Society, 1892–9. He entertained at his country home people in all branches of culture, including Matthew Arnold, John Bright, Benjamin Disraeli, and Henry James. His many books include *Studies in European Politics* (1886), *Ernest Renan: In Memoriam* (1893), and the fourteen volumes of *Notes from a Diary* (1897–1905), in which he provides portraits of the people he had met, with ten entries for Pater. For example, on a visit to Oxford 25–7 September 1875, he spent time with Ingram Bywater,* J. R. Green, Benjamin Jowett, Pater, and Henry Smith. On 26 June 1887, he recorded that 'Pater dined with us', mentioning that, so far, 3,000 copies of *Marius the Epicurean* had been sold. On 4 January 1891 he recorded that 'Pater spent the day with us' and that they went to a Catholic chapel, where Pater talked about the Mass and its 'wealth of suggestion'.

GRAY, JOHN MILLER (1850–94), art critic, antiquarian, and administrator, was the first curator of the Scottish National Portrait Gallery. Miller left school early because his father (a shawl manufacturer) had been ruined by the failure of the Western Bank of Scotland; in 1866 he apprenticed as a clerk in the Bank of Scotland, while devoting his leisure time to books about art, with a view to making portraiture his specialty; during his vacations, he travelled to art galleries and historic churches in London and Paris. Modelling his critical style on Pater's aesthetic criticism, Gray contributed notices of exhibitions and reviews of books to the leading periodicals in Edinburgh and London, starting in 1872 with the *Edinburgh Courant*. A brilliant conversationalist, he expanded his circle of acquaintances to include Robert Browning, Edward Burne-Jones, William Bell Scott, and Frederick Wedmore. Officials who were establishing the Scottish National Portrait Gallery appointed Gray the director (1884–90) because they were impressed with his criticism, and because Pater and others provided testimonials expressing their high regard for Gray's accomplishments. His book-length publications include *David Scott, R.S.A., and his Works* (1884) and *James and William Tassie* (1894). Gray and Pater met in Oxford on 1 June 1878; Gray sent Pater samples of his art criticism, and Pater sent him short critiques of these samples. Gray reviewed 'The Child in the House' in the *Academy*, August 1878 (see *CW* iii), and wrote the enthusiastic reviews of *Marius the Epicurean* that appeared in the *Academy* and *Edinburgh Courant*.

GREEN, CHARLOTTE SYMONDS (1842–1929), was an educational reformer and nurse who assisted in the preparation of two learned men's writings. She was born in Bristol, the daughter of a successful physician and the sister of John Addington Symonds; in 1871 she married her brother's friend Thomas Hill Green (1836–82), the Balliol philosopher. Together they championed the causes of better education for young people and women's rights for a university education (she worked with Clara Pater* on several fundraising and reform campaigns). In the early 1870s, the Greens, Mary and T. Humphry Ward,* and Pater and his sisters were friends and neighbours on Bradmore Road, Oxford. After Thomas Green's death in 1882, Charlotte helped R. L. Nettleship to assemble her husband's writings. She then trained as a nurse in Oxford and London (Benjamin Jowett* arranged for her to work with Florence Nightingale). She helped Jowett in his later years to organize his papers. She nursed Jowett twice, and Pater in the summer of 1894. After Pater's death, she assisted Clara and Hester.* From the late 1880s onwards, Charlotte was personally and financially supportive of Somerville College and St Anne's College. She served as a member of Somerville Council in 1884 and as Vice-President from 1908 to 1926, when she became a life member. She was awarded the degree of MA *honoris causa* in 1921, the year after Oxford opened its degrees to women.

GROVE, SIR GEORGE (1820–1900), made his mark as a civil engineer and then as a musicologist and editor. Grove became secretary to the Society of Arts in 1850 and secretary to the Crystal Palace Company in 1852. From 1856 to 1896, he wrote analytical programme notes for the Crystal Palace concerts. He edited *Macmillan's Magazine* from May 1866 to April 1883, printing Pater's 'Romanticism' and 'The Child in the House'. He also served as the first director of the Royal College of Music, 1883–94, and published the *Dictionary of Music and Musicians*, 4 vols (1878–89), a classic still known as the 'Grove' and still reprinted. He was knighted in 1883. His analyses of Beethoven's symphonies appeared in book form in 1896.

HARDINGE, WILLIAM MONEY (1854–1916), poet and novelist, studied classics at Balliol College, Oxford, 1873–6. By all accounts he enjoyed shocking people, advertising his homosexuality in words and deeds. Early in 1874 Hardinge and Pater developed a close relationship, which was brought to the attention of Benjamin Jowett,* then Master of Balliol. According to some reports, W. H. Mallock,* another Balliol undergraduate and Hardinge's friend, gave Jowett several letters that Pater had written to Hardinge, allegedly signed 'Yours lovingly'. Jowett interviewed both parties: loath to ruin the life of a talented young man, he urged Hardinge to spend the next nine months at home under his father's supervision. Yet Jowett excoriated Pater, threatening to make the letters public if ever Pater stood for a university office. Pater and Hardinge were caricatured as Mr Rose the aesthete and Robert Leslie, respectively, in Mallock's satirical novel, *The New Republic* (1877). Hardinge left Oxford in 1876, the year he won the Newdigate Prize for a poem entitled 'Troy'; in the 1880s he penned romantic novels. Violet Paget* recalls meeting Hardinge when she dined with the Paters on 22 July 1886 (see *VLL*, 224).

HARRIS, JAMES FRANK THOMAS (1856–1931), Irish-American journalist, editor, and publisher, was born in Galway, Ireland, the son of Welsh parents. Harris migrated to the United States in 1871, working his way from New York City to Lawrence, Kansas, where he studied law, 1874–5, at the University of Kansas. Disliking the legal profession, he travelled to Europe, determined to be a scholar, attending classes in language and literature at Heidelberg, Berlin, and Göttingen. In 1882 he settled in London as a journalist; he served as editor of the *Evening News*, 1883–6, the *Fortnightly Review*, 1886–94, and the *Saturday Review*, 1894–8, before writing fiction (*The Bomb*, 1908), biographical sketches (*Contemporary Portraits*, 1915; 1919), full-scale biographies of Shakespeare (1909), Oscar Wilde* (1916), and George Bernard Shaw (1931), and a multi-volume autobiography, *My Life and Loves* (1922–7). Four works by Pater appeared in the *Fortnightly Review* while Harris was editor. Harris and Pater probably met in February or March 1886, at the behest of Oscar Wilde, a mutual friend. Harris mentions Pater seven times in *My Life and Loves*; his biographical sketch, 'Walter Pater', in the second series of *Contemporary Portraits* (1919), is not a vivid picture of their relationship. Harris claims that he and Pater dined a dozen times or more together (with such guests as George Meredith and Wilde) before Pater invited him to tea and then much later to dinner with his sisters. Harris attended Pater's lecture on Prosper Mérimée at the London Institute, 24 November 1890.

HOPKINS, S.J., GERARD MANLEY (1844–89), poet and priest, achieved fame posthumously. While he studied classics at Balliol College, Oxford, 1863–7, he met eminent 'high' Anglican churchmen such as Edward Pusey and Henry Parry Liddon,* and forged a friendship with Robert Bridges (who proved to be vital to the development of his poetry). Benjamin Jowett* was his principal tutor. Pater 'coached' Hopkins from April 1866 to June 1867 (the essays Hopkins wrote for Pater have been published). Caught up in the aftermath of the Oxford Movement, Hopkins converted to Roman Catholicism in 1866. From September 1867 to April 1868, Hopkins taught at John Henry Newman's school for Catholic boys in Birmingham, and it was there that he developed his theory of 'inscape' and 'instress'. In June 1868 he lunched with Pater in London and visited the studio of Simeon Solomon.* In September 1868 Hopkins joined the Society of Jesus. During the first seven years of his Jesuit training, he did not write poetry; however, a shipwreck that claimed the lives of five Franciscan nuns inspired 'The Wreck of the Deutschland' (1876). Thereafter, his poems in 'sprung rhythm' conveyed his profound attachment to nature's 'pied beauty' and its Creator. When he served at

St Aloysius's Church, Oxford, from December 1878 to October 1879, Hopkins dined with Pater several times. He helped to establish the Oxford University Catholic Society in 1878; members included Hartwell Grissell (see Pater's letter to Grissell). Hopkins lived in various communities in England and Scotland as parish priest and taught classics at Stonyhurst College, Lancashire, 1882–4; in 1884, he was transferred to Dublin to teach classics at University College and serve as a Fellow of the Royal University of Ireland. He died of typhoid. Bridges, who became Poet Laureate in 1913, edited the first volume of Hopkins's poetry in 1918.

HORNE, HERBERT PERCY (1864–1916), poet, architect, art historian, and collector, played an important role in the development of the Arts and Crafts Movement. Horne articled with a relative, George Vigers, a London architect; in the early 1880s, he joined Arthur H. Mackmurdo (1851–1942), an architect, designer, and social reformer who was starting his own studio. Inspired by John Ruskin and William Morris, Mackmurdo, Horne, and Selwyn Image (1849–1930), a designer, established the Century Guild of Artists for the purpose of uniting the arts. Taking their cue from Morris and Co. (1861–1940), members of the Guild designed buildings and produced home furnishings such as wallpapers, fabrics, metal-work, stained glass, and furniture. Horne helped to launch the *Century Guild Hobby Horse*, an arts and literature periodical, 1884–94; he edited the journal from 1886 to 1891, and its successor, the *Hobby Horse*, from 1893 to 1894, and also contributed poetry and articles, especially on the Renaissance and seventeenth-century English culture. (Reading Pater's *The Renaissance* helped Horne to formulate his own aesthetic theories and practices.) After dissolving the partnership with Mackmurdo in 1890, Horne opened his own architectural business, designing buildings in a *quattrocento* style. After the demise of the *Hobby Horse* in 1894, he abandoned poetry, architecture, and decorative work, and concentrated on antiquarian interests, writing for such periodicals as the *Saturday Review*. In 1904, he settled in Florence permanently, developing his skills as an art dealer (sometimes partnering with Roger Fry and Bernard Berenson). Pater and Horne met in the 1880s. Horne dedicated his principal art-historical work, *Alessandro Filipepi, commonly called Sandro Botticelli, Painter of Florence* (1908), to Pater.

JOHNSON, LIONEL PIGOT (1867–1902), poet and critic, attended New College, Oxford, 1886–90; he was tutored and strongly influenced by Pater. When he graduated in 1890, he joined Herbert Horne,* Selwyn Image, and Arthur Mackmurdo, members of the Century Guild, in London. His health was undermined by alcohol and his pattern of working or walking through the night and sleeping late into the day. In 1891 he converted to the Roman Catholic faith and introduced Oscar Wilde* to Lord Alfred Douglas. His own homosexuality was strictly repressed. With Ernest Dowson, Arthur Symons,* and W. B. Yeats, Johnson was involved in the Rhymers' Club and became a regular contributor to the *Academy*, the *Anti-Jacobin*, and the *Daily Chronicle*, and wrote occasionally for the *Pageant*, the *Savoy*, the *Speaker*, and the *Spectator*. His first book, *The Art of Thomas Hardy* (1894), was among the first to consider the novel seriously as an art form. Johnson's poetic reputation was confirmed by his *Poems* in 1895; *Ireland, with Other Poems* (1897) explores his triad of passions: Catholicism, classicism, and Celtic culture. His obituary of Pater for the *Fortnightly Review*, September 1894, pays homage in the periodical in which so many of Pater's ground-breaking essays had been published. Johnson assisted Charles Shadwell* in sifting through Pater's literary remains and advised him in the preparation of three posthumous volumes he published.

JOWETT, BENJAMIN (1817–93), classical scholar, theologian, and translator, was one of the great educators of the Victorian era and one of the major reformers at Oxford. Jowett attended Oxford's Balliol College, 1836–9, and became Fellow (1838) and Tutor (1842) of the college. He became an Anglican priest in 1845. He soon earned acclaim as a teacher and scholar. During the late 1840s he studied the works of G. W. F. Hegel and Plato. With A. P. Stanley, a close friend, he worked on a series of commentaries on the epistles of St Paul; Jowett's ensuing volume (1855) offended conservative theologians and philologists. In 1850, Jowett and Stanley contributed to the government's Royal Commission on reforming the universities of Oxford and Cambridge. Jowett recommended measures such as opening fellowships to competition, improving education in the colleges, abolishing tests of orthodoxy, and enabling poorer students to attend the university. Despite opposition fuelled by his unorthodox religious views, in 1855 Jowett was appointed Regius Professor of Greek. He tried to clarify his religious views in 'On the Interpretation of Scripture', his article for *Essays and Reviews* (1860), one of the most controversial books in the country. The authors maintained that it was time to subject the Bible to scientific enquiry and critical scholarship. The book was condemned by a meeting of bishops in 1861 and by the Synod of the Church of England in 1864. Jowett enjoyed tutoring undergraduates, coaching, for example, Pater and Ingram Bywater* during Lent term 1861. Jowett was elected Master of Balliol in 1870 and later served as Vice-Chancellor of the University, 1882–6. His many publications include translations of the dialogues of Plato, of Aristotle's *Politics*, and of Thucydides. A number of Jowett's sermons appeared posthumously, including *College Sermons*, ed. W. H. Freemantle (1895). His candid opinions about life at Balliol and in Oxford are best expressed in letters he wrote to his close friend Florence Nightingale (*Dear Miss Nightingale: A Selection of Benjamin Jowett's Letters to Florence Nightingale 1860–1893*, 1987).

LEE, VERNON, see PAGET, VIOLET

LEE-HAMILTON, JACOB EUGENE (1845–1907), poet and novelist, was the older half-brother of Violet Paget* (who wrote under the pseudonym Vernon Lee). Lee-Hamilton read modern languages at Oriel College, Oxford, 1864–6, but left university without taking a degree. For the next two years, he spent term-time in Oxford (writing home with news of his academic activities and suggesting projects that would stimulate his half-sister's intellectual development) and summer with his family at the watering-holes at Baden, Brussels, and Nice. He entered the British diplomatic service in 1869 and served in embassies in Paris and Lisbon. In 1875 he suffered a breakdown in health and resigned; for the next twenty years a painful spinal complaint made any form of active life impossible. The Paget family settled in Florence, where his mother and his half-sister looked after him. Confined to bed, he wrote verse, employing his half-sister as his amanuensis, and achieved success with his third volume, *The New Medusa, and Other Poems* (1882). (Violet Paget was instrumental in negotiating the publication of his books.) In a letter to Paget dated 18 November [1882], Pater acknowledged that he liked the book very much. Lee-Hamilton's room became a centre of cosmopolitan society; visitors included American, British, French, and Italian authors. Under the care of Dr Erb, a Heidelberg-based doctor, his health improved in 1893; he regained mobility and returned to ordinary life. Lee-Hamilton travelled to the United States in 1898, where he visited Edith Wharton, and married Annie E. Holdsworth (1860–1917), an Anglo-Caribbean novelist and feminist, and settled in an Italian villa.

LIDDON, HENRY PARRY (1829–90), was one of the last great Victorian pulpit preachers of the Church of England. Liddon secured a Studentship to Christ Church, Oxford, 1846–50, where he was mentored by two leaders of the Oxford (or Tractarian) Movement (1833–45), John Keble (1792–1866), clergyman and poet, and Edward Bouverie Pusey (1800–82), theologian. Liddon was ordained a priest in 1853. Parish work proved difficult, due to his health; consequently, he pursued situations emphasizing mental effort. He served as Vice-Principal of the new theological college at

Cuddesden, Oxfordshire, 1854–9, and Vice-Principal of St Edmund Hall, Oxford, 1859–62. At the Hall he delivered a series of Sunday evening lectures on the New Testament (1859–69), which attracted many undergraduates, including Gerard Manley Hopkins.* To these lectures he brought his gifts of spiritual earnestness, theological knowledge, and rhetorical skill. Liddon championed the Tractarian principles of his mentors and challenged the Broad Church school espoused by such figures as Benjamin Jowett.* Illness forced Liddon to resign from St Edmund Hall; he then took rooms at Christ Church, assuming responsibility for the pastoral care of undergraduates. In 1866, his Bampton Lectures, devoted to the divinity of Christ, increased his fame as a preacher of eloquence, passion, and intelligence. He served as a canon at St Paul's Cathedral, 1870–90, Ireland Professor of Exegesis of Holy Scripture, Oxford, 1870–82, and select preacher at Oxford, 1863, 1870, 1877, and 1884. Mary Arnold Ward* described Liddon as 'the arch wire-puller and ecclesiastical intriguer in University forces' with 'perfect rhetoric'. Liddon published fourteen volumes of his sermons, and biographies of W. K. Hamilton, the Bishop of Salisbury (1869), and Pusey (1893–97).

MACCOLL, DUGALD SUTHERLAND (1859–1948), Scottish art critic, author, and painter, studied at London University and Lincoln College, Oxford, 1876–84, earning the Newdigate poetry prize for 'The Fall of Carthage' in 1882. At this time his cultural heroes were Matthew Arnold, John Ruskin, and Walter Pater. During 1887–9 MacColl visited the major galleries of Europe to prepare for a career in art. From 1890–6 he served as art critic for the *Spectator*, championing the work of the Impressionists. After retiring for a year from the *Spectator* to paint watercolours, he returned to journalism in 1896. Frank Harris* asked him to be a regular contributor to the *Saturday Review*, a position he kept until 1906. From 1901 to 1905 he served as editor of the *Architectural Review*. He was Keeper of the Tate Gallery, 1906–11, and of the Wallace Collection, 1911–24. His publications include *Nineteenth Century Art* (1902) and *Confessions of a Keeper and Other Papers* (1931). MacColl met Pater when he was an undergraduate at Lincoln College; he attended Pater's lectures on Plato's *Republic* at Brasenose. As one of the co-founders and editors of the *Oxford Magazine*, he solicited at least one contribution from Pater.

MACMILLAN AND CO., the eminent publishing house, was founded in 1843 by DANIEL MACMILLAN (1813–57) and his brother ALEXANDER MACMILLAN (1818–96). Daniel apprenticed in the bookselling trade in Irvine, Glasgow, Cambridge, and London. After working as a teacher, clerk, and sailor, Alexander joined his brother in London in 1839. Three years later, they launched their own bookselling and publishing business in Cambridge, but sold it within a year. By 1845, however, Macmillan, Barclay, and Macmillan (their new venture) was flourishing in Cambridge; in addition to providing academic books, they developed a literary list including Charles Kingsley (1855), Thomas Hughes (1859), Francis Turner Palgrave (1861), Christina Rossetti (1862), Matthew Arnold (1865), Lewis Carroll (1865), Walter Pater (1872), Henry James (1879), Thomas Hardy (1886), and Alfred Tennyson (1884). Daniel married Frances Orridge in 1850; their two sons, Frederick* and Maurice,* became partners in the firm. Alexander married Caroline Brimley in 1851; they had five children, including Malcolm* and George.* Caroline Macmillan died in 1871; Alexander married Jeanne Barbe Pignatel in 1872 and they had two children. Alexander launched *Macmillan's Magazine* in 1859. The firm moved its headquarters to London in 1863; a nephew, Robert Bowes,* managed the book retailing business in Cambridge (which became Macmillan and Bowes). George Lillie Craik* became a partner in 1865; he supervised the firm's financial affairs. In 1869, Macmillan and Co. opened a New York City office under the management of George Brett.* Pater first met Alexander Macmillan in June 1872; his correspondence with the firm spans twenty-two years. After Pater's death in August 1894, the Macmillans were very solicitous of his sisters Clara* and Hester.*

MACMILLAN, FREDERICK ORRIDGE (1851–1936), the eldest son of Frances and Daniel Macmillan* and the father of a future prime minister, Harold Macmillan, trained at the headquarters of the firm at Cambridge and at its branch in New York. In 1874 Frederick married Georgina Elizabeth Warrin, of Newtown, Long Island, and in 1876 returned to England as a partner, one of the few publishers who had first-hand knowledge of all the technical features of the profession. A man of taste and sound judgement, he followed his uncle's lead in building up a world-wide organization with branches in Australia, Canada, and India. He played a leading role in establishing the 'net book agreement' in 1890 and in framing the Copyright Act of 1911. Macmillan also served as President of the Publishers' Association in 1900, 1911, and 1912. He was interested not only in the Booksellers' Provident Institution, of which he was a trustee, and the Royal Literary Fund, of which he was a council member, but also in the welfare of the National Hospital for Paralysis, of which he was chair of the board. He was knighted in 1909.

MACMILLAN, GEORGE AUGUSTIN (1855–1936), the second son of Caroline and Alexander Macmillan,* attended Eton, 1868–73. With Oscar Wilde,* George travelled to Greece in spring 1877 in the company of

J. P. Mahaffy (1839–1919), Professor of Ancient History at Trinity College, Dublin. George became a partner in the firm in 1879, taking a special interest in classical studies. Together with Mahaffy and Revd A. H. Sayce (1845–1933), Oxford's Professor of Assyriology, George played an important role in establishing the Society for the Promotion of Hellenic Studies (1879); he also helped to establish (1886) the British School of Archaeology at Athens. In 1879 he married Margaret Helen Lucas; the couple had one son and one daughter.

MACMILLAN, MALCOLM KINGSLEY (1852–89), the eldest son of Caroline and Alexander Macmillan,* studied classics at Balliol College, Oxford, 1875–9. Malcolm joined the firm in the early 1870s as a trainee but owing to poor health played little part in its activities. Instead, he spent much of his time studying and travelling. He is thought to be the author of *Dragonet the Jester*, a novel about the Fens (a marshy region of eastern England) set during the seventeenth century, which appeared under the Macmillan imprint in 1886. Malcolm disappeared (and was presumed to have died) walking on Mount Olympus in July 1889.

MACMILLAN, MAURICE CRAWFORD (1853–1936), the second son of Frances and Daniel Macmillan,* attended Christ's College, Cambridge, 1871–5. He served as a classics master at St Paul's School from 1877 to 1883, and produced an educational manual, *First Latin Grammar* (1879), which appeared under the Macmillan imprint. He joined the family business as a partner in 1883, assuming responsibility for the development of the firm's educational business, at home and abroad; he toured India, Australia, and Egypt. He put into practice some of the ideas that had been stirring in Alexander's head for forty years, taking a position in 1889 as an educational agent for India and opening in 1901 a branch in Bombay.

MADAN, FALCONER (1851–1935), librarian and bibliographer, attended Brasenose College, Oxford, 1870–5, and subsequently served as Lecturer (1875–9) and Fellow (1876–80 and 1889–1912) of the college and as the university's Lecturer in Mediaeval Paleography, 1889–1913. He was the Sandars Reader in Bibliography at Cambridge from 1909. Madan made his mark as Sub-Librarian of the Bodleian Library, 1880–1912, where he undertook the task of cataloguing manuscripts, and succeeded E. W. B. Nicholson as Librarian, 1912–19. His publications include *Oxford Books: A Bibliography of Printed Works relating to the University and City of Oxford or Printed or Published there, with Appendixes, Annals, and Illustrations*, 2 vols (1912), *The Daniel Press: Memorials of C. H. O. Daniel with a Bibliography of the Press, 1845–1919* (1921), *Oxford outside the*

Guide-Books (1923), and *A Handbook of the Literature of C. L. Dodgson* (1931). Contemporaries regarded Madan, a 'scholar of the old school', as one the 'personalities' of the university. He and Pater were close friends during the latter's final years.

MALLOCK, WILLIAM HURRELL (1849–1923), a political and religious polemicist, grew up in Devonshire, a member of the landed gentry. He attended Balliol College, 1869–74, with a view to entering the Diplomatic Service. Instead, he developed a passion for poetry, and won the Newdigate Prize in 1871. Disillusioned with the Oxford liberalism of Benjamin Jowett* and Pater in particular, he set out to produce an account of his intellectual experiences, modelling his narrative on the methods employed by Thomas Love Peacock among others. Mallock published *The New Republic* in *Belgravia*, June to December 1876, and then in book form (in two volumes) in March 1877. His satirical formula is simple enough: a number of eminent Victorians collect at a country house, with Mr Luke standing in as Matthew Arnold; Donald Gordon, Thomas Carlyle; Dr Jenkinson, Benjamin Jowett; Mr Rose, Pater; Lady Grace, Emilia Pattison.* While these figures discuss the religious and social problems of the day, Mallock provides thinly veiled parodies of their opinions, manners, and behaviour. Mr Rose reveals a fondness for such classical figures and texts as Socrates and the *Phaedrus*, by which Mallock suggests the latter's pagan sexual preferences, and the ethos of Greek *paiderastia*. The narrative also features the antipathy that Dr Jenkinson and Mr Rose feel for one another. Thomas Wright maintained that Mallock and Pater met in Oxford, possibly at a salon at Lincoln College, hosted by Emilia and Mark Pattison.* Pater admired the young writer's cleverness but considered the Rose caricature to be unscrupulous. A prolific writer, Mallock produced satirical works of fiction and serious non-fiction in which he defended conservative social, religious, political, and economic theories and practices; his autobiography, *Memoirs of Life and Literature*, was published in 1920.

MCQUEEN, JOHN RAINIER (1840–1912), known familiarly as René, had a privileged upbringing in a wealthy military family. He and Pater met at the King's School, Canterbury; together with Henry Dombrain, they were close friends from 1855 to 1858. All three men attended Oxford, 1858–62, but the friendship between McQueen and Pater ended before graduation: when Pater, despite religious doubts, suggested he would seek ordination as a means of acquiring an academic position, McQueen, an ardent Anglican, reported him to the Bishop of London, Revd Archibald Tait. McQueen studied law and history at Oxford, but after graduation he did not pursue a career. In 1865, he moved to Yell, one of the northern Shetland islands, where he established a pseudo-feudal lairdship for two decades and served as a justice of the peace. In 1872, he married a distant cousin, Mary Rainier; they separated several years later. In 1887, McQueen returned to Chailey, in east Sussex, to live in his ancestral home. McQueen was a major source for Pater biographer Thomas Wright.*

MOORE, GEORGE AUGUSTUS (1852–1933), Anglo-Irish poet, playwright, critic, and novelist, has been described as a 'literary chameleon'. Initially, Moore settled in Paris in 1873 to study painting. Three years later, when he resolved to become a writer, he studied contemporary French literature and met artists and writers at cafés. His first volumes of poetry, *Flowers of Passion* (1878) and *Pagan Poems* (1881), were meant to shock. Later he presented himself as a playwright and then as a critic, 1881–93, promoting Impressionism in painting (Édouard Manet and Edgar Degas) and Naturalism in fiction (Émile Zola). Many of these articles were reprinted as *Modern Painting* (1893), which Pater reviewed favourably (see *CW* vi). Moore next turned to story-telling, wanting to produce 'aesthetic' novels free of sentimentalizing and moralizing. His works include *A Modern Lover* (1883) and *Esther Waters* (1894). During the Irish literary revival he was active as stage director, playwright, and short-story writer. Moore and Pater met in June 1885 at the home of author A. Mary F. Robinson, a neighbour who lived at 10 Earl's Terrace, Kensington (*VLL*, 123). Moore's social aggressiveness made Pater uneasy; they did not become friends. The two were estranged after the publication of *Confessions of a Young Man* (1888), a copy of which was sent to Pater with a request that he review the work. Pater, however, found much of it too provocative (see letter of 4 March 1888). Nonetheless, Moore regarded Pater as 'the greatest master of English prose'.

MORLEY, JOHN, 1st VISCOUNT MORLEY OF BLACKBURN (1838–1923), journalist, biographer, and politician, attended Lincoln College, Oxford, 1856–9, planning to become a clergyman. Instead, he abandoned orthodox Christianity, settled in London to take up the law, but eventually resolved to make his way as a writer. Morley contributed to such periodicals as the *Leader* and the *Saturday Review*, and edited the *Fortnightly Review*, 1867–82. The eminent liberal authors he published included Matthew Arnold, Frederic Harrison, J. S. Mill, Pater, Herbert Spencer, Leslie Stephen, and A. C. Swinburne.* During the early 1880s, Morley edited the *Pall Mall Gazette* and *Macmillan's Magazine*. For many years, he also edited the 'English Men of Letters' series for Macmillan. From 1883 to 1895 Morley served as the Liberal MP for Newcastle-upon-Tyne; in Gladstone's government he supported Home Rule and served as Chief Secretary for Ireland, 1886 and 1892–5, and Secretary of State for India, 1905–10 and 1911. In 1908 he moved to the House of Lords as Viscount Morley of Blackburn, and from 1910 to 1914 served as Lord President of the Council (he resigned to protest Great Britain's involvement in the First World War). A prolific writer, Morley produced biographies of Edmund Burke (1867), Voltaire (1872), Jean-Jacques Rousseau (1873), and W. E. Gladstone (1903). Morley and Pater met late in the 1860s, but little is known about their friendship. As editor of the *Fortnightly Review*, Morley published thirteen essays by Pater (see *CW* v and vi); in his favourable review of *Studies in the History of the Renaissance* (1873), he calls attention to the aesthetic movement as a cultural phenomenon.

MOULTON, ELLEN LOUISE CHANDLER (1835–1908), American poet, story-teller, and critic, was home-schooled in Pomfret, Connecticut; at Pomfret's Christ Church School her classmates included J. M. Whistler,* a life-long friend. She was fourteen when she published her first poem. At the age of eighteen, she published a collection of stories and verse, *This, That, and the Other* (1854), which sold 20,000 copies. In 1855 she married William Moulton, the Boston publisher. Her salon in Boston included leading artists, musicians, and writers such as J. G. Whittier, H. W. Longfellow, and Oliver Wendell Holmes. Her publications include novels, children's stories, poetry, and critiques of the American literary scene for the *New York Tribune*, 1870–6, and the *Boston Herald*, 1886–92. From 1876 Moulton divided her time between Boston and London, where her salon included Edmund Gosse,* A. Mary F. Robinson, Olive Schreiner, William Sharp,* A. C. Swinburne,* Whistler, and Oscar Wilde.* Moulton and Pater may have met late in 1888 or early in 1889, possibly at the home of A. Mary F. Robinson. Moulton recalled having lunch with Pater in 1889, and on that occasion met Gabriel Sarrazin, the French critic.

OTTLEY, MARY KAY, *née* ALEXANDER (May) (1872–1939), teacher and author, attended Somerville College, Oxford, 1891–4. During the years 1885–94 Clara Pater* served as Tutor and Vice-Principal of the college; the two became close friends. Ottley taught English literature and history in public and private schools and wrote for such magazines as *Hearth and Home*, the *World of Dress*, and *Myra's Journal*. As 'Deborah Primrose', the name of the clergyman's wife in Oliver Goldsmith's *Vicar of Wakefield* (1766), Ottley published *A Modern Boetia: Pictures from Life in a Country Parish* (1904) and *Beauty of Figure: How to Acquire and Retain It by Means of Easy and Practical Home Exercises* (1905). In 1897 she married the Revd Robert Ottley (1856–1933), a theologian, who had attended the King's

School, Canterbury, 1873-7, and Pembroke College, Oxford, 1877-80. The couple had five daughters. Robert served as Student and Tutor of Christ Church, Oxford, 1879-86; Regius Professor of Moral and Pastoral Theology at Oxford, 1903; and Canon of Christ Church, 1903. He also served as Anniversary Preacher at the King's School on Annual Speech Day, 30 July 1891, when Pater visited the school. In 1922 May inherited Hester Pater's entire estate, including Walter's autograph manuscripts and books. After her death, the Pater materials were inherited by her daughter, Constance Mary Ottley (1898-1981), a surgeon. Ottley recorded her recollections of the Paters in the preface to her 1931 edition of 'Imaginary Portraits. II. An English Poet. By Walter Pater' in the *Fortnightly Review* (see *CW* iii).

PAGET, VIOLET (*pseud.* VERNON LEE; 1856-1935), art historian, short-story writer, critic, and travel writer, grew up (along with her half-brother, Eugene Lee-Hamilton*) in a peripatetic blended family; they spent spring and summer in northern Europe (Paris) and autumn and winter in southern Europe (Rome). Paget was fluent in English, German, French, and Italian. She spent most of her adult life in Florence, making sojourns in England. Her first book, *Studies of the Eighteenth Century in Italy* (1880), yielded invitations to literary and artistic circles when she visited London in 1881; admirers included Robert Browning, Henry James, and Pater. Throughout the 1880s and the 1890s she published supernatural and historical short fiction, as well as essays on religious belief, aesthetics, and literary criticism. Her satirical novel *Miss Brown* (1884) contains thinly disguised caricatures of leading London artistic and literary figures (and ruined some friendships). With Clementina (Kit) Anstruther-Thomson (1857-1921), the Scottish painter, she undertook practical experiments to document physiological responses to art, while also studying the latest books on artistic perception in the fields of psychology and physiology. Their co-authored study, *Beauty and Ugliness and Other Studies in Psychological Aesthetics* (1912), marked a new aesthetics of empathy. Lee's *The Handling of Words and Other Studies in Literary Psychology* (1923) looked ahead to the 'new criticism', while *Music and its Lovers: An Empirical Study of Emotional and Imaginative Responses to Music* (1932) introduced terminology and perspectives from the visual arts into the aesthetics of music. She published seven collections of travel essays, from *Limbo and other Essays* (1897) to *The Golden Keys and other Essays on the Genius Loci* (1925). Paget and Pater met at a dinner party in Oxford hosted by Mary* and Humphry Ward* on 18 July 1881. Paget attended a dinner party given by the Paters two days later; the guests included Falconer

Madan* and Mary and Mabel Robinson. Some of the longest letters Pater wrote are to Paget; she stayed with Pater and his sisters several times. Paget found the Paters 'extremely hospitable and kind' and they found her extremely clever. She dedicated *Euphorion: Being Studies of the Antique and the Mediaeval in the Renaissance* (1884) to Pater, and often acknowledged his influence; Pater favourably reviewed her volume entitled *Juvenilia* (1887) in the *Pall Mall Gazette* (see *CW* v).

PATER, CLARA ANN (1841–1910), tutor and women's educational rights advocate, was the younger sister of Hester Pater,* William Pater,* and Walter Pater. Clara, who studied privately with tutors, was thirteen when she and her siblings were orphaned. Their aunt 'Bessie' Pater became principal caregiver. When Walter went to Oxford in 1858, Hester and Clara moved with their aunt to Germany, completing their education in a British 'colony' in Heidelberg, 1858–61, where Pater spent Christmas, and then in Dresden for part of 1862. For the most part the Pater sisters studied 'informally'; presumably they became proficient in German and advertised themselves as 'refined young women from England' in the local newspapers. After their aunt died in 1862, Clara and Hester returned to England; they lived in London with their cousin Foster Pater; in Sidmouth, 1865–7; and in Hastings, 1867–9. In London, Clara worked as a private German tutor; in the mid-1870s, she studied Latin and Greek. In 1873, Clara took up the cause of women's higher education at Oxford, serving first as a member of the Lectures for Women Committee and then the Association for Promoting Higher Education for Women. The latter, founded in 1879, lobbied for and established women's colleges (Somerville, St Anne's, and Lady Margaret Hall). Clara served Somerville in several capacities: as Deputy Principal in autumn 1880, Acting Principal 1885–6, Vice-Principal in 1886, Classics Tutor from 1885, and Resident Tutor for the West Building from 1887 until she resigned in June 1894; after Walter's death, she and Hester returned to London, where Clara continued to work as a private tutor. From 1898 to 1902 she was a Tutor in Greek and Latin at King's College, where her students included Virginia Stephen (Woolf). Apparently, the Pater sisters attended dinner parties in Bloomsbury as late as 1905. Clara Pater died of cancer on 9 August 1910, leaving an estate, comprised of manuscripts and books worth £50 1s 8d, to Hester.

PATER, HESTER MARIA (1837–1922), the sister of William Pater,* Walter Pater, and Clara Pater,* was in fact the centre of the Pater family; the sisters created a home for their brother, first in Oxford, 1869–85, in London, 1885–93, and again in Oxford, 1893–4, which they made comfortable and aesthetic in every respect. The three siblings were inseparable. Seemingly the more domestic of the two sisters, Hester acted as hostess; visitors commented on the excellence of her coffee and needlework. After Walter's death in 1894, Hester and Clara concentrated on safeguarding their brother's literary reputation (the trials of Oscar Wilde* generated an anxiety about all things aesthetic that extended into the new century). In addition, they faced a grim future financially, and so exploited opportunities to benefit financially from the sale of their brother's publications. The Civil List Pension of £50 each—obtained on their behalf by Edmund Gosse*—defrayed only a portion of their expenses. Taking their cue from literary advisers Charles Shadwell* and Gosse, they pursued a policy of printing nothing that might injure Walter's literary reputation, and attending to such matters as printing and binding. They denied biographer Thomas Wright* access to Walter's letters and instead sanctioned A. C. Benson's volume. Clara opposed the publication of any of Walter's manuscripts after the publication of 'Shadows of Events', chapter vi of *Gaston de Latour*, but Hester judged the unpublished manuscripts 'too interesting to be lost', and tried to publish a number of them. She died on 5 August 1922, leaving her estate (including books, manuscripts, and other items from the Pater household) to May Ottley.* Hester was buried beside her brother and sister in Holywell Cemetery, Oxford.

PATER, WILLIAM THOMPSON (1835–87), the oldest of the Pater siblings, remains a shadowy figure (Thomas Wright,* among other biographers, learned very little about William). William left school in 1851 to pursue office work, but changed directions and followed his father, uncle, and grandfather in becoming a doctor. He was admitted to the Royal College of Surgeons at Canterbury on 23 December 1857. According to reports, he was a handsome man. He served as Assistant Medical Officer at the County Lunatic Asylum at Fareham, Hampshire, from July 1865 to spring 1874, and as Medical Officer and Superintendent of the County Lunatic Asylum at Stafford from May 1874 until shortly before he died, a bachelor, in April 1887, leaving his possessions to Hester and Clara. Pater dedicated *Appreciations, with an Essay on Style* (1889) to William.

PATTISON, EMILY/EMILIA FRANCIS STRONG, see DILKE, EMILIA

PATTISON, MARK (1813–84), historian and biographer, was a major force in the modernization of the University of Oxford. After graduating from Oriel College in 1836, he fell under the spell of the Tractarians, John Henry Newman especially, and abandoned the Evangelicalism of his youth, but he stopped short of following Newman into the Church of Rome. He became a Fellow and Tutor of Lincoln College in 1839 and 1842 respectively, and was ordained an Anglican priest in 1843. He met his obligations with enthusiasm, determined to become an inspiring teacher and an influential writer. In 1855 he resigned his tutorship to concentrate on becoming a serious scholar, which meant travelling and studying Continental systems of higher education. Eventually he judged that a university should not be an ecclesiastical, socially exclusive institution devoted to teaching (understood as 'cramming'), but instead an institution devoted to learning (understood as 'developing the whole person'). Researching the lives of Isaac Casaubon (1559–1614) and Joseph Scaliger (1540–1609), scholars who had devoted their lives to recovering classical learning, became his life's work. Pattison earned acclaim as a scholar who produced important texts in such fields as the history of ideas. To *Essays and Reviews*, the controversial collection of essays by liberal Anglicans (1860), he contributed 'Tendencies of Religious Thought in England, 1688–1750s'. In 1861 Pattison became Rector of Lincoln College and married Emilia Francis Strong (see Dilke, Emilia*). Together, they turned the Rector's lodgings into a social and intellectual centre where Ingram Bywater* and Pater would socialize with such personalities as Robert Browning, George Eliot, Edmund Gosse,* Henry James, Hippolyte Taine, and Mary Arnold Ward* and her husband Humphry.* Ill-health prevented Pattison from undertaking serious study during the last months of his life; instead, he dictated his reminiscences, *Memoirs* (1885), which were edited by his wife.

RAFFALOVICH, MARC ANDRÉ (1864–1934), poet, novelist, and critic, was the youngest child born into a wealthy Russian-Jewish family who had migrated from Odessa to Paris in 1863 rather than convert to Christianity by decree. With his governess Raffalovich moved to England in 1882, and enrolled at Balliol College. When illness forced him to abandon his studies, he settled in London, and resolved to become a writer. Oscar Wilde* and others ridiculed him for pushing himself into literary circles by hosting elaborate dinner parties. Undeterred, he wrote reviews and critical articles, five volumes of homoerotic poetry, and two novels, including *A Willing Exile* (1890), in which he caricatured the engagement and marriage of Constance Lloyd and Oscar Wilde. In 1892, Arthur Symons* introduced Raffalovich to the love of his life, John Henry Gray (1866–1934), a young poet, short-story writer, and translator. After converting to Roman Catholicism and financing Gray's studies in Rome to become a priest, Raffalovich followed Gray to a posting in Edinburgh in 1907, and helped to finance the construction of St Peter's church (where Gray served as parish priest). Under the pseudonym Alexander Michaelson,

Raffalovich published *Uranism and Unisexuality: A Study of Different Manifestations of Sexual Instinct* (1896). He and Pater met in Oxford in 1882; their cordial friendship lasted until Pater's death. Pater reviewed Raffalovich's *It is Thyself* (1889) in the *Pall Mall Gazette* (see *CW* v); Raffalovich published his recollections of Pater under the name Alexander Michaelson in *Blackfriars*, 9 (1928). After Pater's death, and with Raffalovich's assistance, the Dominicans acquired the house at 64 St Giles, Oxford, the last residence of the Paters; it is now a Dominican friary.

RITCHIE, LADY ANNE ISABELLA, née THACKERAY (1837–1919), novelist and editor, was the eldest surviving daughter of William Makepeace Thackeray (1811–63) and his wife, Isabella Gethin Creagh Shawe. By 1850, her father celebrated his success as a writer by acquiring a house in London's Kensington district. In her memoirs, Annie paints a lively picture of home life, including such visiting personalities as Alfred Tennyson and Thomas Carlyle. As they grew older, the girls accompanied their father on trips abroad; invariably Annie served as his amanuensis. As editor of the *Cornhill Magazine*, William Thackeray shepherded Annie's first piece of journalism through the press. In 1867 her sister Harriet (Minny) (1839–75) married Leslie Stephen; Annie would become the aunt of Virginia Stephen Woolf. In 1877 Annie married her cousin Richmond Thackeray Ritchie (1854–1912), seventeen years younger (he later distinguished himself as a civil servant); they had two children. Annie Thackeray published her first novel, *The Story of Elizabeth*, in 1863. *The Village on the Cliff* (1867) was her first major success. In the late 1880s, Annie Ritchie began editing her father's papers; she was also a vivid memoirist: see *Chapters from some Memoirs* (1894).

SHADWELL, CHARLES LANCELOT (1840–1919), scholar and administrator, was the grandson of Sir Lancelot Shadwell, the last Vice-Chancellor of England. Shadwell attended Christ Church, Oxford, 1859–63, taking a first in classics and a second in law and history. Before his last exams Shadwell studied privately with Pater: in due course the two became close friends. They joined the Old Mortality essay society, where Pater read the paper entitled 'Diaphaneitè' (1864), very likely composed with Shadwell in mind (see *CW* v); they toured Italy together during the summer of 1865. Pater dedicated *The Renaissance* to Shadwell. In 1864, he was elected Fellow of Oriel College, one of the first colleges to allow Fellows to marry. He was called to the Bar at Lincoln's Inn in 1872 but instead returned to Oriel, serving as the college's Lecturer in Jurisprudence (1865–75), Treasurer (1874–87), and Provost (1905–14). His extensive knowledge of the college's history is evident in his *Registrum Orielense, 1500–1900*

(2 vols, 1893, 1902). His verse translation of Dante's *Purgatorio* features an introduction by Pater (1892; see *CW* vi). After Pater's death, Shadwell served as literary executor, and was a friend and adviser to Clara* and Hester Pater.* He edited the volumes *Greek Studies* (1895), *Miscellaneous Studies* (1895), and the unfinished *Gaston de Latour* (1896). Shadwell assisted A. C. Benson in producing his biography of Pater but refused to assist Thomas Wright.*

SHARP, WILLIAM (1855–1905), earned acclaim as a poet, critic, biographer, and editor, and as 'Fiona Macleod', his female alter ego, who published mainly on Celtic subjects (he published forty volumes or editions under his own name and more than ten volumes under the name Macleod). After working as a clerk in Glasgow, Sharp moved to London in 1878 as a clerk, but hoping to publish a work of some significance. He contributed poems and articles to the leading journals; through Dante Gabriel Rossetti, he met Ford Madox Brown, Robert Browning, William Holman Hunt, George Meredith, William Morris, Pater, William Bell Scott, A. C. Swinburne,* and Theodore Watts, who encouraged him in his writing. By 1882, Sharp was earning his living by writing: as a poet, and as a critic and editor, publishing biographical studies of Dante Rossetti (1882), Percy Bysshe Shelley (1887), Robert Browning (1889), and others. In 1892, he edited and composed (under various pseudonyms) the *Pagan Review*, a journal central to the New Paganism movement. Together with Patrick Geddes he headed the Evergreen Circle, concerned with developing a Scottish Celticism to recapture Edinburgh's status as a metropolis of European stature. Sharp and Pater met at a dinner party in London in 1882; Pater wrote Sharp several uncharacteristically long letters during the 1880s. *Dante Gabriel Rossetti: A Record and a Study* (1882), Sharp's first book, was inspired by Pater. Sharp published favourable reviews of *Marius the Epicurean* and of *Appreciations*, and dedicated his second volume of poems, *Earth's Voices: Transcripts from Nature, Sospitra, and Other Poems* (1884) to Pater. Pater sent a presentation copy of *Imaginary Portraits* (1887) to Sharp and supported his application for the Chair of English Literature at the University of London in 1889. In 1884 Sharp married a cousin, Elizabeth Amelia Sharp, who became his literary partner. After the late 1880s the two men saw little of each other; Sharp spent much time abroad in Europe and in the United States.

SOLOMON, SIMEON (1840–1905), painter and draughtsman, was the youngest in a prominent family of artists. Solomon studied with his brother Abraham and later with masters at the Royal Academy Schools. Many of his early works, 1856–63, depict Old Testament subjects in emotionally charged situations. Joining the Pre-Raphaelite circle in 1857 resulted in an expansion of his aesthetic theories and practices; D. G. Rossetti and Edward Burne-Jones held Solomon's work in high esteem, and the Royal Academy exhibited *Isaac Offered* in 1858. Meeting A. C. Swinburne* in 1863 resulted in a clarification of his aesthetics; he was inspired by Swinburne's cosmopolitanism. Solomon turned to mythical or classical subjects, Hellenic as well as Hebraic, with a view to exploring such themes as same-sex desire. In 1868, Pater took former student Gerard Manley Hopkins* to visit Solomon's studio. Two paintings of Bacchus, *Love in Autumn* (1866) and *Bacchus* (1867), drew public attention and Pater's admiration (expressed in 'A Study of Dionysus. I. The Spiritual Form of Fire and Dew', 1876; see *CW* viii). Pater purchased Solomon's *Chanting the Gospel* (1867); Solomon dedicated his drawing *The Bride, the Bridegroom, and Friend of the Bridegroom* (1868) to Pater, and in 1872 executed a drawing of Pater at Brasenose. In February 1873 Solomon was arrested in London and charged with buggery, generating great anxiety among his family and friends. Pater contacted Rebecca Solomon, who hoped for her brother's 'ultimate recovery and rehabilitation'. One year later, when Solomon was arrested in Paris, a guilty verdict resulted in a three-month prison term and ended his public career. Although he continued to sell paintings privately, he became itinerant, and an alcoholic, working at one point as a shoelace vendor and another as a sidewalk artist in London's Bayswater district. Intermittently, he lived in workhouses. In the 1890s, his art was championed by Herbert Horne,* editor of the *Hobby Horse*. Solomon died in St Giles's Workhouse from heart failure brought on by alcoholism.

SWINBURNE, ALGERNON CHARLES (1837–1909), poet and critic, contributed to the formulation of Pre-Raphaelitism, aestheticism, and decadence. Swinburne studied Classics at Balliol College, Oxford, 1856–60, where he chafed at academic regulations and concentrated on writing poetry, preparing essays he would read at the Old Mortality society (1856–66), and socialized with the Pre-Raphaelite circle of D. G. Rossetti, William Morris, and Edward Burne-Jones, who were then decorating the walls of the Oxford Union debating hall with murals depicting King Arthur and the Knights of the Round Table (1857–9). Swinburne settled in London in 1860 to devote his life to writing. *Atalanta in Calydon* (1865), a verse-drama styled after Aeschylus, brought him wide acclaim; *Poems and Ballads* (1866), in which he explored lesbianism, hermaphroditism, necrophilia, and sadomasochism, set off a critical storm. After advocating art for art's sake in numerous essays and his full-length study *William*

Blake: A Critical Essay (1868), Swinburne turned to political topics such as the cause of Italian nationalism (*Songs before Sunrise*, 1871). Swinburne and Pater probably met in January 1863, at an Old Mortality meeting. A decade later, when Simeon Solomon* was arrested, Swinburne was keen to disavow their friend, but Pater was not.

SYMONDS, JOHN ADDINGTON (1840–93), poet, historian, and biographer, was an advocate of sexual reform. The son of an eminent physician, Symonds read Classics at Balliol College, 1858–62, where he studied with Benjamin Jowett* and Thomas Hill Green (who married Symonds's sister Charlotte (see Green, Charlotte*) in 1871). Symonds became a Fellow of Magdalen College, but resigned when rumours of sexual impropriety circulated. After travelling in Switzerland and Italy for his health, he settled in London, intent on becoming a lawyer. In 1864 he married Catherine North (1837–1913), daughter of a Liberal MP for Hastings, with whom he had four daughters. In 1869 the couple agreed to live platonically; in 1877 the family moved to Davos Platz, Switzerland, where they lived until Symonds died. When diagnosed with tuberculosis in 1865, he reinvented himself as an independent scholar. His many publications included 'Uranian' poetry (*Animi Figura*, 1882); cultural history (*The Renaissance in Italy* in seven volumes, 1875–86); literary criticism (*Studies of the Greek Poets*, 1873); life-writing (*Michelangelo Buonarroti* (1893); as well as translation studies and travel writing. In *A Problem in Greek Ethics* (1883) he argues that some forms of male–male desire were similar to the *paiderastia* of the ancient Greeks; see also *A Problem in Modern Ethics* (1891). Symonds and Pater met in Oxford early in 1860, but developed a mutual dislike. Nevertheless, Symonds reviewed *Studies in the History of the Renaissance* (1873) favourably in the *Academy*, 25 March 1873, and Pater reviewed Symonds's *The Age of the Despots* (the first volume of *Renaissance in Italy*, 1876–86) favourably (see *CW* v). In 1877 both men were unsuccessful candidates for the office of Oxford's Professor of Poetry.

SYMONS, ARTHUR WILLIAM (1865–1945), poet, translator, critic, and travel writer, served as a conduit among decadence, symbolism, and modernism. Early on, Symons resolved to be a writer; his apprenticeship included producing poetry and criticism in the manner of Robert Browning and Pater. Joining the Browning Society enabled Symons to establish important literary and social contacts. His first academic book, *Introduction to the Study of Browning* (1886), was praised by Pater and Browning himself. Symons's first volume of poetry, *Days and Nights* (1889), was dedicated 'in all gratitude and admiration' to Pater, who urged the Macmillans to publish it (for Pater's review, see *CW* v). In 1890

Symons joined the Rhymers' Club; his friendship with W. B. Yeats resulted in a mutually productive literary relationship. Symons emerged as a leading figure espousing 'art for art's sake'; in 1893, his influential essay 'The Decadent Movement in Literature' delineated the verse and prose of Huysmans, Goncourt, Maeterlinck, Mallarmé, and Verlaine. Revised in 1900 as *The Symbolist Movement in Literature*, the book was dedicated to Yeats as 'the chief representative of that movement in our country'. T. S. Eliot praised Symons's work as a 'revelation' that affected the course of his life. He remained productive—writing plays and reviews, producing translations in several languages, preparing a book on William Blake—until 1908, when he suffered a mental breakdown. Although he recovered by 1910, his later publications bear no resemblance to his work of the 1880s and 1890s. Symons and Pater began corresponding in 1886 (see letter dated 2 December [1886]); they met in London on 7 August 1888. Pater became a mentor, critiquing manuscripts and championing Symons's work. Symons attended Pater's lectures on Prosper Mérimée in 1890 and Raphael in 1892. The relationship cooled after 1890, but Symons continued to regard himself a disciple after Pater's death, reprinting memorial articles in such volumes as *A Study of Walter Pater* (1932).

WARD, MARY AUGUSTA, née ARNOLD (1851–1920), novelist, educational reformer, and philanthropist, was the eldest daughter of Julia Sorell Arnold and Thomas Arnold and niece of Matthew Arnold. She was born in New Zealand, but raised in England in the Lake District and then Oxford. Senior academics, including Mark Pattison,* mentored her. When Pattison advised her to choose a subject that captivated her and to become an 'authority' in it, she decided to become an expert on the Spanish language and history. In April 1872, she married T. Humphry Ward,* formerly one of Pater's pupils and latterly one of his colleagues. For nine years, the Wards resided on Bradmore Road in north Oxford, where their neighbours and friends included the Paters and Charlotte* and T. H. Green. During this period Ward produced nearly 200 entries on Spanish ecclesiastics for *A Dictionary of Christian Biography*, and many articles on historical and literary topics for leading newspapers and periodicals. In 1873 Ward founded (with Clara Pater*) the Lectures for Women Committee, which in 1878 expanded into the Association for the Education of Women. Their activities led to the establishment of Somerville Hall (later, College), St Anne's, and Lady Margaret Hall. The Wards moved to London in November 1881; Humphry took a position with *The Times*, and Mary, using the name Mrs Humphry Ward, published novels such as *Miss Bretherton* (1884), *Robert Elsmere* (1888), *David*

Grieve (1892), and *Marcella* (1894). In May 1885 Ward reviewed *Marius the Epicurean* favourably for *Macmillan's Magazine*; Pater reviewed *Robert Elsmere* in 1888 for *The Guardian* (see *CW* v). Walter, Hester, and Clara are fondly sketched in Ward's *A Writer's Recollections* (1918). Ward's philanthropy and administrative skills led to the development of 'settlements' for the working-class of London's St Pancras area. Feminist friends and colleagues were dismayed, however, when, as of 1908, Ward championed the Women's Anti-Suffrage Association.

WARD, THOMAS HUMPHRY (1845–1926), journalist, art critic, and editor, studied at Brasenose College, 1864-8. Ward attended Pater's first course of lectures on 'The History of Philosophy', delivered at the college in 1867. He regarded these lectures as 'an extraordinary stimulus': they could be classified, he later observed, with those of William Newman on Greek history and Sir Henry Maine on Roman law. After graduating, Ward served as Fellow and Tutor of the college, 1869-81; students packed his lectures, whatever the topic: ancient Greece, the Italian Renaissance, or the age of Chaucer. In April 1872 he married Mary Augusta Arnold*; from 1872 to 1881 the couple lived in north Oxford, near Pater and his sisters and Charlotte* and T. H. Green. The couple pursued literary interests, raised three children, and entertained friends and colleagues. Ward was not content with academia, however; in November 1881 he and his family moved to London so that he could take a position with *The Times*. In addition to his journalism, Ward edited *The English Poets*, 4 vols (1880), for which Pater produced the introduction for the poetry of S. T. Coleridge and of D. G. Rossetti. Ward also edited the popular 'English Men of Letters' series for Macmillan, and *Selections from the English Poets*. The Wards were good friends of Henry Olive Daniel* and his wife Emily.

WHISTLER, JAMES MCNEILL (1834–1903), American painter, etcher, and lithographer, dominated the art world during the late nineteenth century. He moved to Europe in 1855, determined to be a bohemian artist. Settling in Paris, he attended classes at the École Impériale et Spéciale de Dessin and the Académie Gleyre, and learned from the aesthetic of landscape painter Gustave Courbet. Whistler moved to London in 1859, where he developed a passion for the Thames. With *Symphony in White, No. 1: The White Girl* (1861-2), Whistler challenged viewers conditioned to expect narrative canvases. Critics dismissed the painting as 'bizarre'. Inspired by the stylized simplicity, graceful design, and tonal harmonies of Japanese woodblock prints, Whistler produced paintings such as *Nocturne: Blue and Gold, Old Battersea Bridge* (1872-5) and *Arrangement in Grey and Black, No. 1: Portrait of the Artist's Mother* (1871). *Nocturne in Black and*

Gold: The Falling Rocket (1872–7) was reviled by John Ruskin in 1877; Whistler sued for libel. He won the notorious 1878 *Whistler v. Ruskin* trial but was bankrupted by the proceedings. Whistler adopted Charles Baudelaire's concept of the artist as dandy, in possession of the 'characteristic quality of opposition and revolt'. In 1885 he delivered his 'Ten O'Clock' lecture in London, Cambridge, and Oxford to refute Ruskin's doctrines. *The Gentle Art of Making Enemies* (1890) records Whistler's quarrels with individuals and newspapers. In 1888, Whistler married Beatrice (Trixie) Godwin, the widow of architect E. W. Godwin. Pater regarded Whistler, Alphonse Legros, and Edward Burne-Jones as the leading painters of the age (see *CW* vi and x). Whistler and Pater moved in social and intellectual circles that overlapped; they may have met, at least once. Pater likely attended the 'Ten O'Clock Lecture', presented at the Town Hall, Oxford, on 30 April 1885, and the dinner organized to honour Whistler, held at the Criterion Restaurant, London, on 1 May 1889.

WILDE, OSCAR FINGAL O'FLAHERTIE WILLS (1854–1900), Irish poet, critic, novelist, and playwright, was the doyen of the aesthetic and decadent movements. He studied classics at Trinity College, Dublin, 1871–4, and Magdalen College, Oxford, 1874–9, winning prizes at both institutions. Unable to obtain a fellowship at Oxford, he moved to London, determined to become a celebrity. Gilbert and Sullivan satirized his aesthetic posturing in their comic opera *Patience* (1881). Under the auspices of D'Oyly Carte, the producer of *Patience*, Wilde toured the United States and Canada in 1882 and the United Kingdom and Ireland, 1883–4, lecturing on aestheticism. In 1884 he married Constance Lloyd; the couple had two sons. Later, the dandy turned to journalism (he edited *Woman's World*, 1887–9) and wrote children's stories. During the period 1888–95, Wilde created the works for which he is best remembered: *The Picture of Dorian Gray* (1890), *Lady Windermere's Fan* (1892), and *The Importance of Being Earnest* (1895). Three trials in 1895 ended his career: his libel action against the Marquess of Queensberry, the father of his lover, Lord Alfred Douglas (1870–1945), which Wilde lost; the first prosecution for 'gross indecency' which resulted in an acquittal; and the second, in which he was found guilty and sentenced to two years in prison with hard labour (see Wilde's *Ballad of Reading Gaol* and *De Profundis*). After prison, he went into exile in Europe, and died in Paris of meningitis. Wilde and Pater were introduced in Oxford in October 1877; they met often during Wilde's final year at Oxford and occasionally over the course of the next twelve years. Wilde enthusiastically reviewed *Imaginary Portraits* (1887) and *Appreciations* (1889); Pater reviewed *The Picture of Dorian Gray* guardedly for *The Bookman* (see *CW* vi).

WRIGHT, THOMAS (1859–1936), schoolmaster, historian, biographer, and literary enthusiast, studied classics at Derbyshire's Buxton College, 1873–81; he later founded and operated the Cowper School, a private school located in Olney, Buckinghamshire. In addition to writing poetry and fiction, Wright produced local histories and biographies to help promote Olney's heritage. Like his mentor, the investigative journalist William Thomas Stead (1849–1912), Wright sought out and interviewed his subject's relatives and acquaintances. As a matter of principle, he rejected the popular belief that a writer's 'work' belonged to the public and the 'life' belonged to the author. With an eye for sensation, he produced the lives of such figures as Daniel Defoe (1894), Edward FitzGerald (1904), Richard Burton (1906), John Payne (1919), William Blake (1929), and Charles Dickens (1935), filling his accounts with anecdotes and interviews. His motto was: 'Truth at all costs'. As well, he founded a number of societies, including the Cowper Society (1900), the John Payne Society (1905), and the Blake Society (1912). In 1903 Wright embarked on the life of Pater, encouraged by the fact that he knew several members of the extended Pater family in Buckinghamshire. He contacted Macmillan and Co. and Pater's sisters, presenting them with an outline of the 'revelatory' biography he had in mind, one which would provide the history of Pater's 'intimate friendships'. George Macmillan* urged Clara* and Hester* to avoid this 'bookmaker', and they rejected his proposal. Undaunted, Wright pressed on with his research, locating individuals and collecting information. He based volume one on the information supplied by John Rainier McQueen,* who knew Pater intimately during the years from 1855 to 1860, when the two were students at the King's School and then Oxford. McQueen's account, however, conveyed by letters and responses to questionnaires written fifty years after the events he describes, is poorly documented. Wright based volume two on the information supplied by Richard C. Jackson (1851–1923), the eccentric churchman and literary dilettante who claimed to have been Pater's closest friend from the late 1870s and the model for Marius the Epicurean. *The Life of Walter Pater* (1907), lavishly illustrated, appeared on 14 February 1907.

Critical Introduction

> It might even be said that the trial-task of criticism, in regard to literature and art no less than to philosophy begins exactly where the estimate of general conditions, of the conditions common to all the products of this or that particular age—of the 'environmental'—leaves off, and we touch what is unique in the individual genius which contrived after all, by force of will to have its own masterful way with that environment.
>
> *Plato and Platonism* (1893)

By a strange irony, Walter Pater, one of the most subjective of prose writers of the Victorian era, stands apart as one of the most enigmatic; because of his reserved nature and secluded way of life, his contemporaries in Oxford and London regarded him as an enigma, the subject of legends and rumours. Speaking for many of his close friends and acquaintances, Edmund Gosse, William Sharp, and Arthur Symons predicted that, as a literary figure represented by relatively few letters and no diaries, Pater would grow more and more shadowy. As late as 1948, it was possible to declare that '[n]o English writer of the nineteenth century stands so much in need of rehabilitation as Walter Pater'.[1] Critical interest in his life and work has intensified considerably since then; however, situating him with any precision in the cultural history of the nineteenth century remains a challenge, not only because he left few primary biographical sources but also because in his work he addresses a range of subjects that lie in a grey area of scholarship, between criticism and creation. To paraphrase Ian Fletcher,[2] few readers are equipped to appreciate Pater's many accomplishments: as a classics scholar; critic of architecture, fiction, mythology, painting, poetry, sculpture, and theatre; philosopher of aesthetics; and writer of ruminative fiction, but something more or less than this (creative non-fiction). In short, Pater earned distinction in several fields of intellectual endeavour, especially as the central figure of the aesthetic movement, that loosely organized intellectual and artistic project that flourished in

England during the 1870s and 1880s. The members of this enterprise promoted the ideal of 'art for art's sake', rejecting the notion that art should have a political, religious, or social purpose. Aesthetes such as the Pre-Raphaelites, Algernon Charles Swinburne, Simeon Solomon, James McNeill Whistler, Oscar Wilde, Aubrey Beardsley, and Max Beerbohm took part in this initiative with a view to elevating taste and championing beauty as the basic principles in art and in life. Ultimately, these figures deemed the intellectual, literary, and philosophical outlook of the Greeks as nothing less than the fundamental guide to an aesthetic approach to life.

This volume reproduces 381 letters that were written by Pater during the period from 9 May 1859 to 30 July 1894. In addition, the volume includes eighty-two letters that were written by members of Macmillan and Co. to Pater; fifty-three letters that were written by Macmillan and Co. to the Pater sisters, Hester and Clara; twenty-one letters written by Clara Pater to the Macmillans and to friends; twenty-seven letters written by Hester to the Macmillans and to friends; and twelve letters written by others (Field, Gosse, Shadwell, Symons, Wordsworth, and Wright) until 1919—yielding a total of 576 letters. I reproduce all the complete and fragmentary items of correspondence that have appeared in biographies, memoirs, and miscellaneous works. Letters written by other correspondents have been included because they serve as a source of biographical, historical, literary, and social information. In preparing this volume, I build on four sources: *Letters of Walter Pater*, ed. Lawrence Evans (1970), which reproduces 266 letters written by Pater and six letters written by others during the period 4 October 1859 to 10 July 1905, yielding a total of 278 letters; Hiroko Hagiwara, *Walter Pater and his Circle*, introduced by Tatsuhiko Arakawa (1984), which reproduces thirteen letters written by Clara Pater to Macmillan and Co.; *Walter Pater: A Life Remembered*, ed. Robert M. Seiler (1987), which reproduces ten letters written by Clara and Hester Pater to Thomas Wright; and *The Book Beautiful: Walter Pater and the House of Macmillan*, ed. Robert M. Seiler (1999), which reproduces 189 letters exchanged between Pater and Macmillan and Co. regarding the design and production of his books.

INTELLECTUAL AWAKENING

Walter Pater was the third child and the second son born to Maria Pater, *née* Hill (1801–54), a homemaker, and Richard Glode Pater (1796–1842), a surgeon dedicated to helping the poor. The family lived at 1 Honduras Terrace, Commercial Road, Stepney, a riverside district in what is now the

London borough of Tower Hamlets. Maria, 'a rather faint figure to her own children',[3] and Richard, 'a tall, grave figure, a little cold and severe',[4] had four children: William (1835–87), who later qualified as a surgeon; Hester (1837–1922), who became an accomplished homemaker; Walter (1839–94), who as an adolescent decided to live the life of the mind; and Clara (1841–1910), who later distinguished herself as a tutor in classics and administrator at Somerville College, Oxford. By 1854, the sense of home that Pater had formed had been shattered by the deaths of four members of the family: his father on 28 January 1842; his uncle William on 19 September 1845; his paternal grandmother on 21 February 1848; and his mother on 25 February 1854. Understandably, he later developed the conviction that life is not only brief but also that its tenure is arbitrary: that it might end at any time and without an apparent cause. In due course, he reasoned that one should live intensely.[5]

In the paragraphs that follow I trace the intellectual journey that Pater took from devout pupil at the King's School, Canterbury, to free-thinking undergraduate at Queen's College, Oxford, where in aesthetic contemplation he discovered a means of self-development; chronicle the inception, production, revision, and promotion of Pater's many-faceted texts, published as well as unpublished; assess the integrity of the collection of letters reproduced here, in terms of completeness and comprehensiveness; and delineate the image of Pater as a teacher, writer, and mentor conveyed by the correspondence. These letters, together with the editor's introduction and annotations, paint a picture of the aesthete living with his sisters, negotiating the grind of academic life, and pursuing his literary career. They help us develop an appreciation for the self-fashioning by which he shaped his life and his work, as well as his long commitment to living life in the spirit of art.

During the years 1842 to 1853 Pater lived with his family at Chase Side, a market town near Enfield; he spent his days reading voraciously and thinking about the Church, an interest that may have been prompted by the headmaster of the Enfield Grammar School, where he was a pupil. He enjoyed 'playing at being a clergyman'.[6] From 1853 to 1858, when the family lived at Harbledown, a village near Canterbury, Pater attended the King's School, Canterbury.[7] On a visit to Hursley, Hampshire, on 25 February 1854, the young Pater met the vicar of the parish, the poet and theologian John Keble, one of the leaders of the Oxford Movement. On walks they discussed such mutual enthusiasms as the works of philosopher and theologian Richard Hooker. Interestingly, Keble encouraged the young Pater in his aspiration to become a clergyman.[8] Shortly after entering the Sixth Form, Pater experienced an 'intellectual awakening',[9] which rendered the world a place of many possibilities. Suddenly, it had become obvious to him that, despite his lack of wealth, or important family connections, or powerful external support, he could make his mark, quite possibly as a writer. During his apprenticeship, he would write poetry and, most importantly, undertake a self-directed reading programme so as to discover words, images, and sounds, not to mention rhetorical strategies, that he could utilize in his own compositions.[10]

During the first phase of this intellectual programme, 1857–60, Pater focused on the works of modern British authors.[11] A close friend and fellow undergraduate at Queen's College, Oxford, Ingram Bywater (1840–1915), who became a renowned classical scholar (see Biographical Register), recalled that Pater 'devoured' all the serious literature of the period: 'His reading was extraordinarily wide—I think he would have done better in the examinations if it had been less so—and he was full of ability. At first his interests were theological, but in this respect his mind soon underwent a change, and he became more literary and philosophical.'[12] One influence at work was the charismatic William Wolfe Capes (1834–1914), Fellow, Tutor, and Lecturer at Queen's College, 1856–70, with whom Pater and Bywater studied. Capes enriched his lectures on early Roman history, the history of philosophy from Heraclitus to Mill, ethics, and logic with digests of European literature; apparently, he encouraged students to read widely and to think critically.[13] Capes's lectures on Francis Bacon would have a lasting influence on Pater.

The changes that were modernizing the older British universities were also shaping Pater. At issue was the question: what role should the university play in society?[14] Two positions vied for pre-eminence. One, championed by Benjamin Jowett (1817–93), classical scholar (see Biographical Register), favoured the transmission of accepted knowledge, and regarded the study of ancient languages and literatures as the best preparation for lawyers, politicians, and civil servants. The other position, championed by Mark Pattison (1813–84), classical scholar and critic (see Biographical Register), favoured the pursuit of research and the search for new knowledge. The University of Oxford Act 1854 (and the University of Cambridge Act 1856), ushered in such reforms as democratizing university government, including reducing the influence of the heads of colleges, and framing new constitutions that would free the colleges from the ties which bound them to families, places, and schools; re-organizing the professorial systems; opening fellowships and scholarships to free competition; allowing Non-Conformists to take the BA degree without religious tests;[15] and removing the obligation that Fellows take holy orders.[16] The Examination Statute of 1850 emphasized a shift in the *Literae Humaniores* curriculum, making proficiency in Greek and Latin the focus of the examination in the second year (Moderations), and knowledge of ancient history and philosophy the basis for the examinations in the final year (Greats). Jowett added Plato's *Republic* and Bacon's *Novum Organum* (1620) to the list of standard texts and stressed teaching the history of philosophy as part of the apparatus of philosophy. In this way, Jowett addressed the question that was perplexing Pater, namely, how should one live in the modern world?[17]

It is likely that Bacon was the first philosopher Pater studied in depth and that subsequently he read philosophy from a Baconian perspective.[18] According to Bacon, knowledge may be gathered from the past via tradition, but it must be accumulated and augmented by personal observation. He judged induction to be the best method of investigation. Later, while articulating his own philosophical perspective, Pater would express (as his own) ideas that derived from *Novum Organum*, notably the application of the Baconian inductive method in aesthetic criticism in the 'Preface' to *Studies in the History of the Renaissance* (1873; see *CW* i). The perspective from which he judges philosophies in *Marius the Epicurean* (1885) and in *Gaston de Latour* (1896) is undoubtedly Bacon's (see *CW* ii, iv). Several fundamental principles that inform Pater's writings (the suggestion that one's temperament and one's philosophy are connected) derive from *Novum Organum*, including Pater's impatience with systems (at least after 1868) and metaphysics, and his assumption that, in spite of the errors generated by perception, a return to 'sensuous perception' as a basis of all understanding offers the only hope for mental progress.

Two public intellectuals who were exercising a spell over Oxford piqued Pater's interest: Matthew Arnold (1822–88), poet, critic, and Professor of Poetry, 1857–67, and John Ruskin (1819–1900), art and social critic and Oxford's Slade Professor of Fine Art, 1869–77 and 1883–5.[19] Pater attended several of Arnold's lectures, notably 'On the Modern Element in Literature', the inaugural talk delivered in November 1857, and on 'Pagan and Modern Religious Sentiment', delivered in March 1864 (Pater enjoyed the latter's 'onslaught on the Philistines').[20] Hellenism, by way of the Italian Renaissance, and Romanticism, as propounded by Ruskin and Arnold, were indispensable sources for Pater's own distinctive formulation of Hellenism and aestheticism.[21]

Texts produced by prominent liberal churchmen such as Charles Kingsley, F. D. Maurice, and A. P. Stanley topped Pater's list of works warranting attention—and gradually, they shook Pater's faith in Christianity.[22] A major influence at this time, Frederick Denison Maurice (1805–72), clergyman and theologian, had founded the Christian Socialism movement.

He also achieved acclaim as a preacher who delivered sermons to working men and as a writer who challenged orthodoxy in his pamphlets and books (*Theological Essays*, 1853). Pater often attended service at the chapels at Lincoln's Inn Square and St Peter, London, so that he could hear Maurice preach. Apparently, Pater shocked acquaintances by saying that it would be fun to be ordained without believing a single word of Christian doctrine.[23]

Three texts that appeared during the period of February 1859 to March 1860 exposed the conflict between the teachings of the Bible and the lessons of science.[24] In *On Liberty* (1859), written by John Stuart Mill (1806–73), utilitarian philosopher and political economist, and his wife Harriet Taylor, Pater read that freedom of opinion and discussion is essential in the search for truth, and that freedom to act in all self-regarding matters and bearing the consequences of that activity is essential for building character.[25] In developing this view, the authors drew on such German intellectuals as Wilhelm von Humboldt (1767–1835), Prussian philosopher, linguist, and diplomat, who stressed the right to and the duty of self-development. Humboldt maintained that, to develop one's full powers in a harmonious and balanced way, one has to know what human nature has been and could be: the sensible individual in search of *Bildung* or self-cultivation should concentrate on the Greeks, the most independent, sensitive, and creative of civilizations.

Whereas *On Liberty* celebrated the individual, stressing the duty of the individual to pursue self-development, Charles Darwin's *On the Origin of Species* (1859) celebrated process, displacing the individual from her or his unique place in the universe. Pater and his friends at Queen's College discussed the work with passion;[26] they were intrigued by how Darwin (1809–82), naturalist, geologist, and biologist, had addressed such fundamental questions as how species are formed, and had developed the theory of natural selection as the process for preserving and accumulating minor advantageous variations within living systems. Like many people, Pater became agnostic when he realized that life on earth evolved (that there was no need for an ultimate Creator). In due course, he pointed to evolutionary theory as confirmation of the Heraclitean flux[27] and utilized it in his formulation of aestheticism.

Essays and Reviews (1860), a collection of theological studies produced by seven liberal Anglican churchmen, sought to empower the lay person by demonstrating a free and critical study of such topics as the predictive character of Old Testament prophecies, the impossibility of miracles, the nature of the national church, Mosaic cosmogony, evidential theology of the eighteenth century, and biblical hermeneutics. Bywater recalled that the volume had caught the attention of all the undergraduates who were wrestling with the works of the major intellectuals of the time.[28] *Essays and Reviews* set off a huge controversy that extended into the 1870s.[29]

Meditating on these topics soon became meditating on modernity and, by implication, the individual living under conditions of modernity. Artists and writers who produced social criticism thought of the age as a period of transition, associated with historical trends including industrial capitalism, revolutionary politics, and cultural changes.[30] Liberal thinkers of the period also embraced a new Hellenism as a force of renewal, a new version of Graeco-Roman culture of the classical period, one that would ameliorate the contemporary human condition of 'psychic fragmentation and cultural stagnation' generated by progressive rationalism and rapid industrialization and urbanization. Acknowledging one's doubts, Pater had learned, represents an important step in one's intellectual quest. The older Pater would observe that one class of minds believed that the sacred story could not be true, whereas another class of minds could not be sure that the sacred story was false.[31] Increasingly, he identified with thinkers of the second group.

Pater launched the second phase of his programme of self-directed reading during the Long Vacation of 1860; while vacationing with his family in Heidelberg, he learned German with a view to studying the major German and English empirical philosophers of the eighteenth and nineteenth centuries, plus selected classical philosophers, primarily Plato.[32] Pater was anxious to examine the works of Johann Wolfgang von Goethe (1749–1832), German poet, playwright, novelist, scientist, and civil servant, the true illustration of the 'speculative' temper and his theory of how life should be lived.

Interest in things German ran high in Oxford at this time, thanks to Germanophiles who exploited German ideas of personal culture when formulating antidotes to the ugly materialism that had accompanied the industrial revolution.[33] Pater's philosophical turn grew out of his reading of Thomas Carlyle (1795–1881), Scottish historian and biographer, who acknowledged that he had learned German as a young man believing that studying the major works of German literature and philosophy would help him overcome his religious doubt.[34] In Goethe, Carlyle found 'a mind... gaining a more and more perfect dominion of its world'.[35] A leading champion of the poet, Carlyle translated two of Goethe's novels, *Wilhelm Meister's Apprenticeship* (1824) and *Wilhelm Meister's Travels* (1827), produced a biography of Goethe's close friend, Friedrich Schiller (1825), and edited an anthology of German writers (1827). In German Idealism Carlyle saw a necessary alternative to British empiricism.

During October 1860 Pater examined *Dichtung und Wahrheit*, known to English-speaking readers as *Poetry and Truth*, which Goethe published in three parts, 1811–14 and 1830–1. In this fictionalized autobiography Goethe chronicles his life from his childhood in Frankfurt; his youth in Leipzig and Strasbourg, where he studied law and gained notoriety for his extra-curricular activities, such as pursuing classical studies (and discovering the work of Johann Joachim Winckelmann [1717–68], art historian and archaeologist[36]), developing his talents as poet, playwright, and novelist, and falling in love; his early manhood in Frankfurt and Darmstadt, where he gained widespread acclaim with the publication of *The Sorrows of Young Werther* (1774), and the days in 1775, when he joined the court at Weimar as a civil servant. Importantly, the narrative illustrates the concept of *Bildung* or self-cultivation at work,[37] the literary possibilities of which Pater explored in texts such as 'The Child in the House' and *Marius the Epicurean*.[38]

In Goethe Pater discovered the last Renaissance man, the embodiment of the Greek culture that constitutes 'that complex, many-sided movement'.[39] Like Goethe, Pater would come to regard culture as an agent of transformation, for the individual and for society. Goethe believed that culture would raise humanity to its full powers, and that there was no cultural form equal to that of art. As Goethe observes, 'true poetry is that which, like a worldly gospel, can by its inner serenity and outward calm free us from the burdens which press upon us';[40] Pater concludes *The Renaissance* with a similar observation: 'For our one chance lies in expanding that interval, in getting as many pulsations as possible into the given time.... Of such wisdom, the poetic passion, the desire of beauty, the love of art for its own sake, has most. For art comes to you proposing frankly to give nothing but the highest quality to your moments as they pass, and simply for those moments' sake' (*CW* i).

Additionally, the older Pater would share with Goethe an affection for the *Bildungsroman*, the literary form Goethe more or less invented in *Wilhelm Meisters Lehrjahre*, a loose framework of a journey across various settings and through various trials and tribulations, as the protagonist explores, inwardly and outwardly, what Meister calls his self-cultivation and personal development. The older Pater would employ the form several times, starting with 'The Child in the House' (1878) and later in *Marius the Epicurean* (1885), wherein a young Roman is in pursuit of a congenial religion or philosophy at a time of change.

During Lent Term 1861, Pater studied Greek with Balliol Fellow Benjamin Jowett, who 'coached' promising students for free.[41] Jowett had a gift for enabling students to think for themselves: he critiqued their work without discouraging them, and in setting lofty goals he inspired a strong belief in powers yet to be developed.[42] Jowett is said to have told Pater: 'I think you have a mind that will come to great eminence'.[43] (Among Pater's friends and acquaintances, those who were or would be tutored by Jowett included Algernon Swinburne, John Addington Symonds, and Gerard Manley Hopkins.) While studying for Greats, which he sat in spring 1862, Pater continued to accumulate the philosophical materials that would support his writings for the rest of his career, much of it empirical in orientation.[44] A close friend recalled that, during the course of 1861, he 'devoured' works by Thomas Hobbes, John Locke, George Berkeley, and David Hume,[45] figures who, as Kate Hext suggests, helped Pater understand the nature of the individual in the modern world.[46] During the Long Vacation of 1862, he tackled *Phänomenologie des Geistes* (1806), the first major philosophic work by German philosopher George Wilhelm Friedrich Hegel (1770–1831).[47] In this volume, known to English readers as *The Phenomenology of Spirit*, Pater found a thoroughgoing 'developmental interpretation of the human mind'.[48] As commentators point out, Hegel provides a novel picture of the relation of mind to world and of how individuals relate to each other.

Pater graduated from Queen's with his BA in the summer of 1862. For three years, until he was appointed to Brasenose College, he supported himself by tutoring private students. The year 1863 represented a significant milestone in Pater's life; in discovering aesthetics, he discovered his subject, bringing the second stage of his programme to an end, and, in due course, he followed the example of Goethe and became an aesthete.[49] Hegel's *Vorlesungen über die Ästhetik* (1835), known in English as *Lectures on Aesthetics*, provided Pater with basic ideas concerning such matters as the historical development of art, the relationship of art forms to historical periods, the relationship of art to nature, the difference between the mind of the artist and the mind of the philosopher, the relationship of the critic to art, and the kind of subjectivity that is desirable in criticism.[50] Subsequently, Pater would conceptualize the evolution of art in terms of a movement towards greater subjectivity, drawing on Hegel's triads or styles of art.

Pater had realized that, in the modern world, aesthetic contemplation could serve as an agent for self-cultivation and personal development.[51] Becoming an aesthete meant becoming a connoisseur as well as a prose artist. As a connoisseur, he would study and collect prints and as a prose artist he would write about works of art and produce works of fiction and what we would call creative non-fiction. He would use materials from artists' lives and works similar to the way in which Robert Browning fictionalized 'Fra Lippo Lippi' and 'Andrea del Sarto' in his dramatic monologues.[52]

As Billie Andrew Inman summarizes, by 1868 Pater had not only assimilated Hegel's and Friedrich Schiller's ideas on aesthetics, Edgar Quinet's and Jules Michelet's orientation in history, and Ernest Renan's eclectic mode of thought, but was also in command of a wide range of references—classical, German, French, and English—that is astounding, Inman points out, when one realizes that this was the fruit of only six years of research.[53]

THE LITERARY CAREER

On 5 February 1864, Pater was elected Fellow at Brasenose College, thanks to his grasp of German philosophy (it was a rare non-clerical position).[54] He served Brasenose in several capacities, all the while making his way as a cultural critic.[55] Initially, Pater produced review essays and articles, as opposed to the heavily documented monographs that conventional academics of the time were generating,[56] and, like other writers of the period, he recycled these pieces in book form.[57] He sent his first compositions— 'Coleridge's Writings' (1866), 'Winkelmann' (1867), 'Poems by William Morris' (1868)—to the *Westminster Review*, associated with John Stuart Mill and philosophical radicalism.[58] From 1869 he diversified, publishing in such periodicals as the *Fortnightly Review*, which featured signed articles surveying current social and cultural matters, as well as critiques of new books. Pater's association with the journal proved fruitful indeed: he refined his critical method, calling it aesthetic criticism, the foundation for which he laid in the essay on Winckelmann, and he published several articles from 1869 to 1871 on the culture of the Italian Renaissance, thereby establishing a theme for his first book. In all of these works he introduced a group of related topics he would explore throughout his career, including human isolation within the 'flux', the relative spirit of the modern world, the importance of temperament, and the significance of the Hellenic ideal. Importantly, he developed the 'self-conscious' and 'carefully-measured' prose style that readers would find beguiling.[59]

In the first of his review essays, 'Coleridge's Writings', Pater examines Coleridge's 'intellectual position' in terms of the conflict between the pursuit of the 'absolute', a quest characteristic of ancient thought, and the cultivation of the 'relative' spirit, a quest characteristic of modern thought. According to the modern spirit, one can know nothing rightly except relatively, that is, under very specific conditions. Rejecting Coleridge's critical method (the attempt to define the universal element in any artistic effort), Pater posits the empirical test of an individual's response to a work.

Importantly, he rejects orthodox Christianity because the worship of sorrow frustrates creativity.

His second essay puts Winckelmann into intellectual perspective, with J. W. von Goethe in the foreground. The German Hellenist stands apart from Pater's other Renaissance types, who exude the sense of discovering in the classical world something new with the possibility of renewed creation; Winckelmann exudes the sense of recovering something lost, that is, the Greek ideal. That Pater identifies with the persona of Winckelmann as scholar and writer and pagan becomes obvious.[60] Winckelmann's affinity with paganism enabled him to apprehend Hellenic art not in the abstract but in the concrete; when he moved to Rome he could 'finger' those marble classical male nudes without shame. In a word, appreciating the beauty of the male form is the key to appreciating Greek art.

In his third essay, 'Poems by William Morris', Pater takes as his point of departure an observation he made in the Winckelmann essay: what modern art should be doing in the service of culture is to rearrange the details of modern life so as to reflect it, thereby satisfying the human spirit; what the spirit needs in the face of modern life is a sense of freedom. Morris's narrative poems exude the pagan spirit: 'the sense of death and the desire of beauty; the desire of beauty quickened by the sense of death' (*CW* v). The last paragraphs of the essay, reading like a manifesto for the liberation of the human spirit from the trammels of the modern world, observe that modern empirical science has atomized life so completely that one feels caught up in 'a magic web' of necessity or natural law, which has produced a psychological paralysis. The solution is to make life as intense and as complete as possible by experiencing 'the love of art for art's sake' (*CW* v), since art provides the most appropriate objects for 'impassioned contemplation' ('On Wordsworth' *CW* v).

In December 1869, Pater sub-leased the house at 2 Bradmore Road, located in the suburb that was built in north Oxford on land adjacent to University Parks.[61] Pater and his sisters, Hester and Clara, turned the house into an aesthetic home.[62] (Their neighbours on Bradmore Road included Mary and Humphry Ward and Charlotte and Thomas Green.[63]) With his domestic life comfortably settled, he blossomed 'into considerable sociability, entertaining and being entertained in the cordial Oxford way'.[64]

Early in June 1872, Pater called on Alexander Macmillan (see Biographical Register), determined to persuade Macmillan and Co. to publish a collection of essays that explored the culture of the Renaissance, a topic that was enjoying immense popularity.[65] As a riposte to John Ruskin, who referred to the Renaissance as a period of artistic and moral decline, Pater's project had special gravitas.[66] With this meeting the aspiring author and the established publisher launched a long and fruitful relationship, as demonstrated in their correspondence.[67] On 29 June, Pater mailed Macmillan a prospectus for the proposed volume, enclosing the Winckelmann essay (from the *Westminster Review*), four essays that had appeared in the *Fortnightly Review*, and an essay in manuscript. Macmillan studied the essays with interest and proposed, on 2 July 1872, to publish a handsome octavo volume and terms of 'half profits'. Pater accepted this proposal, resolved to produce a volume that appealed to the eye and the mind, and promised to complete the essays over the summer. In September, Macmillan and Co. sent Pater printed specimens of the essays; Pater studied these, and in a letter to Alexander Macmillan complained that, in terms of presentation, they were unsuitable for the book he had in mind: 'Some of the essays are so short, and all of them in some ways so slight, that I think the only suitable form would be a small volume, costing about five shillings' (letter to Macmillan, 21 September [1872]). As well, he mentioned that he wanted to make suggestions with regard to such matters as the printing and the binding.

As the letters in this collection show, Pater played an active role in these negotiations, attending to every detail of manufacture in the interest of producing a technically and aesthetically pleasing book. In doing so, Pater had joined a handful of writers and artists and small publishers who were inaugurating a new era in book design, hoping to bring all the elements of the book into harmony. In deeming the book 'an aesthetic object' Pater may well have taken his cue from Dante Gabriel Rossetti (1828–82), poet and painter, co-founder of the Pre-Raphaelite Brotherhood. In due course, *Studies in the History of the Renaissance* was issued in March 1873. During Pater's lifetime, the book went through four editions.

The volume is the work of a young man eager to make his mark. Pater not only challenges individual judgements that his distinguished elders take as settled, but also modifies the aesthetics that make their judgements possible. Importantly, he formulates (in the chapter on Luca della Robbia) a romantic or expressive theory of art; that is, he challenges Ruskin's notion, conveyed in Volume I of *Modern Painters* (1843–60), that art is 'a noble and expressive language'. Whereas Ruskin stresses the didactic function of art, arguing that the painter gathers and arranges the facts of nature (natural objects for Ruskin symbolize the divinity of God) so as to induce 'noble emotions' in the spectators, Pater argues that if a work of art is to have an aesthetic as distinct from a historical value (Ruskin's sense of the transcription of natural facts), it must exhibit something individual, the impress of the artist's temper and personality. Importantly, Pater formulates 'aesthetic criticism' as a way of liberating the appreciation of art from moral considerations. In this enterprise, he draws on Matthew Arnold, who in the first series of *Essays in Criticism* (1865) suggests that the goal in all branches of knowledge is 'to see the object as in itself it really is'. In the 'Preface' to his own volume, Pater differentiates himself from Arnold, asserting that in 'aesthetic criticism the first step is to know one's own impression as it really is, to discriminate it, to realize it distinctly'. In this respect, he shifts critical attention to the circumstances that mould the artist's genius, as well as the force of the artist's personality that resists these circumstances.[68]

The first book by a relatively unknown writer, *Studies in the History of the Renaissance* generated as much censure as praise.[69] Some reviewers found the essays pleasant and instructive; others judged them to be 'pretentious' and 'artificial'. Specialists took a dim view of the volume as historical scholarship. Most notably, conservative observers in Oxford generated considerable hostility towards the work, especially towards the *carpe diem* theme of the 'Conclusion'.[70] Several colleagues, such as Benjamin Jowett, spoke of Pater as a 'demoralizing moralizer'.[71] In a letter to Pater, 17 March 1873, John Wordsworth, a former pupil and then Chaplain at Brasenose College, complained about the pain the philosophy expressed in the 'Conclusion' caused him and other readers.

More than a decade passed before Pater published another book. Edmund Gosse explained Pater's lack of production in terms of 'the painful slowness of his methods of composition, which were "a travail and an agony"',[72] whereas biographer A. C. Benson explained the silence in terms of the onerous demands of Pater's duties as Tutor and Lecturer at Brasenose, for which he was not fully equipped.[73] Actually, Pater produced thirteen articles on various subjects between 1873 and 1885, but, as his correspondence reveals, this number tells only part of the story.[74] During these years of 'experimentation' he made false starts in several different directions, including searching for a 'safe' subject with which to restore his reputation as a writer; revising his work in order to clarify his meaning and to remove grounds for offence; soliciting reviews from fellow-writers in order to ensure that the reception of his works was largely favourable; expressing his gratitude to friends and acquaintances who had praised his works in print; and distancing himself from the aesthetic movement.

In the 1870s, Pater made plans for a book on English literature. His essay on William Wordsworth, which appeared in the *Fortnightly Review* for April 1874, was regarded by some commentators as one of his finest pieces of criticism (see *CW* v). He 'leaked' word to the press, indicating that he was planning to produce a book of 'aesthetic studies' of Shakespeare. The *Academy* announced in November 1874 that Pater intended 'to continue his short aesthetic studies of Shakespeare's plays in *The Fortnightly*, the present month's piece on *Measure for Measure* being the first of a series that will some day make a book';[75] weeks later, the *Academy* announced that his next 'study' for the *Fortnightly Review* would be on *Love's Labour's Lost*.[76] In due course, however, this project collapsed. By November 1875, Pater was contemplating producing a volume of Greek studies. Over the next three years he wrote two two-part essays: 'The Myth of Demeter and Persephone', which he delivered (in November 1875) as a lecture, and 'A Study of Dionysus'. The first part of the lecture appeared in the *Fortnightly Review* in January 1876; the second, in February.

On 13 November 1876, Alexander Macmillan suggested that Pater pursue his plan to issue a new, revised edition of his Renaissance studies. Pater agreed to this proposal, stating that he wanted to add some new material to the volume and to modify a number of passages. A number of important changes were considered, including giving the volume a new title, *The Renaissance: Studies in Art and Poetry* (1877); toning down expressions of aestheticism; excising passages that were plainly provocative or critical of religion; and omitting the 'Conclusion' because (as he argued later) 'it might possibly mislead some of those young men into whose hands it might fall'. Cumulatively, these revisions left 'hardly a page untouched'.[77]

Next, Pater proposed (in his letter of 1 October 1878 to Alexander Macmillan) to publish a volume of miscellaneous essays collected from various periodicals. This book, provisionally entitled *The School of Giorgione, and other Studies*, was to include essays on Giorgione, Wordsworth, Demeter and Persephone, Dionysus, Romanticism, *Love's Labour's Lost*, *Measure for Measure*, and Charles Lamb. The following day, Macmillan wrote to say that he would be very glad to publish this new volume of essays, 'exactly uniform' with the second edition of *The Renaissance* because that volume embodied his aesthetic intentions regarding book design. Pater felt especially confident about this project, and again approached the *Academy* and the *Athenaeum*, both of which announced (5 October 1878) that this new volume could be expected early in the following year. On 18 November 1878, he wrote to say that the book was ready to be printed, but five days later he asked Macmillan to change the title to read: *Dionysus and other Studies*. The paper was specially made and proof copies were printed later that month, but surprisingly, when he revised the proofs, Pater changed his mind and decided to stop the publication of this volume altogether (see letter to Macmillan, 30 November [1878]).

Early in 1878, Pater developed the 'imaginary portrait', and decided to make this hybrid form the centre of his creative work.[78] This genre grew out of the technique he had employed in his Renaissance studies to 'realize' the personality behind a philosophical idea or a work of art. In essays on Leonardo da Vinci, Luca della Robbia, and Winckelmann, he sketched 'real lives' imaginatively, situating them as characters in narratives. (The dramatic monologues of Robert Browning, the literary portraits of Charles Augustin Sainte-Beuve, and the imaginary conversations of Walter Savage Landor may all have served as inspiration.) Pater planned to produce a series of short fictional portraits, each more or less complete in itself. He sent the first, 'Imaginary Portraits. I. The Child in the House', to George Grove on 17 April 1878; it appeared in *Macmillan's Magazine* in August 1878 (and republished years later in book form as *An Imaginary Portrait: The Child in the House* in 1894; see *CW* iii). The subject of this fictionalized autobiographical portrait, a man in his thirties named Florian Deleal, reflects on the impact of childhood experiences on his personality and sensibility; he focuses on what Pater calls 'that process of brain-building by which we are, each one of us, what we are'. He began working on the second, 'An English Poet', between 1878 and 1879,[79] but abandoned it; in 1931 it was published by May Ottley (*CW* iii), who had been a pupil of Clara Pater. Producing imaginary portraits proved to be a congenial and transgeneric enterprise; Pater incorporated aspects of art and literary criticism, biography, confessional texts, history, myth, portraiture, philosophy, and travelogue into his narratives, which focused on young, imaginary, as opposed to historical (and mostly male) protagonists, many of whom are destined for a sudden, early death.

Pater began researching his second book, *Marius the Epicurean* (1885), in the early 1880s, perhaps the spring of 1881. He spent seven weeks from December 1882 through January 1883 in Rome and Naples, collecting material for a work that would both complete the project he had begun with 'The Child in the House', a study of an artistic personality, and clear up any misunderstandings generated by the 'Conclusion' to his first volume. The project is first mentioned in a letter dated 22 July [1883] to his close friend and confidante Violet Paget (1856–1935), the essayist and novelist who wrote under the pseudonym 'Vernon Lee' (see Biographical Register); Pater states that he wants to complete the first half of this extended 'imaginary portrait' set in the era of Marcus Aurelius by the end of the Long Vacation. In *Marius the Epicurean*, Pater charts the intellectual development of a young Roman who searches for a 'principle of conduct' he can live by.[80] In setting this 'interior drama' or spiritual autobiography in Rome during the second century CE, Pater exploits the resources of a long tradition, namely, the comparison between the Antonine 'past' and the late-Victorian 'present',[81] thereby establishing a context for exploring the possibility of religious belief during an age of transition, the intellectual climate of which is made up of an almost bewildering number of intellectual and ethical systems.[82] *Marius*, published in two volumes, was issued on 4 March 1885. Readers on both sides of the Atlantic took up *Marius* with respect, fascinated as well as perplexed by the complex work.[83]

To celebrate the publication of the book, Pater moved to London, where he leased the house at 12 Earl's Terrace, Kensington; he lived here with his sisters until the end of July 1893. Richard Aldington was among the first to observe that Pater felt it necessary to 'step beyond the jealous professionalism of Oxford to a wider and worldlier audience'.[84] He threw himself into writing articles and book reviews for a variety of magazines and newspapers, which he recycled in book form. As the correspondence demonstrates, he expended considerable energy on these projects during the last decade of his life, finding himself 'overburdened' and 'overworked'.[85]

During the period 1885–93, Pater produced eighteen book reviews, four articles, five book chapters, five lectures, and ten imaginary portraits, many of which appeared in a variety of newspapers and periodicals. From March 1885 to May 1887, he concentrated on 'imaginary portraits', publishing one portrait a year in *Macmillan's Magazine*. Originally, he planned to include 'The Child in the House' (1878) in this volume, but found that it required too many alterations. Macmillan issued *Imaginary Portraits* in an edition of 1,000 copies on 24 May 1887, and a second edition of 1,200 copies in November 1890. Pater's third book generated much less discussion than had the previous volumes;[86] some commentators identified the autobiographical dimension as the work's distinctive merit, while others claimed that the work represented the fusion of Pater's insight and imagination.

Very likely, Pater began work on *Gaston de Latour* (1896), the second volume in his proposed trilogy, shortly after completing *Marius the Epicurean*.[87] This book-length imaginary portrait was to feature a counterpart to Marius in sixteenth-century France. Pater published the first five chapters in *Macmillan's Magazine* from June to October 1888, and the greater part of chapter 7 ('The Lower Pantheism') as 'Giordano Bruno' in the *Fortnightly Review*, August 1889. (When he abandoned the work—complicated in historical setting and crowded with many personalities—he concentrated instead on one of the most difficult compositions he had undertaken, the essay on 'Style', published in the *Fortnightly Review* for December 1888.) Pater continued to work on the novel intermittently until his death. The chapters that had been published, together with one chapter in manuscript, were issued (1896) by Macmillan and Co. in book form, edited by Charles Lancelot Shadwell, Pater's long-time friend and literary executor.

Pater tried again to publish a collection of miscellaneous essays in June 1888, hoping to please the widest possible cross-section of the reading public. He proposed that this book, provisionally entitled *On Style, with other studies in Literature*, should be printed before the first of November 1888, and should appear in all respects similar to the third edition of *The Renaissance*. He collected eleven of his essays on English literature, together with three essays on Shakespeare, which had appeared in a variety of periodicals. He included two theoretical essays: 'Style' (the opening text) and 'Romanticism' (the concluding text, but renamed 'Postscript'). In these studies he outlines his conception of the literary critic, taking John Henry Newman[88] and Matthew Arnold[89] as his points of departure, thereby challenging two pre-eminent interpreters of British culture. Macmillan released this collection of essays under the title of *Appreciations, with an Essay on Style* on 15 November 1889. The book sold rapidly.

Almost immediately, Pater revived his campaign to secure a favourable public image. Two considerations motivated him: the response to *Imaginary Portraits* had not been as enthusiastic as he had hoped, and he felt uneasy about issuing a collection of previously published essays that spanned his entire literary career, including such a controversial composition as 'Aesthetic Poetry'. Consequently, he solicited sympathetic notices and reviews from friends, and in each instance thanked the reviewer. Reviewers on both sides of the Atlantic greeted *Appreciations* with mixed feelings.[90]

In December 1890, Pater began writing lectures on Plato and pre-Socratic and Socratic philosophy, and on 21 January 1892 he delivered the first of the series to Oxford undergraduates. Characteristically, he tried to publish the work in parts. He sent chapters to journalist Percy William Bunting (1836–1911), who edited the *Contemporary Review* (1882–1911). In his letter, Pater remarked: 'I have treated the subject in as popular a manner as I could' (dated 21 December [1891]). Macmillan drew up a contract for *Plato and Platonism* on 13 December 1892, awarding Pater an additional bonus of 10 per cent of the American sales. The book was issued on 9 February 1893. Interestingly, Pater thought that if any of his books were to survive, it would be this one.[91] He hoped that his lectures would 'interest' more students of philosophy than had attended his lectures in Oxford. What he produced, as several commentators pointed out, was not simply a study of philosophy, as contemporary scholars understood the term, but a portrait of a philosopher emerging from his cultural environment. The influence of Pythagoras, Parmenides, and Heraclitus on Plato is traced, showing how Plato transformed their disparate ideas into a unified whole. The goal of criticism, Pater maintains, is to determine where 'environment' leaves off and personality (or genius) begins. Almost imperceptibly, Pater glides over Plato's metaphysics in order to get to the latter's aesthetics, so that he can show how Plato anticipates modern thought.[92] In the end, this Plato, like Pater's Wordsworth, resembles Pater himself, namely, a relativist.

Pater experienced some apprehension about the critical reception of this book. Three days after it appeared, Pater sent a copy to a friend, James R. Thursfield (1840–1923), a naval historian and journalist, who was in charge of the 'Books of the Week' section of *The Times*. Thursfield's unsigned review in that newspaper appeared 16 February 1893. Pater also contacted another friend, Dugald Sutherland MacColl (1859–1948), art critic for the *Spectator*, who later told the following story: '*Plato* appeared, and one morning I was called from a scandalously late bath by a visitor. It was Pater with a copy in his hand. He gave me this, and explained that he was concerned about its reception by the reviewers. Could I arrange to deal with it in the *Spectator*? I stammered my astonishment that he should care what any reviewer said, and urged the difficulty of invading [R. H.] Hutton's domain. It would fall, I was certain, into more competent hands, but I would find some less preoccupied corner to say my modest word.'[93] It is likely that Pater prompted two other friends to review the volume: Richard Le Gallienne, who produced the unsigned review that appeared in the *Star*, 23 February 1893, and Edmund Gosse, who produced the signed review for *The New Review*, April 1893. Clearly, as late as 1893, Pater was sensitive to disapproval and suspicion.

THE LETTERS

In letter-writing Pater exercised restraint, understanding that all the arts served as modes of 'self-portraiture' and, as a consequence, that self-portraiture had best be undertaken indirectly. A. C. Benson claimed that Pater wrote few letters, whereas Thomas Wright insisted that Pater wrote many letters, as many as 400 to one friend.[94] If, as Lawrence Evans speculated, we assume that from the age of nineteen Pater wrote at least one letter per week, Pater would have written more than 1,800 letters— that is, over and above the business letters, acknowledgements, and polite social notes that form a major part of this collection. The letters that have survived seem all the fewer in comparison with the correspondence of such figures as George Eliot (4,060), Henry James (10,500), William Morris (2,400), D. G. Rossetti (5,800), A. C. Swinburne (2,000), J. A. Symonds (2,117), J. M. Whistler (10,000), and Oscar Wilde (1,398).[95]

The paucity of surviving letters might also confirm the traditional view that, compared with other major Victorian prose writers, Pater lived a singularly uneventful life.[96] It is fair to suggest, however, that the collection of letters in this volume by no means represents the probable shape of Pater's total correspondence. Some friendships are more fully documented than others, and some arrangements for the publication of his essays and books are recorded more accurately than others. Many more letters have survived from some periods of Pater's life than from others. It is instructive to consider the distribution of the letters, which provides an indication of where they shed most, and where least, light on various aspects of his life. To begin with, no letters to his nearest relatives—to his Aunt Bessie, who for eight years acted as head of the family, to his brother William, or to his sisters—have survived. The letters he must have written to Hester and Clara when separated from them so often during his undergraduate years, and apparently for some time thereafter, have been lost. A single letter (dated 30 April [1887]) on mourning paper to a cousin, Frederic Loudon Pater (1838–1901), a merchant, is all that remains of his family correspondence.

The number of surviving letters sent to any given correspondent is a dubious index of the intimacy between Pater and that correspondent. On the one hand, there are seven letters to Louise Chandler Moulton, with whom Pater was only slightly acquainted; and these seven may be all that Pater ever wrote to her. On the other hand, there are only five letters to Mary Arnold Ward, who knew Pater well for more than twenty years. It seems that, as a matter of principle, some friends never kept letters, while others destroyed their personal correspondence; still others, like Arthur Symons, to whom Pater wrote fifty or sixty letters, saved all the memorabilia that came their way. No letters to such close friends as F. W. Bussell, Ingram Bywater, Sidney Colvin, Mandell Creighton, Andrew Lang, Mark Pattison, A. Mary F. Robinson, and Simeon Solomon have survived; there is one letter apiece to such friends as Gerard Manley Hopkins, Charles Shadwell, A. C. Swinburne, and T. Humphry Ward; and there are two letters apiece to such close friends as C. H. O. Daniel, Emilia Pattison (later, Lady Dilke), and Lionel Johnson. The distribution of letters to other correspondents can be represented as follows: George Moore (three), Marc André Raffalovich (four), Oscar Browning (five), Michael Field (eight), Mountstuart Grant Duff (eight), Douglas Ainslie (nine), Violet Paget (nine), Oscar Wilde (ten), William Sharp (twelve), Herbert Horne (seventeen), Edmund Gosse (nineteen), and Arthur Symons (twenty-six).

The case is similar with Pater's business correspondence. His negotiations and dealings with his publisher Alexander Macmillan are well documented up to 1885, but after that year, surprisingly, only two of his letters to Macmillan and Co. survive, although thirty-nine of their letters to Pater over the following nine years have been preserved (see *TBB*). If one judges from the instance of Percy W. Bunting (three letters) and William Canton (nineteen) of the *Contemporary Review*, Pater's letters to the editors of journals in which he published his essays and fiction would seem to have been a sizeable portion of his correspondence. But in addition to Bunting and Canton, only John Chapman (three) of the *Westminster Review*, George Grove (four) of *Macmillan's Magazine*, and James Knowles (five) of *The Nineteenth Century* are represented here. The letters to an editor who would likely have shed light on Pater's development, those to John Morley (two) of the *Fortnightly Review* during the years 1869 to 1871, when four essays later collected in *Studies in the History of the Renaissance* were published there, are, for the most part, under-represented. And there are no letters to editors about his contributions to the *Academy*, the *Athenaeum*, *The Bookman*, *The Guardian*, *Harper's*, *The New Review*, the *Oxford Magazine*, the *Pall Mall Gazette*, or *Scribner's*—nor any to Morley's successors at the *Fortnightly* or to George Grove's at *Macmillan's Magazine*.

Some periods of Pater's life are better documented than others. The years from May 1859 to February 1873 (when *Studies in the History of the Renaissance* appeared), and from April 1873 to July 1885 (the years between Pater's first book and his second) are represented by twenty-nine and 112 letters respectively, whereas the years from August 1885 to the end of July 1894, the London period, are represented by 221 letters. For three years—1861, 1869, and 1870—there are no letters that can be dated with any reasonable probability. Relatively long personal letters are scarce throughout Pater's lifetime, but they occupy a prominent place in the early 1880s, the first years of his friendships with Violet Paget and William Sharp. During the London years, there are frequent brief messages on correspondence cards; discursive personal letters almost disappear when, by spending term-time in Oxford and certain weekends and the vacations in London, Pater was easily able to meet most of his friends and acquaintances. Thus, although more correspondence survives from this decade than from any other, the notes and letters between 1885 and 1893 are on the whole less substantial and informative.

THE IMAGE

To the surprise of some admirers, the prose artist did not become a model letter-writer. Commentators have lamented that Pater was no John Keats, an exemplary correspondent, no George Moore, a prolific one, and no James Joyce, a revealing one.[97] They observe that, while Pater read with great pleasure the correspondence of such figures as Gustave Flaubert, Charles Lamb, Michel de Montaigne, Blaise Pascal, and J. J. Winckelmann, he refrained from putting the lessons he learned in reading these collections into practice.[98] After all, they point out, he studied the correspondence of Flaubert during the years 1886–8, when he was preparing his essay on 'Style'. Now and again Pater acknowledged that he was a 'reluctant' correspondent, but by this he meant that, like many of his contemporaries, he postponed writing in the hope that at a later date inspiration would yield a letter of some length and interest. It is fair to say that letter-writing was not his favourite means of communication.

These concerns notwithstanding, the letters convey the most vivid image we have of Pater the public person bent on establishing and maintaining his reputation as an intellectual and writer, and Pater the private person, the head of a small household bent on providing for his sisters. As indicated earlier, more letters of the former category have surfaced than of the latter. It must be noted that the image of Pater that emerges from the letters in this volume is more complex than the image of Pater that emerges from *The Book Beautiful: Walter Pater and the House of Macmillan*: this revised Pater is an intellectual entrepreneur who, at every opportunity, reaffirmed his reputation as a scholar-artist. The present collection reminds us that, first and foremost, Pater was an Oxford don who met his obligations conscientiously;[99] many letters feature him negotiating his duties as a university teacher, ruminating on matters related to teaching, research (roughly speaking) and writing, and committee work. Evidence also suggests that he devoted considerable time to mentoring young, emerging writers and responding to inquiries sent by unknown admirers.

During the years 1864–74, Pater's 'unconventionality' attracted attention. The cavalier, if not iconoclastic, attitude he exhibited in his conversations and in his first essays revealed the antipathy he felt for authority, especially for the intellectual and moral forms he had encountered at the university.[100] According to reports, admirers in small circles in Oxford and London associated the name of W. H. Pater with a new and daring philosophy and a remarkable prose style.[101] In social interactions he presented himself as an amusing conversationalist.[102] T. Humphry Ward, a student at Brasenose College, 1864–8, recalled that this 'curiosity of admiration' became general when the essay on Leonardo da Vinci (1869) appeared.[103] Among the distinguished guests who assembled at the Rector's lodgings at Lincoln College, hosted by Emilia and Mark Pattison, Pater was known for his paradoxes and often mordant wit. The target of his jibes tended to be religion, especially Anglican orthodoxy. Mary Ward recalled a dinner party in the early 1870s at the Pater home during which 'a great tumult arose over a statement he made to the High Church wife of a well-known professor. Apparently, Pater had been in some way pressed controversially beyond the point of wisdom, and had said suddenly that no reasonable person could govern their lives by the opinions of a man who had died eighteen centuries ago. The Professor and his wife—I look back on them with the warmest affection—departed hurriedly, in agitation; and the rest of us only gradually found out what had happened.'[104]

Meanwhile, Pater declared his heterodoxy on 1 May 1869 when he discarded 'the ordinary academic attire of the period' and appeared at the 'private view' of the Royal Academy (advertised in *The Times*, 3 May 1869, 3) in a top hat, high stiff collar, silk tie of brilliant apple green, dog-skin gloves, dark-striped trousers, and patent leather boots.[105] Like Lord Byron and Matthew Arnold before him, and Oscar Wilde after him, Pater adopted the persona of the dandy, a figure of sartorial elegance, humorous and philosophical in demeanour, who poked fun at the hypocrisy of society via the paradoxes and epigrams he uttered in public; in this spirit, he ceased considering himself a 'provincial philosopher', but rather regarded himself as a cosmopolitan commentator on the fine arts. Similarly, an image of Pater at work as a writer deliberating boldly on such matters as the inception, composition, publication, promotion, and reception of his works,[106] emerges from many letters. In these letters he communicates with editors and publishers with regard to correcting proofs, attending to the design and the layout of texts, selecting copy for advertisements, signing contracts, and soliciting reviews of his books. We see him closely monitoring the production of his books, especially the early ones, involving himself in the process to an extent far greater than that achieved by many of his contemporaries.

The self-assertive Pater of the years 1864–73 gave way to the more reflective Pater of the years 1874–8.[107] Pater's 'flippant conversation' and the transgressive arguments of *Studies in the History of the Renaissance* elicited suspicion if not hostility from clerics in Oxford. Moreover, early in February 1874, suggestions that Pater was romantically involved with a Balliol College undergraduate named William Money Hardinge reached the authorities, notably Jowett, who threatened to make public the letters the two had exchanged if Pater ever attempted to stand for university office.[108] Apparently Pater's nature changed under this strain.[109] As well, at some point during the spring or summer of 1875, rumours reached Pater that he was being criticized for having encouraged a young man to read Théophile Gautier's infamous *Mademoiselle de Maupin*, during a visit to

Oscar Browning at Eton. Two years later, he was ruthlessly caricatured in *The New Republic* (1877), W. H. Mallock's novel satirizing a number of eminent Victorians, including Matthew Arnold, T. H. Huxley, Benjamin Jowett, Pater, and John Ruskin, which was initially serialized in *Belgravia* from June to December 1876. Pater comes across rather badly as Mr Rose, the arch-aesthete who always talks about 'self-indulgence and art'. Not surprisingly, Pater developed the theme of victimization in his writings during these years, repeating the image of the soul or body being torn to pieces.[110]

Despite Jowett's threat to make public the letters written to Hardinge, Pater sought university appointments, with a view to augmenting his meagre income. Early in 1874, he tried but failed to secure the position of Junior Proctor (a university-wide academic officer that it was Brasenose's turn to fill), thanks in large part to Jowett, who had taken up 'a line of definite opposition to Pater'.[111] The office went to his former student and colleague John Wordsworth. Early in 1877 Pater allowed his name to stand as candidate for the office of Professor of Poetry, only to withdraw from the field when opposition developed. In November 1884, he angled for and in fact secured the position of Curator of the University Galleries.[112] Early in 1885, he allowed his name to stand as candidate for Oxford's Slade Professor of Fine Art, an office held by Ruskin from 1869 to 1879 and from 1883 to 1885. Pater's expectations collapsed when news circulated that Ruskin had endorsed the candidacy of Hubert von Herkhomer (1849–1914), the Bavarian-born painter, illustrator, and printmaker.[113]

Evidence suggests that Pater also took committee work seriously.[114] Records show that he attended meetings, including those considering the merger of Lincoln College and Brasenose in 1878 and the design and construction of the New Quad in 1880. Brasenose colleague and close friend, Falconer Madan (see Biographical Register), documented these meetings.[115] After viewing various records, Ian Fletcher concluded that Pater's administrative powers were minor: for one thing, he tended to be rather vague.[116] Several contemporaries thought differently, however, because Pater not only served as Curator of the University Galleries but was also a member of the Library Committee of the Oxford Union in 1891.[117] He did not attend the opening of the Shelley Memorial at University College, under the auspices of Lady Shelley, on the afternoon of 14 June 1893 because he was attending a special meeting of the Principal and Fellows of Brasenose College, which had been called to consider the changes to be made to the College statutes.[118]

Many letters show Pater engaged in public relations, networking with established writers, and mentoring emerging talents. An avid reader of periodicals, he acknowledged the work of his colleagues that appeared in such 'intellectual' journals as the *Westminster Review* and the *Fortnightly Review*. These include the letters he wrote to Edmund Gosse, dated 4 November 1882, wishing the latter good luck with his book on D. G. Rossetti; to George Moore, dated [c.9 August 1887], stating that he had been reading *Confessions of a Young Man* (1888) with great interest; and to William Canton, dated 22 January [1892], affirming that he was reading his volume of poetry with great pleasure.

As well, many letters show Pater acknowledging the presentation copies of texts that young writers had sent him. As Oxford don and London man of letters he took an interest in undergraduates in part because, as William Sharp put it, they exuded energy and optimism.[119] Sharp's comment should be weighed in the context of Violet Paget's observation that a gentle sadness pervaded the Pater household.[120] For example, on 7 December [1872] he wrote to Swinburne to state that he enjoyed reading the verses included in the memorial volume for Théophile Gautier, *Le tombeau de Théophile Gautier*. Writers sent Pater approximately forty volumes, and in each case he crafted an appropriate response. Several of the volumes sent to him were dedicated to him: for example, William Sharp dedicated his life of D. G. Rossetti (1886) to Pater (see letter, 17 February 1886), and Arthur Symons dedicated *Days and Nights* (1889) to Pater (see letter, 21 November [1888]). Again, Pater crafted responses that conveyed the honour he felt.

Pater also assessed manuscripts and advocated for young writers, especially admirers who had recently sent him copies of their publications: these included Oscar Wilde, Marc André Raffalovich, W. B. Scott, Violet Paget, George Moore, Arthur Symons, Michael Field, Lionel Johnson, J. M. Gray, Richard Le Gallienne, Douglas Ainslie, and A. C. Benson.[121] In some of these letters, he lifted what Moore called his 'mask' to discuss their work and to reflect on his own. He encouraged them, critiqued their manuscripts, and in a couple of instances contacted a publisher on their behalf and wrote testimonials respectively.[122] In other letters Pater asked Macmillan and Co. to send an admirer a copy of his latest book.[123]

The public Pater shifts into the private Pater and back again. Evidence suggests that Pater's interest in, and kindness towards, other people was 'plain and effortless'.[124] Despite being judged shy by some of his contemporaries, he enjoyed socializing immensely. In many letters he conveyed the desire to meet, or acknowledged the pleasure he had in meeting, a correspondent. Interestingly, when he corresponded with writers from abroad, such as Paul Bourget,[125] and up-and-coming British writers such as Clyde Fitch,[126] he invited them to visit him in Oxford or London when they were in the area. These invitations were 'general' in wording (I hope to see you some day) or specific (Will you dine with us on Friday?). Now and then he invited a close friend, such as Oscar Browning, William Sharp, Edmund Gosse, or Marc André Raffalovich, who looked up to him as 'master', to visit him at Brasenose, where he had a spare room.

As the examples mentioned suggest, Pater cultivated a substantial social life. Ordinarily this meant arranging and attending social events: extending and responding to invitations to have lunch or tea or dinner, at home or at college primarily (see letter to Mountstaurt Grant Duff, 23 June [1887]). He would have tea with Oscar Wilde; lunch with Arthur Galton, Marc André Raffalovich, or Arthur Symons; and dinner with Douglas Ainslie, Oscar Browning, Edmund Gosse, Gerard Manley Hopkins, Herbert Horne, or D. S. MacColl. Violet Paget notes that, in June 1893, the Paters hosted a tea that featured twenty-four women and one man— Pater himself.[127]

As well, Pater enjoyed attending cultural events with friends, including art exhibitions. The correspondence during the 1880s includes three invitations of this sort, including one invitation he sent on 4 July [1884] to Marc André Raffalovich to go to the theatre. Now and then acquaintances met him as he wandered through the Greek Galleries at the British Museum. In addition, the letters show that he enjoyed walking in Oxford every day at about 5 pm, a fact reported by Hopkins among others and confirmed by the invitation he extended to Oscar Wilde on 15 November 1877. William Sharp recalled fondly the walks they took in Christ Church Meadows and by the banks of the Cherwell.[128]

Occasionally in a missive Pater shares a confidence or reveals an aspect of his inner life. One thinks of the letter to Oscar Browning, dated spring or summer 1875, explaining that he was concerned about the tenor and substance of his friend's letter. On a more mundane level, Pater often lamented that he was a bad letter-writer, admitting that he had been neglectful because he was overwhelmed with work, undertaken and promised (see letters dated 29 December 1888, 18 October 1890, 17 January 18[94], 19 May 1894), or suggesting that he read little contemporary English literature (5 July 1891, 9 August 1891).

The defensiveness, if not the diffidence, we see in the rhetorical manoeuvres undertaken by Pater when revising texts is also apparent in Pater's letter-writing persona, 1885–93.[129] Many observers have remarked on the note of 'weary courtesy' detected in his manner,[130] as if his motto were (to cite Lawrence Evans): 'I am utterly purposed that my mouth shall not offend',[131] the words of a favourite passage from the Book of Common Prayer (Psalm 17:3). The statement, slightly altered, serves as the motto for the Raphael essay (1892; see *CW* vi). What might be called a strategy of 'studied blandness' runs throughout the correspondence. The manner seems to have satisfied many but not all of his correspondents. When rereading the letter dated 4 March [1888], George Moore found himself less and less certain that Pater had paid him a compliment.[132] By the same token, Katharine Bradley flew into a rage when she read the letter dated 9 August [1890]; Pater, obviously struggling to find a compliment, simply writes that *The Tragic Mary* is 'a sterling piece of literary work'.

The so-called blandness that has been detected in the letters signals not only Pater's defensiveness but also his aversion to communicating by means of letters. Even with friends who were especially close he felt constrained in committing himself to pen and paper. Reducing the stress that he experienced in everyday life meant cultivating a circle of sympathetic and young admirers. With Emilia Pattison, Oscar Wilde, Violet Paget, William Sharp, Lionel Johnson, Arthur Symons, and F. W. Bussell he lowered his guard: he shared their concerns and spoke about himself and his ambitions. Commentators were mistaken in declaring that Pater 'could not be intimate'.[133] As Evans points out, intimacy for Pater usually required special circumstances as well as a special effort. Interestingly, Johnson maintained that, initially, it was the atmosphere of London that lifted Pater's spirits; when he visited the Paters in Kensington on 30 March 1889 Johnson found his host in 'radiant' and 'delightful' spirit.[134]

EXACTING EXPLORATIONS

From an early age, Pater dreamed of enjoying an intellectual life, whether as a clergyman or as a scholar; disillusioned with orthodox Christianity, he chose the latter career when the opportunity presented itself. His approach to the academic profession differed from that being developed by his colleagues. In his essay on 'Style', Pater characterized the literary artist as a scholar, stressing the notion that writing that aims at beauty must be exacting in self-exploration. With this dictum in mind, and convinced that imaginative prose was the special art of the modern world, he fashioned himself not as a conventional scholar, but as a prose artist. Pater poured himself into his creative non-fiction and fiction, regarding letter-writing to be of secondary importance. As we have seen, this has puzzled commentators.[135] While these observations have more than a little validity, the letters printed in this volume constitute a valuable resource for appreciating the artist and the man. The would-be biographer faces the challenge of grasping the character of a person who seemingly lived a rather uneventful life, and who, by design, discouraged an examination of his private life. Fortunately, however, his letters are more revealing as life documents than commentators in the past have maintained.

Alarmed by the disapproval he had met early in his career, Pater retreated from the boldness of his earlier conversations and writings, and in his letters he adopted a rhetorical strategy aimed at achieving his professional ends as completely as possible in a rather hostile world. The image that emerges from the letters printed in this volume is not simply that of the intellectual entrepreneur who promoted his reputation as a scholar-artist; rather, the image is that of the esteemed scholar-artist who made every effort to socialize with a small circle of friends and to mentor young writers. The letters that could be categorized as personal clearly reveal this social dimension of Pater's life and work. As well, one is struck by the time and effort Pater put into responding to the queries posted by anonymous admirers.

While in much of his extant, largely professional, correspondence, Pater fashions a persona that is cautious, one that he judges will achieve his professional ends by giving the reader no cause for offence, at times he drops his mask just enough to allow those correspondents with whom he feels safe to glimpse his face. Indeed, what emerges from a careful reading of all his letters is 'a wise, grave passiveness, a gentle susceptibility, a kind of soft impressionability; that he tried to keep, and did keep'.[136] Yet, given his reserved nature and the constraints he lived under, it is in his imaginative prose that we see him most clearly. In his correspondence, he could express himself indirectly, fashioning himself 'as a permanently significant symbolical figure: the most complete, the least trivial, of the aesthetic man'.[137]

Appendix A lists letters and provides information regarding letters that Pater is known to have written, but of which not even a phrase has survived. Such a list yields a better approximation of what was, at one time, the totality of Pater's correspondence. Appendix B lists the recipients of Pater's letters, and those of Clara and Hester Pater, included in this volume. Appendix C lists the individuals and the institutions that have provided me with copies of manuscript letters.

Notes

[1] Herbert Read, 'Walter Pater', *The Tenth Muse: Essays in Criticism* (London: Routledge & Kegan Paul, 1957), 58.
[2] Ian Fletcher, *Walter Pater* (London: Longmans Group, 1959; revised 1971), 1.
[3] Michael Levey, *The Case of Walter Pater* (London: Thames and Hudson, 1978), 29.
[4] Thomas Wright, *The Life of Walter Pater*, 2 vols (London: Everett, 1907), 1: 15.

[5] See Denis Donoghue, *Walter Pater: Lover of Strange Souls* (New York: Alfred Knopf, 1995), 24–5.
[6] Wright, *Life*, 1: 19–26, 43–4.
[7] Wright, *Life*, 1: 64–9.
[8] Wright, *Life*, 1: 77–8.
[9] Gosse, 'Walter Pater: A Portrait', *Contemporary Review*, 66 (Dec. 1894), 797–8.
[10] See Billie Andrew Inman, *Walter Pater's Reading: A Bibliography of his Library Borrowings and Literary References, 1858–1873* (New York: Garland, 1981), ix–xxix.
[11] Wright, *Life*, 1: 172–9.
[12] Bywater, qtd in William Walrond Jackson, *Ingram Bywater: The Memoir of an Oxford Scholar, 1840–1914* (Oxford: Clarendon, 1917), 196–7.
[13] Wright, *Life*, 1: 154–6.
[14] See Jackson, *Ingram Bywater*, 23–9; W. R. Ward, *Victorian Oxford* (London: Frank Cass, 1965), 193–202; A. J. Engel, *From Clergyman to Don: The Rise of the Academic Profession in the Nineteenth Century* (Oxford: Clarendon, 1983), 56–77.
[15] All university students had to endorse the tenets of the Church of England by signing the 'Thirty-Nine Articles' of faith when matriculating (entering the university as a full member) and graduating. In June 1871, the University Tests Act removed religious tests for all higher degrees at British universities.
[16] See Ward, *Victorian Oxford*, 213–24; Engel, *From Clergyman to Don*, 106–55; William F. Shuter, *Rereading Walter Pater* (Cambridge: Cambridge University Press, 1997), 79–80.
[17] Pater rephrases the question in 'Winckelmann': 'And what does the spirit need in the face of modern life?' (see *CW* i). See Kate Hext, *Walter Pater: Individualism and Aesthetic Philosophy* (Edinburgh: Edinburgh University Press, 2013), 8.
[18] Inman, *Walter Pater's Reading*, 29–31.
[19] Mrs Humphry Ward, *A Writer's Recollections*, 2 vols (New York and London: Harper and Bros., 1918), 1: 51, 55–6. See Mary Arnold Ward in the Biographical Register.
[20] Wright, *Life*, 1: 173.
[21] See Stefano Evangelista, 'The German Roots of British Aestheticism: Pater's "Winckelmann", Goethe's Winckelmann, and Pater's Goethe', *Anglo-German Affinities and Antipathies*, ed. Rüdiger Görner (Munich: Ludicium, 2004), 57–70.
[22] Wright, *Life*, 1: 167–71.
[23] Qtd in Wright, *Life*, 1: 188.
[24] According to Inman, Pater wrestled with such fundamental questions as: what is knowledge? See *Walter Pater's Reading*, xi.
[25] Pater read Mill's work assiduously, subscribing to the latter's dictum that thinking individuals must follow reason as far as the faculty would carry them. Benson, *Walter Pater*, 194.
[26] Wright, *Life*, 1: 174, 203–4. On 30 June 1860, the Oxford University Museum was the site of a famous debate about *On the Origin of Species*. Participants included Darwin apologist Thomas Huxley, Benjamin Brodie, Joseph Dalton Hooker, Robert FitzRoy, and the Bishop of Oxford, Samuel Wilberforce, who was fiercely critical of evolutionary theory. The event is now known as the Huxley-Wilberforce debate.
[27] For Pater's response to the pre-Socratic philosopher's theories, see *The Renaissance*, especially the 'Conclusion' (*CW* i) and *Plato and Platonism* (*CW* vii).
[28] Bywater, qtd in Jackson, *Ingram Bywater*, 197.
[29] See Victor Shea and William Whitla, 'Part One: Reading "An Epoch in the History of Opinion" ', in *Essays and Reviews: The 1860 Text and its Reading*, ed. Shea and Whitla (Charlottesville, Va.: University Press of Virginia, 2000), 3–126. Contributors included Frederick Temple, Baden Powell, Mark Pattison, and Benjamin Jowett; several were accused of heresy. See also Alvar Ellegard, *Darwin and the General Reader* (Chicago: University of Chicago Press, 1958), 27, 106; Josef L. Altholz, 'A Tale of Two Controversies: Darwinism and the Debate over *Essays and Reviews*', *Church History*, 63.1 (Mar. 1994), 50–9.

[30] See David DeLaura, *Hebrew and Hellene in Victorian England: Newman, Arnold, and Pater* (Austin: University of Texas Press, 1969), 181–91; Linda Dowling, *Hellenism and Homosexuality in Victorian Oxford* (Ithaca, N.Y.: Cornell University Press, 1994), 59–66; Stefano Evangelista, '"Life in the Whole": Goethe and English Aestheticism', *Publications of the English Goethe Society*, 82.3 (Dec. 2013), 183–5.

[31] See Pater's review of *Robert Elsmere* by Mary Arnold Ward (1888), *CW* v.

[32] Wright, *Life*, 1: 145–54. It was Socrates who was supposed to have declared, at his trial, that the unexamined life is not worth living. For a discussion of those who pursued philosophy as a way of life, including Socrates, Montaigne, and Nietzsche, see Richard Wollheim, 'Walter Pater: From Philosophy to Art', *Comparative Criticism*, 17 (1995), 21–40; and Alexander Nehamas, *The Art of Living: Socratic Reflections from Plato to Foucault* (Berkeley: University of California Press, 1998).

[33] Gosse, 'Walter Pater: A Portrait', 795–810. See also Kit Andrews, 'Walter Pater as Oxford Hegelian: *Plato and Platonism*, and T. H. Green's *Prolegomena to Ethics*', *Journal of the History of Ideas*, 72.3 (July 2011), 437–59.

[34] Inman, *Walter Pater's Reading*, x.

[35] See Thomas Carlyle, 'Goethe's Helena', *Foreign Review*, 1 (Apr. 1828), 429–68; 'Goethe', *Foreign Review*, 2 (July 1828), 80–127; 'Death of Goethe', *New Monthly Magazine*, 34 (June 1832), 507–12.

[36] Pater's 1867 essay, 'Winckelmann', became the last chapter in *The Renaissance*; see *CW* i.

[37] W. H. Bruford, *The German Tradition of Self-Cultivation: 'Bildung' from Humboldt to Thomas Mann* (Cambridge: Cambridge University Press, 1975), 14–18; W. H. Bruford, 'Goethe, Walter Pater, and "the Aesthetic Consciousness"', *Festschrift for E. W. Herd*, ed. August Obermayer (Dunedin: University of Otago Press, 1980), 44–54.

[38] In *Poetry and Truth* Pater discovered a formative influence that he acknowledged throughout his career. See DeLaura, *Hebrew and Hellene*, 207–22; Bruford, 'Goethe, Walter Pater, and "the Aesthetic Consciousness"', 44–54; Donald D. Stone, 'Goethe and the Victorians', *Carlyle Annual*, 13 (1992/93), 17–34; Hext, *Walter Pater: Individualism and Aesthetic Philosophy*, 147–55.

[39] See 'Winckelmann', *CW* i.

[40] Johann Wolfgang von Goethe, *Poetry and Truth: From my own Life*, trans. Minna Steele Smith, 2 vols (London: G. Bell, 1913), 1: 122–3.

[41] See Pater's letter to Lewis Campbell, 6 May 1894.

[42] Geoffrey Faber, *Jowett: A Portrait with Background* (London: Faber, 1957), 166–7; Lesley Higgins, 'Hopkins and "The Jowler"', *Texas Studies in Literature and Language*, 31 (Spring 1989), 143–67.

[43] Qtd in Benson, *Walter Pater*, 9.

[44] Inman, *Walter Pater's Reading*, xi.

[45] Bywater, qtd in Jackson, *Ingram Bywater*, 79.

[46] Hext, *Walter Pater: Individualism and Aesthetic Philosophy*, 24–7.

[47] Bywater, qtd in Jackson, *Ingram Bywater*, 79.

[48] Inman, *Walter Pater's Reading*, 32–4.

[49] See Linda Dowling, 'The Aesthete and the Eighteenth-Century', *Victorian Studies*, 20.4 (Summer 1977), 357–77. One can read the rich texture of Pater's aesthetic prose as a 'mask' worn to conceal his sexual identity. Increasingly, commentators have subjected his texts to queer readings, illustrating his evolving hermeneutic practice. Linda Dowling, Herbert Sussman, and Stefano Evangelista take as their point of departure the premise that a full understanding of Pater's homoeroticism is fundamental to interpreting his *oeuvre*. For a discussion of aesthetic criticism as a form of self-portraiture, see Evangelista, who in 'Walter Pater Unmasked: Impressionistic Criticism and the Gender of Aesthetic Writing', *Literature Compass*, 1.1 (Dec. 2004), 1–4, argues that Pater's writings bring together the autobiographical element of critical impressionism and the pleasure of aesthetic criticism in a way that reveals the critic as a sexually desiring subject.

[50] Inman, *Walter Pater's Reading*, 49.
[51] Hext, *Walter Pater: Individualism and Aesthetic Philosophy*, 1–24.
[52] Inman, *Walter Pater's Reading*, ix–xv, xxv.
[53] Inman, *Walter Pater's Reading*, xi–xii.
[54] Wright, *Life*, 1: 211.
[55] Benson, *Walter Pater*, 183–4.
[56] Pater and Oscar Wilde situated themselves in opposition to authority as it was being established in movements towards the institutionalization of knowledge and the professionalization of disciplines. See Ian Small, *Conditions for Criticism: Authority, Knowledge, and Literature in the Late Nineteenth-Century* (Oxford: Clarendon, 1991), 31–63, 64–88, 91–111, 112–30.
[57] See Laurel Brake, *Subjugated Knowledges: Journalism, Gender, and Literature in the Nineteenth Century* (New York: New York University Press, 1994), 16.
[58] Policies governing how authors contributed reviews and articles varied from periodical to periodical. See Brake, *Subjugated Knowledges*, 1–35, and the Critical Introduction to *CW* v.
[59] J. B. Bullen, *The Myth of the Renaissance in Nineteenth-Century Writing* (Oxford: Clarendon, 1994), 280.
[60] Benson, *Walter Pater*, 29.
[61] Tanis Hinchcliffe, *North Oxford* (New Haven: Yale University Press, 1992), 38–64.
[62] Mrs Humphry Ward, *A Writer's Recollections*, 1: 123–4.
[63] See Lesley Higgins, 'Living Effectively: Charlotte Green and Walter Pater', *Studies in Walter Pater and Aestheticism*, 2 (Autumn 2016), 57–70.
[64] Gosse, 'Walter Pater: A Portrait', 801–2.
[65] Hilary Fraser, *The Victorians and Renaissance Italy* (Oxford: Blackwell, 1992).
[66] See J. B. Bullen, 'Pater and Ruskin on Michelangelo: Two Contrasting Views', *Prose Studies*, 4.1 (1981), 55–73; Wendell Harris, 'Ruskin and Pater—Hebrew and Hellene—Explore the Renaissance', *Clio*, 17.2 (1988), 173–85; J. B. Bullen, 'The Historiography of *Studies in the History of the Renaissance*', in *Pater in the 1990s*, ed. Laurel Brake and Ian Small (Greensboro, N.C.: ELT Press, 1991), 155–67; Fraser, *The Victorians and Renaissance Italy*, 213–34; Kenneth Daley, *The Rescue of Romanticism: Walter Pater and John Ruskin* (Athens, Oh.: Ohio University Press, 2001), 51–86.
[67] For an account of Pater's relationship with the firm, together with an analysis of how Pater monitored the production of his publications, see Robert Seiler, *The Book Beautiful: Walter Pater and the House of Macmillan* (London: Athlone Press, 1999).
[68] For a discussion of aesthetic criticism as a vehicle for creative self-portraiture, see Stefano Evangelista and Katherine Harloe, 'Pater's "Winckelmann"', in *Pater the Classicist: Classical Scholarship, Reception, and Aestheticism*, ed. Charles Martindale, Stefano Evangelista, and Elizabeth Prettejohn (Oxford: Oxford University Press, 2017), 63–80.
[69] For the critics' initial response to this volume, see *Walter Pater: The Critical Heritage*, ed. Robert M. Seiler (London: Routledge and Kegan Paul, 1980), and *The Reception of Walter Pater in Europe*, ed. Stephen Bann (London: Thoemmes Continuum, 2004).
[70] The 'Conclusion' consists of the last seven paragraphs of 'Poems by William Morris', carefully revised. See *CW* i.
[71] Qtd in Sharp, 'Some Personal Reminiscences of Walter Pater', *Atlantic Monthly*, 74 (Dec. 1894), 811.
[72] Gosse, 'Walter Pater: A Portrait', 804, 806.
[73] Benson, *Walter Pater*, 59.
[74] See *CW* v.
[75] *Academy*, 7 Nov. 1874, 506.
[76] *Academy*, 12 Dec. 1874, 630.
[77] Donald L. Hill, Critical Notes for Walter Pater, *The Renaissance*, ed. Donald L. Hill (Berkeley: University of California Press, 1980), 282–3.
[78] See the Critical Introduction to Lene Østermark-Johansen's edition of Pater's *Imaginary Portraits* (*CW* iii). See also Elisa Bizzotto, 'The Imaginary Portrait: Pater's

Contribution to a Literary Genre', in *Transparencies of Desire*, ed. Laurel Brake, Lesley Higgins, and Carolyn Williams (Greensboro, N.C.: ELT Press, 2002), 213–23.

[79] Germain d'Hangest, *Walter Pater. L'homme et l'oeuvre*, 2 vols (Paris: Didier, 1961), 2: 317.

[80] Benson, *Walter Pater*, 89–90.

[81] Historians such as Edward Gibbon, author of *The History of the Decline and Fall of the Roman Empire* (1776–88), regarded life in Rome under Marcus Aurelius Antonius as an idyllic moment in human history. From the middle of the nineteenth century, however, B. G. Niebuhr and Theodor Mommsen questioned the lessons that Gibbon and others had proposed. In this tradition, Pater's *Marius the Epicurean* is not only an imaginative re-creation of Antonine Rome, but a critique of Antonine Stoicism and a subtle analysis of Victorian England. Fletcher, *Walter Pater*, 30–1.

[82] In the letter to Paget dated 22 July [1883], Pater explains that he regards completing *Marius the Epicurean* as 'a sort of duty'; 'there is a fourth sort of religious phase possible for the modern mind, over and above those presented in your late admirable paper in the *Contemporary*, the conditions of which phase it is the main object of my design to convey.' See Vernon Lee, 'The Portrait Art of the Renaissance', *Cornhill Magazine*, 47 (May 1883), 564–81, and 'The Responsibilities of Unbelief: A Conversation between Three Rationalists', *Contemporary Review*, 43 (May 1883), 685–710.

[83] See Seiler, *Walter Pater: A Life Remembered*, 113–61.

[84] Richard Aldington, ed., 'Introduction', *Walter Pater: Selected Works* (London: William Heinemann, 1948), 13.

[85] See Monsman, *Walter Pater*, 105; Levey, *The Case of Walter Pater*, 173.

[86] See Seiler, *Walter Pater: A Life Remembered*, 162–93.

[87] Benson, *Walter Pater*, 140. See Gerald Monsman's Critical Introduction to *Gaston de Latour* (*CW* iv).

[88] DeLaura, *Hebrew and Hellene*, 329–38. For Pater's unpublished essay on Newman, see *CW* x.

[89] Laurel Brake, *Walter Pater* (Plymouth: Northcote House, 1994), 47.

[90] See Seiler, *Walter Pater: A Life Remembered*, 194–241.

[91] Benson, *Walter Pater*, 162.

[92] Donoghue, *Walter Pater: Lover of Strange Souls*, 250–3.

[93] D. S. MacColl, 'A Batch of Memories. XII. Walter Pater', *Week-End Review*, 4 (Dec. 1931), 759–60.

[94] Benson, *Walter Pater*, 185; Wright, *Life of Walter Pater*, 1: ix. The alleged friend, Richard Jackson, was never a reliable source.

[95] The trials of Oscar Wilde concentrated public attention on homosexuality, and thus intensified assertions of its 'indecency' (Wilde was convicted of 'gross indecency' according to the Labouchere amendment of the Criminal Law Amendment Act, 1885). In this context, Pater's sisters, Hester and Clara, blocked attempts to scrutinize their brother's private life and may have destroyed invaluable documents, including correspondence.

[96] Lawrence Evans, 'Walter Pater', *Victorian Prose: A Guide to Research*, ed. David DeLaura (New York: Modern Language Association, 1973), 329.

[97] Robert M. Scotto, review of *Letters of Walter Pater* by Lawrence Evans, *English Literature in Transition*, 142 (1971), 151–2.

[98] See Pater's review, *Pall Mall Gazette*, 25 Aug. 1888, 1–2 (*CW* v).

[99] William F. Shuter, 'Pater as Don', *Prose Studies*, 11.1 (1988), 41–60.

[100] Small, *Conditions for Criticism*, 91–111.

[101] T. Humphry Ward, qtd in Benson, *Walter Pater*, 22.

[102] Benson, *Walter Pater*, 32.

[103] T. Humphry Ward, 'Reminiscences. Brasenose, 1864–72', *Brasenose College Quatercentenary Monographs*, 2 vols (Oxford: Clarendon, 1909), 2: part 2, 74.

[104] Mrs Humphry Ward, *A Writer's Recollections*, 121.

[105] See Gosse, 'Walter Pater: A Portrait', 801.

[106] See Laurel Brake, *Print in Transition: Studies in Media and Book History* (London: Palgrave, 2001), 185.

[107] See d'Hangest, *Walter Pater. L'homme et l'oeuvre*, 1: 220–40; and Lesley Higgins, 'Pater and the "Laws" of Victorian Iconography', *Journal of Pre-Raphaelite Studies*, ns 19 (Fall 2010), 66–82.

[108] See Billie Andrew Inman, 'Estrangement and Connection: Walter Pater, Benjamin Jowett, and William M. Hardinge', in *Pater in the 1990s*, ed. Laurel Brake and Ian Small (Greensboro, N.C.: ELT Press, 1991), 1–20.

[109] See Inman, 'Estrangement and Connection', and Seiler, *Walter Pater: A Life Remembered*, 253–61. But see also Lesley Higgins and David Latham, 'Privileging the Later Pater: The Choice of Copy-Text for the *Collected Works*', in *Testing New Opinions and Courting New Impressions: New Perspectives on Walter Pater*, ed. Anne-Florence Gillard-Estrada, Martine Lambert-Charbonnier, and Charlotte Ribeyrol (New York: Routledge, 2018), 37–50, who argue that a change is not visible in the collations of his prose: 'Too much has been made of a timid Pater withdrawing his controversial "Conclusion"... and not enough credit is given to the courageous Pater who restored it in the subsequent editions despite Benjamin Jowett's threat to expose Pater's scandalous affair with a student' (38).

[110] Inman, *Walter Pater and His Reading*, 16–20.

[111] Benson, *Walter Pater*, 54–8; Wright, *Life of Walter Pater*, 1: 255–6.

[112] See *The Times*, 6 Nov. 1884, 10.

[113] See Vernon Lee, *Vernon Lee's Letters*, ed. Irene Cooper Willis (London: privately printed, 1937), 178, 192.

[114] Benson, *Walter Pater*, 23.

[115] See Seiler, *Walter Pater: A Life Remembered*, 57–61.

[116] Fletcher, *Walter Pater*, 6.

[117] Brake, *Walter Pater*, 13.

[118] Wright, *Life of Walter Pater*, 2: 193–4.

[119] Sharp, 'Some Personal Reminiscences', 802, 804–5.

[120] Lee, *Letters of Vernon Lee*, 147, 223.

[121] See Levey, *The Case of Walter Pater*, 171; Brake, *Walter Pater*, 14.

[122] For examples, see letters to Symons, 17 July [1888], 2 Aug. [1888], and 2 Oct. [1888].

[123] See letters to Sharp, 23 May [1887], and to Michael Field, 1 Mar. [1893].

[124] Fletcher, *Walter Pater*, 9.

[125] See letter to Paul Bourget, 2 Jan. [1884], and to L. C. Moulton, 31 [July 1889].

[126] See letter to Clyde Fitch, 1 Aug. 1890, and to P. M. Watkins, 24 Apr. [1894].

[127] Lee, *Letters of Vernon Lee*, 348.

[128] Sharp, 'Some Personal Reminiscences', 807.

[129] See Evans, Introduction, *Letters of Walter Pater*, xxiii.

[130] Unnamed source, qtd in Benson, *Walter Pater*, 180.

[131] Evans, Introduction, *Letters of Walter Pater*, xxiii.

[132] See George Moore, *Avowals* (London: William Heinemann, 1924), 196–8.

[133] See Benson, *Walter Pater*, 185.

[134] Qtd from Johnson's letter to Arthur Galton, 2 Apr. 1889, in Arthur W. Patrick, *Lionel Johnson. Poète et critique* (Paris: L. Rodstein, 1939), 20–1.

[135] See John Coates, 'Controversial Aspects of Pater's "Style"', *Papers on Language & Literature*, 40.4 (Fall 2004), 384–411; Stefano Evangelista, 'Walter Pater Unmasked', 1–4.

[136] T. H. Warren, qtd in Benson, *Walter Pater*, 175.

[137] Fletcher, *Walter Pater*, 46.

Textual Introduction

The major problem in preparing this edition of Walter Pater's correspondence has been the challenge of determining when the letters were composed; like many of his contemporaries, including Oscar Wilde, Pater rarely dated his letters. Very few letters bear, in his hand, the year in which they were written. Some letters give the day of the week only, and others give no indication of the date (or the place) whatever. Some letters have been dated on the basis of internal evidence, such as postmarks, although occasionally letters have been put into wrong envelopes; others have been dated on the basis of external evidence, such as contemporary endorsements and cross-references. When internal evidence is deemed inadequate, a date can be conjectured with considerable reliability on the basis of the characteristics of the handwriting and/or the characteristics of the stationery used. In tackling this problem, I found the work of Lawrence Evans a valuable resource.

Pater's handwriting (almost always legible) changed appreciably over the course of his adult life,[1] as the samples provided in figures 1, 2, 3, and 4 make clear. At first childish in character, illustrated by a stiff verticality of the handwriting in the letters he wrote on Oxford Union stationery during the 1860s (fig. 1), his writing style matured, illustrated by the graceful script in the letters he wrote from about 1870 to 1887 (fig. 2). Arguably, this abrupt change suggests a new sense of purpose. It must also be noted that, generally speaking, Pater's sentences flow from one to another with few textual alterations; characteristically, he uses commas before predicates, semi-colons and colons freely, and question marks rarely. He wrote some letters in haste, complaining that he was overburdened with work promised or underway (see letter to Barrington, 2 December [1890]). During the late 1880s (fig. 3), however, the handwriting began to grow irregular, at first intermittently during the period when Pater experienced gout, and eventually as a matter of course so that his script in his final years (fig. 4) can be clearly distinguished from what it had

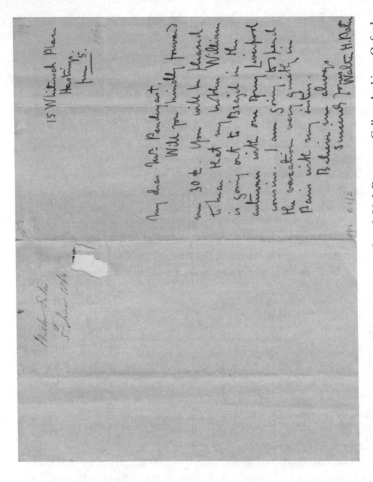

Figure 1. Walter Pater to John Pendergast, 5 June [1864]. Brasenose College Archives, Oxford. Courtesy of the Principal and Fellows of Brasenose College, Oxford.

been before 1887. It should be noted that no date in this edition has been assigned solely on the basis of the characteristics of the handwriting, but they have contributed to the attribution in some doubtful cases, all of which are indicated in the notes.

Interestingly, Pater varied his signature several times. Between 1859 and 1877 he consistently signed his letters 'W. H. Pater', and continued to do so, inconsistently, later in life. From 1877, he infrequently signed letters 'W. H. Pater' and 'Walter H. Pater' but showed a decided preference for 'Walter Pater' (one 1887 letter, to Horne, is signed 'W. Pater'). As a mark of familiarity, he signed himself 'W. P.' in the letter to Emily Daniel, [April or May 1894].

Evans recorded the details of many manuscript letters, including the dimensions of the stationery used, colour, watermarks, ink, and the character of the handwriting; and for certain periods of Pater's life, definite and exclusive scribal patterns.[2] Evidence suggests that Pater used a number of white correspondence cards, approximately 11.5 by 9.2 cm, with rectangular (instead of the usual rounded) corners and plain (as opposed to gilt) edges, which seem to belong only to the autumn and winter of 1886–7. Between November 1889 and the spring of 1890, he had a set of mottled grey-green cards, measuring 11.4 by 8.9 cm, with rounded corners and gilt edges, which he apparently used only in notes written from his residence in the Kensington district of London. He also used white stationery measuring 11.2 by 17.9 cm and watermarked 'Herculaneum | Note Paper' only between the summer of 1891 and March of 1892, in letters he wrote from his residence in Kensington (in the absence of any internal evidence that might dispute the date, the year 1891 or 1892 is supplied in brackets, without a question mark). Some other types of card or letter paper cannot be restricted to periods so distinctly, but still may suggest a two- or three-year span, where otherwise there might be nothing but the characteristics of handwriting to establish a probable date.

Assigning dates has thus been a matter of considering internal evidence, handwriting characteristics, and cross-references. All dates supplied editorially are enclosed within square brackets, for example, 9 May [1859]; doubtful ones are followed by a question mark. It might be thought that the extensive Pater literature would answer many dating problems, but Pater's early biographers ignored the matter. Like many people, he occasionally mis-dated a letter, especially at the beginning of a new year or a new month. In such cases I have corrected the date in square brackets in the headnote, with a note explaining the correction. In cases where my dating is conjectural, I have placed the letters in the most likely positions in the sequence.

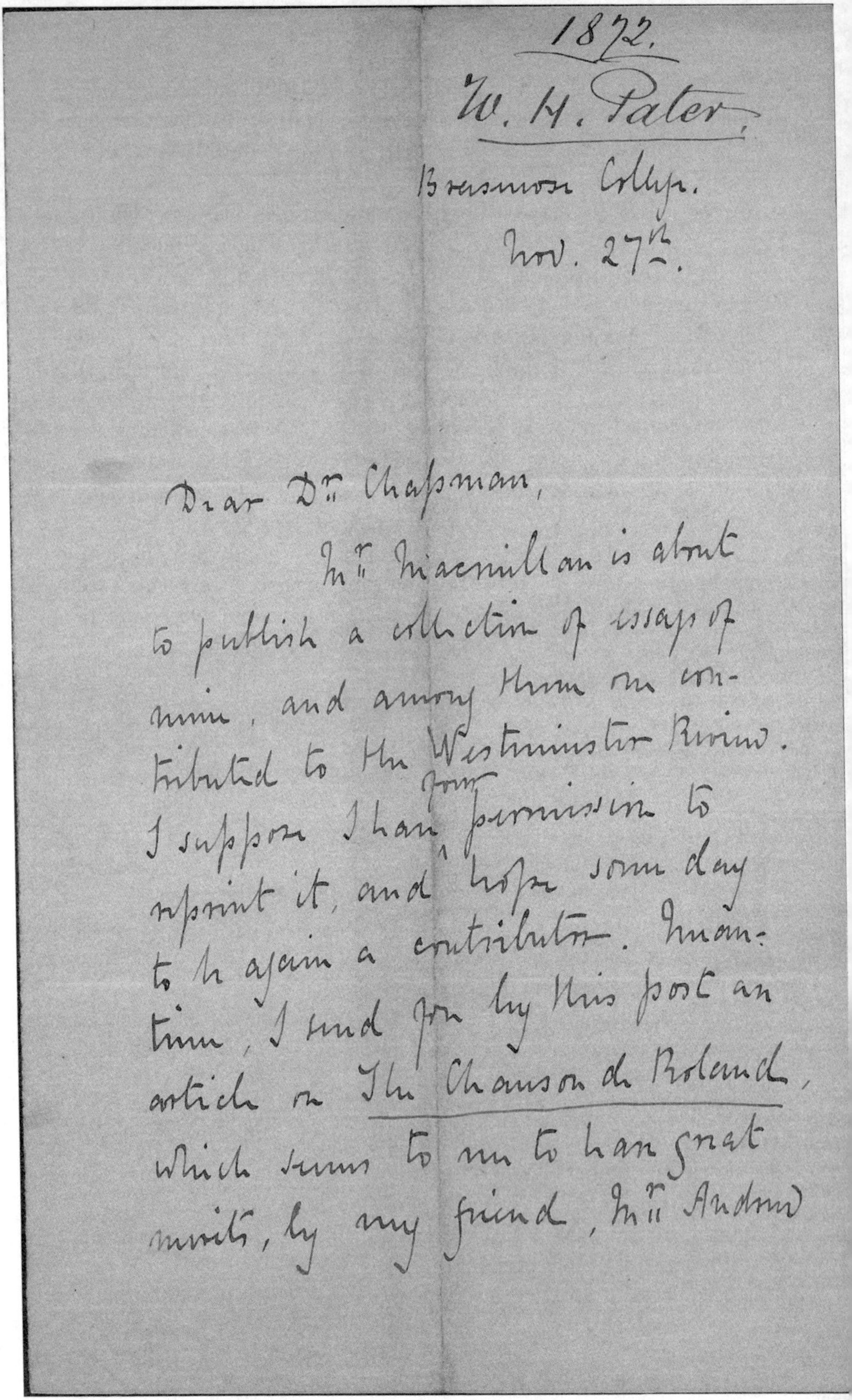

1872.

W. H. Pater

Brasenose College.

Nov. 27th.

Dear Dr Chapman,

Mr Macmillan is about to publish a collection of essays of mine, and among them one contributed to the Westminster Review. I suppose I have your permission to reprint it, and hope some day to be again a contributor. In the mean time, I send you by this post an article on The Chanson de Roland, which seems to me to have great merits, by my friend, Mr Andrew

Figure 2. Walter Pater to John Chapman, 27 November 1872. Yale University, New Haven, Connecticut. Courtesy of Beinecke Rare Book and Manuscript Library, Yale University.

Lang, Fellow of Merton College, the author of a volume of translations from French poets &c. which you may have seen. He is now at Cannes, and has entrusted the article to me, hoping that you might be able to find a place for it in the Westminster Review.

Believe me always
Very sincerely yours
W. H. Pater.

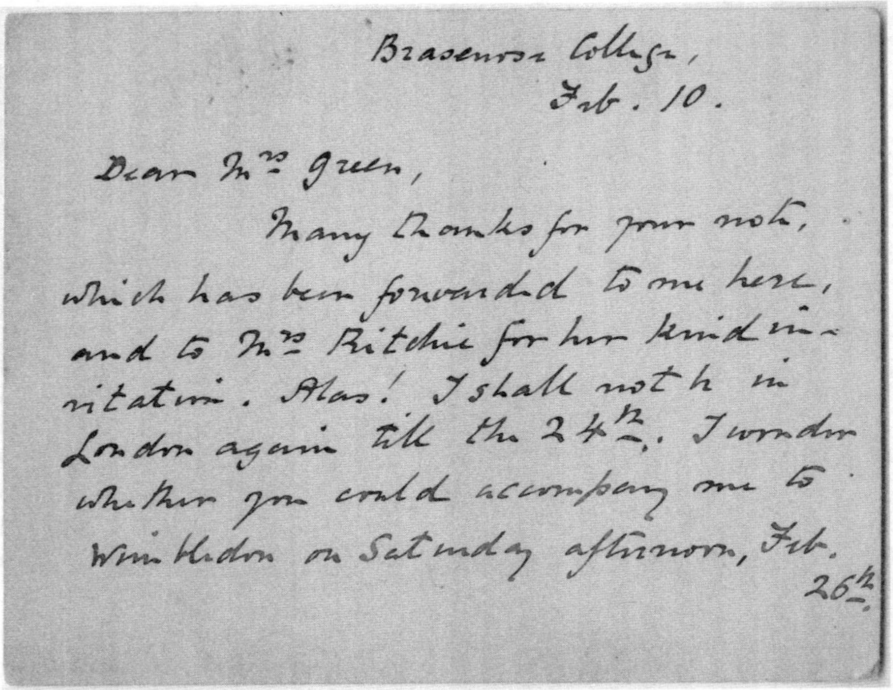

Brasenose College,
Feb. 10.

Dear Mrs Green,

Many thanks for your note, which has been forwarded to me here, and to Mrs Ritchie for her kind invitation. Alas! I shall not be in London again till the 24th. I wonder whether you could accompany me to Winchester on Saturday afternoon, Feb. 26th.

Figure 3. Walter Pater to Charlotte Symonds Green, 10 February [1887]. Bates College, Lewiston, Maine. Courtesy of Bates College, Lewiston, Maine.

It would give me great pleasure
if you could, suppose next day
were convenient to 3 = Ritchie.
I am reading Brownings and Rossetti
which will perhaps a little publicise
and hope to bring it you when
I come to London.

Very faithfully yours
Walter Pater.

YORK April 5th 1894.

Dear Mr Lane,

My sisters have seen the drawing, and think it so unlike me that the publication of it must be given up. I am very sorry; but, if Rothenstein thinks it worth while, would sit to him again. I am

Figure 4. Walter Pater to John Lane, 5 April 1894. Brasenose College Archives, Oxford. Courtesy of the Principal and Fellows of Brasenose College, Oxford.

going to Glasgow for a
dyne, and am taking
some of those northern
cathedral towns on my
way there, and write
as best I may to catch
the post.

By the way, the few
lines I sent you à propos
of Mr. Bussell might be
abbreviated, by the omission
of "his friends", to "instruct".
Believe me
Very sincerely yours
Walter Pater.

When converting the textual elements and the non-textual elements (such as drawings) in the original documents into readable, publishable, typescript form, I employ the diplomatic mode of transcription: reproducing as accurately as possible the texts as they appear in the manuscripts while maintaining readability for current audiences. Formulated by G. Thomas Tanselle, textual critic and bibliographer, and Robert H. Hirst, general editor (since 1980) of the Mark Twain Project,[3] this approach seeks to capture the creative process at work in the production of original documents. The rationale can be summarized simply: when transcribing carefully what appears on the page, the editor is being faithful to the letter-writer's intention; when employing the diplomatic mode of transcription, the editor enables the reader to approximate the experience of reading the original holograph letters.[4] In producing what can be called a 'plain-text' edition, the editor strives to represent the meaningful elements of original documents, employing an editorial apparatus to represent the alterations the author has made, including corrections, cancellations, and insertions, and thus conveying the creative process at work in the production of the hand-written documents (the system of symbols I employ throughout this volume is described later in this Textual Introduction). Plain-text editing, which stresses reliability, can be contrasted with 'clear-text' editing, the object of which is to produce a printed text that is free of editorial apparatus and commentary (emendations and annotations to clear-text editions, if provided, are usually found at the end of those editions, with line and page references to the text). Plain-text editing is vital to producing (as in the present case) an edition of correspondence that is inclusive, reliable, and readable. Most importantly, the plain-text editor focuses attention on what appears on the page: preserving the idiosyncrasies of the letter-writer and, in this case, the practices of the Victorian age.

For decades, editors modified—modernized—their texts for the sake of readability: translating hand-written letters into printed texts meant editing them to read as one reads a printed book (with few brackets and annotations).[5] Like a growing number of Anglo-American editors, I have taken my cue from plain-text editors and resisted the temptation to make readability my chief concern, bearing in mind the view (advanced by Tanselle among others) that, in capitalizing proper nouns and the first letters of sentences; expanding abbreviations and contractions; correcting mistakes in spelling, punctuation, and paragraphing; and regularizing indentations, the editor distorts the content as well as the character of the original text.[6]

The headnote to each letter conveys several pieces of information: (a) the name of the addressee rendered in the shortest form consistent with easy identification; (b) the date of composition, with approximate date in square brackets, and question marks indicating elements that are in doubt; (c) the source of the text, including the location of the original; (d) the medium employed, for example, correspondence card or college letterhead, where applicable; (e) details emerging from the envelope, including the name of the addressee and his or her address, postmarks, and any alterations; and (f) details of previous publication, where applicable.

I take the texts of the letters from Pater's own manuscript letters or facsimiles of them wherever possible. If this has not been possible, I have employed reliable transcriptions in other hands or typescripts. When I have taken a text from a published source, such as a memoir or a scholarly journal, I have reproduced the body of the letter as it appeared in that publication. Descriptions of passages from Pater's letters excerpted from various contemporary texts, such as biographies and memoirs, and from catalogues issued by booksellers and antiquarians, such as Pater's letter dated [*c*.3 August 1887] to George Moore, appear in italics.

The letters are published in the standard format, according to Pater's usual, but not invariable, practice: the address and the date (on one line) and the closing and the signature (on separate lines) are printed flush right, whereas the salutation and the postscript are printed flush left. It should be noted that the words introducing passages obtained from printed sources (diaries, journals, memoirs, periodicals, and newspapers) and from fugitive Pater letters are italicized, such as the letter to George Moore dated [*c*.3 August 1887]. If the date is a matter of conjecture, it is preceded by a question mark. The elements of letters that have been drawn from published sources, where the heading or the closing (judging by its deviation from Pater's normal practice) has been altered by the writer or the editor, have been rearranged to conform to Pater's customary practice. All postscripts have been placed after the closing, regardless of their position on the manuscript. The letters have been arranged in a chronological order for ease of reference.

The following practices have shaped this volume:

1. *Abbreviations* such as 'Esq.', 'MS.', 'obedt', 'shd', 'wh', 'wd', and 'yrs', and contractions, which might have been expanded, have in fact been printed as they appear in the manuscripts. Accordingly, the ampersand [&] has been retained.
2. *Angle brackets* have been employed to indicate that a single letter, a digit, or a punctuation mark has been crossed out: <m>.
3. *Cancellations*, if legible, are represented by strike-throughs: ~~revose~~. Double-cancellations, plus false starts and apparent slips of the pen, have not been recorded.
4. *Capitalization* is retained as found in the original manuscripts. The capitalization of such letters as 'b', 'c', 'k', 'p', 's', and 'w' is often a matter of judgement.

5. *Foreign words* are printed in italics, unless the whole letter is in, for example, French.
6. *Hash marks* [#, ##, ###] indicate illegible letters.
7. *Interlineations* (substitutions, alternatives, augmentations) are inserted into the text by means of angled brackets: \only/.
8. *Lacunae* and *illegible cancellations* are indicated by square brackets with an approximation of the interval, rounded off to the closest 0.5 cm. Thus, [3 cm] indicates a lacuna of that length (Pater's 'the' is typically about this length).
9. *Paragraphing* is retained as found in manuscripts and printed sources.
10. Pater's *punctuation*, including instances where he puts a comma before the predicate and uses a dash instead of a full stop, has been retained. Now and then Pater employs a dash for a full-stop. Sometimes, he leaves spaces between sentences. These too have been rendered as found.
11. All *quotations*, English or foreign, are given as they appear. In some instances, correct versions are given in the notes; in others, the fact of inaccuracy is only mentioned.
12. *Spelling* is retained as written in the original documents, for example, Shakespere, even in instances that are inconsistent or idiosyncratic. Misspelled words are not marked with an editorial [sic]. If the sense of a word is obscured through misspelling, the meaning is clarified in a footnote.
13. *Square brackets* enclose all interpolated matter. In several instances square brackets indicate (a) emendations or comments that have been added to the text, such as [Walt] Whitman or [this portion of the letter was torn off]; (b) uncertainty of a word or a phrase, as in [?] Wednesday; (c) words or phrases that appear to be in error but are not, for example, [sic], which is employed rarely; and (d) the measurements of a space that was left blank by Pater, such as [2 cm].
14. *Superscripts* employed by Pater and many contemporaries, in such cases as the raised r, rs, and th (M^r, M^{rs}, and 26th) are not employed here; the superscript position is a flourish of penmanship, a convention that needs no documentation.
15. *Underlining*, especially the titles of periodicals and books, is rendered as *italics*. No indication is given of the words that have more than one underlining.
16. *Vertical bars* have been used in the headnotes to indicate line-divisions in text, for example, marking off address and date, as in Brasenose College, | Oxford. | May 18th.

The Explanatory Notes, which follow individual letters, reconstruct the personal and historical contexts in which the correspondence was produced. More 'recovery' annotation than 'explanatory' annotation, to use the terminology introduced by Arthur Friedman,[7] the notes concentrate on identifying people, places, and events that are mentioned in the letters;

on elucidating allusions, references, and quotations; and on translating foreign words and phrases. Biographical information emphasizes the individual's relationship with Pater. I have minimized the cross-referencing, believing that the Index will serve the reader most effectively.

The Biographical Register provides more particulars concerning Pater's major correspondents, including information about the nature of their relationships. (Not finding a name or term in the Index means that I have failed to make the necessary identification.)

A list of now lost letters Pater is known to have written is featured in Appendix A. I give the name of the correspondent, the date (if possible), the source, and whatever information is provided elsewhere in this volume.

Notes

[1] See Lawrence Evans, *LWP*, xliii–xliv; Inman, *Walter Pater's Reading*, 8–9. At least one expert found in Pater's handwriting good evidence of an individual who was a disciplined thinker and an affectionate companion. See Mary L. Bisland, 'An Essay in Graphology', *Book Buyer*, 11 (1894), 429–32.

[2] See *LWP*, xliii–xliv.

[3] See Samuel Eliot Morison, 'The Editing and Printing of Manuscripts', *Harvard Guide to American History*, ed. Oscar Handlin et al. (Cambridge, Mass.: Belknap Press, 1954), 95–104; G. Thomas Tanselle, 'The Editing of Historical Documents', *Studies in Bibliography*, 31 (1978), 1–56; and Michael E. Stevens and Steven B. Burg, *Editing Historical Documents: A Handbook of Practice* (Walnut Creek, Calif.: Altamira, 1997), 71–84, for whom the idiosyncratic elements of style and language are essential characteristics of such private documents as diaries, letters, and notebooks. See also Robert Halsband, 'Editing the Letters of Letter-Writers', *Studies in Bibliography*, 11 (1958), 25–37; Gillian Hughes, 'Editing the Letters of a Scottish Author', *Studies in Scottish Literature*, 39.1 (2013), 31–7; and Amanda Gagel, 'Letters as Critical Texts', *Scholarly Editing*, 36 (2015), 1–20.

[4] Pierre G. Walker and Greg W. Zacharias, 'Editing the Complete Letters of Henry James', *Palgrave Advances in Henry James Studies*, ed. Peter Rawlings (Houndmills, Hampshire: Palgrave Macmillan, 2007), 239–62; Stevens and Burg, *Editing Historical Documents*. See also G. Thomas Tanselle, 'Textual Criticism and Deconstruction', *Studies in Bibliography*, 43 (1990), 1–33; Jerome McGann, *The Textual Condition* (Princeton, N.J.: Princeton University Press, 1991).

[5] Cecil Y. Lang observes: 'In transcribing and annotating these letters, I have always tried to make readability my first concern, preferring it, in a few instances, even to consistency.' See *The Swinburne Letters*, ed. Cecil Y. Lang, 6 vols (New Haven: Yale University Press, 1959–62), 1: xlix.

[6] Tanselle, 'The Editing of Historical Documents', 48–50.

[7] Arthur Friedman, 'Principles of Historical Annotation in Critical Editions of Modern Texts', *English Institute Annual* (New York: Columbia University Press, 1942), 115–28. Friedman contrasts two classes of annotation: (a) notes of 'recovery', which provide information familiar to contemporary readers, and (b) notes of 'explanation', which aim to make a text more intelligible by showing its relationship to earlier texts. See also Ian Small, 'The Editor as Annotator as Ideal Reader', in *The Theory and Practice of Text-Editing*, ed. Ian Small and Marcus Nash (Cambridge: Cambridge University Press, 1991), 186–209, and John H. Middendorf, 'Eighteenth-Century English Literature', in *Scholarly Editing: A Guide to Research*, ed. D. C. Greetham (New York: Garland, 1994), 283–307.

Correspondence

1859

To G. FURLEY,[1] 9 May [1859]
MS.: Archives, the King's School, Canterbury. On Oxford Union stationery.

Queen's Coll: | Oxford. | May 9:

Dear Sir,

I shall be much obliged if you will send me at your convenience the second moiety of the King's School exhibition[2] which I hold. I believe it becomes due about this time.

I am

Your obedt servant
W. H. Pater.

G. Furley Esq:

---

[1] It is not clear why Pater wrote to George Furley (1817–98), an attorney, and not to his brother William Henry Furley (1802–59), a banker who served as the treasurer of 'The Society of Gentlemen Educated at Canterbury School' (see next note). George Furley was elected mayor of Canterbury in 1850, and his name was added to 'The Society of Gentlemen' on 2 May 1859, the week before Pater's letter.

[2] 'Moiety' means portion. A group of the King's School graduates formed the 'Society of Gentlemen Educated at Canterbury School' in 1712, later renamed 'The King's School Feast Society', to support students who attended the universities of Oxford and Cambridge with exhibitions (scholarships). The society created two exhibitions of £60 in 1829 and four exhibitions of £60 in 1844, to be held for four years. Exhibitioners were elected, as vacancies occurred, by a process of examination. Members would meet annually to attend a service at the Cathedral, at which a clergyman who had been brought up at the school delivered a sermon (a forerunner of today's Commemoration Day sermon); to listen to speeches or extracts from plays given by the boys; to award exhibitions (or grants); and to salute the recipients at a dinner. The Headmaster would deliver his farewell comments at this time (in 1864, the Exhibition Fund Committee took over the task of raising funds for boys going to university). The Revd G. A. Ellicott, Professor of Divinity, King's College, London, examined the exhibition candidates in 1858, and recommended in favour of Pater. Pater left the King's School in 1858 with prizes in Latin scholarship and ecclesiastical history, together with an exhibition of £60 a year for three years and a prize of £30 for books. The McQueen family probably gave him a gift of £40. See A. C. Benson, *Walter Pater* (London: Macmillan, 1906), 8–9; Thomas Wright, *The Life of Walter Pater*, 2 vols (London: Everett, 1907), 1: 139–40; Robert M. Seiler, *Walter Pater: A Life Remembered* (Calgary, Alberta: University of Calgary Press, 1987), 245. Records show that Pater was entitled to the following funds administered by the Society of Gentlemen: £30 (exhibition) in 1858, plus Dr Shepherd's gift of £30; £48 (exhibition) in 1859; £36 (exhibition) in 1860; £60 (exhibition) in 1861; and £18 (exhibition) in 1862, for a total of £192 (exhibition only). See also C. E. Woodruff and H. J. Cape, *Schola Regia Cantuariensis: A History of Canterbury School, Commonly called The King's School* (London: Mitchell Hughes & Clarke, 1908).

To G. FURLEY, 24 May [1859]
MS.: Archives, the King's School, Canterbury. On Oxford Union stationery.

                                    Queen's Coll: | Oxford. | May 24:

Dear Sir,

    I am afraid a note I wrote you about a fortnight ago has by some means missed its destination. I shall feel much obliged if you will forward me at your earliest convenience the second moiety of the King's School exhibition which I think has become due.

    I think the most available way would be to pay it [in to] the Old Bank in Oxford.

                                                      Your obedt servant
                                                             W. H. Pater.

G. Furley Esq:

To T. N. WIGHTWICK,[1] 1 June [1859]
MS.: Archives, the King's School, Canterbury. On Oxford Union stationery.

                                    Queen's Coll: | Oxford. | June 1:

Dear Sir,

    Mr. Furley informs me that you have succeeded his brother as treasurer for the King's School Society. I shall feel much obliged if you will send me the second moiety of the exhibition which I hold, and which, if I mistake not, became due at Easter. I think the most convenient way would be to have it paid into the Old Bank in Oxford.

    I am

                                                        Your obedt servant
                                                             W. H. Pater.

W. [sic] Wightwick Esq:

---

[1] Thomas Norman Wightwick (1818–87), a solicitor in Canterbury, served as mayor in the late 1850s and early 1860s. He succeeded William Henry Furley as treasurer of 'The Society of Gentlemen Educated at Canterbury School'.

To T. N. WIGHTWICK, 3 June [1859]
MS.: Archives, the King's School, Canterbury. On Oxford Union stationery.

Queen's Coll. | June 3.

Dear Sir,

I beg to acknowledge the receipt of a bank bill for 30£, with many thanks.

Your obedt servant
W. H. Pater.

W. J. [sic] Wightwick Esq:

To T. N. WIGHTWICK, 18 October [1859]
MS.: Archives, the King's School, Canterbury. On Oxford Union stationery.

Queen's Coll. | Oxford. | Oct. 18.

Dear Sir,

I shall be much obliged if you will send me the portion of the King's School exhibition which becomes due about this time, by an order on the Old Bank in Oxford.

Your obedt servant
W. H. Pater.

W. [sic] Wightwick Esq.

To JOHN PENDERGAST,[1] 24 October [1859]
MS.: Bodleian Library. Envelope: J. Pendergast Esq. | 37 Colet Place | Commercial Road | London E. Postmark: F OXFORD OC 24 59. Printed in *LWP*.

Queen's Coll: | Oct. 24.

My dear Mr. Pendergast,

I arrived here last week after a wet and disagreeable journey, having left all well at Heidelberg.[2] I have just received my half-year's money from Canterbury,[3] but there is a deduction of 12£ from the full amount, so that I shall be glad if you will kindly send me 20£.

William[4] is at Portsmouth with his regiment unless he has shifted his quarters lately,—he never informs us of any of his movements. I daresay you saw by the papers the death of my Aunt Anne at Weston.[5]

Believe me

Very sincerely your's
W. H. Pater.

[1] John Pendergast (1815?–93), a London conveyancer, was one of the three executors and trustees of the estate of Maria Hill Pater (1800?–54), Pater's mother. Pendergast became a member of Gray's Inn in 1843. His offices and residence on Commercial Road, Stepney, London were not far from where Richard Glode Pater (1796?–1842), Pater's father, and William Grange Pater (1799?–1845), Pater's uncle, had practised medicine.

[2] Pater's aunt Bessey (also Bessie), Hester Elizabeth Mary Pater (1793–1862), had settled in Heidelberg in 1858, with Pater's sisters Hester and Clara (see Biographical Register). Pater spent the Long Vacation of 1859 with them. See Wright, 1: 178–9, 181–4; Billie Andrew Inman, 'Tracing the Pater Legacy', Parts 1 and 2, *Pater Newsletter*, 11 and 32 (Spring 1983/ Winter 1995): 31; 3–8.

[3] A 'commoner' at the Queen's College, Oxford, Pater held an exhibition (scholarship), worth £60 per year for three years, from the King's School, Canterbury.

[4] William Thompson Pater (1835–87), Pater's older brother (see Biographical Register).

[5] Anne Pater, third sister of Pater's grandfather, John Thompson Pater (1766–1812), died on 23 Sept. 1850, at the age of eighty, in Weston Underwood, Buckinghamshire.

1860

To T. N. WIGHTWICK, 29 March [1860]
MS.: Archives, the King's School, Canterbury. On Oxford Union stationery.

Queen's Coll. | Oxford. | Mar. 29.

Dear Sir,

I shall feel much obliged if you will remit the moiety of the King's School exhibition which becomes due at this time.

Your obedt servant
W. H. Pater.

To S. W. WIGHTWICK, 17 October [1860]
MS.: Archives, the King's School, Canterbury. On Oxford Union stationery.

Queen's Coll. | Oxford. | Oct. 17.

Dear Sir,

I shall feel much obliged if you will send me the moiety of the King's School exhibition money which becomes due at about this time.

Your obedt servant
W. H. Pater.

T. N. Wightwick Esq.

1862

To JOHN PENDERGAST, 8 December [1862]
Text: *Sotheran's Price Current of Literature*, 827 (1931), 95. Printed in *LWP*.

Queen's, | Dec. 8.

... I am going to take my B. A. degree on Thursday.[1]... My friends here advise me to try for a fellowship, but this is uncertain—anyhow I shall take orders in the spring, probably for a London curacy.[2]...

---

[1] Pater took his BA on Thursday, 11 Dec. 1862.
[2] Wright explains that Pater's estranged friend, John Rainier McQueen (see Biographical Register), shocked at Pater's persistence in seeking holy orders despite indications of apostasy, and acting on the advice of Henry Parry Liddon (1829–90), one of the leading Anglican clergyman in Oxford (see Biographical Register), wrote in Dec. 1862 to the Bishop of London, the Revd Archibald Campbell Tait, to prevent Pater's ordination (Wright, 1: 207). Pater did not abandon the plan, however, until after the summer of 1863, when he competed unsuccessfully for a clerical fellowship at Oxford's Trinity College. He also failed to obtain a clerical fellowship at Brasenose College, Oxford in Jan. 1863; later, on 5 Feb. 1864, he sought and obtained a non-clerical fellowship at Brasenose. See also letter to Pendergast, 8 Apr. [1863].

1863

To JOHN PENDERGAST, 8 April [1863]
MS.: Bodleian Library. Envelope: J. Pendergast Esq. | 37 Colet Place | Commercial Rd. | London E. Postmark: N OXFORD AP 8 63. Mourning paper.[1] Printed in *LWP*.

Apr. 8.

My dear Mr. Pendergast,

I enclose the receipt for 10£ with many thanks for the account. I hope I shall not need to touch my share of the Trust fund, but I shall have pleasure in calling as you mention when I go back to London. Will you be kind enough to pay the interest of this to my Sisters with what they receive on their share. Unless I gain a fellowship within the next two or three months I shall take a curacy. At present I have some pupils who reduce the expense of staying here.

I am happy to say that Clara[2] is getting better.

With best wishes for your health, and thanks for your long-continued kindness,
Believe me

Very sincerely yours
W. H. Pater.

[1] Elizabeth Pater. Pater's 'Aunt Bessie', died in Dresden on 28 Dec. 1862. Wright's account of Pater being summoned to Dresden from a holiday spent with cousins in London is probably correct, although his source, apparently one of Pater's cousins, places Bessie's death during the following Easter season (Wright, 1: 209–19).

[2] Pater's sister, Clara Ann Pater (1841–1910), an academic and women's educational rights advocate (see Biographical Register).

To JOHN PENDERGAST, 25 November [1863]
MS.: Brasenose College. Printed in *LWP*.

9 Grove St.[1] | Oxford. | Nov. 25.

My dear Mr. Pendergast,

Will you kindly send me what remains of my share of my mother's property—I think a little over 30£. I expect to be in London in a few weeks and shall then have the pleasure of calling on you.
Always

Very sincerely yours
W. H. Pater.

[1] After taking his degree, Pater remained in Oxford, tutoring privately, while trying for a college fellowship. According to Edmund Gosse (see Biographical Register), Pater took lodgings in the High Street in this period. But Grove Street (now called Magpie Lane) was a very short street, just off 'the High', and 9 Grove Street may well have been Pater's address throughout the interval between taking his degree and moving into Brasenose College as a Fellow in 1864.

1864

To JOHN PENDERGAST, 5 June [1864]
MS.: Brasenose College. Printed in *LWP*.

15 Whiterock Place.[1] | Hastings. | June 5.

My dear Mr. Pendergast,

Will you kindly forward me 30£.[2] You will be pleased to hear that my brother William is going out to Brazil in the autumn with one of my Liverpool cousins.[3] I am going to spend the vacation very quietly in Paris with my sisters.[4]

Believe me always

Sincerely yours
Walter H. Pater.

[1] White Rock Place was a street crowded with shops and lodging-houses in the fashionable seaside town of Hastings, East Sussex. Mary Ann Matthews kept a lodging-house at number 15.

[2] On 9 June 1864 Pater wrote to Pendergast from Hastings to acknowledge the receipt of £30. The letter is listed as item 1288 in *Sotheran's Price Current of Literature*, no. 827, 95.

[3] Pater's father's cousin, Joseph Pater (1799?–1862), was connected with Samuel Johnston & Co. of Liverpool, merchants, who carried on a lucrative trade with Brazil. Joseph Pater had three sons by his first marriage who were old enough to make the voyage; of these, the eldest, Thompson Pater (1835?–93), was most likely William's prospective companion. Thompson Pater became a merchant and was resident in Brazil by 1870; whether he and William actually made the voyage in 1864 has not been determined. See letter to F. L. Pater, 30 Apr. [1887].

[4] On 1 Aug. 1864 Pater wrote to Pendergast from 414 rue St Honoré, Paris, asking for a further sum of £40. The letter is listed as item 1289 in the *Sotheran's* catalogue. See n. 2.

1865

To CHARLES SHADWELL,[1] 31 December [1865?][2]
MS.: Brasenose College. Printed in *LWP*.

50 Jermyn St. W. | Dec. 31st.

My dear Shadwell,

Should you be in London any time within the next week or ten days you will find me at the above address. Although you talked of returning to Oxford about this time I still have hopes of seeing you here.

Yours ever
W. H. Pater.

[1] Charles Lancelot Shadwell (1840–1919), scholar and administrator, was a Fellow of Oriel College and a member of the Old Mortality essay society (see Biographical Register).

[2] The letter is on a half-sheet, torn so as to leave of the faintly watermarked date only '186' and a fragment of the fourth numeral, which appears to be 5. In 1865 the Jermyn Street address, near Piccadilly Circus, was that of a tailor's shop, over which one Wortley Stuart kept a lodging house. Pater had evidently taken a room, or rooms, for the end of the Christmas vacation, for himself and his sisters.

1866

To [CHARLES GORDON?] BROWNE,[1] [1866–67?][2]
MS.: Brasenose College. Printed in *LWP*.

B. N. C. | Friday.

Dear Browne,

Will you lunch with me tomorrow at 1.30?

Yours ever
W. H. Pater

[1] Possibly Charles Gordon Browne (1845–1920), who studied at Balliol College, 1864–7. He may have been sent to Pater for 'coaching' for the final 'Greats' examinations by classical scholar, theologian, and translator Benjamin Jowett (1817–93), Fellow of Balliol College from 1838 (see Biographical Register). Ordained an Anglican priest in 1872, Browne served as curate of St Peter's, Bournemouth, Dorset, 1876–80; assistant curate, Clewer House of Mercy, 1882–8; and rector of Lympstone, Devon, 1892–1910. With the Revd Oswald J. Reichel (a friend of Pater's during their undergraduate years at Queen's College) he translated St Gregory Nazianzen. He published *Instructions in the Way of Life: An Attempt to Reply to Some Practical and Theological Questions* (London: J. Masters, 1881). Another possibility, not quite as strong, is Henry Llewelyn Browne (1840?–86), who studied at Jesus College, 1859–63. Browne served as a Fellow of Queen's College, 1866–76, when he was a member of the Old Mortality essay society. He served as rector of Hampton Poyle, Oxfordshire, 1875–6, and vicar of Monk Sherborne, Dorset, 1876–86.
[2] The handwriting dates this letter in the later 1860s.

To JOHN PENDERGAST, 17 July [1866]
MS.: Bischoff Research Collection, Gonzaga University.

Clifton Cottage[1] | Sidmouth | July 17th.

Dear Mr. Pendergast,

I enclose the Insurance Office paper,[2] filled up as you suggest. I think you mentioned the sum of 25£ as the annual premium. Perhaps you will take this from the small sum of mine you have in your possession when required. I fear I am giving you a great deal of trouble on my account.
With best thanks—
I remain

Very sincerely yours
W. H. Pater.

[1] Possibly a stuccoed thatched house (with a sea-view) on Peak Hill Road, East Devon, now a historical landmark.
[2] The enclosure is missing.

To JOHN CHAPMAN,[1] 12 November [1866]
MS.: University of Michigan. Endorsed: 12 November 1866. Printed in *LWP*.

Brasenose College. | Nov. 12th

My dear Dr. Chapman,

I shall be very glad to have my article inserted in the January number.[2] There are however a good many minute corrections which I should like to make in it; and I shall therefore be glad, if it is not giving you too much trouble, if you will return me the MS. for that purpose, and also let me know on what day it will be necessary to forward it to you for the press.

Believe me

Very truly yours
Walter H. Pater.

---

[1] John Chapman (1821–94), publisher, author, and physician, was the proprietor and editor (1851–94) of the *Westminster Review*; he published three review essays by Pater between Jan. 1866 and Oct. 1868, starting with 'Coleridge's Writings', 85 (Jan. 1866), 106–32. See Biographical Register.

[2] 'Winckelmann', *Westminster Review*, 87 (Jan. 1867), 80–110.

1867

To EDWARD HARTOPP CRADOCK,[1] 2 March [1867][2]
MS.: Brasenose College. Printed in *LWP*.

B. N. C. | March 2nd.

Dear Mr. Principal,

I have taken some days to consider the proposal you lately made me, and have now to inform you that I shall be happy to undertake the duties proposed, at least for a time.

Believe me

Very truly yours
W. H. Pater.

---

[1] The Revd Edward Hartopp Grove, subsequently Hartopp Cradock, D.D. (1810–86), cleric and administrator, attended Balliol College, Oxford, 1827–31, was elected Fellow of Brasenose in 1833. For Brasenose he held several offices, including Senior Bursar (1839–43) and Vice-Principal (1843–4). In 1844 he married the Hon. Harriet Lister, one of Queen Victoria's maids of honour and a novelist. Cradock served as the Principal of Brasenose 1853–86. Religious frictions diminished during his administration and the number of students who matriculated at the college tripled. J. Mordaunt Crook, *Brasenose: The Biography of an Oxford College* (Oxford: Oxford University Press, 2008), 299. In 1849, he changed his name from Grove to Cradock on inheriting property from Sir Edmund Cradock Hartopp, a maternal uncle.

[2] The handwriting belongs to the late 1860s. It seems likely that the 'duties proposed' are those of college lecturer. Pater delivered his first lectures at Brasenose in the spring of 1867 (see Benson, 20).

1868

To JOHN CHAPMAN, 23 July [1868]
MS.: Fales Collection, New York University. Endorsed: 23 July 1868. Printed in *LWP*.

                                  27 Westmorland Place.[1] | Bayswater. | July 23rd.

Dear Dr. Chapman,

    I intend to leave London on the 1st of August. I shall be abroad for about five weeks and then return to Oxford, where you might send the proof of my article.[2] If you could let me have it in type to take abroad with me I might improve it by many minute corrections.

    My friend Mr. Colvin,[3] of whom I spoke to you, had not time to see you before going away to the country. I advised him however to communicate with you and should he do so you will not be surprised.

    When I saw you, you spoke of my doing part of the general reviews at the end of the W. R. I may now say that I shall be very glad to undertake the division on Belles Lettres, or perhaps after a trial at this the philosophical division, if you please, when you have a vacancy.[4]

    I should like to hear whether you can let me have the article in type to take away with me, and remain

                                                             Very truly yours
                                                              W. H. Pater.

---

[1] According to the Post Office's London Directory, 1868, this was the private residence of a Mrs Lane. Although not listed among boarding- or lodging-house keepers, Mrs Lane may have let a few rooms, just as many of her neighbours on the street did.

[2] 'Poems by William Morris', *Westminster Review*, 90 (Oct. 1868), 300–12.

[3] Sidney Colvin (1845–1927), art critic, biographer, and administrator. See Biographical Register.

[4] There is no evidence that Pater ever contributed again to the *Westminster Review*. See also letter to Chapman, 27 Nov. [1872].

1871

To JOHN MORLEY,[1] 16 November [1871?][2]
MS.: Brasenose College. Printed in *LWP*.

Bradmore Road.[3] | Nov. 16.

My dear Morley,

Many thanks for the cheque. I hope to send you another article, or at all events a long letter, soon; meantime with kind regards to Mrs. Morley, believe me

Very sincerely yours
W. H. Pater.

---

[1] John Morley, 1st Viscount Morley of Blackburn (1838–1923), journalist, biographer, and politician. See Biographical Register.

[2] The letter belongs to the period after Morley's marriage to Rose Mary Ayling (1840–1923) in May 1870 and before the Paters left their residence in Bradmore Road (occupied since 1869) in the summer of 1885. Evans chose 1871 as the probable date (1874 and 1876 being next in order of likelihood) on the basis of the handwriting, the stationery, and the publication of 'The Poetry of Michelangelo', *Fortnightly Review*, ns 16 (Nov. 1871), 559–70. This was Pater's fourth contribution to the periodical.

[3] On 3 Dec. 1869 Pater sub-leased a semi-detached house at 2 Bradmore Road, and with his sisters he lived here until Aug. 1885. Mary Augusta Ward (1851–1920) and her husband, T. Humphry Ward (1845–1926), lived at 17 (formerly 5) Bradmore Road from 1872 to 1881; Charlotte and T. H. Green were also neighbours (see Biographical Register). Bradmore Road offers an entrance to Norham Manor estate, a residential suburb in central North Oxford, just north of the Oxford University Parks and bounded by the River Cherwell to the east and the Oxford canal to the west, an estate which was designed (from 1860) by architect William Wilkinson (1819–1901), who served as the supervisor, on land owned by St John's College. Wilkinson's colleague, Frederick Codd, designed nos 1–2 and 13–17 on Bradmore Road for tradesmen and academics: large, gabled villas of brick (set off by prominent stone dressing), Italianate and Gothic Revival styles predominating, each set in a spacious garden surrounded by low boundary walls and railings along tree-lined avenues. See Tanis Hinchcliffe, *North Oxford* (New Haven: Yale University Press, 1992), 65–89.

1872

To EDMUND GOSSE,[1] 8 March [1872]
MS.: Brotherton Collection, University of Leeds. Printed in *LWP*.

Bradmore Road. | Oxford. | March 8th.

My dear Mr. Gosse,

Accept my best thanks for your beautiful volume.[2] Some of the poems I had already read with great pleasure, but I am glad to have the volume by me that I may read it with more leisure. I had intended to buy it before I saw you. I had much pleasure in making your acquaintance and hope to meet again. My kind regards to Mr. and Mrs. Scott[3] when you see them.

Very truly yours
W. H. Pater.

[1] Edmund Gosse (1849–1928), poet, critic, and biographer. See Biographical Register.
[2] Apparently, *Madrigals, Songs and Sonnets* (London: Longmans, Green, 1870). Of the poems in this volume, thirty-two were written by Gosse, the rest by J. A. Blaikie.
[3] In 1894 Gosse recalled meeting Pater in the studio of William Bell Scott (1811–90), Scottish poet and painter, in 1872. See Gosse, 'Walter Pater: A Portrait', *Contemporary Review*, 66 (Dec. 1894), 795–810. For Scott, see letter to Scott, 18 June [1872–73], n. 1.

To [WILLIAM BELL?] SCOTT,[1] 18 June [1872–3?][2]
Text: Maggs Bros. *Catalogue* no. 326 (1914), 114.

Oxford, | June 18.

My dear Scott,

...there is much here which I think you would be pleased to see....

[1] William Bell Scott (1811–90), Scottish poet and painter, hovered at the periphery of Pre-Raphaelite art and literature. Scott honed his poetic and artistic powers in London, 1837–42, and made a name for himself as master of the Government School of Design in Newcastle-upon-Tyne, 1843–64. Sir Walter Trevelyan and Pauline, Lady Trevelyan, née Jermyn (1816–66), who presided over a salon that included John Ruskin, the Brownings, Thomas Carlyle, and various Pre-Raphaelites, asked him to decorate their home, Wallington Hall, with a series of eight panels illustrating key moments in Northumberland history, 1857–61. The only comparable decorative scheme undertaken at the time was the series of murals painted by a group of Pre-Raphaelite artists on the walls of the Oxford Union Library featuring scenes from Arthurian legends (1857–9). Alice Boyd (1825–97), daughter of the 12th Laird of Penkill, asked Scott to decorate the great circular staircase at her ancestral home, Penkill Castle, Ayrshire; this notable project included a group of murals (1865–8), the subject being *The*

Kingis Quair, a Scottish poem ostensibly written by James I; see John Batchelor, *Lady Trevelyan and the Pre-Raphaelite Brotherhood* (London: Chatto & Windus, 2006), 124-44. In 1864 Scott returned to London, and in 1870, he acquired 92 Cheyne Walk, Chelsea, becoming a neighbour of D. G. Rossetti, who lived at 16 Cheyne Walk. Scott painted pictures, murals, and portraits; produced several volumes of poetry and many texts on art and literature; and edited and illustrated volumes of Romantic poetry. While defending the Pre-Raphaelites in his letter to *The Times*, 13 May 1851, Ruskin said nothing about Scott's work or that of Ford Madox Brown; in his letter to the *Pall Mall Gazette*, 13 Jan. 1875, Ruskin referred to Scott as a member of that unfortunate class of artists who suppose they have genius. Scott's *Autobiographical Notes*, ed. W. Minto, 2 vols (London: James R. Osgood, McIllvaine, 1892), became the subject of controversy because it betrays bitterness and disappointment; people complained that Scott bolstered his own reputation while belittling the reputation of others. Although Pater and Scott moved in overlapping social and intellectual circles (A. C. Swinburne, William Minto, and Simeon Solomon), Pater is not mentioned in Scott's autobiography.

[2] Pater's correspondence indicates that he was friendly with Scott from Mar. 1872 through Sept. 1887 (see letter to Gosse, 8 Mar. 1872, n. 3, and letters to Scott, 30 Apr. [1882] and 23 Sept. 1887). This now lost letter is placed here, after his letter to Gosse, as a reminder that his friendship with Scott began no later than 1872.

To ALEXANDER MACMILLAN,[1] 29 June [1872]
Text: Charles Morgan, *The House of Macmillan, 1843-1943* (London: Macmillan, 1943), 104. Printed in *LWP* and *TBB*.

Brasenose College. | June 29th.

Dear Sir,

I send you by this post the papers of which I spoke when I called on you in London and must apologize for not having sent them before.

The paper in MS.[2] has not been published hitherto, that on Winckelmann appeared in the *Westminster Review* and the other four in the *Fortnightly*.[3] I enclose a table of the proposed series which I hope to complete by the end of the long Vacation, with a short Preface. I think in the form in which I should like the essays to appear they would make a book of about 300 pages. Of the ten essays five only will have appeared before.[4] With many thanks for the kindness with which you have consented to consider my proposal,[5]

I am, dear Sir,

Faithfully yours
W. H. Pater.

[1] Alexander Macmillan (1818-96), publisher. See Biographical Register.
[2] The essay in question may have been 'Aucassin and Nicolette', 'Luca della Robbia', or 'Joachim du Bellay', all of which are dated 1872 in the third and later editions of *The Renaissance*; or it may have been the 'rejected essay' mentioned in a letter to Macmillan, 2 Nov. [1872].

³ 'Notes on Leonardo da Vinci', *Fortnightly Review*, ns 12 (Nov. 1869), 494–508; 'A Fragment on Sandro Botticelli', ns 14 (Aug. 1870), 155–60; 'Pico della Mirandola', ns 16 (Oct. 1871), 377–86; and 'The Poetry of Michelangelo', ns 16 (Nov. 1871), 559–70.
⁴ The table is not printed by Morgan. If Pater includes the Preface among the five new essays, one essay is still unaccounted for; since it must have been unpublished at the time, it cannot be the 'Conclusion', which had appeared as the last section (309–12) of 'Poems by William Morris' (see letter to Chapman, 23 July [1868]). Pater makes no mention of the Morris essay, which probably means that he was working on 'Aucassin and Nicolette', 'Luca della Robbia', and 'Joachim du Bellay', which are dated 1872 in the third and fourth editions of *The Renaissance*. The essay in question was set up in type, and then cancelled by Pater late in Oct. 1872; on 28 Oct. 1872, George Lillie Craik, acting for Macmillan and Co., wrote to him: 'The Essay you refer to was printed, but in deference to your wish it shall be cancelled.' Two days later Craik wrote again, telling Pater that the essay was being returned to him so that he could 'embody parts of it in the Preface'. Lawrence Evans has argued that the essay in question may have been 'The School of Giorgione', theoretical portions of which enlarge on the doctrine advanced in the 'Preface'. The essay on Giorgione appeared in the *Fortnightly Review*, ns 28 (Oct. 1877), 526–38, and later in the third edition (1888) of *The Renaissance*. Brake has suggested that the essay in question was the essay entitled 'Arezzo'; Laurel Brake, 'A Commentary on "Arezzo": An Unpublished Manuscript by Walter Pater', *Review of English Studies*, ns 27 (Aug. 1976), 266–76. Inman, in *Walter Pater's Reading*, 264–6, has argued convincingly that the paper in manuscript was the essay on Wordsworth, parts of which were also incorporated into the Preface to illustrate the idea that only some of an author's works bear 'the virtue, the active principle'. See 'On Wordsworth', *Fortnightly Review*, ns 21 (Apr. 1874), 455–65 (*CW* v).
⁵ On 2 July 1872 Macmillan wrote to Pater, accepting his essays for publication, risking any loss, and offering equal shares in any profits.

To WALTER PATER, 2 July [1872]
MS.: British Library. Printed in *TBB*.

W. H. Pater Esq., | Brasenose College, | Oxford.

July 2.

Dear Sir,

I have been reading your essays on art subjects with very considerable interest, and shall feel pleasure and honour in publishing them. I am also so far encouraged [to hope] that it may also be profitable to at least some small extent that I am willing to risk the cost of publishing your volume, sharing equally with profits, if they should accrue, and ~~being~~ bearing loss, should an inappreciative public leave us with loss. I thought of a handsome 8 oc.¹ volume. As soon as you decide that these terms will satisfy you and you are ready to print we can consult on the points of style etc.

Yours sincerely,
A. Macmillan.

¹ Octavo (8vo), an economical size for a book and typical for works of prose (folio is the largest; then quarto, octavo, and duodecimo).

To ALEXANDER MACMILLAN, 21 September [1872]
MS.: British Library. Printed in *LWP* and *TBB*.

Brasenose College. | Sept. 21.

Dear Sir,

I have received a printed specimen of the essays, but regret to say not in the form which I think most suitable for the book. Some of the essays are so short, and all of them in some ways so slight, that I think the only suitable form would be a small volume, costing about five shillings; and I should like to make some suggestions on the binding and some other points.[1]

I will use the copy now sent for corrections, which will save the printers some trouble. I expect to get the remaining essays finished very soon—in two or three weeks—and hope then to have the pleasure of calling on you with them, if you will make an appointment with me for the purpose.

Believe me

Very faithfully yours
W. H. Pater.

---

[1] Macmillan thought otherwise, and on 24 Sept. [1872] wrote that he preferred an octavo volume, and would explain why when Pater came to see him. Macmillan Letter Book XX.

To WALTER PATER, 24 September [1872]
MS.: British Library. Printed in *TBB*.

W. H. Pater Esq., | Brasenose College, | Oxford.
Sept. 24.

My Dear Sir,

I shall be glad to see you about the form and binding of your essays any day you can fix. I am here generally from 10:00 until 5:00, except on Saturday, when I leave about 2:00. I shall be glad to meet your wishes as far as possible, but my experience leads me to think that an 8oc. volume is most suitable for such a book as yours. But I will give you my reasons when we meet. Of course I am very anxious that your book should be a success in our hands.

Yours very truly,
A. Macmillan.

To WALTER PATER, 28 October [1872]
MS.: British Library. Printed in *TBB*.

W. H. Pater Esq.
Oct. 28.

Dear Sir,

In Mr. Macmillan's absence I am answering your letter. The essay you refer to was printed, but in compliance with your wishes it shall be cancelled.[1] This however reduces the book to 210 pages, a smaller book than might have been advisable. I suppose you have no other matter that can be added?

Yours very truly,
G. Lillie Craik.[2]

---

[1] The unnamed essay may have been an early version of 'The School of Giorgione', parts of which were folded into the Preface. The essay appeared in the *Fortnightly Review*, ns 28 (Oct. 1877), 526–38, and was added to the third edition (1888) of *The Renaissance*. Kenneth Clark describes the essay as the most original in the whole collection: 'To suggest that the basic beauty of a picture was like "a space of fallen light, caught as in the colours of an eastern carpet", and that its value increased insofar as it aspired towards the condition of music, was to go beyond the most adventurous critics of the next generation. . . . We ask if Pater, with his keen sense of tradition, could really have invented such a revolutionary doctrine; and the answer is, I think, that he did.' Clark compares similar ideas in John Ruskin, Théophile Gautier, and Charles Baudelaire, but finds them random and under-developed: 'None of the critics come to the point which Pater saw so clearly.' *The Renaissance: Studies In Art and Poetry*, ed. Kenneth Clark (London: Collins, 1961), 20–3. See also Hill in Pater, *The Renaissance*, ed. Donald L. Hill (Berkeley: University of California Press, 1980), 384–5.

[2] George Lillie Craik (1837–1905), publisher, became a partner at Macmillan and Co. in 1865. See Biographical Register.

To WALTER PATER, 30 October [1872]
MS.: British Library. Printed in *TBB*.

W. H. Pater Esq.

Oct. 30.

Dear Sir,

The essay [will be] sent to you in order that you [can] embody parts of it in the preface. It will be necessary for you to revise the proofs in small instalments in order that the postscript of the book may be printed [well] before the rest is in type. In this way a smaller quantity of type is employed. It is in every way a convenience.

Yours faithfully,
G. Lillie Craik.

To ALEXANDER MACMILLAN, 2 November [1872]
MS.: British Library. Extracts printed in Morgan, *The House of Macmillan*, 105; printed in full in *LWP* and *TBB*.

Brasenose. | Nov. 2nd.

Dear Mr. Macmillan,

I have not yet received the Preface and the rejected essay,[1] which were to be returned to me for the alteration of the former. I should be glad to have them as soon as possible; and hope to send you in a day or two an additional essay, to form the conclusion of the series.

I like the look of the page very much, but not altogether the paper. It has occurred to me that the old-fashioned binding in paste-board with paper back and printed title, usual, I think, about thirty years ago, but not yet gone quite out of use, would be an economical, and very pretty binding for my book. It would, I am sure, be much approved of by many persons of taste, among whom the sale of my book would probably in the first instance be. I have just had in my hands an old book so bound, the paste-board covers of a greyish-blue, and the paper back olive green; nothing could be prettier or more simple; and I should be very glad if you could indulge me in this particular.

I do not know whether without adding to the expense of publication, the present paper might be changed for paper with rough edges and showing the water-mark; but suppose not.

I will send you on Monday the proofs I have already received with corrections, and remain

Very sincerely yours
W. H. Pater.

[1] See letters to Macmillan, 29 June [1872], and to Pater, 28 Oct. [1872].

To WALTER PATER, 7 November [1872]
MS.: British Library. Printed in *TBB*.

W. H. Pater Esq.

Nov. 7.

Dear Mr. Pater,

I wished to have seen you when I was in Oxford yesterday, but our train was an hour late, so that I was little more than in time for [Mr. Combe's][1] funeral. I meant to speak to you about the binding, which you wish: paper boards and labels. This will be a serious drawback to book sellers keeping it in stock, as these kinds of covers are so apt to get soiled and spoiled. Besides, I don't like it anyway. It is like a recurrence to the *fig-leaf.* The cloth in gilt is infinitely more useful and surely not less beautiful. Please don't wish for it.

The alterations in the chaptering will I fear cause a good deal of additional expense, as I suspect the cut [alters] the paging, but the type itself will be distributed. Perhaps you might go to the Press and see how this can best be adjusted. Mr. Wheeler[2] will give you every attention.

Yours very truly,
A. Macmillan.

---

[1] Thomas Combe (1797–1872), from 1841 Printer to the Clarendon Press, was a valued friend of Daniel Macmillan (see George Macmillan, *Letters of Alexander Macmillan* [London: Macmillan, 1908], xxxiv) and later Alexander Macmillan. As chief manager, he displayed considerable expertise and financial skill. In 1855 he bought the paper mill at Wolvercote in order to enable the Press to compete with greater ease. This venture proved to be highly successful, and Combe amassed a fortune of £80,000. He built the chapel attached to the Radcliffe Infirmary, as well as the church of St Barnabas. He was a major patron of the Pre-Raphaelites, owning among other paintings Holman Hunt's *The Light of the World* (1851–3), which his widow gave to Keble College. Combe died suddenly on 30 Oct. 1872.

[2] Rowland Wheeler (1826–98) devoted most of his life to the Clarendon Press, where he worked as compositor, proof-reader, and manager of the composing room. A man of extraordinary vigour, he was for many years chief of the staff of teachers who conducted evening classes at the firm as well as one of its Sunday school teachers.

To ALEXANDER MACMILLAN, 11 November [1872]
MS.: British Library. Extracts are printed in Morgan, 105 and 106; printed in full in *LWP* and *TBB*.

Brasenose. | Nov. 11th.

Dear Mr. Macmillan,

I was disappointed at the contents of your letter,[1] as the cover I wish for had occurred to me as a way of giving my book the artistic appearance which I am sure is necessary for it, without the expense and trouble of an unusual form of binding. I fancy that if I saw you I could persuade you to think the old-fashioned binding in boards as pretty as it seems to me. The objection as to its liability to be soiled might be met by the paper wrapper for packing, now not uncommon. Something not quite in the ordinary way is, I must repeat, very necessary in a volume the contents of which are so unpretending as in mine, and which is intended in the first instance for a comparatively small section of readers. For a book on art to be bound quite in the ordinary way is, it seems to me, behind the times; and the difficulty of getting a book bound in cloth so as to be at all artistic, and indeed not quite the other way, is very great.

I prefer in all cases the paper label, as the lettering is necessarily clumsy on a cloth binding, especially when as in this case the volume is a thin one.

I have been to the Press and find that the paging may be set right with little trouble, and spoke to Mr. Hall,[2] in the absence of Mr. Wheeler, about the paper.[3] I should like, with your permission, to select the kind of paper I think nicest, providing it is not more expensive than that ordinarily used.

Believe me

Very sincerely yours
W. H. Pater.

[1] Macmillan had travelled to Oxford (see letter to Pater, 7 Nov. [1872]) for a funeral on 6 Nov. 1872, meaning also to see Pater about the binding; because his train was late, he had to write, instead, the next day.

[2] Edward Pickard Hall (1808–86), superintendent of the Bible Press, 1862–81, was responsible for labour relations at the Clarendon Press (see following note). He was also organist and choirmaster at East Farleigh and founder of the Oxford Churchmen's Union. *The Renaissance* was printed by Thomas Combe, E. Bensley Gardner, Edward Pickard Hall, and John Stacey, Printers to the University until 1884, when the partnership was dissolved. The 'Press' is 'The Clarendon Press', which became the Oxford University Press when printing moved from the Sheldonian Theatre to the Clarendon Building, Broad Street, in 1713. The name came from the funds that were generated by the Earl of Clarendon's *History of the Rebellion and Civil Wars in England* (1704), the perpetual copyright of which was given to the Press by his son. It is now the publishing department of OUP in charge of its learned publications.

[3] Macmillan had asked Pater to see Mr Wheeler about re-pagination, after the cancellation of an essay (see letter to Pater, 7 Nov. [1872]).

To WALTER PATER, 12 November [1872]
MS.: British Library. Printed in George A. Macmillan, *Letters of Alexander Macmillan*, 266–7, and *TBB*.

W. H. Pater Esq.

Nov. 12.

Dear Mr. Pater,

I don't think you would convince me that paper covers are more beautiful than cloth, and they certainly are very much less useful. I am speaking with recent experience when I say that it would interfere with the sale of the book, as booksellers won't keep them, even with the paper cover. My friend Mr. Maclehose[1] of Glasgow published *Olrig Grange* in this fashion at first and has been obliged to abandon it for cloth. He still uses paper labels and gives a duplicate label to be stuck on when the old gets dirty! This is droll to say the least of it. The bookseller or possessor has to remove the old one and get paste, which he possibly has not at hand, and repaste the clean one on. The [recurrence] has nothing admirable in it to [use]. The use of inferior unuseful materials cannot be needful to the realisation of any art which is of much value, at least I cannot see how. Gold lettering on cloth was an immense advance on the old paper boards and was welcomed as such. I remember the period of change. I still possess books which are done up in smooth cloth with paper label and value them historically, just as I would value Adam's original fig-leaf, if I could find it.

But I will most gladly cede my tastes to yours as far as possible. I send you by this post a book in a style of binding which I devised for the author and which he liked. His tastes were 'artistic'. He is an intimate friend of Mr. Burne Jones and others who think in that line. Also, the paper of the book is made to imitate the old wire wove paper which can only now be got in this mock rib, which is really rather pleasant to my own eye. If you like the paper, let me know at once, as it will have to be made on purpose. Perhaps we can meditate on the binding a little further.

Yours very truly,
A. Macmillan.

[1] James Maclehose (1810–85), friend and confidant of Daniel and Alexander Macmillan for fifty years, founded (with Robert Nelson) a publishing business in Glasgow in 1838. From 1841, when Nelson retired, Maclehose carried on the business in his own name. He was appointed bookseller (1862) and publisher (1871) to the University of Glasgow. In 1881, his nephews, Robert Maclehose and James J. Maclehose, were admitted as partners, and the firm was renamed James Maclehose and Sons. On 6 Mar. 1886 James Maclehose's third son Norman married Alexander Macmillan's daughter Olive. The reference is to *Olrig Grange*, a poem by W. C. Smith, published by Maclehose in 1872. See *TBB*, 150.

To ALEXANDER MACMILLAN, 13 November [1872]
MS.: British Library. Printed in Morgan, 106, *LWP,* and *TBB*.

Brasenose. | Nov. 13th.

Dear Mr. Macmillan,

The volume you send seems to me a beautiful specimen of printing, and I should much like to have the same sort of paper.[1] I like the black cloth cover, and think, with some modifications, about which I will write shortly, it will do very well for my book.

Believe me,

Yours very truly
W. H. Pater.

[1] In his letter of 12 Nov., Macmillan argued forcibly for cloth binding.

To JOHN CHAPMAN, 27 November [1872]
MS.: Yale University. Endorsed: 1872. Printed in *LWP*.

Brasenose College. | Nov. 27th.

Dear Dr. Chapman,

Mr. Macmillan is about to publish a collection of essays of mine, and among them one contributed to the Westminster Review. I suppose I have \your/ permission to reprint it, and hope someday to be again a contributor.[1] Meantime, I send you by this post an article on *The Chanson de Roland*, which seems to me to have great merits, by my friend, Mr. Andrew Lang,[2] Fellow of Merton College, the author of a volume of translations from French poets &.c. which you may have seen. He is now at Cannes, and has entrusted the article to me, hoping that you might be able to find a place for it in the Westminster Review.[3]

Believe me always

Very sincerely yours
W. H. Pater.

---

[1] Despite expressing this sentiment, Pater never again contributed to the *Westminster Review*. He found a more satisfactory outlet in the *Fortnightly Review*, where he was not bound by the requirements of a formal review-essay, and where his work appeared under his signature.

[2] Andrew Lang (1844–1912), a polymath, studied classics at Balliol College, 1865–8, and served as Fellow of Merton College, 1868–75, where he developed a keen interest in the Renaissance. He then moved to London and married Leonora Blanche Alleyne, a writer and translator. He contributed reviews and articles to newspapers and periodicals, making a name for himself in such diverse fields as anthropology, classical scholarship (translations of Homer and Theocritus), Scottish history and biography, and modern literature. Lang is best remembered for collecting, translating, and publishing folk and fairy tales. Pater refers to Lang's first publication, *Ballads and Lyrics of Old France* (London: Longmans, Green, 1872), which featured translations of verse by Villon, Ronsard, and du Bellay and original verse by Lang, confirming his knowledge of old French literature and a mastery of such forms as the ballade, triolet, and rondeau. Pater sent Lang a presentation copy of *The Renaissance*; a footnote to the third edition (1888) acknowledges a translation of the story of Aucassin and Nicolette 'from the ingenious and versatile pen of Mr Andrew Lang' (*CW* i). See Robert Crawford, 'Pater's Renaissance, Andrew Lang, and Anthropological Romanticism', *English Literary History*, 53.4 (Winter 1986), 849–79.

[3] An unsigned review of Léon Gautier, *La chanson de Roland*, 2 vols (Tours: Alfred Mame et fils, 1872), appeared in the *Westminster Review*, 100 (July 1873), 32–44.

To WALTER PATER, 29 November [1872]
MS.: British Library. Printed in *TBB*.

W. H. Pater Esq.

Nov. 29.

Dear Mr. Pater,

I accepted the black [vignette] as a not unusual or unbeautiful variety on a title page, but have no special enthusiasm for it and very gladly accept your decision on the subject.

Yours very truly,
A. Macmillan.

To ALGERNON CHARLES SWINBURNE,[1] 9 December [1872]
MS.: British Library, Ashley Collection. Printed in *LWP*.

B. N. C. | Dec. 9th.

My dear Swinburne,

I have been very busy during the last week, as I always am at this time. However, at last I have found time to read in peace, and with much enjoyment, your beautiful French verses on Gautier,[2] which I now return, with best thanks, and apologies for having kept them so long. The English sonnet[3] I suppose I may keep, and am always

Very sincerely yours
W. H. Pater.

---

[1] Algernon Charles Swinburne (1837–1909), poet and critic, exerted a major influence on Pater. See Biographical Register. In French authors such as novelist Théophile Gautier (1811–72), author of *Mademoiselle de Maupin* (1835), and poet Charles Baudelaire (1821–67), author of *Les fleurs du mal* (1857), Swinburne found inspiration for formulating an art for art's sake aesthetic.

[2] In Nov. 1872, for a memorial volume, *Le tombeau de Théophile Gautier*, ed. Alphonse Lemerre (Paris: A. Lemerre, 1873), Swinburne composed ten poems, two each in English and French, one in Latin, and five in Greek. The two French poems he sent to Pater are 'Ode' and 'Sonnet', both printed in *Poems and Ballads*, 2nd series (London: Chatto & Windus, 1878).

[3] 'Sonnet (with a copy of "Mademoiselle de Maupin")' appeared in the *Fortnightly Review*, ns 13 (Jan. 1873), 68–73.

To RODEN NOEL,[1] 29 December [1872]
Text: Christie's Catalogue, Sale 7574, Lot 89, 20 November 1992. Fragments of an autograph letter, signed 'W. H. Pater'. Two and one-half pages, 8vo, integral second leaf laid down on larger sheet.

...I have been very busy for many weeks past and must make many apologies for not having long since acknowledged the 'Red Flag',[2] which you so kindly sent me, much of which however I had read with great pleasure.... I am not one of those who think political questions an unfit subject for poetry, a point which I think Swinburne [settled conclusively] in his article 'L'année terrible'[3].... *Pater spends a page commenting on five poems in the book and closes....* Excuse all this. I should much like some day to accept the kind invitation in a former note of yours....

[1] Roden Berkeley Wriothesley Noel (1834–94), poet and critic, was a godchild of Queen Victoria. Noel attended Trinity College, Cambridge, where he made his mark as a member of the Cambridge Apostles. He travelled to the Middle East, 1858–60, with his close friend Horatio Forbes Brown (1854–1926), who became an eminent Scottish historian and produced the first biography (1895) of John Addington Symonds (1840–93) (see Biographical Register). From 1867–71 Noel served as a groom of the Privy Chamber in Ordinary to Queen Victoria. During the late 1860s, he added Symonds to his circle of close friends. Noel's poetry volumes include *Beatrice, and Other Poems* (London: Macmillan, 1868) and *A Little Child's Monument* (London: C. K. Paul, 1881); his criticism includes *Essays upon Poets and Poetry* (London: K. Paul, Trench, 1886). Edward Elgar turned Noel's poem, 'Sea Slumber Song', into the first of his song-cycle, *Sea Pictures*.
[2] In 'The Red Flag', *The Red Flag, and Other Poems* (London: Strahan, 1872), the speaker meditates on freedom and slavery.
[3] Swinburne modifies his stand on the art for art's sake doctrine he had expressed in his monograph *William Blake, A Critical Essay* (London: John Camden Hotton, 1868). In the article on 'Victor Hugo. L'année terrible', *Fortnightly Review*, ns 12 (Sept. 1872), 243–67 (rptd in *Essays and Studies*, 1875), he claims that '[n]o work of art has any worth in it that is not done on the absolute terms of art...; on the other hand we refuse to admit that art of the highest kind may not ally itself with moral or religious passion, with the ethics or the politics of a nation or an age'.

1873

To WALTER PATER, 3 January [1873]
MS.: British Library. Printed in *TBB*.

W. H. Pater Esq.

> Jan. 3.

Dear Sir,

We enclose a form of agreement[1] for your *Studies in the Renaissance*. The copy we have signed is for you to keep, the other is for you to sign and return to us.

> Yours faithfully,
> Macmillan and Co.

[1] According to this agreement, dated 4 Jan. 1873, Macmillan and Co. contracted to publish at its own expense *Studies in the History of the Renaissance* on condition that, after deducting expenses, the profits remaining would be divided equally. See Brit. Lib. Add. MS. 55030, fol. 8.

To WALTER PATER, 12 February [1873]
MS.: British Library. Printed in *TBB*.

W. H. Pater Esq., | Brasenose College, | Oxford.

> Feb. 12.

My dear Mr. Pater,

We have been stifled in the issue of your book by being unable to get a further supply of the cloth you approved of, as I also did. It was ordered by our binder five weeks since in advance, and the maker cannot supply it, or promise when. Might we use our own design in the proper colour? We have some more, but the bulk of the edition will be in a somewhat different colour, which I hope you will like. [It won't] do to delay longer.

Sidney Colvin[1] writes me that his paper is ready and waiting.

> Yours very sincerely,
> Alex Macmillan.

[1] Colvin (1845-1927) was an art critic, biographer, and administrator. See Biographical Register.

To ALEXANDER MACMILLAN, 18 February [1873]
MS.: British Library. Printed in *LWP* and *TBB*.

Brasenose College, | Oxford. | Feb. 18.

Dear Mr. Macmillan,

I was sorry to hear of the change in the binding, not only as undesirable in itself, but as not likely to be a change for the better. I should have preferred a quite different colour *of the same character* rather than any ordinary green cloth. However, I think you were quite right not to delay the book longer. How many copies are there altogether in the original binding? I still require four copies of the book, one of which might be in the new colour.

Very sincerely yours
W. H. Pater.

To WALTER PATER, 19 February [1873]
MS.: British Library. Printed in *TBB*.

W. H. Pater Esq., | Brasenose College, | Oxford.

Feb. 19.

Dear Mr. Pater,

I am glad to tell you that just after I had written my last letter to you our binder sent down word to say that at last the proper cloth had come, so that the whole edition can be bound in its own cloth.

So the matter is now settled as we had originally agreed.

Yours very truly,
A. Macmillan.

To WALTER PATER, 17 March 1873
Text: E[dward]. W[illiam]. Watson, *Life of Bishop John Wordsworth*[1] (London: Longmans, Green, 1915), 89-91. Watson provides the date. Printed in *LWP*.

You will, I think, hardly be surprised at my writing to you in reference to a subject which has been much in my thoughts of late. I mean your book of studies in the History of the Renaissance. No one can admire more than I do the beauty of style and the felicity of thought by which it is distinguished, but I must add that no one can be more grieved than I am at the conclusions at which you represent yourself as having arrived. I owe so much to you in times past, and have so much to thank you for as a colleague more recently, that I am very much pained in making this avowal. But after a perusal of the book I cannot disguise from myself that the concluding pages adequately sum up the philosophy of the whole; and that that philosophy is an assertion, that no fixed principles either of religion or morality can be regarded as certain, that the only thing worth living for is momentary enjoyment (of course of a high and subtle kind) and that probably or certainly the soul dissolves at death into elements which are destined never to reunite. I believe you will acknowledge that this is a fair statement of your position. If it is not, I shall be only too happy to be disabused of my misconceptions. I am aware that the concluding pages are, with small exceptions, taken from a review of Morris's poems published in 1868 in *The Westminster Review*. But that article was anonymous, whereas this appears under your own name as a Fellow of Brasenose and as the mature result of your studies in an important period of history. If you had not reprinted it with your name no one would, I presume, have had a right to remonstrate with you on the subject, but now the case appears to be different; and I should be faithless to myself and to the beliefs which I hold, if in the position in which I find myself as tutor next in standing to yourself I were to let your book pass without a word. My object in writing is not to attempt argument on the conclusions, nor simply to let you know the pain they have caused me and I know also many others. Could you indeed have known the dangers into which you were likely to lead minds weaker than your own, you would, I believe, have paused. Could you have known the grief your words would be to many of your Oxford contemporaries you might even have found no ignoble pleasure in refraining from uttering them. But you may have already weighed these considerations and have set them aside, and when they are pressed upon you you may take your stand on your right under the University Tests Act to teach and publish whatever you please.[2] I must then, however unwillingly, accept the same ground. The difference of opinion which you must be well aware has for some time existed between us must, I fear, become public and avowed, and it may be my duty to oppose you, I hope always within the limits of courtesy and moderation, yet openly and without reserve. It is a painful result to arrive at, but one which I hope you will not resent as unfair. At any rate, before it goes any further, I think it right to let you know my feeling and to ask if you have any reply to make to my letter. On one practical point perhaps you will allow me to ask a favour. Would you object to give up to myself or to the other tutors (if they will take it) your share in the Divinity Examination in Collections?[3] This is probably the last time in which the old system will be in force, and it would be, I confess, a relief to my mind if you would consent to do so.

[1] Revd John Wordsworth (1843–1911), ecclesiastic and theological scholar, was the grandnephew of William Wordsworth. He attended New College, Oxford, 1861–5; served as Fellow (1867) and Chaplain (1868) of Brasenose College, and was ordained priest in 1869. In 1881 he was the Bampton Lecturer. He was also Fellow of Oriel College and Oriel Professor of the Interpretation of the Holy Scriptures (1883–5). Wordsworth achieved distinction as the Bishop of Salisbury (1885–1911). His many publications include *Fragments and Specimens of Early Latin* (Oxford: James Parker, 1874) and *The Gospel according to St. Matthew, from the St. Germain MS* (Oxford: Clarendon Press, 1883). For one term, late in his undergraduate years, Wordsworth was Pater's private pupil; both men belonged to the Old Mortality essay society. See Gerald Monsman, 'Old Mortality at Oxford', *Studies in Philology*, 67 (July 1970), 359–89. When, on 25 Feb. 1874, it was the privilege of Brasenose to nominate a University proctor, Pater would normally, by virtue of seniority, have received the nomination. The college, however, selected Wordsworth instead, possibly under pressure from Benjamin Jowett (1817–93), Master of Balliol College from 1870 (see Biographical Register), who had grown suspicious of Pater's moral character and teaching. The election was a bitter rebuff to Pater.

[2] The Universities Test Act 1871, which removed religious 'tests' (signing the Thirty-Nine Articles of the Church of England) for all university degrees, except in divinity, was the second major step in the secularization of the universities (the removal of tests for matriculation and bachelors' degrees was decreed by the University Act 1851). By section 3 of the 1871 Act (34 Vict. c. 26), no person teaching in any university could be required 'to subscribe any article or formulary of faith, or to make any declaration or take any oath respecting his religious belief or profession, or to conform to any religious observance, or to attend or abstain from attending any form of public worship, or to belong to any specified church, sect, or denomination'. Pater had been obliged to subscribe to the Thirty-Nine Articles on taking his MA in 1865.

[3] A written examination in the Greek text of the New Testament, usually taken by students in their second year; typically followed by a *viva voce* (oral examination). The divinity examination in Collections was retained until 1931, on a non-denominational basis, as a prerequisite to the BA.

To JOHN MORLEY, [*c*.1 April 1873]
Text: F[rancis]. W[rigley]. Hirst, *Early Life and Letters of John Morley*, 2 vols (London: Macmillan, 1927), 1: 240. Printed in *LWP*.

Pater thanks Morley for your explanation of my ethical point of view, to which I fancy some readers have given a prominence I did not mean it to have.[1]

[1] Morley's review of *Studies in the History of the Renaissance*, 'Mr. Pater's Essays', *Fortnightly Review*, ns 19 (Apr. 1873), 469–77, praises Pater's work as 'the most remarkable example of [a] younger movement towards a fresh and inner criticism' (471). Morley notes the philosophy of the 'Conclusion' as 'worth attention' (474), although he does not wholly agree with it. Morley was rebuked by some, however, for what they thought was his endorsement of Pater's views: see Hirst, *Early Life and Letters*, 1: 240, and Z., 'Modern Cyrenaicism', *Examiner*, 12 Apr. 1873, 381–2; and Morley's 'Reply to "Z."', *Examiner*, 19 Apr. 1873, 410.

1874

To AN UNKNOWN CORRESPONDENT, 14 January [1874]¹
MS.: Daichi Ishikawa.

Bradmore Road. | Oxford. | Jan 14.

My dear Sir,

I was pleased to know that as I gathered from your note, you liked my book, which is the only one I have published.

Believe me

Yours truly
W. H. Pater.

---

[1] This date (added by another hand) is confirmed by internal evidence.

1875

To FREDERICK JAMES FURNIVALL,[1] 18 May [1875][2]
MS.: Huntington Library. Printed in *LWP*.

Bradmore Road. | May 18.

My dear Furnivall,

I ought to have written before, but have been exceptionally busy and also away from Oxford. I should like much to edit a play of Shakspere, e.g. Romeo and Juliet, for schoolboys, but see no prospect of my having time to do so for a long while to come, so must deny myself the pleasure of saying and fancying that I will do so.

Indeed, I have not yet had time to read over again my notes on L. L. L.[3] but hope to recover some lost time in the long vacation.

Always very sincerely yours
W. H. Pater.

---

[1] Professional English studies found inspiration in two main elements: the new scientific philology and the movement for adult education; the two streams converged in the person of Frederick James Furnivall (1825–1910), philologist, textual scholar, and editor. A brilliant student of languages, science, and theology, Furnivall nevertheless read mathematics at Trinity Hall, Cambridge, 1842–6, studied law at Lincoln's Inn, London, and practised law 1849–70. In the spirit of Christian socialism, he joined J. M. Ludlow, F. D. Maurice, Charles Kingsley, and Thomas Hughes in founding the Working Men's College, London, 1854, where he lectured on English grammar and literature. As a member of the Philological Society from 1853 to 1910, Furnivall supported its proposal to reform spelling and to create a wholly new dictionary (in 1876 Oxford University Press took over the enterprise, the credit for bringing the project to fruition going to James Murray). He formed the Early English Text Society in 1864 (devoting forty years to the organization, as director and editor) and by 1867 he had launched a second series to include reprints of the earliest English printers. By 1910 the Society had issued 140 volumes in the original series and 107 in the extra series. He also established the Chaucer Society and the Ballad Society in 1868, and the New Shakspere Society in 1873. From 1880–9 he organized the production of photographic facsimiles of the Shakespeare quartos in forty-three volumes (and wrote critical introductions for eight volumes). In 1881 he founded the Browning Society with Emily Hickey (1845–1924), arranging stage productions of several of Browning's plays, and the Shelley Society in 1886. Pater did not join the New Shakspere Society or any of the other literary societies Furnivall established. See the notes for Pater's Shakespeare essays, *CW* vi.

[2] Pater's reference to his 'notes' would seem to date this letter in advance of 13 Apr. 1878, when a paper of his on *Love's Labour's Lost* was read (the records do not indicate by whom) before the New Shakspere Society. This paper was evidently the first version of an essay, 'On Love's Labours [sic] Lost', *Macmillan's Magazine*, 53 (Dec. 1885), 89–91, and later collected (as 'Love's Labours Lost') in *Appreciations*, where it is dated 1878. The 1875 date for the letter is more likely than 1876 or 1877 because Pater had then recently been reported as

preparing, with a book in view, a series of Shakespeare studies, begun with the publication of 'A Fragment on *Measure for Measure*', *Fortnightly Review*, ns 22 (Nov. 1874), 652–8. See the announcement of a study of *Love's Labour's Lost*, *Academy*, 7 Nov. 1874, 506, and 12 Dec. 1874, 630; and see *CW* vi.
  [3] William Shakespeare, *Love's Labour's Lost*.

To OSCAR BROWNING,[1] [Spring or Summer 1875?]
Text: H[ugh]. E[velyn]. Wortham, *Oscar Browning* (London: Constable, 1927), 59. Printed in *LWP*.

My dear Browning,

I was not at all amused but much pained at the letters you enclose.[2] You heard all I said to Graham. I think it is not possible that I mentioned the book in question. I should greatly disapprove its being lent to any boy or young man, or even allowed in his way, and it would be quite impossible for me to recommend it to anybody. I read it years ago but do not possess it.[3] Please give an unqualified denial to the statement that I approved anything of the kind. Such statements misrepresent and pain me profoundly.... I remember that, the subject arising in the natural course of conversation, I mentioned an innocent sort of ghost story by Gautier as a very good specimen of its kind. I am sorry now that I did so, as I can only suppose that the report in question arose in this way.[4]

  [1] Oscar Browning (1837–1923), historian, biographer, and educator, co-founder (1891), and first Principal (1891–1909) of the Cambridge University Day Training College. See Biographical Register. The letter was written between the spring of 1872, when William Graham, the boy concerned, entered Eton, and Sept. 1875, when he accidentally drowned. Evans preferred 1875 on the chance that Pater's visit to Eton may be that of which he speaks in letter to Browning, [early Oct.? 1875], and/or the reason for his having been 'away from Oxford' in a letter to Furnivall, 18 May [1875].
  [2] According to Wortham, James Fitzjames Stephen (1829–94) heard from his brother, Leslie Stephen (1832–1904), that Browning had lent a copy of Gautier's *Mademoiselle de Maupin* (1834) to an Eton boy; having a son, James Kenneth Stephen (1859–92), in Browning's house at Eton, Stephen was concerned, and wrote to ask if the report were true. Stephen had come across the book by accident years before, and regarded it as 'nothing more than a mass of obscenity'. Browning assured him it was not. 'In another note', Wortham observes, 'Stephen says that though he does not wish to mention names, a man called Pater, whom he does not know, was reported as "approving the supposed proceeding".' It is the letters that passed between himself and Stephen that Browning, amused, sends to Pater. Wortham, *Oscar Browning*, 59.
  [3] At one time Pater certainly possessed a copy of the book, for in 1885 Gosse noticed Pater's 'curiously marked copy' in Sidney Colvin's Cambridge lodgings (Gosse, letter to Nellie Gosse, Trin[ity] Coll[ege], 1 Nov. 1885, Cambridge University Library MS. Add. 7020).
  [4] The story of the rumour is told by Wortham, *Oscar Browning*, 60. There had been a water-party, presumably at Eton; young Graham showed a remarkable knowledge of current French novelists, discussing Prosper Mérimée and Gautier with Browning and Pater and

some women. The next day, Pater, speaking to one of these women, praised Graham's accomplishments, 'adding that when a boy of his tender years showed any kind of literary taste it was generally for poetry of a commonplace nature, such as Alfred Tennyson's!' The story was repeated to Annie Thackeray, Lady Ritchie (1837–1919) (see Biographical Register), who in turn told her brother-in-law, Leslie Stephen.

To MOUNTSTUART GRANT DUFF,[1] 4 October [1875][2]
MS.: Brasenose College. The body of the letter is printed in Maggs Bros., *Catalogue* no. 863 (1959), 50. Printed in *LWP*.

Brasenose. | Oct. 4.

Dear Mr. Grant Duff,

I have received the chrysoberyl[3] quite safely, and with much pleasure. Accept my best thanks for your kindness in sending it. I think it a very beautiful stone, and find the green colour in it quite discernible.

Believe me

Yours very truly
W. H. Pater.

[1] Mountstuart Elphinstone Grant Duff (1829–1906), Scottish politician, administrator, and author. See Biographical Register. Scattered throughout the fourteen volumes of *Notes from a Diary, 1851–1872*, 14 vols (London: John Murray, 1897–1905) are ten personal references to Pater.
[2] According to *Notes from a Diary*, Grant Duff spent some time in Oxford in May 1874, when he visited Pater, and in Sept. 1875, when he visited Henry John Smith (1826–83), mathematician, Oxford's Savilian Chair of Geometry, and as of 1874, Keeper of the University Museum; according to an entry for this period Pater lunched with them on 26 Sept. The proximity of the dates is suggestive.
[3] A hard, tough, durable gem, valuable in some of its forms.

To OSCAR BROWNING, [early October? 1875][1]
Text: Wortham, *Oscar Browning*, 132. Printed in *LWP*.

All I can say is, that you know how much I admired your work at Eton when I was with you in the summer, and I was very glad to hear, not for your own sake only but on public grounds, that you had decided not to leave Eton without a struggle.

[1] Browning was dismissed from Eton on 16 Sept. 1875; see Biographical Register. Regarding Browning's 'struggle', see Wortham, *Oscar Browning*, 126–41; Ian Anstruther, *Oscar Browning: A Biography* (London: John Murray, 1983), 65–6, 68–80. Pater's letter was prompted in part by his having just met one of Browning's former pupils, who was 'enthusiastic in his favour' (Wortham, 132).

1876

To GEORGE SAINTSBURY,[1] [early February 1876]
Text: George Saintsbury, *A History of English Prose Rhythm* (London: Macmillan, 1912), 421. Printed in *LWP*.

When Saintsbury remarked in a Fortnightly Review *essay[2] that 'the care of the paragraph was one of Mr. Pater's first and greatest anxieties', Pater wrote to Saintsbury expressing his 'special gratification'.*

[1] George Edward Saintsbury (1845–1933), journalist, literary critic, and literary historian, attended Merton College, Oxford, 1864–8. Unable to secure a fellowship, he left Oxford to work as a schoolmaster (1868–76) and then, in London, as a reviewer (1876–95). He contributed to the leading newspapers and periodicals, including the *Fortnightly Review* and *Macmillan's Magazine*. In 1895, he succeeded David Masson (1822–1907), the Scottish biographer, critic, and journalist, as Professor of Rhetoric and English Literature at Edinburgh. His wide variety of books include *A Short History of French Literature* (1882), *A Short History of English Literature* (1898), and *A History of Criticism and Literary Taste*, 3 vols (1902–4). Saintsbury and Pater met at Merton in the late 1860s, through a mutual friend, the Revd Mandell Creighton (1843–1901), the Anglican prelate and historian, who was a Merton Fellow (1867–75) and the Dixie Professor (1884–91) of Ecclesiastical History at Cambridge. (Pater's sister Clara campaigned for women's educational rights with Creighton's wife, Louise.) Pater reviewed Saintsbury's *Specimens of English Prose Style: From Malory to Macaulay* (London: Kegan Paul, Trench, 1885) in *The Guardian*, 17 Feb. 1886, 246–7 (see *CW* v), and Saintsbury recorded his recollections of Pater in 'Walter Pater', *The Bookman*, 30 (Aug. 1906), 165–70.
[2] Saintsbury, 'Modern English Prose', *Fortnightly Review*, ns 25 (Feb. 1876), 243–69.

To WALTER PATER, 13 November 1876
MS.: British Library. Printed in *TBB*.

W. H. Pater Esq., | Brasenose College. | Oxford.

                                                            Nov: 13. 1876

Dear Mr. Pater,

About a new edition of your Essays? You spoke of altering some and adding some. I think a new revised edition might do.

                                                            Yours very truly,
                                                            Alex Macmillan.

To ALEXANDER MACMILLAN, 15 November [1876]
MS.: British Library. Printed in *LWP* and *TBB*.

Brasenose. | Nov. 15.

Dear Mr. Macmillan,

I shall be very glad to have a new and revised edition of my essays, adding a small quantity of new matter, and making a good many alterations, so that the book would be of the size of the present.[1] I should like the new edition to be as perfect as possible, as regards paper etc. with an engraved vignette, as I once suggested to you. I hope to be in London about Xmas, and will call on you on the subject. It might be ready by about March or April. Should you wish to put it in a list of books, I think the title ought to be as follows. *The Renaissance, a Series of Studies in Art and Poetry, A new Edition, etc*. Also, perhaps the price might be raised.[2]

With many thanks, I am

Very sincerely yours
W. H. Pater.

[1] Macmillan had proposed a new edition of *The Renaissance* in a note to Pater dated 13 Nov. 1876 (Letter Book XXVIII). Among the alterations Pater had mentioned was eliminating the 'Conclusion'. The essay on 'Aucassin and Nicolette' was enlarged by a discussion of '*Li Amitiez de Ami et Amile*', and retitled 'Two Early French Stories'.

[2] In 1877 the book was retitled *The Renaissance: Studies in Art and Poetry*. Critics such as Emilia Pattison (Dilke; see Biographical Register) had called attention to the misleading use of 'History' in the original title. The second edition sold for 10s. 6d.; the first, for 7s. 6d.

To WALTER PATER, 30 November 1876
MS.: British Library. Printed in *TBB*.

W. H. Pater Esq.

Nov 30. 1876

Dear Mr. Pater,

I am not sure whether I told you not to speak about a new edition of your book, as if a [word] gets abroad of one, it is likely to paralyse the sale of the present one.

I shall be very glad to see you when you are in town. [Then] we can discuss the details you mention.

Yours very sincerely,
Alex Macmillan.

1877

To ALEXANDER MACMILLAN, 30 January [1877]
MS.: British Library. Printed in *LWP* and *TBB*.

Bradmore Road. | Oxford. | Jan. 30.

Dear Mr. Macmillan,

I had hoped to have written to you before now, but have been much occupied with an examination since the beginning of term. Of the two specimen pages, I enclose the one I think preferable. I should like the line under the heading, and the number of the essay omitted. The page might, I think, be shortened by one line. This would increase, instead of slightly diminishing, the number of pages in the first edition, besides improving the look of the page, which to my eye is the better for a broad space at the foot. I shall be quite ready to send to you, or take to the press here, the corrected copy, as soon as I have heard from you, and will send you, as soon as I can, the corrected title and notices of the press, for advertisement.

I shall look out for the proof of the vignette, and specimens of binding, and I think the title on the back would perhaps be neatest in print on white paper.

The engraving from Theologia Germanica arrived quite safe. Many thanks for that and cheque.[1]

Believe me

Very sincerely yours
W. H. Pater.

---

[1] *Theologia Germanica: Which setteth forth many fair lineaments of divine truth, and saith very lofty and lovely things touching a perfect life*, a fourteenth-century German devotional work (edited by Franz Pfeiffer and translated from the German by Susanna Winkworth, with a Preface by Charles Kingsley), was published by Macmillan in 1874. Pater alludes to an engraving by C. H. Jeens on the title-page of the head and shoulders of Christ, blindfolded and wearing the crown of thorns. The cheque was probably the firm's annual payment to Pater, representing half profits on the sale of *Studies in the History of the Renaissance* during 1876. During the 1860s and 1870s, Charles Henry Jeens (1827–79), engraver, produced many beautiful vignettes and portraits for Macmillan, especially for their 'Golden Treasury' and 'Scientific Worthies' publications. The portrait of Daniel Macmillan which serves as the frontispiece to Thomas Hughes's *Memoir of Daniel Macmillan* (London: Macmillan, 1883) was engraved on steel by Jeens, after a painting by Lowes Dickinson.

To WALTER PATER, 1 February 1877
MS.: British Library. Printed in *TBB*.

W. H. Pater Esqre. | Bradmore Road | Oxford.

Feb. 1. 1877

Dear Mr. Pater,

I have instructed the printer to go on print[ing] with a page such as you decide on. We are also ordering the paper & our burden is looking after the cloth & I hope we will succeed. Mr. Jeens[1] too is at work on the little vignette but you will hardly see a proof for six weeks or so.

Yours very sincerely,
Alex Macmillan.

[1] See letter to Macmillan, 30 Jan. [1877], n. 1.

To EDMUND GOSSE, 5 February [1877]
MS.: Brotherton Collection, University of Leeds. Printed in *LWP*.

Bradmore Road. | Oxford. | Feb. 5.

My dear Gosse,

Since my return to Oxford I have been almost entirely occupied with an examination, otherwise I should have written to you before now. We hope you have not forgotten your promise to come and stay a few days with us, and that you will be able to fulfil it soon. Would Saturday, Feb. 17. suit you?[1] By that time, we may perhaps have pleasant weather. My sisters join me in kind regards, and beg me to say that it will give us great pleasure to receive you and Mrs. Gosse on that day, or any subsequent day that may be most convenient to you.[2] Hoping to hear from you soon,
I remain

Very sincerely yours
W. H. Pater.

[1] The Gosses were in Oxford by 18 Feb. 1877, for on that day Mark Pattison (see Biographical Register) noted in his diary that he found Gosse at the Paters' when he paid an afternoon call on them 'by special request' (Bodleian MS. Pattison 130, fol. 169).
[2] Gosse's circle widened considerably when he met such figures as painter Ford Madox Brown (1821–93), famous for *Work* (1852–65) and *The Last of England* (1852–5), and William Bell Scott (1811–90), Scottish poet and painter (see letter to Scott, 18 June [1872–3], n. 1).

To CHARLES ROWLEY,[1] 12 February [1877?]
MS.: Manchester Central Library. Printed in George P. Landow, 'Walter Pater to Charles Rowley', *Notes and Queries*, ns 22.10 (October 1975), 44.

Brasenose | Feb. 12

Dear Sir,

Many thanks for the programme[2] of your company. My means are too limited to permit me to be of much help to you as a purchaser, though I should be glad to hear when you publish anything of Mr. D. G. Rossetti's. I should think your most practical plan would be to apply to Mr. Ryan.[3]

Pray excuse my delay in answering your letter and believe me

Faithfully yours
W. H. Pater.

C. Rowley Esq.

[1] Charles Rowley (1839–1933), the Manchester-based picture frame-maker, socialist, author, and philanthropist, apprenticed with his father, a major print-seller and picture frame-maker who had exhibited at the International Exhibition in London, 1862, and at the Universal Exhibition in Paris, 1867. Under the pseudonym 'Roland Gilderoy', and inspired by John Ruskin, Rowley reviewed art exhibitions during the 1870s, praising the work of D. G. Rossetti, Frederic Shields, Edward Burne-Jones, and Ford Madox Brown. As managing director of Charles Rowley, 1874–1909, he promoted the sale of works by these artists, many of whom he had met through Ruskin. See Oswald Doughty, *A Victorian Romantic: Dante Gabriel Rossetti* (London: Oxford University Press, 1960). In 1875 Rowley became a member of Manchester City Council, and led campaigns for 'healthy lives, healthy homes, and healthy surroundings'. See Rowley, *Fifty Years of Ancoats* (Manchester: privately printed, 1899) and *Fifty Years of Work without Wages* (London: Hodder and Stoughton, 1911), 97–9, 114–15. According to Landow, Rowley had written to Pater about the English Picture Publishing Company, the Manchester-based firm that had been organized (under the influence of Ford Madox Brown) for the purpose of publishing photographic reproductions of contemporary and earlier British artwork. Initially, D. G. Rossetti opposed the plan, but by autumn 1876 the company's pamphlets were featuring samples of his work.
[2] This circular is missing.
[3] Unknown.

To WALTER PATER, 14 February 1877
MS.: British Library. Printed in *TBB*.

W. H. Pater Esqre. | Bradmore Road | Oxford

Feb. 14 1877

Dear Mr. Pater,

After many trials the enclosed[1] are the results of what can be done in the way of reproducing your colour. The lightest is the nearest, but the *texture* makes such a difference in the affect to the eye that I cannot say whether the result might not be nearer your wishes if we might put a graining on the cloth instead of leaving it smooth.

When you are next in town we can talk it over.

Yours very truly,
Alex Macmillan.

[1] The enclosure is missing.

To ALEXANDER MACMILLAN, 24 February [1877]
MS.: British Library. Printed in *LWP* and *TBB*.

Bradmore Road. | Feb. 24.

Dear Mr. Macmillan,

I have nearly finished correcting the proofs, so that they might begin printing in about a week from this time, if the paper can be sent. I like one of the specimens of binding, but think perhaps one of those you have in use already e.g. Green's Stray Studies,[1] might do still better. I hope to be in town at the beginning of the vacation and will call on you about it. Meantime could you ascertain from Mr. Jeens[2] the exact size of the vignette, as the Title-page must be made up accordingly.

Very sincerely yours
W. H. Pater.

How many copies are to be printed? I should propose 1000 instead of 1250, as before.[3]

P. S. I am anxious that the new edition should appear as soon as possible, and I will write myself to Mr. Jeens about the size of the vignette, which will be more direct and save you the trouble.

[1] John Richard Green's *Stray Studies from England and Italy* (London: Macmillan, 1876) was bound in the dark blue-green cloth that would be used by Macmillan for all of Pater's subsequent volumes published in his lifetime, except the second edition of *Marius the Epicurean*. Alexander Macmillan met John Green (1837–83), a historian, early in 1862 and they became close friends. For a time, Green was curate and vicar of two East End London parishes and then librarian at Lambeth. When he developed tuberculosis in 1869, all active work became impossible. Macmillan published Green's bestseller, *A Short History of the English People*, in 1874, the first complete history of England from a societal and geographical perspective; 35,000 copies of this work were sold by Mar. 1876. See Graves, *Life and Letters of Alexander Macmillan* (London: Macmillan, 1910), 325.

[2] Charles Henry Jeens engraved historical and genre subjects from contemporary painters, postal stamps for the colonies, U.S. Confederate banknotes, and did much work for Macmillan (see letter to Macmillan, 30 Jan. [1877]). The vignette, which was added to the title page of the second edition of *The Renaissance* (1877), and to the page facing the title-

page of later editions, was taken from the Leonardesque drawing no. 2252 in the Louvre, *Head of a Youth*. Pater seems to have this drawing in mind when, in the essay on Leonardo, he refers to 'a little drawing in red chalk which everyone will remember who has examined at all carefully the drawings by old masters at the Louvre. It is a face of doubtful sex, set in the shadow of its own hair, the cheek-line in high light against it, with something voluptuous and full in the eyelids and the lips' (see *CW* i).

[3] Macmillan stuck to his plan of 1,250 copies; see next letter.

To WALTER PATER, 26 February 1877
MS.: British Library. Printed in *TBB*.

W. H. Pater Esqre. | 22 Bradmore Road | Oxford

Feb. 26. 1877

Dear Mr. Pater,

As the paper we are to use is an unusual size we have to order it to be made, and the exact quantity needed. We are writing to the Press to ask how many pages exactly the book now comes to. When we know this we will order paper & get it in a week or ten days.

I think I would prefer to print 1250 copies. The last 250 make a considerable difference in the money result & they are sure to sell. Could you kindly send me back the specimens of cloth[1] as we want them for another book. I shall be glad if you adopt the colour of Green's *Stray Studies*, which I think very good. I also am writing to Mr. Jeens to say that it is important to get the vignette early.

Yours very sincerely,
Alex Macmillan.

[1] The specimens are missing.

To ALEXANDER MACMILLAN, 6 March [1877]
MS.: British Library. Printed in *LWP* and *TBB*.

Bradmore Road. | Mar. 6.

My dear Mr. Macmillan,

My book will be ready for printing in a few days. But Mr. Jeens has not yet answered my letter.[1] Could you ascertain, and let me know, the exact size of the vignette, as it is impossible to make up the title-page properly without knowing that.

Very sincerely yours
W. H. Pater.

[1] Jeens had been very ill; see next letter.

To WALTER PATER, 7 March 1877
MS.: British Library. Printed in *TBB*.

W. H. Pater Esqre. | Bradmore Road | Oxford

March 7. 1877

Dear Mr. Pater,

The paper is ordered for your book, & as soon as the printer has it he can begin printing. This we [hope] will be in a few days.

Mr. Jeens has been seriously ill, dangerously I fear. But he is sticking to his work, & when I saw him on Saturday he hoped to be able to answer your letter yesterday. As the title page is the last thing printed in a book I don't like to hurry him, as he had hoped to get the plate done in a fortnight or so.

When do you come to town? I want to show you an actual book bound in the cloth that was made after your colour. You could hardly judge of it from the bits you saw. I cannot well send the book by post.

Yours very truly,
Alex Macmillan.

To ALEXANDER MACMILLAN, 10 March [1877]
MS.: British Library. Printed in *LWP* and *TBB*.

Bradmore Road. | Mar. 10.

Dear Mr. Macmillan,

I hope to be in London the week after next and will make an appointment to see you. As I am anxious for the book to appear as soon as possible, perhaps you would give the printers a hint to that effect. I enclose the exact form of an advertisement which I should be glad to have inserted, as soon as possible, in your list of forthcoming books, in the Pall Mall Gazette for instance, with an extract which I have copied accurately from John Morley's article on my Essays in the Fortnightly Review for April, 1873.[1] I will bring you, when I come to see you, some other press notices for a longer advertisement.

Believe me

Very sincerely yours
W. H. Pater.

I hope to finish and print before long, my essays on Demeter and Dionysus,[2] and should like to talk to you about the same.

[1] See [John Morley], 'Mr. Pater's Essays', 469–77.
[2] Pater delivered the lecture 'Demeter and Persephone: A Study in Art Mythology' at the Birmingham and Midland Institute on 29 Nov. 1875. It was subsequently published in two parts: 'The Myth of Demeter and Persephone', *Fortnightly Review*, ns 25 (Jan. 1876), 82–95, and *Fortnightly Review*, ns 25 (Feb. 1876), 260–76. Pater revised this essay with a view to publishing it, together with 'A Study of Dionysus'. See letter to Macmillan, 18 Nov. [1878]. See *CW* viii.

To WALTER PATER, 12 March 1877
MS.: British Library. Printed in *TBB*.

W. H. Pater Esqre. | Bradmore Road | Oxford

March 12. 1877

Dear Mr. Pater,

An advertisement such as you send with the long extract would cost about 25/– if properly displayed in the Pall Mall. This I don't think we should spend before the book is published. We can announce the coming of the Edition in the gossip of the Athenaeum & the Academy of this week & this would attract notice. Don't you think that the *subject* of the vignette should be given? I remember that it is a head by Leonardo & is in the Louvre, but I can't recall the subject. Can you tell me by return of post?

I shall be very glad to see you when you come to town, and shall be delighted to negotiate with [you] for the Essays on Demeter & Dionysus.

Yours very truly,
A. Macmillan.

To ALEXANDER MACMILLAN, 13 March [1877]
MS.: British Library. Printed in *LWP* and *TBB*.

Bradmore Road. | Mar. 13.

Dear Mr. Macmillan,

I daresay you are right: but I am anxious that the book should be thoroughly advertised when it does appear.[1] The subject of the vignette has no recognised name, being only a small drawing;—the words of the advertisement might run,—'with a vignette after Leonardo da Vinci, engraved by Jeens'; and in any gossip on the subject it might be described as being from a favourite drawing by L. da V. in the Louvre.

Unless I hear from you to the contrary I hope to call on you on Tuesday next.[2]

Very sincerely yours
W. H. Pater.

[1] The second edition of *The Renaissance* was advertised in the *Athenaeum*, 19 May 1877, 631; in the *Pall Mall Gazette*, 24 May 1877, 13; and in the *Saturday Review*, 26 May 1877, 654. Each notice reprinted an excerpt from Morley's appreciative article. Upon discovering a mistake in referring to the old (and misleading) title, Pater arranged for a fourth notice to appear in the *Pall Mall Gazette*, 31 May 1877, 13. This one reprinted two comments praising Pater's criticism.
[2] 20 Mar. 1877.

To WALTER PATER, 14 March [1877]
MS.: British Library. Printed in *TBB*.

Mar. 14.

Dear Mr. Pater,

If you can fix what hours on Tuesday—between 11:00 and 4:00—you will call I will be careful to be in and free.

Yours very truly,
Alex Macmillan.

To ALEXANDER MACMILLAN, 31 March [1877]
MS.: British Library. Printed in *LWP* and *TBB*.

Bradmore Road. | Mar. 31.

Dear Mr. Macmillan,

I have received the proof of the vignette, and think it the most exquisite thing I have seen for a long time—a perfect reproduction of the beauty of the original, and absolutely satisfactory in the exactness and delicacy of its execution. My sincere thanks to Mr. Jeens. I should like to see an impression in red, that I may judge the colour. I suppose it ought to have a morsel of tissue paper inserted to cover it; and lest the monogram should rub it, that must be removed to some other place in the volume. I enclose a pattern for the lettering of the back;[1] I think the letters ought to be perfectly plain, but as thin and delicate as possible.

I think you told me you had thoughts of publishing a translation of Schnaase's History of Sculpture.² In that case I daresay you are already provided with a translator. If not I should venture to recommend one of my sisters,³ to whom I fancy I could give some real assistance in the work.

Very sincerely yours
W. H. Pater.

---

¹ The enclosure is missing.

² This is a reference to Karl Julius Ferdinand Schnaase (1798–1875), *Geschichte der bildenden Künste* {*History of the Fine Arts*}, 7 vols, ed. W. Lubke (Dusseldorf: J. Buddeus, 1843–64). As a law student at Heidelberg, Schnasse attended the lectures of Georg Wilhelm Friedrich Hegel; in 1818, he followed Hegel to Berlin, where he obtained his law degree. Considered the first history of art, Schnaase's study has not been translated in English.

³ Probably Clara Pater (see Biographical Register).

To ALEXANDER MACMILLAN, 9 April [1877]
MS.: British Library. Printed in *LWP* and *TBB*.

Bradmore Road. | Ap. 9.

Dear Mr. Macmillan,

I return by this post the proof of the vignette which I think on the whole the best in colour. I think it very beautiful. The others I should like to keep as specimens, unless they are wanted. The purple ones, seem to me wonderful reproductions of some tints used by Bartolozzi¹ and that set, though perhaps the engraving seems to lose some of its delicacy in them.

Very sincerely yours
W. H. Pater.

---

¹ Francesco Bartolozzi, RA (1728–1815), the son of a Florentine goldsmith, made a name for himself in England as an engraver of exquisitely finished plates. Shortly after his arrival in 1764, he was appointed engraver to George III, and in 1768 he helped found the Royal Academy. Bartolozzi produced a prodigious number of plates that capture (in the stipple engraving technique) the spirit of the Old Masters as well as of the leading painters of the day. In 1802 he was appointed Director of the National Academy of Lisbon.

To WALTER PATER, 10 April 1877
MS.: British Library. Printed in *TBB*.

W. H. Pater Esqre. | Bradmore Road | Oxford

April 10. 1877

Dear Mr. Pater,

The colour you chose is what we had liked, so we gladly adopt it. By all means keep the specimens.

Jeens' account of how he did this work is curious. He found it impossible to copy the photo, or indeed do any work on the steel while looking at it. The spots and blotches perplexed him, so he just 'learnt it by heart' and said all off without ever looking at the photo again.

Yours very sincerely,
Alex Macmillan.

To ALEXANDER MACMILLAN, 26 April [1877]
MS.: British Library. Printed in *LWP* and *TBB*.

Bradmore Road. | Ap. 26.

Dear Mr. Macmillan,

I find the binding perfectly satisfactory; with print, paper and vignette, it makes a quite typical book. But there are some points to notice—The title-page is insecurely fixed—came out, as you see, without pulling. There is a curious irregularity in the folding of the sheets, which makes the margins unequal, and produces an odd appearance on the upper edge of the volume. Please to notice also the irregularity of pp. VIII and IX; and that the whole of the *Preface* is printed on a different level from the rest of the book. I trust this is an accident of this particular copy. Alas! also, for the hands of bookbinders, which are apt to tarnish a little title-page, and the last page of all, where you will notice also an irregularity similar to that of p. IX. On the *title-page*, it seems to me that the letters are not bitten in enough. I thought the vignette was to be *pasted* on, though perhaps it is well enough as it is—looks very beautiful. I think it was a pity the attribution to Leonardo da Vinci was omitted, and that Jeens's own name might have been much more distinctly visible. Also, in this copy, the vignette is printed awry, and not, as it ought to be, exactly midway between the printing immediately above and below it.

Please don't forget my suggestions about advertising; and I should be glad if the book could be got out as soon as possible, and also if you will kindly send me, when it is ready, the number of copies for presentation you usually allow.

I am working at the other volume proposed,[1] and am

Very sincerely yours
W. H. Pater.

---

[1] Pater and Macmillan met in London on 20 Mar. 1877 to discuss his proposed new book, 'The School of Giorgione and other Studies', the contents of which are listed in letter to Macmillan, 1 Oct. [1878].

To EDMUND GOSSE, 25 May [1877]
MS.: Brotherton Collection, University of Leeds. Printed in *LWP*.

Bradmore Road. | May 25.

My dear Gosse,

It will give us great pleasure to see you and Mrs. Gosse on Saturday, June 2, and we hope you will be able to stay with us several days. I wish to ask some friends to meet you on *Monday* evening, and should be glad if you could let me have a line to say that we may reckon on your being able to stay at least so long.

Very sincerely yours
W. H. Pater.

To WALTER PATER, 30 May 1877
MS.: British Library. Printed in *TBB*.

May 30. 1877

Dear Mr. Pater,

We are sending you six copies of your book by rail today. People seem to like the look of the book very much. I do think it fulfils your ideal of being 'dainty'.

My daughter[1] greatly enjoyed your kind hospitality and that of your sisters. I do hope they will come & see us on your return to England.[2]

Yours very sincerely,
Alex Macmillan.

---

[1] Margaret Anne Macmillan (1857–1935) married Louis Dyer (1851–1908), an American writer and academic, who studied at Balliol College 1874–8, where he was friends with Margaret's brother Malcolm (see entry in Biographical Register). He taught Greek and

Latin at Harvard from 1877 to 1887, when he moved to Oxford. For many years he acted as an unofficial liaison between the university and the young American students who were attending Oxford under the Rhodes Foundation. Dyer published a short, sympathetic account of Pater's life and work in the *Nation*, 23 Aug. 1894, 137–79. Margaret helped Graves prepare the *Life and Letters of Alexander Macmillan* (1910).

[2] Pater and his sisters toured Normandy, Brittany, and the Loire Valley from Aug. to Sept. 1877.

To OSCAR WILDE,[1] 14 July [1877]
MS.: Miriam Lutcher Stark Library, Harry Ransom Center, University of Texas.[2] Printed in *LWP* and (with some changes) in *The Complete Letters of Oscar Wilde*, ed. Merlin Holland and Rupert Hart-Davis (London: Fourth Estate, 2000), 59.

Bradmore Road. | Oxford. | July 14

Dear Mr. Wilde,

Accept my best thanks for the Magazine and your letter. Your excellent article on the Grosvenor Gallery[3] I read with very great pleasure;[4] it makes me much wish to make your acquaintance, and I hope you will give me an early call on your return to Oxford.

I should much like to talk over some of the points with you, though on the whole I think your criticism very just, and it is certainly very pleasantly expressed. It shows that you possess some beautiful, and for your age quite exceptionally cultivated, tastes, and a considerable knowledge also of many beautiful things. I hope you will write a great deal in time to come.

Very truly yours
Walter Pater.

[1] Oscar Wilde (1854–1900), Irish poet, critic, novelist, and playwright. See Biographical Register and Matthew Sturgis, *Oscar: A Life* (London: Head of Zeus, 2018).

[2] Wilde was overjoyed with this, his first letter from Pater, and he copied it (somewhat inaccurately) in a letter of 19 July 1877 to his friend William Welsford Ward (1854–1932), who (following his father) became a solicitor in Bristol. This is the earliest known letter to bear the signature 'Walter Pater'.

[3] From the mid-1800s the demand for exhibition sites intensified. Young artists complained that their works found no place on the walls of the Royal Academy (RA), which, since 1768 (when it was founded), had served as the chief venue in London dedicated to instruction and exhibition. In 1863 the government appointed a Royal Commission to determine whether or not the RA was fulfilling its role as champion of national art; nothing came of the matter. For the report, see the *Edinburgh Review*, 242 (Oct. 1863), 483–507. Sir Coutts Lindsay (1824–1913), artist, collector, and impresario, and his wife, Blanche, Lady Lindsay (1844–1912), artist, musician, and writer, resolved to fill the gap, establishing the Grosvenor Gallery (1877–90) at 135–7 New Bond Street, London. Erected at a cost of £100,000, the gallery opened to the public on 1 May 1877. See [Tom Taylor], 'The Grosvenor Gallery', *The Times*, 10 May 1877, 6; Virginia Surtees, *Lindsay Coutts, 1824–1913* (London: Michael Russell, 1993). From 1878, J. Comyns Carr and Charles Edward Hallé acted as directors; their avant-garde measures included staging elaborate openings; inviting artists to choose the exhibition pieces, rather than organizing a jury to judge works submitted by artists; and

installing pictures according to aesthetic principles. Initially the Grosvenor served as the focus of the aesthetic movement, featuring works by Edward Burne-Jones, Louise Jopling, Frederic Leighton, Edward Poynter, Marie Spartali Stillman, George Frederic Watts, and James McNeill Whistler (see Biographical Register). Various people mocked 'the Palace of Art', including George Du Maurier, who in *Punch* lampooned the affectations of people who adopted the new religion of art, and W. S. Gilbert and Arthur Sullivan, who in *Patience*, their comic opera, satirized aesthetes (first performed at the Opera Comique, 23 Apr. 1881, it moved to the Savoy Theatre on 10 Oct. 1881).

⁴ Wilde's signed article, 'The Grosvenor Gallery', appeared in the *Dublin University Magazine*, 90 (July 1877), 118–26; it was his first published art criticism.

To EDMUND GOSSE, 10 September [1877]
MS.: British Library, Ashley Collection.¹ Printed in *LWP*.

Bradmore Road. | Sept. 10.

My dear Gosse,

We have just returned here from our little tour in France, and I am reminded that I have not yet thanked you for sending me your very adequate and charming article in the 'Cornhill',² which I had already read, but was very glad to receive from yourself. I hope that in spite of bad weather you have been able to write a good deal this summer. This sample makes me feel more than ever that such a book as you have proposed, on poetic execution in general, would be \a/ most effective contribution to literature.

The restoration-mania, (I mean architectural restoration,) rages in France almost as fiercely, and even with more total suppression of intelligence, than in England. However, not too troubled by this, nor at all by the politics which I suppose were something below a very agreeable surface of things,³ we saw a great deal that pleased us very much, in the way of scenery and architecture, our journey comprehending those places in Normandy, Brittany, and on the Loire, which had lain out of the way of our previous excursions, including Azay-le-Rideau, the most perfect of all those Loire Châteaux, concerning which Mrs. Mark Pattison seems, if I may judge from a rather rapid glance only at present, to have been writing well.⁴ I don't know whether you know these French places much, but we find always great pleasure in adding to our experiences of them, and return always, a little tired indeed, but with our minds pleasantly full of memories of stained glass, old tapestries, and new wild flowers. Don't trouble to answer this letter till you feel inclined, as it is only a late 'thank-you' for your essay, and, with our united kind regards to you and Mrs. Gosse, believe me

Very sincerely yours
W. H. Pater.

¹ Most of the penultimate sentence is quoted by Gosse in 'Walter Pater: A Portrait', 795–810, and rptd in *Critical Kit-Kats* (London: Heinemann, 1896), 241–71.
² 'A Plea for Certain Exotic Forms of Verse', *Cornhill Magazine*, 26 (July 1877), 53–71. The article is signed 'E. W. G'.
³ Summer 1877 was disruptive for the Third Republic of France. In an effort to restore a conservative majority in the Oct. elections, President Marie Edmé Patrice Maurice de MacMahon (1808–93) exercised severe restrictive measures on the press. Republicans answered with protests, threats, and manifestos, and eventually won a decisive electoral victory.
⁴ 'French Châteaux of the Renaissance (1460–1547)', *Contemporary Review*, 30 (Sept. 1877), 579–97. A revised version of the article was later incorporated as ch. 2 in Emilia Pattison's *The Renaissance of Art in France*, 2 vols (London: C. Kegan Paul, 1879).

To [H. G.] GRISSELL,¹ Wednesday [Autumn 1877?]
MS.: Daichi Ishikawa.

B. N. C. | Wednesday.

My dear Grissell,

I should have liked much to come to the meeting in your rooms this evening, but am engaged to dine out and fear I shall hardly get away in time.² With many thanks

Very truly yours
Walter Pater.

¹ Hartwell de la Garde Grissell (1839–1907), antiquarian, attended Brasenose College from 1859 to 1866. In the early 1860s he was influenced by Revd Henry Parry Liddon (see Biographical Register). Grissell embarked on a series of 'liturgical studies' (as he called them), publishing *Ritual Inaccuracies: Or Errors commonly made in the Celebration of the Holy Eucharist* (1865). Yet, after debating the 'Catholic' nature of the Church of England with Roman Catholic priests, he converted to Roman Catholicism on 2 Mar. 1868 and moved to Rome, where he became a personal friend of Pope Leo XIII (the Pope appointed him the first non-Italian chamberlain). Late in 1870, Grissell returned to Oxford and took a house at 60 High Street, where he set up a private oratory. In autumn 1877, when news that an Oxford High Church Society was being formed and that John Henry Newman (1801–90) was to be elected the first honorary Fellow of Trinity College, Grissell campaigned to renew Roman Catholicism in Oxford. The Catholic Club was established in Mar. 1878 by Grissell, the Revd Fr Thomas Brown Parkinson, S.J. (b. 1819), parish priest at St Aloysius (25 Woodstock Road), Gerard Manley Hopkins, S.J. (see Biographical Register), Oliver Rodie Vassall, and others. See Anthony Bischoff, S.J., *St. Aloysius: The First Eighty Years, 1875–1955* (Oxford: Oxford University Press, 1955), 9–10. The Catholic Club was re-named the Oxford University Newman Society in 1888.
² Possibly one of the meetings Grissell organized in the autumn of 1877 with a view to discussing the Catholic Club.

To OSCAR WILDE, 15 November [1877]
MS.: William Andrews Clark Memorial Library, University of California at Los Angeles. Printed in *LWP*.

B. N. C. | Nov. 15.

My dear Wilde,

I send 'Trois Contes'[1]—also the book you lent me, for which many thanks, though I don't care about it. Come for a walk any afternoon you like to name, and believe me

Yours ever
W. H. Pater.

[1] Gustave Flaubert's *Trois contes* (Paris: G. Charpentier, 1877) contains three tales: '*Un coeur simple*', '*La légende de Saint Julien l'Hospitalier*', and '*Hérodias*'; the latter had an important influence on Wilde's *Salome* (Paris: Libraire de l'Art Indépendent, 1893). Pater's copy of *Trois contes*, 2nd edn (Paris: G. Charpentier, 1877), was subsequently owned by May Ottley (see letter to Clara Pater, 11 June 1903, and Biographical Register). The title of the book that Wilde sent to Pater is unknown.

To OSCAR WILDE, 27 November [1877]
MS.: William Andrews Clark Memorial Library, University of California at Los Angeles. Printed in *LWP*.

Nov. 27.

My dear Wilde,

It will give me much pleasure to come to you tomorrow—Wednesday—at 4 o'clock.

Yours ever
W. H. Pater.

1878

To ALEXANDER MACMILLAN, 23 January [1878]
MS.: British Library. Printed in *LWP* and *TBB*.

22 Bradmore Road.[1] | Jan. 23.

My dear Mr. Macmillan,

I beg to acknowledge a cheque for 4.17.8, with many thanks.[2] I had hoped to be able to call on you before this, having never thanked you for your kind invitation to myself and my sisters, of which we hope to avail ourselves some time in the warmer weather.

I suppose Malcolm[3] will be resident again this term, and hope he will give me a call.

With very kind regards, I remain

Sincerely yours
W. H. Pater.

[1] An examination of Oxford directories for 1869–85, the years of the Paters' residence in Bradmore Road, reveals much confusion about the numbering of the houses. At the start of 1878 a numbering system was instituted by which the Paters' house, previously unnumbered, became no. 22. The system was abandoned after a year, however, and by 1882 the present number system was established; the house occupied by the Paters for sixteen years became, as it remains, no. 2. Thus, the address '22 Bradmore Road' appears only in letters of 1878.

[2] Probably Pater's account for 1877; the small stipend suggests that he may have received a considerable advance on the sales of his new edition.

[3] Malcolm Kingsley Macmillan (1852–89), eldest son of the publisher (see Biographical Register).

To OSCAR WILDE, 25 January [1878]
MS.: William Andrews Clark Memorial Library, University of California at Los Angeles. Printed in *LWP*.

22 Bradmore Road. | Jan. 25.

My dear Wilde,

Many thanks for the photograph[1] which I am very glad to have, but had previously obtained, with its fellow, from Guggenheim.[2] It came just before I was starting for London, and I was so busy then, that I hope you will forgive my not [thanking you] for it till now, when I hope also soon to see you.

Very sincerely yours
W. H. Pater.

¹ Possibly the photograph, 'Oscar Wilde When at Oxford', 1878 (J. Guggenheim, photo, Oxford), reproduced in Robert H. Sherard, *Oscar Wilde: The Story of an Unhappy Friendship* (London: Greening, 1905), opposite 48.

² Julius (Jules) Nicholas Franz Guggenheim (1820–89), a Hungarian photographer, emigrated to Great Britain in 1848; he operated a business at 56 High Street, Oxford, 1863–85. Several of his sons became photographers, and worked in Oxfordshire (see advertisements in the *Radcliffe*, 10 May 1869, 68; *Oxford Undergraduate's Journal*, 5 June 1873, 14; and *Photographic News*, 16 Feb. 1877, 84).

To OSCAR WILDE, [30 January? 1878]¹
MS.: William Andrews Clark Memorial Library, University of California at Los Angeles. Printed in *LWP*.

22 Bradmore Road. | Wednesday.

My dear Wilde,

Can you come to tea with me tomorrow at 4 o'clock, or any time later you like? I have been ill and confined to the house, but am better today. I have been much disappointed not to have seen you before now.

Very sincerely yours
W. H. Pater.

¹ This note and an undated note [5 Feb.? 1878] seem to follow logically upon the letter dated 25 Jan. [1878]; there is no evidence against dates in Hilary term, 1878. The 30th, the third Wednesday of term, was the first Wednesday after letter dated 25 Jan. [1878]. The allusion to his illness makes the 29th highly unlikely for the letter dated [5 Feb.? 1878], which probably followed on the next Tuesday, 5 Feb. 1878. This letter is printed in facsimile by Robert Sherard, *The Real Oscar Wilde* (London: T. Werner Laurie, 1916), 387.

To EDMUND GOSSE, 31 January [1878]
MS.: Brotherton Collection, University of Leeds. Printed in *LWP*.

22 Bradmore Rd. | Jan. 31.

My dear Gosse,

We are much charmed by, and thank you much for the 'Unknown Lover,' and Preface.¹

With very kind regards,

Yours ever truly
W. H. Pater.

¹ Gosse's drama, *The Unknown Lover: A Drama for Private Acting* (London: Chatto & Windus, 1878), appeared in Jan. 1878. Prefixed to the play is 'An Essay on the Chamber Drama in England'.

To ALEXANDER MACMILLAN, 31 January [1878]
MS.: British Library. Printed in *LWP* and *TBB*.

22 Bradmore Rd. | Oxford. | Jan. 31.

Dear Mr. Macmillan,

A second copy of 'Mirage'[1] has just reached me. I read the first with very great pleasure, and acknowledged it in a letter which I hope reached you, for the writer. If this second copy was sent by mistake I will return it; but, not hearing from you, shall hand it on, some time, to a friend.[2]

Very sincerely yours
W. H. Pater.

[1] Julia Constance Fletcher (1858–1938), a novelist, playwright, and literary critic, was the daughter of an American clergyman and his Swiss wife; she grew up in Italy. She published six novels and several plays under the pseudonym of George Fleming. Commentators praised her first novel, *A Nile Novel* (London: Macmillan, 1876), for its presentation of character, especially female characters, and its beautiful prose. Wilde met her in Rome in spring 1877; she studied Wilde as a character, attracted by his aesthetic lifestyle, dandyish dress, and outrageous talk, and within weeks wrote *Mirage*, which was published in three volumes by Macmillan (Dec. 1877; the minor character, Claude Davenant, a young Oxford poet and aesthete, is based on Wilde). Fletcher dedicated the book 'To Walter H. Pater, Author of "Studies in the History of the Renaissance", with profound admiration for the rare and exquisite quality of his work', and also took her epigraph from the 'Winckelmann' essay. Although she lived most of her life in Venice (because of her mother's poor health), Fletcher lived for long periods in London during the 1880s and 1890s. Her papers, possibly including letters from Pater and Wilde, as well as from Robert Browning, William Henley, Henry James, and Rudyard Kipling, have never been found. For her connections with Wilde and Pater, see the letter to Fletcher, 21 June [1882].

[2] The second copy was sent by mistake (see letter to Pater, 1 Feb. 1878). Writing for his father the next day, George A. Macmillan asked Pater to send it on, with his father's regards, to Mary Arnold Ward. Letter Book XXXII.

To WALTER PATER, 1 February 1878
MS.: British Library. Printed in *TBB*.

Feb. 1. 1878

Dear Mr. Pater,

In answer to your letter of this morning my father asks me to say that the second copy of 'Mirage' was sent by mistake. If you have no special object in view for it he would be glad if you would send it with his kind regards to Mrs. Humphry Ward.[1]

I am

Yours very truly,
George A. Macmillan.

[1] The novelist Mary Augusta Arnold Ward (1851–1920); see Biographical Register.

To OSCAR WILDE, [5 February? 1878]
MS.: William Andrews Clark Memorial Library, University of California at Los Angeles. Printed in *LWP*.

22 Bradmore Road. | Tuesday.

My dear Wilde,

I had hoped to see you again before this. Will you come to tea with me today or tomorrow at 4, or 4.30.

Yours ever
W. H. Pater.

To OSCAR BROWNING,[1] 13 March [1878]
MS.: Archive Centre, King's College, Cambridge, Papers of Oscar Browning, OB/1/1248/A. Printed in Lene Østermark-Johansen, ' "Don't forget your promise to come soon": Seven Unpublished Letters from Walter Pater to Oscar Browning', *Pater Newsletter*, 59/60 (Fall/Spring 2011), 23.

22 Bradmore Rd. | Mar. 13.

My dear Browning,

I enclose all the papers of general questions wh. I can just now find.

I enjoyed my visit to Cambridge, very much, through your kindness, and look back to it with great pleasure; and returned to Oxford much better than when I left as I had really been ill.[2]

Don't forget your promise to come here soon. It will give me great pleasure to receive you almost whenever you like.

Very sincerely yours
W. H. Pater.

---

[1] Oscar Browning (1837–1923), historian, biographer, and educator; see Biographical Register.
[2] See letter to Wilde, [30 Jan.? 1878].

To OSCAR BROWNING, 30 March [1878]
MS.: Archive Centre, King's College, Cambridge, Papers of Oscar Browning, OB/1/1248/A. On the stationery of the Oxford Union Society, with crest. Printed in Østermark-Johansen, 'Don't forget your promise', 23–4.

22 Bradmore Rd. | Mar. 30.

My dear Browning,

So many people are away just now that it would be hardly possible to get you full statistics of the new buildings here. I don't think those at Ch. Ch.[1] would be so much of a parallel to those you contemplate, as the new buildings at New College. The buildings now in progress at Ch. Ch. aim only at decoration, though, I believe, costly. The New College buildings which have been opened within the last two or three years contain, besides undergraduates' rooms, houses for married fellows.[2] Alfred Robinson[3] would be the best man to consult for exact details about them. The Bursar under whom they were commenced is no longer resident. The new buildings at Balliol, though I fancy they add something to the accommodation there, only replaced old ones. I think New College would be almost precisely a parallel case to yours at King's College.

Ever very sincerely yours
W. H. Pater.

[1] Christ Church College, Oxford.
[2] George Gilbert Scott (1811–78), an architect, advocated the Gothic Revival style; the new building for New College, which he designed, was completed in 1873. Two more staircases, plus accommodation for a married tutor, were added in 1875–7.
[3] Alfred Robinson (1841–95) studied classics and mathematics at University College, Oxford, 1861–4, before serving as Fellow (from 1865), Tutor (1865–75), and Senior Bursar (from 1875) of New College. Reforming the college absorbed much of Robinson's time and energy: he took an active interest in such matters as erecting new buildings and restoring the chapel, increasing the number of Fellows, initiating (in concert with Balliol College) the system of intercollegiate lectures, expanding the student population, and creating a number of new scholarships.

To GEORGE GROVE,[1] 17 April [1878]
MS.: British Library. Printed in *LWP* and *TBB*.

22 Bradmore Road. | Oxford. | Ap. 17.

Dear Mr. Grove,

I send you by this post a MS. entitled 'The House and the Child',[2] and should be pleased if you should like to have it for *Macmillan's Magazine*. It is not, as you may perhaps fancy, the first part of a work of fiction, but is meant to be complete in itself; though the first of a series, as I hope, with some real kind of sequence in them, and which I should be glad to send to you. I call the MS. a portrait, and mean readers, as they might do on seeing a portrait, to begin speculating—what came of him?

Very truly yours
W. H. Pater.

[1] George Grove (1820–1900), editor, musicologist, and administrator; see Biographical Register.
[2] Published as 'Imaginary Portraits. I. The Child in the House', *Macmillan's Magazine*, 38 (Aug. 1878), 313–21, and reprinted as a book, *An Imaginary Portrait: The Child in the House* (1894), shortly before Pater's death. See *CW* iii.

To OSCAR BROWNING, 23 April [1878]
MS.: Archive Centre, King's College, Cambridge, Papers of Oscar Browning, OB/1/1248/A. Printed in Østermark-Johansen, 'Don't forget your promise', 24.

22 Bradmore Road. | Ap. 23.

My dear Browning,

It will give me much pleasure to see you, and receive you in my small quarters, at the time you propose. I shall expect you on Sat. May 4th, or earlier, if you like.

Yours very truly
W. H. Pater.

To OSCAR BROWNING, 3 May [1878]
MS.: Archive Centre, King's College, Cambridge, Papers of Oscar Browning, OB/1/1248/A. On paper with the Brasenose College crest. Printed in Østermark-Johansen, 'Don't forget your promise', 24–5.

22 Bradmore Road. | May 3.

My dear Browning,

I am looking forward to seeing you tomorrow. There is a good train from Cambridge at 2:00 but come earlier if you can. You had best come straight to my house. I have some men dining with me to meet on Monday, so that I hope, as I concluded from your letter, that you will be able to stay till Tuesday. We dine at 7 on Saturday.

Yours ever
W. H. Pater.

To GEORGE GROVE, 12 May [1878]
MS.: British Library. Printed in *LWP* and *TBB*.

22 Bradmore Road, | Oxford. | May 12.

Dear Mr. Grove,

I have just sent the corrected proofs of my article to the Printers and told them I should like to have a revise. Also, I should prefer the article to appear without signature.

Yours very truly
W. H. Pater.

To OSCAR BROWNING, 20 May [1878]
MS.: Archive Centre, King's College, Cambridge, Papers of Oscar Browning, OB/1/1248/A. Printed in Østermark-Johansen, 'Don't forget your promise', 26.

B. N. C. | May 20.

My dear Browning,

I hear from Sayce[1] that the meeting about the *Scholarships*[2] will take place in London at a time and place not yet settled. There will be no meeting at Queen's; only, Colvin[3] and Newton[4] are, I believe, coming to give evidence before a committee, of which Magrath[5] is a member, about an *Archaeological Museum*.[6]

Please let me know a day or two before you come. I can give you a bed if you like.

Very sincerely yours
W. H. Pater.

---

[1] Revd Archibald Henry Sayce (1845–1933), an Assyriologist, developed a passion for the culture of ancient Mesopotamia in his youth. He studied with experts who became close friends, starting with John Earle (1824–1903), Rawlinson and Bosworth Professor of Anglo-Saxon at Oxford, who introduced him to the work of F. Max Müller (1823–1900), the Oxford-based German philologist and Orientalist, with a view to mastering the writing systems of Egypt and Assyria. Sayce matriculated at Brasenose College, Oxford, but attended Queen's College 1865–9. He served as Deputy Professor of Comparative Philology at Oxford from 1876–90, and Examiner, from 1877, in the new School of Theology. He resigned his university offices, except his fellowship, in 1891 so that he could devote all his time to archaeological research and writing (and spending the winters on the Nile). In his *Reminiscences* (London: Macmillan, 1923), Sayce provides details of his friendships with such figures as Ingram Bywater, Sidney Colvin, Walter Pater, Mark Pattison, T. Humphry Ward, and Oscar Wilde.

[2] This matter is not clear.

[3] Sidney Colvin (1845–1927), art critic, biographer, and administrator. See Biographical Register.

⁴ Sir Charles Thomas Newton (1816–94), archaeologist and diplomat, was a student at Christ Church, Oxford, where he befriended John Ruskin. Newton served as assistant in the Department of Antiquities at the British Museum, 1840–52; in 1852, he was vice-consul at Mytilene, with the goal of exploring the coasts and islands of Asia Minor. As the British ambassador at Constantinople, he uncovered in 1852–7 inscriptions on the island of Kalymnos and discovered the remains of the mausoleum of Halicarnassus, one of the seven wonders of the ancient world. From 1860–85 he was Keeper of the British Museum, responsible for re-organizing the department of antiquities. Newton was also Yates Professor of Classical Archaeology at the University of London, 1880–8. Publications include *Essays on Art and Archaeology* (1886). For Pater's indebtedness to Newton's archaeological reports, see Linda Dowling, 'Walter Pater and Archaeology: The Reconciliation with Earth', *Victorian Studies*, 31 (Winter 1988), 209–31; Lesley Higgins, 'But who is "She"?: Female Subjectivity in Pater's Writings', *Nineteenth-Century Prose*, 24.2 (Fall 1997), 37–65; and Lene Østermark-Johansen, *Walter Pater and the Language of Sculpture* (Farnham: Ashgate, 2011), 232–8.

⁵ John Richard Magrath (1839–1930), academic and administrator, became Fellow (1860), Tutor (1864), Dean (1864–7), Chaplain (1867–78), Bursar (1874–8), Pro-Provost (1877), and then Provost (1878–1930) of Queen's College, Oxford. He was a member of the Hebdomadal Council (1878–99), Curator of the University Chest (1885–1908), a Delegate of the Oxford University Press (1894–1920), and University Vice-Chancellor (1894–8). In addition, Magrath served as an alderman in Oxford, 1889–95.

⁶ The Ashmolean Museum, Oxford, was built on Beaumont Street between Apr. 1841 and Aug. 1845 to a design by Charles Robert Cockerell (1788–1863). One wing houses the Taylor Institution, the university's modern languages faculty, and the other houses the extensive collections of archaeological specimens and fine art (including one of the best collections of Pre-Raphaelite art). Between 1886–94 the facility was expanded to the north of the original galleries to house the Archaeological and Tradescant Collections; in 1908, the facility became the Ashmolean Museum of Art and Archaeology.

To OSCAR WILDE, 10 June [1878]
MS.: William Andrews Clark Memorial Library, University of California at Los Angeles. Printed in *LWP*.

22 Bradmore Road. | June 10.

My dear Wilde,

I stupidly forgot yesterday that we have some people coming here to dine on Monday, so that I shall be, with much regret, unable to accept your kind invitation. It would give me much pleasure, however, if you would bring Miss Fletcher[1] and her party, to lunch with me in the Common Room at B. N. C. on Thursday, June 20th, at 1.30., if they stay so long; if not, I would try to fix an earlier day.

Also I forgot to thank you for your poem in the 'Irish Monthly',[2] which has I think many great beauties, and real music and impulse in it.

In haste,

Ever yours
W. H. Pater.

[1] Julia Fletcher (see letter to Macmillan, 31 Jan. [1878], n. 1) wrote to Wilde from London on Wed., 12 June 1878, congratulating him on winning the Newdigate prize for his poem, 'Ravenna'. 'We shall go up [to Oxford] Sunday morning by a train that leaves Paddington at 10 o'clock—and stay until Tuesday night.... And will you, if you see him, tell Mr. Pater of our arrival? I should write to him but I don't know how to sign myself.' Her letter is in the Wilde Collection at the Clark Library. Wilde, who met Fletcher in Rome, in spring 1877, was much impressed by her cleverness, charm, and beauty. He may well have introduced her to Pater's works, for he wrote to W. W. Ward on 19 July 1877 that he had not yet sent her some articles by Pater that he had promised; see Holland and Hart-Davis, eds, *Complete Letters of Oscar Wilde*, 57–9.

[2] Wilde, 'Magdalen Walks', *Irish Monthly*, 6 (Apr. 1878), 211.

To GEORGE GROVE, 11 June [1878]
MS.: British Library. Printed in *LWP* and *TBB*.

George Grove Esq.

22 Bradmore Road, | Oxford. | June 11.

Dear Mr. Grove,

I have sent the corrected version of my paper[1] for Macmillan back to Messrs. Clay and Sons,[2] and have restored the signature, as you proposed. With many thanks for your letters, I am

Very sincerely yours
W. H. Pater.

Geo. Grove, Esq.

[1] Pater's earliest work of fiction was published as 'Imaginary Portraits. I. The Child in the House' in *Macmillan's Magazine*, 37 (Aug. 1878), 313–21, and issued as a book in 1894 by the Daniel Press. See *CW* iii.

[2] The Clays of Bungay, Suffolk, printed a wide range of books and periodicals for the leading publishers of the day, including Richard Bentley, Archibald Constable, J. M. Dent, Ward Lock, Macmillan, and George Routledge. Richard Clay (1789–1877) founded the firm in 1827, when he took over a printing business in London. The business prospered and became renowned for its expert printing of wood engravings. When Clay retired in 1868, a new partnership was formed under the name R. Clay, Sons and Taylor. The Clays printed a wide range of books and three periodicals for Macmillan: *Macmillan's Magazine* (1859–1907), *Nature* (1869–1920), and *Journal of Hellenic Studies* (1880–1956).

To JOHN MILLER GRAY,[1] [August? 1878][2]
Text: *John Miller Gray: Memoir and Remains*, ed. J. Balfour Paul and W. R. Macdonald, 2 vols (Edinburgh: David Douglas, 1895), 1: 42–3. Printed in *LWP*.

Many thanks for your charming fragments of criticism, which ought, I think, to go finally into some large and complete work of criticism. You seem to me to have real possession of many important principles—in speaking of Whistler's exhibition,³ for instance—and unite them to a style which seems to me at once highly picturesque, finished, and temperate. Thank you also for your appreciation of my article in Macmillan—I value it much—the appreciation, I mean....⁴

¹ John Miller Gray (1850–94), Scottish art critic, antiquarian, and administrator. See Biographical Register.
² Paul and Macdonald (1: 42) give the year as 1878; the reference to 'The Child in the House' places the date after 1 Aug.; and if Gray wrote the notice mentioned in n. 4, after 17 Aug.
³ James McNeill Whistler (1834–1903), American painter, etcher, and lithographer. See Biographical Register.
⁴ Gray appears to have sent Pater a few works of criticism from the *Academy* and the *Edinburgh Courant*, to which Gray was contributing regularly at this time. These included 'Mr. Whistler's Exhibition', just mentioned, and the 'appreciation' of 'The Child in the House', which may be the unsigned notice by Gray that appeared in the *Academy*, 17 Aug. 1878, 166.

To WALTER PATER, 2 September 1878
MS.: British Library.

Sept 2nd 1878

Dear W. Pater,

Thank you very much for your letter. I am off to America on Thursday¹ till about the middle of November. When you have more MS. ready please send it *here* to W. Jack Esq.² who will act for me in my absence.

I am delighted to think that you are going on with the series.

Yours faithfully,
G. Grove.

W. H. Walter Pater Esq.

¹ 5 Sept. 1878.
² Not identified.

To ALEXANDER MACMILLAN, 1 October [1878]
MS.: British Library. Printed in *LWP* and *TBB*.

22 Bradmore Road. | Oxford. | Oct. 1.

Dear Mr. Macmillan,

I propose to print a volume of essays from the 'Fortnightly' etc. and should be glad if you would take it on the same terms as my former volume, to the second edition of which I should like it to correspond in type etc. It might appear at the beginning of next year; and I will, if you like, call on you, at the beginning of November about it.[1] Meantime perhaps it might be got into type. I propose to call it,

'The School of Giorgione, and other studies.'

and give, opposite, a list of contents. I think it would be a volume of about 300 pages.

Very sincerely yours
W. H. Pater.

Contents[2]

The School of Giorgione.
Wordsworth.
The Myth of Demeter—

1. The Homeric Hymn.
2. Demeter and Persephone.

The Myth of Dionysus—

1. The spiritual form of fire and dew.
2. The Bacchanals of Euripides.

Romanticism.
On 'Love's Labour [sic] Lost'.
On 'Measure for Measure'.
The Character of the Humourist—*Charles Lamb*.

---

[1] Pater probably called on Saturday, 2 Nov., for Macmillan wrote him on 30 Oct. 1878 that he would be glad to see him then, about noon. Letter Book XXXV.

[2] Only 'The Bacchanals of Euripides' and the essay on Shakespeare's *Love's Labour's Lost* were unpublished. References to the first publication of most of the others have already been given in the notes. Those not yet mentioned are 'On Wordsworth' and 'The Character of the Humourist: Charles Lamb', *Fortnightly Review*, ns 21 (Apr. 1874), 455–65, and ns 30 (Oct. 1878), 466–74, respectively, and 'Romanticism', *Macmillan's Magazine*, 35 (Nov. 1876), 64–70. All the essays on English literature were collected in *Appreciations*, in which a version of 'Romanticism' appears as the 'Postscript'. See *CW* v and vi.

To WALTER PATER, 2 October 1878
MS.: British Library. Printed *TBB*.

W. H. Pater Esqre. | 22 Bradmore Road | Oxford

Oct. 2. 1878

Dear Mr. Pater,

We shall be very glad to undertake the publication of your new volume of essays on the same terms as we did your studies in the Renaissance.

We will print it as before at the Clarendon Press and we are writing to the Printers there to say that you are ready to supply them with copy as soon as they like to begin, and that it is to be printed exactly uniform with the second edition of your 'Studies'.

We will send a paragraph to the *Athenaeum* & *Academy* saying that it is coming & giving them the [title] as you give it.

I shall be very glad to see you when you come to London.

Very sincerely yours,
Alex Macmillan.

To WALTER PATER, 30 October 1878
MS.: British Library. Printed in *TBB*.

W. H. Pater | 22 Bradmore Road

Oct: 30. 1878

Dear Mr. Pater,

I shall be very glad to see you on Saturday about noon.[1] The press has not given us the exact number of pages so that we may order the paper which is rather peculiar, but we are writing them today.

Very sincerely yours,
Alex Macmillan.

[1] 2 Nov. 1878.

To ALEXANDER MACMILLAN, 13 November [1878]
MS.: British Library. Printed in *LWP* and *TBB*.

22 Bradmore Road. | Nov. 13.

Dear Mr. Macmillan,

Accept my best thanks for the beautiful copy of Milton, and for the 'Europeans',[1] which I am reading slowly, as it deserves, with immense enjoyment of its delicate beauty. It makes most other literature seem rather vulgar.

Will you kindly give directions that the paper should be sent as soon as possible to the Oxford Press,[2] for my Essays; as they are now ready to begin printing.[3] I suppose there will be no delay in the binding; and will send, in a few days, a note about the advertisements for the end of the volume.

Very sincerely yours
W. H. Pater.

[1] The 'Milton' was probably *Milton's Poetical Works*, ed. David Masson (London: Macmillan, 1877), an inexpensive popular edition in Macmillan's Globe series, but one which was also available in a more elegant format, with gilt edges and various calf or morocco bindings. Henry James's *The Europeans: A Sketch* was issued by Macmillan on 28 Sept. 1878.

[2] Oxford University Press, a department of the university, is wholly owned by 'the Chancellor, Masters, and Scholars'. It has been suggested that the first book was printed in 1478, although the continuous history of the press dates from 1858, when the university approved a loan of £100 to a local bookseller, Joseph Barnes, to set up a press. The first volume printed by Barnes was John Case's book on Aristotle's *Ethics*. Over the next thirty-three years, Barnes produced some 300 books, mostly tracts or sermons; see Peter Sutcliffe, *The Oxford University Press: An Informal History* (Oxford: Clarendon Press, 1978), xiv–xv. In 1863, Alexander Macmillan was appointed Publisher to the University of Oxford, a post he held until 1880, when the Delegates of the University Press abandoned the system of employing a private publisher to manage their publications (see *A Bibliographical Catalogue of Macmillan and Co.'s Publications from 1843 to 1889* (London: Macmillan, 1891), vi.

[3] The page proofs were already begun, and perhaps completed, for in 1882 (see letter to Sharp, 4 Nov. 1882) Pater gave William Sharp proofs of 'The School of Giorgione', paginated 157–84. See Elizabeth A. Sharp, *William Sharp (Fiona Macleod): A Memoir* (London: William Heinemann, 1910), 211. The proofs had been printed at the Clarendon Press on 12 Nov. 1878.

To WALTER PATER, 16 November 1878
MS.: British Library. Printed in *TBB*.

Walter Pater Esq.

> Nov: 16. 1878

Dear Mr. Pater,

The paper for your book had to be specially made. It was ordered as soon as we had a clear idea of the size of the book. We expect it in the printers' hands early next week. We will do all we can to get your book out early. Have you given the printers your title-page yet? They will send us a proof of it & from this we fix the latter on the outside. When we get this we can have all ready so that the binding causes no delay.

With kind regards

> Yours very sincerely,
> Alex Macmillan.

To ALEXANDER MACMILLAN, 18 November [1878]
MS.: British Library. Printed in *LWP* and *TBB*.

> 22 Bradmore Road. | Nov. 18.

Dear Mr. Macmillan,

I enclose a selection of 'Opinions of the Press', which I should like to appear as an advertisement, at the end of my new volume.[1] They might, I think, occupy two pages, in the order which I have given; and be followed by the advertisements of 'Belles Lettres', which appear in 'Mirage' etc.; of course, omitting from the latter, the advertisement of my book, now there. Would you let me have a proof of the 'Opinions', I enclose?

Many thanks for your letter.[2] I will take the title-page etc. to the Press, almost immediately.

I should like the lettering on the back to be precisely as before, in type and arrangement—with, at the top,

DIONYSUS
AND
OTHER STUDIES

Believe me

> Very sincerely yours
> W. H. Pater.

---

[1] The enclosure is missing.
[2] See letter to Pater, 16 Nov. 1878.

To ALEXANDER MACMILLAN, 30 November [1878]
MS.: British Library. Printed in *LWP* and *TBB*.

22 Bradmore Road. | Nov. 30.

Dear Mr. Macmillan,

I find more and more, as I revise the proofs of my essays, so many inadequacies that I feel compelled, very reluctantly, to give up the publication of them for the present. You will of course let me know all the cost of setting up in type, for which of course I will immediately repay you. The paper which I fancy has not yet arrived, may, I suppose, be used for some other book. I hope you will forgive me all the trouble I have given you. But, sincerely, I think it would be a mistake to publish the essays in their present form; some day they may take a better and more complete form. Please send me a line of assent at once.[1]

With many apologies,

Very sincerely yours
W. H. Pater.

P. S. Please do not announce, in any way, that the book is not to be published.

---

[1] Pater's decision to cancel this collection of essays coincided with the heated debates over the aesthetics and the economics of art that dominated the Whistler *v.* Ruskin trial, 25 and 26 Nov. 1878, which were aired in newspapers. See *The Times*, 27 Nov. 1878, 9; Laurel Brake, 'After *Studies*: Walter Pater's Cancelled Book, Or *Dionysus* and Gay Discourse in the 1870s', *Beauty and the Beast*, ed. P. Liebregts and Wim Tigges (Amsterdam: Rodopi, 1996), 115–26.

To WALTER PATER, 2 December 1878
MS.: British Library. Printed in *TBB*.

W. H. Pater Esqre. | 22 Bradmore Road | Oxford

Dec. 2 1878

Dear Mr. Pater,

Please don't! At least wait a little till we have gone carefully over the proofs. There is no reason so far as I have seen for your apprehension. I think this will be a quite worthy successor of your 'Renaissance'. The paper is in the printers' hands, but of course we could arrange that. But it would be awkward to answer the many questions that would come to us as 'Why is Pater's book not forthcoming'? Let us wait a little at best.

Yours very sincerely,
Alex Macmillan.

To GEORGE GROVE, 4 December [1878]
MS.: British Library. Printed in *LWP* and *TBB*.

22 Bradmore Road. | Dec. 4.

Dear Mr. Grove,

I am glad to hear of your safe return.¹ Many thanks for your letter. I fear I shall not be able to send you another instalment just yet, as I have found it necessary to take up again, some work I thought I had finished, of another sort.²

I heard a conversation among some musical people the other night about your Musical Dictionary, which made me put your article on Beethoven, down among things to be read.

Very truly yours
W. H. Pater.

---

¹ From a trip to the United States and Canada; Grove had left England on 5 Sept. and returned on 14 Nov.

² Pater had informed Grove earlier that he was working on another instalment for the series of which 'The Child in the House' was meant to have been the first; Grove had written to him on 2 Sept. 1878, asking him to send the material to Grove's assistant during his absence (Letter Book XXXIV). The incomplete second instalment is evidently 'An English Poet'; see *CW* iii and x. The work Pater had to take up was probably the revision of the essays in the volume he had just abandoned. It may, however, have been the refurbishing of the lectures he was delivering on the 'History of Greek Art, with Books I, V, VI of Pausanias'; some of these lectures furnished the basis for three articles that appeared a year later in the *Fortnightly Review*: 'The Beginnings of Greek Sculpture. I. The Heroic Age of Greek Art', ns 33 (Feb. 1880), 190–207; 'The Beginnings of Greek Sculpture. II. The Age of Graven Images', ns 33 (Mar. 1880), 422–34; and 'The Marbles of Aegina', ns 33 (Apr. 1880), 540–8; see *CW* viii.

To WALTER PATER, 5 December 1878
MS.: British Library. Printed in *TBB*.

W. H. Pater Esq. | 22 Bradmore Road | Oxford

Dec. 5. 1878

Dear Mr. Pater,

I have had a note from the Clarendon Press, and £35. would cover the printer's expenses. We had sent down paper which cost us £39. & part of which they had 'wetted ready for working' before you called. The paper is peculiar and was made specially for this book, but we will most likely be able to use it somehow. If I find we incur any loss I will tell you hereafter.

Would you like the type taken down at once?

I am rather sorry about the matter, but you clearly are the final judge & [I submit.]

Very sincerely yours,
Alex Macmillan.

To ALEXANDER MACMILLAN, 9 December [1878]
MS.: British Library. Printed in *LWP* and *TBB*.

22 Bradmore Road. | Dec. 9.

Dear Mr. Macmillan,

I enclose a cheque for 35.£. You will let me know if you incur any expense about the paper. I am sorry to have given you so much trouble for nothing.

Very sincerely yours
W. H. Pater.

P. S. I should like the type to be broken up.
Alex. Macmillan Esq. | Bedford St., Covent Garden, | London. W. C.

To WALTER PATER, 11 December 1878
MS.: British Library. Printed in *TBB*.

W. H. Pater Esqre. | Bradmore Road | Oxford

Dec. 11. 1878

My dear Mr. Pater,

I enclose [a] receipt for the printing expenses of the discarded Dionysus. I cannot but feel he is rather hardly treated by his father, but of course the father in this case is the judge, a Brutus come to judgment & execution too. The paper question must stand over for a time. If we sustain any loss over it we will let you know by & by. It is a peculiar paper & we will have a look about us to see how we can use it. If we can without actual loss we will leave you free.

Very sincerely yours,
Alex Macmillan.

We are ordering the type to be taken down.

1879

To AN UNKNOWN CORRESPONDENT,[1] 4 January [1879?]
MS.: The University of Kansas.

Brasenose College. | Jan. 4th.

My dear Sir,

The copy of 'Savonarola'[2] which you kindly sent me some weeks ago reached me at a very busy time or I should have written before now to thank you for what it gave me great pleasure to receive. I have now had time to read it \'Savonarola'/ with much enjoyment, and admire greatly the really dramatic picture it presents of a period which strongly interests me. Its subject is one which at this time interests a very large number of people, and it strikes me that there is a classical finish and definiteness of effect, about your work, which must make it a favourite with all such. Accept my sincere thanks for it, and believe me

Faithfully yours
W. H. Pater.

Should you at any time visit Oxford, it would give me much pleasure to see you.

---

[1] Possibly William Robinson Clark (1829–1912), the acclaimed Scottish-Canadian theologian. Clark attended King's College, Aberdeen, graduating BA in 1848. Clark served as minister for the Congregationalist church at Lymington, Hampshire, 1854-6. After converting to the Church of England and taking holy orders, he served as Dean of Taunton and Prebendary of Wells Cathedral, Somerset, 1859-80. His talents attracted attention; he frequently preached in St Paul's Cathedral and Westminster Abbey. Meanwhile, he attended Hertford College, Oxford, graduating BA in 1864, and spent two years in London working on literary projects. He emigrated to Canada in 1882, where he became Professor of Mental and Moral Philosophy at Trinity College, and Professor of Theology, at the University of Toronto, 1883 to 1908. Clark served as a Fellow (and later President) of the Royal Society of Canada and as a founding member of the Empire Club. He married three times and fathered twelve children. Clark produced many volumes on biographical, theological, and literary subjects, which appeared in the United Kingdom, Canada, and the United States. Presumably, he sent Pater a copy of *Savonarola: His Life and Times* (London: Society for Promoting Christian Knowledge, 1878) late in 1878.

[2] Pater encountered Girolamo Savonarola (1452–98), the charismatic Dominican friar, reformer, and martyr, in George Eliot's historical novel, *Romola* (1863), a study of life in Renaissance Florence narrated from artistic, religious, and social perspectives. Romola, the female protagonist, meets several leading figures of the day, including Savonarola, who engineered the overthrow of the Medici in 1494 and initiated the incineration of secular art (the 'Bonfire of the Vanities') in 1497 and 1498. Pater developed an admiration for the rebel against established authority; in 'Winckelmann' (Jan. 1867), for example, he explained that Savonarola developed 'a new organ for the human spirit'. See Donald L. Hill, 'Pater's Debt to *Romola*', *Nineteenth-Century Fiction*, 22 (Mar. 1968), 361–77.

To F. G. ELLERTON,¹ [January 1879 to April 1889?]
MS.: Bates College. Printed in *LWP*.

B. N. C. | Thursday

Dear Mr. Ellerton,

I shall hope to have the pleasure of seeing you tomorrow (Friday) at 1.15.

Very truly yours
Walter Pater.

[1] The Revd Francis George Ellerton (1861–1943) studied at Hertford College, Oxford, 1879–84. He was ordained in 1887 and served (from 1890) as vicar of Warmingham, Cheshire, Ellesmore, Salop, and Tardebigge, Bromsgrove. Bernard Richards has pointed out that Ellerton comments on the 'lunch' Pater alludes to in a letter (17 Dec. 1896) written to John Cann Bailey (1864–1931), literary critic, lecturer, and administrator. Ellerton wrote: 'Dear Pater. Never, never, shall I forget my lunch with him and the two fair American girls and their very American Dragon, in his rooms at B. N. C. How he soliloquized of the Campo Santo and the fair flowers planted long ago by dead hands—"and they linger yet"; and how as he looked out of his window he felt that if Dante came to Oxford he *must* have passed under his window. And how the Dragon tried to be intense on the colour and shimmer of a jelly he had provided for her delectation. And how I explained to the fairer of the girls in the Library that... but certainly here *parlons* {we speak}'. Qtd in *John Bailey 1864–1931, Letters and Diaries*, ed. by his Wife (London: John Murray, 1935), 58–9. The Americans have not been identified. The reference to Campo Santo suggests that Pater was reproducing a passage from his essay on Pico della Mirandola; it could be argued that Pater was being fanciful, because Brasenose College was founded in 1509 and the room looking onto Radcliffe Square in which Pater taught was constructed in the sixteenth century, about 200 years after the death of Dante in 1321.

To OSCAR BROWNING, 17 February [1879]
MS.: Archive Centre, King's College, Cambridge, Papers of Oscar Browning, OB/1/1248/A. Printed in Østermark-Johansen, 'Don't forget your promise', 27.

B. N. C. | Feb. 17.

My dear Browning,

The Principal¹ had a severe illness last term, but seems now, I am glad to say, almost recovered, and I hope it may be long before we think about his successor. The special rumour² you speak of \was/ absolutely new to me, and arose, I imagine, out of ### mere speculation following on Dr Percival's³ appointment to a headship. We expect Colvin⁴ here today à propos of the proposed archaeological school.

In haste,

Very sincerely yours
W. H. Pater.

[1] The Revd Edward Hartopp Cradock (1810–86), classical scholar, was Principal of Brasenose College from 1853 to 1886, managing the institution with fairness and compassion. It has been said that Cradock devoted more time and energy to organized sports than to promoting intellectual pursuits (Crook, *Brasenose*, 247–8).

[2] The reference is not clear.

[3] The Revd John Percival (1834–1918), churchman and schoolmaster, studied classics and mathematics at Queen's College 1854–8. He was then elected Fellow of the college. He became a deacon in 1860 and a priest in 1861. He served as the first Headmaster of Clifton College, 1862–79, turning the institution into a premier public school; President of Trinity College, Oxford, 1879–87; Headmaster of Rugby School, 1887–95; and Bishop of Hereford, 1895–1917. He championed two causes: higher education for women (chairing the committee that established Somerville Hall in 1879) and university extension in general.

[4] Sidney Colvin (1845–1927), art critic, biographer, and administrator. See Biographical Register.

To GERARD MANLEY HOPKINS,[1] 20 May [1879][2]
MS.: Bodleian Library. Printed in *LWP*.

Bradmore Road. | May 20.

My dear Hopkins,

It will give me great pleasure to accept your kind invitation to dinner on Thursday[3] at 5.30.

Very sincerely yours
W. H. Pater.

[1] Revd Fr Gerard Manley Hopkins, S.J. (1844–89), poet and priest. See Biographical Register.

[2] From Dec. 1878 to Oct. 1879, Hopkins was assistant curate at St Aloysius Church (est. in 1875 as the Jesuit parish for central Oxford); he dined with Pater and the Paters several times (including 11 Feb. 1879). On the back of Pater's note, Hopkins drafted verses for 'On a Piece of Music'. Months after leaving Oxford, he informed a friend: 'Pater was one of the men I saw most of.' Hopkins, *Correspondence*, 2 vols, ed. R. K. R. Thornton and Catherine Phillips (Oxford: Oxford University Press, 2013), 1: 396.

[3] 22 May 1879.

To ALEXANDER MACMILLAN, 4 June [1879]
MS.: British Library. Printed in *LWP* and *TBB*.

A. Macmillan Esq.

Brasenose. | June 4.

Dear Mr. Macmillan,

A friend of mine, E. S. Dodgson[1] of New College, is anxious to make and publish a translation of Dante's 'Convito',[2] and I believe he has written to you on the subject. He is very enthusiastic about Dante and I think really knows a good deal about him. There seems to be so wide an interest felt just now on the subject of Dante that I should think a well-made translation of the 'Convito' might sell fairly. If you should feel inclined to encourage my young friend, would you propose that he should write a short introduction, explaining the place of the 'Convito' in Dante's writings, and also that the translation should be as carefully finished as possible, without haste?

Very sincerely yours
W. H. Pater.

[1] Edward Spencer Dodgson (1857–1922) was a cousin of Charles Lutwidge Dodgson (1832–98), pseud. Lewis Carroll, author, mathematician, and photographer. After spending several years in New Zealand and Brazil, Dodgson became active in Basque studies. He was elected an honorary member of the Real Academia de la Historia of Madrid, and received an honorary MA from Oxford in 1907. Little is known of his relationship with Pater.

[2] Dodgson wrote on 2 June, and George A. Macmillan answered three days later, with an invitation to talk over the proposal in London. See Alexander Macmillan's letter to Pater, 5 June 1879, suggesting his reservations. Dodgson never published a translation.

To WALTER PATER, 5 June 1879
MS.: British Library. Printed in *TBB*.

W. H. Pater Esqre. | Brasenose College | Oxford

June 5. 1879

Dear Mr. Pater,

I am afraid I must say that a translation of Dante's 'Cantos' by itself would have little chance of success. If it were possible to get a complete translation of all the minor works, and make them range with such a translation of the 'Commedia' as Dr. John Carlyle[1] has partly done it might be worth considering. The 'New Life' has been excellently well done by C. E. Norton[2] ranging with Longfellow's translation,[3] and the Poems from it and the Convito were done by Lyell[4] to range with Cary's[5] and Miss Rossetti[6] in her 'Shadow of Dante' gives a good deal from both the Convito & the Vita Nuova. If Mr. Dodgson happened to be in London I should like to see & talk the whole matter over with him, if he would write & make an appointment.

Very sincerely yours,
Alex Macmillan.

[1] *Dante's Divine Comedy: The Inferno, a literal prose translation*, by John Aitken Carlyle (London: Chapman and Hall, 1847).

[2] *The New Life of Dante Alighieri*, trans. Charles Eliot Norton (Boston: Ticknor and Fields, 1867).

[3] *The Divine Comedy of Dante Alighieri*, trans. Henry Wadsworth Longfellow, 3 vols (London: Routledge, 1867).

[4] *The Poems of the Vita Nuova and Convito*, trans. C. Lyell (London: C. F. Molini, 1842).

[5] *The Vision: or Hell, Purgatory, and Paradise of Dante Alighieri*, trans. Revd H. F. Cary, 3 vols (London: Taylor and Hessey, 1819).

[6] Maria Francesca Rossetti, *A Shadow of Dante: Being an Essay towards Studying Himself, His World, and his Pilgrimage* (London: Rivingtons, 1871). Rossetti (1827–76), author and Anglican nun, was the sister of Christina, Dante Gabriel, and William Michael Rossetti.

1880

To T. H. S. ESCOTT,[1] 8 April [1880?][2]
MS.: British Library Lib. Add. MS. 58789, fol. 70. Paper: white, folded, watermarked BASKERVILLE, vellum wove, colophon. Printed in Peter Vernon, 'Walter Pater to Thomas Escott: A New Letter', *Notes and Queries*, ns 30.4 (August 1983), 311.

22 Bradmore Road, | Oxford | April 8th.

Dear Escott,

I daresay you will be surprised to hear that I am so little in London that your letter of Jan. 15, has only just reached me. I called on you at the Thatched House Club[3] just before leaving town to congratulate you on the success of your recent work,[4] and was in London again for last Sunday, when it occurred to me to ask for letters at my club,[5] as it is not the custom there to forward them, and I then received your very kind invitation. I shall be in town again in the course of summer, and hope then to see you. Should you be visiting Oxford, it will give me great pleasure to see you. Come and dine with me, either at the above address, where I spend a great part of the vacation with my sisters, or at my old rooms at Brasenose— Only send me a line beforehand, and believe me

Very truly yours
W. H. Pater.

---

[1] Thomas Hay Sweet Escott (1844–1924) began a career in academia, serving (1866–73) as a Lecturer in Logic and Deputy Professor of Classics at King's College, London, and preparing editions of the satirists Juvenal and Persius. Yet he found his real vocation in journalism, writing daily for the *Standard* (from 1866) and the *World* (from 1874). He succeeded John Morley as editor (1882–6) of the *Fortnightly Review*. He published many volumes, including *Masters of English Journalism: A Study of Personal Forces* (London: T. Fisher Unwin, 1911). Pater tutored Escott for the final honour schools, 1862–4; they remained friends, and Escott assisted Wright in preparing *The Life of Walter Pater* (1907).

[2] Judging by the address and the internal evidence.

[3] St James Street. For comments on the club, see Escott's volume, *Club Makers and Club Members* (London: T., 1914), 140–31, 281–5.

[4] Probably the publication of his volume, *England: Its People, Polity, and Pursuits*, 2 vols (London: Cassell, Peter, 1879).

[5] Pater and Sidney Colvin (1845–1927), art critic, biographer, and administrator (see Biographical Register) were elected members of the New (later the Savile) Club in 1869.

To OSCAR BROWNING, 13 May [1880]
MS.: Archive Centre, King's College, Cambridge, Papers of Oscar Browning, OB/l/1248/A. Printed in Østermark-Johansen, 'Don't forget your promise', 28.

Brasenose. | May 13.

My dear Browning,

I am living in college, and shall be very pleased to give you a bed here on Saturday and Sunday. I shall #### ask some young people to meet you at breakfast on Sunday morning.[1] Could you stay over Monday; I should much like to ask Paton[2] and Barnes[3] to meet you at dinner on that day; if so, send me a line by return of post.

Very sincerely yours
W. H. Pater.

[1] Pater may have organized these events to mark his friend's recent achievements: Browning had been appointed Lecturer for the Teachers' Training Syndicate for the year 1880–1, his subject being 'The History of Education'; his third book, *Modern France: 1814–1879* (London: Longmans, 1880), was to be released early that summer. For Browning's favourable account of his visit (15–16 May 1880) to Oxford as Pater's guest, possibly the last time they met socially, see his *Memories of Sixty Years at Eton, Cambridge, and Elsewhere* (London: Bodley Head, 1910), 289.

[2] William Roger Paton (1857–1921), Scottish classical scholar and epigraphist, was a former pupil of Browning's. He joined the Hellenic Society in 1881 and edited and translated several Greek texts, including five volumes of *The Greek Anthology* (1915–18) for the Loeb Library.

[3] Unidentified.

To MR BARNES,[1] 15 May [1880]
MS.: Francis O'Gorman. Autograph letter, signed; one-page 8vo. Printed in Francis O'Gorman, 'Walter Pater and Oscar Browning: The "Last" Meeting', *Journal of Pre-Raphaelite Studies*, ns 20 (Fall 2011), 72–6.

B. N. C. | May 15.

Dear Mr Barnes,

Will you lunch with me here tomorrow (Sunday) at 1.30. to meet Oscar Browning?

Yours very truly
W. H. Pater.

[1] Unidentified. See letter to Browning, 13 May [1880].

To J. R. THURSFIELD,¹ 26 July [1880]
MS.: Brasenose College. Printed in *LWP*.

Bradmore Road. | July 26.

My dear Thursfield,

I have just despatched to your address an old pair of silver salt-cellars, which I hope you will think pretty, and kindly accept as a slight token of my sincere friendship, and congratulations on the approaching event. With best wishes for your happiness and kind regards to your mother, in which my sisters join,
    I remain

Very sincerely yours
W. H. Pater.

¹ James Richard Thursfield (1840–1923), naval historian and journalist, attended Corpus Christi College, Oxford, 1859–63, and served as Fellow, Tutor, Dean, and Lecturer of Jesus College, 1864–81. He joined *The Times* as a leader writer and later editor of the 'Books of the Week' section; in 1902 he served as the first editor of the *Times Literary Supplement*. His own books include *Peel* (London: Macmillan, 1891) in the English Statesmen series, and, with George Sydenham Clarke, *The Navy and The Nation: Naval Warfare and Imperial Defence* (London: J. Murray, 1897). Thursfield and Pater may have met as undergraduates in the early 1860s; friends in common included Ingram Bywater, Edward Caird, Louise and Mandel Creighton, Emily and C. H. O. Daniel, Lionel Johnson, and Mary and T. Humphry Ward. Pater persuaded Thursfield to write a favourable review of *Plato and Platonism* (*CW* vii) in *The Times*, 10 Feb. 1893, 12. Thursfield concluded: '[We] cannot readily recall a work dealing with Plato as a man and a thinker which is at once more suggestive in its presentation and more attractive in its style.' He also wrote an obituary of Pater in *The Times*, 31 July 1894, 10.

To CHARLES HENRY OLIVE DANIEL,¹ 23 November [1880]
MS.: The Huntington Library. A portion is printed in W[illiam]. W[alrond]. Jackson, 'Memoir', in Falconer Madon, *The Daniel Press: Memorials of C. H. O. Daniel with a Bibliography of the Press, 1845–1919* (Oxford: Daniel Press, 1921), 85–6. Jackson provides the date. Printed in *LWP*.

B. N. C. | Nov. 23.

My dear Daniel,

I shall prize the 'Colloquies',² which you so kindly brought me, greatly. It is, I suppose, the most exquisite specimen of printing I have seen. Accept my best thanks.

I am much tempted to ~~join~~ \take part/ in \the making of/ your proposed baby-house,³ and like the idea of it very much, but at the moment feel very barren on the subject. Perhaps however if my contribution was to be by way of preface, it might be actually printed last, so that I might tell you in or after the vacation, and have a preliminary look at the other contents—only, of course, you must not delay your plan on my account.

Have you ever seen Colvin's[4] very pretty book on 'Children in Italian and English Design'? Earle's 'Micro-ie'[5] I have not read, but should be glad to. Has Dodgson[6] of Ch. Ch. occurred to you as a possible contributor?

Yours very sincerely
W. H. Pater.

---

[1] The Revd Charles Henry Olive Daniel (1836–1919), printer and man of letters. See Biographical Register.

[2] A limited edition of forty copies of *Desiderii Erasmii Colloquia* was printed at the Daniel Press in 1880.

[3] The 'project' became *The Garland of Rachel* (Oxford: H. Daniel, 1881), a collection of eighteen poems by friends of the Daniels such as Robert Bridges, Lewis Carroll, Austin Dobson, A. Mary F. Robinson, Edmund Gosse, John Addington Symonds, and T. Humphry Ward, published to celebrate the first birthday of their first child, Rachel Anne Olive Daniel (b. 27 Sept. 1880). Thirty-six copies were printed. See Harry Morgan Ayres, 'Lewis Carroll and *The Garland of Rachel*', *Huntington Library Quarterly*, 5.1 (Oct. 1941), 141–5.

[4] Sidney Colvin (1845–1927), art critic, biographer, and administrator; see Biographical Register. *Children in Italian and English Design* was published by Seeley, Jackson, and Halliday in 1872.

[5] John Earle (1601–65), an Anglican divine, was known for his eloquent and powerful preaching. Earle served as Fellow of Merton College, Oxford, the Chancellor (from 1643) of Salisbury Cathedral, and the Bishop (from 1662) of Worcester. He published *Micro-Cosmographie, or a Peece of the World Discovered; in Essayes and Characters* (London: William Stansby, 1628), humorous reflections on the manners of the time that were frequently reprinted.

[6] Charles Lutwidge Dodgson (1832–98), mathematician and logician, taught at Christ Church, Oxford, from 1855 to 1881. As Lewis Carroll, he was famous as the author of *Alice's Adventures in Wonderland* (1865) and its sequel, *Through the Looking Glass* (1871). According to Thomas Wright, Pater and Dodgson were friends, the former much appreciating the latter's humour (Wright, 1: 240).

To CHARLES HENRY OLIVE DANIEL, 18 December [1880]
MS.: Huntington Library.

22 Bradmore Road. | Dec. 18.

My dear Daniel,

I have been thinking over your proposal,[1] and find that I liked the notion of it so much as to be tempted to keep the matter open when I ought, in fairness to you, to have declined what thus is now [no] small prospect of my being able to fulfil. It would take me a long time to satisfy myself in the little composition you require—long time, in proportion to the due brevity of the result; and meantime yourself, who have conceived the whole pretty design, would I am sure be better able than any one else to introduce your composers gracefully. I should have been pleased and proud to contribute, had I seen my way; but must, in justice to you, ask you to take the will for the deed, together with my best wishes for Rachel—the infant and the book.

I had written the above more than a week ago, but did not send it because I fancied you would be very busy just then. I must now add my sincere fond wishes for yourself, and remain

Very truly yours
Walter H. Pater.

[1] See letter to Daniel, 23 Nov. [1880].

1881

To EDMUND GOSSE, 29 January [1881]
MS.: British Library, Ashley Collection. Printed in *LWP*.

Brasenose. | Jan. 29.

My dear Gosse,

I feel quite ashamed for having kept Miss Robinson's Poems so long, and now send it by post, with this.[1] The fact is I had hoped to return it in person, and the book went with me to London the other day for that purpose; but what with the bad weather, and the quantity we had to do during our short stay, added to one of my sisters being far from well all through it, I had to leave without seeing you, to my great regret. Many thanks for the loan of the poems, which I, and some others here, much enjoyed especially the 'Ballad of Heroes'.

Oddly enough, I was on the very point of writing to recommend to your notice a volume of translations by my friend A. J. Butler, from the Greek Anthology, wh. Kegan Paul will publish in a few days, under the title of 'Amaranth and Asphodel'.[2] The writer is a very distinguished Oxford scholar, at present, as tutor to the son of \the/ Khedive, making, I believe, very charming experiences of Egypt. I cannot but think that his translations will have great merit; and should you see them, and feel pleased, I think you would be doing a good service by expressing your favourable opinion about them, as a master of all metrical perfection, in the Academy or elsewhere.

I am sorry to say that my sister Tottie[3] will have to be very careful of her health for some time to come. With our united kind regards to you and Mrs. Gosse,
    I remain

Very truly yours
W. H. Pater.

Excuse my bad, hasty writing.

[1] Agnes Mary Frances Robinson (1857–1944), poet, translator, essayist, and biographer, and her younger sister, Frances Mabel Robinson (1858–1954), novelist, grew up in a wealthy, intellectual environment. Their father, George T. Robinson, F.S.A. (1828–97), architect and interior decorator, designed the Bolton Market Mall (1855). During the 1880s the Robinsons,

who lived in Gower Street and then in Earl's Terrace, London, entertained the painters and writers of the Pre-Raphaelite movement (see Sharp, 'Some Personal Reminiscence of Walter Pater', 801–14). Robinson established her reputation with her first book of verse, *A Handful of Honeysuckle* (London: C. Kegan Paul, 1878); it includes 'A Ballad of Heroes', which Pater enjoyed. From 1880 to 1887 she regarded Violet Paget (see Biographical Register) as her closest friend and John Addington Symonds her literary mentor. In 1888 Mary married James Darmesteter (1849–94), Distinguished Professor at the Collège de France, and founder of *Revue de Paris*.

[2] Alfred Joshua Butler (1850–1936), scholar, antiquary, and administrator, taught at Worcester College, Oxford, before he was elected Fellow (1877-1920) of Brasenose. In 1880, he went to Egypt for a year as tutor to the sons of the Khedive (ruler of Egypt and Ottoman viceroy), the eldest of whom became Khedive in 1892. Butler also served as Curator of the University Galleries and visitor (from 1887) of the Ashmolean Museum, and sat on the Hebdomadal Council, 1899–1905. His publications include *Amaranth and Asphodel: Songs from the Greek Anthology* (London: C. Kegan Paul, 1881), and *The Ancient Coptic Churches of Egypt* (Oxford: Clarendon Press, 1884).

[3] Hester Pater, Pater's sister. See Biographical Register.

To EDMUND GOSSE, 25 February [1881]
MS.: British Library, Ashley Collection.

22 Bradmore Road. | Feb. 25.

My dear Gosse,

I don't know what Morley's[1] principle of selection is, but think that on any principle he might well be glad to have you and your proposed 'life'. Certainly I think you ~~would~~ might write and lay your proposal before him. He has been making a change of residence,—I have not yet heard whither—but believe to Wimbledon; but he may always be addressed at the Athenaeum Club.

My sisters join me in kind regards to yourself and Mrs. Gosse.

Very sincerely yours
W. H. Pater.

I think you won't find Morley at all 'terrible'.

[1] John Morley, 1st Viscount Morley of Blackburn (1838–1923), journalist, biographer, and politician (see Biographical Register), commissioned Gosse to prepare the life of Thomas Gray (1716–71), poet and scholar, for the English Men of Letters series, which Morley edited 1878–92 for Macmillan.

To ALFRED JOSHUA BUTLER,[1] 31 March [1881]
Text: A. J. Butler, Preface, *Amaranth and Asphodel: Poems from the Greek Anthology* (Oxford: Basil Blackwell, 1922), x.[2] Printed in *LWP*.

2 Bradmore Road, Oxford | Mar. 31 [1881]

My dear Butler,

I have been reading your translations with extreme pleasure at so much skill in both Greek and English. Your versions, while they seem very close to the original, make in themselves a delightful book of verse.

I am sending a copy to E. W. Gosse, who is I think a master in all metrical secrets, and delighting also in all Greek things, will I feel sure be pleased with your work; also to one or two others to whom I am glad to have the opportunity of making a little present.

I was very pleased to hear that you had decided to return to Oxford, and hope you will be always very far from regretting your severance from the lotuses and the gold of Egypt, for the share of which, however, in the genesis of your charming little book I, for one, am grateful.

Believe me,

Very sincerely yours,
W. H. Pater.

[1] See letter to Gosse, 29 Jan. [1881], n. 2.

[2] In this volume, a revised and expanded version of *Amaranth and Asphodel: Songs from the Greek Anthology*, Butler prints Pater's letter in the Preface. The 'treasured' letter from 'so great a writer' encouraged Butler to republish (ix). See letter to Gosse, 29 Jan. [1881].

To RICHARD CLAVERHOUSE JEBB,[1] 31 March [1881]
MS.: Library Special Collections, Charles E. Young Research Library, UCLA.

Brasenose College. | Mar. 31. [1881]

Dear Professor Jebb,

I send you by this post ~~as~~ a small volume of translations by a friend of mine,[2] who was a very distinguished undergraduate here and of whom I believe Mr Raper[3] entertains a high opinion. They seem to me very pleasing and vigorous. The writer is away from England as tutor to the son of the Khedive[4] and I am therefore anxious to bring it to the notice of one or two I hope it may have the good fortune to please.

Believe me

Very truly yours
W. H. Pater.

¹ Richard Claverhouse Jebb (1841–1905), a Scottish classical scholar, was educated at Charterhouse School and Trinity College, Cambridge. He became a Fellow of Trinity in 1863, and subsequently held positions at Cambridge and the University of Glasgow. In 1891, he was elected the member of Parliament for Cambridge University; he was knighted in 1900. His translations were highly regarded, beginning with *Translations into Greek and Latin* (1873).
² Alfred Butler (1850–1936); see letter of 31 Mar. [1881], n. 1 and 2. The letter to Jebb was found in a copy of Butler's *Amaranth and Asphodel: Songs from the Greek Anthology* (London: C. Kegan Paul, 1881).
³ Robert William Raper (1842–1915), classicist and conservationist, was Senior Fellow, Vice-President, and Bursar of Trinity College, Oxford, where Butler also studied before becoming a Fellow of Brasenose.
⁴ A Persian word before it was adopted into Turkish, 'khedive' was an honorific title for grand viziers and sultans of the Ottoman Empire, and used by the viceroy of Egypt from 1805, when Muhammad Ali Pasha (1769–1849) was recognized as the governor of Egypt (recently recaptured from Napoleon's control), and 1914. Ali's great-grandson, Mohamed Tewfik Pasha (1853–1892) was Khedive of Egypt and the Sudan from 1879–92. Butler's *Amaranth and Asphodel: Songs from the Greek Anthology*, referenced in Pater's letter (and within which it was found), was dedicated to 'His Highness the Khedive of Egypt'.

To AN UNKNOWN CORRESPONDENT,¹ 4 May [1881?]
MS.: Northwestern University. Printed in *LWP*.

Brasenose College. | May 4.

Dear Sir,

Accept my sincere thanks for the present of your charming volume of poems.

Should you at any time visit Oxford, I hope you will give me the favour of a call, and remain

Yours very truly
W. H. Pater

¹ Evidence, especially the handwriting and the signature, suggests a date between 1870 and 1885. As Evans points out, the watermark is the same as that of a letter to Gosse, 29 Jan. [1881].

To JOHN MILLER GRAY, [November 1881?]¹
Text: *John Miller Gray: Memoir and Remains*, eds, Balfour Paul and W. R. Macdonald, 1:46. Printed in *LWP*.

Thank you very much for your charming article on David Scott, which I have read with great pleasure and interest.... I hope you will do much more of such excellent work as that paper. I am very pleased to hear of your continued memory of and interest in my projected series of Imaginary Portraits, one of which I have now seriously on hand.² I have been looking over it, but find it is still too much a matter of shorthand notes at present, or I would very gladly send it you, and should value your remarks upon it....

¹ Dated from Pater's reference to Gray's article, 'David Scott, R.S.A.', *Blackwood's Edinburgh Magazine*, 130 (Nov. 1881), 589–611. David Scott (1806–49), Scottish historical painter, was the older brother of William Bell Scott (1811–90), poet and painter (see letter to Scott, 30 Apr. [1882]). David Scott is remembered for such works as *Vasco da Gama Encountering the Spirit of the Storm* (1842). See *Tait's Edinburgh Magazine*, 16 (1849), 269.
² The reference is uncertain. The strongest possibility is 'An English Poet', dating from 1878 and terminating in mid-sentence (*CW* iii). The portrait 'on hand' might also have been a first version of *Marius the Epicurean*, which is dated '1881–1884' in the second (1885) and third editions. The earliest indisputable reference to the composition of *Marius*, however, is Vernon Lee's letter of 24 July 1882, where she refers to him doing 'something... in the way of a novel about the time of Marcus Aurelius'. See *VLL*, 105.

To MR BARNETT,[1] 22 November [1881?][2]
MS.: Brasenose College.

B. N. C. | Nov. 22.

My dear Barnett,

Alas! I find myself unable to tell you any thing about the Arthurian localities, or where to get any sort of detailed information on the subject. I have always thought that Tennyson[3] had realised his scenes for himself and remember a description in him of Camelot, which seemed to have exactly the air of Winchester about it. There is an interesting essay, (though with little or nothing as to this point,) on the Arthurian Legend, at the end of Renan's Essais de Morale et de Critique.[4]

In great haste,

Ever yours truly
W. H. Pater.

¹ Possibly John Francis Barnett (1837–1916), composer and teacher. Barnett set out to become a concert pianist: he studied at the Royal Academy of Music, London, and in Germany, playing at the Gewandhaus, Leipzig, in 1860. He made a name for himself, however, as a composer of such compositions as *The Ancient Mariner*, a choral work (1867), and *The Winter's Tale*, an orchestral work (1873). Barnett became Professor at the Guildhall School of Music and at the Royal College of Music.
² Dated on the basis of the handwriting.
³ Pater's high regard for the poetry of Alfred, Lord Tennyson (1809–92) dates from his school days. On 5 Aug. 1858, his last Speech Day at the King's School, Pater recited a portion of 'Morte d'Arthur' (Wright, 1: 138). Pater regarded Tennyson as a prototypical Pre-Raphaelite, an artist of landscape and picturesque detail. In a conversation with William Sharp, he explained that Tennyson had imposed 'a new and exigent conception of poetic art and has profoundly affected a technique not only of contemporary poetry, but of that which is yet unwritten' (Sharp, 803). Pater expanded this notion in 'Style' (1888), where

he points out that Tennyson treats life nobly in his poetry (see *CW* vi), and in 'The Genius of Plato' (1892), where he observes that when one reads the speculative poetry of Wordsworth or Tennyson, one realizes that 'a great metaphysical force has come into the language, which is by no means purely technical or scholastic' (*CW* vii). See letter to Canton, 12 Oct. [1892].

⁴ Pater's interest in the work of Ernest Renan (1823–92), French philologist and historian, dates from 1865. Samuel Wright noted (in a letter dated 27 May 1977 to Billie Andrew Inman) that in 1965 he had seen several Renan volumes in the collection of texts once owned by Pater, texts which were then in the possession of May Ottley. See Inman, 'Tracing the Pater Legacy' (1983), 4; 'Tracing the Pater Legacy, Part II' (1995), 3–8. These books included *Essais de morale et de critique* (1859), *Vie de Jésus* (1863), and *Les apôtres* (1866). In this letter, Pater refers to Renan, 'La poésie des races celtiques', *Essais de morale et de critique* (Paris: Calmann-Lévy, 1859), 375–456.

To EDWARD HARTOPP CRADOCK, [26 November? 1881]
MS.: Brasenose College. Printed in *LWP*.

Brasenose. | Sunday.

My dear Principal,

I enclose Mr. Jackson's letter.¹ The rise in the architect's estimate is, I suppose, what almost invariably happens. I think all would agree that the whole work projected ought to be pushed forward as quickly as is possible with fairness to the various calls on the resources of the college.

Perhaps the 'scullery block' is not the least important part of the whole. I have noticed this term more than ever what can only be called the unseemly squalor of our back quadrangle, occasioned in a great measure by the crowding and general inadequacy in our domestic arrangements.

With many thanks

Ever yours truly
W. H. Pater.

¹ This letter, now missing, probably refers to the estimate submitted by Thomas Graham Jackson (1835–1924), architect, outlined in a letter dated 23 Nov. 1881 (MS.: Brasenose College) for the construction of new buildings at Brasenose College between 1882 and 1889. Jackson articled with George Gilbert Scott and set up his own practice in 1862; he was a Fellow of Wadham, 1863–80. Professionally he concentrated on restoring and adding to schools, libraries, churches, and colleges, working in the Gothic Revival style. His first major success was the Examination Schools building, Oxford, 1876–85. He also published many volumes documenting architectural history, including *Modern Gothic Architecture* (London: H. S. King, 1873).

Brasenose's income was on the rise in that era; the college had secured several properties on Oxford's High Street. Jackson was commissioned to design the New Quadrangle. Builders executed the first stage of Jackson's plan in two stages: staircases X and XI during 1881–3, and staircase IX, 1886–7. These alterations included twenty-two new undergraduate quarters, two lecture rooms, and an undergraduate reading room, soon to become the college's first Junior Common Room. Pater argued that 'a new kitchen should be built to the west of the buttery, leaving room for a spacious new quadrangle, unencumbered by the old service buildings' (qtd in Crook, *Brasenose*, 292). This arrangement would have given the chapel greater prominence. Jackson explained that 'the present kitchen is the most convenient place for the Hall.... When stripped of its ugly outbuildings... [it will be] a very picturesque mass of building' (qtd in Crook, *Brasenose*, 292). After Cradock's death in 1886, college officials decided to launch the next stage of the scheme, which meant building the Principal's lodgings as part of a new entrance. In two phases, 1887–90 and 1909–11, modifications included the lodgings, the new entrance tower, and staircase XIII; then Broadgate, Amsterdam, and staircase XII. The challenge, as Crook puts it, was to 'create a powerful college image without destroying the random balance of the High Street' (293).

To HENRY JAMES NICOLL,[1] 28 November 1881
Text: Maggs Bros. *Catalogue* no. 459 (1925), 216. Printed in *LWP*.

...Besides my volume of 'Studies on [sic] the Renaissance', published in 1873, of which a second edition appeared in 1877, I may mention, among my writings, the following contributions to Magazines and Reviews:—

Coleridge's Writings. Westminster Review, Jan., 1866.
William Wordsworth. Fortnightly Review, April, 1874.
A Fragment on 'Measure for Measure'. Fortnightly, Nov., 1874.
The Myth of Demeter and Persephone. Parts 1 and 2. Fortnightly, Jan. and Feb., 1876.

...A large part of my Renaissance Studies had previously appeared in Reviews or Magazines, among others that on Botticelli,[2] which I believe to be the first notice in English of that old painter. It preceded Mr. Ruskin's lectures on the same subject by I believe two years....

---

[1] Henry James Nicoll (1858–85), a journalist, is identified in the Maggs catalogue as the recipient of this letter, dated 'Oxford, 28th November (1881)'. Pater is replying to Nicoll's request for a biographical notice of himself and a list of his publications. The information was used by Nicoll in his notice of Pater in *Landmarks of English Literature* (London: John Hogg, 1883), 440–1.

[2] Pater's essay on Botticelli appeared in the *Fortnightly Review*, ns 8 (Aug. 1870), 155–60, and was reprinted in *Studies in the History of the Renaissance* (1873). In the 'Epilogue' (1883) to vol. 2 of *Modern Painters*, Ruskin (incorrectly) claims: 'it was left to me, and to me alone, first to discern, and then to teach...the excellency and supremacy of five great painters, despised until I spoke of them—Turner, Tintoret, Luini, Botticelli, and Carpaccio'. *Works of John Ruskin*, ed. E. T. Cook and Alexander Wedderburn (1903–12), 4: 355. Ruskin's editors note that his 'first mention of Botticelli was in a lecture delivered at Oxford during the Lent Term, 1871'. See also *Fors Clavigera*, Letter 22.41.

1882

To VIOLET PAGET,[1] 26 March [1882]
MS.: Colby College. Printed in *LWP*.

Bradmore Road. | Oxford. | Mar. 26.

My dear Miss Paget,

I received 'Belcaro'[2] duly, several weeks ago, and have not written to thank you for it before this, only because I wished to read it carefully first; such thorough and well-considered literary work as yours being far too rare, and too enjoyable, to be disposed of in a hurry. I suppose it is always hazardous to express what one has to say indirectly and allusively, by the sort of literary stratagem of which the Platonic Dialogues are the great example; but I think your device, in setting your essays in the way you have done, very successfully carried out; and to me it is certainly very pleasant in effect.

The book, as a whole, and almost always in its parts, has left on my mind a wonderfully rich impression of a world of all sorts of delightful things, under the action of a powerful intelligence. The union of extensive knowledge and imaginative power, which your writing presents, is certainly a very rare one, and of course could hardly exist without an unusual power of expression, in which, if I might make ## \one/ exception, there is perhaps at times a little crowding. I think you would find instances when you have admitted alternative<s> images and expressions, the weaker of which might have been dismissed. I think, especially in 'Kreisler', you have lighted on sound and wholesome truth, and was very glad to read your powerful description of the 'Stregozzo', which seems to me so little known, yet in its way so wonderful a piece of work.[3]

I am doubtful whether we shall find it prudent to venture to Italy in the summer vacation; but, if not, hope to have a month or two at Rome next spring. Meantime, I hope we may meet in your proposed visit to England.

With sincere wishes for the success of your present and future work, and thanking you for the pleasure and profit afforded me by 'Belcaro', I remain

Very sincerely yours
Walter H. Pater.

[1] Violet Paget, pseud. Vernon Lee (1856–1935), art historian, novelist, and critic. See Biographical Register.

² Vernon Lee, *Belcaro: Being Essays on Sundry Aesthetical Questions* (London: W. Satchell, 1881).
³ 'Chapelmeister Kreisler. A Study of Musical Romanticists', chapter 5 of *Belcaro*, attacks a conceptualist approach to the aesthetics of music. 'Lo Stregozzo' or 'The Witches' Procession' is the title of an arresting image depicting an array of enigmatic skeletal creatures and demon-like humans making their way through a marshy landscape. It survives as a copper engraving (c.1520), very likely produced by Roman craftsmen associated with Raphael, such as Marcantonio Raimondi (c.1480–c.1534) or his student, Agostino de' Musi, also known as Agostino Veneziano (c.1490–c.1540). The identity of the draughtsman responsible for the preliminary sketch is also uncertain: Raphael, Giulio Romano, Baldassarre Peruzzi, and Girolamo Genga have been suggested. 'It is perhaps the highest achievement of great art in the direction of the supernatural', Paget argues (*Belcaro*, 89). Her discussion of 'Lo Stregozzo' appears in chapter 4, 'Faustus and Helena: Notes on the Supernatural in Art'. See Patricia Emison, 'Truth and Bizzarria in an Engraving of Lo Stregozzo', *Art Bulletin*, 81.4 (Dec. 1999), 623–36.

To WILLIAM BELL SCOTT,¹ 30 April [1882]
MS.: Colbeck Collection, University of British Columbia.

Oxford | 30 April. 82

My dear Scott,

Accept my very best thanks for the gift² of one of the most charming books I have come across for some time. \In/ the vignettes and many of the verses, so simple in form and expression, yet so suggestive of further thoughts, you seem to have caught much of what is most delightful in Blake,³ \though/ with much added [store] of your own. I am glad to recognise in the 'Norns watering Issdrasill',⁴ the beautiful poem which I remember having you recite some years ago. I shall put the book away with what I value.

I had just written this when I read your letter of April 27. It adds to the value of the book. The account you give me of your motive in these poems agrees mainly with what would be my own theory about them. Pattison⁵ writes well about Milton, but I could hardly tell what amount of interest he might have in quite modern poetry.

Excuse the shortness of my letter, as it at least gives you my \freshest/ impressions of your latest work, and with our united kind regards to you and Mrs. Scott, believe me

Very sincerely yours
Walter H. Pater.

¹ William Bell Scott (1811–90), Scottish poet and painter. See letter to Scott, 18 June [1872–73], n. 1.
² *A Poet's Harvest Home: Being one Hundred Short Poems* (London: Elliot Stock, 1882), appeared on 8 Apr. 1882. The poems, Scott explains in his autobiography, are meant to express 'the mental state of the day in the simplest terms'.

[3] Scott, who found inspiration in William Blake (1757–1827), poet, painter, printmaker, and a crucial figure in the poetry and visual art of the Romantic age, published *William Blake: Etchings from his Works* (London: Chatto and Windus, 1878).
[4] 'The Norns Watering Yggdrasill', *A Poet's Harvest Home*, 34–6. In Norse mythology, the Norns are goddesses of Fate; the Yggdrasill is the world tree, a giant ash supporting the universe.
[5] Mark Pattison (1813–84), historian and biographer, served as Fellow (from 1839), Tutor (from 1843), and Rector (from 1861) of Lincoln College. See Biographical Register. Pattison, a close friend, had just published *Milton* (London: Macmillan, 1879), which appeared in the English Men of Letters series, and produced an introductory essay for a selection of Milton's poetry, which appeared in *The English Poets: Selections with Critical Introductions*, ed. T. Humphry Ward, 4 vols (London: Macmillan, 1880), 2: 293–305.

To DUGALD SUTHERLAND MACCOLL,[1] 20 May [1882][2]
MS.: Library, University of Glasgow. Printed in John J. Conlon, 'Three Letters of Walter Pater', *Notes and Queries*, ns 22.3 (August 1978), 317–18.

2 Bradmore Road. | May 20.

Dear Mr. MacColl,

Will you give me the pleasure of your company, at the address above, on Friday May 26, at 8:30.

Very truly yours
W. H. Pater.

R.S.V.P.

[1] Dugald Sutherland MacColl (1859–1948), Scottish art critic, author, and painter. See Biographical Register.
[2] Dates relevant to MacColl's attendance at Oxford and Pater's tenancy at Bradmore Road point to 1882 as the year, and Saturday as the day.

To JULIA CONSTANCE FLETCHER,[1] 21 June [1882][2]
MS.: Archives, the King's School, Canterbury.

Bradmore Road. | June 21st.

My dear Miss Fletcher,

It will give me and my sister much pleasure to accept your kind invitation on Saturday, July 1st.

There seems to be a good deal to see and hear in London just now, and perhaps we may have a little summer-like weather at last. I am sorry to miss Mr. Benson;³ and with sincere ##### thanks for your note, and our united kind regards to yourself,

I remain

Very sincerely yours,
W. H. Pater.

We go to London tomorrow, and shall be at 25 Montague Place, Russell Square.

---

¹ Julia Constance Fletcher (1853-1938), a novelist, playwright, and literary critic (see letter to Macmillan, 31 Jan. [1878], n. 1).
² 1 July fell on a Saturday in 1876 and in 1882.
³ Julia and her step-father, Eugene Benson (1839-1938), the American painter and art critic (see letter to Macmillan, 31 Jan. [1878]), travelled to London on literary matters.

To WILLIAM SHARP,¹ 30 July [1882]
Text: Elizabeth A. Sharp, *William Sharp (Fiona Macleod)*, 73. Printed in *LWP*.

2 Bradmore Road. | July 30th.

My dear Sharp,

Since you have been here I have been reading your poems with great enjoyment.² The presence of philosophical, as in 'The New Hope' and of such original, and at the same time perfectly natural motives as 'Motherhood' is certainly a remarkable thing among younger English poets, especially when united with a command of rhythmical and verbal form like yours. The poem 'Motherhood' is of course a bold one; but it expresses, as I think, with perfect purity, a thought, which all who can do so are the better for meditating on it. The 'Transcripts from Nature' seem to me precisely all, and no more than (and just how is the test of excellence in such things) what little pictures in verse ought to be.

Very sincerely yours,
Walter Pater.

---

¹ William Sharp (1855-1905), Scottish poet, biographer, and editor. In 1891 Sharp adopted the pseudonym 'Fiona Macleod'. See Biographical Register.
² Sharp stayed with Pater for three or four days late in July 1882. His recollections of the visit, his first to Oxford, can be found in Sharp, 'Some Personal', 801-14, rptd Mrs William Sharp, *Papers Critical & Reminiscent*, 187-228. Sharp's volume of poetry is *The Human Inheritance, The New Hope, Motherhood* (London: Elliot Stock, 1882).

To WILLIAM SHARP, 4 November 1882
Text: Elizabeth A. Sharp, 67–8.[1] Printed in *LWP*.

2 Bradmore Road, | Oxford. | Nov. 4, 1882

My dear Sharp,

(I think we have known each other long enough to drop the 'Mr.') I read your letter with great pleasure, and thank you very much for it. Your friendly interest in my various essays I value highly. I have really worked hard for now many years at these prose essays, and it is a real encouragement to hear such good things said of them by one of the most original of young English poets. It will be a singular pleasure to me to be connected, in a sense, in your book on Rossetti, with one I admired so greatly.[2] I wish the book all the success both the subject and the writer deserve.

You encourage me to do what I have sometimes thought of doing, when I have got on a little further with the work I have actually on hand—viz. to complete the various series of which the papers I have printed in the *Fortnightly*[3] are parts. The list you sent me is complete with the exception of an article on Coleridge in the *Westminster* of January, 1866, with much of which, both as to matter and manner, I should now be greatly dissatisfied. The article is concerned with S. T. C.'s prose; but, corrected, might be put alongside of the criticism on his verse which I made for Ward's 'English Poets'.[4] I can only say that should you finish the paper you speak of on these essays, your critical approval will be of great service to me with the reading public.[5]

I find I have by me a second copy of the paper on Giorgione, revised in print, which I send by this post,[6] and hope you will kindly accept. It was reprinted some time ago when I thought of collecting that and other papers into a volume. I am pleased to hear that you remember with pleasure your flying visit to Oxford;[7] and hope you will come for a longer stay in term time early next year.[8]

At the end of this month I hope to leave for seven weeks in Italy, chiefly at Rome, where I have never yet been. We went to Cornwall for our summer holiday, but though that country is certainly very singular and beautiful, I found there not a tithe of the stimulus to one's imagination which I have sometimes experienced in quite unrenowned places abroad.

I should be delighted with a copy of the Rossetti volume from yourself; but it is a volume I should have in any case purchased, and I hope it may appear in time to be my companion on my contemplated journey.

Very sincerely yours,
Walter H. Pater.

[1] Another version of most of the text, with some striking differences, appears in *Papers Critical and Reminiscent by William Sharp*, ed. Elizabeth A. Sharp, 209–10, which in turn differs slightly from that given in William Sharp's essay in the *Atlantic Monthly*, 74 (Dec. 1894), 801–14. Sharp's variations, however, appear to be his own tampering—especially the variant 'the strongest and most original' for 'one of the most original of young English poets'. He gives the date as 5 Nov.

[2] Sharp had written to Pater that he intended to use, in his discussion of D. G. Rossetti's prose works, a passage from Pater's essay on Leonardo, to exemplify what he meant by poetic prose (Mrs William Sharp, *Papers Critical and Reminiscent*, 208). The extract appears in Sharp's *Dante Gabriel Rossetti: A Record and a Study* (London: Macmillan, 1882), 275, along with passages from Walter Raleigh, Thomas De Quincey, and Ruskin.

[3] Pater was at work on *Marius*. Elizabeth Sharp's variant (209) may be a correction of Pater, if Pater overlooked 'Romanticism', *Macmillan's Magazine*, 35 (Nov. 1876), 64–70, 'Imaginary Portraits. I. The Child in the House', *Macmillan's Magazine*, 38 (Aug. 1878), 313–21, and 'Poems by William Morris', *Westminster Review*, 90 (Oct. 1868), 300–12. The essays would have made up three series: one on Greek art and mythology, one on English literature, and one on 'imaginary portraits'. Of these, only the second (*Appreciations*) was ever completed; *Imaginary Portraits* (1887) was not what Pater originally intended (see letter to Grove, 17 Apr. [1878]).

[4] The essay on Coleridge in *Appreciations* combines a revised version of 'Coleridge's Writings', *Westminster Review*, ns 29 (Jan. 1866), 106–32, with the Introduction to selected poems of Coleridge contributed to *The English Poets*, ed. T. Humphry Ward, 4 vols (London: Macmillan, 1880), 4: 102–14 (see *CW* vi).

[5] Apparently, this paper was never written. Sharp did, however, get the chance to express his enthusiasm for Pater's writings in two reviews of *Marius* (see letter to Sharp, 1 Mar. 1885).

[6] The sentence 'I find...send' was revised by Sharp: 'As to the paper on Giorgione which I read to you in manuscript, I find I have by me a second copy of the proof, which I have revised and sent' (Mrs William Sharp, *Papers Critical & Reminiscent*, 210).

[7] The phrase 'with pleasure your flying visit' was revised by Sharp: 'with so much pleasure your visit' (Elizabeth A. Sharp, 210).

[8] Sharp did not come in 1883, but paid his second visit to Pater in Oxford in late spring 1884 (Elizabeth A. Sharp, 208).

To VIOLET PAGET, 18 November [1882]
MS.: Henry W. and Albert A. Berg Collection, New York Public Library. Printed in *LWP*.

2 Bradmore Road | Nov. 18.

My dear Miss Paget,

I ought to have written long ago to thank you for the photograph of the drawing of yourself and the Fraser's Magazine.[1] I thought the likeness a real one. The drawing is certainly picturesque, though startling and very French. The draughtsman must certainly be a powerful workman. Your ghost-story in Fraser I have read twice. We all ## enjoyed its charming portraiture of Italian things and ways, which real knowledge could alone have made possible; and it has many dexterous points \which add to its effect of reality,/ e.g. that the phantom is beheld through the oeil de boeuf,[2] making it \felt/ somehow as a less incredible vision. On the whole it struck me as like a very good French piece of work, again. You know that is high approval from me; and this reminds me that Merimée's tale,[3] (it is certainly his,) may be found in the volume named at the end of this paper— I haven't it at hand, and must look for it in the library. Thank you most of all, for the 'New Medusa',[4] which we like very much. The first piece is, indeed, in its kind, as touching as anything I know; and the tales told, have a really imaginative boldness which puts them, I think, beside Browning's, but with a simplicity not often his. It is a very real and original contribution to poetry, and I hope your brother may do more.

I hope also to make his acquaintance, if we come to Florence; as I think we may next year, towards autumn.[5] At present, I expect to leave Oxford, for 6 or 7 weeks at Rome and Naples, in about a fortnight. On mature thought we have decided not to venture thither in the hot weather, and also that my sisters would not make much of such a visit in the middle of winter; and as I wish to put off my first visit to Rome no longer, I take this opportunity.

We were glad to hear of the Lemons[6] so charmingly at work, and I shall look out with much pleasure for your joint work on the little old French book.[7] Thank you very much; but don't trouble yourself any further about the Villa Lemmi[8] photographs, as I shall pass through Paris myself on my way to Italy. We often speak of your visit here in the summer.[9] What a fund of conversation we had! Lately the weather has been very damp, in all sorts of ways, binding up one's arteries, and making me very long in writing this letter.

We had however last night one of the prettiest auroras I have ever seen—a large part of the sky almost as bright as day with sheets and beams of light, milky or faintly coloured; and all in delicately elusive motion: it was like the *making* of opal or mother-of-pearl. My sisters join in kind regards,

Yours very sincerely
Walter Pater.
T. O.

Either appended to the volume which contains 'Colomba'—or, in a volume of 'Nouvelles—Carmen', etc. I can't lay hand on either, but am sure on the main point.

---

[1] Neither the photograph nor the drawing has been traced. Vernon Lee's story, 'Apollo the Fiddler: A Chapter on Artistic Anachronism', appeared in *Fraser's Magazine*, ns 26 (July 1882), 52–67.

² *Oeil-en-boeuf* is an architectural term for an 'ox-eye' or small, oval window located in a building's upper storey.

³ Probably '*La Vénus d'Ille*' (1837) by Prosper Mérimée (1803–70). It was subsequently reprinted, with '*Les Âmes du Purgatoire*', in *Colomba* (Paris: Maulde et Renou pour Magen et Comon, 1841), to which Pater intends to refer in his postscript to this letter. Mérimée's tale, a story of pagan gods' survival in other ages, has affinities with stories by Paget and Pater.

⁴ Eugene Lee-Hamilton (1845–1907), poet and novelist, was Paget's half-brother. See Biographical Register. With the publication of *The New Medusa, and Other Poems* (London: Elliot Stock, 1882) his work began to attract critical attention.

⁵ The trip was not made; Pater remained in Oxford to work on *Marius*. Instead, Paget planned to visit the Paters on 20 July 1883 (see letter to Paget, 22 July [1883]).

⁶ Arthur D. Lemon (1850–1912), a painter, and his wife Blanche, friends of Paget. See Vernon Lee, *Hauntings and Other Fantastic Tales*, ed. Catherine Maxwell and Patricia Pulham (Peterborough, Ont.: Broadview Press, 2006), 37, n.1.

⁷ The 'French book' is unidentified.

⁸ In 1881 two frescoes by Sandro Botticelli, which had been discovered eight years earlier in the Florentine villa of Dr Petronio Lemmi, were purchased by the French government, and in Mar. 1882 placed on exhibition in the Louvre. Painted between 1485 and 1490, the frescoes represent Giovanna and Lorenzo Tornabuoni with Venus and the Three Graces. See Lee, 'Botticelli at the Villa Lemmi', *Cornhill Magazine*, 46 (Aug. 1882), 159–73; rptd in *Juvenilia: Being a Second Series of Essays on Sundry Aesthetical Questions*, 2 vols (London: T. Fisher Unwin, 1887), 1: 79–129.

⁹ Paget visited the Paters on 13 Aug. 1882; for her account of the visit, see *VLL*, 109–10.

To EDWARD WILLIAMS BYRON NICHOLSON,¹ 27 November [1882]
Text: Maggs Bros. *Catalogue* no. 396 (Autumn 1920), 176. This fragment is printed in *LWP*.

November 27th.

...Many thanks for 'Jim Lord', which I have read with much enjoyment. I shall put it by with my other literary curiosities....

¹ Edward Williams Byron Nicholson (1849–1912), scholar and librarian, attended Trinity College, Oxford, 1867–71. He became the honorary Librarian of the Oxford Union Society in 1872, Principal Librarian of the London Institute in 1873, and, thanks to the support of Benjamin Jowett (see Biographical Register), of the Bodleian Library in 1882. His literary work focused on classical literature and comparative philology, but he earned a reputation for writing limericks. His popular *Jim Lord: A Poem* (Oxford: privately printed, 1882), about a cat, went through three editions in three years.

1883

To WILLIAM SHARP, 15 January 1883
Text: Elizabeth A. Sharp, 69. Printed in *LWP*.

2 Bradmore Road, | Jan. 15, 1883.

My dear Sharp,

Thank you very sincerely for the copy of your book,[1] with the fine impression of the beautiful frontispiece, which reached me yesterday. One copy of the book I had already obtained through a bookseller in Rome, and read it there with much admiration of its wealth of ideas and expression, and its abundance of interesting information. Thank you also sincerely, for the pleasant things you have said about myself;[2] all the pleasanter for being said in connection with the subject of Rossetti, whose genius and work I esteemed so greatly. I am glad to hear that the book is having the large sale it deserves. Your letter of December 24th, was forwarded to me at Rome, with the kind invitation I should have been delighted to accept had it been possible, and which I hope you will let me profit by some other time. Then, I heard from my sisters, of your search for me in London, and was very sorry to have missed you there. I shall be delighted to see you here; and can give you a bed at Brasenose, where I shall reside this term.

Thank you again for the pleasure your book has given, and will give me, in future reading. Excuse this hurried letter, and
Believe me,

Very sincerely yours,
Walter Pater.

[1] *Dante Gabriel Rossetti: A Record and a Study* (London: Macmillan, 1882).
[2] Sharp applies to a painting by D. G. Rossetti a sentence from Pater's essay on Michelangelo, and refers to Pater as 'one of the most masterly and cultivated art-writers of our time' (115).

To DUGALD SUTHERLAND MACCOLL, 8 February [1883][1]
MS.: Library, University of Glasgow. Printed in Conlon, 'Three Letters of Walter Pater', 318.

B. N. C. | Feb. 8

Dear Mr. MacColl,

From what I have heard, I fancy 'Love in Idleness'[2] is a good piece of work, and should be tempted to undertake what you propose, if it were not fairer both to you and the authors, not to do so. My hands are full of work, which has been interrupted in various ways this term, and I might find myself unable to complete the notice you want in anything like reasonable time. I hope therefore you will let me contribute something else at some future time, and meantime wish you all success in your undertaking. I was sorry not to have seen you on Thursday, and hope we may meet soon.

Very sincerely yours
Walter H. Pater.

[1] MacColl likely stopped at Pater's rooms at Brasenose on Thursday, 1 Feb., and left word proposing the review.
[2] *Love in Idleness: A Volume of Poems* (London: Kegan Paul, Trench, 1883) was published anonymously by J. W. Mackail, H. C. Beeching, and J. B. B. Nichols in Feb. 1883. See the next two letters for the progress of Pater's review.

To DUGALD SUTHERLAND MACCOLL, [14 or 21 February 1883][1]
MS.: Library, University of Glasgow. Printed in Conlon, 'Three Letters of Walter Pater', 318.

B. N. C. | Wednesday.

Dear Mr. MacColl,

If you have not yet found a reviewer of 'Love in Idleness', would you kindly let me have the volume?

Very truly yours
Walter Pater.

[1] Since Pater's review appeared on Wednesday, 7 Mar., and neither his habitual working methods nor the time needed to see the review through the press could allow for a date of 28 Feb. for the Wednesday in question, 14 or 21 Feb. is the more likely date, with 14 Feb. the most likely. Pater's (unsigned) review appeared as 'Love in Idleness', *Oxford Magazine*, 7 Mar. 1883, 144–5. See *CW* v.

HESTER PATER to VIOLET PAGET, 24 February [1883]
MS.: Colby College. Printed in *LWP*.

2 Bradmore Rd | Feb. 24th.

My dear Miss Paget,

The flowers were a pleasant surprise, many thanks for them, it was so kind of you to think of sending them. They look very Italian with their rich colours in an Indian turquoise vase. Our poor pale primroses and snowdrops look like gohsts [sic] beside them. Walter enjoyed his visit to Rome very much. He was very much obliged for the introductions you sent him and was very sorry he had no time to use any. A month is a short time to see much of Rome. He found he had to give all his time to the galleries and churches and was so tired in the evening he was quite unfit for social intercourse.[1] We are looking forward to coming to Florence this year in the beginning of September. I am afraid it will not be the best time to see it, and that you will not be there then, which will be a disappointment. Perhaps we may see you in England before that.

With love

Yours most sincerely
Hester M. Pater.

My brother desires [to send] kindest regards.

[1] This may be in part a rationalization, for Pater was notoriously shy with most strangers, and especially so when out of England. See, for example, Mandell Creighton's letter to Gosse, 19 Nov. 1894, in Louise Creighton, ed., *The Life and Letters of Mandell Creighton*, 2 vols (London: Longmans, Green, 1904), 2: 111. Creighton adds that 'Pater when he travelled with his sisters always left a place if anyone staying in the hotel spoke to him'.

To JOHN WILLIAM MACKAIL,[1] [late February? 1883]
MS.: Private. Printed in *LWP*.

I have been reading Love in Idleness very carefully today!....

Ever yours truly
Walter Pater.

[1] John William Mackail (1859-1945), Scottish classical scholar, literary critic, poet, and biographer, studied at Balliol College, Oxford, 1877–82, and may have helped Benjamin Jowett (see Biographical Register) with his work on Plato and Aristotle during this period. Mackail served as a Balliol Fellow, 1882–4; as a secretary in the Education Department of the Privy Council, 1884–1903; Assistant Secretary of the Privy Council, 1903–5; Oxford Professor of Poetry, 1906–11; and President of the British Academy, 1932–6. His scholarly

work includes studies of Virgil, lectures on classical subjects, and his lives of British poets, especially of William Morris (1899). He married Margaret Burne-Jones, the daughter of Georgiana and Edward Burne-Jones. With his friends Henry Charles Beeching (1859–1919) and John Bowyer Buchanan Nichols (1859–1939) Mackail produced *Love in Idleness* (see letter to MacColl, 8 Feb. [1883], n. 2), a volume of poetry published anonymously in Feb. 1883. Pater's letter praising the volume almost surely precedes his favourable review in the *Oxford Magazine*, 7 Mar. 1883, 144–5. (See *CW* v.) Mackail returned the compliment, reviewing *Marius* in the *Oxford Magazine*, 29 Apr. 1885, 191–2, and 6 May 1885, 207–8.

To T. HUMPHRY WARD,[1] 5 March [1883]
MS.: Private. Envelope: T. H. Ward Esq. | 61 Russell Square | London. W. C. Postmark: OXFORD R MR 5 83. Printed in *LWP*.

B. N. C. | Mar. 5.

My dear Ward,

Many thanks for your letter, which I have been unable to answer before. I think I shall be able to do what you propose for your new edition,[2] but can't feel quite certain for a day or two; if *not*, I will let you know when you come to Oxford and I hope we shall have the pleasure of seeing you and Mrs. Ward.

Very sincerely yours
W. H. Pater.

[1] T. Humphry Ward (1845–1926), journalist, art critic, and editor (see Biographical Register).
[2] Pater contributed an introductory essay on Dante Gabriel Rossetti, and a selection of his poems, for the second edition of Ward's anthology, *The English Poets: Selections*, 4 vols (London: Macmillan, 1883), 4: 633–41 (and in subsequent editions); it is reprinted in *Appreciations* (1889; see *CW* vi).

To FALCONER MADAN,[1] 5 April [1883?][2]
MS.: Bodleian Library. Printed in *LWP*.

2 Bradmore Road. | April 5.

My dear Madan,

Your (I doubt not, just) reproaches make me wish I could afford to make a present of the little volume[3] to the Bodleian. On the other hand, a remark as to what you would yourself do, make [sic] me decide on keeping it. Meantime, keep it till you have done with it, and copy as much of it as you like. With many thanks for the trouble you have so kindly taken for me,
 I remain

Very sincerely yours
W. H. Pater.

[1] Falconer Madan (1851–1935), librarian and bibliographer, formerly a student at Brasenose College. See Biographical Register.
[2] The letter is filed in Nicholson's Miscellaneous Correspondence for 1888–90, but the Bradmore Road address requires a date no later than 1885. As the stationery is the same as that Pater used in letter to Ward, 5 Mar. [1883], seems most probable.
[3] The 'little volume' remains unidentified.

To VIOLET PAGET, 10 June [1883]
MS.: Colby College. Postcard addressed: Miss Paget | 5 Via Garibaldi | Florence | Italy. Postmark: OXFORD JU 11 83. Printed in *LWP*.

June 10.

My dear Miss Paget,

I have just read your letter to my Sister, and find that you are probably leaving Florence this week. I meant to have written at length a few days hence, to tell you how much interested I had been ~~in~~ by your papers in the Cornhill and Contemp[orar]y.[1] But I am going to London for a day or two tomorrow, and have only time to send this card to catch you before you leave Italy. We are looking forward to 'Ottilie'.[2] I am sorry to say that in consequence of the illness of ~~our~~ my Brother my Sister Clara is away from home. Notwithstanding that, we hope we shall have the pleasure of seeing you here.

W. H. Pater.

[1] 'The Portrait Art of the Renaissance', *Cornhill Magazine*, 47 (May 1883), 564–81; and 'The Responsibilities of Unbelief: A Conversation between Three Rationalists', *Contemporary Review*, 43 (May 1883), 685–710. The former was revised and reprinted by Vernon Lee in *Euphorion: Being Studies of the Antique and the Mediaeval in the Renaissance*, 2 vols (London: T. Fisher Unwin, 1884), 2: 3–45; the latter in *Baldwin: Being Dialogues on Views and Aspirations* (London: T. Fisher Unwin, 1886), 15–73.
[2] T. Fisher Unwin published Paget's short narrative, *Ottilie: An Eighteenth Century Idyll*, in the autumn 1883.

To VIOLET PAGET, 22 July [1883]
MS.: Colby College. Printed in *LWP*.

2 Bradmore Road. | July 22.

My dear Miss Paget,

We are much disappointed not to have the pleasure of seeing you here this week. We had looked forward to your visit as a particularly refreshing incident after what has been a depressing time to us, and myself in particular had much to say about work I have in hand, and, better still, about your own work. I am thankful to say the accounts of my brother, with whom my sister Clara is still absent, have been of late hopeful; though I am afraid my sisters, at all events, will not be able to leave England this summer. I hope however you may still be able to spend a few days with us.[1] I fear there is no place near here which could be fairly recommended for your villeggiatura,[2] although on selfish grounds we wish there were. Winchester and Salisbury are both noble places, and with quietly charming surroundings, but I know them only as a mere passing visitor. I believe the regions about Wantage on the Berkshire Downs, not far from here, are healthy, bright-looking, and with a sort of historic interest.

I am very glad to hear you are going to collect those papers which I have admired so much from time to time. They certainly deserve republication, and I shall be pleased and proud at your dedicating them to me, and thus in a way associating me in your so rapidly growing literary fame. I feel great interest in all you write, and am really grateful for the pleasure thereby. The title of your proposed volume is I think ben trovato.[3]

I write so few letters! and this strikes me as a very stiff one, after yours. Your letters always greatly interest us—me, and my sister, who hopes with me that we shall see you here later in the summer, and some time or other (it is all one can say just now) in Italy.

I have hopes of completing one half of my present chief work—an Imaginary Portrait of a peculiar type of mind in the time of Marcus Aurelius[4]—by the end of this Vacation, and meant to have asked you to look at some of the MS. perhaps. I am wishing to get the whole completed, as I have visions of many smaller pieces of work the composition of which would be actually pleasanter to me. However, I regard this present matter as a sort of duty. For, you know, I think that there is a fourth sort of religious phase possible for the modern mind, over and above those presented in your late admirable paper in the Contemporary, the conditions of which \phase/ it is the main object of my design to convey.[5]

With sincere kind regards from my sister, I remain

Ever yours truly
Walter Pater.

---

[1] There is no evidence that Paget was able to visit the Paters in Oxford during 1883.

[2] A country residence used for a holiday.

[3] '[Even] if it is not true, it is very well invented.' Paget collected seven essays in *Euphorion: Being Studies of the Antique and the Mediaeval in the Renaissance* (1884), adding to them an Introduction written in Sept. 1882 and an epilogue dated Jan. 1884. Her title alludes to the second part of Goethe's *Faust*, in which the child Euphorion, son of Faust and Helen of Troy, symbolizes the union of the classical and the medieval. The book is dedicated 'to Walter Pater, in appreciation of that which, in expounding the beautiful

things of the past, he has added to the beautiful things of the present'. See letter to Paget, 4 June [1884].

⁴ *Marius the Epicurean* (*CW* ii).

⁵ 'The Responsibilities of Unbelief' (see letter to Paget, 10 June [1883], n. 1) features three speakers: Rheinhardt, an 'optimistic Voltairean' and intellectual epicure; Vere, an 'aesthetic pessimist'; and Baldwin, the positivist and 'militant, humanitarian atheist'. Baldwin's opinions seem to be those of Eugene Lee-Hamilton, although Gunn identifies Baldwin with Paget herself; Gunn, *Vernon Lee: Violet Paget* (London: Oxford University Press, 1964), 112. Rheinhardt accuses Vere of having 'scornfully decided that no Catholicism more recent than that of St Theresa deserved the attention of the real aesthetic pessimist' (685). After that Baldwin delivers a lengthy speech on atheism; no priest ever came to him 'spoiling for a pleasant chat' (696).

1884

To PAUL BOURGET,[1] 2 January [1884]
MS.: Bourget Archive, Fels Library, Paris. The letter (with no envelope) is written on light grey paper measuring 10.1 x 12.7 cm. Printed in Bénédicte Coste, 'Two Unpublished Letters from Walter Pater to Paul Bourget', *Pater Newsletter*, 61/62 (Spring/Fall 2012), 7–8.

2 Bradmore Road | Oxford | Jan 2.

My dear Mr Bourget,

I ought to have thanked you earlier for so kindly sending me your most interesting volume of Essays.[2] But it reached me at a moment when I had much work on hand and I was forced to put it aside to enjoy at leisure. I have just finished a careful reading of it with great delight at the acuteness of its analysis, the variety of its appreciations, its mastery of great masters in literature, and the finished hand and power of its style, so rare, alas! in contemporary English prose.

It is certainly more stimulation of thought than any book I have read for some time past, and I feel that I shall go back to its pages, again and again when I need intellectual stimulus, with full confidence of finding it there. Your essay on Stendhal,[3] especially, brought me many new lights upon him, and has ~~taken~~ already taken me all through Le 'Rouge et Noir', with even greater interest than of old. I hope you will visit Oxford again before long, or at any rate to have the pleasure of meeting you in Paris,[4] some time this year. With best wishes for you on its [reception], I am

Very truly yours
Walter Pater.

---

[1] Paul Bourget (1852–1935), French novelist and critic (see Biographical Register). Bourget probably met Pater through Ingram Bywater and Mark Pattison. He judged Pater to be the 'most refined of contemporary English prose-writers'. Bourget, *Études et Portraits* (Paris: Alphonse Lemerre, 1906), 304. Pater was not in the best of spirits. Work on *Marius the Epicurean* was moving more slowly than he had anticipated and throughout June and July William Pater's health had deteriorated (Hester and Clara took turns looking after him).

[2] Pater received a copy of the *Essais* (Paris: Alphonse Lemerre, 1883) in mid-Oct. 1883 (Coste, 'Two Unpublished Letters', 8).

[3] Bourget's portrait of Stendhal (Marie-Henri Beyle, author of *Le rouge et le noir*, known in English as *The Red and Black*, 1830), appears in *Essais* (1883), 253–323.

[4] There is no evidence of such a meeting.

To MARC ANDRÉ RAFFALOVICH,[1] 25 April [1884]
MS.: Blackfriars Priory, Oxford. Envelope: André Raffalovich Esq. | 1 Albert Hall Mansions | Kensington Gore | London SW. Postmark: OXFORD AP 25 84. Paper: small blue watermarked 'GC'. Tucked into a copy of *The Renaissance* (1893). Printed in Peter J. Vernon, 'Pater's Letters to André Raffalovich', *English Literature in Transition*, 26.3 (1983), 193.

B. N. C. | Ap. 25.

My dear Raffalovich,

I ought to have thanked you long since for your two charming sonnets in MS.[2] and the French critique,[3] which I read with great interest and pleasure. Though you may differ from some of the writer's points, you must have been pleased with criticism, at once so careful, and so friendly and appreciative. I have been very busy here with my MSS.[4] this vacation, though I managed to get away to London for a short visit, and had some hopes of being able to call on you at Kensington. That I must now hope to do at some not distant time, and meantime thank you sincerely for your kind invitation, and all the kind expressions in your letter.

Always very sincerely yours
Walter Pater.

[1] Marc André Raffalovich (1864–1934), poet, novelist, and critic (see Biographical Register).
[2] Probably the two sonnets entitled 'To One of My Readers' and 'To One of My Readers: A Sequel', printed in *Cyril and Lionel* (London: Kegan Paul, 1884), 1 and 87. Vernon, 'Pater's Letters', 196, n. 15.
[3] Untraced.
[4] Pater was trying to complete *Marius the Epicurean* (pub. Mar. 1885).

To WILLIAM SHARP, 28 May [1884]
Text: Elizabeth A. Sharp, 99–100. Printed in *LWP*.

2 Bradmore Road, | May 28th.

My dear Sharp,

I was just thinking of sending off my long-delayed acknowledgement of your charming volume, with its friendly dedication[1] (which I take as a great compliment, and sincerely thank you for) when your post card arrived. These new poems must, I feel sure, add much to your poetic reputation. I have just finished my first reading of them; but feel that I shall have to go back many times to appreciate all their complex harmonies of sense and rhythm. On a first superficial reading, I incline to think that the marks of power cluster most about the poem of *Sospitra*. Also, I prefer the *Transcripts from Nature*, to the various poems included in *Earth's Voices*, admirable as I think many of the latter to be, e.g., The Song of the Flowers, The Field Mouse, The Song of the Thrush, The Cry of the Tiger, The Chant of the Lion, The Hymn of the Autumn. This looks shamefully matter-of-fact. But then, you asked me to tell you precisely which I preferred. *The Shadowed Souls*, among the short pieces, I find very beautiful. The whole volume seems to me distinguishable among latter-day poetry for its cheerfulness and animation, and of course the Australian pieces are delightfully novel and fresh. Many thanks, again, from

Yours very sincerely
Walter H. Pater.

[1] Sharp's second volume of poetry, *Earth's Voices, Transcripts from Nature, Sospitra, and Other Poems* (London: Elliott Stock, 1884), is 'Dedicated in High Esteem and in Personal Regard to my friend, Walter H. Pater, Fellow of Brasenose College, Oxford, Author of "Studies in the History of the Renaissance", Etc.'

To VIOLET PAGET, 4 June [1884]
MS.: Colby College. Printed in *LWP*.

2 Bradmore Road. | June 4th.

My dear Miss Paget,

Euphorion arrived last Saturday. It is a very great pleasure to me to find myself associated with literary work so delightful and so excellent as yours, and I thank you sincerely for your generous and graceful dedication to myself.[1]

I have had time for a current reading of the greater part of it, and a very careful reading of some particular portions, e.g. the essay on 'Portrait Art', which struck me much when I got \a/ ### #### peep of it in a magazine.[2] It is, I think, a typical example of the peculiar excellencies of your work. There are three things which especially impress me, and I should think others, in these two volumes; as in your previous aesthetic writings, though now, certainly, in a heightened and strengthened way—

1. Very remarkable learning: by which I mean far more than an extensive knowledge of books and direct personal acquaintance with 'Italy's self'—learning, in the sense in which it is above all characteristic of Browning. I mean that these essays of yours are evidence of a very great variety and richness of intellectual stock—apprehensions, sympathies, and personal

observations of all kinds—such as make the criticism of art and poetry a real part of the 'criticism of life'.

2—Very remarkable power of style—full of poetic charm, without which, certainly, no handling of such subjects as yours could be appropriate—imagination, justly expressive, sustained and firm—as women's style so seldom is.

3ly—That that admirable power of writing is evidenced, in this book, in the treatment of very difficult matter. It is not *easy* to do what you have done in the essay on 'Portrait Art', for instance—to make, viz. *intellectual theorems* seem like the life's essence of the concrete, sensuous objects, from which they have been abstracted. I always welcome this evidence of intellectual structure in a poetic of or imaginative piece of criticism, as I think it a very rare thing, and it is also an effect I have myself endeavoured after, and so come to know its difficulties.

The sense of power comes out increasingly, in a second reading of your work; and this is of a [sic] course of a chief sign of good writing. I therefore look forward to much enjoyment in reading Euphorion, again and again. I find in it, not historic merely historic learning dominated by ideas, which is certainly a good thing; but ideas gathering themselves a visible presence out of historic fact, which to me, at least, is a far more interesting thing. Forgive this very lengthy way of saying that I sincerely congratulate \you/ on your success in this book.

It will give us great pleasure to see you at Commemoration,[3] which however will, I believe, not be a particularly showy one this year. The chief day is Wednesday, June 18th. But the solemnities are supposed to begin on the preceding Sunday. We shall be very pleased to welcome you for as many days as you can spare from London.[4] We have none of us any other sort of engagements at that time. Please let us have a few lines to tell us when we may expect you, and with our united kind regards, believe me

Very sincerely yours
Walter Pater.

[1] See letter to Paget, 22 July [1883], n. 3.
[2] See letter to Paget, 10 June [1883], n. 1.
[3] Commemoration ceremonies (including concerts, sports events, and white-tie balls) are held at the end of Trinity term to honour the university's founders and benefactors. These week-long ceremonies are held on a three-year cycle so that all undergraduates (and their families) can attend the festivities at least once.
[4] Paget stayed with the Paters 18–21 June; during her visit she heard Pater read from *Marius*. See her account in *VLL*, 146–8.

HESTER PATER TO VIOLET PAGET, 6 June [1884]
MS.: Colby College.

2 Bradmore Rd | June 6th

Dear Miss Paget,

I heard from Mr. Sharp that you were expected in London at the beginning of this week and I have been hoping to hear from you telling us when we might expect to see you. I wrote to Florence but I am afraid you perhaps did not receive any letter before you left. I don't know if you would like to come to Commemoration which is on the 17th of June and the two days before. Hoping to hear from you soon
Believe me

Yours very sincerely
H. W. Pater.

To WALTER PATER, 9 June 1884
MS.: British Library. Printed in *TBB*.

W. H. Pater Esqre. | 2 Bradmore Road | Oxford

June 9 | 1884

Dear Mr. Pater,

The first chapters, pp. 1–31, of 'Marius', have duly reached us. I hope to see Morley[1] tomorrow or next day & will put it in his hands, and try to discuss it with him, if I can find time to read it, as I hope to do, before I see him.

Ever truly yours,
Alex Macmillan.

---

[1] John Morley, 1st Viscount Morley of Blackburn (1838–1923), journalist, biographer, and radical politician, was the editor of *Macmillan's Magazine*. See Biographical Register.

To MARC ANDRÉ RAFFALOVICH, 4 July [1884]
Text: Christie's Catalogue, Sale 7574, Lot 90, 20 November 1992. Listed as autograph letter, signed; 3 pages, 12 mo.

...I should be very pleased to spend the evening with yourself, or go to the play, if you like. I have seen The Rivals[1].... I return to Oxford on

Saturday... and should be disappointed to leave London without seeing you.... I have just received your second note. It would have been very nice to go with you to Twelfth Night.² Alas! I am engaged on the 11th.... I shall probably see it some other night. Don't mind about going to the Play. I should be very pleased to pass the evening with you quietly.

¹ A production of *The Rivals*, a comedy of manners by Richard Brinsley Sheridan, directed by S. B. Bancroft and featuring Johnston Forbes-Robertson, ran at the Haymarket Theatre from 3 May to 19 July 1884.
² An acclaimed production of Shakespeare's *Twelfth Night*, directed by Henry Irving and featuring Ellen Terry as Viola, Fred Terry as Sebastian, and Henry Irving as Malvolio, was performed at the Lyceum Theatre from 5 July to 25 Aug. 1884.

To MADAME MARIE RAFFALOVICH, [July 1884?]¹
Text: Christie's Catalogue, 20 November 1992, Sale 7574, Lot 90. Listed as autograph letter, signed; 3 pages, 12 mo.

...I take this opportunity of telling you how much pleasure I have found in the acquaintance of your son André, for whom I hope all the happiness in life which his charming character, and interesting mind, deserves. Should you ever visit Oxford, it will be an honour to make you acquainted with its remarkable objects....

¹ The letters to Raffalovich, 25 Apr. [1884] and 4 July [1884], surfaced at the same time. Internal evidence suggests the order provided here.

To PAUL BOURGET, 2 August [1884]
MS.: Bourget Archive, Fels Library, Paris. The letter¹ (with no envelope) is written on white paper measuring 11.2 x 17.9 cm. Printed in Coste, 'Two Unpublished Letters', 9.

2 Bradmore Road | Oxford | Aug 2nd

My dear Mr Bourget,

I hoped to have thanked you before for so kindly sending me your new volume.² It interested me much to see your hand in a new kind of work, and I must congratulate you on what seems to me your great success in it. I put it with the best things I know in French fiction—itself so perfect after its kind, and mean to take it away, for second reading, among my summer-holiday books. I had some hopes of seeing you in London[.]³ Miss Paget⁴ has since furnished me with this address to which I send this. I leave Oxford, for some places in Sussex,⁵ on Thursday, and hope to return home somewhere about September 15th. Should you be in England, and inclined to ~~be in~~ spend a few days in Oxford, after that date, it would be a great pleasure to me to see you here, if you will occupy my spare bed-room.[6] In that case, please send me a line addressed to me here.

Very sincerely yours
Walter Pater.

[1] The letter was discovered in a presentation copy of *The Renaissance* (1877) that Pater had given to Bourget.

[2] Probably *L'irréparable* (1884), the story about an upper-class, free-thinking young woman (her family had neglected to educate her to the ways of the world) who takes her own life on her wedding night, overcome by the memory of being raped, the 'irreparable' act of the title. In response to George Moore's novel, *A Mere Accident* (London: Vizetelly, 1887), which deals with the rape of a young woman, Pater claimed that 'descriptions of violent incidents and abnormal states of mind do not serve the purpose of art' (see letter to Moore, [*c*.3 Aug. 1887]).

[3] If Pater and Bourget did not meet in Oxford, they may have met in London, where the latter stayed from 15 Jul. to the end of Sept. to examine D. G. Rossetti's paintings and to meet artists and writers, including Oscar Wilde, John Singer Sargent, and Henry James. His observations appeared as 'Notes sur l'Angleterre' in the autumn issue of *Journal des Débats*. Bourget also visited Canterbury and Oxford at the end of Aug. (Coste, 10).

[4] John Singer Sargent (1856–1925), the American painter, hosted a tea party on 3 July 1884; the guests included Henry James and Pater. Sargent introduced Paul Bourget to Violet Paget (Vernon Lee) in London on 20 July 1884, although Bourget and Paget may have met in Paris (Coste, 10). Sargent settled in London in 1885, where he painted the portraits of celebrities, American and British. Bourget and Paget met again at his studio on 22 July. See Gordon W. Smith, trans. and ed., 'Letters from Paul Bourget to Vernon Lee', *Colby Library Quarterly*, 3.15 (Aug. 1954), 236–44.

[5] Details of this excursion have not emerged.

[6] As Coste points out, this invitation suggests a degree of intimacy. If they did meet, they likely met in London. Gradually, the writers drifted apart; Bourget spent more and more time in Venice and Rome, writing and entertaining celebrities. In 1885–93 Pater commuted between Oxford and London, overwhelmed by work promised or nearly completed. See Coste, 'Two Unpublished Letters', 11–14.

To ALEXANDER MACMILLAN, 9 September [1884]
MS.: British Library. Printed in *LWP* and *TBB*.

2 Bradmore Road. | Oxford. | Sept. 9.

My dear Mr. Macmillan

I was not surprised that Morley was unable to take my M.S. for the magazine,[1] its unfitness for serial publication having sometimes occurred to me, though for some reasons I should have preferred that mode. I am now thinking of offering it to a publisher with a view to its appearing in the spring. I should feel much honoured if you could take it. It would be pleasing to me in many ways; and the convenience of printing in Oxford, great.

I wonder whether you could take it on slightly more favourable terms than in the case of my former volume.² Excuse the plainness of my question. I had thoughts of asking Morley to consult you on the matter, but it seems unfair to poach on his already so much occupied time.

I should like the book to appear early in the year, and would call on you about it, if necessary.³

Believe me

Very sincerely yours
W. H. Pater.

¹ John Morley (see Biographical Register) succeeded George Grove as editor of *Macmillan's Magazine*, holding the office from May 1883 to summer 1885. Pater had hoped to publish *Marius* serially in the magazine, and had submitted his first two chapters before 9 June. On 10 June 1884 George A. Macmillan sent Morley the chapters 'intended, as you will remember, for the Magazine'. Letter Book XLV.

² Macmillan replied on 11 Sept. (Letter Book XLVI) that he 'would greatly like' to publish *Marius*, and expressed hope that its sale would exceed that of Pater's *Renaissance*. While unwilling to grant Pater better terms than half-profits, the rationale of which he explained at length, he offered to pay £50 at once on account, 'agreeing that whether your share reaches this amount or not it will still be yours'.

³ Macmillan wrote on 31 Oct. (Letter Book XLVI), making an appointment for Monday morning, 3 Nov.

To WALTER PATER, 11 September 1884
MS.: British Library. Printed in *TBB*.

W. H. Pater Esqre. | 2 Bradmore Road | Oxford

Sept. 11. 1884

My dear Mr. Pater,

I would greatly like to publish your new book, and I am inclined to hope that its sales would be larger than the Essays; but that is uncertain, and I don't feel that we could offer any terms beyond those on which we published your 'Essays'. That is equal division of profits. But we are willing to pay you, on publication, the sum of Fifty Pounds on account of your half share of profits, agreeing that whether your share reaches this amount or not it will still be yours.

I suspect that authors do not realize that in the case of half profit arrangements the publisher only charges the actual cost of production & advertisements. House rent, clerks' salaries, our own time, thought, correspondence—whatever they are worth are supposed to be paid out of *our* share of profits. I am fully & keenly aware how little the money result ever is to writers like yourself [who] by careful elaboration of thought & skill work out results that have intellectual value. But I think we do our best for the *higher* literature, as distinguished from the merely popular.

With all kind regards,

Very faithfully yours,
Alex Macmillan.

We shall be glad to have your copy soon & arrange for a delicate & dainty form of book & also early publication.

To ALEXANDER MACMILLAN, 14 September [1884]
MS.: British Library. Printed in *LWP* and *TBB*.

2 Bradmore Road. | Sept. 14.

My dear Mr. Macmillan,

Many thanks for your letter. I shall be very pleased to accept your offer, and sincerely hope you will lose nothing by it. I am not one of those (if such there be) who complain of the useful office of the Publisher; and I know not how long ago I formed the ambition that *you* should publish what I might write as I glanced over the fascinating list of your publications in the "higher" literature—certainly, before I could afford to buy them.

The M.S. will not be quite complete till the end of October, at earliest, when it shall be duly delivered to you. I suppose three months will be sufficient for the printing, and that the book might appear in February. Three quarters of the whole are ready, and the printing might begin at once, if necessary.

I should like the volume to be, in size, quality of paper, and binding, precisely similar to the second edition of my Essays, which, though simple in form, is, I think, a model of what such a book should be, as regards that matter.

Ever

Very sincerely yours
W. H. Pater.

To MARC ANDRÉ RAFFALOVICH, 15 September [1884]
MS.: Blackfriars Priory, Oxford. Envelope: André Raffalovich Esq. | 1 Albert Hall Mansions | Kensington Gore | London SW. | Postmark: Oxford SP 15 84. Paper: small blue watermarked. Tucked into a copy of *Greek Studies* (London, 1908). Printed in Vernon, 'Pater's Letters to André Raffalovich', 194.

2 Bradmore Road, | Oxford | Sept. 15

My dear Mr Raffalovich,

    When I last saw you, you promised to come and stay with me here for a few days. I should be very pleased if you could do so. I am afraid Oxford is rather dull for visitors just now. But if you don't mind risking that, your visit would be to me a very pleasant episode in this quiet time. Let me have a line, and believe me

Very sincerely yours
Walter Pater.

To WALTER PATER, 31 October 1884
MS.: British Library. Printed in *TBB*.

Walter Pater Esqre. | 2 Bradmore Road | Oxford

Oct. 31. 1884

My dear Mr. Pater,

    I shall be very glad to see you here on Monday [morning]. I generally reach [the office] a little before 11 a.m.

Yours very truly,
Alex Macmillan.

To WALTER PATER, 20 November 1884
MS.: British Library. Printed in *TBB*.

Walter Pater Esqre. | 2 Bradmore Road, | Oxford.

Nov: 20. 1884

My dear Mr. Pater,

    We are writing to the Press telling them that we are anxious that your book should be hastened on. But you are on the spot & please add personal emphasis to our communication.

We do not order paper till we have received the first sheet marked finally for press. Will you kindly give them your information & when they send it to us we will return it with our instructions as to number & paper, at once.

Very sincerely yours,
Alex Macmillan.

To VIOLET PAGET, 4 December [1884]
MS.: Colby College. Printed in *LWP*.

2 Bradmore Road. | Dec. 4.

My dear Miss Paget,

Miss Brown arrived safely some days ago, and I have already read the greater part of it with much interest and amusement.[1] # I send only brief thanks now in answer to your card of this morning, hoping to write at length before long. Brief thanks also to your brother for the new volume of his poems, which reached me a day or two ago.[2] I lighted at once \upon/, and have read twice, a powerful ballad—'Hunting the King'.

I am very busy correcting the proofs of my new book, but hope soon to have a little more time at my command.

Very sincerely yours
Walter Pater.

[1] Vernon Lee's [Violet Paget's] *Miss Brown: A Novel* (Edinburgh: W. Blackwood and Sons, 1884), published in three volumes on 29 Nov. 1884, is a satire on the excesses of aestheticism. For an account of the novel, and of the reactions of Pater and Henry James, see Gunn, *Vernon Lee*, 98–107.

[2] Eugene Lee-Hamilton, *Apollo and Marsyas, and Other Poems* (London: Elliott Stock, 1884).

To MARY ARNOLD WARD,[1] 15 December [1884]
MS.: Mary Moorman. Printed in *LWP*.

Bradmore Road. | Dec. 15.

My dear Mrs. Ward,

Accept my sincere thanks at last, for your charming and touching book,[2] which I have read with the greatest relish for its literary finish, its dainty natural description, and the accomplished skill in the management of plot which seems to promise much for future work of a larger scope—larger, I mean, in quantity; in quality it could scarcely be better. It seems to me to fulfil one's notion of a masterly sketch—a sketch, because it is plain that you had carefully limited your design from the first—and masterly, because, within this limited outline, all the various elements of interest are so admirably proportioned to each other. I hope to read it over again soon.

Very sincerely yours
Walter Pater.

[1] Mary Arnold Ward (1851–1920), novelist, philanthropist, and political lobbyist (see Biographical Register).
[2] The one-volume novel, *Miss Bretherton* (London: Macmillan, 1884), appeared in Nov. 1884 under the name Mrs Humphry Ward.

To WALTER PATER, 17 December 1884
MS.: British Library. Printed in *TBB*.

Walter Pater Esqre. | 2 Bradmore Road | Oxford

Dec. 17. 1884

Dear Mr. Pater,

The paper for your book is ordered & will be in the printers' hands early in January. We are working for publication[1] about the end of January, so as to be ready for the Lent Term & the London Post Christmas Season. I have read the proof copy. It seems to me excellent & rare. Perhaps too fine for a wide popularity. We'll see. But we are hopeful of adequate sale for a book treating out of the way material. Malcolm[2] has read it with great interest.

Very sincerely yours,
Alex Macmillan.

[1] *Marius* appeared on 4 Mar. 1885. See letter to Pater, 6 Feb. 1885.
[2] Malcolm Macmillan (see Biographical Register).

1885

To FREDERICK WEDMORE,[1] 31 January [1885]
MS.: Brasenose College. Envelope: Frederick Wedmore Esq. | Fine Art Society | 148 New Bond Street | London. Postmark: OXFORD A FE 2 85. Printed in *LWP*.

Brasenose– | Jan. 31.

Dear Mr. Wedmore,

One line to thank you for a very pleasant hour over your Notes on the French painters[2]— I wish I could manage to see the exhibition.

Very truly yours
Walter Pater.

---

[1] Frederick Wedmore (1844–1921), an art critic, worked for newspapers in Bristol and London, including the *Spectator* from 1868 and the *Standard* from 1878. In 1878, he defended Ruskin's position against James McNeill Whistler (1834–1903), the American painter (see Biographical Register), and introduced the French Impressionists to English readers; see 'The Impressionists', *Fortnightly Review*, ns 33 (Jan. 1883), 75–82. His novels include *Pastorals of France* (London: Richard Bentley and Son, 1877), and his art criticism includes *Four Masters of Etching* (London: Fine Art Society, 1883), *Whistler's Etchings: A Study and a Catalogue* (London: A. W. Thibaudeau, 1886), and *Turner and Ruskin: An Exposition of the Works of Turner from the Writings of Ruskin* (London: George Allen, 1900). Wedmore 'discovered' Pater in 1873 while visiting John Addington Symonds; he perused Symonds's copy of *Studies in the History of the Renaissance* and described the 'mark' the work and its author were making in Oxford. He recalled meeting Pater in Oxford, at the home of Mary and T. Humphry Ward, where Pater expressed admiration for Wedmore's *Pastorals of France*. The two became close friends, with Wedmore visiting the Paters in Oxford and London. For his 'portrait' of Pater, see his *Memories* (London: Methuen, 1912), 156–65.

[2] *Notes by Mr. Wedmore on French Eighteenth Century Art* (London: Fine Art Society, 1885). Wedmore mentions Jean-Antoine Watteau's connection with Jean-Baptiste Pater (8). This brochure may have influenced Pater's 'A Prince of Court Painters', first published in *Macmillan's Magazine*, 52 (Oct. 1885), 401–14, and later included in *Imaginary Portraits* (1887). See *CW* iii.

To WALTER PATER, 6 February 1885
MS.: British Library. Printed in *TBB*.

Walter Pater Esq. | 2 Bradmore Road | Oxford

Feb. 6 1885

Dear Mr. Pater,

We had a dummy copy of your book put into cloth to show the general effect of the binding. We are sending it by today's post. We are writing to urge the printers to get on with the book. Nothing could be gained by binding volume 1 separately. Our binder could bind a thousand volumes as quickly as 100.

Very sincerely yours,
Alex Macmillan.

To WALTER PATER, 16 February 1885
MS.: British Library. Printed in *TBB*.

Walter Pater Esq. | 2 Bradmore Road | Oxford

Feb. 16 1885

My dear Mr. Pater,

We will attend to your wish that the boards are not too heavy. Your presentation list will be attended to. We hope to publish about this 20th.

Very sincerely yours,
Alex Macmillan.

To WILLIAM SHARP, 1 March 1885
Text: Elizabeth A. Sharp, 104–5.[1] Printed in *LWP*.

2 Bradmore Road. | March 1, 1885.

My dear Sharp,

I have read your article in *The Athenaeum*[2] with very real pleasure; feeling criticism, at once so independent and so sympathetic, to be a reward for all the long labours the book has cost me. You seem to me to have struck a note [of] criticism not merely pleasant but judicious; and there are one or two important points—literary ones—on which you have said precisely what I should have wished, and thought it important for me, to have said. Thank you sincerely for your friendly work! Also, for your letter, and promise of the other notices, which I shall look out for,[3] and greatly value. I was much pleased also that Mrs. Sharp had been so much interested in my writing. It is always a sign to me that I have to some extent succeeded in my literary aim when I gain the approval of accomplished women.

I should be glad, and feel it a great compliment, to have Marius translated into German, on whatever terms your friend likes—provided of course that Macmillan approves.[4] I will ask him his views on this point.

As regards the ethical drift of *Marius*, I should like to talk to you, if you were here. I *did* mean it to be more anti-Epicurean than it has struck you as being.[5] In one way however I am glad you have mistaken me a little on this point, as I had some fears that I might seem to be pleading for a formal thesis, or 'parti pris'.[6] Be assured how cheering your praise—praise from so genuine and accomplished a fellow-workman—has been to me. Such recognition is especially a help to one whose work is so exclusively personal and solitary as the kind of literary work, which I feel I can do best, must be.

I fancied you spoke of bringing your wife to Oxford this term; and wish we had a room to offer you. But I think you know that we have at most only room for a single visitor. It will however give my sisters great pleasure to make the acquaintance of Mrs. Sharp. Only let us know a week or so, if possible, before you come to Oxford, that we may see as much of you as possible:[7] and with our united kind regards, believe me, my dear Sharp,

> Very sincerely yours,
> Walter Pater.

I hope that in generosity to me you are not wasting too much of the time that belongs to your own original work. I have told Macmillan to send you a properly bound copy of Marius, with only a few misprints.

---

[1] As with the letter to Sharp, 4 Nov. 1882, Sharp's version of the text differs somewhat from his wife's (see Elizabeth A. Sharp, 212–14). Again, Evans follows her rendering, except for the paragraphing and one word, indicated in n. 3. He indicates the only major variant in n. 4.

[2] Sharp's review of *Marius* appeared in the *Athenaeum*, 28 Feb. 1885, 271–3. He also reviewed the book at greater length in *Time*, ns 1 (Mar. 1885), 341–54; rptd Elizabeth A. Sharp, 229–40. Both notices appeared prematurely; Sharp worked from revised proofs furnished by Pater. *Marius* was issued on 4 Mar. 1885, and Macmillan wrote to Pater that day regretting these premature articles.

[3] 'Thank you...look out for,'. These two sentences are revised by Elizabeth A. Sharp: 'I thank you sincerely for your friendly work; also for your letter and the other article, which I shall look forward to,' (Elizabeth A. Sharp, 213).

[4] A translation of *The Renaissance* by Wilhelm Schölermann was published in Leipzig in 1902, but whether he was Sharp's friend who proposed to translate *Marius* in 1885 is not clear. The Macmillan Letter Books contain no correspondence on the subject.

[5] Sharp is uncertain 'if it has been Mr. Pater's intention to offer an apology for the higher Epicureanism' (272). He does, however, refer to Pater himself as 'in our own day the chief English exponent of the central doctrine of Epicurus' (271).

[6] *Parti pris* ('decision taken') is a preconceived idea, organizing thought, or bias.

[7] The Sharps visited in the early summer of 1885; for a short account of their visit, see Elizabeth A. Sharp, 120.

To WALTER PATER, 4 March 1885
MS.: British Library. Printed in *TBB*.

Walter Pater Esq. | 2 Bradmore Road | Oxford

March 4 1885

My dear Mr. Pater,

Marius is in the hands of the trade today. Our first subscription was not large. But that does not count for much. The reviewers, and especially the cultivated readers, tell most.

The premature notice in the Athenaeum & in Time is rather unfortunate. We take pains that all papers have their copies for review as nearly as possible at the same time. We certainly sent early copies to neither the Athenaeum nor Time. How did they get them?

It probably won't matter much, but the other papers, if they notice it, will certainly feel irritated.

I hope the look of the book pleases you.

Very sincerely yours,
Alex Macmillan.

To WALTER PATER, 16 March 1885
MS.: British Library. Printed in *TBB*.

Walter Pater Esq. | 2 Bradmore Road | Oxford

March 16 1885

My dear Mr. Pater,

We have already made our extract from The Saturday Review.[1] It is shorter than yours & we think not less effective, and it will cost less. But if you much prefer your own we will use it.

We are sending the book to Prof. Nettleship.[2]

Very truly yours,
Alex Macmillan.

---

[1] Probably a reference to the review of *Marius* that appeared in the *Saturday Review*, 14 Mar. 1885, 351–2.

[2] Henry Nettleship (1839–93), Latin scholar and academic reformer, read classics at Corpus Christi College, Oxford, 1858–61. He served various colleges, including as Fellow of Lincoln College, 1862–70, until his marriage to Mathilda Steel; subsequently, he was Assistant Master at Harrow, 1868–73; Fellow, Tutor, and Librarian at Corpus Christi College, 1873–8.

In 1878 he was elected Corpus Professor of Latin at Oxford, a position he held until his death. He took a keen interest in the educational advancement of women and believed that a university should be devoted to teaching as well as research. His publications include a revised edition of Conington's *Virgil* (London: Bell, 1883–98), and *Lectures and Essays on Subjects Concerned with Latin Literature and Scholarship* (Oxford: Clarendon Press, 1885). The Nettleships lived at 17 Bradmore Road.

To PERCY EWING MATHESON, 16 March [1885?]
Text: Maggs Bros. *Catalogue* no. 349 (1916), 98.

March 16th.

Dear Matheson,[1]

...Many thanks for it and for the trouble you have taken. I should much like Ritchie to do it, if he will....

[1] In 1884–5, Percy Ewing Matheson (1859–1946), scholar and translator, served as editor of the *Oxford Magazine*; David George Ritchie (1853–1903), philosopher, was a frequent contributor of reviews to that journal. Pater may have been recommending Ritchie as a reviewer for *Marius* (reviewed for the *Oxford Magazine* by J. W. Mackail); a stronger possibility is that Matheson had asked Pater to review Mark Pattison's newly published *Memoirs* (1885) and that Pater had recommended Ritchie instead. Pattison's book is reviewed anonymously in the *Oxford Magazine*, 22 Apr. 1885, 175–7, the first issue of the magazine to appear after 16 March.

To JOHN MILLER GRAY, 24 March 1885
Text: *John Miller Gray: Memoir and Remains*, 1: 51–2. Printed in *LWP*.

My dear Mr. Gray,

It gives me extreme pleasure to know from your generous article on it in the *Academy* that my new book has not disappointed you—one of the most valued of my readers.[1] Of three or four very friendly recognitions of my work, yours is the most complete, and it is a great encouragement to me to receive a criticism so kindly in what is itself so graceful a piece of writing.

I was very glad to find in your letter of Feb. 23rd that your office in the National Portrait Gallery[2] was what you had hoped to find it, and wish all prosperity to your own literary and artistic work. Excuse this brief note. It seems gracelessly little after your good work and trouble for me, but I cannot delay these few lines of acknowledgment.

Always very sincerely yours,
Walter Pater.

[1] Gray's enthusiastic review of *Marius* was the leading article in the *Academy*, 21 Mar. 1885, 197–9; he also reviewed the novel in the *Edinburgh Courant*, 4 Apr. 1885, 3. This second review is reprinted in *John Miller Gray*, 2: 3–9.

² When Gray applied in 1884 for the curatorship of the Scottish National Portrait Gallery, Pater (and Robert Browning, among others) wrote a testimonial, expressing 'the high opinion he had been led to form of his [Gray's] ability and accomplishments' (*John Miller Gray*, 1: 49).

To EDMUND GOSSE, 31 March [1885]
MS.: Brotherton Collection, University of Leeds. Printed in *LWP*.

2 Bradmore Road. | March 31.

My dear Gosse,

I was much pleased by your letter.¹ With thanks for that, and congratulations on what I hear of the great success of your lectures at Cambridge,² I remain

Ever sincerely yours
Walter Pater.

¹ Presumably congratulating Pater on *Marius*; Gosse had received a presentation copy.
² Gosse, the Clark Lecturer at Cambridge University, 1884–9, was repeating a series of lectures first given in the United States (see Biographical Register). They were subsequently published as *From Shakespeare to Pope: An Inquiry into the Causes and Phenomena of the Rise of Classical Poetry in England* (Cambridge: Cambridge University Press, 1885). See also letter to Gosse, 24 Oct. [1886].

To CHARLES EDWARD SAYLE,¹ 22 May [1885]²
MS.: Bates College. Most of the first sentence is printed in Emily Driscoll, *Autographs and Manuscripts*, Supplementary List no. 9 (October 1968), 27. Printed in *LWP*.

B. N. C. | May 22.

Dear Sir,

I can remember, at the moment, no authority but Sismondi;³ but doubt not there are more recent ones in German and Italian. If you like to call on me, at 2 Bradmore Road, some afternoon, I should be very pleased to see you.

Faithfully yours
Walter Pater.

¹ Charles Edward Sayle (1864–1924), poet, librarian, and bibliographer, studied classics at New College, Oxford, 1883–7. While still an undergraduate, Sayle published (anonymously) *Bertha: A Story of Love* (Kegan Paul, Trench, 1885), a volume of 'Uranian' poems, and

Wiclif: An Historical Drama (Oxford: James Thornton, 1887). Sayle was 'sent down' for the academic year 1885–6 because of a sexual liaison he had with another undergraduate. In 1889 he joined St John's College, Cambridge, where he catalogued books in the library, and in 1893 he joined the staff of the University of Cambridge Library, achieving some distinction as cataloguer and editor of rare books, notably *Early English Printed Books in the University Library, Cambridge, 1475–1640*, 4 vols (1900–7). According to reports, Sayle inspired many budding bibliographers before the Great War, including A. W. Pollard and R. B. McKerrow. In addition, he wrote articles and reviews for periodicals, produced two more volumes of poetry, edited two anthologies of poetry, and composed inscriptions for memorials erected to the dead of the Great War. Sayle's circles included Lionel Johnson (see Biographical Register), Michael Ernest Sadler (1861–1943), historian, educator, and administrator (see letter to Sadler, 5 Mar. [1892]), Arthur Galton (see Biographical Register), Ernest Dowson (1867–1900), poet, novelist, and short-story writer, and A. C. Benson (see Biographical Register). Sayle and Pater probably met in June; evidence confirms that Pater and Johnson met a couple of years later, in 1887, in Galton's rooms at New College. See J. C. T. Oates, 'Charles Edward Sayle', *Transactions of the Cambridge Bibliographical Society*, 8.2 (1982), 236–69.

[2] This letter and the letter to Sayle, [27 May? 1885] are written on the same grey paper, 10.2 x 12.7 cm, as are the letters to Wedmore, 31 Jan. [1885], Gosse, 31 Mar. [1885], Ward, 2 June [1885], Nicholson, 7 June [1885], and Alexander Macmillan, 16 June [1885].

[3] The context, and Pater's interest in the early Italian Renaissance, suggest that his reference may be to *Histoire des républiques italiennes du moyen âge*, 16 vols (Paris: H. Nicolle, 1809–18) by the Swiss historian and economist J. C. L. Simonde de Sismondi (1773–1842).

To CHARLES EDWARD SAYLE, [27 May? 1885][1]
MS.: Bates College. Printed in *LWP*.

Bradmore Road. | Wednesday.

Dear Mr. Sayle,

I am sorry I was not at home when you called. I shall be at home tomorrow at 5.30. and should be pleased to see you then.

Very truly yours
W. H. Pater.

[1] This letter was probably written soon after the letter to Sayle, 22 May [1885]; 27 May was the first Wednesday following 22 May 1885.

To MARY ARNOLD WARD, 2 June [1885]
MS.: Mary Moorman. Printed in *LWP*.

2 Bradmore Road. | June 2nd.

My dear Mrs. Ward,

I have read your paper on Marius in 'Macmillan',[1] and cannot help sending a few lines to tell you how much it has pleased me. To be really understood by a critic at once so accomplished and so generous as yourself, is a real reward for all one's labours. When one has taken pains about a piece of work, it is certainly pleasant to have a criticism upon it which is itself so graceful and painstaking.

Coming from one who, like yourself, has really mastered those matters, the objections you have urged, are also full of import and interest to me. The chief of them, I feel I must try to deal with before very long.[2] Meantime, my sincere thanks for all your care for my work: I only hope it has not taken too much time from your own varied and admirable literary work.

We were much pleased to hear you were better. Believe me, with our united kind regards, ever

Very sincerely yours
Walter Pater.

[1] Ward's review of *Marius* appeared in *Macmillan's Magazine*, 52 (June 1885), 132–9.

[2] According to Ward, 'what makes the great psychological interest of the book, while it constitutes what seems to us its principal intellectual weakness, is the further application of this Epicurean principle of an aesthetic loss and gain not only to morals, but [also] to religion'. She adds that 'acquiescence in the religious order, which a man finds about him, opens for opportunities of feeling and sensation which would otherwise be denied him, provides him with a fresh series of "exquisite moments"' (137). Ultimately Ward contrasts this attitude unfavourably with the more strenuous temper of Arthur Hugh Clough, who, she argues, sought 'no personal ease or relief at the expense of truth, and... put no fairy tales knowingly into the place which belongs to realities' (138). For all the numerous revisions made in *Marius* in the third edition (1892), Pater scarcely seems to 'deal with' Ward's objection; his reply may perhaps be found in unpublished essays that treat the question of religious assent (see his manuscripts, *CW* x). Pater's continuing difference with Ward on these matters is evident in the letter to Ward, 23 Dec. 1885, and in his review of *Robert Elsmere* in *The Guardian*, 28 Mar. 1888, 468–9. See *CW* v.

To EDWARD WILLIAMS BYRON NICHOLSON, 7 June [1885][1]
MS.: Bodleian Library. Printed in *LWP*.

B. N. C. | June 7.

Dear Nicholson,

The bearer, Mr. J. M. Gray, Curator of the Scottish National Portrait Gallery, is desirous of seeing the works—paintings or engravings—which bear on Scotch art.

Very truly yours

W. H. Pater.

[1] Gray was admitted to the Bodleian Library on 8 June 1885; the Library Register notes that he was recommended by Pater.

To WALTER PATER, 11 June [1885]
MS.: British Library. Printed in *TBB*.

June 11 5

Dear Sir,

We are pleased to be able to report that the 1st edition of 'Marius the Epicurean' is all but exhausted. Our idea about a second edition[1] is that it should be not cheap, but at a rather less price than the present one. It might be printed in the same type as at present on a paper of the same size but thinner, & published in one volume, or it might be printed in two pretty little volumes like the 2nd edition of 'John Inglesant',[2] the so-called 'Eversley Edition'[3] of Kingsley's novels & several other books we have published recently. The advantage of the former plan would be that the book would be uniform with your 'Renaissance' but we think the two small volumes would be prettier. We shall be glad to know your views on the subject & also whether you will have any corrections or alterations to make before reprinting.

We are

Yours truly,
Macmillan and Co.

[1] The second edition of *Marius the Epicurean* was released on 12 Nov. 1885.

[2] Joseph Henry Shorthouse (1834–1903), chemical manufacturer and novelist, was a Quaker by upbringing. He self-published *John Inglesant* (1880). Mary Ward sent a copy to Alexander Macmillan, whose firm published it in 1881. The novel surpassed all expectations, selling nearly 9,000 copies during the first year. The edition printed on hand-made paper was produced in July 1882.

[3] The Eversley series began in 1881 with a special edition of Charles Kingsley's *Alton Locke, Tailor and Poet*, 2 vols (London: Chapman and Hall, 1850). Alexander Macmillan thought Kingsley (1819–75) was 'one of the noblest men' he had ever known (Graves, *Life and Letters of Alexander Macmillan*, 329). The Eversley series eventually included almost 200 volumes. For *Marius*, Pater chose the second alternative, the two-volume edition, and the new (2nd) edition appeared on 12 Nov. 1885, selling for 12s. Evans points out that the first had sold for a guinea.

To ALEXANDER MACMILLAN, 16 June [1885]
MS.: British Library. Printed in *LWP* and *TBB*.

2 Bradmore Road. | Oxford | June 16th.

Dear Mr. Macmillan,

I am pleased to hear that the first edition of 'Marius' is all but exhausted, and should be glad to proceed with the second edition.

There are many minute corrections to make,[1] but I could send away the first sheets, thus corrected, at once to the printers. Two volumes would, I think, be best—of the size of the 'Eversley' Kingsley. If the present paging were exactly followed, we should have two volumes of about 250 pages; with a fair margin, if type of the size of Kingsley were used. I think a volume of that size should be not stumpy; so that a thinner kind of paper than before might be used—the nicest paper you have in use, not above the average price.

Might it be printed by Clark or your London printers?[2] I think the Oxford printing, as exemplified in the first edition, far from what it might be. Of course I could correct the proofs by post, either sheet by sheet, or all together, according to the convenience of the printers.

As to binding, I feel uncertain. I think it should be something quite distinct from that of the larger edition. It has occurred to me that cloth binding of the colour enclosed,[3] with yellowish white vellum back, would look well. I suppose it would be impracticable to bind in oriental silk of that colour, which can be obtained at very moderate cost. What do you think of the old-fashioned binding in boards? or wholly in thin vellum?

What do you think the price of the book should be—about 12 shillings? With many thanks, I remain

Very sincerely yours
Walter Pater.

Alex. Macmillan Esq.,
for Messrs. Macmillan and Co.

P. T. O.

I think the paper on which Miss Bretherton[4] is printed good, for ordinary paper. Do you ever use paper like the morsel enclosed?

---

[1] Almost immediately after the publication of *Marius*, Pater began to revise the book; he made more than a hundred alterations, primarily in word order and punctuation. They are insignificant, however, in comparison to the 6,000 textual changes he made for the third edition (1892). See Edmund Chandler, *Pater on Style* (Copenhagen: Rosenkilde and Bagger, 1958), 24–5, and *CW* ii.

[2] R. and R. Clark printed many books issued by Macmillan, including the first editions of *Imaginary Portraits* and *Appreciations*, as well as the third edition of *The Renaissance*. The firm, founded in Edinburgh in 1846 by Robert Clark (1825–94), established a reputation for high quality work in 1852, when it printed an edition of Sir Walter Scott's Waverley novels for Adam and Charles Black. For many years, it printed books for the leading publishing houses of the day, including Constable, Macmillan, and Penguin. Thomas Hardy and Bernard Shaw, among other writers, thought highly of the firm. In 1946, the company became printers to the newly founded University of Edinburgh Press.

[3] Pinned to the letter are a piece of chartreuse fabric and a small triangle of white paper.

[4] The story of *Miss Bretherton* (the artistic growth of a beautiful young actress whose natural gifts are supplemented by an intellectual understanding of drama) was suggested to Mary Arnold Ward (see Biographical Register) by the success in 1883 of an actress, Mary Anderson. On Morley's suggestion, Macmillan published the book, Ward's first novel, Dec. 1884.

To MOUNTSTUART GRANT DUFF, 9 August [1885]
MS.: Sheila Sokolov Grant. Printed in *LWP*.

Brasenose College. | Aug. 9th.

My dear Mr. Grant Duff,

Accept one line of sincere thanks for your kind appreciation[1] of my work—appreciation, which I greatly value. There were some tiresome misprints, and some mistakes, in the first edition of 'Marius', which I have corrected in the second edition which I hope will soon be ready.

We were sincerely grieved to hear of Mrs. Pattison's illness,[2] but hope by this time she is again able to enjoy her visit.

Ever

Very truly yours
Walter Pater.

[1] His appreciation has not been found.
[2] A recurring 'nervous illness' (so diagnosed) troubled Emily Pattison, later Lady Dilke (1840–1904), art historian, critic, and trade unionist (see Biographical Register), forcing her to spend part of the year abroad.

To WALTER PATER, 16 September [1885]
MS.: British Library. Printed in *TBB*.

Sept. 16 5

Dear Mr. Pater,

I send the 'dummy' copy of Marius by this post that you may see how the label on the back will look. The printers have omitted 'Vol. I' but that can easily be put right.

I am

Yours truly,
Frederick Macmillan.

To ALBERT FORBES SIEVEKING,[1] 18 October [1885]
MS.: Sir Rupert Hart-Davis. Printed in *LWP*.

12 Earl's Terrace. | Kensington.[2] | Oct. 18.

Dear Sieveking,

Many thanks for the little book, with your M.S. notes.[3] I shall read it and them with much interest, and return it to you.

I go to Oxford tomorrow; and I had hoped to be able to call on you in Essex Street before doing so. I shall hope to see you some day during term, when I come up to London.

Ever

Very truly yours
Walter Pater.

[1] Albert Forbes Sieveking (1857–1951), solicitor and miscellaneous writer, and the son of Sir Edward Sieveking, Physician-in-Ordinary to Queen Victoria. Sieveking became a solicitor in 1881 and practised law in London until 1913. He served as the Librarian of the Imperial War Museum, 1917–21. He edited *In Praise of Gardens: A Prose Cento, collected and in part Englished* (London: Elliott Stock, 1885) and *Gardens Ancient and Modern: An Epitome of the Literature of the Garden-Art* (London: J. M. Dent, 1899), which reprints five passages from the works of Pater, and *The Sentiment of the Sword: A Country-House Dialogue* (London: Horace Cox, 1911). There is no further record of his acquaintance or friendship with Pater.

[2] The Paters moved to this London address in Aug. 1885; it remained their home until the end of July 1893.

[3] A pencilled notation on the manuscript, presumably by Sieveking, identifies the book as Jules Barbey d'Aurevilly, *Du dandysme et de G. Brummell*, of which three French editions had been published: Caen: B. Mancel, 1845; Paris: Poulet-Malassis, 1861; and Paris: Lemerre, 1879. The first English translation is Jules Barbey d'Aurevilly, *Of Dandyism and of George Brummell*, trans. Douglas Ainslie (London: J. M. Dent, 1897). Grant Duff Douglas Ainslie (1865–1948) was a Scottish poet, diplomat, translator, and critic (see Biographical Register).

To WALTER PATER, 5 November [1885]
MS.: British Library. Printed in *TBB*.

Nov. 5 5

Dear Mr. Pater,

We shall publish the second edition of *Marius* on Friday week.[1] We were delayed very much by the paper which had to be made in Holland and it seemed impossible to get the phlegmatic Dutchmen to hurry themselves.

You shall have a copy as early as possible. I am,

Yours very truly,
Frederick Macmillan.

[1] The second edition of *Marius the Epicurean* appeared on 12 Nov. 1885.

To WALTER PATER, 25 November [1885]
MS.: British Library. Printed in *TBB*.

Nov. 25 5

Dear Mr. Pater,

I am glad you like the appearance of the second edition of 'Marius'. I am sending you by this post a copy of an edition that we have printed for America. It will not be on sale in this country.

I am glad to find that Mr. [Knowles][1] has secured a charming paper[2] from you for the next number of 'Macmillan'. I hope that you will find it possible to be a frequent contributor.

Believe me

Yours sincerely,
Frederick Macmillan.

---

[1] James Thomas Knowles (1831–1908), architect and editor, apprenticed with his father in 1846 and studied evenings at University College, London. He became an Associate (1853) and a Fellow (1870) of the Royal Institute of British Architects. Knowles edited the *Contemporary Review*, 1870–7, and founded and edited *The Nineteenth Century*, 1877, in order 'to provide a platform from which men of all parties and persuasions might address the public in their own names'. Knowles gave up architecture in 1883.

[2] Pater published 'On Love's Labours Lost' in *Macmillan's Magazine* in Dec. 1885. See *CW* v.

To DUGALD SUTHERLAND MACCOLL,[1] 2 December [1885]
MS.: Leonard S. Elton. Printed in *LWP*.

B. N. C. | Dec. 2nd.

Dear MacColl,

Will you dine with us at 12 Earl's Terrace, Kensington, on Saturday, Dec. 19th, at 7.30. Please send answer to me here.

Very sincerely yours
Walter Pater.

---

[1] Dugald Sutherland MacColl (1859–1948), Scottish art critic, author, and painter; see Biographical Register.

To ROBERT DUDLEY ADAMS,[1] 5 December [1885]
MS.: National Library of New Zealand.

Brasenose Colle, | Dec. 5th.

My dear Sir,

Be assured my long delay in answering your letter of Aug. 8th—your most kind and interesting letter, is no measure of the value I set on your friendly interest in my work. The fact is, I thought your warm expressions of sympathy in regard to it deserved a longer and more careful letter than I was able to write, (having my hands very full of various work,) or indeed have time for now. Still I don't like to wear an appearance of unthankfulness any longer, and must ask you to accept this brief assurance that I greatly value your very good opinion.

The good and sympathetic review of 'Marius',[2] which you forwarded, arrived duly; and I had much pleasure in reading it. Your own promised work, however, has not yet come to London; and I shall therefore seek to be possessed of it in some other way. Pardon my saying that your letter, apart from its kind expressions about myself, excited in me a lively interest as to the writer; and I have no doubt it would be largely increased by the reading of your poems. It would indeed be a pleasure to think that any work of mine would encourage the spiritual side of a life, spent so much in actual business as you describe yours to be. On the other hand; I suppose it often happens that hours which must be snatched from alien employment often tell more for our best development than our uninterrupted leisure for the things our minds are really most akin to. In my case, you have my sincere best wishes for your success in whatever you do. Should you come to England, I hope we may make acquaintance in person. During University Term-time I am to be found for the most part, at Brasenose College; at other times in London, at no. 12 Earl's Terrace, Kensington.

Believe me

Very truly and gratefully yours
Walter Pater.

[1] Robert Dudley Adams, née Herbert (1829–1912), connoisseur, studied law, and served as private secretary to the Hon. Sidney Herbert, Minister at War. In 1851 he settled in New South Wales, where he engaged in business and pastoral pursuits, and contributed to newspapers and magazines, including the *Empire* and the *Sydney Morning Herald*. He published a volume of poetry, *The Song of the Stars and other Poems* (London: Cassell, Petter, Galpin, 1882), which appeared under the nom de plume 'Alpha Crucis', and served on the New South Wales Exhibition Commissions. Ian A. Gordon explains that Adams wrote to many literary figures (to whom he sent copies of his poetry; he often received presentation copies in return). Gordon speculates that Adams collected autograph letters, valuing the signatures. Ian A. Gordon, 'Three New Letters of Matthew Arnold', *Modern Language Notes*, 56 (Nov. 1941), 552–4.

[2] This review has not been located.

To MARY ARNOLD WARD, 23 December 1885[1]
Text: Benson, 199–200. Printed in *LWP*.

I find a store of general interest in *Amiel*, (take at random, e.g., the shrewd criticism of Quinet,)[2] which must attract all those who care for literature; while for the moralist and the student of religion he presents the additional attraction of yet another thoroughly original and individual witness to experiences on the subject they care most for. For myself, I gather from your well-meditated introduction, that I shall think, on finishing the book, that there was still something *Amiel* might have added to those elements of natural religion, (so to call it, for want of a better expression,) which he was able to accept, at times with full belief, and always with the sort of hope which is a great factor in life. To my mind, the beliefs, and the function in the world, of the historic church, form just one of those obscure but all-important possibilities, which the human mind is powerless effectively to dismiss from itself;[3] and might wisely accept, in the first place, as a workable hypothesis. The supposed facts on which Christianity rests, utterly incapable as they have become of any ordinary test, seem to me matters of very much the same sort of assent we give to any assumption, in the strict and ultimate sense, moral. The question whether those facts were real will, I think, always continue to be what I should call one of the *natural* questions of the human mind.

---

[1] So dated in Benson, who introduces this fragment with the following words: 'He wrote Mrs. Humphry Ward a very interesting letter on 23 Dec. 1885, on receiving from her as a Christmas gift her newly published translation of *Amiel's Journal*. After congratulating her on the admirable literary grace of the translation, he continued...' (Benson, 199). Most of the extract also appears, with some variations, in Ward, *A Writer's Recollections*, 210.

[2] According to Thomas Escott (1844–1924), a journalist (see letter to Escott, 8 Apr. [1880?]), the Revd William Wolfe Capes (1834–1914) encouraged independent thought among his students at Queen's College, including Pater, and peppered his lectures with digressions on contemporary European authors, including Edgar Quinet and Jules Michelet. Quinet (1813–75), French poet, historian, and politician, championed liberalism and republicanism. Quinet found inspiration in the philosophy of Johann Gottfried von Herder (1744–1803), the leader of the *Sturm und Drang* {storm and stress, drive} movement. He translated Herder's work into French. From Feb. 1865 to Dec. 1872, Pater visited the Taylor Institution library and borrowed volumes 2 and 5 of Quinet's collected works, volumes dealing with the Jesuits and the revolution in thinking when the medieval mind discovered pagan art, and volumes 10, 14, and 15 of Michelet's *Histoire de France*, dealing with conflicts between Catholics and Huguenots, Louis XIV, and the Regency (1715–23).

[3] Compare with chapters 1 and 2, 'A Clerk in Orders' and 'Our Lady's Church', *Gaston de Latour*; see *CW* iv: 37–60. See also Pater's review of Ward's *Robert Elsmere*, *CW* v.

1886

To CARL WILHELM ERNST,¹ 28 January [1886]²
MS.: Columbia University. Printed in *LWP*.

Brasenose College, | Oxford, | Jan. 28th.

My dear Sir,

   Accept my sincere thanks for your kind letter, and interesting notices of my book. Be assured I greatly value your good opinion of it. In answer to your inquiries, I send, over-leaf, a list of my chief contributions to periodicals. I was born in London, in 1839: was educated at the King's School, Canterbury: took my degree, in second class, in 186<6>\2/: ~~and~~ was elected a Fellow of Brasenose College, in 1864: and have been continuously, since about that time, one of its Lecturers.

   I may add that 'Marius' is designed to be the first of a kind of a trilogy, or triplet, of works of a similar character; dealing with the same problems, under altered historical conditions. The period of the second of the series would be at the end of the 16th century, and the place France: of the third, the time, probably the end of the last century—and the scene, England.³

   With renewed thanks for your friendly interest in my work, and apologies for my delay in acknowledgment, I remain

Very faithfully yours
Walter Pater.

The 2nd edition of 'Marius', for sale in England, price 12 \s./, is, I think, a very *pretty looking* pair of volumes.

C. W. Ernst Esq.

Contributed⁴ to the Fortnightly Review—
Wordsworth: April, 1874.
On 'Measure for Measure': November, 1874.
Demeter & Persephone: January & February, 1876.
Dionysus: December, 1876.
The School of Giorgione: November, 1877.
Charles Lamb: October, 1878.
The Beginnings of Greek Sculpture: February & March, 1880.
The Marbles of Aegina: April, 1880.

———————

Contributed to Macmillan's Magazine—
Romanticism: November, 1876.

The Child in the House: August, 1878.
A Picture of Court Painters: October, 1885.
On 'Love's Labours Lost': December, 1885.

I also wrote the essays on Coleridge and on D. G. Rossetti, in Ward's English Poets.

---

[1] Carl Wilhelm Ernst (1845–1919), a journalist, grew up in Hanover, Germany, and settled in the United States in 1863. He studied theology then served as a Lutheran minister, first in Illinois and then in Rhode Island. When he left the ministry, he earned an MA at Brown University (1875). He moved to Boston in 1879, where he worked as a journalist, and married Abbie Snow Hart, daughter of mayor Thomas N. Hart in 1885, and became the mayor's secretary, 1889. He published several volumes, including *The Constitutional History of Boston: An Essay* (1894).
[2] So dated by another hand.
[3] The second volume was to have been *Gaston de Latour*. Its first five chapters appeared in *Macmillan's Magazine*, 58 (June–Oct. 1888), 152–60, 222–9, 258–66, 393–400, 472–80; and the substance of chapter 7 as 'Giordano Bruno', in *Fortnightly Review*, ns 46 (Aug. 1889), 234–44. See *CW* iv. That Pater also planned a third volume in the series was not known until the discovery of this letter and the letter to Withers, 13 Mar. [1886]. Among the Harvard manuscripts, however, are a few pages of notes, headed 'Thistle', bMS Eng 1150 (31), which may well have been meant for this unwritten work. See *CW* x.
[4] This list appears on the third page of the letter.

To WILLIAM SHARP, [17 February 1886]
Text: Elizabeth A. Sharp, 116.[1] Printed in *LWP*.

...Your own beautiful dedication to D. G. R. seems to me *perfect*, and brought back, with great freshness, all I have felt, and so sincerely, about him and his work....

[1] According to Elizabeth A. Sharp, the letter refers to *Sonnets of This Century*, ed. and arranged by William Sharp (London: Walter Scott, 1886), which was released on 25 Jan. The volume was dedicated to Dante Gabriel Rossetti. Elizabeth Sharp comments that, '[t]o Walter Pater the Introductory Essay was "most pleasing and informing"', then quotes the sentence given above.

To WILLIAM STANLEY WITHERS,[1] 13 March [1886]
MS.: Manchester Central Library. Printed in *LWP*.

Brasenose College, | Oxford. | March 13.

Dear Sir,

Many thanks for your letter of March 7. It would have given me great pleasure to accept your proposal to lecture at Sale. But the truth is, my time is wholly occupied just now, in completing many unfinished pieces of literary work.

Be assured, I value greatly your kind expression of interest in my writings. 'Marius' is meant to be the first of a kind of trilogy of works, dealing with similar problems, under different historical conditions: in France, at the end of the 16th century; and in England, at the end of the 18th.

Should you visit Oxford at any time, I should be much pleased if you would give me a call. I am to be found at the address above, during the greater part of Term time.

Believe me, dear Sir,

Very truly yours
Walter Pater.

[1] William Stanley Withers (1862–1927), collector, was the Registrar of the Royal Manchester (now Royal Northern) College of Music from 1893 (when it was founded) to 1927. During World War I, he served as the Acting Principal and produced a history of the institution. It is not clear who was invited to lecture at Sale (a town in Trafford, Greater Manchester) before Pater.

To HELEN TROWER, 12 April [1886–93]
Ref.: Sotheby, Wilkinson & Hodge Catalogue (Sale of 27–29 July 1921), 86; and *American Book-Prices Current*, 55 (1949), 492.

Subject: Pater states that he is unable to accept an invitation to a dinner party hosted by Helen and Henry Seymour Trower and refers to going to Oxford for some months.

The letter is written from 12 Earl's Terrace—hence the dating (it can be assumed from the identity of dates and addresses that the letters listed in his sources are one and the same). Helen Trower's presentation copy of the 1888 Renaissance *is in the possession of Brasenose College.*

To LADY DILKE,[1] 27 May [1886]
MS.: British Library. A brief fragment was printed (and misquoted) by Sir Charles W. Dilke, 'Memoir', prefixed to Lady Dilke's *The Book of the Spiritual Life* (London: J. Murray, 1905), 90. Printed in *LWP*.

B. N. C. | May 27.

My dear Lady Dilke,

For a week past, day after day, something has prevented my fulfilling the pleasant duty of a few words of thanks for your new book which duly came to hand, and for the great pleasure it has given me.² The stories were certainly far too good to leave unprinted, and I can sincerely congratulate you on your success in this new line of literature. The combined care and simplicity of these charming pieces of writing, together with their intellectual weight of purpose, make them worthy of your pen: and then!—you, or your publishers, or both, have succeeded in making the volume charming in appearance. My best thanks for so choice a specimen of it. Ever, my dear Lady Dilke,

Very sincerely yours
Walter Pater.

¹ Emilia Francis Strong Pattison (1840–1904), art historian, critic, and trade unionist, widowed in 1884, married Charles Dilke in Oct. 1885. See Biographical Register.
² *The Shrine of Death and Other Stories* (London: George Routledge & Sons, 1886), a collection of nine allegorical fantasies. Sir Charles Dilke wrote that Lady Dilke kept three letters—Pater's and two others—in her copy of *The Shrine*. He adds that 'Pater differed from some of the newspaper critics, who thought the stories overwrought'. Qtd in Lady Dilke, *The Book of the Spiritual Life*, 90.

To ISABELLA STEWART GARDNER,¹ 1 October [1886]
MS: Archives, Isabella Stewart Gardner Museum, Boston.

12 Earl's Terrace | Kensington, W. | Oct. 1.

Dear Mrs. Gardner,

I greatly value the opinion of cultivated Americans in all matters of art and literature, and was much pleased to hear that you like my writings. I have been away from England, and only heard on my return, from our charming host of two months ago,² that you desired a bit of my writing to put into Marius.³ Why not put this there, and so record a very pleasant evening in a delightful house?

Please don't forget, when you come to England again, that my address in London is as above, and believe me,

Very truly yours,
Walter Pater.

¹ Isabella Stewart Gardner (1840–1924) was an American art collector, patron of artists, and philanthropist. From the late 1860s, she travelled extensively. When Gardner and her husband John visited London from 1 to 21 July 1886, Henry James introduced her to John Singer Sargent (the painter had met Pater by 1884; see above, 147, n. 4). Gardner and Sargent became friends and she was one of his most important American patrons. (Sargent's 1888 portrait of Gardner is housed in the Metropolitan Museum of Art, New York.) Gardner began collecting art seriously in the 1890s, sometimes on the advice of Bernard Berenson.

The Isabella Stewart Gardner Museum in Boston, designed to resemble a Renaissance Venetian palace, opened in 1903.

[2] Unknown. According to the travel diaries of John Lowell Gardner, on Tuesday, 13 July they 'Lunched with H. James. Miss Paget [Vernon Lee]. Mrs. Lawrence. Mrs. Mason. Mr. Roberts.' Pater is not mentioned in their diaries. None of Pater's letters from July to Sept. 1886 are extant.

[3] Gardner's copy of *Marius the Epicurean*, now housed in the Gardner Museum, is inscribed 'I. S. Gardner. | June, 1885'.

To MARC ANDRÉ RAFFALOVICH, 11 October [1886][1]
MS.: Blackfriars Priory, Oxford. Written on the front and the back of a correspondence card. Printed in Vernon, 'Pater's Letters to André Raffalovich', 194–5.

12 Earl's Terrace | October 11.

My dear Raffalovich,

Sincere thanks for your kind letter and thought of me. I leave for Oxford on Monday evening Oct. 18, but shall have much pleasure in lunching with you that day. Douglas Ainslie[2] is going away to Dresden very soon, for the winter.[3] He is dining with me tomorrow & I shall give him your message. I [have] no doubt he would be very pleased to come, but believe he leaves on Wednesday or Thursday. With our united very kind regards to yourself and Miss Gribbell.[4]

Ever

Very truly yours
Walter Pater.

My compliments to Madame Raffalovich.[5]

[1] Vernon determined the date by cross-referencing the dates in this letter with that of the letter to Ainslie, 6 Oct. [1887?] (Vernon, 'Pater's Letters to André Raffalovich', 197, n. 19).

[2] See letter to Ainslie, 7 June [1887].

[3] Probably visiting Mrs Greg, a friend of his uncle, Sir Mountstuart Elphinstone Grant Duff (1829–1906), Scottish politician and author (see Biographical Register). Grant Duff visited her in Dresden on 23 Oct. 1887. See Gosse, *Notes from a Diary, 1886-1888*, 201.

[4] Florence Truscott Gribbell, Raffalovich's governess in Paris and later his housekeeper in London from 1882 until her death in 1930, was a woman of ambition and strength. From indications in the diaries of Michael Field, Raffalovich and Gray were somewhat in awe of her. Vernon, 'Pater's Letters to André Raffalovich', 197, n. 22.

[5] Raffalovich's mother, Marie Raffalovich (1832–1921), a woman of great intelligence and beauty, was a friend of Ernest Renan and Claude Bernard. For many years she held a salon at 19 Avenue Hoche, Paris.

To EDMUND GOSSE, 24 October [1886]
MS.: Brotherton Collection, University of Leeds. On a correspondence card. Printed in *LWP*.

B. N. C. | Oct. 24.

My dear Gosse,

Many thanks for the copy of your letter to the Athenaeum.[1] It gave me sincere pleasure to see your ponderous antagonist so lightly, gracefully, promptly, overturned. With best wishes for the continued prosperity of your admirable book, and your work generally,
Believe me ever

Very truly yours
Walter Pater.

[1] Gosse wrote two letters, one to *The Times*, 19 Oct. 1886, 6, and one to the *Athenaeum*, 23 Oct. 1886, 534–5, in response to an attack launched against *From Shakespeare to Pope* (1885) by John Churton Collins (1848–1908), literary critic, extension lecturer, and polemicist (see Biographical Register). Gosse's book was based on his Clark Lectures at Trinity College, Cambridge, Michaelmas term 1884, and at the Lowell Institute at Boston, and repeated under the auspices of the Lowell Institute at Cornell, Harvard, and Yale, during the winter of 1884–5. Collins regarded Gosse as an amiable dilettante. When Cambridge University Press released Gosse's lectures in book form in Oct. 1885, Collins seized the opportunity to support his campaign to persuade officials at Oxford and Cambridge to teach English literature as an academic discipline. His review article in the *Quarterly Review*, 163 (Oct. 1886), 289–309, attacked 'both Gosse's social success among the literati and his ability to persuade academics that he was a scholar of consequence'. The attack left Gosse hurt, bewildered, indignant. His letters in *The Times* and the *Athenaeum* defended his scholarship and explained how hurtful this betrayal by a friend had been. This attempt to answer Collins's charges was not as successful as Pater believed. When the editor of the *Athenaeum* offered Collins space to reply, Collins concentrated on Gosse's errors and inaccuracies. Yet, Collins's attack aroused widespread sympathy for Gosse. Arnold, Browning, Swinburne, Tennyson, and others assisted with letters of support to newspapers and magazines, and authorities at Cambridge renewed his appointment. R. S. Ralston, as the spokesman for Trinity College, declared that 'Trinity is not willing to be dictated to by Mr. Collins, by the *World*, by the *Pall Mall Gazette*, or, indeed, by any other authority except its Visitor, the Queen' (*Athenaeum*, 6 Nov. 1886, 601).

To HERBERT HORNE,[1] 25 October [1886]
MS.: Mark Samuels Lasner Collection, University of Delaware. On a correspondence card. Printed in *LWP*.

B. N. C. | Oct. 25.

My dear Sir,

The 'Hobby Horse'[2] duly arrived. Your own learned and picturesque study on Inigo Jones I read with great interest.[3] It is certainly a delightful addition to one's knowledge of old London. I was also much struck by the fine illustration from Blake.

Accept my sincere thanks, and believe me

Very truly yours
Walter Pater.

¹ Herbert Percy Horne (1864–1916), poet, architect, typographer, and art historian, helped shape the Arts and Crafts Movement. See Biographical Register.

² Published quarterly from Apr. 1884 to Oct. 1894, the *Century Guild Hobby Horse* was the first major periodical committed to the visual arts (Arthur Mackmurdo founded the Guild; Horne served as the editor of the journal). Contributors included Selwyn Image, Oscar Wilde, and William De Morgan.

³ 'A Study of Certain Buildings Designed by Inigo Jones and yet Remaining in London', *Century Guild Hobby Horse*, 1 (Oct. 1886), 123–39. Facing page 121 of this number is a 'Facsimile of William Blake's broadsheet of "Little Tom the Sailor", from a unique copy, by kind permission of H. H. Gilchrist, Esq.'. Inigo Jones (1573–1652) was the first significant English architect to employ Vitruvian rules of proportion and symmetry to buildings.

To THE PALL MALL GAZETTE,¹ 27 November 1886
Text: *Pall Mall Gazette*, 27 November 1886, 1–2. Printed in *LWP*.

You have asked me to express an opinion on a proposal to establish here a School of English Literature. I have long had an interest in the teaching of young men at Oxford, and in the study of English literature; and proposals similar to this have from time to time occurred to me. The university has done little for English literature by way of direct teaching. Its indirect encouragement of what is best in English literature has, I think, been immense, as regards both the appreciation of what is old and the initiation of what is new. The university has been enabled to exercise this influence mainly as a consequence of its abundant and disinterested devotion, in the face of much opposition, to Greek and Latin literature—to the study of those literary productions wherein lie the sources of all our most salutary literary traditions, and which must always remain typical standards in literature, of a stirring interest in the matter together with absolute correctness in the form. I should, therefore, be no advocate for any plan of introducing English literature into the course of university studies which seemed likely to throw into the background that study of classical literature which has proved so effective for the maintenance of what is excellent in our own. On the other hand, much probably might be done for the expansion and enlivening of classical study itself by a larger infusion into it of those literary interests which modern literature, in particular, has developed; and a closer connection of it, if this be practicable, with the study of great modern works (classical literature and the literature of modern Europe having, in truth, an organic unity); above all, by the maintenance, at its highest possible level, of the purely literary character of those literary exercises in which the classical examination mainly consists.

An examination seems to run the risk of two opposite defects. Many of those who most truly enjoy this or that special study are jealous of examinations in it. The 'fine flower' of English poetry, or Latin oratory, or Greek art, might fade for them, in the long, pedantic, mechanical discipline (perhaps the 'cram') which is the necessary accompaniment of a system of examination; indispensable as that may nevertheless be for certain purposes. Intelligent Englishmen resort naturally for a liberal pleasure to their own literature. Why transform into a difficult exercise what is natural virtue in them? On the other hand, there are those who might give the preference to these studies for their fancied easiness, and welcome such a change in the interest of that desire to facilitate things, at any cost, the tendency of which is to suppress every kind of excellence born of strenuous labour, and, in literature especially, to promote what is lax and slipshod, alike in thought and expression. That is the last thing we require from the university, in an age already overloaded with the heavy, incondite, 'brute matter' of knowledge, and too bustling in its habits to think of that just management of its material which is precisely what we admire in the Greek and Latin writers. Much, then, would depend upon the details of the proposed scheme; that scheme itself possessing, perhaps, a more general interest than usually belongs to matters of the kind. Certainly it would show a poor sense of responsibility towards the interests of literature if one judged such a proposal as this on any other ground than its own intrinsic reasonableness.

---

[1] The chief article in the *Quarterly Review* for Oct. 1886 featured John Churton Collins's attack on the teaching of English literature at the universities (see letter to Gosse, 24 Oct. [1886]). The author was first thought to be Alfred Austin, but Collins was soon identified after the article generated a commotion in literary circles. Like other publications, the *Pall Mall Gazette* reported almost daily on the controversy (see 'The Literary Duel and its Lessons', *Pall Mall Gazette*, 30 Oct. 1886, 1). From 22 Oct. 1886 to 21 Jan. 1887 the paper ran a series of twelve articles entitled 'English at the Universities', showcasing eminent figures (including E. B. Benson, the Archbishop of Canterbury, F. J. Furnivall, W. E. Gladstone, T. H. Huxley, Max Müller, and Pater) who reflected on the much-debated question of whether or not the study of English literature should be established at Oxford and Cambridge. 'English at the Universities. IV' on 27 Nov. featured Pater and Frederic William Myers (1843–1901), the poet, classicist, and philologist. Pater approaches the topic as an 'interdisciplinary' academic, a teacher of philosophy who regards English literature as part of 'an organic unity' with other subjects, including the study of the Classics, philosophy, and European literature; he had already indicated his perspective in 'English Literature: Four Books for Students of English Literature', *The Guardian*, 17 Feb. 1886, 3–26; see *CW* v. Schools of English literature were eventually established at Oxford, in 1893, and at Cambridge, in 1917.

To ARTHUR SYMONS,[1] 2 December [1886]
Text: Transcript by Roger Lhombreaud.[2] Printed in *LWP*.

Brasenose College. | Dec. 2nd.

Dear Sir,

Accept my sincere thanks for your very interesting and useful volume on Browning, one of my best-loved writers.[3]

I have left Bradmore Road some time since; and my present address is as above, during the University term-time; otherwise, at 12, Earl's Terrace, Kensington; where I should be much pleased to make your acquaintance, should you be able at any time to give me a call. I am generally at home on Monday afternoons, when in London.

Very truly yours
Walter Pater.

[1] Arthur Symons (1865–1945), poet, critic, translator, and editor (see Biographical Register).
[2] In 1951 Roger Lhombreaud was given access to many of Symons's papers by Symons's sister-in-law, Lucy Featherston. Among them he found five letters from Pater (see letters to Symons, 2 Dec. [1886], 29 Oct. [1888], 23 Jan. [1889], [24 Mar. 1889], and 17 Jan. [1894], transcripts of which he gave to Lawrence Evans. About half of the letter dated 2 Dec. [1886] is quoted by Symons in 'Some Browning Reminiscences', *North American Review*, 204 (Oct. 1916), 603.
[3] *An Introduction to the Study of Browning* (London: Cassell, 1886), Symons's first book. In *A Study of Walter Pater* (London: C. J. Sawyer, 1932), 99, Symons notes that this letter was the first he received from Pater.

To HAROLD A. PETO,[1] 5 December [1886]
MS.: Brasenose College. Envelope: Harold A. Peto Esq. | 9 Collingham Gardens | S.W. Postmark: KENSINGTON BX JA 5 87. On a correspondence card.

12 Earl's Terrace, | Dec. 5.

Dear Mr. Peto,

I regret extremely not to be able to accept your kind invitation for Jan. 20th, as I have to return to Oxford on the 17th, and should not be able to be here again so soon after.

With many thanks,

Very sincerely yours
Walter Pater.

[1] Harold Ainsworth Peto (1854–1933), architect and garden designer, trained with J. Clements, in Suffolk, and worked with Karslake and Mortimer, London, before forming a partnership (1876–92) with Ernest George (1839–1922), architect and landscape and architectural watercolourist. The firm was immensely successful, designing and building prestigious mansions, including Collingham Gardens (1881–84), Kensington. He was elected Associate (1881) and Fellow (1884) of the Royal Institute of British Architects. Peto travelled widely, noting innovations in design and technology (elevators, steam heating, ventilation, sanitation) and introducing them into some of the commissions he and George carried out. He resigned from the partnership in 1892 and turned his attention to designing gardens and garden buildings.

To MARC ANDRÉ RAFFALOVICH, 11 December [1886]
MS.: Blackfriars Priory, Oxford. On the front and the back of a correspondence card. Printed in Vernon, 'Pater's Letters to André Raffalovich', 195.

12 Earl's Terrace | Dec. 11th.

My dear Raffalovich,

Your quaintly arranged book[1] arrived yesterday. Many thanks! I have already found much in it that is charming and original, and reminds me very pleasantly of the author. Mrs. Churson[2] seems to me to strike a new and very interesting note in poetry. I think some day you ought to expand this 'First Book'[3] into one almost six times as long. The mélange of sentiment and satire it presents is to me very fascinating. Much of it, however, is obscure. Sometimes, on the other hand, you seem to me to reach a quite perfect expression of difficult ideas; e.g. the stanza on the top of page 145.[4] I think that perfectly expressed. There is a pleasant sense of flowers and gaiety everywhere in the volume, together with the suggestion of a capacity for serious things. Excuse these first thoughts, and believe me

Most truly yours
Walter Pater.

[1] *In Fancy Dress* (London: Walter Scott, 1886).
[2] 'Mrs. Churson', a poem from *In Fancy Dress*, 123–46.
[3] 'Mrs. Churson' consists of an introductory stanza and bk 1 only.
[4] The stanza reads:

> He did not seek the end before beginning,
> And could be happy with a scarlet kiss,
> The first, and think the second worth the winning,
> More than the stern delight, analysis,
> Whose votaries beginning reach the end,
> And in the lover see the treacherous friend.
> Raffalovich, *In Fancy Dress*, 145.

To EDMUND GOSSE, 31 December [1886–92?]¹
Text: Maggs Bros. *Catalogue* no. 497 (1927), 204.

Dec. 31st.

...I enclose a little book which my friend, who came with me to see you, has asked me to forward....

[1] The letter is written on a correspondence card, and thus probably belongs to the period of Pater's residence in Kensington. It has been impossible to identify the friend or the book.

1887

To [?] HAROLD E. BOULTON,[1] 8 February [1887?][2]
MS.: Brasenose College. On a correspondence card. Printed in *LWP*.

B. N. C. | Feb. 8.

My dear Boulton,

I found your letters on my return to Oxford last night, and am sorry I was away when you were here. I hope to send you the MS. tomorrow afternoon.[3]

Very sincerely yours

Walter Pater.

[1] Possibly Sir Harold Edward Boulton (1859–1935), who was known as a poet and athlete while studying at Balliol College, 1878–81. He was one of the founders of *Waifs and Strays*, a students' arts magazine (June 1879–Feb. 1882). In 1884, he helped to establish Oxford House, in London's Bethnal Green area, a 'settlement' for the underprivileged. Boulton was a noted philanthropist and folklorist. The salutation suggests that Pater and his correspondent were good friends. Billie Inman conjectured that the recipient was Matthew Piers Watt Boulton (1820–94), classicist, amateur scientist, and inventor. Inman, 'Pater's Letters', 408.
[2] The letter can be dated 1887 because it was written on the same kind of correspondence card as the notes to Gosse, 24 Oct. [1886], Horne, 25 Oct. [1886], and Green, 10 Feb. [1887].
[3] Unidentified. Boulton published several essays in the *Fortnightly Review*: 'Houseless at Night', Feb. 1887; 'The Housing of the Poor', Feb. 1888, and 'A London House of Shelter', Feb. 1894.

To CHARLOTTE GREEN,[1] 10 February [1887]
MS.: Bates College. On a correspondence card. Printed in *LWP*.

Brasenose College, | Feb. 10.

Dear Mrs. Green,

Many thanks for your note, which has been forwarded to me here, and to Mrs. Ritchie[2] for her kind invitation. Alas! I shall not be in London again till the 24th. I wonder whether you could accompany me to Wimbledon on Saturday afternoon, Feb. 26th. It would give me great pleasure if you could, supposing that day were convenient to Mrs. Ritchie. I am reading Browning's new volume,[3] which well repays a little patience, and hope to bring it [to] you when I come to London.

Very faithfully yours
Walter Pater.

[1] Charlotte Byron Green, *née* Symonds (1842–1929), was an advocate for women's education; see Biographical Register.
[2] Anne Isabella Thackeray Ritchie (1837–1919), author; see Biographical Register. At the time of this letter she was residing at Southmead, the Wimbledon home of her mother-in-law.
[3] *Parleyings with Certain People of Importance in their Day* (London: Smith, Elder, 1887) appeared on 28 Jan.; Robert Browning was then seventy-five. In this volume of blank verse he reflects on a number of historical figures, including Bernard de Mandeville, Daniel Bartoli, and Christopher Smart. The phrase 'certain people of importance' derives from Dante's *La vita nuova*.

To AN UNKNOWN CORRESPONDENT, 18 March [1887?][1]
MS.: Alex Wong.

12 Earl's Terrace, W. | March 18th.

Dear Sir,

The prize essays,[2] four in number, accompany this: also the Latin verses. No Latin essays have been sent in. When you have done with them, kindly forward them to Mr. A. Godley,[3] at Magdalen College.

Faithfully yours
Walter Pater.

[1] This date is confirmed by the handwriting and by internal evidence.
[2] Presumably a reference to the Chancellor's Prizes, specifically to three categories: Latin Essay, Latin Verse, and English Essay. The *Oxford Magazine*, 4 May 1887, 166, notes that no award was made for composition in the first category.
[3] Alfred Denis Godley (1856–1925), classical scholar and writer, attended Balliol College, Oxford, 1874–8, where he won prizes for prose and poetry. After teaching classics at Bradfield College, Berkshire, 1879–82, he returned to Oxford in 1883, where he became Fellow and Tutor of Magdalen College, a post he held until he retired in 1912. Godley served as examiner for the classical Moderations programme at Magdalen College and for classical scholarships and prizes at the university (*The Times*, 29 July 1925, 16). The office of university Public Orator, which he occupied 1910–20, provided a significant venue for displaying his elegant command of Latin. His publications include editions and translations of Herodotus, Tacitus, and Horace, and volumes of poetry, such as *Lyra frivola* (London: Methuen, 1899).

To HAROLD A. PETO, 6 April [?1887]
MS: Archives, Isabella Stewart Gardner Museum, Boston. On a correspondence card.

12 Earl's Terrace | April 6.

My dear Peto,[1]

I shall think it very kind if you will speed the enclosed[2] on its second journey to America.

Very sincerely yours
Walter Pater.

[1] This more familiar salutation suggests a date subsequent to the letter of 5 Dec. [1886] to 'Dear Mr. Peto'.

[2] Unknown. It is possible that Pater was asking Peto to forward a letter to Isabella Stewart Gardner (see letter to Stewart, 1 Oct. [1886]).

To WALTER PATER, 12 April [1887]
MS.: British Library. Printed in *TBB*.

April 12 7

Dear Mr. Pater,

We found that there was no paper of the necessary size and quality for your book[1] to be bought ready made and I have therefore ordered a supply which will be in the printers' hands by the middle of next week without fail. You will not have been able to correct the proof sheets before then so no time will be lost.

I am

Yours very truly,
Frederick Macmillan.

Walter Pater Esq.
12 Earl's Terrace.

[1] *Imaginary Portraits* was published on 24 May 1887. See *CW* iii.

To WALTER PATER, 15 April [1887]
MS.: British Library. Printed in *TBB*.

April 15 7

Dear Mr. Pater,

I enclose a specimen of the type we propose to use for your new book. It will make 180 pages like this.

I also send a proof of the advertisement that has been set up for the May number of 'Macmillan'. It is very ugly and will have to be altered: if the extracts from the Reviews could be cut down it would be easier to make the advertisement look well. At present it is too crowded.

Believe me

Yours very truly,
Frederick Macmillan.

Walter Pater Esq.

To ARTHUR SYMONS, 19 April [1887]
MS.: University of Kansas. Envelope: Arthur Symons Esq. | Nuneaton. Postmark: KENSINGTON BX APR 19 W. On a correspondence card.

12 Earl's Terrace, W. | April 19.

Dear Mr. Symons,

Accept my sincere thanks for so generously sending me a copy of your 'Massinger'.[1] It is a charming volume in appearance, and your Introduction has struck me as a really interesting and graceful piece of criticism. I shall value it; and hope before long to make your acquaintance personally.

Very truly yours
Walter Pater.

---

[1] *Philip Massinger*, ed. Arthur Symons (London: T. Fisher Unwin, 1887), appeared (Apr.) in Unwin's Mermaid series, which reprinted texts from Elizabethan, Jacobean, and Restoration drama. See Symons's letter dated 26 Apr. 1887 to James Dykes Campbell, in *Arthur Symons: Selected Letters, 1880–1935*, ed. Karl Beckson and John M. Munro (Iowa City: University of Iowa Press, 1989), 24–6. See also the *Leeds Mercury*, 20 Apr. 1887, 3.

To FREDERIC LOUDON PATER,[1] 30 April [1887]
MS.: University of California at Los Angeles. On mourning paper. Printed in *LWP*.

12 Earl's Terrace, W. | April 30th.

Dear Fred,

Accept my sincere thanks for your kind letter. During the last four months my dear Brother's illness had taken a most serious turn, and about a month ago he felt obliged to resign his post at Stafford. He had been, with one or other of my sisters, at Hastings for many weeks past; and came to lodgings in London about a fortnight, or more, ago, partly for the sake of medical advice. He left us to our great grief on Sunday last, with less suffering than there might have been in a disease of that kind.[2] To the last he was hopeful and cheerful in moments of relief.

He was interred on Wednesday, at the cemetery, Highgate—a place associated with my memories of him as a boy. It would have been undesirable to delay the funeral; and only a few friends besides ourselves were present. Yourself, however, your brother, and others to whom he was attached, were in my thoughts about that time.

Our united thanks to you: also to Cousin Anne and Eleanor[3] for their kind messages, with sincere regards.

Very sincerely yours
W. H. Pater.

---

[1] Frederic Loudon Pater (1838–1901), merchant, was the second son of Joseph Pater of Liverpool, also a merchant of Liverpool, and cousin to Pater, William, Hester, and Clara. His brother, mentioned in the letter, was William Pater.

[2] William Thompson Pater died of heart disease on 24 Apr. 1887. Michael Levey notes that the words 'disease' and 'dropsy' appear on the death certificate (Levey, *The Case of Walter Pater* [London: Thames and Hudson, 1978], 220). *Appreciations* (1889) is dedicated to his memory (*CW* vi).

[3] Apparently, Ann Nash Pater (1810?–98), aunt to Frederic Pater and cousin to Richard Pater, Pater's father; and Eleanor Pater Comber (1837?–1925), sister to Frederic. The death of Ann Nash Pater, as indicated on her tombstone, was 5 Sept. 1898. The tombstone indicating the death of Eleanor Pater Comber has not been found.

To EDMUND GOSSE, 7 May [1887]

MS.: Brasenose College. Envelope: Edmund Gosse Esq. | Trinity College | Cambridge. Postmark: OXFORD W MY 7 87. On mourning paper. Printed in *LWP*.

B. N. C. | May 7th.

My dear Gosse,

Accept my warm thanks for your kind and tempting invitation, which has been forwarded to me here. Alas! we have been in much trouble lately in consequence of the death of my Brother, after a long and trying illness, and I hardly feel in the mood for visiting just at present.

On and about the ~~26th~~ \21st/, I must be in London. But I shall not forget your kind proposal to come to Cambridge; which, especially as your guest, I feel sure I should greatly enjoy, and hope to remind you of it at some future, but I hope not distant time.

With kind regards,

Ever very sincerely yours
Walter Pater.

To WILLIAM SHARP, 23 May [1887]

MS.: Brasenose College. On mourning paper. Printed in *LWP*.

12 Earl's Terrace, | Kensington. | May 23.

My dear Sharp,

Many thanks for your letter. My book[1] will be out tomorrow, and I have directed a copy of it to be sent to you, which please accept with very kind regards. I pondered the inclusion among the other pieces of the 'Child in the House', but found it would need many alterations, which I felt disinclined to make just then. I hope it may be included in some future similar series.

I leave for Oxford this evening, but hope to be here again before long. Very kind regards to Mrs. Sharp. Ever

Very sincerely yours
Walter Pater.

We lost my poor Brother about four weeks since.

---

[1] *Imaginary Portraits* appeared on 24 May 1887 (see *CW* iii).

To DOUGLAS AINSLIE,[1] 7 June [1887]
MS.: Bates College. On a correspondence card. Printed in *LWP*.

B. N. C. | June 7th.

Dear Mr. Ainslie,

I found your note on my return from London last night. It is undated; but I fancy *Friday* means Friday *June 10th*; in that case, I shall have much pleasure in lunching with you on that day.

Very truly yours
Walter Pater.

[1] Grant Duff Douglas Ainslie (1865–1948), Scottish poet, diplomat, translator, and critic (see Biographical Register).

To AN UNKNOWN CORRESPONDENT, 9 June [1887]
MS.: Brasenose College. On a postcard.

Brasenose College, | June 9th.

My dear Sir,

Thank you sincerely for your enthusiastic praise of 'Marius'. I have just published another book, entitled 'Imaginary Portraits'. I have seen Cambridge, and thought it a very beautiful place, though in a different way from Oxford. Should you ever be here, give me a call at Brasenose, where I am to be found during the greater part of term-time, and believe me

Very truly yours
Walter Pater.

To HERBERT HORNE, 17 June [1887]
MS.: Mark Samuels Lasner Collection, University of Delaware. On a correspondence card. Printed in *LWP*.

12 Earl's Terrace, | Kensington. W. | June 17.

My dear Mr. Horne,

I arrived here yesterday, and hoped to come to you in the evening as you so kindly proposed, but found it impossible. I hope I may have the pleasure some other time. Many thanks to you and Mr. Mackmurdo,[1] with kind regards.

Very sincerely yours
Walter Pater.

[1] Arthur Heygate Mackmurdo (1851–1942), architect, designer, and social reformer, helped to shape the Arts and Crafts Movement. In 1869, he apprenticed with architect Thomas Chatfield Clarke, and in 1873 worked for James Brooks, the Gothic Revival architect. That same year, he attended John Ruskin's School of Drawing and Fine Art, Oxford, and travelled with Ruskin to Italy in 1874. The following year he opened his own architectural practice in London. In 1877 he joined William Morris, Philip Webb, and others to organize the Society for the Protection of Ancient Buildings. With his friend Selwyn Image, he founded the Century Guild of Artists in 1882, producing wallpapers, fabrics, metal-work, and furniture. He took on Herbert Horne (1864–1916), poet, architect, and art historian (see Biographical Register) as a pupil (then a partner, in 1885). Although the Guild broke up in 1892, members remained in close association afterwards. Mackmurdo published *Wren's City Churches* (London: Hazell, Watson, and Viney, 1883), the first manifestation of Art Nouveau in Britain and Europe. From 1888, he concentrated on architectural work.

To SIR MOUNTSTUART GRANT DUFF, 23 June [1887][1]
MS.: Sheila Sokolov Grant. Printed in *LWP*.

12 Earl's Terrace, W. | June 23rd.

Dear Sir Mountstuart Grant-Duff,

It will give me great pleasure to accept your kind invitation on Sunday next at 8 o'clock.

Believe me

Very sincerely yours
Walter Pater.

[1] The year is pencilled on the MS., presumably by Grant Duff. In his diary entry for Sunday, 26 June 1887, Duff notes: 'Mr. Pater dined with us, and told me that about 3,000 copies of *Marius* had been sold, which seems to be thought a fair amount for a book of that character.' See Grant Duff, *Notes from a Diary 1886–1888*, 1: 144.

To HERBERT HORNE, [3 August 1887][1]
MS.: Mark Samuels Lasner Collection, University of Delaware. On a correspondence card. Printed in *LWP*.

Dear Mr. Horne,

I am just going into the country for a short time. Otherwise, I should have liked to accept your kind invitation.

Very truly yours
W. Pater.

In haste.

[1] The date is pencilled on the MS., presumably based on the postmark.

To GEORGE MOORE,[1] [c.3 August 1887]
Text: Paraphrased in George Moore, 'Avowals. VI. Walter Pater', *Pall Mall Magazine*, 33 (August 1904), 532.[2] Printed in *LWP*.

...*Pater wrote back—the letter he wrote was at once grave and timid—reproving me a little, I think; for after saying that he could not review the book in the* Guardian, *he said that the object of such writing was not very clear to him. Object was not the word—what word could he have used? Perhaps it was purpose, for certainly the purpose of such a story could not have been clear to him.... Without any stress of expression, he made me understand very well that descriptions of violent incidents and abnormal states of mind do not serve the purpose of art, the purpose of art not being to astonish or to perplex. He made me understand that the object of art is to help us to forget the crude and the violent, to lead us towards certain normal aspects of nature....*

[1] George Augustus Moore (1852–1933), Anglo-Irish poet, playwright, critic, and novelist (see Biographical Register).
[2] This, the earliest text, is preferable to the revised versions in *Avowals*, because of its greater specificity. Moore confesses that he lost both this letter and the letter dated [c.9 Aug. 1887]. In the *Pall Mall Magazine*, 33 (Aug. 1904), 527–33, he introduces his paraphrase with these words: 'remembering that he wrote essays for the *Guardian*, I sent him a book about a girl who met an ugly accident on the Sussex downs.' The book Moore invited Pater to review was his naturalistic novel, *A Mere Accident* (London: Vizetelly, 1887), the story of an ascetic young man who seeks to bury his homosexual inclinations in a loveless marriage; the 'ugly accident' alluded to is the rape of the heroine by a tramp. Moore omitted the novel from later editions of his works.

To ARTHUR SYMONS, 9 August [1887]
MS.: Roger A. Lhombreaud. Addressed: Arthur Symons Esq. | Coton Road | Nuneaton. Postmark: PADDINGTON L5 AU 9 87. Printed in *LWP*.

12 Earl's Terrace, W. | Aug. 9th.

My dear Mr. Symons,

Accept my sincere thanks for your letter of July 30th and for so kindly sending me your article in 'Time', which I have read carefully and on the whole with much pleasure.[1] It strikes me as the work of a really critical mind and a well-skilled pen, and I feel grateful for it. I was sorry not to have seen you when you called here, and hope I may have the pleasure of meeting you here or in Oxford before long. Don't forget me when you visit either place next; and, if you can, drop me a line beforehand.

I start in a few days for a holiday of five weeks or so in France.

Success to your own most interesting literary work.

Very sincerely yours
Walter Pater.

[1] Symons's review of *Imaginary Portraits* (1887) appeared in *Time*, ns 6 (Aug. 1887), 157–62. Symons is enthusiastic, yet he makes the familiar charge that Pater failed to endow his characters with effective, independent life.

To GEORGE MOORE, [*c*.9 August 1887]
MS.: Morgan Library & Museum (MA 4500). Written on a correspondence card. Paraphrased in *LWP*. Printed in Inman, 'Pater's Letters at Pierpont Library', *English Literature in Transition*, 34.4 (1991), 410–12.

12 Earl's Terrace, W.

My dear Moore,

I have just seen, by accident, a chapter of your 'Confessions of a young man',[1] and have read it with great admiration of its freshness and gaiety, only enhanced by a touch of satire which runs through it. Your critical lights by the way are of great interest. After my unsympathetic letter the other day,[2] I can't help sending a hurried line to tell you this.
Ever

Very truly yours
Walter Pater.

[1] Chapters 3 and 4 of Moore's novel, *Confessions of a Young Man* (1888), appeared in the same issue of *Time*, ns 6 (Aug. 1887), as Symons's review of *Imaginary Portraits*. Billie Andrew Inman suggests that after he acknowledged receiving the review, Pater took the opportunity to write to Moore. See Inman, 'Pater's Letters at the Pierpont Library', 411.
[2] See above.

To WILLIAM BELL SCOTT,[1] 23 September [1887]
MS.: Mark Samuels Lasner Collection, University of Delaware.

12 Earl's Terrace, W. | Sept. 23.

My dear Scott,

I ought to have written weeks and weeks ago to thank you for your kind and valuable present of the 'Illustrations to the King's Quair'.[2] It reached me at a very busy moment, and then came my summer holiday in France, from which I returned here not long since. Accept my sincere thanks now, though so late. I read with great interest the charming souvenirs of your introduction; and think the illustrations themselves a genuine addition to poetic art. It is well that they should have been etched for the sake of a larger number than can have the opportunity of seeing the originals. For subject and treatment, I think I like no. ii best. It seems to carry out certain delightful veins of sentiment to their [utmost] expression. Accept our united kind regards to yourself, to Mrs. Scott and Miss Boyd, and believe me

Very truly yours
Walter Pater.

[1] William Bell Scott (1811–90), Scottish poet and painter, was a well-known figure hovering at the periphery of Pre-Raphaelite art and literature. See letter to Scott, 18 June [1872–73], n. 1.

[2] Scott produced a series of etchings based on his paintings of the circular staircase at Penkill Castle, 1865–8; he called the work *Illustrations to the Kingis Quair of James I of Scotland* (Edinburgh: privately printed by T. & A. Constable, 1887), and sent copies to his friends and acquaintances. His subject, the *Kingis Quair*, a dream vision in verse written by James I of Scotland, describes how he was captured and imprisoned and how he fell in love with a British noblewoman, Joan Beaufort. It is preserved in the Bodleian Library, MS Arch. Seldon. B. 24.

To HERBERT HORNE, 3 October [1887]
MS.: Mark Samuels Lasner Collection, University of Delaware. On a correspondence card. Printed in *LWP*.

12 Earl's Terrace, | Oct. 3.

My dear Mr. Horne,

Accept my sincere thanks for your pretty edition of Herrick,[1] my acquaintance with whom it will induce me to enlarge, and in reading him I shall look to your notes with great interest. I shall hope to see you before I leave for Oxford, and remain

Very truly yours
Walter Pater.

[1] *Hesperides: Poems by Robert Herrick*, ed. Herbert P. Horne and Introduction by Ernest Rhys (London: W. Scott, 1887) appeared in Sept.

To DOUGLAS AINSLIE, 6 October [1887][1]
MS.: Bates College. On a correspondence card. Printed in *LWP*.

12 Earl's Terrace, W. | Oct. 6th.

My dear Ainslie,

I was pleased to get your note, but alas! we are engaged on Sunday. Please come and dine on Tuesday at 7.30, and give pleasure to

Yours very truly
Walter Pater.

[1] The sequence of dates, as well as the gilt-edged off-white correspondence card used by Pater, suggests 1887. Sunday was 9 Oct.; Tuesday, 11 Oct.

To GEORGE BAINTON,[1] [October 1887–1889?[2]]
Text: George Bainton, *The Art of Authorship: Literary Reminiscences, Methods of Work, and Advice to Young Beginners* (London: James Clarke & Co, 1890), 292–4. Printed in Gerald Monsman, 'Two Pater Letters to George Bainton', *Pater Newsletter*, 63 (Spring 2013), 73–5.

I wish I could send you anything helpful towards the matter on which you have asked my opinion. It would take me a long time to formulate the rules, conscious or unconscious, which I have followed in my humble way. I think they would, one and all, be reducible to *Truthfulness*—truthfulness, I mean, to one's own inward impression. It seems to me that all the excellencies of composition, clearness, subtlety, beauty, freedom, severity, and any others there may be, depend upon the exact propriety with which language follows or shapes itself to the consciousness within. True and good elaboration of style would, in this way, come to be the elaboration, the articulation to oneself of one's own meaning, one's real condition of mind. I suppose this is the true significance of that often quoted saying, that style is the man. Of course models count for much. As beginners, at least, we are all learners. I think Tennyson and Browning, in quite opposite ways, have influenced me more than prose writers. And I have come to think that, on the whole, Newman is our greatest master of prose, partly on account of the variety of his excellence.[3]

[1] Revd George Bainton (1847–1925), who grew up in London, studied to be a minister in the Congregational Church. He and his wife, Mary Cave, had one son, Edgar Leslie Bainton, who became a composer of church music and operatic works. Bainton secured a position at a church in Coventry. From there, he solicited the responses published in *The Art of Authorship*, asking an international array of authors to discuss four topics: their style of writing, advice for training young authors, methods used for literary composition, and the names of those writers who had influenced them. The 178 contributors included Robert Browning, Hall Caine, Marie Corelli, Dinah Maria Craik, Edward Dowden, Francis Galton, Thomas Hardy, Thomas Huxley, Jean Ingelow, Henry James, Benjamin Jowett, Andrew Lang, Vernon Lee, James Russell Lowell, George Meredith, Louise Chandler Moulton, Christina Rossetti, Samuel Smiles, Leslie Stephen, John Addington Symonds, and Hippolyte Taine. Pater's letter appears in the 'Truthfulness to One's Self' section.
[2] Robert Browning and Thomas Hardy replied to Bainton's request in Oct. 1887, Marie Corelli in Sept. 1888. Pater may have been in the second group of authors Bainton contacted. The book was published in May 1890.
[3] For Pater's unfinished essay on 'Cardinal Newman', see *CW* x.

To AN UNKNOWN CORRESPONDENT,[1] [1887–94][2]

MS.: Michael Seeney. The text printed here represents the second and the fourth sections of a piece of paper (twice the size of a correspondence card) that has been folded in half and later torn in half, perhaps by a collector of autographs. This would explain why the first line is partially legible and why there is a gap between the sections.

...your very kind [invitation for] Nov. 4th; but as I come to London chiefly to see my sister I don't like to leave her on the first evening of my visit. I shall therefore hope to make the acquaintance of your...

...old favourite of mine—in France.

With kind regards,

Very sincerely yours
(and with many thanks)
Walter Pater.

Many thanks also for kind thoughts about Pansy![3]

[1] Presumably a casual acquaintance, judging by the tone.
[2] Arguably, Pater wrote this letter during term-time and refers to Hester, the sister who looked after the Pater home, 12 Earl's Terrace, Kensington.
[3] Very likely one of the cats that the Paters owned over the years.

To HERBERT HORNE, 2 November [1887]

MS.: Mark Samuels Lasner Collection, University of Delaware. On a correspondence card. Printed in *LWP*.

B. N. C. | Nov. 2.

My dear Mr. Horne,

I am very sorry not to be able to accept your kind invitation as I am already engaged. Many thanks. I should like much to meet Mr. Selwyn Image,[1] and should be glad if you could bring him some Monday afternoon when I am in London.

I hope the deserved prosperity of the 'Hobby Horse' may continue; but, alas! my hands are so full of work just now that it would be insincere of me to promise anything as you so kindly propose, and I should be so glad to do, were there any likelihood of my being able to fulfil my promise.[2]

Very sincerely yours
Walter Pater.

¹ Selwyn Image (1849–1930), poet and designer, studied at New College, Oxford, 1868–72, during which time he also attended the Ruskin School of Drawing. He was ordained deacon, 1872, and priest, 1873; he later served as curate in several parishes. His designs for stained glass were included in the Paris International Exhibition of 1878. In 1882, he resigned from holy orders and helped Arthur Heygate Mackmurdo (1851–1942), architect, designer, and social reformer, found the Century Guild; in 1884 he helped to establish the *Century Guild Hobby Horse*, which he co-edited, 1886–92, with Herbert Horne (see Biographical Register). Image became Master of the Workers' Guild in 1900 and Slade Professor of Fine Art at Oxford, 1910–16. Horne may have introduced Pater and Image, who contributed a favourable review of *Imaginary Portraits* in the *Century Guild Hobby Horse*, 3 (Jan. 1888), 14–16. Image was one of the few figures to defend Wilde during and after his 1895 trials.
² Pater never contributed to the *Century Guild Hobby Horse*.

To FALCONER MADAN, 13 November [1887]¹
MS.: Bodleian Library. Printed in *LWP*.

B. N. C. | Nov. 13.

My dear Madan,

Sincere thanks for your kindness. The old edition was what I wanted.² It was that in which I read the Life [long] ago and found it so charming that I wished to have a copy on my shelves. I willingly enclose 4 shillings for the same and am glad to have it for so little.

Very sincerely yours
W. H. Pater.

I return the 1848 copy with this.

¹ The year is pencilled on the MS., presumably by Madan; the gilt-edged off-white correspondence card used by Pater at that time supports this conclusion.
² Possibly Thomas Noon Talfourd's *Letters of Charles Lamb, with a Sketch of his Life* (London: Edward Moxon, 1837), the 1848 version of which is entitled *Final Memorials of Charles Lamb*. Pater alludes to Talfourd twice in his essay, 'The Character of the Humourist: Charles Lamb', *Fortnightly Review*, ns 30 (Oct. 1878), 466–74, collected in *Appreciations* (1889); see *CW* vi.

To WALTER PATER, 15 November [1887]
MS.: British Library. Printed in *TBB*.

Nov. 15. 7

Dear Mr. Pater,

I am forwarding the revised copy[1] of your Renaissance to Clark [and] also will send you proofs forthwith. You have not forgotten, I hope, that the Americans are expecting a photograph of you.[2]

Believe me

Yours very truly,
Frederick Macmillan.

[1] The third edition of *The Renaissance*, with the 'Conclusion' restored, appeared late in May or early June 1888. See 'Literary Gossip', *Athenaeum*, 7 Apr. 1888, 437.

[2] The familiar portrait of Pater was taken two years later, in summer 1889, possibly for his fiftieth birthday, by Elliott & Fry, two of the most eminent portrait photographers of the age. It was used as the frontispiece in *Greek Studies* (1895). Little is known about Joseph John Elliott or Clarence Edmund Fry, who formed a partnership in 1863 (dissolved 1893). In 1880, H. Baden Pritchard, editor of *The Year-Book of Photography*, recorded his impressions of their studio on Baker Street; see *The Photographic Studios of Europe* (London: Piper & Carter, 1882), 42–5. The fee was one guinea (somewhat higher than average), which entitled the sitter to eighteen *cartes de visite* or six cabinet photographs after a ten-minute sitting. Fry made every effort to put his sitters at ease before going to the studio. No fewer than seven dressing rooms were fitted up to this end.

To [?] HAROLD E. BOULTON,[1] 17 November [1887]
MS.: Morgan Library & Museum (MA 4500). Printed in Inman, 'Pater's Letters at the Pierpont Library', 407.

B. N. C. | Nov. 17.

My dear Boulton,

It will give me much pleasure to accept your kind invitation tomorrow at 1.30.

Yours very truly
W. H. Pater.

[1] See letter to Boulton above, 8 Feb. [1887?]; 178.

To WILLIAM SHARP, 23 November [1887]
Text: Elizabeth A. Sharp, 133. Printed in *LWP*.

Brasenose College, | Nov. 23d.

My dear Sharp,

I am reading your short life of Shelley[1] with great pleasure and profit. Many thanks for your kindness in sending it. It seems to me that with a full, nay! an enthusiastic, appreciation of Shelley and his work, you unite a shrewdness and good sense rare in those who have treated this subject. And then your book is pleasant and effective, in contrast to a French book on Shelley[2] of which I read reluctantly a good deal lately. Your book leaves a very definite image on the brain.

With sincere kind regards,

Very truly yours
Walter Pater.

[1] William Sharp, *Life of Percy Bysshe Shelley* (London: Walter Scott, 1887), appeared in the Great Writers series, ed. Eric Sutherland Robertson (1857–1926), a Scottish *belle-lettrist* and former editor of the *Magazine of Art*.

[2] Probably Félix Rabbe, *Shelley. Sa vie et ses oeuvres* (Paris: Nouvelle libraire parisenne, 1887).

To MESSRS. R. & R. CLARK,[1] 1 December [1887]
MS.: Brasenose College. Printed in *LWP* and *TBB*.

Brasenose College, | Oxford. | Dec. 1st.

Dear Sir,

I send you by this post some more copy of 'The Renaissance'. I find your compositor has a way of forcing (I think) every chapter to end at the end of a page, which seems to me not desirable: and although some new matter has been added, he has gained by about 4 pages on the original copy, which, as the book is not a long one, is disadvantageous. Please note that the added chapter on *The School of Giorgione* is to be printed *between* those on *Leonardo da Vinci* and *Joachim du Bellay*.[2]

Very truly yours
Walter Pater.

After Saturday, until further notice, my address will be
12 Earl's Terrace | Kensington | London. W.

[1] See letter to Macmillan, 16 June [1885], n. 2.
[2] Pater's recommendations were acted upon: in the third edn of *The Renaissance*, the Preface, 'Conclusion', and four of the nine chapters do not 'end at the end of a page', and 'The School of Giorgione' is inserted as directed.

1888

To ARTHUR SYMONS, 8 January [1888]
MS.: Brasenose College. Envelope: Arthur Symons Esq. | Coton Road | Nuneaton. Postmark: KENSINGTON BX JA 10 [88].[1] Printed in *LWP*.

           12 Earl's Terrace, | Kensington, W. | Jan. 8.
My dear Mr. Symons,

 I feel much flattered at your choosing me as an arbiter in the matter of your literary work, and thank you for the pleasure I have had in reading carefully the two poems you have sent me.[2] I don't use the word 'arbiter', loosely, for 'critic'; but suppose a real controversy, on the question whether you shall spend your best energies in writing verse, between your poetic aspirations on the one side, and prudence (calculating results) on the other. Well! Judging by these two pieces, I should say that you have a poetic talent, remarkable, especially at the present day, for \precise and/ intellectual grasp on a process \the/ matter it deals with. Rossetti, I believe, said that the value of all \every/ artistic product<s> was in direct proportion to the amount of purely intellectual force that went to the initial conception of it;[3] and it and it is just this intellectual \conception/ which seems to me to be so conspicuously wanting in what, in some ways, is the most characteristics verse of our time, especially that of our secondary poets. In your own pieces, particularly in the \your/ MS. 'A Revenge', I find Rossetti's requirement fulfilled, and should anticipate great things from one who has the talent of conceiving his motive with so much firmness and tangibility—with that close logic, if I may say so, which is an element in every genuinely imaginative process. It is clear to me that you aim at this, and it is what gives your verses, to my mind, great interest.

 Otherwise, I think the two pieces of unequal excellence, greatly preferring 'A Revenge' to 'Bell in Camp'. Reserving some doubt whether the watch, as the lover's gift, is not a little bourgeois, I think this piece worthy of any poet. It has that air of concentration and organic unity which I value greatly ## both in prose and verse. 'Bell in Camp' pleases me less, for the same reason which makes me put Rossetti's 'Jenny', and some of Browning's pathetic-satiric pieces below the rank which many assign them. In no one of the poems I am thinking of, is the inherent sordidness of everything in the persons supposed except the one poetic trait then under treatment, quite forgotten. Otherwise, I feel the pathos, the humour, of the piece (in the full sense of the word humour) and the skill with which you have worked out your motive therein.

I think the present age an unfavourable one to poets, at least in England. The young poet comes into a generation which has produced a large amount of first-rate poetry, and an enormous amount of good secondary poetry. You know I give a high place to the literature of prose as a fine art, and therefore hope you won't think me brutal in saying that the admirable qualities of your verse are those also of imaginative prose; as I think is the case also with much of Browning's finest verse. I should say, make prose your principal *metier*, as a man of letters, and publish your verse as a more intimate gift for those who already value you for your pedestrian work in literature. I should think you ought to find no difficulty in finding a publisher for poems such as those you have sent to me.

I am more than ever anxious to meet you. Letters are such poor means of communication. Don't come to London without making an appointment to come and see me here.

Very sincerely yours
Walter Pater.

[1] Symons printed this letter, with a few minor errors, on at least three occasions. In his Introduction to *The Renaissance* (New York: Modern Library, 1919), xvii, he calls this 'the most interesting letter which I ever had from him, the only letter which went to six pages'.

[2] 'A Revenge' and 'Bell in Camp' were included in Symons's first volume of poetry, *Days and Nights* (London: Macmillan, 1889).

[3] 'Conception, my boy, FUNDAMENTAL BRAINWORK, that is what makes the difference in all art. Work your metal as much as you like, but first take care that it is gold and worth working. A Shakspearean sonnet is better than the most perfect form, because Shakspeare wrote it'. Pater read D. G. Rossetti's famous dictum in T. Hall Caine's *Recollections of Dante Gabriel Rossetti* (London: Elliott Stock, 1882), 249.

To WALTER PATER, 18 January [1888]
MS.: British Library. Printed in *TBB*.

Jan. 18. 8

Dear Mr. Pater,

The paper on which the last edition of your 'Studies in the Renaissance' was printed was a rather expensive one, & we cannot get a paper not unlike it in appearance but a good deal cheaper which I cannot half [think] would do so well. I send you a book ('Neaera')[1] printed on this cheap paper that you may judge of its appearance. It would have to be made in a different size & rather thicker for your book but the quality would be the same. The difference in cost will amount to about £15 on the edition. Please let me know what you think about it.

Yours very truly,
Frederick Macmillan.

Walter Pater Esqre.

¹ *Neaera: A Tale of Ancient Rome*, by J. W. Graham, was published by Macmillan in 1886. John William Graham (1859–1932), writer and activist, was Tutor (1886–97) in Mathematics and Principal (1897–1924) of Dalton Hall, the Quaker residence at Owens College (later, the University of Manchester). He was a significant figure in Quaker intellectual life, lecturing and campaigning against vivisection and militarism. His books include *The Destruction of Daylight: A Study of the Smoke Problem* (London: George Allen, 1907).

To HERBERT HORNE, 18 January [1888]
MS.: Mark Samuels Lasner Collection, University of Delaware. On a correspondence card. Printed in *LWP*.

Brasenose College | Oxford. | Jan. 18.

Dear Mr. Horne,

Will you give me the pleasure of your company at dinner on Saturday, Jan. 28, at a quarter before eight: at *12 Earl's Terrace*. Will you forward the accompanying card to Mr. Image, and send reply to the *address above*.

Yours very truly
Walter Pater.

To EDWARD BRADFORD TITCHENER,[1] 18 February [1888][2]
MS.: Cornell University. On correspondence cards.

B. N. C. | Feb. 18.

Dear Mr. Titchener,

I send subjects for an essay.

Yours truly
Walter Pater.

Various Theories of the Origin of Morals:
or, Utilitarianism:
or, Darwinism in Morals.

Plato, viewed in connexion with the intellectual and political influences of his own day.

[1] Edward Titchener (1867–1927), a psychologist, studied at Brasenose 1885–9, and received a 'double first' in classics. He spent an additional year at Oxford, 1890, to study physiology. In Leipzig, he studied under Wilhelm Wundt, earning his PhD in psychology (1892). He then became Assistant Professor of Psychology at Cornell University, where he contributed to the emerging field of structuralism. He delineated his views on the mind in *Experimental Psychology: A Manual of Laboratory Practice*, 4 vols (London: Macmillan, 1901–5) and served as the American editor of *Mind* from 1895 to 1920. Titchener's recollections of Pater's informal lecturing style are invaluable. The classes took place in Pater's rooms; Pater was sitting at the side of an open hearth, before a little table, on which 'lay a neat pile of oblong slips of paper'. Each slip of paper conveyed some aspect of the subject at hand. Pater shuffled the slips this way and that, like a pack of cards, and decided the final arrangement only after testing and re-testing. See Titchener, 'Walter Horatio Pater', *Book Reviews*, 2 (Oct. 1894), 201–5. See also William F. Shuter, 'Pater's Reshuffled Text', *Nineteenth-Century Literature*, 43.4 (1989), 500–25, and *CW* vii.

[2] Dated on the basis of internal evidence, and the letter to Titchener dated 8 May [1888], 201.

To BERNARD BERENSON,[1] 16 February [1888]
MS.: Biblioteca Berenson, Villa I Tatti, Florence. Envelope: To | Mr. Bernhard Berenson | 31 Holywell Street. Printed in *LWP*.

Brasenose College. | Feb. 16.

Dear Sir,

I would gladly admit you to my lectures were they of a public character, or, in the full sense, lectures at all. As a matter of fact they consist of informal instruction to the undergraduates of my college, and the course is now drawing to an end.

Believe me

Very truly yours
Walter Pater.

[1] Bernard Berenson, born Bernhard Valvrojenski (1865–1959), the Lithuanian-American historian of Italian art. Berenson studied at Harvard University, 1884–7, under Charles Eliot Norton and William James, and read Pater and John Addington Symonds with great interest. After graduating, he took the Grand Tour; his interests shifted to the visual arts. In Jan. 1888, he settled in Oxford for a term, where he met Lionel Johnson, Herbert Horne, Jean-Paul Richter (who urged him to read Giovanni Morelli), and Oscar Wilde, whose advances he rejected. He met and fell in love with Mary Whitall Smith, sister of Logan Pearsall Smith and Alys Pearsall Smith (the first wife of Bertrand Russell). Berenson and Mary married in 1900 and settled in Villa I Tatti near Florence, where they developed their brand of connoisseurship, advising major art galleries and art collectors. They collaborated on all aspects of the business; Mary produced the notes that became many of his books, starting with *The Venetian Painters of the Renaissance* (New York and London: G. P. Putnam's Sons, 1894), which was issued under Berenson's name. Although Berenson never met Pater, he constantly read and re-read his writings, clarifying his own ideas and sensations.

To MARY ARNOLD WARD, [26 February? 1888][1]
MS.: Mary Moorman. The last sentence is printed in Mrs Humphry Ward, *A Writer's Recollections* (1918), 245. Printed in *LWP*.

B. N. C. | Sunday.

My dear Mrs. Ward,

One brief word of congratulation on having brought your long labour to so worthy a conclusion as I feel R. E. to be. I am reading it with very great interest and readiness, and shall soon have finished it; and then I hope you will kindly read my longer observations about it.

It is a chef d'oeuvre after its kind, and justifies the care you have devoted to it.

Very sincerely yours
Walter Pater.

[1] Feb. 26 was the first Sunday after the publication of Ward's *Robert Elsmere* (1888) in 3 volumes. The review to which Pater alludes appeared in *The Guardian*, 28 Mar. 1888, 468–9 (see *CW* v). The only other dates possible for this letter are 4, 11, 18, and 25 Mar.

To GEORGE MOORE, 4 March [1888]
MS.: Harvard University.[1] Printed in *LWP*.

Brasenose College, | Mar: 4.

My dear, audacious, Moore,

Many thanks for the 'Confessions', which I have read with great interest, and admiration of your originality—your delightful criticisms—your Aristophanic joy, or at least enjoyment, in life—your unfailing liveliness. Of course, there are many things in the book I don't agree with. But then, in the case of so satiric a book, I suppose one is hardly expected to agree or disagree.—what I cannot doubt of is the literary faculty displayed. 'Thou com'st in such a questionable shape!'[2]—I feel inclined to say, on finishing your book: 'shape'—morally, I mean; not in reference to style.

You speak of my own work very pleasantly,[3] but ## my enjoyment has been independent of that. And still I wonder how much you may be losing, both for yourself and for your writings, by what, in spite of its gaiety and good-nature and genuine sense of the beauty of many things, I must still call a cynical, and therefore exclusive, way of looking at the world. You call it only 'realistic'. Still—!

With sincere wishes for the future success of your most entertaining pen,

Very sincerely yours
Walter Pater.

[1] Moore first printed this letter (somewhat inaccurately) in 'Avowals. VI. Walter Pater', *Pall Mall Magazine*, 33 (Aug. 1904), 527–33, and reprinted it in all editions of *Confessions of a Young Man* issued from 1917 on, and in all editions of *Avowals*. See letter to Moore, [*c*.3 Aug. 1887], n. 2.
[2] Shakespeare, *Hamlet*, I.iv.43.
[3] Moore spends several pages in *Confessions* praising *Marius the Epicurean*, 'the book to which I owe the last temple of my soul' (1888 edn, 288–92; 1937 edn, 139–41).

To WALTER PATER, 12 March [1888]
MS.: British Library. Printed in *TBB*.

Walter Pater Esq.

Mar. 12.

Dear Mr. Pater,

A proof of the steel plate on the title page of your *Renaissance* printed in purple ink was sent to Earl's Terrace last week for your approval. As we have heard nothing from you I presume you must be at Oxford. We shall be glad to know as soon as possible whether the colour is as you wish in order that the printing may proceed.

I am

Yours very truly,
Frederick Macmillan.

To WALTER PATER, 27 March [1888]
MS.: British Library. Printed in *TBB*.

Walter Pater Esq.

Mar. 27.

Dear Mr. Pater,

We sent you another proof of the vignette for the *Renaissance* which I hope you like better than the first. I am afraid it still has something of the roughness of which you complained: this seems to be the fault of the coloured ink.

I am

Yours very truly,
Frederick Macmillan.

To HERBERT HORNE, 3 April [1888][1]
MS.: Mark Samuels Lasner Collection, University of Delaware. On a correspondence card. Printed in *LWP*.

12 Earl's Terrace. | April 3rd.

Dear Mr. Horne,

If you have nothing else to do, will you dine with us on Friday next at 7.30.?

Very sincerely yours
Walter Pater.

[1] The year is pencilled on the MS., presumably from the postmark. 'Friday next' was 6 Apr. 1888.

To DOUGLAS AINSLIE, 5 April [1888?][1]
MS.: Bates College. On a correspondence card. Printed in *LWP*.

12 Earl's Terrace, W. | April 5.

My dear Ainslie,

I grieve to think how long I have left your letter unanswered, having hoped before this at least to have thanked you for it. I can't wait any longer for the opportunity of writing at length; so just send this off, on the chance of its finding you still at Dresden. I shall be in London till April 23; and then at intervals, as usual, during Term time. Your own time at Dresden must be almost at an end, and I suppose you will be returning to England. Come and see me when you come to London, and if possible make an appointment beforehand.

Very sincerely yours
Walter Pater.

[1] The various dates given in the letter, especially 23 Apr., when term began in 1888, and the plain-edged off-white correspondence cards used, suggest 1888. Ainslie may or may not have been in Germany at this time.

To EDWARD BRADFORD TITCHENER, 8 May [1888]
MS.: Cornell University. On correspondence cards.

B. N. C. | May 8th.

Dear Mr. Titchener,

I only found your note last night, on my return here. Please bring two essays on Wednesday, May 16th, at 9 o'clock. I give a subject on the other side.

Very truly yours
Walter Pater.

Plato, viewed in connexion with the intellectual and political influence of his own day.
The dialectic of Pl[ato]:
The Theory of art Pl[ato]:
The Ideal of Republic:

To HERBERT HORNE, 24 May [1888]
MS.: Mark Samuels Lasner Collection, University of Delaware. On a correspondence card. Printed in *LWP*.

Brasenose College, | May 24th.

Dear Mr. Horne,

I only returned to Oxford late last night, and am engaged this evening. Also, I have to attend a meeting at 2 tomorrow.[1] If however you could lunch with me here, quite quietly, tomorrow, at 1 o'clock, it would give me much pleasure to make your acquaintance at last, in person.

Very truly yours
Walter Pater.

[1] Probably one of the college meetings, usually held on Friday afternoon.

To NORMAN MACCOLL,[1] 3 June [1888]
MS.: Steven J. Eisner. Printed in *LWP*.

12 Earl's Terrace. | June 3.

My dear MacColl,

Many thanks for the 'Select Plays of Calderon',[2] which I feel I don't deserve, as I am ignorant of Spanish. I wish I could read Calderon under your guidance, and profit by all the taste and scholarship that would secure. I have been greatly interested in the General Introduction.

With kind regards,

Very sincerely yours
Walter Pater.

[1] Norman MacColl (1843–1904), Scottish editor and Spanish scholar, attended Christ's College and Downing College, Cambridge, 1862–6, becoming a Fellow of Downing College in 1869. MacColl moved to London in 1872, studied law at Lincoln's Inn, and began practising law in 1875. His vocation, however, was journalism; he edited the *Athenaeum* from 1871 to 1900. His wide range of interests included the language and literature of Spain, in particular the work of Miguel de Cervantes Saavedra and Pedro Calderón de la Barca. MacColl published two (unsigned) reviews by Pater in the *Athenaeum*: 'The Complete Poetical Works of William Wordsworth', 26 Feb. 1889, 109–10, and 'Correspondence of Gustave Flaubert', 3 Aug. 1889, 155–6. See *CW* v.
[2] *Select Plays of Calderón*, ed. Norman MacColl (London: Macmillan, 1888). See Cervantes, *Exemplary Novels*, trans. N. MacColl and ed. James Fitzmaurice, 2 vols (Glasgow: Cowans Gray, 1902).

To ARTHUR SYMONS, 3 June [1888][1]
MS.: Sam S. Glass. Printed in *LWP*.

12 Earl's Terrace, | Kensington, W. | June 3.

My dear Mr. Symons,

I meant to thank you weeks ago for so kindly sending me 'Nero and other Plays', with your own interesting contributions.[2] I take this opportunity of thanking you, as I am sending, by this post, a copy of the enlarged edition of my old book on the Renaissance, which I hope you will kindly accept.

When are we to meet? I come to London on June 14th, for about 8 or 9 weeks. Don't forget your promise to let me know when you come to Town. I shall be sincerely disappointed if you come without my seeing you.[3]

Very sincerely yours
Walter Pater.

[1] The letter is accompanied by an envelope that once contained another untraced Pater letter to Symons, postmarked KENSINGTON KZ AU 10 89 W.

[2] *Nero and Other Plays*, ed. Herbert P. Horne, Havelock Ellis, Arthur Symons, and A. Wilson Verity (1888), appeared in the Mermaid series, reprints of texts by Elizabethan, Jacobean, and Restoration dramatists. Havelock Ellis (1859–1939), physician, writer, and social reformer, edited the series, the name of which derives from the Mermaid Tavern in London. Symons edited John Day's *The Parliament of Bees* (London: William Lee, 1641) and *Humour out of Breath* (London: Richard Bradock, 1608).

[3] Symons travelled to London early in Aug., meeting Pater there on 7 Aug. 1888. For his impressions of this visit see his 8 Aug. 1888 letter (mistakenly dated 8 July) to James Dykes Campbell (Brit. Lib. Add. MS. 49522); *Arthur Symons: Selected Letters, 1880–1935*, 39.

To SIR MOUNTSTUART GRANT DUFF, 7 June [1888]
MS.: Sheila Sokolov Grant. Printed in *LWP*.

Brasenose, | June 7th.

Dear Sir Mountstuart,

Your letter has been forwarded to me here. It will give me great pleasure to accept your kind invitation for Tuesday, June 12th. I sometimes, a little to my own surprise, find myself a contributor to The Guardian, where I lately reviewed 'Robert Elsmere'.

I heard you were staying at Mount Carmel[1] last winter. It must be a singular neighbourhood, and I can well believe yielded you many sources of interest besides its obvious ones.

With many thanks,

Very truly yours
Walter Pater.

[1] A coastal mountain range in northern Palestine, now Israel; Mt Carmel is sacred in the Judeo-Christian traditions and for Muslims and Bahá'ís.

To HARRY EDWARD MELVILL,[1] [10 June 1888?][2]
MS.: Brasenose College. On a correspondence card. Printed in *LWP*.

B. N. C. | Sunday.

Dear Mr. Melvill,

I looked for you in your rooms the other day but failed to find you. I am going down sooner than I anticipated, and without meeting you, properly speaking, unless you happen to be able to lunch with me here tomorrow Monday, at 1.30. I should be very glad if you can.

Very truly yours
Walter Pater.

I have been suffering from gout.

[1] Harry Edward Melvill (1866–1931), dandy and raconteur, attended University College, Oxford from 1884 to 1888. He is the original of Hugh Dearborn, the central character in Osbert Sitwell's short story, 'The Machine Breaks Down', in *Triple Fugue* (London: Richards, 1924). One of Dearborn's favourite topics is his recollection of a spring afternoon in Pater's garden; the narrator adds that he has heard that Pater declared, 'That young man will go far!' (180).

[2] The letter clearly belongs to Melvill's undergraduate years; the date is suggested by the letter to Wilde, 12 June [1888], in which Pater also refers to his gout and his impending departure for London.

To OSCAR WILDE, 12 June [1888]
MS.: Princeton University. Printed in *LWP*.

B. N. C. | June 12th.

My dear Wilde,

I am confined to my room with gout, but have been consoling myself with 'The Happy Prince',[1] and feel it would be ungrateful not to send a line to tell you how delightful I have found him and his companions. I hardly know whether to admire more the wise wit of 'The Wonderful Rocket',[2] or the beauty and tenderness of 'The Selfish Giant': the latter certainly is perfect in its kind. Your genuine 'little poems in prose', those at the top of pages 10 and 14, for instance, are gems, and the whole, too brief, book abounds with delicate touches and pure English.

I hope to get away in a day or two, and meantime am a debtor in the matter of letters.

Ever

Very sincerely yours
Walter Pater.

[1] Wilde's *The Happy Prince and Other Tales* (London: David Nutt, 1888) appeared in May.

[2] The title of the story is 'The Remarkable Rocket'. Wilde was delighted with Pater's 'wonderful letter about my prose'. *Complete Letters of Oscar Wilde*, ed. Merlin Holland and Hart-Davis, 219.

To WILLIAM SHARP, [June 1888?][1]
Text: *The Realm*, 25 January 1895, 418. Printed in *LWP*.

... Imagination, *he writes, à propos of the work-in-mass of one of our greatest poets*,—imagination is a Divine gift, as was the Bacchic vine; but each can intoxicate the heedless, and so enslave where it should serve. Therefore, I do not say with you that X. Z. is great because of his magnificent imagination, but because of his magnificently controlled imagination.

... The heir who carefully sets himself to exploit his heritage, to till every barren land, to afforest every waste place, has already expended not the least of his treasures. A more austere judgement, a taste more serene because more severe, would not hasten to enforce from an irresponsible inheritance all that it could possibly be made to surrender: rather, this wiser heir would gladly move patiently through his domain, content if he has his due measure of delight in this grove or on that sunlit slope, content even though there are remoter slopes and still inward groves which he shall never explore, never more than discern, possibly that he shall not even view at all—the not unenviable ignorance of true wisdom.

---

[1] This letter is printed in an unsigned review of *Greek Studies* (1895); the identity of Sharp as the addressee depends on the inked ascription 'By W. S.' on Sharp's own copy of the review, now in the collection at Brasenose College. The date of the letter hinges on internal evidence; if Pater is discussing published comments by Sharp about poetic imagination in general and the work of one English poet ('X. Z.') in particular, he may refer to Sharp's 'Dedicatory Introduction' to *Romantic Ballads and Poems of Phantasy* (London: Walter Scott, 1888), which appeared in June. In this introduction, Sharp celebrates imagination in poetry and eulogizes Coleridge, Keats, D. G. Rossetti (especially), and Morris. But this identification and the date, 1888, are tentative.

To HERBERT HORNE, 17 July [1888]
MS.: Mark Samuels Lasner Collection, University of Delaware. On a correspondence card. Printed in *LWP*.

       12 Earl's Terrace, | Kensington, W. | July 17th.

Dear Horne,

Will you dine with us on Friday, July 27th, at 7.45. I do not know whether Galton[1] will be then in London, nor his present address. The enclosed[2] asks him to dine with me at the same time. Will you kindly forward it to him, and let me have your reply as soon as you can.

            Very sincerely yours
            Walter Pater.

---

[1] Revd Arthur Howard Galton (1852–1921), classicist, critic, and priest (see Biographical Register).
[2] The enclosure is missing.

To ARTHUR SYMONS, 17 July [1888]
MS.: Morgan Library & Museum (MA 4500). On stationery measuring 4 3/8 × 7 ins. when folded. Accompanied by an envelope addressed to 'Arthur Symons, Esq. | Coton Road | Nuneaton. Postmark: LONDON. S.W. | J[U]LY 17 | [18]88' and stamped as received as NUNEATON | A | J[U]LY 17 | [18]88. Printed in Inman, 'Pater's Letters at the Pierpont Library', 412–13.

12 Earl's Terrace, | Kensington, W. | July 17th.

My dear Mr. Symons,

Excuse my delay in answering your letter. I saw Mr. George Macmillan yesterday, and expressed my very high opinion of your powers and performance in poetry and literature generally. I do not know whether my opinion has much weight with the Macmillans;[1] and, of course, all publishers are often inexplicable in their choice and rejection. I can only say that I wish you now and always the success—the high success—you seem to me to merit.

I was much pleased to hear of your proposal to live nearer London, where I remain till about August 13th, ######### when I leave for about six weeks. It seems a long time before we meet. I hope you will some day pay me a visit at Oxford, and remain, in haste,

Very sincerely yours
Walter Pater.

[1] As Inman notes, Pater had considerable influence with the Macmillans. In this case, the firm acted swiftly and efficiently; Symons received a telegram from James Dykes Campbell that *Days and Nights* (1889) had been accepted for publication.

To ARTHUR SYMONS, 2 August [1888]
MS.: Brasenose College. Envelope: Arthur Symons Esq. | Coton Road | Nuneaton. Postmark: KENSINGTON BX AU 2 88 W. Printed in *LWP*.

12 Earl's Terrace | Kensington, W. | Aug. 2.

My dear Mr. Symons,

I was much pleased but not surprised to hear that Macmillan had agreed to take your poems.[1] I wish I could have given an earlier answer to your letter of July 27, which I read with great interest, and have just read over again. I think you have chosen an excellent, because expressive, title for the volume, as you describe it. I should be delighted to read the MS., but am going away for about six weeks on the 13th of this month. I feel the practical difficulty you describe. Might it be solved by placing those extraneous pieces at the end of the volume, distinguishably from its main content? If you still care to send me the volume, or any part of it, (don't do so, unless you have a second copy,) I will take care to return the same before I go away.

Very sincerely yours
Walter Pater.

[1] Published as *Days and Nights* (1889). Symons had asked Pater to intervene; Pater spoke on Symons's behalf to George Augustin Macmillan (1855-1936), the second son of Jeanne and Alexander Macmillan (see Biographical Register). See Symons's letters to James Dykes Campbell, 12 and 18 July 1888, Brit. Lib. Add. MS. 49522.

To EDMUND GOSSE, 7 August [1888]
MS.: Brotherton Collection, University of Leeds. Printed in *LWP*.

12 Earl's Terrace, | Aug. 7th.

My dear Gosse,

Accept my best thanks for the kind present of your life of Congreve.[1] It seems to me to possess in large measure the peculiar excellences of your work, and makes charming reading. A figure practically indistinct, to me at least, becomes very real under your hands.

I leave London shortly for about six weeks,[2] but hope we may meet in the autumn.

With kind regards,

Very sincerely yours
Walter Pater.

[1] Gosse's *Life of William Congreve* (1888) appeared in the Great Writers series, ed. by Eric Sutherland Robertson (see letter to Sharp, 23 Nov. [1887]).
[2] Gosse wrote to his wife Ellen on 'Friday' (probably 10 Aug. 1888) that he had received 'a nice note from Pater. He is off to Switzerland' (Cambridge Univ. Lib. Ms. Add. 7021).

To ARTHUR SYMONS, 11 August [1888]
Text: *Autograph Prices Current*, 3 (1918), 192.

Pater advised Symons 'as to the MS. of some poems', texts intended for Days and Nights (1889).

To WALTER PATER, 30 August [1888]
MS.: British Library. Printed in *TBB*.

Walter Pater Esq.

Aug. 30.

Dear Mr. Pater,

I am sorry to say that I have not been able to send you a copy of the American edition of the *Renaissance*. We sent the whole edition to America with the exception of half a dozen which are imperfect. These are being put right and you shall have one of them in a few days.

I am

Yours very truly,
Frederick Macmillan.

To HERBERT HORNE, 2 October [1888]
MS.: Mark Samuels Lasner Collection, University of Delaware. On a correspondence card. Printed in *LWP*.

12 Earl's Terrace, | Oct. 2.

My dear Horne,

Excuse my long silence. I found your letter, with many others, on my return from abroad, and can't put off just acknowledging it any longer. The Sibyl is, I think, an excellent title,[1] and I was greatly interested in your explanation and defence of the same. I hope the magazine will continue to thrive under it.

I hope we may meet soon, and am

Very sincerely yours
Walter Pater.

---

[1] In the summer and early autumn of 1888 Horne, Galton, and others were considering changing the name of the *Century Guild Hobby Horse*, which some people thought trivialized art and literature. In Greek mythology, the Sibyls were oracular women who resided at holy sites.

To ARTHUR SYMONS, 2 October [1888]
MS.: Morgan Library & Museum (MA 4500). On a correspondence card, accompanied by an envelope addressed to Arthur Symons Esq. | 21 Chandos Road, | Buckingham. Postmark: KENSINGTON OZ OC 2 88 W. Printed in Inman, 'Pater's Letters at the Pierpont Library', 413–14.

12 Earl's Terrace, | Kensington, W. | Oct. 2.

My dear Mr. Symons,

Excuse my long silence. I found your letter, with many others, on my return from abroad. I shall now look with great interest for the proofs of your poems, and should be glad if you would kindly have them sent direct to me, as you propose. Many thanks for the Shakspere pieces,[1] which seem extremely interesting, though I have not had time to go through them properly. With best wishes,

Very sincerely yours
Walter Pater.

[1] These compositions are probably the introductions to *The Winter's Tale* and *Henry VIII* written by Symons for an edition of *The Works of William Shakespeare*, popularly known as 'The Henry Irving Shakespeare' (London: Gresham Publishing, 1888–90), edited by Henry Irving (1838–1905), the celebrated actor-manager, and Frank A. Marshall, with illustrations by Gordon Browne. In his general introduction, 'Shakespeare as Playwright', Irving maintains that the plays should be seen on the stage, as opposed to analysed in print. As Inman points out, Symons informed James Dykes Campbell on 3 Dec. 1887 that he was working on introductions to these plays, the third and fourth he had undertaken for the project. The fifth introduction by Symons, on *Macbeth*, reached Pater on 29 Dec. 1888 (see letter to Symons, 29 Dec. [1888]).

To [?] W. B. SQUIRE,[1] [early October 1888][2]
MS.: Pierpont Library, New York (MA 4500). On a correspondence card. Printed in Inman, 'Pater's Letters at the Pierpont Library', 409–10.

12 Earl's Terrace, | Saturday.

Dear Mr. Squire,

I found your invitation on my return yesterday. There was no need to apologise for asking me to your pleasant party. I am not sure whether you meant Thursday last or next. However, I leave London again on Monday, and should not be able to avail myself of your kindness, for which sincere thanks.

Very truly yours
Walter Pater.

¹ Possibly William Barclay Squire (1855–1927), a musicologist, who joined the British Museum in 1885, and for many years was in charge of Printed Music and Deputy Keeper of Printed Books. His chief interest lay in the bibliographical and historical aspects of music (see his *Catalogue of Printed Music before 1801*, London: Royal College of Music, 1912). Inman makes the case that Squire invited Pater to a party because he was an acquaintance of John Addington Symonds (Symonds and Squire met in Italy in 1888; they exchanged letters and visited one another in 1889.) By late 1887 or early 1888 Symonds was working on a criticism of Pater's essay on Giorgione (which had appeared in the *Fortnightly Review*, ns 22 (Oct. 1877), 526–38).

² See letters to Horne, 2 Oct. [1888], and Symons, 2 Oct. [1888].

To AN UNKNOWN CORRESPONDENT,¹ 28 October 1888
MS.: Ronald J. Kopnicki. On a gilt-edged off-white correspondence card.

Brasenose College | Oct. 28th, 1888

Dear Sir,

Excuse my long delay. I return the post card with words from Lucian.² See 'Marius', 2, p. 179, 1st. edition.

Truly yours
Walter Pater.

—'And we too desire, not a fair one, but the fairest of all. Unless we find him, we shall think we have failed'.³

¹ As Kopnicki explains, evidence points to Charles [Thomas John] Hiatt (1869–1904), collector, critic, and editor. Samuel Wright discusses Charles Hiatt in the *Bibliography of the Writings of Walter Pater* (New York: Garland, 1975), 80. During the late 1880s, this connoisseur collected autographs. He wrote to literary figures, posing questions designed to elicit a personal response—and the desired autograph. He asked Walter Pater to 'write a favourite sentiment from his own writings for a collection of autographs'. Hiatt acknowledged this strategy in 'Walter Pater's Autograph', *Notes and Queries*, 17 July 1897, 45. (Wright reproduces the passage, but gives the date as 17 July 1893.) He asked Thomas Hardy to identify the works that were appearing in serial form. Martin Ray makes this case in 'Thomas Hardy's Letter to Charles Hiatt', *Notes and Queries*, ns 53.3 (Sept. 2006), 338. During the early 1890s Hiatt collected posters, and promoted this activity in articles such as 'The Collecting of Posters: A New Field for the Connoisseur', *Studio*, 1.2 (May 1893), 61–4. He introduced major designers, such as Jules Chéret, and glossed the elements that constituted remarkable specimens. The first international exhibition of artistic pictorial posters produced by French and English designers, held at the Royal Aquarium, Westminster, in 1894, reinforced his message that the poster could be much more than a vehicle for conveying a commercial message. Arguably, Hiatt produced the first history of poster advertising, *Picture Posters: A Short History of the Illustrated Placard* (1895), and edited the first periodical devoted to the medium, *The Poster: An Illustrated Monthly Chronicle*, which served poster collectors from June 1898 to Dec. 1900.

² Lucian (*c*.125–180 CE), Greek rhetorician, was born at Samosata on the Euphrates. He travelled in Greece, Italy, and southern Gaul, earning his living by his declamations. After settling in Athens he devoted himself to philosophy, studying under the Stoic Demonax, and to writing dialogues. Eventually he renounced philosophy as a subject of dialogues (except for the exposure of false practitioners), and turned to the development of a new form of literature, the satirical dialogue, for which he is chiefly famous.

³ Lucian, *Hermotimus*; cited in *Marius*, ch. 24. See *CW* ii.

To ARTHUR SYMONS, 29 October [1888]
Text: Transcript by Roger Lhombreaud. Printed in *LWP*.

Brasenose College, | Oct. 29.

Dear Mr. Symons,

I return the proofs, with, I fear, very categorical answers to your questions. I cannot help thinking you would be wise in omitting 'The Temptation of St. Anthony', on page 55. You might supply its place. 'A Vigil in Lent', page 74, is perhaps open to similar objections. These, I think, might be obviated by a less frequent use of the name of Christ, which seems to me entirely a fault of taste in it. I enclose the MS. poems. 'Corruptio optimi pessima' I don't care for much; but find 'The Knife-Thrower' admirable. By all means include it.[1]

I am greatly struck by the force and clearness and dramatic effect of your work, in this second reading, as indeed I was when I had it in MS.; while the lighter interludes are graceful and pleasant in their turn. It will give me great pleasure to read the remaining proofs, if you don't mind my lengthiness about it—a lengthiness which I must now ask you to pardon with regard to the present instalment, my hands being somewhat burdened with work just now.[2] So believe me

Very sincerely yours
Walter Pater.

---

[1] Apparently, Symons did not heed Pater's advice: he included 'The Temptation of St. Anthony' (perhaps revised in response to Pater's objection) in *Days and Nights* (1889). 'A Vigil in Lent' was also included, and in it the name of Christ is used nine times, six in the petition of the distraught adulteress. Symons agreed with Pater in printing 'The Knife-Thrower' (66–70), and in rejecting '*Corruptio optimi pessima*' {The corruption of the best is the worst [of all corruptions]}. The Latin tag was also the title of several Simeon Solomon sketches of Medusa: *Corruptio Optimi Pessima: Medusa* (1890s, chalk on paper; Neil Bartlett and James Gardiner Collection) and the 1893 woodcut (British Museum no. 1896, 1019.176).

[2] Pater was probably still working on 'Style', which appeared in the *Fortnightly Review*, ns 44 (Dec. 1888), 728–43, and rptd in *Appreciations* (1889); see *CW* vi. Pater once told Symons that this essay was 'the most laborious task he ever set himself to accomplish' (Symons, 61).

To ARTHUR SYMONS, 21 November [1888]
Text: Francis Edwards Catalogue no. 406 (1920), 29. Printed in *LWP*.

Brasenose College, | Nov. 21.

...That you should dedicate to me what I think a very remarkable volume...shall think it a very charming incident in my life....[1]

[1] Symons dedicated *Days and Nights* (1889) to Pater (see letter to Symons, 23 Jan. [1889], n. 1). This lost letter may also have extended or confirmed an invitation to Symons to visit Pater in Oxford; Symons mentions his intention of going in a 19 Nov. 1888 letter to James Dykes Campbell, and describes his visit, during the first week of Dec., in a letter dated 11 Dec. to Campbell (Brit. Lib. Add. MS. 49522). See *Arthur Symons: Selected Letters, 1880–1935*, 40–1.

To HERBERT HORNE, [24 December 1888]
MS.: Mark Samuels Lasner Collection, University of Delaware. On a correspondence card. Printed in *LWP*.

12 Earl's Terrace, W. | Christmas Eve.

My dear Horne,

It seems an age since we met. It will give me much pleasure if you can dine with us on Wednesday, Jan. 2nd, at 8 o'clock, when we expect some other friends.

Very sincerely yours
Walter Pater.

To HERBERT HORNE, 29 December [1888]
MS.: Mark Samuels Lasner Collection, University of Delaware. On a correspondence card. Printed in *LWP*.

12 Earl's Terrace, | Dec. 29.

My dear Horne,

Sincere thanks for your generosity in sending me the Hobby-Horse, which arrived some days since. It is a good number. Your paper on Gibbs I read with great interest, and hope you will do much more of the same kind—also K. Paul's paper on Style, and hope to have a chance of telling him so before long.[1] I am pleased to hear you like my own essay on that subject.

Don't forget Wednesday at 8.

Very sincerely yours
Walter Pater.

[1] The first of three instalments of Horne's 'Some Account of the Life and Public Works of James Gibbs, Architect', *Century Guild Hobby Horse*, 4 (Jan. 1889), 29–36; (Apr. 1889), 71–80; and (July 1889), 110–17. Gibbs (1682–1754), a Scot, studied in Rome with Carlo Fontana, a leading exponent of the Italian Baroque style; when he returned to England, he developed a style in which he synthesized Baroque and Palladian elements,

as in his best-known work, St Martin-in-the-Fields (*c.*1720). Horne printed C. Kegan Paul's lecture, 'On English Prose Style', in the same Jan. issue, 11–26; Paul quotes Pater on Gustave Flaubert and cites Pater as one of four contemporary examples of excellent English prose style: 'While Cardinal Newman and Walter Pater, Thomas Hardy and Hesba Stretton, live among us, each in his or her own way showing the perfection to which, in this age, our language can be wrought, he would be a bold man who would assert that even in the adaptation of sound to sense the art of style has in any degree decayed.' 'Hesba Stretton' was the pseud. of Sarah Smith (1832–1911), an author of children's books who first garnered fame for *Jessica's First Prayer* (1866), which out-sold Carroll's *Alice in Wonderland*.

To ARTHUR SYMONS, 29 December [1888]
MS.: Folger Shakespeare Library. Envelope: Arthur Symons Esq. | 21 Chandos Street | Buckingham. Postmark: KENSINGTON OZ D[E] 29 88 W. On a correspondence card. Printed in *LWP*.

12 Earl's Terrace, | Kensington. W. | Dec. 29th.

My dear Mr. Symons,

Sincere thanks for your letter. Also for the paper on Macbeth,[1] which I shall read with great interest. I have just finished a second reading of your poems, and am otherwise very busy. I too am just completing a brief Shakspere study—The English Kings:—am also at work on a new Portrait—Hippolytus Veiled.[2]

With sincere regards,
Walter Pater.

[1] Symons, 'Critical Remarks', an Introduction to *Macbeth*, *The Works of William Shakespeare*, ed. Henry Irving and Frank A. Marshall, 8 vols (London: Blackie & Sons, 1889), 5: 355–9.

[2] 'Shakspere's English Kings' was published in *Scribner's Magazine*, 5 (Apr. 1889), 506–12, and collected the same year in *Appreciations*; see *CW* vi. 'Hippolytus Veiled: A Study from Euripides', *Macmillan's Magazine*, 60 (Aug. 1889), 294–306, was included by C. L. Shadwell in *Greek Studies* (London: Macmillan, 1895); see *CW* iii, 157–73.

1889

To WALTER PATER, 3 January [1889]
MS.: British Library. Printed in *TBB*.

Jan 3. 9

Dear Mr. Pater,

The post office people in Paris cannot find Mr. [Sarrazin][1] at the address you gave me—11 Rue Troyan. Can you find out where he is? The books meanwhile lie at his disposal in Paris.

I am

Yours very truly,
George A. Macmillan.

W. H. Pater Esq.,
12 Earl's Terrace | Kensington

[1] Possibly Gabriel Sarrazin (1853–1935), a French poet and translator who developed an appreciation for nineteenth-century British and American poetry. He contributed essays on English poets (among them the Pre-Raphaelites) to French periodicals and on French poets to English periodicals. In *Poètes modernes de l'Angleterre* (Paris: Paul Ollendorf, 1885), he introduces to French readers Browning, Keats, W. S. Landor, Shelley, D. G. Rossetti, and A. C. Swinburne. In *La renaissance de la poésie anglaise, 1798–1889* (Paris: Perrin, 1889), he features Browning, Coleridge, Tennyson, Walt Whitman, and Wordsworth. Georges Knopff produced the first French translation of a work by Pater. See letters to Pater, 2 Sept. [1890], and Hester Pater, 18 Jan. [1897].

To AN UNKNOWN CORRESPONDENT,[1] 7 January [1889]
MS.: William Andrews Clark Memorial Library, University of California at Los Angeles.

12 Earl's Terrace, W. | Jan. 7.

Dear Sir,

I would willingly send you a contribution to the 'Fortnightly' if I had anything ready, at all suitable for the purpose. I have on hand a critical article[2] which I had prepared for the 'Fortnightly', in fulfilment of an old promise; but it involves a good deal of reading, and can hardly be finished for some time to come. After your letter, I shall speed the work as much as possible, and hope to send you that and some other papers in the course of the year.

With many thanks,

Very truly yours
Walter Pater.

¹ Presumably Revd John Stuart Verschoyle (1853–1915), Anglo-Irish clergyman, journalist, and editor, who became an Anglican priest and took up an appointment as the curate of the Church of Holy Trinity, Marylebone, London, 1882. Early on, he met Frank Harris (1856–1931), the Irish-American journalist, editor, and publisher (see Biographical Register). Verschoyle served as a confidant and an advisor, editing Harris's submissions to periodicals and introducing Harris to important literary and political figures. Thus Verschoyle played a role in Harris becoming editor of the *London Evening News* in 1883. When Harris was the editor of the *Fortnightly Review*, 1886–94, Verschoyle was the official assistant editor, 1889–91. According to some, Verschoyle did much of the work, soliciting essays and reading proofs. See Esther Rhoads Houghton, 'Verschoyle and the *Fortnightly Review*', *Victorian Periodicals Newsletter*, 3.4 (Nov. 1968), 17–21; Philippa Pullar, *Frank Harris: A Biography* (New York: Simon and Shuster, 1976), 83, 141. He left London to become rector of Creeting St Peter, Suffolk, 1891–3, and later rector of Huish Champflower, Somerset, 1893–1915.

² Possibly 'The Aesthetic Life', Houghton Library bMS 1150 (7); see *CW* x.

To SIR MOUNTSTUART GRANT DUFF, 21 January [1889]¹
MS.: Sheila Sokolov Grant. Printed in *LWP*.

12 Earl's Terrace, W. | Jan: 21.

My dear Sir Mountstuart,

Accept my best thanks for your kind invitation, which reaches me at the moment of my departure for Oxford; otherwise I should have been delighted to accept it. I hope I may have the good-fortune to find you at Twickenham when I return to Town about seven weeks hence, to stay for a considerable time. I should greatly enjoy a talk with you, and am ever

Very sincerely yours
Walter Pater.

¹ The year is pencilled on the MS. In 1889, Monday, 21 Jan. was the first day of Oxford's Hilary term.

To ARTHUR SYMONS, 23 January [1889]
Text: Transcription by Roger Lhombreaud. Printed in *LWP*.

Brasenose College | Jan 23rd.

My dear Mr. Symons,

Your letter of Jan. 22 has been forwarded to me here. I was on the point of writing to you. I think the Title-page satisfactory. I don't like to discuss your too flattering dedication to me, though I feel proud to see it on your charming book, but I agree with you in not liking the German type in union with Roman.[1] My dear Mr. Symons you know already what I think of your work, and I hope to find means of saying what I think in some public print, meantime sincerely wish you success in this volume and all things.

Very sincerely yours
Walter Pater.

[1] Symons asked Macmillan's to set Pater's name in Roman type instead, and sent this note to James Dykes Campbell, asking: 'Did you ever see a more delightful little note?' (postscript [24 Jan.] to letter of 22 Jan. [1889], Brit. Lib. Add. MS. 49523). The dedication of *Days and Nights* reads: 'To Walter Pater in all gratitude and admiration'.

To ARTHUR SYMONS, [11 February 1889]
MS.: Princeton University. On a correspondence card. Envelope: Arthur Symons Esq. | 21 Chandos Road | Buckingham. Postmark: OXFORD X FE 11 89. Printed in *LWP*.

Brasenose College. | Monday

My dear Mr. Symons,

I am going to London on Thursday. But it will give me great pleasure to see you on Wednesday, any time you like.[1] I am engaged to dinner that day, but have no other fixed engagement. Come in time for lunch.

Very sincerely yours
Walter Pater.

I think you mean *the day after tomorrow*. If so, don't write.

[1] Symons wrote to James Dykes Campbell on 24 Feb. 1889: 'Last Wednesday week I spent a delightful day with Pater at Oxford.... I have not had so pleasant a talk with him before, or so long a one. We seem to be quite old friends by this time, & I am getting to like him, as a man, more & more.' Brit. Lib. Add. MS. 49523.

To AN UNKNOWN CORRESPONDENT,[1] 20 February [1889]
MS.: William Andrews Clark Memorial Library, University of California at Los Angeles. The left right-hand and the upper right-hand corners of the letter, which had been folded in two, have been torn off.

[Brasenose] College, | Feb. 20.

[Dear Sir],

A thousand apologies for my delay in answering your letter of last week. During the last month I have been much occupied with various work, and shall not be able to do much to my promised essay on Flaubert[2] for two or three weeks to come. It is a subject which requires a good deal of careful labour, if it is to be dealt with at all adequately. I hope however that the article may [*part missing*] for the May issue [*part missing*] Fortnightly.

I am tempted [*part missing*] proposal that [*part missing*] those two papers on 'aesthetics':[3] but it would be uncandid in me to do so. I have too much work on hand already begun.

With many thanks,

Very truly yours
Walter Pater.

---

[1] The salutation and other parts of the letter are missing. Probably addressed to Revd John Stuart Verschoyle (1853–1915), who served as the assistant editor of the *Fortnightly Review*, 1888–91 (see letter to Unknown Correspondent, 7 Jan. [1889]).

[2] Pater was preoccupied with Flaubert in 1888–9. See Østermark-Johansen, *Walter Pater and the Language of Sculpture*, 308–14. He published 'The Life and Letters of Gustave Flaubert', *Pall Mall Gazette*, 25 Aug. 1888, 1–2; 'Style', *Fortnightly Review*, ns 44 (Dec. 1888), 728–43; 'Correspondence de Gustave Flaubert', *Athenaeum*, 3 Aug. 1889, 155–6 (see *CW* v).

[3] See 'The Aesthetic Life', Houghton Library bMS 1150 (7); *CW* x.

To HERBERT HORNE, [18? March 1889][1]
MS.: Mark Samuels Lasner Collection, University of Delaware. On a correspondence card. Printed in *LWP*.

12 Earl's Terrace, | Kensington, W. | Monday.

My dear Horne,

It seems an age since we met. Could you come and dine with us \quite alone,/ on Wednesday, March 20th, at 7.30.

Very sincerely yours
Walter Pater.

---

[1] The date '19 March 1889' is pencilled on the MS., presumably based on the postmark; however, 19 Mar. was a Tuesday.

To WILLIAM SHARP, [March? 1889][1]
MS.: London University, *Chair of English Literature: Testimonials in favour of Mr. William Sharp* (London: London University, 1889), 32.[2] Printed in *LWP*.

Brasenose College, Oxford.

I have no hesitation in saying that I have formed a high opinion of the ability and attainments of Mr. William Sharp. His enthusiasm for literature is very remarkable, and has made him a laborious student, as well as a clear, effective, ready writer, both in criticism and in the more original departments of literary composition. With a large knowledge of books and of fine arts, he is also intimately in touch with men and things, and would, I think, give taking[3] lectures and stimulate the interest of young students.

Walter Pater, M.A.,
Fellow of Brasenose College.

[1] In Mar. 1889, Sharp presented himself as a candidate for the Chair of English Literature at University College, London, which Henry Morley had just resigned. Several leading figures supported Sharp's candidacy, including Browning, George Meredith, Pater, and William Michael Rossetti. Sharp's health, however, did not allow him to remain in contention; he withdrew his name in May. See Elizabeth A. Sharp, *William Sharp (Fiona Macleod)*, 149.

[2] According to Lawrence Evans, Pater's testimonial can be understood as an enclosure in a letter to Sharp, who compiled and had printed the volume from which this text is drawn. In the heading, closing, and body of this letter I have normalized what seem clear editorial alterations, chiefly in italicizing and capitalizing various words for effect.

[3] Pater suggests that Sharp delivers stimulating lectures that fire the intellectual curiosity of students.

To GEORGE ALLISON ARMOUR,[1] 24 March [1889]
MS.: The Grolier Club, New York.

Brasenose College, | March 24th

My Dear Mr. Armour,

I was much pleased, and felt much honoured, in receiving your valuable present of the Grolier Club edition of the "Philobiblon"[2]—the matter so excellent: the form so exquisite! Accept my sincere thanks, and forgive my delay in the expression of them. Be assured I value greatly this note of interest in my writings.

Should you visit Oxford, let me have the pleasure of making your personal acquaintance, and believe me

Very sincerely yours,
Walter Pater.

[1] George Allison Armour (1856–1936), the son of a Scottish engineer who settled in the United States, enjoyed great success as engineer and businessman. Armour met and became a close friend of Edmund Gosse (see Biographical Register). Gosse's biographer, Evan Charteris, describes Armour as a bibliophile and patron of the arts. In 1885, Armour contributed to the memorial for Thomas Gray at Pembroke College, Cambridge. From 1886, the Gosses and the Armours were close friends.

[2] *The Philobiblon of Richard de Bury*, ed. and trans. by Andrew Fleming West, 3 vols (New York: Grolier Club, 1889). This copy would have been one of an edition of 297 copies on paper and three copies on vellum, of which the first and second volumes were printed in Apr. and the third volume in Dec. 1889. New York's Grolier Club, a society of bibliophiles, was founded in 1884 for aficionados of the graphic arts. It was named after Jean Grolier de Servières, Viscount d'Aguisy (1489–1565), Treasurer General of France. In Pater's library were two volumes of *Philobiblon*, sent to him by Armour, with a presentation letter, on 11 Jan. 1890. For some time the books and letter were in the possession of May Ottley.

To ARTHUR SYMONS, [24 March 1889]
Text: Transcript by Roger Lhombreaud. Printed in *LWP*.

12 Earl's Terrace. | Sunday.

My dear Mr. Symons,

I send you a line to tell you that you will find my view of 'Nights and Days' in yesterday's Pall Mall Gazette[1]—rather hastily expressed I fear.

Yours ever
Walter Pater.

[1] Pater's review of *Days and Nights* (1889), entitled 'A Poet with Something to Say', appeared in the *Pall Mall Gazette*, 23 Mar. 1889, 3. See *CW* v.

To ARTHUR SYMONS, [1? April 1889][1]
MS.: Harvard University. On correspondence cards. Printed in *LWP*.

12 Earl's Terrace.

My dear Mr. Symons,

Many thanks for your letter of March 24th. I was much pleased that you liked my article in the Pall Mall Gazette. The bound copy of your poems has since arrived.[2] My sincere thanks for it, once more—for the inside and outside. In both respects, it makes a charming addition to my shelf of best-valued books. I enclose a paper, from Scribner's Magazine, on 'Shakspere's English Kings', and should be grateful if, at your leisure, you would point out anything that strikes you as behind actual Shaksperian criticism therein, as I intend to include it in my next volume.

I shall be here on the 26th. Will you lunch with me here, on that, or the preceding or following day.³—Let me know, when your plans are fixed.

Very sincerely yours
Walter Pater.

¹ On 5 Apr. 1889 Symons wrote to Michael Field: 'I enclose something else which you may care to see of his: he sent it to me a few days ago. It is from *Scribner's Magazine*. It seems to me a very original handling of a theme difficult to say anything fresh about' (Brit. Lib. Add. MS. 46867, fol. 224). See *Arthur Symons: Selected Letters*, 47. Pater's letter, however, is included in an envelope addressed to Arthur Symons Esq. | Emma place | Bodwin | Cornwall; and postmarked LONDON W AU 14 88 7. This envelope probably once contained the note Pater wrote in sending back Symons's MS., before he left for his European holiday (see letter to Symons, 2 Aug. [1888]).
² At Symons's request, Macmillan had prepared a specially bound presentation copy of *Days and Nights* for Pater. See letter of George A. Macmillan to Symons, 14 Mar. 1889 (Letter Book LVI).
³ Symons lunched with Pater on Thursday, 25 Apr. 1889. See his letter of that date to James Dykes Campbell (Brit. Lib. Add. MS. 49523).

To HERBERT HORNE, [16 April 1889][1]
MS.: Mark Samuels Lasner Collection, University of Delaware. On a correspondence card. Printed in *LWP*.

My dear Horne,

Would you kindly forward this to Galton's London address.[2] Ever

Very sincerely yours
Walter Pater.

Thanks, sincerely, by the way, for the Hobby Horse. Your papers on Gibbs have greatly interested me.[3] I hope we may meet before long.

¹ The date, pencilled on the MS., presumably from the postmark, seems wholly consistent with the contents.
² The enclosure is probably the following letter to Arthur Galton.
³ The second instalment of Horne's essay on Gibbs appeared in the *Century Guild Hobby Horse*, 4 (Apr. 1889), 71–80. See letter to Horne, 29 Dec. [1888].

To ARTHUR GALTON, [16 April 1889]
MS.: Smith College, Northampton, MA. On both sides of a correspondence card.
Envelope: Arthur Galton | 35 Brunswick Gardens, | Kensington, | W. Postmark: LONDON 4 AR 17 89 12.

                                          12 Earl's Terrace, | Kensington, W. | Tuesday.

My dear Galton,

    I have just been reading over again your charming, alas! un-answered letter of April 10th. Shall you be here on Thursday, April 25th; if so come and lunch with us at 2 o'clock. I am expecting A. Symons, author of 'Days and Nights'. You didn't leave your London address yesterday, and I therefore I invoke the kindly assistance of Horne to forward this.[1]

                                                                 Very sincerely yours
                                                                          Walter Pater.

---

[1] See letter to Horne, [16 Apr. 1889].

To AN UNKNOWN CORRESPONDENT,[1] 30 April [1889?][2]
MS.: Gerald Monsman. Printed in *LWP*.

                                                                    Brasenose, | April 30th.

Dear Sir,

    I have just read your letter of March 28th, on my return to Oxford. I wish I could undertake a life for your admirable Series; but, in truth, just now my hands are already so full of work, promised elsewhere, and partly begun, that it would be useless for me to do so, as least at present.

                                                                     Very truly yours
                                                                        Walter Pater.

---

[1] Probably Frank Thomas Marzials (1840–1912), writer, editor, and civil servant, who served as Accountant-General of the Army, 1898–1904. Marzials was decorated for his long service in 1902 and knighted in 1904. He also developed a reputation for his literary and biographical studies; he was co-editor of the Great Writers series for Walter Scott, contributing the lives of Charles Dickens and Victor Hugo. Several of Pater's friends, including Oscar Browning, Edmund Gosse, and William Sharp, were contributors. The letter is enclosed in the same envelope as the letter to Symons, [15 Jan. 1890]; Symons, who had promised but never completed a life of Edgar Allan Poe for the series, urged Marzials to approach Pater, and Marzials passed along to Symons Pater's refusal.

[2] If Marzials's letter was prompted by Symons, it probably belongs during the years of their association, 1888–9. I prefer 1889, as Pater is known to have returned to Oxford later in April that year (see letter to Symons, [1? Apr. 1889]).

To EMILIE ISABEL WILSON BARRINGTON,[1] 17 May [1889]
MS.: Bates College. On a correspondence card. Printed in *LWP*.

B. N. C. | May 17th.

My dear Mrs. Barrington,

Many thanks for your pamphlet, which I brought down here for quiet reading. I have read it carefully, and with great interest and sympathy for so earnest and eloquent a plea for what is permanently desirable, or even indispensable, in life. You write with an air of conviction, which I am sure must stir others at least to reflection, and I hope your work will reach those for whom it was intended.

Ever

Very truly yours
Walter Pater.

[1] Emilie Isabel Barrington, *née* Wilson (1841–1933), amateur artist and writer about art, was educated on the Continent. During her twenties, she devoted herself to feminist and social causes. With Emily Faithfull (1835–95), she advocated expanding opportunities for training and employing women. Later, with Octavia Hill (1835–1912), she hoped to improve the conditions of the working classes through the production and appreciation of art. She studied drawing with Arthur Hughes (1832–1915), Pre-Raphaelite painter and illustrator. After her marriage to Russell Henry Barrington (1840–1916), she established a circle of literary and artistic luminaries. She promoted the work of George Frederic Watts (1817–1904), painter and sculptor (in 1884 she compiled a critical catalogue of his paintings for an exhibition at the Metropolitan Museum of Art, New York), and Frederic Leighton (1830–96), painter and sculptor. She produced many works under the name 'Mrs. Russell Barrington'. In *The Reality of the Spiritual Life* (1889), she argued that 'there is something radically unspiritual in the dogmatic side of Christian teaching'; her pamphlet was reprinted in *A Retrospect and Other Articles* (London: Osgood and McIlvaine, 1896), 325–49. See also *Life, Letters, and Work of Frederic Leighton* (London: G. Allen, 1906), and a biography of Walter Bagehot (London: Longmans, Green, 1914).

To MARIE SPARTALI STILLMAN,[1] 10 June [1889]
MS.: Northwestern University. Printed in *LWP*.

12 Earl's Terrace, | June 10.

Dear Mrs. Stillman,

I have much pleasure in signing the memorial to the Home Secretary, as you propose. Would you kindly add my name; or, if necessary, send the memorial to me, at Brasenose College, Oxford, whither I return this evening. I have always felt very great respect for Dr. Hueffer's[2] work. Believe me

Very sincerely yours
Walter Pater.

[1] Marie Spartali Stillman (1844–1927), a painter, was the daughter of Effie and Michael Spartali (a wealthy merchant and the Greek Consul-General based in London, 1866–82). From 1864–70 she studied with Pre-Raphaelite painter Ford Madox Brown. In her art she concentrated on literary-historical group figures and decorative female heads. She produced more than one hundred works during a career of sixty years, and contributed regularly to exhibitions at the Grosvenor Gallery and its successor, the New Gallery. As well, she served as a model for Brown, Edward Burne-Jones, D. G. Rossetti, and photographer Julia Margaret Cameron. In 1871 she married William J. Stillman (1828–1901), an American journalist, diplomat, and photographer who, with J. Durand, founded and edited *The Crayon*, 'a journal devoted to the graphic arts and the literature related to them'.

[2] In 1889 Stillman, Lucy Madox Brown Rossetti, and others unsuccessfully petitioned the Home Secretary, Henry Matthews, QC, for a Civil List pension for the painter Catherine Madox Brown Hueffer (1850–1927), the daughter of Ford Madox Brown and Emma Hill (b. 1829) and the widow of Francis Hueffer (1845–89), the German-born music critic and librettist. Catherine Heuffer was an artist and a model associated with the Pre-Raphaelites.

To WALTER PATER, 11 June 1889
Text: Draft in Journals of Michael Field,[1] Br. Lib. Add. MS. 46777. Printed in *LWP*.

Blackberry Lodge | Reigate | Surrey | June XI, 1889

Dear Sir,

Ever since the issue of my little volume *Long Ago*,[2] I have had the intention of pleasing myself by offering a copy to you: circumstance alone has intervened. I feel I have hope that you will understand the spirit of my lyrics—you who have sympathy with attempts to reconcile the old and the new, to live as in continuation the beautiful life of Greece. Renaissance is the condition of man's thought which seems to have for you the most exciting charm. What I have aspired to do from Sappho's fragments may therefore somewhat appeal to your sense of survival in human things—to your interest in the shoots and offspring of elder literature.

Sincerely yours,
Michael Field.

[1] Katharine Harris Bradley (1846–1914) and Edith Emma Cooper (1862–1913) published together under the pseudonym of 'Michael Field'; see Biographical Register.

[2] *Long Ago* (London: George Bell and Sons, 1889) represents an extension of Sappho's poetic fragments into lyrics. The edition was limited to a hundred copies.

To ARTHUR SYMONS, [*c.*18 June 1889][1]
Text: Symons, *A Study of Walter Pater*, 100. Printed in *LWP*.

... I take your copy of Shakespeare's sonnets with me, hoping to be able to restore it to you there lest it should get bruised by transit through the post....

[1] Lawrence Evans quotes Symons citing the date as June 1889. The letter seems to have been written in Oxford, just before Pater's return to London. He remained at Brasenose after the end of term on Friday, 7 June 1889, at least as late as 19 June, when he returned a book to the college library. Since May at least, Symons had been trying to induce Pater to write an essay on Shakespeare's sonnets, and sending him material like the book mentioned here. Pater returned this book on 4 July 1889, when Symons visited him in London and found him 'pushing ahead with Gaston' (Symons's letters to James Dykes Campbell of 19 May 1889 and 7 July [1889], Brit. Lib. Add. MS. 49523).

To MESSRS. R. & R. CLARK, [c.20 June 1889][1]
MS.: Brasenose College. Printed in *LWP* and *TBB*.

12 Earl's Terrace, | Kensington, | London. W.

Dear Sir,

Messrs. Macmillan propose that you should print a book of mine, for publication by Nov. 1st, to be entitled,

'On Style,
With other studies in literature'.[2]

The volume is to be precisely similar, in all respects, to the edition of 'The Renaissance', printed by you, in 1888. I am anxious to finish the correction of proofs, and get the whole ready for Press, by August 8th; soon after which I propose to leave England for some weeks. I send, by this post, the first portion of the copy, and will send the remainder in good time. Please send me the proofs at the address above.

Opposite is the list of contents.[3]

Truly yours
Walter Pater.

For
Messrs. R. & R. Clark
42 Hanover St. | Edinburgh.

[1] As proofs of the first forty-eight pages were sent back to Pater early in July (Letter Book LVI), a date around 20 June, perhaps immediately after his return to London, seems reasonable for this letter.
[2] Published as *Appreciations: With an Essay on Style* on, or shortly after, 16 Nov. 1889. See *CW* vi.
[3] The list is missing; the page having been torn off.

To MICHAEL FIELD, 4 July [1889]
MS.: Miriam Lutcher Stark Library, Harry Ransom Center, University of Texas.
Envelope: To | Michael Field Esq. | Blackberry Lodge | Reigate | Surrey.
Postmark: PADDINGTON 5 JY 4 89 B. Printed in *LWP*.

12 Earl's Terrace, | Kensington, W. | July 4th.

Dear Sir,

(I suppose I must say,)[1] how ungratefully long I have been in acknowledging the choice copy of 'Long Ago',[2] which I was much pleased to receive from you, a true poet, as I know I feel it would take me a long time to exhaust their calm Attic wisdom—their sweetness of mind—which has struck me, in pieces like that on page 48, for instance, as their leading characteristic—a golden calmness, which \that/ has determined a similar quality in rhythm and expression. I suppose this is the mood proper to our minds in returning, by conscious effort, to distant worlds of thought or feeling; the more so, if that mood be itself unconscious.

I can but congratulate you on this charming addition to your work; having, too, something of that dramatic aim and power, by which you won your laurels.

It is natural to wish to meet those whose work interests one, and I must therefore add that it would give me great pleasure to see you here, if I had the good chance some day.

With sincere thanks,

Very truly yours
Walter Pater.

---

[1] Pater had been told by Arthur Symons that Michael Field was not a man; but beyond that Symons had disclosed nothing. See Symons's letter to Bradley of 2 Jan. 1889 (Brit. Lib. Add. MS. 46867, fols. 216–18).

[2] A line by the ancient Greek poet Sappho inspired each poem in Fields's *Long Ago* (1889). See letter to Pater, 11 June 1889.

To MICHAEL FIELD, 17 July [1889]
MS.: Miriam Lutcher Stark Library, Harry Ransom Center, University of Texas.
Envelope: To | Michael Field Esq. | Blackberry Lodge | Reigate. Postmark: KENSINGTON KZ JY 17 89 W. Printed in *LWP*.

12 Earl's Terrace, W. | July 17th.

To Michael Field,

Many thanks for your letter. Alas! I shall inevitably be away on Saturday; but shall be at home, about tea-time, 5 o'clock, on Monday, and hope you may be able to give me the pleasure of a call then, as I have a good many engagements in the short time that remains ~~from~~ before I leave town.[1]

Very truly yours
Walter Pater.

[1] Bradley and Cooper visited Pater on Monday, 22 July 1889. In their journal, Cooper describes '[a] serious man, quiet—with blue—constantly kind eyes'. Brit. Lib. Add. MS. 46777, fol. 85. Pater did not include a salutation.

To LOUISE CHANDLER MOULTON,[1] [18 July 1889]
MS.: Library of Congress. Envelope: To | Mrs. Moulton | 17 Langham Street | Portland Place | W. Postmark: KENSINGTON X JY 18 89 W. Printed in *LWP*.

12 Earl's Terrace, W. | Thursday.

My dear Mrs. Moulton,

I regret extremely to be unable to accept your most kind invitation for Friday, July 26th, as I shall have a friend[2] staying with me then for whose entertainment I have already provided at home. It would have been a great pleasure to me to come, and I shall hope to call some Tuesday afternoon before I leave Town.

Very sincerely yours
Walter Pater.

[1] Ellen Louise Chandler Moulton (1835-1908), American poet, storyteller, and critic (see Biographical Register).
[2] Pater's guest remains unidentified.

To LOUISE CHANDLER MOULTON, 31 [July 1889]
MS.: Library of Congress. Envelope: To | Mrs. Moulton | 17 Langham Street | Portland place | W. Postmark: KENSI[NG]TON KZZ JY 31 89 W. Printed in *LWP*.

12 Earl's Terrace, | July 31.

My dear Mrs. Moulton,

I had not forgotten Tuesday—had hoped to call on you yesterday, but have had a friend staying with me for the last week, who has made great demands on my time. I send a few lines now to thank you for your kind reminder just received, and to say that I shall look forward to the pleasure of calling on you on Saturday, at 6 o'clock. If that day should happen not to be convenient to you, kindly send me a post card.

Ever

> Very sincerely yours
> Walter Pater.

To BENJAMIN NATTALI,[1] [6 August 1889?]
MS.: Brasenose College. Printed in *LWP*.

> Tuesday.

Dear Nattali,

It will give me very great pleasure to accept Mrs. Hogge's[2] invitation for tomorrow. I shall be delighted to make her acquaintance.

In great haste,

> Very truly yours
> Walter Pater.

---

[1] Benjamin Nattali (1842–1901), a wealthy antiquarian and art collector, lived not far from Pater in the Kensington district of London. From 1869 to 1887 he was assistant in the Royal Library, Windsor Castle, concerned mainly with the library's art collection (noted for its da Vinci drawings).

[2] Helen Julia Magniac Hogge (1825?–91), a wealthy widow living in Pimlico. Among letters written before Hogge's death, only the letters written to Moulton, 31 [July 1889], and to Madan, 22 July [1890], appear on white letter paper of this particular size. An equally valid and equally uncertain date for this note would be 22 July 1890.

To LOUISE CHANDLER MOULTON, 7 August [1889]
MS.: Library of Congress. Envelope: To | Mrs. Moulton | 17 Langham Street | Portland Road [sic] | W. Postmark: KENSINGTON KZ AU 7 89 W. Printed in *LWP*.

> 12 Earl's Terrace, W. | August 7th.

My dear Mrs. Moulton,

Sincere thanks for your kind invitation. I leave London on Monday; otherwise it would have given me very great pleasure to dine with you and make the acquaintance of Mr. Greenough.[1] I hope to return to London about <O> September 23rd, and that it will not be a whole year before we meet again.

With kind regards,

> Very sincerely yours
> Walter Pater.

¹ Richard Saltonstall Greenough (1819–1904), American sculptor, grew up in a Boston-based family; his brothers Horatio and Henry made their names as sculptor and architect respectively. In 1837, he joined a community of American expatriate artists in Rome; afterwards he divided his time between Europe and America, creating statues and portrait busts, including a bronze statue of Benjamin Franklin (1856) eight feet in height. Greenough was elected Fellow of the American Academy of Arts and Sciences in 1855. He and Moulton were good friends.

To HERBERT HORNE, 9 August [1889]
MS.: Mark Samuels Lasner Collection, University of Delaware. Printed in *LWP*.

12 Earl's Terrace, | August 9.

My dear Horne,

I think it very kind of you to send me this beautiful and characteristic drawing by S. Solomon.¹—Accept my sincere thanks for so choice a gift.²

We hope to leave for the Continent on Monday. Our programme is a little uncertain, and may become more so in execution; but at present we propose to be in Milan for some days about the second week in ~~December~~ September, and it would be very pleasant and interesting to meet you there in one of those grand churches, or the like.³

In any case, I hope you will have a charming visit to Italy, and that I may meet you very soon after our return.

With our kind regards,
Very sincerely yours
Walter Pater.

¹ Simeon Solomon (1840–1905), Pre-Raphaelite painter and draughtsman (see Biographical Register).
² Pater celebrated his fiftieth birthday on Sunday, 4 Aug. 1889; the drawing he mentions (untraced) was almost surely a birthday gift. Herbert Percy Horne (1864–1916), poet, architect, typographer, and art historian, admired Solomon's work; he owned the striking drawing of Pater (1872) now in the Uffizi Gallery, Florence. Horne acted as the artist's informal agent.
³ Grant Duff records in his diary for 13 Oct. 1889: 'A large party with us. Pater talked much of the charms of Bergamo and Brescia, where he has lately been.' See *Notes from a Diary 1889–1891*, 1: 169.

To ARTHUR SYMONS, [10 August 1889]
MS.: Scott Library, York University, Toronto. On a correspondence card.

> 12 Earl's Terrace.

My dear Symons,

Many thanks for your kind thought of me.[1] I regret extremely not to see you on your way through London, but must inevitably be away nearly all Wednesday. Engagements multiply upon me, just at this time.

In great haste,

> Very sincerely yours
> Walter Pater.

---

[1] See letter to Horne, 9 Aug. [1889], n. 2. Very likely the 'kind thought' was a card, letter, or gift marking the occasion of Pater's fiftieth birthday.

To JOHN VERSCHOYLE,[1] 11 August [1889][2]
MS.: William Andrews Clark Memorial Library, University of California at Los Angeles. On a correspondence card.

> 12 Earl's Terrace, W. | August 11th.

My dear Verschoyle,

As I leave England tomorrow for many weeks, I think it right to send a line to tell you that I have received no cheque for my contribution to The Fortnightly.[3]

In great haste,

> Very sincerely yours
> Walter Pater.

---

[1] Revd John Stuart Verschoyle (1853–1915), Anglo-Irish clergyman and journalist, served as the assistant editor of the *Fortnightly Review*, 1889–91 (see letter to Unknown Correspondent, 7 Jan. [1889]).

[2] So dated on the evidence presented in the letter to Horne, 9 Aug. [1889]; 12 Aug. 1889 was a Monday.

[3] 'Giordano Bruno. Paris: 1856' appeared in the *Fortnightly Review*, ns 46 (Aug. 1889), 234–44.

To WALTER PATER, 16 September [1889]
MS.: British Library. Printed in *TBB*.

Sept. 16 9

Dear Mr. Pater,

Clark says that he sent you [?] proofs of the whole of your new book on August 12.13 with some queries & that they have not been returned for press. I expect that you are away; perhaps you will kindly send Clark his proofs as soon as you get back. The paper is all ready & it will take a very short time to [work] it.

I am

Yours very truly,
Frederick Macmillan.

Walter Pater Esq.

To WALTER PATER, 30 September [1889]
MS.: British Library. Printed in *TBB*.

Sept. 30 9

Dear Mr. Pater,

I enclose the annual statement[1] of account & at the same time I send you the final Memoranda of Agreement[2] as arranged. Kindly sign & return one copy of the latter.

I am

Yours very truly,
Frederick Macmillan.

Walter Pater Esq.

[1] This enclosure is missing.
[2] According to this agreement, dated 13 Sept. 1889, Macmillan contracted to publish at its own risk *The Renaissance*, *Marius the Epicurean*, and *Appreciations* on condition that the copyright belong to the publishers and that, after deducting expenses, profits be divided equally. See Brit. Lib. Add. MS. 55030, fol. 52.

To MR BURY, [13 October 1889?]¹
MS.: Archives, the King's School, Canterbury.

B. N. C. | Sunday.

My dear Mr Bury,²

I shall, with much pleasure, expect you to dine in Hall tomorrow, at 7 o'clock.

Sincerely yours
Walter Pater.

---

¹ The handwriting belongs to the period 1888 to 1891. I choose 1889 as the date because the handwriting bears a strong resemblance to, for example, the handwriting in the letter Pater wrote to Benjamin Nattali, dated 6 Aug. [1889?]. Given that Pater writes from Oxford, possibly just after returning from London, and that he speaks of dining 'in Hall', it follows that he is writing in October. In 1889, Michaelmas Term began on 10 Oct. (see *Jackson's Oxford Journal*, 10 Aug. 1889, 5).

² Unknown.

To WALTER PATER, 18 October [1889]
MS.: British Library. Printed in *TBB*.

Oct. 18 9

Dear Mr. Pater,

I understand from Clark that he is still waiting for the return 'for press' of the title page to your new book. I shall be glad if you can send this back as we should like to publish it before the work on Childrens' books etc. begins. When bookshops become crowded with 'Christmas books' serious literature is apt to receive shabby treatment.

I am

Very truly yours
Frederick Macmillan.

Walter Pater Esq.

To ARTHUR SYMONS, 19 October [1889]
MS.: Colin Smythe. On a correspondence card. Envelope postmarked OC 19 89.

Brasenose. Saturday.

My dear Symons,

 I was just about to send you a line. Shall now hope to see you, instead, on Tuesday,[1] preferably. Lunch here, at 1.30.

Ever yours
Walter Pater.

 [1] That is, 22 Oct. 1889.

To LOUISE CHANDLER MOULTON, 30 October [1889]
MS.: Library of Congress. Envelope: To | Mrs. Moulton | Durham House | Chelsea | S.W. Postmark: OXFORD R OC 30 89. Printed in *LWP*.

Brasenose College, | Oxford. | Oct: 30th.

My dear Mrs. Moulton,

 I much wish I could take advantage of your kind note of invitation, which has been transferred to me here, where my residence continues for some weeks to come. I feel I have been very unfortunate this year, with regard to my chance of getting a talk with you: hope, however, you will be in England again, early next year, and am, meantime and always,

Very sincerely yours
Walter Pater.

To WALTER PATER, 1 November [1889]
MS.: British Library. Printed in *TBB*.

Nov 1. 9

Dear Mr. Pater,

 'Appreciations' which is now ready for publication contains 264 pages & makes a goodly volume; I think the price might be 7/6 or 8/6.[1] 'Imaginary Portraits' which is 6/– only contains 186 pages. What are your views?
 I am

Yours very truly
Frederick Macmillan.

Walter Pater Esq.

[1] The prices refer to seven shillings and six pence, and eight shillings and six pence.

To AN UNKNOWN CORRESPONDENT, 12 November [1889?][1]
MS.: Samuel Wright. Printed in *LWP*.

Brasenose College, | Nov: 12th.

Dear Sir,

I see no objection to your using my article on Bruno,[2] in the way you propose. The article is really a chapter from an unfinished work, and had to be cut about for insertion in the Review. This may have given it an inexplicable air, here or there. I shall be interested in seeing your lecture.

Yours truly
Walter Pater.

[1] Much was written and said in 1889 about the Italian Renaissance philosopher Giordano Bruno (1548–1600) because of the furore created by the installation in Rome that year of a statue by Ettore Ferrari (1845–1929) to commemorate Bruno on the location in the Campo de' Fiori where he was burned at the stake by the papal Inquisition in 1600.

[2] Pater's article is 'Giordano Bruno', *Fortnightly Review*, ns 52 (Aug. 1889), 234–44; the full text, from which the article was drawn, is printed as ch. 7, 'The Lower Pantheism', *Gaston de Latour* (see *CW* iv).

To ARTHUR SYMONS, [22? November 1889][1]
MS.: Brasenose College. Written on a correspondence card. Printed in *LWP*.

12 Earl's Terrace, | Kensington, W.

My dear Symons,

I enclose the photograph you so kindly wished to have. It may amuse \you/ to compare therewith the other enclosure.[2]

Very sincerely yours
Walter Pater.

[1] Symons visited Pater in Oxford on Wednesday, 20 Nov. 1889, and had the newspaper cutting (see next note), apparently from Pater, by Saturday (see his letter to James Dykes Campbell of 'Saturday' [23 Nov. 1889], Brit. Lib. Add. MS. 49523).
[2] The 'other enclosure' to which Pater refers is a cutting from the London *Star*, 21 Nov. 1889, 4. Taken from the column, 'Books and Bookmen', it is a short, commendatory notice of *Appreciations* by Clement King Shorter (1857–1926), journalist and editor (see letter to

Unknown Correspondent, 6 June [1892]), and contains a picture of Pater from an engraving based on an early photograph (1870). The photograph Pater sent Symons is missing, but it was probably the well-known Elliott & Fry study, 1889 (see letter to Pater, 15 Nov. [1887], n. 2).

To BERTHA PENROSE LATHBURY,[1] [*c*.24 November 1889][2]
MS.: Brasenose College. On a correspondence card. Printed in *LWP*.

12 Earl's Terrace, W.

My dear Mrs. Lathbury,

I hope Mr. Lathbury is improving steadily,—was sincerely grieved to hear of his illness.

I have asked Macmillan to send you a volume of mine recently published. I think part of its contents may interest you.

Don't be troubled to reply to this, but believe me, with very kind regards,

Sincerely yours
Walter Pater.

[1] Bertha Penrose Lathbury (1846–1934), daughter of Bonamy Price (1807–88), political economist. Price was Drummond Professor of Political Economy at Oxford, 1868–88; on at least one occasion in the early 1870s Pater and Price met at a luncheon or a soirée in north Oxford, where they discussed ecclesiastical matters (see Gosse, 801; Wright, 1: 259–60; James Covert, *A Victorian Marriage: Mandell and Louise Creighton* (London: Hambledon, 2000), 86–8). Bertha married Daniel Conner Lathbury (1831–1922), an ecclesiastical journalist. Lathbury, who attended Brasenose 1850–4, later edited the *Economist* (1878–81), *The Guardian* (1883–99), an Anglican weekly to which Pater contributed nine anonymous reviews between Feb. 1886 and Oct. 1890, and the *Pilot*, 1900–4. Bertha Lathbury made a name for herself as a London hostess, especially in High Church circles, and as the writer of occasional reviews and essays.
[2] The volume 'recently published' and sent by Pater to Lathbury was *Appreciations*, the only one of the three books of his London period to appear at a time when he used mottled grey-green, gilt-edged correspondence cards. Grant Duff received his presentation copy of *Appreciations* by 24 Nov. 1889; I take that date as a reasonable approximation for this note.

To WILLIAM SHARP, 24 November [1889]
MS.: Noel F. Sharp. Printed in *LWP*.

12 Earl's Terrace: | Nov: 24.

My dear Sharp,

Sincere thanks for your most interesting and excellent criticism, itself, in so high a degree, graceful and scholarly.[1] I read it with great pleasure; and shall read it again carefully. Thanks also for your recent letters, which interested me much; though I felt I didn't deserve them; but you know how unfruitful a correspondent I am. I am here on one of my flying visits, but shall look forward to meeting when I return for the vacation next month. Meantime, with kind regards,

> Very sincerely yours
> Walter Pater.

[1] This early review of *Appreciations* has not been traced.

To SAMUEL WADDINGTON,[1] 30 November [1889]
MS.: Brasenose College. The letter is printed and dated 1889 in Samuel Waddington, *Chapters of My Life: An Autobiography* (London: Chapman and Hall, 1909), 36; with a facsimile between pages 36 and 37. Printed in *LWP*.

> Brasenose, | Nov: 30th.

Dear Sir,

It was very kind of you to send me your charming book.[2] Some of the sonnets I knew already, but am glad to possess the entire collection of them. They seem to fulfil the purpose of the sonnet, in embodying a somewhat subtle clause of thought, in perfected words. The Prelude and Epilogue too, are delightful. Many thanks!

> Very sincerely yours
> Walter Pater.

Mr. F. W. Percival[3] is an old friend of mine. I hope we may some day meet.

[1] Samuel Waddington (1844–1923), anthologist, poet, and biographer, studied at Brasenose 1862–5; he admired Pater, but did not form a personal acquaintance with him. From 1868–1906 he worked for the Board of Trade, where he was for some years a colleague of Austin Dobson, Edmund Gosse, and Cosmo Monkhouse. He edited several collections of sonnets and published a critical biography of poet Arthur Clough (1819–61) in 1883.

[2] *A Century of Sonnets* (1889) consists of Waddington's original verse. A number of poems feature scientific subjects and promote rationalist thought (arguing against, for example, 'superstition').

[3] Waddington dedicated his volume to Francis William Percival (1844–1929), a school inspector and examiner in the Education Office who was probably one of Pater's first pupils at Brasenose College, 1863–7. Percival visited Pater at his house in Bradmore Road (Wright, 1: 240). He had numerous interests, including Egyptology and ecclesiology, and was one of the founders of the Society for Psychical Research.

To JOHN VERSCHOYLE, 3 December [1889]
MS.: William Andrews Clark Memorial Library, University of California at Los Angeles. On correspondence cards; the bottom of each card has been torn off.

Brasenose, | Dec: 3rd.

My Dear Verschoyle,

It is ungrateful of me not to have told you before that I thought your article 'In the Forests of Navarro and Aragon' a very fresh and agreeable piece of writing on a delightful, but to me unknown, country.[1] I hope you will write more [of the kind] as I find such reading a very pleasant relaxation.

I wish I could finally disentangle the Aesthetic Life,[2] or my promised article thereon, from my brains; but am unable to do so yet. I must ask you to forgive me once more, and believe me

Very sincerely yours
Walter Pater.

[1] Revd John Verschoyle, 'In the Forests of Navarre and Aragon', *Fortnightly Review*, ns 46 (Oct. 1889), 516–37. See letter to Unknown Correspondent, 7 Jan. [1889].
[2] See 'The Aesthetic Life', Houghton Library bMS Eng 1150 (7); *CW* x.

To WILLIAM SHARP, 3 December [1889]
MS.: Noel F. Sharp. Printed in *LWP*.

Brasenose, | Dec: 3rd.

My dear Sharp,

Sincere thanks! I read yesterday, with great pleasure, in the Glasgow Herald, the so appreciative criticism of my 'Appreciations', by so excellent a critic as yourself.[1]

Yours truly yours
Walter Pater.

[1] Sharp's unsigned review, 'Mr. Pater on Appreciations', *Glasgow Herald*, 28 Nov. 1889, 9. 'To many', Sharp observes, 'this volume will seem to contain the wisest and most significant *urbana scripta* {urbane, elegant writings} of its accomplished author.'

To WALTER PATER, 17 December [1889]
MS.: British Library. Printed in *TBB*.

Walter Pater Esqre. | 12 Earl's Terrace | Kensington | W

                    Dec 17 9

Dear W Pater,

 The words marked by you in the Athenaeum notice shall be used in our advertisements of 'Appreciations' where it is possible.

 I am

                    Yours very truly,
                    Maurice Macmillan.[1]

P. S. I return your copy of the review.

---

[1] Maurice Crawford Macmillan (1853–1936), the second son of Frances and Daniel Macmillan (see Biographical Register).

To WALTER PATER, 23 December [1889]
MS.: British Library. Printed in *TBB*.

                    Dec. 23 89

Dear Mr. Pater,

 We have only 120 copies left of 'Appreciations' and though no doubt the demand will slacken a little after Christmas, we certainly ought to begin upon the reprint without undue delay. Will you therefore let us have by the end of the week a note of any corrections you may wish to make? It would be quite safe to print 1250 copies or even 1500 if you can make up your mind to it. The rapidity of the sale is very encouraging.

 I am

                    Yours very truly,
                    George A. Macmillan.

Walter Pater Esq. | 12 Earl's Terrace.

To DOUGLAS AINSLIE, [c.23 December 1889]¹
MS.: Bates College. On a correspondence card. Printed in *LWP*.

12 Earl's Terrace, | Kensington, W.

Dear Ainslie,

I am sorry not to have seen you these late weeks, and thank you for calling. I hope I may have the pleasure when you return to London, taking it for granted that you are hardly likely to be in Town now. I think the enclosed² may interest you. Don't be troubled to answer this; but believe me, with best Xmas wishes,

Sincerely yours
Walter Pater.

¹ Dated from the Christmas wishes and the mottled grey-green, gilt-edged correspondence cards used.
² The enclosure is missing; it might have been one of two reviews of *Appreciations* that pleased Pater: either William Watson's, in the *Academy*, 21 Dec. 1889, 399–400 (see letter to Cotton, 23 Dec. [1889]), or Arthur Symons's (unsigned) in the *Athenaeum*, 14 Dec. 1889, 813–14.

To JAMES SUTHERLAND COTTON,¹ 23 December [1889]
Text: Maggs Bros. *Catalogue* no. 396 (1920), 176. The catalogue gives the date '23rd December'. Printed in *LWP*.

Dear Mr. Cotton,

Of course I was much pleased with Mr. Watson's paper in the Academy.² His own poetic work is so excellent! I hope I may one day have the pleasure of meeting him....

¹ James Sutherland Cotton (1847–1918), writer and editor, attended Trinity College, Oxford, 1867–70, and was a Fellow and Lecturer of Queen's College, 1871–4. He was called to the Bar of Lincoln's Inn in 1874, but turned instead to journalism: from 1881–96 he edited the *Academy*, encouraging high-quality (signed) articles. Cotton wrote the obituary of Pater for the *Academy*, 11 Aug. 1894, 102.
² John William Watson (1858–1935), poet and critic, published his first volume of verse, *The Prince's Quest, and Other Poems* in 1880, at the age of twenty-two, followed by *Epigrams of Art, Life, and Nature* (1884). *Wordsworth's Grave* (1890) and *Lachrymae Musarum, and Other Poems* (1893). In Watson's signed review of *Appreciations*, which appeared in the *Academy*, 21 Dec. 1889, 399–400, Pater is praised as 'one of the most catholic of living critics, and beyond rivalry the subtlest artist in contemporary English prose' (400).

To HERBERT HORNE, 24 December [1889]
MS.: Mark Samuels Lasner Collection, University of Delaware. On a correspondence card. Printed in *LWP*.

12 Earl's Terrace, | Dec: 24th.

My dear Horne,

Many thanks! It would give me great pleasure to dine with you some time later. I shall look with interest to the new number of The Hobby Horse;[1] meantime, with best Xmas wishes, I remain

Very sincerely yours
Walter Pater.

The enclosed[2] may interest you.

---

[1] Presumably Horne had told Pater that a review of *Appreciations* by Lionel Johnson (see Biographical Register), 'A Note upon Certain Qualities in the Writing of Mr. Pater; as Illustrated by his Recent Book', would appear in the *Century Guild Hobby Horse*, 4 (Jan. 1890), 36–40. For Pater's later reactions, see letter to Johnson, [20 Feb. 1890]).

[2] A pencilled note on the MS. identifies the enclosure (now missing) as Watson's review of *Appreciations*, which appeared in the *Academy* (see letter to Johnson, [20 Feb. 1890]).

1890

To OSCAR WILDE, [4? January 1890][1]
MS.: William Andrews Clark Memorial Library, University of California at Los Angeles. On a correspondence card measuring 11.4 × 8.9 cm. Printed in full (except for the words 'to be able') by Stuart Mason, *Bibliography of Oscar Wilde* (London: T. W. Laurie, 1914), 208. Also printed in *LWP*.

12 Earl's Terrace, W.

My dear Wilde,

It seems an age since we met. I had hoped to be able to call this afternoon. I have been reading the 'Speaker': it seems very clever and excellent, and makes me anxious that should my recent volume be noticed there, it may not fall into unsympathetic hands. If I am intrusive in saying this, I am sure you will forgive me, and believe me, with kind regards,

Very sincerely yours
Walter Pater.

Don't be troubled to answer this.

[1] The *Speaker: A Review of Politics, Letters, Science, and the Arts*, a liberal magazine that was published by Cassell & Co. from 4 Jan. 1890 to 30 Sept. 1899. Advance notices of the new weekly had listed Wilde as a contributor; it is not unreasonable, from what Pater writes, to assume this date for his note. Pater's hint was not wasted: see letter to Wilde, 22 Mar. [1890].

To HERBERT HORNE [early January 1890][1]
MS: Mark Samuels Lasner Collection, University of Delaware. On a correspondence card. Printed in *LWP*.

12 Earl's Terrace.

My dear Horne,

Sincere thanks for your very kind invitation. But I have already an engagement for that evening and am very sorry to be unable to accept. In haste, with kind regards,

Very truly yours
Walter Pater.

[1] The year 1890 is pencilled on the MS., presumably from the postmark. As this correspondence card is mottled grey-green and gilt-edged, I place the note in the winter, during Pater's Christmas vacation.

To SIR MOUNTSTUART GRANT DUFF, 7 January [1890][1]
MS.: Brasenose College. On a mottled-grey correspondence card. Printed in *LWP*.

12 Earl's Terrace, W. | Jan: 7th.

My dear Sir Mountstuart,

I *am* engaged to dine on Saturday evening, and don't like to make an excuse; otherwise, it would have given me great pleasure to accept your so kind invitation. I should much like however, if I may, to dine with you on Sunday, returning here, as I can easily do, that night. I will come as early as possible in the afternoon: only, you must not stay in for me. I am sorry to hear of Lady Grant Duff's illness, and, with our kind regards, am

Very sincerely yours
Walter Pater.

[1] So dated by Grant Duff in a letter of 13 Jan. 1890 to his son, Evelyn Grant Duff (MS.: Sheila Sokolov Grant), listing 'Pater who only dined and went back again' among their visitors since the first of the year.

To ARTHUR SYMONS, [15 January 1890][1]
MS.: Gerald Monsman. Printed in *LWP*.

Brasenose, | Wednesday.

My dear Symons,

Many thanks for your letter; also for the excellent verses on Browning.
I think I shall be here till Wednesday next, inclusive; but on Thursday (tomorrow) and on Tuesday and Wednesday next week, may be engaged from 5 to 6. If you happen to come on either of those days, take the chance of finding me here, a little earlier in the afternoon.

Very sincerely yours
Walter Pater.

[1] Symons was planning two visits, one during the third week of Jan. and one during the fourth, to research Shakespeare's *Henry VIII* in the Bodleian library (see his letter to James Dykes Campbell, 20 Jan. 1890, Brit. Lib. Add. MS. 49523). Presumably Symons wrote to Pater in advance, eliciting this reply. The 'verses on Browning' were Symons's elegy for Robert Browning, 'Dead in Venice. 12 December 1889', *Athenaeum*, 21 Dec. 1889, 860. Pater's letter, however, like the letters dated 3 June [1888] and [1? Apr. 1889], has become associated with the wrong envelope. The envelope is addressed to Arthur Symons Esq. | Coton Road | Nuneaton; and postmarked OXFORD X JU 5 88.

To WALTER PATER, 7 February [1890]
MS.: British Library.

Feb. 7 90

Dear Mr. Pater,

Messrs. Clark inform us that you have not yet sent them a corrected copy of Appreciations.[1] Please do so as soon as possible. The book is quite out of print and the delay cannot fail to be injurious.

I was so glad to hear from Miss Pater[2] that you thought well of my friend Mr. Francis Lucas's poems.[3]

I am

Yours very truly,
George A. Macmillan.

W. H. Pater Esq. | 12 Earl's Terrace

[1] *Appreciations* was released on 15 Nov. 1889; the second edition appeared in May 1890. See *CW* vi.
[2] Clara Pater (see Biographical Register).
[3] Francis Lucas (1830–97) produced one volume, *Sketches of Rural Life and other Poems* (London: Macmillan, 1889), which was printed by R. & R. Clark, Edinburgh, and reprinted in 1897.

To LIONEL JOHNSON,[1] [20 February 1890]
MS.: Brasenose College. On a correspondence card. Printed in *LWP*.[2]

My dear Mr. Johnson,

I have read with great pleasure your careful and scholarly paper on my work; and value it. You write with great refinement: pleasantly, at once, and with a pervading air of thoughtful concentration.

Kindly tell Galton,[3] when you write, that the Hobby Horse was duly received, and greatly liked.

Very truly yours
Walter Pater.

[1] Lionel Pigot Johnson (1867–1902), poet and literary scholar (see Biographical Register).
[2] The story of this letter is told by Arthur W. Patrick in *Lionel Johnson. Poète et critique* (Paris: Rodstein, 1939), 165. Johnson reviewed *Appreciations* ('A Note, upon Certain Qualities in the Writings of Mr. Pater; as Illustrated by his Recent Book') in the *Century Guild Hobby Horse*, 5 (Jan. 1890), 36–40. On hearing about the article from Galton (an assistant editor of the journal), Pater went at once to see Johnson on 18 Feb. Later that day Johnson wrote to

Galton: 'Pater has just left me: your letter sent him round, insisting to know what I had said of him: he was immensely agitated, coming at nine in the morning.' On receiving Johnson's letter, Galton sent Pater a copy of the *Hobby Horse*, which must have arrived on the 20th. Pater then penned this note to Johnson, who in turn wrote the same day to Galton: 'Pater asks me to tell you that he has received the Hobby Horse and greatly likes it.'

[3] Revd Arthur Howard Galton (1852–1921), classicist, critic, and priest, was a close friend of Johnson at New College, Oxford; it was through him that Johnson met Pater in 1887. See Biographical Register; and letter to Horne, 17 July [1888].

To ARTHUR SYMONS, [22 February 1890]
MS.: University of Michigan. Envelope: Arthur Symons Esq. | 21 Chandos Road | Buckingham. Postmark: KENS[IN]GTON X FE 22 90 W. Printed in *LWP*.

My dear Symons,

I am ashamed to find how long your letter of the 10th has remained unanswered, and just send this now to say that, though I cannot make an appointment now, it would give me great pleasure to go and make Mrs. Holman Hunt's[1] acquaintance some day. In haste,

> Very sincerely yours
> Walter Pater.

[1] Marion Edith Hunt, née Waugh (1846–1931) married the Pre-Raphaelite painter William Holman Hunt (1827–1910) in 1875; she was the younger sister of his first wife, Fanny Waugh Hunt (1833–66), who had died in childbirth. (Marrying a dead spouse's sister was illegal in the UK until 1907; the ceremony took place in France.) Marion Hunt was a well-known figure in London society for half a century.

To LOUISE CHANDLER MOULTON, [25 February 1890]
MS.: Library of Congress. Envelope: To | Mrs. Moulton | 28 Rutland Square | Boston | Mass: | U.S.A. Postmark: OXFORD T FE 25 90. The first two sentences, slightly misquoted, are printed by Lilian Whiting, *Louise Chandler Moulton: Poet and Friend* (Boston: Little, Brown, and Company, 1910) and in *LWP*.

My dear Mrs. Moulton,

I read very little contemporary poetry, finding a good deal of it a little *falsetto*[.] I found, however, in your elegant and musical volume,[1] a sincerity, a simplicity, which struck me as constituting a *cachet*, a distinct note. My sister also, \who/ is a good judge of poetry, has also enjoyed the reading of it.

I am a reluctant letter-writer, and when a pleasant book or letter reaches me, sometimes delay acknowledgement in hope of being able to write at greater length. It was so with your volume: but, as you have now supplemented it by your kind notice of my own,[2] I must delay no longer, and ask you to forgive this late but sincere word of thanks for both.

Very truly yours,
Walter Pater.

[1] *In the Garden of Dreams: Lyrics and Sonnets* (Boston: Roberts Brothers, 1889).
[2] Moulton (see letter to Moulton, [18 July 1889]) reviewed *Appreciations* in the Boston *Sunday Herald*, 5 Jan. 1890, 24, praising Pater's style and his 'power of illumination': 'There is no critic writing today who seems to me so helpful and so stimulating as Walter Pater.... We find, instead, the sanest and subtlest appreciation of other men's works, and the clearest insight into the sources of their power. It is criticism with which it is almost a liberal education to be familiar.'

To WALTER PATER, 3 March [1890]
MS.: British Library. Printed in *TBB*.

Re. *Appreciations*

March 3 90

Dear Mr. Pater,

I have come across this card[1] which I ought to have sent you when it first came. I suppose I laid it aside with the at that time not unnatural idea that a new edition would hardly be wanted just yet. Events happily proved otherwise. I only hope it is not too late to correct the statement if it really needs correction. You are I think in direct communication with the printers.

This needs no reply.

Yours very truly,
George A. Macmillan.

Walter Pater Esq. | 12 Earl's Terrace W.

[1] The enclosure is missing.

To OSCAR WILDE, 22 March [1890]
MS.: William Andrews Clark Memorial Library, University of California at Los Angeles. Printed in *LWP*.

12 Earl's Terrace, | March 22.

My dear Wilde,

    I have read your pleasantly written, genial, sensible, criticism in the Speaker with very great pleasure.[1] How friendly of you to have given so much care and time to my book, in the midst of your own work in that prose of which you have become so successful a writer.[2]

    Thank you sincerely. Ever

Most truly yours
Walter Pater.

With kind regards.

---

[1] Wilde's signed review of *Appreciations*, 'Mr. Pater's Last Volume', *Speaker*, 22 Mar. 1890, 319–20, is lavish in praise: 'in Mr. Pater, as in Cardinal Newman, we find the union of personality with perfection'.

[2] Possibly a reference to Wilde's latest project, *The Picture of Dorian Gray*, which initially appeared in *Lippincott's Monthly Magazine*, 46 (July 1890), 3–100.

To MICHAEL FIELD, [12 April 1890]
MS.: Miriam Lutcher Stark Library, Harry Ransom Center, University of Texas. On a correspondence card. Envelope: Michael Field Esq. | Blackberry Lodge | Reigate. Postmark: KENSINGTON BX AP 12 90 W. Printed in *LWP*.

12 Earl's Terrace.

Dear Mr. Michael Field,

    I don't think I can claim any property in so slight a phrase; but ## if so, shall be proud that you should adopt it for the title of your new work; also the quotation for the note.[1] I shall look forward to the appearance of your play with much interest, and am

Very sincerely yours
Walter Pater.

---

[1] John Miller Gray (see letter to Gray, [Aug.? 1878]) had suggested Pater's phrase, 'the tragic Mary', as a title for Michael Field's new play about Mary, Queen of Scots (see letter to Michael Field, 11 June 1889); Bradley and Cooper had gone to Earl's Terrace on 24 Mar. 1890 to ask Pater's permission to use it—but Pater was not home (see Michael Field Papers, Brit. Lib. Add. MS. 46778, fol. 45). The phrase, drawn from Pater's essay on D. G. Rossetti in *Appreciations* (see *CW* vi), is acknowledged in *The Tragic Mary* (London: George Bell, 1890) and its context quoted by Field in an endnote, 261.

To WALTER PATER, 15 April [1890]
MS.: British Library. Printed in *TBB*.

April 15 90

Dear Mr. Pater,

I send you herewith a specimen cover for 'Appreciations' giving only the first title as you suggested. I shall be glad to know by return whether you prefer this to the original arrangement as the copies of the 2nd edition are ready for binding.

Yours very truly,
Frederick Macmillan.

Walter Pater Esq.

To MISS WHITE,[1] 3 May [1890]
Text: Christie's Catalogue, Lot 200, Sale 8942, 17 November 2000.

Brasenose College, | 3 May.

...Pater comments on a passage from Shakespeare's Sonnet 107, 'the prophetic soul / Of the wide world dreaming on things to come',[2] and refers her to Wordsworth.

[1] Unidentified.
[2] The speaker in Sonnet 107 employs astrological conceits to demonstrate the constancy and the eternal nature of his love; his beloved will find his monument in the poem when tyrants and their brass tombs have disappeared.

To WALTER PATER, 30 May [1890]
MS.: British Library. Printed in *TBB*.

May 30

Dear Mr. Pater,

I find that we have less than 40 copies of your 'Imaginary Portraits' left. Would it not be well to be thinking about a new edition?[1]
I am

Yours very truly,
Frederick Macmillan.

Walter Pater Esq.

[1] The second edition was printed in Nov. 1890.

To GEORGE BAINTON,[1] 3 June 1890
MS.: Library Special Collections, Charles E. Young Research Library, UCLA.
Envelope: Revd George Bainton | Coventry. Postmark: OXFORD R JU 3 90.[2]

Brasenose College, | June 3rd.

Dear Mr Bainton,

Many thanks for your letter of April 28th. I have read your ingenious "Art of Authorship"[3] with great interest. I feel sure it will interest and be useful to a large number of readers.

Sincerely yours
Walter Pater.

[1] See letter to Bainton, [Oct. 1887–1889?].
[2] The letter is excerpted in Paul Jordan-Smith, *For the Love of Books: The Adventures of an Impecunious Collector* (Oxford: Oxford University Press, 1934), 274–5, 292–4; printed in Gerald Monsman, 'Two Pater Letters to George Bainton', *Pater Newsletter*, 63 (Spring 2013), 73–5.
[3] Pater contributed a short response for the collection, *The Art of Authorship: Literary Reminiscences, Methods of Work, and Advice to Young Beginners* (London: J. Clarke, 1890); Bainton may have sent him a copy. Melville B. Anderson's review of the book appeared in the *Dial*, 124 (Aug. 1890), 85–7.

To AN UNKNOWN CORRESPONDENT,[1] 3 June [1890?]
MS.: Cynthia Rich Glauber. Printed in *LWP*.

Brasenose College, | June 3rd.

Dear Madam,

I have just found, in a pile of letters awaiting reply, yours of March 5th. Excuse my long delay in acknowledging your kind words. I believe Messrs Elliot[t] and Fry,[2] of Baker Street, London, have a photograph of me. With best wishes,

Faithfully yours
Walter Pater.

[1] Pater's female admirer has not been identified. The date must be after the Elliott & Fry photograph was taken—at some point during the summer of 1889, marking Pater's fiftieth birthday (see letter to Horne, 9 Aug. [1889], n. 2); and perhaps soon after the publication of *Appreciations* (1889) had enlarged his audience. The stationery belongs to 1890 or 1891.
[2] See letter to Pater, 15 Nov. [1887], n. 2, for details regarding the photography studio.

To AN UNKNOWN CORRESPONDENT, 16 June [1890?]
Text: Bonhams Catalogue no. 1793 (22 November 2011). On a correspondence card, a little foxed, neatly inlaid, 8.8 x 11.4 cm.

Brasenose College. | June 16th.

Dear Sir,

Kindly reserve for my proposed lecture[1] the day you have named—Monday, Nov. 24th at 5 pm. With many thanks,

Very faithfully yours
Walter Pater.

[1] Pater presented a lecture on Prosper Mérimée at the Taylor Institution, Oxford, on 17 Nov. 1890, and again at the London Institute, on 24 Nov. 1890. See letter to Wilkinson, [16 Nov. 1890], n. 3. For the published text, see *CW* vi.

To WALTER PATER, 1 July [1890]
MS.: British Library. Printed in *TBB*.

July 1st

Dear Mr. Pater,

We have an order from our New York House for some copies of your 'Studies in the Renaissance' and 'Appreciations' and we propose, with your approval, to print 1000 copies of each book. The price at which we shall sell them will afford a profit of something over £50 to divide. Unless you have any objections we shall proceed at once with the manufacture.

I am

Yours very truly,
Frederick Macmillan.

Walter Pater Esq.

To LOUISE CHANDLER MOULTON, 22 July [1890]
MS.: Library of Congress. Envelope: To | Mrs. Moulton | 11, Weymouth Street | Portland Place | W. Postmark: [KENSINGT]ON DX JY 22 90 W. Printed in *LWP*.

12 Earl's Terrace, | July 22.

My dear Mrs. Moulton,

I enclose a note for Miss Guiney,[1] to be delivered, at the Bodleian Library, to Mr. Madan, one of the Librarians, or in his absence to the Librarian in attendance. I had hoped to be able to call in Weymouth Street ere this, but have been a good deal engaged lately, and also over-powered with work promised, which I should like to finish before I go abroad shortly. I shall try, however, to see you one of these afternoons, and, thanking you sincerely for your kind note, remain

Very truly yours
Walter Pater.

In haste to gain the post.

[1] Louise Imogen Guiney (1861–1920), American poet, essayist, and editor, grew up in Boston and graduated from Elmhurst Academy, Rhode Island, in 1879. She wrote lyrical poetry, starting with *Songs at the Start* (Boston: Cupples, Upham, 1884) and *Goose-Quill Papers* (Boston: Roberts Brothers, 1885). She visited England often during the 1890s, meeting Gosse, W. B. Yeats, and Lionel Johnson. In 1903, Guiney served as Gosse's research assistant, helping him prepare a biography of Jeremy Taylor. The enclosure might have been the letter to Madan, 22 July [1890].

To FALCONER MADAN, 22 July [1890]
MS.: Bodleian Library. Printed in *LWP*.

12 Earl's Terrace, | July 22nd.

My dear Madan,

The bearer, Miss Louise Guiney,[1] a very accomplished American lady, is desirous to make some researches in the Bodleian Library, and has asked me for a line of introduction. Will you kindly do what you can for her.

Very sincerely yours
W. H. Pater.

[1] See letter to Moulton, 22 July [1890].

To CLYDE FITCH,[1] 1 August 1890
Text: Montrose J. Moses and Virginia Gerson, *Clyde Fitch and His Letters* (Boston: Little Brown, 1924), 58. Printed in *LWP*.

12 Earl's Terrace, | August 1, 1890.

Dear Fitch,

Your visit on Sunday[2] gave me great pleasure. We hope to be home again by the end of September. Come and see us then: and kindly accept the enclosed.[3]

Very sincerely yours,
Walter Pater.

[1] William Clyde Fitch (1865–1909), an American playwright, attended Amherst College, 1882–6, where he displayed his virtuosity as an amateur actor. He devoted his life to the theatre, becoming the first American playwright to publish his own plays. A prolific writer, he produced thirty-three original plays, twenty-one adaptations, and five dramatizations of novels, starting with *Beau Brummell* (1890), set in Regency London. His plays gained popularity on both sides of the Atlantic. Travelling in Europe in the summer of 1888, Fitch met Marc André Raffalovich (see Biographical Register) and Oscar Wilde (see Biographical Register) in London and Pater in Oxford. Raffalovich probably introduced Fitch to Wilde. In a letter dated 10 Aug. 1888 Fitch remarked that he planned to stop 'a few days [in October] in Oxford...where I am invited by one of the fellows of Brasenose' (Fitch, *Clyde Fitch and His Letters*, 45). In May 1889, on his next visit to London, Fitch had a brief affair with Wilde. McKenna, *The Secret Life of Oscar Wilde* (New York: Basic Books, 2005), 109–15, 123; Matthew Sturgis, *Oscar: A Life* (London: Head of Zeus, 2018), 383, 384. See also Pater's letter to Fitch dated 4 Jan. [1892].
[2] That is, 27 July 1890.
[3] Moses and Gerson identify the enclosure as an inscribed copy of 'The Child in the House', presumably an offprint of *Macmillan's Magazine* (*Clyde Fitch and His Letters*, 58).

To COVENTRY PATMORE,[1] 5 August [1890]
MS.: Boston College. The final sentence is quoted by Derek Patmore, *The Life and Times of Coventry Patmore* (London: Constable, 1949), 215. Printed in *LWP*.

12 Earl's Terrace, W. | Aug: 5th.

My dear Sir,

I cannot leave England, as I hope to do shortly for some weeks, without sending these few lines to thank you for your most interesting volume of Essays.[2] I thought it extremely kind of you to send it me, though I have been too tardy in telling you so, as I have had much work on my own on hand of late. Those various papers were certainly worth collecting, and make a volume of exceptionally worthy criticism. I was much pleased to find in the architectural ~~styles~~ papers views something like which have sometimes occurred to myself very effectively expressed. Your Essays are one proof more that true poets make excellent critics, and sometimes genuine connoisseurs of art.

Believe me

Very truly yours
Walter Pater.

---

[1] Coventry Patmore (1823–96), poet and essayist, worked in the printed books department of the British Museum Library. He published *The Angel in the House: The Betrothal* (London: John W. Parker, 1854), a sentimental account in verse of his courtship of Emily Augusta Andrews, which became hugely popular. His poetry was admired by many Pre-Raphaelites and Gerard Manley Hopkins. Emily Patmore died in 1862. Two years later, Patmore married Marianne Byles, a Roman Catholic; he then converted. *The Unknown Eros*, a collection of odes, appeared in 1877; he also published prose works such as *Principles in Art* (London: George Bell, 1889) and *Religio Poetae, etc.* (London: George Bell, 1893). Byles died in 1880; the following year, Patmore married Harriet Robson.

[2] Assuming that the 'volume of Essays' is *Religio Poetae*, Derek Patmore dates this letter 1893 (215). *Religio Poetae*, however, contains no essays on architecture. Rather, the book is *Principles in Art*, which appeared in Oct. 1889: it contains three essays that deal with architecture; to one of these, 'Architectural Styles' (160–201), Pater intended to refer directly.

To WALTER PATER, 8 August [1890]
MS.: British Library. Printed in *TBB*.

Aug. 8.

Dear Mr. Pater,

The manager of our American branch[1] has written to order 1000 copies of *Marius* uniform with the editions of *Appreciations* & *The Renaissance* which we are printing for him. Have you any objection to our getting up an edition & if not do you wish to make alterations?

I am

Yours very truly,
Frederick Macmillan.

Walter Pater Esq.

---

[1] In Aug. 1869 Alexander Macmillan (see Biographical Register) sent George Edward Brett (1829–90), bookseller and publisher, to create and manage the New York branch of Macmillan and Co. Brett travelled with a cargo of books and opened the branch office in a private house at 63 Bleecker Street, NYC. The American firm of Messrs. Pott & Amery aided him in this project. Business expanded rapidly, and in 1874, Brett's son, George Platt Brett (1858–1936), joined the staff as a travelling salesman. When Brett senior died in 1890, Brett junior took over. When Macmillan and Co. underwent a re-organization in 1896, the English firm became a limited concern, Macmillan and Co., Ltd., and the American branch was incorporated as the Macmillan Co., a separate entity with Brett as president. See John A. Tebbel, *A History of Book Publishing in the United States*, 3 vols (New York: R. R. Bowker, 1972–8), 2: 354–5.

To MICHAEL FIELD, 9 August [1890]
MS.: Miriam Lutcher Stark Library, Harry Ransom Center, University of Texas. Envelope: Michael Field Esq. | Blackberry Lodge | Reigate. Postmark: KENSINGTON X AU 9 90 W. Printed in *LWP*.

12 Earl's Terrace, | Aug: 9th.

My dear Ladies,

How kind of you! The beautiful book has reached me safely.[1] I have been very busy, and also away from home; otherwise, should have thanked you more promptly. Beautiful it looks, and worthy to contain what I have seen enough of the interior to be assured is a sterling piece of literary work.[2] I feel, however, that I don't deserve this handsome present; being, I suppose, too little a lover of great art, to read dramatic poetry very readily. I look, nevertheless, for great pleasure in reading your work in this form you have made your own after so distinguished a fashion. I am just leaving England for some weeks in hope to see some places, old favourites of mine, in Italy,[3] and with sincere thanks, am

Very truly yours
Walter Pater.

[1] *The Tragic Mary* (1890).
[2] Pater's bland expression infuriated Bradley, who wrote to John Miller Gray on 23 [?] Aug. 1890: 'I will never forgive Mr. Pater for a word of clumsy praise of the T. M. in wh. the word "sterling" occurs.... Nothing offends us except Mr. Pater's "sterling".' MS. letter, Brit. Lib. Add. MS. 45854, fols 54v, 55v.
[3] Apparently, Pater changed his mind, as Michael Field discovered from Horne. On 25 Aug. Bradley wrote in their journal: 'Pater is going to foreswear holiday & finish *Gaston de Latour*—a longer book than *Marius*. He has struck out the Essay on Aesthetic Poetry in *Appreciations* (for 2nd ed.) because it gave offence to some pious person—he is getting hopelessly prudish in literature, & defers to the moral weaknesses of everybody. Deplorable!' Journals of Michael Field, Brit. Lib. Add. MS. 46778, fol. 205.

To WALTER PATER, 27 August [1890]
MS.: British Library. Printed in *TBB*.

Aug. 27

Dear Mr. Pater,

I enclose an application[1] from somebody who wants to translate 'Marius' into French.
I am

Yours very truly,
Frederick Macmillan.

[1] See letter to Pater, 2 Sept. [1890].

To WALTER PATER, 2 September [1890]
MS.: British Library. Printed in *TBB*.

Sept. 2

Dear Mr. Pater,

If you will kindly return M. Lepelletier's[1] letter I will write to him to say that he is at liberty to do what he proposes on condition that he can find a French publisher who will bring out his and will pay you £15 for the right of translation. I mention that modest sum because I don't suppose any foreign publisher will be likely to give it more. Of course whatever we get for the translation will be paid over to you.

I am busy preparing to start for America. We leave London on the 10th inst[ant].

I am

Yours very truly,
Frederick Macmillan.

Walter Pater Esq. | 12 Earl's Terrace

[1] Perhaps a reference to Edmond Adolphe Lepelletier (1846–1913), a French novelist and biographer. During the 1860s, he published a number of articles attacking the regime of Napoléon III, for which he was imprisoned. He was released after the revolution of 4 Sept. 1870, and welcomed the Paris Commune of 1871. He worked in the radical press and wrote biographies of Émile Zola (1908) and Paul Verlaine (1913), a friend. See letter to Hester Pater, 18 Jan. [1897].

To ARTHUR SYMONS, 18 October [1890]
MS.: Harvard University. On a correspondence card. Envelope: Arthur Symons Esq. | 3 Holly Place | Hampstead | London. | N.W. Postmark: OXFORD X OC 18 90. Printed in *LWP*.

Brasenose, | Oct: 18th.

My dear Symons,

Your kind letter of Oct: 13th has been forwarded to me here; where I shall continue (excepting two or three short visits to London) for the remainder of the term. I never got to Italy after all, this summer: instead, finished a paper of Art-Notes in North Italy, by way of prologue to an Imaginary Portrait with Brescia for background.[1] The former will, I think, appear shortly, in one of the monthlies. Glad to hear you are hard at work, and myself overloaded with it, I remain

Very sincerely yours
Walter Pater.

[1] 'Art Notes in North Italy' was published in *The New Review*, 3 (Nov. 1890), 393–403; see *CW* vi. The description of 'an Imaginary Portrait with Brescia for background' refers to the unpublished MS. fragment (now housed at Harvard), 'Gaudioso, the Second'; see *CW* x.

To WALTER PATER, 12 November [1890]
MS.: British Library. Printed in *TBB*.

Nov. 12

Dear Mr. Pater,

Thank you for telling me that the new edition of 'Imaginary Portraits' is out of your hands. We will give the printers the necessary instructions as to the number of copies etc.

Yours very truly,
George A. Macmillan.

Walter Pater Esq. | Brasenose College | Oxford

To JONAS NIEL LYTE WILKINSON,[1] [16 November 1890]
MS.: Miriam Lutcher Stark Library, Harry Ransom Center, University of Texas. On a correspondence card. Envelope: Niel Wilkinson Esq. | 35 Gloucester Gardens | Hyde Park | London. W. Postmark: OXFORD V NO 16 90. Printed in *LWP*.

BRASENOSE COLLEGE, | OXFORD.[2]

Dear Sir,

I believe my lecture on Prosper Mérimée will appear in the Fortnightly Review.[3] I value your kind interest in my writings, and am

Yours truly
Walter Pater.

[1] Jonas Niel Lyte Wilkinson (1859–1902) attended Christ Church, Oxford, from 1878–82. According to the obituary that appeared in the *Teesdale Mercury*, 27 Aug. 1902, 2, Wilkinson lived in London for the rest of his life and devoted much of his time to helping friends edit their books. If and when Wilkinson met Pater is not clear.
[2] This is the earliest instance of Pater using embossed off-white correspondence cards bearing the college name.
[3] The lecture was given twice: at the Taylor Institution, Oxford, on 17 Nov. 1890, and at the London Institute, 24 Nov. 1890. It had been announced both in the *Oxford University Gazette* and in a number of London journals. Many of Pater's friends and acquaintances attended the lecture. After the London lecture, Pater asked if people could hear what he had said, which prompted Oscar Wilde to say, 'We overheard you'. Pater replied, 'Ah, you have a phrase for everything', recognizing Wilde's allusion to J. S. Mill's distinction between poetry and prose. See Richard Ellmann, *Oscar Wilde* (London: Hamish Hamilton, 1987), 84–5.

Michael Field described the lecture in some detail. See *Works and Days: From the Journal of Michael Field*, ed. T. and D. C. Sturge Moore (London: John Murray, 1933), 119–21; and Cooper's diary entry for 24 Nov. 1890, *Works and Days*, Brit. Lib. Add. MS. 46778, fols. 119–20). The lecture, published in the *Fortnightly Review*, ns 54 (Dec. 1890), 852–64, is in *CW* vi.

To FREDERICK WEDMORE, [*c.*22 November 1890?][1]
MS.: Brasenose College. Printed in *LWP*.

My dear Wedmore,

I am extremely sorry not to have a single ticket. It would have been a great encouragement to see you at my lecture.

Yours sincerely
Walter Pater.

[1] The only public lectures Pater is known to have given outside Oxford in the last decade of his life were both delivered in London in late Nov. 1890: that on Wordsworth at Toynbee Hall, 23 Nov., and on Prosper Mérimée at the London Institute, 24 Nov.

To EMILIE ISABEL WILSON BARRINGTON, 2 December [1890]
MS.: Bates College. A portion of the third paragraph is quoted in Emily Driscoll Catalogue no. 20 (1960), 17. Printed in *LWP*.

Brasenose, | Dec: 2nd.

My dear Mrs. Barrington,

I thought it very kind of you to send me your article on Watts and Rossetti;[1] and should have told you so before, had I not been somewhat overburdened with work of various sorts, of late.

Even now, I wish I had had time to study *thoroughly* a piece of writing, which strikes me, after a hasty but very enjoyable reading, as so excellent, so thoroughly felt,—the kind of work, on a fine subject, which could only have been done by one who has really *lived* in art. Some essential things, about art generally, and with special discrimination of those two chosen artists, you seem to me to have said in a most happy and telling way: and, for the most part, I find myself in agreement with you.—You certainly write persuasively.

I don't think your paper too long; and it seems to me to be your own natural way of saying what is really your own. I wouldn't make any structural alterations. Just change a little, in detail, what strikes you, on a leisurely reading, of it, as imperfect expression of your meaning, or in the way.

I thought it very nice of you to come to my lecture;[2] and, grateful for all the kind words of your letter, am

Very sincerely yours
Walter Pater.

[1] Apparently 'The Painted Poetry of Watts and Rossetti', *The Nineteenth Century*, 13 (June 1883), 950–70, a study of G. F. Watts and D. G. Rossetti, later reprinted in *A Retrospect and Other Articles* (London: Osgood, McIllvaine, 1896), 159–94.
[2] The Mérimée lecture at the London Institute; Michael Field notes Barrington's presence in *Works and Days*, 119.

To WALTER PATER, 8 December [1890]
MS.: British Library. Printed in *TBB*.

Dec 8

Dear Mr. Pater,

I am glad to hear that the proofs of 'Marius the Epicurean' have gone back for press. Our people in New York want the book badly.

You told me in July that you did not wish to see proofs of *Appreciation* & the new edition of that book has accordingly been printed off & dispatched to New York.

I am

Yours very truly,
Frederick Macmillan.

Walter Pater Esq.

To SIR MOUNTSTUART GRANT DUFF, 31 December [1890]
MS.: Sheila Sokolov Grant. Printed in *LWP*.

12 Earl's Terrace, W. | Dec: 31st.

My dear Sir Mountstuart,

Sincere thanks for your kind invitation. It will give me much pleasure to see you again. I am writing lectures for my undergraduates—a little against time;[1] but it will be a great refreshment to me to come on Saturday Jan. 3rd, and stay with you till Sunday evening,[2] that I may be here ready for work on Monday morning. With kind regards, and best wishes for the New Year,

Very sincerely yours
Walter Pater.

[1] Pater was to lecture in Hilary term on 'Plato and Platonism'. The lecture series, to be given at noon on Wednesdays, beginning 21 Jan. 1891, was announced in the *Oxford University Gazette*, 19 Jan. 1891, Supplement, 240. See *CW* vii.

[2] Mountstuart Elphinstone Grant Duff (1829–1906), Scottish politician and author (see Biographical Register), lived at York House, Twickenham, from 1876 to 1897. This grand seventeenth-century building (now a heritage site) is set in beautiful grounds on the River Thames. In his diary for 4 Jan. 1891, Grant Duff observes: 'Mr. Pater spent the day with us. He and I went together to the little Catholic Chapel, and he remarked, as we talked about the Mass, on its wonderful wealth of suggestion. Other subjects were Plato, with whom he is, as always, much occupied, and of whose works he thinks a more photographic translation, than we yet have, is a desideratum.' *Notes from a Diary, 1889–1891*, 2: 73.

1891

To ARTHUR SYMONS, 27 January [1891]
MS.: Harvard University. On a correspondence card with College letterhead. Envelope: Arthur Symons Esq. | 21 Chandos Road | Buckingham. Postmark: OXFORD W JA 27 91.[1] Printed in *LWP*.

BRASENOSE COLLEGE, | OXFORD. | Jan: 27th.

My dear Symons,

I should much like:—but am so over-burdened (my time, I mean) just now, with pupils, lectures, and the making thereof, besides my usual literary work, that I can hardly *promise* to be disengaged this week; but am most likely to be so in the afternoon. I go to London on Saturday.[2]

Yours, in great haste,

Ever sincerely
Walter Pater.

[1] A fragment (sixteen words) is printed in Symons, *A Study of Walter Pater*, 100–1.
[2] 'Saturday' refers to 31 Jan. 1891.

To [H. D.] ROLLESTON,[1] 26 May [1891?][2]
MS.: Michael Seeney. On a correspondence card.

B. N. C. | May 26th.

Dear Rolleston,

Will you lunch with me on Saturday at 1.45.

Very sincerely yours
Walter Pater.

[1] Very likely Humphry Davy Rolleston (1862–1944), a physician, who was the eldest son of Grace Davy, daughter of John Davy and niece of Sir Humphry Davy, chemist, and George Rolleston (1829–81), physician, zoologist, and archaeologist. The latter played an important role in promoting the study of science at Oxford. Rolleston junior began his medical studies at St Bartholomew's Hospital, London, in 1881; he also studied at St John's College, Cambridge, 1885–9. He resumed his studies at St Bartholomew's Hospital, and augmented his experience by serving as examiner for various universities, including London and Cambridge, 1886–94, and as curator of the Pathological Museum at St George's Hospital, 1890. He received his MD degree in 1891; at St George's Hospital he was house physician 1893–1918. Rolleston was appointed physician-in-ordinary to King George V, 1923–32, and elected Regius Professor of Physic at Cambridge, 1925–32. The Rollestons were among the Paters' oldest acquaintances in Oxford. George Rolleston and Walter Pater probably met in

the mid-1860s; presumably a mutual friend, possibly Revd Archibald Sayce (1845–1933), Assyriologist, introduced them. The families lived in the same part of Oxford: the Rollestons lived at 2 South Parks Road, 1868–81, close to the Oxford Museum; the Paters lived at 2 Bradmore Road, 1869–85, adjacent to the University Parks.

[2] So dated on the basis of internal and external evidence.

To MR ALLEN,[1] 28 May [1891?]
MS.: Boston Public Library, Artz (Victorine T.) Collection of Literature. Part of the third sentence is printed in Emily Driscoll's *Autographs and Manuscripts*, Supplementary List no. 5 (September 1963), 35. Printed in *LWP*.

B. N. C. | May 28th.

Dear Mr. Allen,

Of course I recollect the pleasure of meeting you, and thank you sincerely for your interesting notice of Mr. Pillian's drawings. I have seen them, and think many of them remarkably beautiful. What a lively sense of architectural line and structure! and as to the surfaces—what a sensitive use alike of bold and delicate colour! The combination of good qualities is certainly a rare one.

Very faithfully yours
Walter Pater.

[1] Several Allens were writing art criticism at this time. The artist in question might have been Henry Pilleau (1815–99), a British painter who specialized in landscapes. Pilleau, who was elected to the Royal Institute of Painters in Water Colours (RI) in 1882, exhibited in the RI's Spring Exhibition of 1891.

To DOUGLAS AINSLIE, [22 June 1891]
MS.: Bates College. On a correspondence card. Printed in *LWP*.

12 Earl's Terrace, W. | Monday.

My dear Ainslie,

F. W. Bussell[1] will be staying with me on Sunday next, June 28th. Could you come to supper with us on that day at 8 o'clock?

Very sincerely yours
Walter Pater.

[1] Revd Frederick William Bussell (1862–1944), clergyman and scholar. See Biographical Register.

To ARTHUR SYMONS, 24 June [1891]
MS.: Roger Lhombreaud. Envelope: Arthur Symons Esq. | Fountain Court | Temple | W. C. Postmark: KEN[SING]TON X JU 24 91 W. Printed in *LWP*.

12 Earl's Terrace, | June 24th.

My dear Symons,

Many thanks for the photograph:[1] I had hoped to see yourself, before this. Artistically, I think it very good indeed; perhaps not quite so good as a likeness.

Very sincerely yours
Walter Pater.

[1] The photograph is missing, but it is probably that of Symons by Frederick Hollyer (1837–1933), engraver and photographer. Hollyer trained as a mezzotint engraver, then took up photography and was soon elected as a member of the Photographic Society of London. During the 1860s, he photographed many sketches by the painter Simeon Solomon, who in 1860 introduced him to other Pre-Raphaelites. For a number of years Hollyer operated a studio in Kensington, then the centre of an artistic circle that included G. F. Watts and Frederic Leighton, making photographic reproductions of their paintings. He also earned a name for himself as a portrait photographer. Symons sent a copy of this photograph to Michael Field in May 1891 (Journals of Michael Field, Brit. Lib. Add. MS. 46779, fol. 81).

To FRANK HARRIS,[1] 5 July [1891]
MS.: Miriam Lutcher Stark Library, Harry Ransom Center, University of Texas. Printed in *LWP*.

12 Earl's Terrace, | July 5th.

Dear Mr. Harris,

I thought it very kind of you to send me your 'Modern Idyll'.[2] I read almost no English fiction, but have read this with great interest, and sense of its freshness, reality, and proportion—the last, \a quality/ so difficult to attain in a short story, and in regard to so complicated a personage as Mr. Letgood. You ought to write more.

Miss Paget[3] is expected here shortly, and will have your letter, and the copy of the Fortnightly.

Very sincerely yours
Walter Pater.

[1] Frank Harris (1856–1931), Irish-American journalist and publisher (see Biographical Register).

² 'A Modern Idyll', *Fortnightly Review*, ns 55 (June 1891), 985–1008, is the story of Revd John Letgood, an eloquent young Baptist preacher in Kansas City 'tempted' by a middle-aged deacon's flirtatious young wife. Harris's short story was dramatized by Arthur Symons as 'The Minister's Call'; the play was staged in Mar. 1892 by the Independent Theatre.

³ Violet Paget [pseud. Vernon Lee]; see Biographical Register and letter to Ainslie, 19 July [1891].

To DOUGLAS AINSLIE, 19 July [1891]
MS.: Northwestern University. Printed in *LWP*.

12 Earl's Terrace, | Kensington, W. | July 19th.

My dear Ainslie,

I had hoped to see you before this. I wonder whether you will be in London so late as Thursday, July 30th. If so, will you dine with me on that day at 7.45. Vernon Lee is coming, and one or two others.¹ Kindly let me have a line.

Very sincerely yours
Walter Pater.

¹ Despite Pater's abrupt departure from London on 28 July (see letter to Moulton, 27 July [1891]), the dinner was held as planned; Vernon Lee wrote to her mother on the 30th that she was to dine at the Paters' that night (see *VLL*, 337).

To DOUGLAS AINSLIE, [27 July 1891]¹
MS.: Northwestern University.

12 Earl's Terrace.

Mr. Douglas Ainslie,

To remind, Thursday, July 30th. Dinner at 7.45.

Very sincerely yours
Walter Pater.

¹ See letter to Moulton, 27 July [1891].

To CICELY MOLESWORTH,[1] 27 July [1891]
MS.: Bates College. Envelope: Miss Molesworth | 19 Sumner Place | Onslow Square | S.W. Postmark: KENSINGTON [E]X JY 27 91 W. Printed in *LWP*.

12 Earl's Terrace, | July 27th.

Dear Miss Molesworth,

I send you, by this post, a novel by Fabre,[2] to whom it may introduce you and Mrs. Molesworth, though it is very far from being his best book. Kindly excuse its soiled condition. —It is the only one of his books I can find. I leave London to-morrow, so don't be troubled to acknowledge it, but believe me, with kind regards,

Sincerely yours
Walter Pater.

[1] Mary Cicely Molesworth (1863–1950), eldest daughter of Mary Louisa Stewart Molesworth (1839–1921), a popular writer of children's fiction who received at her London residence numerous late Victorian writers and aesthetes.

[2] Ferdinand Fabre (1827–98), a French novelist, focused on a realistic portrayal of life of peasants and clergy in the mountain villages of Hérault. *Les Courbezon* (1862), a tale about country priests in the Cévennes, was praised by George Sand and Charles Augustin Sainte-Beuve. In *French Profiles* (New York: Dodd, Mead, 1905), Edmund Gosse attributes his knowledge of Fabre to Pater, who admired *L'Abbé Tigrane, candidat à la papauté* (Paris: Alphonse Lemerre, 1873) more than any work in modern fiction (178–9). The particular book that Pater sent to Molesworth has not been identified; it may have been one of the two novels that he had reviewed in 1889: *Toussaint Galabru* (Paris: G. Charpentier, 1887) or *Norine* (Paris: G. Charpentier, 1889). (See *CW* v.)

To LOUISE CHANDLER MOULTON, 27 July [1891]
MS.: Library of Congress. Envelope: Mrs. Moulton | 23 Weymouth Street | Portland Place | W. Postmark: KENSINGTON EX JY 27 91 W. On a correspondence card. Printed in *LWP*.

12 Earl's Terrace, | July 27th.

My dear Mrs. Moulton,

Alas! for the brief tale of Tuesdays in July. I had hoped to be able to call on you tomorrow, and now unexpectedly have to leave tomorrow morning. Perhaps, however, you may be in London in the autumn.

With very kind regards,

Very sincerely yours
Walter Pater.

To LADY DOROTHY NEVILL,[1] 27 July [1891]
MS.: Bates College. On a correspondence card. Printed in *LWP*.

12 Earl's Terrace, | July 27th.

My dear Lady Dorothy,

I was extremely sorry to be unable to lunch with you today. I send you by this post a volume of French Stories, which I think may please you as it pleased me.[2] The stories are very graceful, and, I think, interesting; certainly original, in matter and form; though they might lie, as people say, on the drawing-room table but for their soiled outside, which I must ask you kindly to excuse. I leave London tomorrow: so don't be troubled to acknowledge this, but believe me, dear Lady Dorothy,

Very truly yours
Walter Pater.

[1] Lady Dorothy Fanny Walpole Nevill (1826–1913), a writer, was one of five children of Mary Fawkener and Horatio Walpole, 3rd Earl of Orford. She was embroiled in a scandal in 1847 with George Smythe MP, heir to a peerage. Smythe refused to marry her; her parents' statements and actions ruined her reputation. In 1847 she married Reginald Henry Nevill (1807–78), a cousin twenty years her senior. The widowed Lady Dorothy cultivated the society of literary and artistic people, including Matthew Arnold, J. A. Froude, Edmund Gosse, and Oscar Wilde. The presentation copy she received of *Imaginary Portraits* is now in the library at Brasenose College.

[2] Possibly the latest volume by Jules Lemaître (1853–1914), French dramatist, novelist, and critic: *Dix contes* (Paris: H. Lecene et H. Oudin, 1890). Of all contemporary French short-story writers, it was Lemaître whom Pater seems most to have admired. See his review of Lemaître's *Serenus. Histoire d'un martyr. Contes d'autrefois et d'aujourd'hui* (Paris: Alphonse Lemerre, 1886) in *Macmillan's Magazine*, 52 (Nov. 1887), 71–80; *CW* v.

To DOUGLAS AINSLIE, 9 August [1891]
MS.: Bates College. A fragment of the first sentence is quoted in Benson, 136, and there dated on Ainslie's authority. Printed in *LWP*.

12 Earl's Terrace, | Aug: 9th.

My dear Ainslie,

I return, with this, the proofs of your play, which I have read with great interest and pleasure, although, as you know, the dramatic form of literature is not what I usually turn to with most readiness. Escarlamonde[1] seems to me to be a very sound performance on a novel subject—well-conceived, and with a good deal of beauty in the execution. Whether or not you decide on publishing it at present, I cannot doubt that it contains proof of your capacity for good literary work. With many thanks,

Very sincerely yours
Walter Pater.

¹ Ainslie's blank-verse drama, written in 1887 and published as *Escarlamonde and Other Poems* (London: George Bell, 1893) in Nov. 1893, is set in Languedoc, France, at the time of the Albigensian persecutions. The play focuses on Escarlamonde, sister to Count Raymond of Toulouse, about whom, according to Ainslie (Benson, 123; cf. Symons, *A Study of Walter Pater*, 104–5), Pater was planning a story for the second volume of *Imaginary Portraits*. Pater's unfinished portrait 'Tibalt the Albigense' (*CW* x) has a similar focus.

To LOUIS DYER,¹ 16 August [1891]
MS.: Miriam Lutcher Stark Library, Harry Ransom Center, University of Texas.
Printed in *LWP*.

12 Earl's Terrace, | Aug: 16th.

Dear Mr. Dyer,

I hope to leave England tomorrow for five or six weeks,² and cannot do so without sending a few lines to thank \you/ for the great pleasure and profit derived from your book,³ which reached me through the kindness of Mr. George Macmillan. It seems to me to be a real and [portion torn off] original contribution [portion torn off] the study of the ancie[nt]⁴ Greeks as a living people, and I congratulate you on its completion. The various studies contained in it gain, of course, much, by connexion with your own personal knowledge of the places concerned. I was pleased to see your friendly references to my own papers on those subjects. You encourage my hope to add to, and polish them, some day.

With kind regards,

Very sincerely yours
Walter Pater.

¹ Louis Dyer (1851–1908), American classical scholar, writer, and lecturer, graduated from Harvard in 1874 and from Balliol College in 1878, where he eventually taught Classics (1893–6). He toured Greece with Malcolm Macmillan in 1887. In Nov. 1889 Dyer married Margaret Anne Macmillan (1857–1935), eldest daughter of Alexander Macmillan; the couple resided in Oxford in the 1890s. He published several volumes, including *The Greek Question and Answer* (Boston: privately printed, 1884). Dyer wrote Pater's obituary for the *Nation*, 23 Aug. 1894, 137–79.
² Violet Paget expected the Paters in Florence on 24–5 Aug. 1891 (*VLL*, 338).
³ *Studies of the Gods in Greece at Certain Sanctuaries Recently Excavated*, a series of lectures given in 1890 at the Lowell Institute, Massachusetts (published by Macmillan in Aug. 1891), features highly complimentary references to Pater, his essays on Demeter, Dionysus, and Euripides (*CW* viii), and *Marius the Epicurean*.
⁴ The upper right-hand corner of fol. 2 is torn, hence the conjectural readings.

To AN UNKNOWN CORRESPONDENT,[1] 2 October [1891?]
MS.: The Mark Samuels Lasner Special Collection, University of Delaware.

12 Earl's Terrace, | Kensington | London. W. | Oct: 2nd.

My dear Madam,

Pray excuse my long delay in acting upon the request with which you honoured me in your letter of June 12th. The letter was overlooked during one of many absences from home this summer and I hope the enclosed,[2] copied from *Men of the Time*, may not come too late to be of use to you.

Kindly send me a copy of your selections when published, and believe me

Very faithfully yours
Walter Pater.

[1] Pater's female admirer and her literary project have not been identified.
[2] On a separate sheet, Pater transcribes (with slight variations) the entry devoted to himself from *Men and Women of the Time: A Dictionary of Contemporaries*, ed. George Washington Moon (London: George Routledge, 1891), 698: 'W. P. was born in London, on Sunday, Aug. 4, The Feast of S. Dominic, 1839, and educated at the King's School Canterbury; he entered the University of Oxford, at Queen's College, in 1858; took B.A. degree (2nd class in Classics) in 1862; was elected to an open Fellowship at Brasenose, in which college he has since held various offices, and took the degree of M.A. in 1865. Mr. P. has made many visits to Italy, France, and Germany. His first contribution to literature was an essay on the Writings of Coleridge in the Westminster Review, Jan: 1866. In ~~17~~ 1873 "The Renaissance" (Macmillan) a series of Studies in Art and Poetry: 5th thousand, 1890. In 1885 appeared "Marius the Epicurean: His Sensations and Ideas", in 2 vols; 4th thousand, 1890. In Jan. 1887, "Imaginary Portraits": 3rd thousand, 1890: "Appreciations", in 1889; 4th thousand, 1890.'

To FRANCIS FORTESCUE URQUHART,[1] 29 October [1891?][2]
MS.: Brasenose College. On a correspondence card. Printed in *LWP*.

B. N. C. | Oct: 29th.

Dear Mr. Urquhart,

Will you lunch with me on Monday next, at 1.30?

Very truly yours
Walter Pater.

[1] Francis Fortescue Urquhart (1868–1934), a historian, read modern history at Balliol, 1890–4, and then served (from 1896) as Fellow and Tutor of Balliol, thus becoming the first Roman Catholic tutor in Oxford since the sixteenth century. Over the years he served as Junior Dean (1896–1907), Domestic Bursar (1907–19), and Dean (1918–34). Pater and Urquhart met in the early 1890s; some of the latter's friends maintained that the young man was the 'original' of Pater's 'Emerald Uthwart', which appeared in *The New Review*, 6 (June 1892), 708–22 (see *CW* iii).

² The letter was written between 1890 and 1893, most likely 1891 or 1892. In Oct. 1890 Urquhart had just arrived at Oxford; if the letter were written in 1893, when the 29th fell on a Sunday, one would expect Pater to say 'tomorrow Monday'. There is, however, no adequate basis for choosing between the remaining alternatives, 1891 (Thursday) or 1892 (Saturday).

To LADY DILKE,¹ 31 October [1891]
MS.: British Library. Printed in *LWP*.

12 Earl's Terrace, W. | Oct: 31st.

My dear Lady Dilke,

I am here for one of my brief visits from Oxford, and find that the kind gift of your book² arrived here some weeks since.

Accept now my best thanks for it. I think it maintains the high interest of its predecessor. I suppose nothing really better can be said of a book—of any work of art with a high purpose—than that it is what it was meant to be; and this book seems to be all yourself.

With very kind regards,

Very sincerely yours
Walter Pater.

¹ Emilia Francis Strong Pattison (1840–1904), art historian, critic, and trade unionist (see Biographical Register and letter to Lady Dilke, 27 May [1886]).
² *The Shrine of Love and Other Stories* (London: George Routledge, 1891). Its 'predecessor' was *The Shrine of Death and Other Stories* (London: George Routledge, 1886). See letter to Lady Dilke, 27 May [1886].

To MARGARET LOUISA WOODS,¹ 7 December [1891]
MS.: Bodleian Library. On College letterhead. Printed in *LWP*.

BRASENOSE COLLEGE, | OXFORD. | Dec: 7th.

My dear Mrs. Woods,

I return 'Hester [sic] Vanhomrigh' herewith.² I have read it far more hurriedly than I should have liked to do with such excellent workmanship as yours; which, however, has left in me an appetite to go over it again with full time and attention. I feel that you have given effective outline to that vague episode in Swift's life,—vague to me it was, I know,—and I suppose that is a legitimate function of the imagination in dealing with matters of historic fact. It is certainly very delightful for the reader, in your successful hands. How crisp and fresh your touch is throughout, in spite of all your knowledge and study of the matter and its time.—Sincere thanks.

I brought a message from my sister in London, and hope it will not be too late to deliver it now. Will you and the President give me the pleasure of your company at dinner, on Tuesday Dec: 22nd, at 7.45. Our address is 12 Earl's Terrace; but kindly send me a line in reply at Brasenose.

Very truly yours
Walter Pater.

---

[1] Margaret Louisa Bradley Woods (1855–1945), poet and novelist, was born in Rugby, Warwickshire, and educated privately. At Oxford she befriended Rhoda Broughton, Mark Pattison, Mary Ward, and Oscar Wilde. In 1879 she married Revd Henry George Woods (1842–1915), who was a Fellow (as of 1865) and later President (1887) of Trinity College, Oxford. Woods made a name for herself as a poet with *Lyrics* (Oxford: H. Daniel, 1888) and the verse-drama *Wilde Justice* (London: Smith, Elder, 1896), and as a novelist with *A Village Tragedy* (London: Richard Bentley, 1889).

[2] Wood's novel, *Esther Vanhomrigh* (London: John Murray, 1891), serialized in *Murray's Magazine*, Jan.–Dec. 1891, was published in three volumes in Nov. 1891. It is a fictionalized account of Jonathan Swift's relationship with Hester Vanhomrigh, the 'Vanessa' of 'Cadenus and Vanessa' (1713).

To PERCY WILLIAM BUNTING,[1] 21 December [1891]
MS.: University of Chicago. Printed in *LWP*.

12 Earl's Terrace, | Kensington, W. | Dec: 21st.

My dear Sir,

I send you, by this post, a MS. on 'The Genius of Plato',[2] which I hope you may find suitable for the Contemporary Review. I have treated the subject in as popular a manner as I could. If you care to have it, I should like it to appear in the February number. I have no other complete copy of the MS.

Please send reply to the address above, and believe me

Very truly yours
Walter Pater.

---

[1] Percy William Bunting (1836–1911), editor and social reformer, attended Pembroke College, Cambridge, 1856–9, and was called to the Bar at Lincoln's Inn in 1862 (he retired in 1895). He edited the *Contemporary Review* (1882–1911), which published four essays by Pater, and the *Methodist Times* (1902–7). In 1892 he was elected to Parliament from East Islington as a Gladstone Liberal.

[2] This essay, which appeared in the *Contemporary Review*, 41 (Feb. 1892), 249–61, was Pater's first contribution to the magazine; slightly revised, it became ch. 6 in *Plato and Platonism*. See *CW* vii.

1892

To CLYDE FITCH, 4 January [1892]
MS.: Amherst College. The letter is printed, with some errors, in Montrose J. Moses and Virginia Gerson, *Clyde Fitch and His Letters*, 73, and *LWP*.

12 Earl's Terrace, | Jan: 4th.

My dear Mr. Fitch,

I thought it extremely kind of you to send me your most charming and effective book, which it has given me great pleasure to read; though I find your friendly dedication of 'An Unchronicled Miracle' to myself more than I deserve.[1] You have been well supported by your illustrator. I sincerely hope you will go on with work like this, on an increasing s[c]ale. It makes a delightful gift-book. Sincere thanks for it, with best wishes for the New Year, from

Yours very truly
Walter Pater.

[1] See letter to Fitch, 1 Aug. 1890. In his book of tales for children, *The Knighting of the Twins, and Ten Other Tales* (Boston: John Wilson, 1891), Fitch dedicated this story to Pater (195). The book was illustrated by Virginia Gerson (1864–1951), author of children's books and a theatrical designer.

To WALTER PATER, 6 January [1892]
MS.: British Library. Printed in *TBB*.

Jan. 6 92

Dear Pater,

The stock of the second edition of 'Marius the Epicurean' is now reduced to something under 60 copies & we ought to be thinking about a third. What do you say to putting it into one volume large crown 8vo. uniform with your three other books? We will of course do what you like, but there seem to me to be advantages in having them all alike.

I take this opportunity of enclosing a cheque for the balance due to you in the course of this month, & wish best wishes for the New Year, remaining

Yours truly,
Frederick Macmillan.

Walter Pater Esqre. | 12 Earl's Terrace | Kensington

To WALTER PATER, 8 January 1892
MS.: British Library. Printed in *TBB*.

8th Jan 1892

Dear Pater,

I see no reason why we should not return to the original form of 'Marius'. I shall be glad to see you and talk it over any day next week except Thursday.

I am

Yours very truly,
Frederick Macmillan.

Walter Pater Esqre. | 12 Earl's Terrace | S.W.

To PERCY WILLIAM BUNTING, 10 January [1892]
MS.: University of Chicago. Printed in *LWP*.

12 Earl's Terrace, W. | Jan: 10th.

My dear Sir,

I have no doubt that you were right. I had not noticed the changes when I read over the proof, which I have just returned to Mr. Canton,[1] corrected.

I am glad you like the article,[2] and have three others; respectively, on

Plato and the doctrine of Motion:
Plato and the doctrine of Rest:
Plato and the doctrine of Music.[3]

Perhaps you might like to have them: perhaps at intervals? Kindly let me know, when you can.

Very truly yours
Walter Pater.

Percy Wm. Bunting Esq:

[1] See letter to Canton, 14 Jan. [1892].
[2] Possibly 'The Genius of Plato'; see letter to Bunting dated 21 Dec. [1891].
[3] All three, published in *Contemporary Review*, became chapters in *Plato and Platonism*. See *CW* vii.

To WILLIAM CANTON,[1] 14 January [1892]
MS.: Brasenose College. Printed in *LWP*.

12 Earl's Terrace, | Kensington, W. | Jan: 14th.

Dear Sir,

Many thanks. I enclose the revise, with a good many improvements. You were quite right, and I have made as many breaks as possible, in throughout. I think, however, the long paragraph, on page 4-5 \2-3/, ought to remain as it is.[2] The changes suggested by Mr. Bunting[3] had been made in the proof.

Yours truly
Walter Pater.

[1] William Canton (1845–1926), poet and editor, was born into a Roman Catholic family of civil servants living in Chusan, China. He studied for the priesthood, but converted to the Protestant faith. He edited the *Glasgow Herald* and was leader writer for the *Glasgow Weekly Herald* before moving to London in 1891, where he served as general manager to the publishing house of Isbister and Company, acting as assistant editor of two Isbister periodicals, the *Contemporary Review* and *Good Words*. His children's books include *The Invisible Playmate: A Story of the Unseen* (London: Isbister, 1894).
[2] The paragraph, beginning 'With Plato it is otherwise...', appears unaltered as the third paragraph of 'The Genius of Plato', *Contemporary Review*, 61 (Feb. 1892), 250–1. See *CW* vii.
[3] See letter to Bunting, 21 Dec. [1891], n. 1.

To WILLIAM CANTON, 22 January [1892]
MS.: Brasenose College. Printed in *LWP*.

12 Earl's Terrace, | Jan: 22nd.

My dear Sir,

I am much pleased that you like this paper on Plato, and my other writings, and think it very kind of you to tell me so. I shall read your volume of poetry[1] with great interest, and thank you sincerely for the gift.

These contributions to the 'Contemporary' are parts of a book on Plato and Platonism I hope to get finished by the end of the year; having some other works near completion, viz. a second series of Imaginary Portraits, and Gaston de Latour, a sort of Marius in France, in the 16th century.[2] Parts of this were published in Macmillan's Magazine some years ago.

The revised proof did not reach me till this morning, and I now return it for Press, and remain

Very sincerely yours
Walter Pater.

[1] See letter to Canton, 28 Jan. [1892].
[2] The last date for which there is indisputable evidence of Pater being at work on *Gaston* is 14 Dec. 1891, when Michael Field was told so by his sisters (see Journals of Michael Field, Brit. Lib. Add. MS. 46778, fol. 261).

To WILLIAM CANTON, 28 January [1892]
MS.: Brasenose College. The second paragraph appears, imperfectly, in Guy D. Canton, ed., *The Poems of William Canton* (London: G. G. Harrap, 1927), 6. Printed in *LWP*.

12 Earl's Terrace, | Jan: 28th.

My dear Sir,

Your book has given me very real pleasure.[1] Parts of it I have read as yet but hastily; but shall return to it often, especially, I think to 'Pearls and Simples', and some of the singularly winning smaller pieces, such as 'A New Poet'. In all the more personal pieces, (personal to yourself I mean,) there is a note of very sincere feeling; and in what might, I suppose, be called the theoretic pieces, a genuine imaginative power, and throughout great command of verse.

I greatly relish an intellectual cast in poetry, such as you have found a way of uniting to real melody and beauty of expression, in those primeval, pre-adamite or pre-historic, subjects. Just there, you seem to me to have struck a distinctly new note. Some, I know, fancy that the material of the poetry of the future will be those half-proved, half-imagined, truths of scientific research into 'origins'. You have certainly made their poetic side your own.

Thank you again for a delightful volume for one's most appreciative moments. I am going to Oxford shortly,[2] for a residence of eight weeks, but shall hope, in one of \my/ flying visits to London, to make your personal acquaintance: meantime
Believe me

Very sincerely yours
Walter Pater.

[1] Canton's first book of verse, *A Lost Epic, and Other Poems* (Edinburgh and London: William Blackwell and Sons, 1887). Many of these poems, rationalistic in temper, are inspired by evolutionary biology and the new scientific cosmology of the later Victorian period.
[2] In 1892, the start of Hilary term (from Jan. to Mar.) was postponed for a fortnight because of an influenza epidemic. See the *Oxford Magazine*, 10 Feb. 1892, 162–3.

To WALTER PATER, 28 January [1892]
MS.: British Library. Printed in *TBB*.

Walter Pater Esq. | 12 Earl's Terrace W.

28 Jan. 92

Dear Pater,

The revised copy for the first volume of 'Marius' has reached me this morning and the new edition shall be put in hand at once. We will follow exactly the type and style of the first edition of 1885. I think that the price might be at least 15/–

I am quite well and back at work again.

With kind regards, believe me

Yours very truly,
Frederick Macmillan.

To MARY ARNOLD WARD [c.1 February 1892][1]
Text: Janet Penrose Trevelyan, *The Life of Mrs. Humphry Ward* (London: Constable, 1923), 99. Printed in *LWP*.

...It seems to me to have all the forces of its predecessor at work in it, with perhaps a mellower kind of art—a more matured power of blending disparate literary gifts in one....

[1] Trevelyan cites this fragment from Pater's letter congratulating Ward on her novel *The History of David Grieve*, 3 vols (London: Smith, Elder, 1892), which was published on 22 Jan. 1892. (See also Mrs Humphry Ward, *A Writer's Recollections*, 1: 283.) Like its 'predecessor', *Robert Elsmere* (1888), *The History of David Grieve* deals with problems of religious assent and ethical conviction in a late Victorian setting.

To WILLIAM CANTON, 20 February [1892]
MS.: Brasenose College. Printed in *LWP*.

12 Earl's Terrace | Kensington, W. | Feb: 20th.

My dear Sir,

I am afraid you must have thought me very neglectful in leaving your last very interesting letter to me unanswered so long. The truth is, I am but a poor letter-writer, and have been away at Oxford, very busy there, from the beginning of the month. I am now here for a day or two, on one of my brief visits, —till Monday: had hoped to be able to call on you. Would you come and see me? I am often in London on Saturdays, and am then always 'at home', from 4 to 7. I expect to be here on alternate Saturdays (from this day) for some time to come, and \it/ would give me very great pleasure to see you.

> Very sincerely yours
> Walter Pater.

To WILLIAM CANTON, 22 February [1892]
MS.: Brasenose College. Printed in *LWP*.

> 12 Earl's Terrace, | Feb: 22nd.

My dear Mr. Canton,

Many thanks. I shall be here, and look forward to see you, on Saturday week, March 5th, at four o'clock, or five, if that would suit you: am just leaving, and write in haste:

> Very sincerely yours
> Walter Pater.

To MICHAEL ERNEST SADLER,[1] 5 March [1892]
MS.: Brasenose College. Printed in *LWP*.

> 12 Earl's Terrace, | March 5th.

Dear Sir,

In reply to your letter of March 1st, I beg to say that it gives me much pleasure to accept the invitation to lecture, on August 2nd, to the University Extension Students, with which the Committee of the Delegates have honoured me.

I would lecture on Raffaelle, his Life and Work,[2] as illustrating the Art of the period which you tell me has been selected as the subject of the chief sequence of lectures.

Believe me with many thanks,

> Faithfully yours
> Walter Pater.

My present address is at B. N. C. Oxford.

¹ Michael Ernest Sadler (1861–1943), historian and educator, studied at Trinity College, Oxford, 1880–2, and admired John Ruskin, the Oxford Slade Professor of Fine Art (1869–79 and 1883–5), who was then lecturing on 'The Art of England'. While a Student (i.e., Fellow) of Christ Church, Sadler served as Secretary (1885–95) of the University Extension programme. Under his leadership, the Extension programme grew enormously, offering nearly 400 courses throughout Great Britain. From 1895 to 1903 he served as Director of the Special Inquiries and Reports in the Education Department. He served as Professor of the 'History and Administration of Education', Victoria University of Manchester, 1903–11, and as Vice-Chancellor of the University of Leeds, 1911–23. Sadler also devoted time and energy to contemporary art, making the acquaintance of the leading artists. He ended his career as Master of University College, Oxford, 1923–34.

² Although Pater planned to lecture on Raphael on 2 Aug. 1892 he lectured instead on Leonardo da Vinci. (The 'chief sequence of lectures' at the fifth Extension summer school in Oxford, 29 July–26 Aug. 1892, dealt with the Renaissance and Reformation.) The Raphael lecture, unfinished by the start of Aug., was completed later in the summer, and published as 'Raphael', *Fortnightly Review*, ns 68 (Oct. 1892), 458–69. See *CW* vi.

To W. GRAHAM ROBERTSON,¹ [21 March 1892]
MS.: Huntington Library. On a correspondence card. Envelope: Graham Robertson Esq. | 23 Rutland Gate | S.W. Postmark: LONDON MR 21 92.

12 Earl's Terrace. | Monday.

Dear Mr. Robertson,

Many thanks. I should have much liked to come, but leave London today. One of my sisters is here, and will, I think, be able and much pleased to accept your kind invitation.

Very truly yours
Walter Pater.

¹ Walford Graham Robertson (1866–1948), painter, poet, playwright, and designer, studied at Eton and later at the Royal College of Art, South Kensington, and earned acclaim in artistic and theatrical circles during the 1880s and 1890s. As a painter, he was somewhat influenced by Albert Moore, but for the most part was faithful to the more poetical side of the Pre-Raphaelite tradition. Robertson produced many book illustrations and designed many stage costumes. He wrote several plays, including a children's play, *Pinkie and the Fairies*, which was produced by Herbert Beerbohm Tree in 1908. Robertson also earned acclaim for his collection of drawings by William Blake. His extensive social circle included Sarah Bernhardt, Henry James, Burne-Jones, Albert Moore, Morris, Pater, John Singer Sargent, Ellen Terry, Whistler, and Wilde. His autobiography *Time Was* (London: Hamish Hamilton, 1931) is a valuable resource.

To WILLIAM CANTON, 27 March [1892]
MS.: Brasenose College. On College letterhead. Printed in *LWP*.

Brasenose College, | Oxford. | March 27th.

My dear Mr. Canton,

Your letter of March 24th has been forwarded to me here. I told you what a poor creature I am in the matter of letter-writing. Pray forgive me. I was disappointed at your not coming that afternoon three weeks ago: had a faint hope you might ~~have called~~ \call/ on Saturday last: meant to have written. However, I shall be at home the next three Saturdays, from 5 to 7. If you could come so far on any one of them, I should be greatly pleased. I believe my Sister is asking several friends to tea on Saturday, April 9th. Could you come that day? R. S. V. P.

Very sincerely yours
Walter Pater.

To FREDERICK MACMILLAN, 3 April [1892]
MS.: British Library. Printed in *LWP* and *TBB*.

12 Earl's Terrace, | April 3rd.

Dear Macmillan,

I enclose a specimen of Mr. C. L. Shadwell's translation of Dante's 'Purgatorio'.[1] Anyone who compares it with the original will, I think, be surprised by its almost literal faithfulness; while it seems to me singularly rhythmical to the ear, and fresh in effect. The metre, as I mentioned, is that of Marvell's Ode; of which that Ode is the only one, or almost the only, example. Mr. Shadwell had reasons for thinking it more suitable for use in an English translation, than the Terza Rima of the original. I think his work very interesting as an experiment in scholarship, and should be glad to tell him you would publish it for him on the terms on which you publish for me.

Very sincerely yours
Walter Pater.

---

[1] Macmillan published Charles Shadwell's translation of Cantos 1–27 of the *Purgatorio* in Nov. 1892. Shadwell's 'Experiment in literal verse translation' is based on the quatrain devised by Andrew Marvell for 'An Horatian Ode upon Cromwell's return from Ireland' (1650). The volume includes a prefatory essay by Pater (see *CW* vi). The reviewer for the *Saturday Review*, 28 Jan. 1893, 106, noted that the book was 'beautifully produced'. What recommends this translation (according to Pater) is 'its union of minute and sensitive fidelity almost to the very syllable of the original, with that general sense of composure and breadth of effect' that marks the great Italian classic (xxv). For Shadwell, see Biographical Register.

To WALTER PATER, 8 April [1892]
MS.: British Library. Printed in *TBB*.

April 8 92

Dear Pater,

I write to say that we shall be happy to undertake the expense of publishing Mr. Shadwell's translation of the 'Purgatorio',[1] dividing with him any profits that may arise from the sale. We think that it ought to be printed in a dainty little volume, & unless Mr. Shadwell & you feel strongly about it we should not advise the inclusion of the text.

I understand that the volume is to have an introduction by you. We can begin printing whenever it is convenient to Mr. Shadwell.

I am

Yours very truly,
Frederick Macmillan.

Walter Pater Esq.

[1] *The Purgatory of Dante Alighieri (Purgatorio 1–27): An Experiment in Literal Verse Translation*, trans. Charles Lancelot Shadwell, with an Introduction by Walter Pater (London: Macmillan, 1892).

To WALTER PATER, 2 May [1892]
MS.: British Library. Printed in *TBB*.

May 2nd 92

Dear Pater,

We agree with you in thinking that 2000 copies of the new edition of 'Marius' had better be printed and I am therefore ordering paper for that number.

I am

Yours very truly,
Frederick Macmillan.

Walter Pater Esq. | Brasenose College | Oxford

To WALTER PATER, 11 May 1892
MS.: British Library. Printed in *TBB*.

May 11. 1892

Dear Pater,

 We are printing in our Classical Series an annotated edition of the Bacchae of Euripides by Professor Tyrrell[1] of Dublin who will at least be known to you by repute as a brilliant scholar. He wishes to reprint as a general introduction to the play your article which appeared in our Magazine for May 1889. He admires it greatly and thinks it would be invaluable for putting his younger readers at the right point of view. I quite agree with him but it is another question whether you care to allow such free use of a paper which I hope you may some day see your way to reprint with some of your other contributions to the study of Greek life and thought. I have never ceased to regret the withdrawal of that volume which was justly printed years ago, containing among other things the beautiful and suggestive essay on Demeter. Do think seriously of such a classical volume, and in the meantime tell me what to say to my friend Professor Tyrrell. I have prepared him for the possibility that you may not care to have more than a few quotations made from the paper in question.

Yours very truly,
George A. Macmillan.

Walter Pater | 12 Earl's Terrace

[1] Robert Yelverton Tyrrell (1844–1914), Irish classical scholar, attended Trinity College, Dublin, from 1860–4 and became Fellow of the college in 1868, Professor of Latin in 1871, Regius Professor of Greek, 1880–98, and Professor of Ancient History, 1900–4. In 1901 he was chosen as one of the first fifty members of the British Academy. Pater's essay, 'The Bacchanals of Euripides', was printed in *The Bacchae of Euripides*, ed. Robert Yelverton Tyrrell (London: Macmillan, 1892), lv–lxxxii. See *CW* viii.

To GEORGE MACMILLAN,[1] 15 May [1892]
MS.: British Library. Printed in *LWP* and *TBB*.

Brasenose College, | Oxford. | May 15.

Dear Macmillan,

 Your letter has been forwarded to me here. Of course I know Professor Tyrrell as a distinguished scholar and excellent writer, and I feel flattered by his proposal to put my paper as an introduction to his edition of the

'Bacchae'.² Kindly tell him so. I will send you a corrected copy of it in a week or ten days, if that will not be too late. It pleases me much that you like those papers of mine, which I should like some day to compile in a small volume, but shall not be able to do so for some time to come. The paper on the 'Bacchae' might thus also be reprinted with the rest. In any case, it would be well disposed of in Professor Tyrrell's volume; I am afraid better than it deserves.

Very sincerely yours
Walter Pater.

¹ An ardent Hellenist, Macmillan was one of the founders and first honorary secretary of the Hellenic Society. See his letter to Pater, 11 May 1892, for his hopes that Pater would 'some day' reprint his essays on Greek life and thought.
² On 27 May (Letter Book LXIV) Macmillan received from Pater the revised text of 'The Bacchanals of Euripides', for reprinting in *The Bacchae of Euripides*, ed. Robert Yelverton Tyrrell (1892), lv–lxxxii. There was some bibliographical confusion about the essay. In his Preface to *Greek Studies*, Shadwell states that it appeared 'with alteration' in Tyrrell's edition; in *Bibliographies of Modern Authors*, Second series (London: John Castle, 1925), C. A. and H. W. Stonehill deny that it was ever printed there. See *CW* viii.

To WALTER PATER, 16 May 1892
MS.: British Library. Printed in *TBB*.

May 16 1892

Dear Pater,

Many thanks for your generous compliance with Professor Tyrrell's wish. It will do quite well if the revised copy of your essay reaches me by about the end of the month. Its appearance in Tyrrell's edition of the Bacchae will of course not prevent its inclusion hereafter in the volume of similar essays which I am glad to know you intend some day to issue.

Yours very truly,
George A. Macmillan.

Walter Pater Esq. | B. N. C. | Oxford.

To WILLIAM CANTON, 17 May [1892]
MS.: Brasenose College. On College letterhead. Printed in *LWP*.

Brasenose College, | Oxford. | May 17th.

Dear Mr. Canton,

I enclose the corrected proof of my paper on 'Lacedaemon'.[1] I found that, like my last paper, it greatly needed subdivision into paragraphs. I suppose this is due to the circumstance that it was written for delivery as a lecture. I have done the best I could to subdivide it.

Very sincerely yours
Walter Pater.

---

[1] Published in the *Contemporary Review*, 61 (June 1892), 791–808; the essay later became ch. 8 of *Plato and Platonism*. See *CW* vii.

To SIR MOUNTSTUART GRANT DUFF, 18 May [1892]
MS.: Sheila Sokolov Grant. Printed in *LWP*.

Brasenose College, | Oxford. | May 18th.

My dear Sir Mountstuart,

Sincere thanks for your notice of Lord Arthur Russell, which I have read with extreme interest.[1] I could hardly claim to be acquainted with him, but remember meeting him at your house.[2]

Ah! what a compliment you pay me.

Ever

Very sincerely yours
Walter Pater.

---

[1] Lord Arthur Edward John Russell (1825–92), politician, was educated by private tutors in Germany, chiefly from 1849 to 1854. He served as private secretary to his uncle, the Liberal Prime Minister Lord John Russell, and sat as Member of Parliament for Tavistock from 1857 to 1885. Grant Duff, a close friend, wrote a memorial article, 'Lord Arthur Russell', for the *Proceedings of the Royal Geographical Society*, 14 (May 1892), 328–34. The 'compliment' to Pater is Grant Duff's suggestion that only the author of *Marius the Epicurean* could successfully describe Lord Arthur.

[2] On 13 Oct. 1889, according to Grant Duff's diary entry for that date.

To WILLIAM CANTON, [21? May 1892][1]
MS.: Brasenose College. On a correspondence card. Printed in *LWP*.

12 Earl's Terrace.

Dear Mr. Canton,

Many thanks for the corrections,[2] to all of which, with one exception, I agree. I am very sorry to have given you the trouble of sending the revise to two places. I suspect the lady you met was Mrs. Kemp-Welch,[3] a neighbour of ours on Campden-Hill, much devoted to nice things.

Very sincerely yours
Walter Pater.

You are right also about the accents.

[1] The first Saturday after the letter to Canton, 17 May [1892], with which this evidently belongs. Evans places this letter after the other, as the 'revise' would logically follow the 'proof' (cf. letters to Urquhart, 29 Oct. [1891?], and Lady Dilke, 31 Oct. [1891]).
[2] In 'Lacedaemon'. See letter to Canton, 17 May [1892].
[3] Wilhelmina Louise Kemp-Welch (1848?–1934), wife of William Kemp-Welch, solicitor, of London.

To MICHAEL FIELD, [late May 1892][1]
MS.: Miriam Lutcher Stark Library, Harry Ransom Center, University of Texas. On College letterhead. Printed in *LWP*.

Brasenose College, | Oxford.

Dear Miss Cooper & Miss Bradley,

Your letter of May 18th has been transported to me here; 'Italian Pictures' remaining, I doubt not, safe at Earl's Terrace, where I shall look forward to find it on my return, a short time hence, to London. Sincere thanks for the gift of it, and for the kind expressions in your letter; which, however, I feel I don't deserve. I read almost no contemporary poetry: have, alas! almost no time to do so; know, however, from past experience, how well worth time and reading is whatever comes from your hands.

Very truly and gratefully yours
Walter Pater.

[1] This letter was probably brought to Pater by his sister Hester, after his visit on the weekend of 21–2 May (assuming that the date for the letter to Canton, 21? May 1892, is correct). Pater is referring to Michael Field's *Sight and Song* (London: Elkin Mathews and John Lane,

1892), which appeared in May. Their poems render impressions of paintings into verse; three focus on works by Jean-Antoine Watteau (1684–1721), the French painter whose brief career generated the revival of interest in colour and movement, and the subject of Pater's 'A Prince of Court Painters' (see *CW* iii).

To WALTER PATER, 27 May 1892
MS.: British Library. Printed in *TBB*.

May 27. 1892

Dear Pater,

Many thanks for your paper on the Bacchae, which I have at once sent on to Professor Tyrrell.

Yours very truly,
George A. Macmillan.

Walter Pater Esq. | Brasenose College | Oxford

To WILLIAM CANTON, [31 May? 1892][1]
MS.: Brasenose College. On correspondence cards. Printed in *LWP*.

12 Earl's Terrace, | Monday.

Dear Mr. Canton,

Many thanks for the Rhymes,[2] which I doubt not will give us pleasant reading; also for your kind proposal. Alas! what with the burden of MSS. and other things, in my limited visits to London I am never able to get out till late in the afternoon, and I am due in Oxford again very soon. You must let me drop in some day at your office, and take the chance of finding you able to see me.

Sincerely yours
Walter Pater.

My sister, and myself if in London, will be at home on Saturdays, for some weeks to come.

---

[1] The reference to Canton's 'kind proposal' places this letter earlier than the letter to Canton, 12 Oct. [1892], but whether in the late spring or early autumn of 1892 is uncertain. Evans takes a late spring date on the assumption that the issue of *Good Words* Pater and Canton discuss (see letter to Canton, 12 Oct. [1892]) is the Aug. number.

[2] Unidentified, but possibly Canton's 'Rhymes about a Little Woman', a series of twelve poems about his infant daughter included in *The Invisible Playmate: A Story of the Unseen* (London: Isbister, 1894); see letter to Canton, 19 May [1894]. The 'Rhymes' may have been printed earlier in an untraced periodical or sent to the Paters in MS. For Canton's 'proposal', see letter to Canton, 12 Oct. [1892].

To AN UNKNOWN CORRESPONDENT,[1] 6 June [1892][2]
MS.: Paul Tucker. Letter written in black ink on white (laid) paper, measuring 22.6 × 18 cm, with no visible watermark. The paper has been folded into four sections, the letter occupying sections one and three. Printed in Paul Tucker, 'An Unpublished Letter of Walter Pater', *Pater Newsletter*, 64 (Fall 2013), 49–66.

12 Earl's Terrace. W. | June 6th.

Dear Sir,

Excuse my delay in replying to your letter of May 28th, which I have just found on my return here. It would have given me great pleasure to contribute to the Illustrated London News, as you so kindly propose, and I hope I may be able to do so some day. At present however, my hands are so full of work already begun, that it would be uncandid to promise anything.

With many thanks,

Sincerely yours
Walter Pater.

---

[1] Possibly Clement King Shorter (1857–1926), journalist and editor, who was remarkable not only for his pioneering work in illustrated journalism, but also for his flair for collecting manuscripts. Shorter worked for several booksellers in London, 1871–6, and as a clerk in the exchequer and audit department at Somerset House, 1877–90. During these years he attended evening classes in language and literature at the Birkbeck Literary and Scientific Institution. In 1888, he turned to journalism, writing for the London *Star*, the *Penny Illustrated Paper*, and the *Illustrated London News*, which he edited 1891–1900. The first illustrated weekly news magazine, the *Illustrated London News* appeared from 1842 to 2003; at its peak, it sold 300,000 copies per week. Contributors included J. M. Barrie, Wilkie Collins, Charles Dickens, Rudyard Kipling, and R. L. Stevenson. It is not clear whether Shorter and Pater ever met. Shorter reviewed *Appreciations* in the London *Star*, 21 Nov. 1889, 4.

[2] So dated by Tucker.

To HERBERT HORNE, 22 June [1892]
MS.: Mark Samuels Lasner Collection, University of Delaware. Printed in *LWP*.

12 Earl's Terrace, | Kensington, W. | June 22nd.

My dear Horne,

It would give us much pleasure if you could dine with us on Wednesday, June 29th at 7.45.

Very truly yours
Walter Pater.

To ARTHUR CHRISTOPHER BENSON,[1] 28 July [1892]
MS.: Mark Samuels Lasner Collection, University of Delaware.

12 Earl's Terrace, | Kensington, W. | July 28th

My dear Mr. Benson,

I thought it very kind of you to send me your 'Cahier Jaune',[2] which I have read with very great pleasure and interest: some of the poems several times over. I read very little modern verse; but it seems to me that you possess a peculiar meditative vein, rare now-a-days; though perhaps, after all, it belongs to the most durable sort of poetry.

'Storm & Tempest', 'All that we know of him', and 'Miserrimus', strike me as perhaps the most beautiful of the series.

Still, our generation has been fertile in good poetry, and writing to one who can write prose as you have done, and who writes from Eton, I cannot help observing that, as it seems to me, the novel of English public school life (though there have been some admirable attempts thereat) is still to be written.[3] I think you might write it.

I hope you will some day let me have the pleasure of making your acquaintance in person.[4] I leave England shortly for six or seven weeks on the Continent, but am otherwise usually at Brasenose during term time, and at other times at the address above. With sincere thanks,

Very truly yours
Walter Pater.

I wonder whether you saw the enclosed. I cannot quite make out whether those who care for my writings care for this. If you could read ~~them~~ it at your leisure, and ~~for~~ send me any observations that may occur to you, frankly, I should be grateful. It is meant to form, with two or three \other/ studies of the kind, a little volume.

---

[1] A. C. Benson (1862–1925), poet, essayist, short-story writer, biographer, and diarist, was the eldest surviving son of Edward White Benson, Archbishop of Canterbury, whose biography he wrote (see Biographical Register). Benson taught classics at Eton from 1885 to 1903 and at Magdalene College, Cambridge, from 1904 to 1925.

[2] *Le cahier jaune. Poems* (Eton: privately printed, 1892) appeared (Jan.) in an edition of 200 copies. Between 1892-1905, Benson published five volumes of poetry, exploring such subjects as nature, the painful brevity of life, the ever-present shadow of death, the joy of companionship, the sustenance of faith, and poets and their art. The verses for which he is best remembered are the lines of 'Land of Hope and Glory' for Edward Elgar's *Pomp and Circumstance*.

[3] To paraphrase Laurel Brake (personal communication, 29 Sept. 2019), Pater's interest in 'English public school life' seems related to his visit on 30 July 1891 to the King's School, Canterbury, where he attended Speech Day, and to the composition inspired by that visit, 'Emerald Uthwart' (1892), regarded as his most autobiographical study since 'The Child in

the House'. 'Emerald Uthwart' appeared (in two parts) in *The New Review*, 6 (June 1892), 708-22, and 7 (July 1892), 42-54, and was rptd in *Miscellaneous Studies* (1895), 198-250. In Jan. 1892, Pater announced that a revised version of his second series of imaginary portraits was 'near completion' (letter to Canton, 22 Jan. [1892]), and he suggested to Frederick Macmillan (see letter to Pater, 14 Dec. [1892]) that the volume would be called *Three Short Stories*, a 'little volume' that would include 'Hippolytus Veiled', 'Emerald Uthwart', and 'Apollo in Picardy' (Benson, 123). Very likely (Brake claims) Pater sent Benson off-prints of these texts.

[4] Benson and Pater met at a luncheon hosted by the former at the National Club, London, in June 1893.

To WILLIAM CANTON, 12 October [1892]
MS.: Brasenose College. On College letterhead. Printed in *LWP*.

BRASENOSE COLLEGE, | OXFORD. | Oct: 12th.

My dear Mr. Canton,

I meant to have written this before I left London,[1] but was overtaken by time. Kindly send the proofs[2] to me here, where I remain for eight weeks, with an occasional day or two in London. It was odd that on ~~going~~ \your/ suggesting something for 'Good Words', ~~that~~ I should pounce on one of the subjects of the current number.[3] I shall hope to write you, though it cannot be [immediately], something else. I read with great interest what came from yourself in that number; and after reading it feel how little you need any prompting from without; though I often feel as you describe. What freedom one feels in working over again some well-used ground!

Judging from what I thought the most effective pieces in your most interesting volume of Poems,[4] I should say that pre-historic man, and what is perhaps in a measure like him, \viz./ unspoiled peasant man, were your proper subjects; but perhaps it is mistaken to abound too much in what comes easiest to us. I think anything like a delicate and really sensitive \treatment/, of England or English things, in prose or verse, very attractive; but how rare it is! Excuse this scrawl, and believe me

Very sincerely yours
Walter Pater.

I will do my best to lighten and popularise my paper, at all points.

[1] Pater may not have left London until late afternoon or early evening on 12 Oct., if he delayed his departure for Tennyson's funeral (the service in Westminster Abbey began at 12:30 pm). Pater had been officially invited to take part in the procession (see 'Tennyson's Funeral', *The Times*, 13 Oct. 1892, 4), but newspaper accounts do not specify whether he was present.
[2] Proofs of 'The Doctrine of Plato', subsequently published as ch. 7 of *Plato and Platonism* (see *CW* vii). See letters to Canton, from 16 Oct. [1892] to 1 Nov. [1892].

[3] Pater's references to various numbers of the Isbister sixpenny monthly, *Good Words*, are confusing, unless he refers to a discussion with Canton in midsummer. The Aug. issue held the second and concluding portion of an informal essay by Canton, 'New Corn from Old Fields', *Good Words*, 33 (Aug. 1892), 545–9, but the Oct. number contains nothing by Canton. The subject in the Aug. number upon which Pater 'pounced' would then be St Hugh of Avalon (see letter to Canton, 23 Oct. [1892]), discussed by H. Donald M. Spence in 'Cloister Life in the Days of Coeur de Lion', *Good Words*, 33 (Aug. 1892), 514–23.
[4] *A Lost Epic, and Other Poems*. See letter to Canton, 23 Jan. [1892].

To WALTER PATER, 12 October [1892]
MS.: British Library. Printed in *TBB*.

Oct. 12th 92

My dear Pater,

There is one point I omitted to mention the other day when you told me about your new volume on 'Plato',[1] and that is with regard to the American sale. Under the new copyright law[2] it is necessary that in order to obtain protection a book should be printed in the United States, and it would I think be a mistake to leave your book open to the pirates. I suggest that you should allow us to print and publish an edition through our New York House. The terms that we should propose for this American edition are a royalty of 10% of the retail price on all copies sold.

I am

Yours very truly,
Frederick Macmillan.

Walter Pater Esq. | Brasenose College | Oxford

[1] Pater began writing his lectures for *Plato and Platonism* in Dec. 1890 (Benson, 156, 163–8), and delivered them at noon each Wednesday of the Hilary term, beginning 21 Jan. 1891.
[2] See letter to Hester Pater, 16 Sept. 1910.

To WILLIAM CANTON, 16 October [1892]
MS.: Brasenose College. On College letterhead. Printed in *LWP*.

BRASENOSE COLLEGE, | OXFORD. | Oct: 16th.

My dear Mr. Canton,

Sincere thanks for your letter and the proofs. I have looked over the latter, and now feel convinced they are unfit for publication in that way, and can only offer my apologies for troubling you, and putting the Contemporary to the expense of printing the article. I hope when my book on Plato comes out you may find time to glance at it, and that I may some day be able to contribute something more suitable to the review.[1] I shall think over the other matter contained in your letter, and remain with kind regards

Very truly yours
Walter Pater.

[1] Pater's next contribution (the last during his lifetime) was 'The Age of Athletic Prizemen: A Chapter in Greek Art', *Contemporary Review*, 65 (Feb. 1894), 242–56, later included by Shadwell in *Greek Studies* (see *CW* viii). The 'other matter' in Canton's letter was probably a request that Pater should reconsider doing an article on St Hugh for *Good Words*. See letter to Canton, 23 Oct. [1892].

To WILLIAM CANTON, 23 October [1892]
MS.: Brasenose College. On College letterhead. Printed in *LWP*.

BRASENOSE COLLEGE, | OXFORD. | Oct: 23rd.

My dear Mr. Canton,

I have written to Mr. Bunting to accept his proposal to print my paper on Plato after all. Would you read my letter to him enclosed; and then kindly have it put in the post.

I am still dubious about St. Hugh,[1] but will do my best to fulfil my promise by that or some other suitable contribution. I suppose you might include me in your list of contributors to future Good Words, without specifying the subject.

Sincere thanks for the trouble you have taken about my essay.

Very truly yours
Walter Pater.

[1] St Hugh of Avalon (*c*.1140–1200), a Carthusian monk, became Bishop of Lincoln in 1186. He was canonized in 1220, and his tomb at Lincoln became second only to that of St Thomas à Becket in Canterbury as a place of popular devotion in late medieval England. The Brasenose chapel is dedicated to him and St Chad. There is no evidence, however, that Pater ever began an essay on this topic, and he never contributed to *Good Words*.

To PERCY WILLIAM BUNTING, 1 November [1892]
MS.: University of Chicago. On College letterhead. Printed in *LWP*.

BRASENOSE COLLEGE, | OXFORD. | Nov: 1st.

Dear Mr. Bunting,

    I greatly value your judgment in such matters, and was very glad you found my paper on The Doctrine of Plato interesting, as I hope to print it soon in a volume. I feel, however, covered with confusion in saying that, on looking over the paper again with a view to its publication in the Contemporary, I feel more convinced than ever that it is unsuitable for publication in that form. For one thing, it is very long, and yet I find it hardly possible to curtail it. I think, in the case of average readers, it might prejudice both my volume and your review. As a month remains, I feel I shall not be putting you to inconvenience, and [hope] you will forgive me having troubled you in the matter.

    Don't be troubled to answer this, and believe me

Very sincerely yours
Walter Pater.

To WILLIAM CANTON, 1 November [1892]
MS.: Brasenose College. On College letterhead. Printed in *LWP*.

BRASENOSE COLLEGE, | OXFORD. | Nov: 1st.

My dear Mr. Canton,

    You will think me a most capricious, but I hope not very troublesome creature, for I have just written to Mr. Bunting to \say/ that on looking over it again I am more convinced than ever that my last paper on Plato is unsuitable for the Review, and might prejudice both that and my proposed volume with average readers. For one thing, it is very long, and yet capable of only a very slight amount of curtailment.

    I saw you had advertised me for 'Good Words',[1] and will make an effort to fulfil my promise in that matter.

    I was much encouraged by your good opinion of that last MS. of mine, with a view to its publication in my proposed volume on Plato; and with many thanks am

Very sincerely yours
Walter Pater.

¹ The first advertisement listing Pater as a future contributor to *Good Words* can be found in 'Messrs. Isbister's New List', *Athenaeum*, 3 Dec. 1892, 760, where he is cited among those who are to furnish 'biographical, travel, and scientific papers'. But Isbister also issued a prospectus for the 1893 volume, and it may be to it that Pater refers.

To WALTER PATER, 11 November [1892]
MS.: British Library. Printed in *TBB*.

Nov. 11th 92

My dear Pater,

Mr. Shadwell wishes us to ask you how many copies of his translation of Dante you will accept for yourself. Please let me know.

Yours very truly,
Frederick Macmillan.

Walter Pater Esq. | Brasenose College | Oxford.

To THE PALL MALL GAZETTE,¹ 14 November 1892
Text: 'Should the Laureateship be Abolished? Opinions on the Subject by Men of Letters', *Pall Mall Gazette*, 14 November 1892, 1–2.

Dear Sir,

In reply to your very courteous letter,² I beg to say that I have been so much occupied with various work here during the last few weeks that I feel quite unprepared to offer you anything worth your having on the question of the Laureateship, which I know has been much debated of late in the Press and elsewhere. Otherwise, it would have given me much pleasure to concur in the request from yourself.

Faithfully yours
Walter Pater.

¹ This letter was solicited by Henry John ('Harry') Cockayne Cust (1861–1917), poet, editor, and politician. Cust attended Trinity College, Cambridge, 1881–4, where he was elected a member of the Apostles; he was admitted to the Inner Temple, but was never called to the Bar. Instead, he turned to politics, serving as MP for Stamford, Lincolnshire, 1890–5 and 1900–6. He edited the *Pall Mall Gazette*, 1892–6, transforming it into the best evening newspaper of the period, featuring Rudyard Kipling, G. B. Shaw, and H. G. Wells. During the Great War he was active in propaganda for the British government. In 1893, Cust married Emmeline Mary Elizabeth Welby-Gregory, the daughter of Victoria, Lady Welby, the language philosopher.

² Commentators had been discussing the office of the poet laureate for some time before Alfred, Lord Tennyson died on 6 Oct. 1892. After Tennyson's death, Cust asked writers and

intellectuals to respond to two questions: should the office of the laureateship be abolished or continued? And if the latter, who should succeed Tennyson? On 24 Nov. the editor printed eleven letters by such figures as Edward Dowden, T. H. Huxley, Max Müller, and Pater. Six indicated that the office of the laureate should be continued, one indicated that it should be abolished, and four wrote that they were unable to express a view. No one would name a successor. Alfred Austin (1835–1913) served as the laureate from 1896 to 1913.

To RICHARD LE GALLIENNE,[1] 16 November [1892]
MS.: Fales Collection, New York University. Envelope: Richard Le Gallienne Esq. | Meadowsweet | Church Road | Hanwell, W. Postmark: OX[FO]RD 5[?] NO 17 92. Printed in Warren Herendeen, 'Three Unpublished Letters by Walter Pater', *Review of English Studies*, 20.77 (January 1969), 64–5, and in *LWP*.

BRASENOSE COLLEGE, | OXFORD. | Nov: 16th.

Dear Mr. Le Gallienne,

I thought it extremely kind of you to send me your very charming book.[2] With its blending of poetry and delicate humour, of analysis and construction, it strikes me as being a very original piece of work, and I look forward to the pleasure of reading it a second time. Sincere thanks for it.

I was glad to make your acquaintance that evening at Mr. Daniel's, and hope it may be renewed a few weeks hence in London.

I should have acknowledged your kind letter of Nov: 5th before this, but have been very busy of late: could not, however, put off any longer these poor words of thanks, from

Very sincerely yours
Walter Pater.

[1] Richard Thomas Le Gallienne (1866–1947), poet and critic, was born in Liverpool. Two events spurred his ambition to become a professional writer: an 1883 lecture given by Oscar Wilde in Birkenhead and an 1886 meeting with Oliver Wendell Holmes in Liverpool. His volume *My Ladies' Sonnets* ([Liverpool]: privately printed, 1887) and book reviews in the *Academy* attracted the encouragement of John Lane. In 1891 Le Gallienne succeeded Clement Shorter as literary critic for the London *Star*, writing under the name of 'Logroller'; the following year he became a reader for the Bodley Head publishing firm. He contributed to *The Book of the Rhymers' Club* (1892) and *The Second Book of the Rhymers' Club* (1894), and to all four volumes of *The Yellow Book*. Le Gallienne always stated that he greatly admired Pater. They met in Oct. 1892 at an Oxford dinner party given by C. H. O. Daniel (see Biographical Register); he recorded his impressions of this first meeting in *The Romantic '90s* (Garden City: Doubleday Page, 1925), 97–105.

[2] *The Book-Bills of Narcissus* (London: Frank Murray, 1891). In this thinly veiled autobiographical narrative, reading *Marius the Epicurean* marks an important stage in Narcissus' spiritual life.

To WALTER PATER, 2 December [1892]
MS.: British Library. Printed in *TBB*.

Dec. 2nd 92

My dear Pater,

When do you think you will be able to send us corrected proofs of your new book from which the American edition can be printed? We ought to have them in good time, because in order to obtain copyright in the United States, the American edition must be published simultaneously with the English one, and I want to give our people there time to get it nicely printed.
I am

Yours truly,
Frederick Macmillan.

Walter Pater Esq. | Brasenose College | Oxford

To WALTER PATER, 13 December [1892]
MS.: British Library. Printed in *TBB*.

Dec. 13 92

My dear Pater,

We are sending the order to Oxford to print 2000 copies of the book on Plato, which I think was what you arranged with my cousin. But as he is not here today I think it best to tell you this in case there should be any mistake. The paper will be sent as soon as we know the quantity required.

Yours very truly,
George A. Macmillan.

Walter Pater Esq. | 12 Earl's Terrace, | Kensington

To EDMUND GOSSE, [13 December? 1892][1]
MS.: Brotherton Collection, University of Leeds. Printed in *LWP*.

12 Earl's Terrace | Tuesday.

My dear Gosse,

I hoped to have thanked you before this in writing for your charming 'Narcisse',[2] also for your kind letter of the other day. If you happen to be disengaged on Thursday, and would come and dine with me at 7.45, I might thank you in person—in any case, sincere thanks! Would you let me have a post-card by return.

Very sincerely yours
Walter Pater.

---

[1] This date, pencilled on the MS. with a question mark, seems logical, and consistent with letter to Gosse, 17 Dec. [1892].

[2] *The Secret of Narcisse: A Romance* (London: William Heinemann, 1892) was published in Nov. 1892.

To WALTER PATER, 14 December [1892]
MS.: British Library. Printed in *TBB*.

Dec. 14 92

My dear Pater,

I enclose a formal memorandum of agreement[1] (in duplicate) for 'Plato & Platonism'. Will you kindly sign & return one copy.

I suppose you will not begin printing 'Three Short Stories'[2] until this book is quite out of your hands.

Believe me

Yours very truly,
Frederick Macmillan.

Walter Pater Esq. | 12 Earl's Terrace

---

[1] According to this agreement, dated 13 Dec. 1892, Macmillan contracted to publish at its own risk *Plato and Platonism* on condition that the copyright belong to the publishers and that, after deducting expenses, profits be divided equally. This agreement also covered the American edition, for which Pater was to be paid a royalty of 10 per cent of the retail price per copy. See Brit. Lib. Add. MS. 55030, fol. 57.

[2] Pater regarded the 'imaginary portrait' as his literary *métier*. In 1890 he contemplated publishing a second series. Writing in the *Monthly Review* for Sept. 1906, Arthur Symons points out that Pater meant to include 'Hippolytus Veiled', a study based on Giovanni Moroni's 'Portrait of a Tailor', and a modern study. According to A. C. Benson, the project to which Macmillan refers would have included 'Hippolytus Veiled', 'Emerald Uthwart', and 'Apollo in Picardy' (Benson, 123). See *CW* iii.

To EDMUND GOSSE, 17 December [1892]
MS.: Brotherton Collection, University of Leeds. Printed in *LWP*.

12 Earl's Terrace, | Dec: 17th.

My dear Gosse,

How ungrateful I have been! I had looked for the appearance of your Romance with great interest. You had talked about it, you know, when I last saw you.[1] Your books are always extremely pleasant reading; and this one, which I have read with far more ease than I usually find in reading English fiction, is perhaps the most pleasant of your books,— one of the pleasantest books, in fact, which I have come across for a good long time. Accept my thanks for it. I seem to see the inside of Bar[2] as distinctly as I saw its outline against the evening sky last autumn, passing on the railway. You make me feel that I ~~have~~ ought to have stayed there. I think you have thoroughly succeeded in working out a really delightful conception. Give us more of the like. But this too seems ungrateful.

Sincerely yours
Walter Pater.

[1] Evidently, Gosse had been unable to accept Pater's invitation to dinner on Thursday, 15 Dec. (see letter to Gosse, [13 Dec.? 1892]). Pater may have last seen Gosse and heard him talk about *Narcisse* when he dined with the Gosses in London on 27 July 1892 ('The Book of Gosse', Cambridge University Library MS. Add. 7034, fol. 93).

[2] Bar-le-Duc, a town east of Paris, was once the seat of the Duchy of Bar. *The Secret of Narcisse: A Romance* is set there in the middle of the sixteenth century.

1893

To JAMES RICHARD THURSFIELD, 12 February [1893][1]
MS.: Brasenose College. On College letterhead. Printed in *LWP*.

BRASENOSE COLLEGE, | OXFORD. | Feb: 12th.

Dear Thursfield,

Macmillan has just published for me a volume on 'Plato and Platonism'. I daresay you would have come across it in any case, but venture to send you a few lines on the subject, as I think if you have time to look at it, you may like it, or some part of it. Don't be troubled to answer this.

Sincerely yours
Walter Pater.

[1] James Thursfield (see letter to Thursfield, 26 July [1880]) was in charge of the 'Books of the Week' section of *The Times*. A favourable, unsigned notice of *Plato and Platonism* appeared in the column for 16 Feb. 1893, 12. 'We cannot', the reviewer states, 'readily recall a work dealing with Plato as a man and a thinker which is at once more suggestive in presentation and more attractive in style'.

To RICHARD LE GALLIENNE, [*c*.25 February 1893][1]
MS.: Fales Collection, New York University. Printed in Herendeen, 'Three Unpublished Letters of Walter Pater', 64, and in *LWP*.

12 Earl's Terrace.

Dear Mr. Le Gallienne,

One line of thanks. I had already read your most interesting but too generous notice of my book.

Sincere thanks.

Very truly yours
Walter Pater.

[1] Under the columnist's pseudonym, 'Logroller', Le Gallienne enthusiastically reviewed *Plato and Platonism* in the London *Star*, 23 Feb. 1893, 2.

To MICHAEL FIELD, 1 March [1893]
MS.: Miriam Lutcher Stark Library, Harry Ransom Center, University of Texas.
Printed in *LWP*.

12 Earl's Terrace, | March 1st.

Dear Miss Bradley and Miss Cooper,

I have been unwell, and able to read and write very little. I hope this may excuse my long delay in thanking you for your beautiful book.[1] Sincere thanks for that, and its predecessor. I have asked Macmillan to send you a book of mine on Plato, some of which I hope you may like, if you have time to look at it. Don't be troubled to answer this,[2] and believe me,

Very truly yours
Walter Pater.

[1] *Stephania: A Trialogue* (London: Elkin Mathews & John Lane, 1892) appeared in Jan., with a frontispiece designed by Selwyn Image. Its 'predecessor' was *Sight and Song* (see letter to Michael Field, [late May 1892]).

[2] Two barely legible, incomplete, and undated drafts of Michael Field's perceptive letter of thanks can be found in the Bodleian Library, MS. Eng. Letters d. 120.

To EDMUND GOSSE, 30 March [1893]
Text: *The Library of Edmund Gosse*, ed. E. H. M. Cox (London: Dulau, 1924), 196.
Printed in *LWP*.

12 Earl's Terrace, | March 30th.

My dear Gosse,

Of course I read your very skilful paper in the 'New Review'[1] with great pleasure, and thank you sincerely for the pains you have taken with it. Though it is all about my own very limited self and production, I think the general reader of the 'Review' will not find it in the way; so much of your own good work and charming manner of saying things have you put into it. I hope to give good heed to your friendly advice on some points,[2] and that my *next book* will be 'really good', as an excellent painter told me he always felt when he had finished a thing.

Very sincerely yours
Walter Pater.

[1] Edmund Gosse, 'Mr. Walter Pater on Platonism', *The New Review*, 8 (Apr. 1893), 419–29.

[2] Gosse gives almost no advice. Knowing little about Plato, he satisfies himself with a largely 'appreciative' summary of *Plato and Platonism*. His only censure is that 'occasionally...the deprecating parenthesis is too often introduced' (421).

To HENRY COCKAYNE CUST,¹ 4 May [1893]
Text: Christie's Catalogue, Sale 7574, Lot 91, 20 November 1992. Printed in J. W. Robertson Scott, *The Life and Death of a Newspaper* (London: Methuen, 1952), 370.

...I shall be willing to write an article on Dante's Pilgrim's Progress,² on the terms you propose. Kindly send me the book....

¹ Henry John ('Harry') Cockayne Cust (1861–1917) was a poet, editor, and politician; he edited the *Pall Mall Gazette*, 1892–6 (see letter to *Pall Mall Gazette*, 14 Nov. 1892).
² Very likely a work by Emelia Russell Gurney (1823–96), activist, patron, and benefactor: *Dante's Pilgrim's Progress* (London: Elliot Stock, 1893). The article was never written.

To HENRY COCKAYNE CUST, 9 May [1893]
Text: Christie's Catalogue, Sale 7574, Lot 91, 20 November 1992.

...I should not be able to review the Sceptics of the Renaissance,¹ as it is a very lengthy work to read. Meantime, my friend, Mr. F. W. [Bussell]² happened to see the book, and is anxious to write an article on it, which, he is very competent. Do you approve of this? If so, do not reply to him. I would send you that article, and my own, when they are ready—two or three weeks hence....

¹ Possibly John Owen, *The Sceptics of the French Renaissance* (London: Swan Sonnenschein, 1893).
² Frederick William Bussell, Pater's friend and colleague (see Biographical Register).

To HENRY COCKAYNE CUST, 19 May [1893]
Text: Christie's Catalogue, Sale 7574, Lot 91, 20 November 1992.

...I am suffering from an attack of gout, and very far from able to do my usual amount of work. I have therefore thought it best to return the books on Dante,¹ that you may put them into the hands of some one who could review them without further delay. Pray excuse this failure to do what I promised....

¹ The article proposed may be a review of Shadwell's translation of Dante's *Purgatory* or an essay on Dante and medieval art, of which an incomplete draft is among the Harvard MSS (see *CW* x).

To LIONEL JOHNSON,[1] [May 1893?][2]
Text: [Lionel Johnson], 'For a Little Clan', *Academy*, 23 October 1900, 314. Printed in *LWP*.

...By the way, I was much pleased with a poem of yours I read in the -----. A certain firmness and definition in the sentiment there expressed, congruous with the thoughtful finish of the manner, mark it very distinctly....

[1] Pater met Johnson (see Biographical Register) in 1887, in the rooms of the Revd Arthur Galton (see letter to Horne, 17 July [1888], n. 1).

[2] This date depends on the periodical whose title Johnson excised when publishing this fragment of Pater's letter. Johnson's poem, 'A Friend', was first published in Lord Alfred Douglas's *Spirit Lamp*, 4 (May 1893), 18–19. The *Spirit Lamp* is the only journal in which Johnson is known to have published verse whose title (after the Wilde trials) could plausibly have occasioned embarrassment. See *The Complete Poems by Lionel Johnson*, ed. Ian Fletcher (London: Unicorn Press, 1953), 9–10.

To WALTER PATER, 7 June [1893]
MS.: British Library. Printed in *TBB*.

Walter Pater Esq., | Brasenose College, | Oxford.

June 7.

Dear Pater,

We have received from America an elaborate thesis on Plato's Theory of Education in the Republic. I wonder whether you would be willing to read the MS. for us and advise us as to its publication? Our usual fee for such advice is £2.2. The author, A. Guyot Cameron,[1] is a Professor at Yale. May I send you the MS.?

Yours very truly,
George A. Macmillan.

[1] Arnold Guyot Cameron (1864–1947), an American editor, studied modern languages at Princeton, and then taught at Yale, 1892–7, and Princeton, 1897–1905. He gave up teaching to write on economic and international matters for the *Wall Street Journal*. Cameron never published the book mentioned in Macmillan's letter.

To EDMUND GOSSE, 10 June [1893]
MS.: Brotherton Collection, University of Leeds. On College letterhead. Printed in *LWP*.

BRASENOSE COLLEGE, | OXFORD. | June 10th.

My dear Gosse,

In consequence of an important college meeting I shall not be able to be present at the ceremony at University.[1] It will give me real pleasure, however, to see you here at dinner, at 7 o'clock. I have already read a great part of your excellent book, so kindly sent me.[2] I find it full of your acute judgments, \of/ the urbanity also, the lightness of touch, one looks for from you. It has greatly interested me. Sincere thanks for it.

Unless I hear to the contrary, I shall look forward to see you on Wednesday, at 7. With kind regards,

Very sincerely yours
Walter Pater.

[1] On 14 June 1893, the Principal and Fellows of Brasenose held a special meeting (almost three hours in length) regarding changes to the College statutes. The 'ceremony' in question was the official unveiling of the memorial to the poet Percy Bysshe Shelley (1792–1822), which was presented to University College by the poet's mother, Lady Elizabeth Shelley. According to a report in *The Times*, 15 June 1893, 11, a large company of dignitaries assembled to witness the official unveiling of the monument by sculptor Onslow Ford (1852–1901). In 1904, Edmund Gosse told Thomas Wright (see Biographical Register) that Pater had not been invited (Wright, 2: 193).

[2] The book alluded to here, *Questions at Issue* (London: William Heinemann, 1893), reprints thirteen essays (nearly half were first published in American periodicals) featuring Gosse (see Biographical Register) ruminating on literary controversies. See Evan Charteris, *The Life and Letters of Sir Edmund Gosse* (London: William Heinemann, 1931), 134–5; Anthony Kearney, 'Settling Scores: Gosse on Mallock and Pater', *Pater Newsletter*, 63 (Spring 2013), 67–71. Gosse and Pater enjoyed a close friendship, unwavering in their mutual regard and concern for each other's literary fortune. In 'Making a Name in Literature' (115–33), Gosse considers the ways in which a literary reputation is formed (and destroyed) via the institution of reviewing, the 'private conversation among leaders of opinion', and 'the instinctive attraction which leads the general public to discover for itself what is calculated to give it pleasure'. Gosse also recalls setbacks suffered from hostile reviewers such as John Churton Collins (see Biographical Register), who caustically dismissed Gosse's *From Shakespeare to Pope* (1885), the subject of Pater's letter to Gosse, 26 Oct. [1886]. In 'Making a Name in Literature', Gosse makes disparaging remarks about a writer (unnamed in the essay) contemporaries would recognize as W. H. Mallock (see Biographical Register), instrumental in bringing about two scandals that touched Pater. See Laurel Brake, 'Judas and the Widow: Thomas Wright and A. C. Benson as Biographers of Walter Pater', *Prose Studies*, 4 (1981), 39–54; Seiler, *Walter Pater: A Life Remembered*, 253–60; Billie Andrew Inman, 'Estrangement and Connection: Walter Pater, Benjamin Jowett, and William M. Hardinge', in *Pater in the 1990s*, 1–13.

To WALTER PATER, 12 June [1893]
MS.: British Library. Printed in *TBB*.

W. H. Pater Esq.

                                                    June 12.

Dear Pater,

Many thanks. The MS.[1] goes today. Your opinion will be regarded as in strict confidence.

                                        Yours very truly,
                                        George A. Macmillan.

[1] 'The Purpose and Plan of Plato's Theory of Education in the *Republic*', a PhD thesis (1891) by A. Guyot Cameron; see letter to Pater, 7 June [1893].

To EDMUND GOSSE, 16 June [1893]
MS.: Brasenose College. Envelope: Edmund Gosse Esq: | 29 Delamere Terrace | Westbourne Park | London. W. Postmark: OXFORD Y JU 16 93. On a correspondence card. Printed in *LWP*.

                                        B. N. C. | June 16th.

My dear Gosse,

Sincere thanks. I, and others, were greatly pleased to see you. I leave for London on Monday; but my coming and going will be a little uncertain.

                                        Very sincerely yours
                                        Walter Pater.

To EDMUND GOSSE, [20 June? 1893][1]
MS.: Brotherton Collection, University of Leeds. On a correspondence card. Printed in *LWP*.

                        12 Earl's Terrace, | Kensington, W.

My dear Gosse,

I ought to have answered your kind invitation last night, but was extremely tired. I could lunch with you on Thursday the 29th.

                                        Very sincerely yours
                                        Walter Pater.

[1] The conjectured date is pencilled on the MS. Gosse gave a luncheon at the National Club, London, on Thursday, 29 June 1893. Among his nine guests were Walter Pater, Thomas Hardy, and A. C. Benson, their names appearing in *The Book of Gosse*, Cambridge University Library MS. Add. 7034, fol. 103.

To DOUGLAS AINSLIE, [1 July 1893]
MS.: Bates College. Printed in *LWP*.

12 Earl's Terrace | Saturday.

My dear Ainslie,

If this should find you disengaged, I shall think it very kind if you will dine with me on Monday, July 3rd, at 7.45.

Very sincerely yours
Walter Pater.

To GRAHAM WALFORD ROBERTSON,[1] 1 July [1893]
MS.: Harvard University. Envelope: Graham Robertson Esq: | 23 Rutland Gate | W. Postmark: KENSINGTON KZ JY 1 93 W. Printed in *LWP*.

12 Earl's Terrace | Saturday.

Dear Mr. Robertson,

If this should find you disengaged, I shall think it very kind if you will dine with me on Monday, July 3rd, to meet two or three friends, at 7.45.[2]

Very truly yours
Walter Pater.

[1] See letter to Robertson, [21 Mar. 1892]. In his autobiography, *Time Was*, Robertson refers to dining 'sometimes... en famille' with the Paters and refers to Pater as 'a kind friend' (96).
[2] Among those who dined with Pater on 3 July 1893 were Violet Paget, her friend Clementine ('Kit') Anstruther-Thomson, and J. S. Cotton (see *VLL*, 349).

To EDWARD VINCENT EYRE,[1] July [1893]
Text: *Church and Parish Chronicle* [of Holy Redeemer, Clerkenwell], 5 (September 1894), 3. Printed in *LWP*.

July 1st.

My dear Sir,

I thought it very kind of you to invite me to the meeting in aid of the completion of your Church, and regret to find that I shall not be able to come, though I should have felt hardly worthy to speak on such a subject.

I am one of those who think that when Gothic may perhaps have fallen into disuse again everywhere else, it will still continue to be our *sacred* style of architecture. Nevertheless when I first entered your Church at Clerkenwell, it seemed to me that a very successful experiment had been made in the application or re-application of quite another sort of architecture to Church purposes. It made one think how some of the Renaissance Churches of Venice, or Wren's London Churches must have looked when they were fresh and clean; and it would be interesting to see it completed after the plan which commended itself to the devout genius of Mr. Sedding.[2]

What a help to the people who live about it such a Church as yours, so fair and cheerful and full of light, with its round of beautiful services must be! Religion, I sometimes think, is the only way in which poetry can really reach the hard-worked poor; and how largely the movement in which your Church takes part has developed the capacities of our national religion towards that effect. One is reminded of the Franciscan movement in Italy long ago. That too, though 'wedded to poverty', bequeathed to those who have leisure to think about such things, a world of beautiful religious art.

There was certainly something very touching and attractive, very winning in the Sunday Morning services (more particularly when one found them in a neighbourhood like that) when I have visited your Church sometimes. Of course I know how much more than all this the Church of the Holy Redeemer is to yourself and others—designed, as I once heard you say, to afford to those who frequent it, 'all the fullness and beauty of the catholic religion'; and I desire sincerely God's blessing upon it [and your own zealous work in and about it].[3] Forgive my frank words, and believe me

Very truly yours
Walter Pater.

The Rev. E. V. Eyre

[1] Revd Edward Vincent Eyre (1851–1925) studied at Corpus Christi College, Oxford, 1870–4. He was, from 1888–1904, vicar of the high Anglican Church of the Holy Redeemer in London's Clerkenwell district. Eyre invited Pater to speak on Tuesday afternoon, 4 July 1893, at a West End meeting on behalf of the parish's building fund. This letter was read at the meeting. Pater's name remains on the church's memorial book, and prayers are offered for him every year on the anniversary of his death.

[2] John Dando Sedding (1838–91), an architect, studied with George Edmund Street (1824–81), the Gothic Revival specialist, from 1858–64. One of his first projects was St Martin's, an Anglo-Catholic church in Cheshire, completed in 1872. The interior was

designed by William Morris. The firm designed (in the Italian style) the Church of Our Most Holy Redeemer, which was started in 1887–8. It remained incomplete until 1894–5, when the east end was extended by Sedding's former assistant, Henry Wilson (1864–1934).

[3] The passage in brackets appears in the MS. draft of this letter at Harvard University, and may have been omitted by the Revd Eyre in 1894.

To ARTHUR WAUGH,[1] 5 July [1893?][2]
Text: The *Critic*, 11 August 1894, 93. Printed in *LWP*.

12 Earl's Terrace, | July 5th.

Dear Mr. Waugh,

I ought to have answered your letter before. I never quite like photographs of myself, but send you the latest taken of me. I leave London in a day or two; but should you be staying at Oxford at any time, it would give me great pleasure to see you. With kind regards,

Very truly yours
Walter Pater.

[1] Arthur Waugh (1866–1943), writer, editor, and publisher, studied at New College, Oxford, 1885–9, and won the Newdigate prize for poetry. He served as the London correspondent to the *Critic* (New York), 1890–7, and as a literary critic for the *Daily Telegraph*, 1901–31. With the help of his cousin and mentor, Edmund Gosse (see Biographical Register), he secured a contract with William Heinemann to write a biography of Tennyson (1892). From 1902 to 1931, Waugh was the managing director and chair of Chapman and Hall. In 1893 he married Catherine Charlotte Raban; their two sons, Alex and Evelyn, both became writers. Waugh wrote an unsigned obituary of Pater ('London Letter', *Critic*, 1 Sept. 1894, 145–6) in which the facsimile text of this letter appears.

[2] Dated from characteristics of the handwriting and the strong possibility that the mention of his soon leaving London refers to Pater's removal from Earl's Terrace at the end of July 1893 (see letter to Gosse, 13 July [1893]).

To EDMUND GOSSE, 13 July [1893]
MS.: British Library, Ashley Collection. Printed in *LWP*.

12 Earl's Terrace | July 13th.

My dear Gosse,

Sincere thanks for your letter, and kindness in the matter of the Library Committee. I hope you will not think me ungrateful when I tell you that I have just written to the Secretary to decline.[1] The fact is, I should never be able to attend the meetings, and in that case I think it would be unfair to the subscribers if I occupied the place of some one who could attend them, and be useful to the Library. If they don't think so now, they would very soon. I am nevertheless, be assured, quite alive to the compliment you and others have paid me.

I leave London in a little more than two weeks, and find much to do in that short time. My new Oxford address is 64 St. Giles's;[2] where, or at B. N. C., I could give you a bed, and should be much pleased to see you. We shall take a few weeks to get settled; after which we propose to be abroad for about a month, hoping to return to Oxford in the beginning of October.

Believe me, my dear Gosse, with kind regards,

Very sincerely yours
Walter Pater.

---

[1] Gosse was an active member of the London Library; it was probably at his instigation that the Committee invited Pater to serve. The *Athenaeum* printed the following notice: 'Mr. Walter Pater has been chosen to fill the vacancy created in the Committee of the London Library by the election of Mr. Leslie Stephen to succeed Lord Tennyson as President of that institution.' 'Literary Gossip', *Athenaeum*, 15 July 1893, 98–9. Pater's letter to the Secretary (apparently later destroyed) was read to the Committee on 24 July 1893.

[2] It was in this house (no longer standing) that Pater died on 30 July 1894.

To WILLIAM CANTON, 18 October [1893]
MS.: Brasenose College. On College letterhead. Printed in *LWP*.

BRASENOSE COLLEGE, | OXFORD. | Oct: 18th.

My dear Mr. Canton,

I found your letter on my return from the continent,—from France, where I have been studying some fine old churches, of which I am my mind is rather full just now. I have given up my house in Kensington, and my permanent address is as above.

I am afraid my promise about St. Hugh was a rash one. Pray forgive me. I hope, however, to send you something acceptable for 'Good Words', by and bye. I am just finishing a paper on a Greek Art subject which I should like to find a place in the 'Contemporary' for December.[1]

By the way, I wish, both for his sake and that of the public, you could \get/ something in the way of articles for the Contemporary or Good Words, from my friend, the Rev. F. W. Bussell, of this college,—an article, e.g. in his popular style, on Marcus Aurelius or Julian, or any of the later Greek or Latin writers of the decadent or semi-christian type.[2] He has a vivid hold on this class of interesting persons. Mr. Bussell is very distinguished here, and is a young man with a real touch of genius, but a little too reluctant, it seems to me, to address the general public. Many thanks for your kind letters, from

Very sincerely yours
Walter Pater.

Ask F. W. B. to send you a short sabbatic reading on Cyprian for Good Words, or an article on Latin Literature in the second century for the Contemporary. You would be tapping a new vein, if I may use what I suppose is a mixed metaphor.

---

¹ See letter to Canton, 7 Nov. [1893].
² Neither the *Contemporary Review* nor *Good Words* published anything by Bussell in 1893 or 1894.

To WALTER PATER, 30 October 1893
MS.: British Library. Printed in *TBB*.

W. H. Pater Esq., | Brasenose College, | Oxford.

Oct. 30.

Dear Pater,

My cousin is not here today so I opened your letter. Your request for copies of the *Renaissance* shall be duly attended to when the book is ready, but the title page is not yet printed off and I enclose herewith two specimens¹ that you may say whether you prefer the lighter or the darker impression.

With kind regards, I am

Yours very truly,
George A. Macmillan.

---

¹ These specimen pages are missing.

To WILLIAM CANTON, 7 November [1893]
MS.: Brasenose College. Printed in *LWP*.

Brasenose College | Nov: 7th.

My dear Mr. Canton,

Sincere thanks for your kind letter. I am much pleased that you like 'Apollo in Picardy'.¹ I send to your address by this post a MS. for the Contemporary Review.² Would you kindly transfer it to Mr. Bunting? If he cares to have it, I should like a proof soon, as I fear the MS. is obscure in parts, and it would be desirable to correct the proof carefully.

A young friend, and former pupil, of mine, Mr. K. McMaster,³ \(*not* Mr. Bussell,)/ proposes to send a paper, for inspection, to the Editor of the Contemporary, and I have promised to mention this. I think he has very considerable, though perhaps immature, abilities, and I shall tell him to send his MS. under cover to you.

Many thanks for your kind suggestions on the matter of publishing. I do not think I could leave Macmillan except for very substantial reasons. But alas! I have nothing in book form nearly ready for publication at present.

Very sincerely yours
Walter Pater.

[1] In *Harper's New Monthly Magazine*, 87 (Nov. 1893), 949–57.
[2] 'The Age of Athletic Prizemen: A Chapter in Greek Art', *Contemporary Review*, 65 (Feb. 1894), 242–56; see *CW* viii.
[3] Kenneth Hovil McMaster (1870–1948) studied at Brasenose College, 1889-94. He became a priest in the Church of England in 1899 and the rector of St Augustine, Kilburn, in 1900. Nothing by him appeared in the *Contemporary Review* for 1893 or 1894.

To WILLIAM CANTON, 20 November [1893]
MS.: Princeton University. Printed in *LWP*.

B. N. C. | Nov: 20th.

My dear Mr. Canton,

I enclose the proof corrected. I hope you will like the essay. Many thanks for your letter: I shall not forget about the C. R.[1]

Very sincerely yours
Walter Pater.

[1] The *Contemporary Review*.

To WILLIAM ROTHENSTEIN,[1] [23 November 1893]
MS.: Harvard University. Printed in *LWP*.

B. N. C. | Thursday.

Dear Mr. Rothenstein,

Sincere thanks. I am sorry, in consequence of an engagement here, to be unable to hear Verlaine lecture,[2] as I had hoped to do.

Very truly yours
Walter Pater.

[1] William Rothenstein (1872–1945), artist, educator, and writer, studied at the Slade School of Art, London, and the Académie Julian, Paris. In the autumn of 1893 John Lane (see letters to Lane, [25 Mar. 1894] and 5 Apr. 1894) commissioned Rothenstein to produce

a set of lithographs of prominent Oxonians. During the 1890s he exhibited at the New English Art Club, London, and contributed to *The Yellow Book* and the *Savoy*. He was Professor of Civic Art at Sheffield University, 1917–26, and Principal of the Royal College of Art, London, 1920–35. His achievements include his series of portraits: *Oxford Characters: Twenty-Four Lithographs by Will Rothenstein*, with text by F. York Powell (1896), *Twelve Portraits* (1929), and *Contemporaries* (1937).

[2] Paul Verlaine visited England for the fourth and last time during the autumn of 1893, under the auspices of Frederick York-Powell, Arthur Symons, and Rothenstein. Verlaine's London lecture (at Barnard's Inn, High Holborn) on 21 Nov. was delivered in 'a low, monotonous, and trembling voice' to an audience of artists, critics, musicians, and poets, including Ernest Dowson, Edmund Gosse, Frank Harris, William Heinemann, Herbert Horne, Selwyn Image, and John Lane. See *The Times*, 22 Nov. 1893, 5. On 23 Nov. Verlaine lectured in Oxford to a small audience in a room behind Blackwell's bookshop.

To WILLIAM CANTON, 17 December [1893]
MS.: Princeton University. Printed in *LWP*.

Brasenose College | Oxford. | Dec: 17th.

My dear Mr. Canton,

I enclose the corrected proof.[1] Please tell Mr. Bunting, with my kind regards, that I shall be glad to see it in the Jan.? number. I am confined to the house with bronchitis.

Very sincerely yours
Walter Pater.

[1] 'The Age of Athletic Prizemen: A Chapter in Greek Art', *Contemporary Review*, 65 (Feb. 1894), 242–56.

To WILLIAM CANTON, [late December? 1893][1]
MS.: Princeton University. Printed in *LWP*.

My dear Canton,

There are two more corrections I should like to make in the proof.
On page 5, last line of paragraph, for *deflowered*, read *slighted*. page 10, fourteenth line from the end, for *get*, read *pass*.

Very sincerely yours
Walter Pater.

[1] So dated because this note appears to follow soon upon the letter to Canton, 17 Dec. [1893]. The second correction stands in the printed text of 'The Age of Athletic Prizemen' (251); but Pater changed his mind again about the first—the printed text reads 'dishonoured'.

1894

To FREDERICK WEDMORE, 4 January [1894]
MS.: Brasenose College. Printed in *LWP*.

                                                  64 St. Giles's | Oxford. | Jan: 4th.

My dear Wedmore,

    You must think me a very ungrateful person for leaving so long unanswered your kind letter of two months ago. The fact, my removal here involved a great deal of fatiguing business. After that, I went abroad; and on my return found large arrears of letters, etc. being always a poor correspondent. Since then I have been laid up with a very disagreeable attack of influenza, or something of the sort.

    I was glad to hear of a new edition of your two exquisite little books.[1] They make a very pretty volume, also, in their new [sic]. I greatly admire both 'Renunciations' and its predecessor, and indeed your work generally. Your short stories seem to me unique, and I hope you will write more of them. Though perhaps a little too persistently sad, they delight me as specimens of literary art, perfect in their way, and according to their own intention. Should you be visiting Oxford at any time, I hope you will let me know a day or two before, and do me the pleasure of lunching or dining with me.

    With all good wishes for the new year,

                                                             Very truly yours
                                                              Walter Pater.

---

[1] Elkin Mathews and John Lane published a double volume of Wedmore's stories, *Pastorals of France* [and] *Renunciations* in Nov. 1893. From the beginning, Pater had liked *Pastorals of France* (1877). See Wedmore, *Memories* (London: Methuen, 1912), 156–65. *Renunciations*, which also contains three tales of a strongly pathetic and sentimental cast, was first published in Jan. 1893.

To WILLIAM ROTHENSTEIN, [16 January 1894?][1]
MS.: Harvard University. Printed in *LWP*.

B. N. C. | Tuesday.

Dear Mr. Rothenstein,

I have very few hours at my disposal this week; but if you would really like me to do so, should be very willing to sit to you for an hour, tomorrow at 12, or on Thursday at 4, in my room *here*.

Will you dine with me at *64 St. Giles's*, and meet Mr. Bussell, on Friday at 7.30. In haste,

Sincerely yours
Walter Pater.

R. S. V. P.

---

[1] From Rothenstein's *Men and Memories*, 2 vols (London: Faber, 1931), 1: 155–6, it seems likely that he drew both Bussell and Pater during Hilary term 1894. Jan. 16 was the first Tuesday of term; Pater's reference to his busy programme accords with the start of term and with letter to Symons, 17 Jan. [1894]. It is possible, however, that this note was written as early as 16 Oct. 1893 or as late as 27 Feb. 1894.

To ARTHUR SYMONS, 17 January [1894]
Text: Transcript by Roger Lhombreaud. Printed in *LWP*.

B. N. C. | Jan. 17th.

My dear Mr. Symons,

I have been overwhelmed with ink work during the last few days. Pray excuse my delay in answering your letter. I should have much liked to do what you therein propose,[1] but it would be simply uncandid in me to the new magazine, and especially to your own contributions, and wish it all success. Kindly tell Mr. Harland[2] this, and, with many thanks to him and to yourself, believe me,

Very sincerely yours
Walter Pater.

---

[1] Symons, acting on behalf of Harland, likely asked Pater to contribute to the first number of *The Yellow Book*. Pater eventually allowed his name to appear among those of future contributors in the prospectus (Mar. 1894) for the new magazine, but died before publishing in it.

[2] Henry Harland (1861–1905), an American novelist and editor, settled in London in 1889, where he entertained many artists and writers, including Edmund Gosse. Harland's novels include *Grandison Mather: Or an Account of the Fortunes of Mr. and Mrs. Thomas*

Gardiner (New York: Cassell, 1889), *Two Voices* (New York: Cassell, 1890), and *Mea Culpa: A Woman's Last Word* (New York: J. W. Lovell, 1891). He edited *The Yellow Book*, published 1894–7 by Elkin Mathews and John Lane.

To JAMES THOMAS KNOWLES, 22 January [1894]
MS.: Northwestern University. Printed in *LWP*.

Brasenose College, | Jan: 22nd.

Dear Mr. Knowles,

I send you, by this post, a short paper on *Notre-Dame d'Amiens*, which I think you may find suitable for the Nineteenth Century.[1] It is of the first of a series, to be ready at intervals, on 'Some Great Churches of France';[2] but it might appear without the general title. Would you kindly read it.

I have given up my house in Kensington, and my address is that above. Believe me

Very truly yours
Walter Pater.

James Knowles Esq:

[1] The essay appeared as 'Some Great Churches of France. I. Notre-Dame d'Amiens', *The Nineteenth Century*, 35 (Mar. 1894), 481–8. See *CW* vi.
[2] The second essay, on 'Vézelay', was published, in *The Nineteenth Century*, 35 (June 1894), 963–70 (see *CW* vi; and see letters to Knowles, 20 Mar. [1894] and 2 May [1894]). Pater began the third, on 'Notre-Dame de Troyes', a partial MS. draft of which survives. See *CW* x.

To JAMES THOMAS KNOWLES, 28 January [1894]
MS.: Northwestern University. Printed in *LWP*.

Brasenose College, | Jan: 28th.

Dear Mr. Knowles,

Many thanks for your kind reply. I am glad you approve of my paper,[1] especially as your opinion is that of an expert. When you print it please send the proof to the address above.

Very truly yours
Walter Pater.

[1] See letter to Knowles, 22 Jan. [1894].

To JAMES THOMAS KNOWLES, 21 February [1894]
MS.: Northwestern University. Printed in *LWP*.

B. N. C. | Feb: 21st.

Dear Mr. Knowles,

I enclose the proof of my paper,[1] finally corrected.

Very truly yours
Walter Pater.

---

[1] 'Some Great Churches of France. I. Notre-Dame d'Amiens'; see letter to Knowles, 22 Jan. [1894].

To FALCONER MADAN, [1 March 1894][1]
MS.: Bodleian Library. Printed in *LWP*.

B. N. C. | Thursday.

Dear Madan,

George Armour[2] of Chicago, with whom I think you are acquainted, dines in Hall this evening. I hope you may be coming. Don't answer this.

Yours very truly
Walter Pater.

---

[1] The date is pencilled on the MS.

[2] George Allison Armour (1856–1936), the son of a Scottish engineer, settled in the United States (see letter to Armour, 24 Mar. [1889], n. 1).

To EMILY DANIEL,[1] 11 March [1894]
MS.: Worcester College, Oxford. Printed in *LWP*.

64 St. Giles's | March 11th.

My dear Mrs. Daniel,

It was with great interest that I read your kind and witty letter. I should think it an honour to contribute, as you propose, to what I know will be so exquisite a volume, and for so excellent a purpose.[2] Only, if it be possible! I have, however, undertaken to do a great deal during the course of the next few months. Kindly tell me by what day, at the latest, the little notice of Lovelace must be ready for printing.

Very sincerely yours
Walter Pater.

P. S. I meant to have posted this yesterday, but it was delayed, and I have now looked at two or three things about Lovelace which convince me that to say anything new about him it would be necessary to read carefully the whole of his work. Brief notices of his more popular pieces have already been well done, e.g. in 'Ward's English Poets'. I fear it is hopeless for me to do anything worth your having *in time*; though I should have liked extremely to participate in your work.

[1] Emily Crabb Daniel, née Olive (1852?–1933), book-binder, printer, and illustrator, was the wife of Worcester College Fellow and publisher C. H. O. Daniel (see Biographical Register). She initiated editorial projects to raise funds for various worthy projects.

[2] This letter was inserted in a copy of Antony à Wood's *Life of Lovelace* (Oxford: Daniel Press, 1896). Richard Lovelace (1617–57) was a Cavalier poet. It seems likely that this edition, first planned in 1894 to include a short introduction by Pater, would have been sold in June at a parish benefit. See also letters to Daniel, [Apr. or May 1894] and 19 June [1894].

To WILLIAM ROTHENSTEIN, 11 March [1894]
MS.: Harvard University. Printed in William Rothenstein, *Men and Memories: Recollections of William Rothenstein, 1872-1900*, 2 vols (London: Faber and Faber, 1931), 1: 156 (with minor errors), and *LWP*.

64 St. Giles's | Oxford. | March 11th.

My dear Rothenstein,

I thought your drawing of me a clever likeness, but doubt very much whether my sister, whom I have told about it will like it; in which case I would rather not have it published.[1] I therefore write at once, to save you needless trouble ~~at~~ \about/ it. Put off the reproduction of the drawing till you come to Oxford again, and then let us see it. I think your likeness of Bussell most excellent, and shall value it. It presents just the look I think so fine in him, and have \not/ seen in his photographs. I should have liked to be coupled with him, and am very sorry not to be. I think however you ought to publish him at once, with some other companion; and \I/ will send you my four or five lines for him soon.

With sincere thanks for the trouble you have taken about me, I remain

Very truly yours
Walter Pater.

[1] In *Men and Memories*, 1: 155–7, Rothenstein tells of Pater's opposition to its publication and transcribes part of a note he received from the printer Thomas Way: 'We have just had a visit from Mr Lane.... He came expressly to say that no more proofs were to be pulled from the Pater. I understand Pater has used great stress as to what he will do if it is published.' In a letter to Lane, [25 Mar. 1894], however, Pater appears more reasonable. The

drawing did not appear until Lionel Johnson persuaded Clara and Hester Pater to have it included in Rothenstein, Part VI, *Oxford Characters: A Series of Lithographs* (London: Bodley Head, 1893–5), together with the drawing of F. W. Bussell, for which Pater had prepared a text.

To JOHN LANE,[1] 15 March [1894]
MS.: Morgan Library & Museum (MA 4500). Printed in Inman, 'Pater's Letters at the Pierpont Library', 415.

64 St. Giles's | Oxford. | March 15th.

Dear Mr Lane,

When my friend, Mr Rothenstein, left me the other day, I understood that the lithograph of his drawing would be submitted to me for approval, before publication. He tells me, however, that the printing of it is begun, and refers me to yourself. The fact is, I think it is a very unpleasing likeness of me, and am certain my friends here will dislike it even more than I do. I am sure I only have to tell you this, to prevent the further printing or publication of it in any way.

I must add that Mr. Rothenstein's drawing of Mr. Bussell is a really good likeness; and will, I feel confident, be very popular in Oxford. I should be glad to send you a few lines to accompany it, as soon as you please, if you desire that I should do so.

Believe me

Very truly yours
Walter Pater.

R. S. V. P.

---

[1] John Lane (1854–1925), publisher, entered the book trade in the mid-1880s; a chance meeting with Elkin Mathews (1851–1921) resulted in the founding of the Bodley Head Press in 1887, a firm initially devoted to the antiquarian book trade. Within a few years the Bodley Head was publishing limited editions that appealed to a sophisticated market, attracting such authors and illustrators as Oscar Wilde, George Egerton (Mary Dunne Bright), Richard Le Gallienne, Aubrey Beardsley, and Charles Rickets. Mathews terminated the partnership in 1894; Lane retained the firm's imprint, and in 1896 opened a New York branch. Lane launched the 'decadent' *The Yellow Book* in 1894, but the uproar generated by Wilde's trials in 1895 hastened the end of the publication in 1897.

To JAMES THOMAS KNOWLES, 20 March [1894]
MS.: Northwestern University. Printed in *LWP*.

Brasenose College, | March 20th.

Dear Mr. Knowles,

I beg to acknowledge receipt of cheque, with many thanks. I hope to send you shortly no. 2 on Vézelay,[1] for use when you think fit.

Very sincerely yours
Walter Pater.

[1] 'Some Great Churches of France. II. Vézelay', *The Nineteenth Century*, 35 (June 1894), 963–70. See *CW* vi.

To JOHN LANE,[1] [25 March 1894]
MS.: Brasenose College. Envelope: John Lane Esq: | Kingswood Park | near Bristol. Postmark: OXFORD B MR 26 94. Printed in *LWP*.

64 St. Giles's | Oxford | Easter Day.

Dear Mr. Lane,

I fancied, rightly, that your delay in reply was caused by absence from London. Many thanks for the trouble you are taking about the drawing. I leave Oxford for three weeks on Wednesday morning for the North of England, and shall be moving about from place to place, so that I fear it will hardly be practicable for me to inspect the drawing. My sisters however will be in London, from the middle of this week for some time onward, and will be glad to call at the Bodley Head for the purpose of looking at the work for me, on Friday or Saturday next. I will abide by their decision in the matter. I should much like to be a companion to Mr. Bussell, as you suggest; but if my likeness is withdrawn, hope you will find him some other companion, and not delay publishing him, as the likeness is a very happy one, and will, I am sure, be welcome in Oxford. I enclose a few lines to introduce him;[2] and with sincere regret to have thus troubled you about myself, remain

Very truly yours
Walter Pater.

[1] See letter to Lane, 15 Mar. [1894].
[2] Enclosed is Pater's MS. draft for the text that appeared facing Bussell's portrait in *Oxford Characters*: 'Mr. F. W. Bussell, Fellow of B. N. C., B. D. and Mus: Bac: is as young as he looks here. He was early distinguished in the University, and has already preached some

remarkable sermons in Saint Mary's pulpit. His friends love him; and he is popular with the Undergraduates whom he instructs. His versatility is considerable; but he is above all a student, with something like genius for classical literature, especially for the early \Christian/ theology, and late \Pagan/ philosophy, of the imperial age, which he reads as other people read the newspapers. His expression after some hours of such reading \is/ ~~has been~~ here recorded by ~~Mr. Rothenstein~~ with remarkable fineness. He is capable of much.'

To JOHN LANE, 5 April 1894
MS.: Brasenose College. On the stationery of the Royal Station Hotel, York. Printed in *LWP*.

YORK | April 5th. 1894.

Dear Mr. Lane,

My sisters have seen the drawing, and think it so unlike me that the publication of it must be given up. I am very sorry; but, if Rothenstein thinks it worth while, would sit to him again. I am going to Glasgow for a degree,[1] and am taking [in] some of these Northern cathedral towns on my way there, and write as best I may to catch the post.

By the way, the few lines I sent you à propos of Mr. Bussell might be abbreviated, by the [revision] of 'His friends', to 'instructs'.

Believe me

Very sincerely yours
Walter Pater.

[1] On 13 Apr. 1894 the University of Glasgow conferred the honorary LLD degrees on Edward Caird, Master of Balliol; Walter H. Pater, MA, Fellow, Dean, and Lecturer, Brasenose; Alexander B. W. Kennedy, FRS, President of the Institute of Mechanical Engineers; and F. McLean, MA, FRAS, of Tunbridge Wells, known for his research into the spectroscope (see the *Glasgow Herald*, 17 Mar. 1894, 6, and *Pall Mall Gazette*, 31 Mar. 1894, 8). The degree was the only such honour Pater received.

To PHILIP MORGAN WATKINS,[1] 24 April [1894]
MS.: Brasenose College. Printed in *LWP*.

B. N. C. | April 24th.

My dear Watkins,

May 11th, 12th, and 24th, are degree-days. Let me know, a few days before, which you select. I shall have much pleasure in seeing you again.

Very sincerely yours
Walter Pater.

[1] Philip Morgan Watkins (1867–1959), educator, studied at Brasenose, 1887–91, and then tutored privately for two years. Ordained in the Church of England in 1894, Watkins served as the curate at Tideswell, Derbyshire, 1893–5. While making plans to visit Oxford to receive his MA, he evidently wrote to Pater, and elicited this reply. From 1897, Watkins served as a schoolmaster in Caterham, Surrey, and published *Rules for Latin Prose*.

To EMILY DANIEL, [April or May 1894][1]
MS.: Worcester College, Oxford. Printed in *LWP*.

My dear Mrs. Daniel,

I am afraid you will find 'Hippolytus', which I send you in a revised MS. copy,[2] too long; longer than I thought. If you prefer the 'Child', I should have to revise it for you, within the next few days.[3]

Sincerely yours
W. P.

[1] This letter precedes the one Emily Daniel wrote to Pater on 2 June 1894 (MS.: Worcester College) announcing she is sending the first copy of Pater's *An Imaginary Portrait: The Child in the House* (1894), the well-known text first entitled 'Imaginary Portraits. I. The Child in the House', which had appeared in *Macmillan's Magazine*, 38 (Aug. 1878), together with a note of thanks (MS.: Worcester College). Emily and her husband, C. H. O. Daniel (see Biographical Register), were on friendly terms with Pater; the impetus for publishing this work seems to have come from Emily. Apparently, she wished to print a piece by Pater, and he suggested 'Hippolytus Veiled', but this was found to be too long. In the end Daniel printed in Fell's old-faced type an edition of 250 copies on French hand-made paper, binding each volume with blue-grey paper covers and numbering each by hand. Information about the Press can be found in *The Daniel Press: Memorials of C. H. O. Daniel with a Bibliography of the Press 1845–1919* (Oxford: Daniel Press, 1921). The foreword of the book was written by C. H. Wilkinson (Worcester College) and the bibliography was compiled by Falconer Madan. Pater revised this 'portrait' for the Daniel Press publication, and Worcester College has a copy of the text as it appeared in *Macmillan's Magazine* in 1878, with the author's corrections (Worcester College YC 12 20(f)). Advertisements indicate that the book was issued on 12 June 1894 at a Venetian Fête at Worcester College Gardens, for the benefit of the Parish of St Thomas the Martyr, Oxford, and that orders could be sent to Mrs Daniel (for reports on the event, see *The Times*, 11 Aug. 1894, 2; the *Oxford Magazine*, 13 June 1894, 1; and the *Nation*, 23 Aug. 1894, 143). The book was an instant success: every copy was sold within an hour of the opening. See Samuel Wright, *A Bibliography*, 94–6; see also Lene Østermark-Johansen, 'The Daniel Press Edition of Walter Pater's Last Book', *Journal of Pre-Raphaelite Studies*, ns 25 (Fall 2016), 73–86. Wilde bought one of the copies and presented it to his wife, Constance Lloyd (this volume, in the British Library, shelf-mark Eccles 477, bears the following inscription: 'To Constance, from Oscar, July 1894'). See *CW* iii and letters to Daniel, 19 June [1894], and Symons, [late June 1894].

[2] This revised MS. copy of 'Hippolytus Veiled' is the text printed in *Greek Studies*. In the Preface to that volume, Shadwell states: 'It was afterwards [after 1889] rewritten, but with only a few substantial alterations, in Mr. Pater's own hand, with a view, probably, of republishing it with other essays. This last revise has been followed in the text now printed' (3). See *CW* iii.

[3] Pater's revised text, an offprint of the *Macmillan's Magazine* version with corrections and changes in his hand, is housed in the library of Worcester College.

To JAMES THOMAS KNOWLES, 2 May [1894]
MS.: Northwestern University. Printed in *LWP*.

Brasenose College, | May 2nd.

Dear Mr. Knowles,

I send you by this post, as I proposed, no. 2 of The Great French Churches.[1]

Very truly yours
Walter Pater.

[1] See letter to Knowles, 20 Mar. [1894].

To LEWIS CAMPBELL,[1] 6 May 1894
MS.: Wright MSS., 1878–1907, Lilly Library, Indiana University. Printed in *LWP*.[2]

B. N. C. | May 6, 1894.

My dear Campbell,

You have asked me to write a few lines 'describing the impression' Jowett made on out-College, i.e. non-Balliol men when he taught the University for nothing. Like many others I [received] much kindness & help from him when I was reading for my degree (1860 to 1862) & afterwards. A large number of his hours in every week of Term time must have been spent in the private teaching of undergrads, not of his own College, over & above his lectures, which of course were open to all. They found him a very encouraging but really critical judge of their work—essays, and the like—listening from 7.30–10.30 to a pupil, or a pair of pupils, for half an hour in turn. Of course many availed themselves of the, I believe, unprecedented offer to receive exercises in Greek or English in this way, & on the part of one whose fame among the youth, though he was then something of a recluse, was already established. Such fame rested on his great originality as a writer & thinker. He seemed to have taken the measure not merely of all opinions, but of all possible ones, & to have put the last refinements on literary expression. The charm of that was enhanced by a certain mystery about his own philosophic & other opinions. You know at that time his writings were thought by some to be obscure. These impressions of him had been derived from his Essays on St. Paul's Epistles,[3] which at that time were much read and pondered by the more intellectual sort of undergraduates. When he lectured on Plato, it was a fascinating thing to see those qualities as if in the act of creation, his lectures being informal, unwritten, and seemingly unpremeditated, but with many a long-remembered gem of expression, or delightfully novel idea, which seemed to be lying in wait whenever, at a loss for a moment in his somewhat hesitating discourse, he opened a book of loose notes. They passed very soon into other note-books all over the University; the larger part, but I think not all of them, into his published introductions to the *Dialogues*. Ever since I heard it, I have been longing to read a very dainty dialogue on language, which formed one of his lectures, a sort of 'New Cratylus'. Excuse the length to which my 'brief' remarks have run. On this closely-written sheet there is only room to sign myself

Very sincerely yours
Walter Pater.

[1] Revd Lewis Campbell (1830–1908), Scottish classical scholar and cleric, studied at the University of Glasgow, 1846–9, Trinity College, Oxford, 1849–50, and Balliol, 1850–2, where Jowett was his tutor (see Biographical Register). He was a Fellow and Tutor of Queen's College, Oxford, 1855–8 (the year that Pater arrived at Queen's). After working as a vicar for five years, he was named Professor of Greek at the University of St Andrews; he taught there until 1894, when he was elected honorary Fellow of Balliol. Campbell published editions of Sophocles and Plato, and with E. A. Abbott, *The Life and Letters of Benjamin Jowett* (London: John Murray, 1897). Campbell and Pater were long acquainted. When Campbell reviewed *Plato and Platonism* (1893) for the *Classical Review*, 7 (1893), 263–6, he judged it 'a brilliant critical essay'. For Wright's biography of Pater, Campbell furnished a few recollections: 'Pater's conversation always seemed to me more interesting than his books. Such easy flow of perfect expression, often paradoxical, but always suggestive. His personal excellence, his kindness and devotion to home duties were well-known to all his friends' (qtd in Wright, 2: 212).

[2] A rough draft of this letter is among the Pater MSS. at Harvard. See *CW* x.

[3] Jowett, *The Epistles of St. Paul to the Thessalonians, Galatians, Romans, with critical notes and dissertations*, 2 vols (London: John Murray, 1855).

To WILLIAM CANTON, 19 May [1894]
MS.: Bates College. A brief extract is printed in Maggs Bros. *Catalogue* no. 870 (1960), 44. Printed in *LWP*.

B. N. C. | May 19th.

My dear Mr. Canton,

Accept my sincere thanks, though so late, for the kind present of your charming, touching, little volume, which I have been studying this afternoon with much enjoyment.[1]

I have been, and am, very busy; so much \so/ as to seem, I am afraid, neglectful of my friends, and their kindness, so cannot put off thanking you till I could write at length. Excuse, then, this too brief acknowledgement, and, with renewed thanks, believe me

Very sincerely yours
Walter Pater.

I find in your book the impress of genuine feeling, though of an original kind; and the simple delicacy of your writing matches it.

[1] Canton's *The Invisible Playmate: A Story of the Unseen* (1894), which appeared in April (see letter to Canton, [31 May? 1892]).

To EMILY DANIEL, 19 June [1894]
MS.: Worcester College, Oxford. Printed in *LWP*.

B. N. C. | June 19th.

My dear Mrs. Daniel,

Many thanks for your kind letter of June 14th. I called at Worcester House, and found you had taken flight for a few days: meant to have tried again today, but am prevented by gout. I hardly like to accept the cheque, and shall hope to see you soon. Meantime with sincere congratulations on the success of the Fête,[1] I remain

Very truly yours
Walter Pater.

It is a great privilege for my poor little piece to have been so daintily attired by printer and binder.

[1] C. H. O. Daniel had printed 250 copies of 'The Child in the House' as *An Imaginary Portrait: The Child in the House* by Walter Pater, selling these (at six shillings per copy) at a fundraising party held in Worcester College Gardens, Oxford, on 12 June 1894. See letters to Daniel, [Apr. or May 1894], and Symons, [late June 1894], n. 2.

To ARTHUR SYMONS, [late June 1894][1]
MS.: Mark Samuels Lasner Collection, University of Delaware. On a correspondence card.

My dear Symons,
  You are very welcome to the enclosed.[2] With kind regards,

Very sincerely yours,
W. P.

[1] So dated on the basis of the handwriting and internal evidence.
[2] Mark Samuels Lasner notes that the card was tucked into a copy of *An Imaginary Portrait: The Child in the House* (1894). See letters to Daniel, [Apr. or May 1894] and 19 June [1894].

To T. HERBERT WARREN,[1] 6 July [1894]
MS.: Brodie/Warren Collection, Magdalen College, Oxford.

64 St. Giles' | July 6th.

My dear Warren,

Sincere thanks for your kind and interesting letter. I should have answered it before this, but have not been able. I have been confined to bed for two weeks with rheumatic gout, and though I am now sitting up still feel unfitted to do much. I was pleased to hear that you like my little piece from the Worcester Press.[2] I did not mean it, however, to be in any sense a formal publication. It was written and printed fifteen years ago, and now I am almost afraid of looking at it.

Your suggestion for a Philosophy of Translation seems to me a very sound and interesting one. I hope you will mature and execute it, as I can think of no one now more fitted for such a work than yourself.

I remain here till the end of the month, having promised two lectures to the Extension Students,[3] one of which however, in consequence of this illness, will fall through. I have just written, very humbly, to Mr. Sadler,[4] to tell him so.

Very sincerely yours
Walter Pater.

[1] Thomas Herbert Warren (1853–1930), scholar and administrator, attended Balliol College, 1872–6, where he quickly made a name for himself, winning the Hertford Scholarship (1873) and the Craven Scholarship (1878). A major influence on his development during this period was the recently elected Master of Balliol, Benjamin Jowett (see Biographical Register). Warren was elected Fellow (1877), Tutor (1878), and President (1885–1928) of Magdalen College, Oxford, where, like his mentor, he laboured indefatigably to increase the college's intellectual and social standing. He also served as Vice-Chancellor of the university, 1906–10, and Professor of Poetry, 1911–16. He published an edition of the first five books of Plato's *Republic* in 1888 and volumes of poetry, including *By Severn Sea, and Other Poems* (Oxford: H. Daniel, 1897) and *The Death of Virgil: A Dramatic Narrative* (Oxford: B. H. Blackwood; London: John Murray, 1907). Warren and Pater were close friends from the early 1870s. Warren provided A. C. Benson with his impressions of Pater lecturing on Prosper Mérimée at the Taylor Institution, Oxford, on 15 Nov. 1890, a presentation which Pater repeated at the London Institute on 24 Nov. 1890 (Benson, 159).
[2] See letter to Daniel, [Apr. or May 1894].
[3] Pater planned to deliver lectures on Peter Paul Rubens (1577–1640), the Flemish Baroque painter, on 28 July 1894, and on Blaise Pascal (1623–62), French mathematician, physicist, inventor, and Christian philosopher, on 30 July at the Sixth Summer Session of the University Extension, Oxford. For the text of 'Pascal', see *CW* x.
[4] See letter to Sadler, 5 Mar. [1892].

LETTERS 1894–1919

After the Death of Walter Pater

Illness bothered Pater during his final year. Bronchitis incapacitated him for part of December 1893. By 4 January 1894 he announced that he felt better, but 'not entirely fit'. As the new term got underway, he complained that he was overwhelmed with work, undertaken and promised. He felt well enough in April to travel to Glasgow, where he received an honorary LLD degree. Gout, however, incapacitated Pater in June, preventing him from working as usual and walking about Oxford with friends and colleagues. Then rheumatic fever confined him to bed; he was nursed by his sisters and a family friend, Charlotte Symonds Green (see Biographical Register). By 29 July it appeared that he had recovered sufficiently to relax on the main floor with his sisters, discussing such topics as the trip they were supposed to make the next day to Devon (they had arranged to stay at an old farmhouse owned by his friend and colleague, F. W. Bussell). On 30 July, at 10 a.m., he descended the stairs, coughed, experienced a heart attack, and died. Officials granted Clara Pater the Letters of Administration and valued Pater's estate at £2,599 4s 3d (Levey, *The Case of Walter Pater*, 202–13).

1894

EDMUND GOSSE to WILLIAM MORRIS COLLES,[1] 8 August 1894
MS.: Bates College. Printed in *LWP*.

29 Delamere Terrace, | Westbourne Square, W. | 8.8.94

Dear Colles

I am writing on behalf of the sisters of my late friend Walter Pater.

Their search among their brother's papers has resulted in the discovery that he has only left one solitary MS. in a publishable state. This is an Essay on Rubens, in his characteristic manner, an admirable thing, to which he had just put the finishing touches when his final illness attacked him. It is between 6000 and 7000 words in length.[2]

The ladies are in great need of money, and it has occurred to me that you could do better for them than anyone else. There must, surely, be a great competition for the very last and only remaining work by so eminent a writer.

Will you kindly tell me what you think. What do you say to the 'Pall Mall Magazine'?

Kindly let me hear from you without delay, as I leave town for Switzerland at the end of this week.

Yours very sincerely
Edmund Gosse.

[1] William Morris Colles (1855–1926), Anglo-Irish journalist and literary barrister, went to Emmanuel College, Cambridge, 1874–7, and was admitted to the Bar, London, in 1880. Colles found his vocation in journalism, however, for a number of years serving as leader-writer for the *Standard*, the popular morning newspaper. Concerned about the difficulties writers experience in trying to retain control of their work, in 1872 he joined the Copyright Association, and in 1884, the Society of Authors, a trade union that was founded to protect the rights and interests of professional writers, illustrators, and literary translators. He founded and managed the Authors' Syndicate (1890–1926), established for the purpose of offering writers direct contact with editors and publishers. Colles devoted himself to getting fair terms for authors with their editors and publishers by making proper contracts on their behalf and finding the best markets for their works. He represented many eminent authors, including Arnold Bennett, George Gissing, Somerset Maugham, and Mary Arnold Ward (see Biographical Register). With Henry Cresswell, he prepared *Success in Literature* (New York: Duffield, 1911), a handbook offering the would-be writer a compendium of hints and useful information culled from successful writers.

[2] No trace has been found of this MS., nor is it mentioned in any published study of Pater. Pater was scheduled to lecture on Rubens for the University Extension programme in Oxford on Saturday, 28 July 1894.

CLARA PATER to GEORGE MACMILLAN, 13 August [1894]
MS.: British Library. On mourning paper. Printed in Hagiwara and *TBB*.

25 Horton Street | Kensington W. | Aug. 13

Dear Mr. Macmillan,

My sister & I both thank you sincerely for your very kind letter of sympathy. It was such a sudden and unexpected shock, for we had every reason to think he would quite recover. We are quite overwhelmed with sorrow.

We have to make a statement at the Probate Office of everything that is due to my Brother. Would you be so kind as to tell us the amount due to him from you from July 1893 to July 1894.

With kind regards to Mrs. Macmillan and yourself,
I am

Yours very truly,
Clara Pater.

GEORGE MACMILLAN to CLARA PATER, 16 August 1894
MS.: British Library. Printed in *TBB*.

Aug. 16. 1894

Dear Miss Pater,

My cousin who is in Yorkshire has sent me your letter of the 13th. I am afraid it will take a few days for us to make out with approximate correctness what sum would have been due to your brother on account of sales during the year end June 30, but you shall have the information as soon as possible. I think you will also be asked to state the value of his books for probate purposes, so when I write I will name what seems to us a fair sum based upon the average of several years' sales.

With kind regards, I am

Yours very truly,
George A. Macmillan.

Miss Pater | 25 Horton St. | Kensington
P. S. May I add that if there is an idea of collecting unpublished papers whether in MS. or otherwise it would be a great pleasure to us to publish them.

GEORGE MACMILLAN to CLARA PATER, 17 August [1894]
MS.: British Library. Printed in *TBB*.

Aug 17 94

Dear Miss Pater,

I am now able to say that the amount due for your brother's books in January next will be £110. We should estimate his interest in all the books for probate purposes and apart from the sum due at £175. The sales have been very steady for some years but it is impossible to say how long they will remain so when the influence of his personality is withdrawn.

With kind regards, I remain

Yours very truly,
George A. Macmillan.

Miss Pater | 25 Horton St.

CHARLES SHADWELL to CLARA PATER, 7 September 1894
MS.: British Library. Printed in Hagiwara.

Freewin Hall, | Oxford. | 7 Sept. 1894

Dear Miss Pater,

I send you a letter of introduction to Mr. Galpin,[1] who I think will do the business you want of him as well as any one in Oxford.

I also send the catalogue of the contents of the portmanteaux,[2] which will remain here and be at your disposal whenever you wish for it.

The articles on 'Dionysus' and on 'Demeter and Persephone' should, I think, be printed in slip form, so that they can be connected from the proof of 1878. 'The 'Bacchanals' was revised in 1887 and requires no attention. The 'Hippolytus Veiled' has been partly corrected in M.S. but the alterations are very few, and, if necessary can be introduced on an ordinary proof: I doubt whether they were even finally decided upon.

There is a fragment only of an 'Introduction to Greek Studies' (in Packet 2) intended to preface the papers on Greek art: but it cannot now be used.

Believe me

Very truly yours,
Charles L. Shadwell.

[1] Possibly H. F. Galpin, a solicitor, who had an office at 43 Cornmarket Street, Oxford, identified in *The Law Times*, 7 Apr. 1894, 536, or Charles Alexander Galpin, auctioneer and surveyor, who conducted business as Galpin & Son at 4 Western Road and 36 Pembroke Street, in Oxford.

[2] The list is missing.

MACMILLAN AND CO. to HESTER PATER, 11 September [1894]
MS.: British Library. Printed in *TBB*.

Miss Hester M. Pater | 5 Alfred Street | St. Giles | Oxford

Sept. 11 94

Madam,

Mr. Frederick Macmillan will be able to see you at three o'clock to-morrow, Wednesday, as you propose.

Yours very truly,
Macmillan and Co.

FREDERICK MACMILLAN to HESTER PATER, 12 September [1894]
MS.: British Library. Printed in *TBB*.

Sept 12 94

Dear Miss Pater,

I write to say that I shall be here tomorrow (Thursday) morning at 11:00 o'[clock], & shall be very glad to see you on the subject of the volume of collected papers.[1]

I am

Yours sincerely,
Frederick Macmillan.

Miss Pater | 5 Alfred St. | St. Giles | Oxford

[1] *Greek Studies* appeared on 12 Jan. 1895. The essays are featured in *CW* viii, *Classical Studies*, except for 'Hippolytus Veiled: A Study from Euripides', in *CW* iii.

FREDERICK MACMILLAN to HESTER PATER, 13 September [1894]
MS. British Library. Printed in *TBB*.

Sept. 13 94

Dear Miss Pater,

I enclose a formal Memorandum of Agreement[1] for the three new volumes of collected papers. If you or your sister will kindly sign & return it I will send you a duplicate signed by ourselves.

I am

Yours truly,
Frederick Macmillan.

Miss Pater | 64 St. Giles | Oxford

[1] According to this agreement, dated 13 Sept. 1894, the publishers agreed to publish at their own risk *Greek Studies* (1895) and two other volumes of uncollected papers by Walter Pater on condition that the copyright belong to the publishers and that, after deducting expenses, profits be divided equally. This agreement also covered the American edition, for which Clara and Hester Pater were to be paid a royalty of 10 per cent of the retail price per copy. See Brit. Lib. Add. MS. 55030, fol. 65.

CLARA PATER to ALFRED JOSHUA BUTLER,[1] 14 September [1894]
MS.: British Library. Printed in Hagiwara.

5 Alfred Street | Sep. 14

Dear Mr. Butler,

The things we are going to leave in the college, are the carpet, curtains, sofa, chairs, window cushions, long table, book-case, scuttle (not fender) and everything in the bed-room. Should we send a valuer, or is that done by the college? Thank you for your letter. We leave Oxford on Monday morning.

Yours sincerely,
C. Pater.

The things inside the drawers we wish to give to Walker[2]

[1] See letter to Gosse, 29 Jan. [1881], n. 2.
[2] Clara Pater left 'the minor contents' of her brother's rooms (such as clothing of various kinds, including coats and boots) to Francis Walker (1856–1934), a fourth-generation servant. Walker assumed the duties of 'messenger' at Brasenose in 1873, and those of 'bedmaker' in 1881, a position he held until 1915. Older members of the college described him as a very brisk, smart servant, who could intimidate new students. Georgina Edwards, Archivist, Brasenose College, notes that his salary in 1873 was £35 per year and by 1911 it was more than £60. See *The Brazen Nose*, 5 (June 1934), 346; Crook, *Brasenose*, 281.

CLARA PATER to ALFRED JOSHUA BUTLER, 15 September [1894]
MS.: British Library. Printed in Hagiwara.

5 Alfred Street | Sep. 15

Dear Mr. Butler,

We found the keys, that is two keys, which the porter said were the keys of the Library & the New Gate, and put them in the table drawer where the others are. The things in the drawers, are all clothing of various kinds; these & books, & some coats in the hanging cupboard, we have told Walker he may have. In the cupboard there are hanging a gown & cap, surplice & two hoods, which we have asked Mr. Bussell to take—May they remain there till he comes up, or else be put in his room. Thank you for seeing the valuation.

Yours very truly
C. Pater.

FREDERICK MACMILLAN to HESTER PATER, 18 September [1894]
MS.: British Library. Printed in *TBB*.

Sept 18 94

Dear Miss Pater,

Messrs. Warne and Co.[1] the publishers of a book called 'Half Hours with the Best Authors' have asked us to give them permission to make an extract of about nine pages in length from W. Pater's paper on Botticelli in the volume of 'Studies in the Renaissance'. Will you please let me know whether you would like this permission to be given or [withheld]? On the whole I think I should be inclined to allow them to make use of the [extract] on the [premise] that it could hardly injure the sale of the book & that its effect on your brother's reputation would be good rather than bad. But if you have the least feeling that you would rather not give the permission, please say so & I will refuse it.

Believe me

Yours sincerely,
Frederick Macmillan.

Miss Pater | Oxford

[1] Frederick Warne (1825–1901), bookseller and publisher, was privately educated in London. In 1839 he joined his eldest brother William in the bookselling and publishing firm that had been established by their brother-in-law George Routledge (1812–88), and in 1851 became partner in the firm, which was renamed Routledge, Warne, and Routledge in 1858. In 1865 the company was divided into two houses: George Routledge and Sons and Frederick Warne and Company. Warne pioneered inexpensive, high-quality, colour-illustrated picture-books for children, starting with the Aunt Louisa's London Toy Books series; thereafter he published works by Edward Lear, Walter Crane, and Kate Greenaway. By the late 1880s Warne and Co. had opened a branch in New York and had acquired the British rights to several family magazines, all of which published serialized works. In 1894 Warne left the company to his three sons. In 1902 the firm introduced Beatrix Potter's *The Tale of Peter Rabbit*.

HESTER PATER to FREDERICK MACMILLAN, [*c*.19 September 1894][1]
MS.: British Library. Printed in *TBB*.

11 Victoria Grove | Gloucester Road | W.

Dear Mr. Macmillan,

We should like the extract from Botticelli to be put into 'Half Hours with the best Authors' as it seems to us as to you, that it might add to our brother's reputation, and a wider knowledge of his writings. We are sending the agreement and the only photograph of my brother we have.[2] We should like to know if you think it a good enough likeness to use as a frontispiece for the book, and whether it would be reproduced satisfactorily. We are staying at the above address for another week, when [?] we get into our house.

Believe me,

Yours sincerely,
Hester M. Pater.

P. S. We should like the original photograph returned to us after the reproduction has been made.

[1] The date '1894' has been pencilled in by another hand.
[2] A reference to the Elliott & Fry portrait.

FREDERICK MACMILLAN to HESTER PATER, 20 September [1894]
MS.: British Library. Printed in *TBB*.

Sept 20 94

Dear Miss Pater,

I am obliged to you for the Agreement, & enclose a duplicate signed by ourselves.

I think that the photograph of your brother will reproduce very well & that it will make an attractive frontispiece for the new volume[1] which many of his admirers will be glad to have. We will make a photogravure plate from it & let you have it back again.

I am

Yours sincerely,
Frederick Macmillan.

Miss Pater | 11 Victoria Grove | Gloucester Road | W

[1] *Greek Studies* (1895); see *CW* viii.

FREDERICK MACMILLAN to HESTER PATER, 28 September [1894]
MS.: British Library. Printed in *TBB*.

Sept. 28th 94

Dear Miss Pater,

On looking at the enclosed I cannot say there seems to me to be too much shoulder. If, however, you think there is, will you kindly say what you would like to have omitted and we will have it done.

Believe me,

Yours very truly,
Frederick Macmillan.

Miss Pater | 11 Victoria Grove | Gloucester Road | W

FREDERICK MACMILLAN to HESTER PATER, 2 October [1894]
MS.: British Library. Printed in *TBB*.

Oct 2nd 94

Dear Miss Pater,

I shall be happy to see you tomorrow (Wednesday) at twelve o'clock.
I am

Yours very truly,
Frederick Macmillan.

Miss Pater | 11 Victoria Grove | Gloucester Road | W.

CLARA PATER to T. HERBERT WARREN,[1] 9 October [1894]
MS.: Brodie/Warren Papers, Magdalen College, Oxford.

6 Canning Place[2] | Kensington Gate W | Oct. 9.

My dear Mr. President,

My sister or I would have written before this to thank you for your kind letter of sympathy, but we heard that you were in Switzerland & were not quite sure where a letter would find you.

If anything could comfort us in our grievous loss it would be the affection & appreciation which his friends have shown for him, and your letter is one of those we both value most.

Mr. Shadwell tells us that you are going to be so kind as to help him, as we wished, in looking over the material for two or three books which we hope may be published.

We are very sorry to leave Oxford without saying goodbye, but most of our friends were away—indeed we were sorry to leave at all, but we felt that to go on living there without him would be quite unbearable to us.

I hope when we come to Oxford we shall see you & Mrs. Warren and if you should be in this neighbourhood when we are a little more settled it would give us the most sincere pleasure to see you.

With kindest regards from my sister
I am

Yours sincerely
Clara A. Pater.

[1] Thomas Herbert Warren (1853–1930), scholar and administrator, served as President of Magdalen College, Oxford, 1885–1928.

[2] Shortly after Pater's death, Clara and Hester moved to this address; the following notice was circulated: 'MISS CLARA PATER, late Tutor of Somerville College and Lecturer of the Association for the Education of Women, Oxford, prepares pupils for London, Oxford, and Cambridge Examinations, in Classics and German.—6 Canning Place, Kensington Gate, London, W' (see the *Journal of Education*, 1 Oct. 1894, 537). Hester Pater remained at this address until her death in 1922.

CLARA PATER to ALFRED JOSHUA BUTLER, 10 October [1894]
MS.: British Library. Printed in Hagiwara.

6 Canning Place | Kensington W | Oct. 10

Dear Mr. Butler,

Will you kindly give the china & glass you speak of to Walker. The above is our permanent address so will you send the cheque here, made payable to me, as I am administratrix. We hope a volume of my brother's classical essays will be brought out this autumn. There is to be a vignette portrait as frontispiece done from a photograph—finding from one specimen we have seen it [sic] will be a very excellent likeness—it seemed to us better than the photograph. We are still in a good deal of confusion, but when we are settled should be so pleased to see you if you were in this neighbourhood at any time. With my sister's kindest regards to yourself & Mrs. Butler.

Believe me

Yours very sincerely
Clara A. Pater.

CLARA PATER to ALFRED JOSHUA BUTLER, 12 October [1894]
MS.: British Library. Printed in Hagiwara.

6 Canning Place | Kensington W | Oct. 12

Dear Mr. Butler,

I enclose the script, with many thanks to give you all the trouble you have taken.

Yours very sincerely
C. A. Pater.

FREDERICK MACMILLAN to HESTER PATER, 15 October [1894]
MS.: British Library. Printed in *TBB*.

Oct 15th 94

Dear Miss Pater,

I send herewith a proof of the photogravure plate[1] which seems to me very good. I also return the original photograph.

I am

Yours very truly,
Frederick Macmillan.

Miss Pater | 11 Victoria Grove | Gloucester Road | W

[1] This plate is missing.

FREDERICK MACMILLAN to HESTER PATER, 17 October [1894]
MS.: British Library. Printed in *TBB*.

Oct. 17 94

Dear Miss Pater,

We will have the portrait printed in a warm brown ink & will let you see it. I hope we shall manage to please you as I should like to use the plate which I must say seemed to me to be if anything a better likeness than the photograph from which it is taken.

I am

Yours sincerely,
Frederick Macmillan.

Miss Pater | 6 Canning Place | Kensington Gate

HESTER PATER to MICHAEL FIELD, 9 November [1894]
MS.: Miriam Lutcher Stark Library, Harry Ransom Center, University of Texas.

6 Canning Place | Kensington Gate | Nov. 9th

My dear Michael Field,

I want to thank you for your kind letter of sympathy which has been so long unanswered.

We have really had so much to do in all ways, so much business writing, and all the trouble of finding, and settling, in a new home that that must be my excuse. The loss of our dear brother has made a hole in our life that one feels can never be bridged over. So much that gave pleasure ## seems now unmeaning and all the satisfaction and happiness gone out of it.

We hope to see all our friends in a little time as we are now pretty well settled. My sister desires her kindest remembrances.
Believe me

Affectionately yours
Hester M. Pater.

1895

CLARA PATER to EDMUND GOSSE, 25 January 1895
MS.: Bodleian Library. Printed in *LWP* and Hagiwara.

6 Canning Place | Jan. 25 | 1895

My dear Mr. Gosse

We could not possibly part with the Pascal manuscript for money. It is the last thing Walter wrote and was writing even during his illness, and so is precious to us. But as we know your friendship for him, and are sure you would value and cherish it, you shall have it bye and bye as a gift. It will be wanted by Mr. Shadwell in bringing out the next volume of Essays, as he would naturally like to make his own emendations from the original M.S. rather than from the printed article. But after that, all the M.S.S. will be returned to us, & we will hand that one to you. I shall be interested to see how you have got over the difficulties, which I am sure were very great ones, and making it a readable article. If it had not been as you say, a labour of love, I don't know how we could thank you enough for the time & trouble you have spent on it.

All the reviews we have seen of the *Greek Studies*,[1] including your own,[2] have given us great pleasure—so far the book has certainly been well received. With kind regards

I am

Very sincerely yours
Clara Pater.

[1] Gosse edited Pater's essay on Blaise Pascal (1623–62), French mathematician and theologian, for publication in the *Contemporary Review*, 47 (Feb. 1895), 168–81; later Shadwell included the text in *Miscellaneous Studies*. The sisters did give the MS. to Gosse (see letter to Gosse, 13 Nov. 1895); it is now housed in the Bodleian Library, MS. Don.d.84 (see *CW* x).

[2] Untraced. *Greek Studies* appeared on 12 Jan. 1895.

HESTER PATER to CHARLES SHADWELL, 12 May [1895?]
MS.: Brotherton Collection, University of Leeds.

6 Canning Place | May 12th.

Dear Mr. Shadwell,

We wrote to ask Mr. Macmillan if he had any objection to Dr. Daniel printing 'Aesthetic Poetry'. He has no objection. So will you kindly tell Mr. Daniel that we shall be very pleased for him to print it in his charming style.[1] Thank you for the trouble you took about 'Marius the Epicurean'.

Yours very sincerely
H. M. Pater.

[1] See letter to Clara Pater, 11 May 1903, n. 1.

CLARA PATER to EDMUND GOSSE, 13 November 1895
MS.: Bodleian Library. Printed in Hagiwara.

6 Canning Place W. | Nov. 13 1895.

Dear Mr. Gosse,

I am just sending off the 'Pascal' manuscript,[1] which please accept with many thanks for all the trouble you took with it.

It has been very much praised in one of the papers, so I am glad we published it, in spite of its incompleteness.

With best regards to you both. Believe me

Yours very sincerely
Clara Pater.

[1] See letter to Gosse, 25 Jan. 1895, n. 1.

1896

CLARA PATER to EDMUND GOSSE, 24 June 1896
MS.: Brotherton Collection, University of Leeds.

6 Canning Place | June 24 1896

Dear Mr. Gosse,

I am sorry not to have replied to your letter before, but my sister was away & I waited to hear what she said about it. We do not see any reason why you should not do as you propose about the Essays in the 'Guardian'. They would make a pretty little booklet & interest his admirers, & I do not think he would have liked them published in any more formal manner, as he would have written them with less care than more important things. As you say, a private edition would not affect the interests of his publisher, even if later on any more fragments should be published, which however we do not intend at present.

With kind regards

Yours very sincerely
Clara Pater.

HESTER PATER to EDMUND GOSSE, 9 November [1896]
MS.: Brotherton Collection, University of Leeds.

6 Canning Place | Nov 9th.

Dear Mr. Gosse,

The articles make a sweet little book. The binding is most charming. I should think people will like to have it. Many thanks for sending us the copies and so many. I shall much like reading the articles again.

My sister joins me in kind regards.

With yours very sincerely
Hester M. Pater.

CLARA PATER to FATHER CONGREVE,[1] 17 December [1896]
MS.: Bodleian Library. Printed in Hagiwara.

6 Canning Place | Dec. 17

My Dear Father,

I am sending a gravure made from the only photograph of my brother that we have, for unfortunately he had the negatives destroyed. This is not good, and is the frontispiece of one of the books, so that Fr. Conver's friend[2] may have it already—but if he thinks she would care for it, she is very welcome.

All that he wrote has now been collected from the magazines, put together. Since his death three volumes have been brought out, 'Greek Studies', 'Miscellaneous Studies', and an unfinished fragment 'Gaston de Latour'. I very much wish we had a better photograph both for our own sakes, and also to give to kind people who wish for them—We have of course some juvenile ones but they are not of the same interest.

I hope you are well, it seems a long time since you have taken a Quiet Day in London, I always look for such announcements, hoping to see your name.

I felt much sympathy for friend Miss Gurney,[3] though I have never seen her, her brother is a great loss.

Is Miss Béliz[4] still living? if so will you kindly use the enclosed[5] for her, or any other person you may know of—

Yours very sincerely
Clara Pater.

[1] Unidentified.
[2] Unidentified.
[3] Possibly Emilia Russell Gurney: see letter to Cust, 4 May [1893], n. 2.
[4] Unidentified.
[5] Missing.

1897

FREDERICK MACMILLAN to HESTER PATER, 18 January [1897]
MS.: British Library. Printed in *TBB*.

Jan. 18 1897

Dear Miss Pater,

I enclose a letter[1] from a Belgian gentleman asking the conditions on which he may publish a French translation of 'Imaginary Portraits'. As the book appeared so long ago as 1887 the right of translation which can only be reserved for ten years has almost become common property. If a translation appears before the expiration of ten years there will be a copyright [in it and] is a question for you to consider whether it would be best to sell the right to this gentleman for a small sum (I don't suppose he would give much) or whether it would be better to let the right of translation lapse so that it might be open to anybody to publish as many translations as he pleased. From certain points of view it might seem that it [was bad] for your brother's literary reputation that the foreign translation of this work should be open to everyone. Of course if you could sell the right of translation for a large sum it would be another matter. But I do not think you could get more than £10 for it.

I am,

Yours very truly
Frederick Macmillan.

Miss Pater

[1] The enclosure is missing. Possibly Georges Knopff (1860–1927), a Belgian translator, who translated Arthur Symons's chapter on Pater from *Studies in Two Literatures* (1897) and 'Sebastien van Storck', which appeared in the *Mercure de France* for Feb. 1898 and July 1898 respectively, and *Portraits imaginaires*, introduced by Arthur Symons (Paris: Société Mercure de France, 1899). For a discussion of Pater's French translators, see Emily Eells, '"Influence Occulte": The Reception of Pater's Work in France before 1922', *The Reception of Walter Pater in Europe*, ed. Stephen Bann (London: Thoemmes Continuum, 2004), 87–116.

HESTER PATER to MICHAEL FIELD, 19 June [1897]
MS.: Miriam Lutcher Stark Library, Harry Ransom Center, University of Texas.

6 Canning Place | June 19th.

My dear Michael Field,

In answer to your kind letter, there were very few copies of the 'Essays from the Guardian' printed as we did not wish them to be publicly known. They were written without signature and not revised and our publisher for many reasons thought it was not desirable.

If I ever hear of one to be had I will let you know.

I hope you will come and see us in the autumn when we shall be at home.

With kindest remembrances to Miss Cooper

Believe me

Yours very sincerely
Hester M. Pater.

FREDERICK MACMILLAN to HESTER PATER, 31 August [1897]
MS.: British Library. Printed in *TBB*.

Aug 31 97

Dear Miss Pater,

I enclose a letter from a man who wishes to know if he can purchase copies of the *Essays from The Guardian*. I think you told me that you had a few copies which you would sell for two guineas. If this is the case will you kindly communicate with Mr. Allen.[1]

I am

Yours very truly,
Frederick Macmillan.

Miss Pater | 6 Canning Place | Kensington Gate. W.

[1] Unidentified, but see letter of 3 May [1890].

1898

GEORGE MACMILLAN to HESTER PATER, 22 March [1898]
MS.: British Library. Printed in *TBB*.

March 22 98

Dear Miss Pater,

Have you still any copies to dispose of of your brother's Essays from the Guardian? I ask for an old friend, Mr. Robert Maclehose,[1] bookseller and publisher in Glasgow who is particularly anxious to secure a copy (presumably for a customer) and is willing to pay a good price for it. Hoping you will be in a position to oblige him (and me).

I am

Yours very truly,
George A. Macmillan.

Miss Pater

[1] Robert MacLehose (1820–1910), Scottish bookseller and publisher, spent his early years as assistant to his elder brother, James MacLehose (see letter to Pater, 12 Nov. [1872], n. 1), bookseller and publisher. In 1850, he started his own business in Ayr, Ayrshire. Later, he added printing to his business (he produced a number of volumes on hand-presses). In 1872 he acquired the printing business of George Richardson of Glasgow, and that year he became Printer to the University of Glasgow. In 1894, his nephews took over the business.

MAURICE MACMILLAN to HESTER PATER, 14 May 1898
MS.: British Library. This letter (typed) is printed in *TBB*.

Miss Pater. | 6 Canning Place | Kensington Gate, W.

14th May 1898.

Dear Miss Pater,
 I enclose a letter[1] received this morning. There are some questions which you perhaps might be willing to answer. I should think that the right of translation into French must have elapsed by this time. I do not know whether any translation has already been made. At any rate it is not possible to obtain any money for the right, but we or you will write to our correspondent and give him permission. I send the letter however to you on account of the personal matters which we cannot answer.
 I am,

Yours very truly,
Maurice Macmillan [signed].

[1] The letter mentioned is missing.

1899

CLARA PATER to MRS. WOODWARD,[1] 20 February 1899
MS.: Bodleian Library. Printed in Hagiwara.

6 Canning Place | Kensington | London | Feb. 20 | 1899

Dear Madam,
 Thank you for your kind note. It is always a pleasure to have any kind appreciation of my brother's work.
 I heard that you had expressed a wish to have something in his handwriting, so send you two little slips of paper: he used to make notes of any little things he wished to remember on scraps of paper, and not in a pocketbook. We have many such, but most are not legible as they were hastily scribbled, and only meant for himself.
 La B. on one piece means La Beauce a part of France which he liked very much.
 I wish I had something long and more coherent to offer you but he left very little writing.

Believe me

> Sincerely yours
> Clara Pater.

[1] This admirer has not been identified.

MACMILLAN AND CO. to HESTER PATER, 2 June [1899]
MS.: British Library. Printed in *TBB*.

2nd June 99

Dear Madam,

An American firm of Publishers proposes to introduce into Great Britain a work which they have already issued in the United States entitled 'The International Library of Famous Literature'[1] comprised in twenty volumes, and made up of extracts from the works of various writers of all ages—amongst which is one from 'Marius the Epicurean'.

We have been applied to and have given permission for the use of this extract as we cannot think that its appearance in a work of this nature, which is only to be sold in complete sets at a high price, will have any injurious effects upon the sale of Mr. Pater's book. As however, the proprietors have made no payment for the right to use this extract we beg to enclose for the acceptance of the Misses Pater a cheque[2] representing their share in it.

> Yours faithfully,
> Macmillan and Co. Ltd.

Miss Pater

[1] *The International Library of Famous Literature, selections from the world's great writers, ancient, mediaeval, and modern, with biographical and explanatory notes and critical essays by many eminent writers*, ed. Richard Garnett, in association with Léon Vallée, Alois Brandl, and Donald G. Mitchell, 20 vols (London: The Standard, 1899), featured excerpts from the work of such writers as Nathan Haskell Dole, Forrest Morgan, and Caroline Ticknor. Produced by the International Library Company (Boston and London), the set contains about 500 full-page illustrations. A selection from *Marius the Epicurean*, entitled 'Marcus Aurelius at Home', appeared in 3: 1293–1304.
[2] The enclosure is missing.

1900

FREDERICK MACMILLAN to HESTER PATER, 24 January 1900
MS.: British Library. Printed in *TBB*.

Jan. 24 1900

Dear Miss Pater,

You may possibly have seen the so-called *Edition de Luxe*[1] of the works of Lamb, Tennyson & Kipling which we have published during the last two years. These books are very handsome in appearance & profitable to publish as the number of copies printed is limited and they are consequently at once bought up by collectors—people who regard books as bric-a-brac. We have been thinking of following up the books we have already published by an edition of your brother's writings in the same style—that is if we have your approval & consent.

We should propose to put the shortest books, 'Imaginary Portraits' & 'Gaston de Latour' into 1 volume & the series would then be contained in eight volumes of about 300 pages each in type like that of the enclosed specimen.[2]

I shall be glad to know what you think of the idea, and also whether you would care to add to the Edition the little collection of reviews from 'The Guardian' which Mr. Gosse published.

I am

Yours very truly,
Frederick Macmillan.

Miss Pater

[1] The *Edition de Luxe* for Pater, in 775 sets, was issued on 4 Sept. 1901, together with 1,000 copies of *Essays from 'The Guardian'*, which was printed from the private edition of 1896.
[2] The sample is missing.

HESTER PATER to FREDERICK MACMILLAN, 25 January [1900]
MS.: British Library. Printed in *TBB*.

Jan. 25.

Dear Mr. Macmillan,

We should very much like to have the *Edition de Luxe* produced and I should think your suggestion of putting *Imaginary Portraits* and *Gaston de Latour* together in one volume and so making a set of eight would be a very good arrangement. The specimen leaf enclosed[1] we like very much, both type and paper. We have not happened to see the Lamb or Tennyson so may we call on you some day soon and see the binding? As the books have sold so well for the last few years, do you think you could see your way to allowing us a larger share of the profits in future with this new edition? With regard to the reviews from *The Guardian*, we would rather not have them included, as they were never revised or intended for further publication.

With kind regards,

Very sincerely yours
H. M. Pater.

¹ The enclosure is missing.

FREDERICK MACMILLAN to HESTER PATER, 31 January 1900
MS.: British Library. Printed in *TBB*.

Miss Pater, | 6 Canning Place, | Kensington, W.

Jan. 31. 1900

Dear Miss Pater,

I am very glad to hear that you approve of the scheme for an *Edition de Luxe* of your brother's works.

I regret that we do not see our way to make any alteration in the terms upon which his books are published, but if it will be a convenience to you in any way we are quite willing to make you an offer of a lump sum of money for this particular *Edition de Luxe* to be paid on publication. I am unable to say what sum we could give as we have not yet decided of how many copies the edition is to consist.

I am

Yours very truly,
Frederick Macmillan.

CLARA PATER to FREDERICK MACMILLAN, 1 February [1900]
MS.: British Library. Printed in *TBB*.

Feb. 1.

Dear Mr. Macmillan,

We do not at all desire the lump sum for the *Edition de Luxe* suggested in your letter. We should prefer to have the same arrangement for that as for the other books.

But we have long thought that, for a writer of reputation, half profits were not permanently satisfactory terms.

Yours sincerely
Clara A. Pater.

FREDERICK MACMILLAN to HESTER PATER, 2 February 1900
MS.: British Library. Printed in *TBB*.

Miss Pater, | 6 Canning Place, | W.

Feb. 2nd. 1900

Dear Miss Pater,

If you and your sister wish it we shall be quite willing to alter the arrangement for your brother's books from half profits to a royalty of 20% (twenty per cent) of the advertised price. There is perhaps some advantage in the royalty system inasmuch as the returns to the author's representatives are more regular in amount.

Kindly consider this matter at your leisure & let me know your views. If we made the alteration it might as well run from the 1st of July last.

I am,

Yours very truly,
Frederick Macmillan.

CLARA PATER to FREDERICK MACMILLAN, 6 February [1900]
MS.: British Library. Printed in *TBB*.

Feb. 6.

Dear Mr. Macmillan,

We have considered your suggestion of a royalty of twenty per cent instead of half profits and we do not see that it would be any advantage to us or worthwhile to make the alteration.

When I said that the present arrangement was unsatisfactory I meant that half profits were very well to begin with, but now that my brother's books are so well known and have been selling so well for the last five years, we think it only reasonable that in the future we should have a larger proportion of the profits.

We consider that two thirds would be a satisfactory arrangement.

I am

Yours sincerely
Clara A. Pater.

FREDERICK MACMILLAN to HESTER PATER, 8 February 1900
MS.: British Library. Printed in *TBB*.

Miss Pater, | 6 Canning Place, | Kensington, W.

Feb. 8. 1900

Dear Miss Pater,

I am sorry that we do not see our way to make any alteration in the terms on which we publish your brother's books. At the same time I should like you to understand exactly what the conditions are. As you know, the profits that we divide with you are the gross profits, that is to say out of our share we have to pay all the expenses of selling the books, which, with the large organization that we have for such a purpose, I need not point out are very heavy. Roughly speaking, we may say that supposing the profits to be divided amount to £100, £50 of which go to you & £50 to us, our share is reduced to £25 by the cost of business expenses, that is to say although our gross share of the profits is £50, what we actually get is only £25. Some publishers make a charge for working expenses in the general account, so that the amount to be divided is reduced thereby. This is a perfectly legitimate method of procedure, but as a matter of fact we have never done it and have always divided up the gross profits with our authors.

I am,

Yours very truly,
Frederick Macmillan.

FREDERICK MACMILLAN to HESTER PATER, 23 May [1900]
MS.: British Library. Printed in *TBB*.

May 23 0

Dear Miss Pater,

I find that the plate from which the portrait of your brother was printed for the frontispiece of *Greek Studies* is a good deal worn & that in order to get a satisfactory result we ought to have a new one for the *Edition de Luxe*. Can you for this purpose lend me a copy of the photograph from which the plate was made? It will of course be returned to you when done with.

I am,

Yours very truly,
Frederick Macmillan.

Miss Pater

FREDERICK MACMILLAN to HESTER PATER, 25 May 1900
MS.: British Library. Printed in *TBB*.

Miss Pater, | 6 Canning Place, | Kensington Gate, W.

May 25. 1900

Dear Miss Pater,

I think we had certainly better have the portrait of your brother which appeared in *Greek Studies* for the *Edition de Luxe*, for it is in itself an admirable one. If you would like to have some other portraits reproduced in addition to this to be used as frontispieces to the other volumes we shall be glad to engrave them if you will let us have say two others that you consider good. It would no doubt interest purchasers of the book to have portraits of him at various ages.

I am,

Yours very truly,
Frederick Macmillan.

FREDERICK MACMILLAN to HESTER PATER, 5 June 1900
MS.: British Library. Printed in *TBB*.

Miss Pater, | 6 Canning Place, | Kensington Gate, W.

June 5th. 1900

Dear Miss Pater,

I am afraid that the enclosed photographs[1] are too faint to enable us to make satisfactory plates from them and we had better therefore confine ourselves to the portrait which appeared in *Greek Studies*. We will make a new plate of this from the negative as soon as it comes from Mr. Hollyer.[2]

I am,

Yours very truly,
Frederick Macmillan.

---

[1] The enclosures are missing.
[2] See letter to Symons, [22? Nov. 1889], n. 1.

1901

FREDERICK MACMILLAN to HESTER PATER, 25 February 1901
MS.: British Library. Typed letter. Printed in *TBB*.

Miss Pater, | 6 Canning Place, | Kensington Gate, W.

Feb. 25. 1901

Dear Miss Pater,

I ought to have written to you before this with reference to the proposed reprint of *Essays from The Guardian*. I find that if set in the type of the accompanying specimen page[1] we might manage to make a volume of 174 pages. We should propose to issue the book independently of the *Edition de Luxe* but to bind it uniform with that series so that people wishing to make their sets complete could purchase it. The price would have to be less than the volumes of the *E. de L.* I think it might be 7/6.[2] If you approve we will proceed with printing so that the book may be ready to issue after the last of the *E. de L.* has appeared.

I am,

Yours very truly,
Frederick Macmillan.

[1] The enclosure is missing.
[2] 7/6 is seven shillings and sixpence.

CLARA PATER to FREDERICK MACMILLAN, 27 February 1901
MS.: British Library. Printed in Hagiwara and in *TBB*.

6 Canning Place W. | Feb. 27 | 1901

Dear Mr. Macmillan,

We think your proposal with regard to the issue of *Essays from 'The Guardian'* is a very good one. Certainly the price should not be more than 7/6. May we have the original copy back again, at your convenience?

Yours very truly,
Clara Pater.

FREDERICK MACMILLAN to CLARA PATER, 28 February 1901
MS.: British Library. Printed in *TBB*.

Miss Pater, | 6 Canning Place, W.

Feb. 28. 1901.

Dear Miss Pater,

I will let you have back the copy of 'Essays from the Guardian' as soon as it is finished with, but we must have it for some little time to print from. I am telling the printers to be careful and not to injure it in any way.

I am,

Yours very truly,
Frederick Macmillan.

FREDERICK MACMILLAN to CLARA PATER, 7 June 1901
MS.: British Library. Printed in *TBB*.

Miss Pater, | 6 Canning Place, | Kensington, W.

June 7. 1901.

Dear Miss Pater,

A London bookseller who is much interested in Mr. Pater's writings has sent us the enclosed list of articles[1] by him which he says he has been able to trace in various periodicals, and none of which are included in the recently published *Edition de Luxe*. Our friend wishes to know whether it would be worth while to make up another volume containing these papers. I shall be much obliged if you will think this over and will consult somebody such as Mr. Shadwell on the subject. It may be that these articles have already been considered, and that you & Mr. Shadwell concluded that they had better not be reprinted.

I am,

Yours very truly,
Frederick Macmillan.

---

[1] The enclosure is missing. Arthur Symons (see Biographical Register) produced one of the first lists of the signed and unsigned reviews that make up Pater's literary journalism; Symons started collecting details as early as Jan. 1887 (see Karl Beckson, *Arthur Symons: A Life* (Oxford: Clarendon Press, 1987), 36, 339, n. 35). Many of the fugitive pieces were reprinted in *Uncollected Essays* (Portland, ME: Thomas B. Mosher, 1903) and *Sketches and Reviews* (New York: Boni and Liveright, 1919); see *CW* v and vi. See also letter to Thomas Wright, 27 Aug. 1906.

CLARA PATER to FREDERICK MACMILLAN, 12 June 1901
MS.: British Library. Printed in *TBB*.

6 Canning Place W. | June 12. 1901

Dear Mr. Macmillan,

All the articles in the list you sent us were considered by us and Mr. Shadwell some time back, when you may remember there was some talk of publishing all the scraps that could be traced.

We still think it best to adhere to the decision we came to then, & not publish anything more. These articles are very slight, & would not make a volume of any size, many are not signed, & were never intended to be brought out.

Yours sincerely
Clara Pater.

FREDERICK MACMILLAN to CLARA PATER, 17 June 1901
MS.: British Library. Printed in *TBB*.

Miss Pater, | 6 Canning Place, | Kensington Gate, W.

June 17. 1901.

Dear Miss Pater,

Will you kindly send me back the list of the articles by Mr. Pater which I sent you the other day as I must return it to the man from whom it came. I will explain to him that they are not to be reprinted.

I am,

Yours very truly,
Frederick Macmillan.

FREDERICK MACMILLAN to CLARA PATER, 21 September [1901]
MS.: British Library. Printed in *TBB*.

Sept. 21 1

Dear Miss Pater,

I return the copy of the original reprint of 'Essays from The Guardian' which you kindly lent us for our edition.

By the way am I right in thinking that Mr. Gosse asked you for permission to print a second 1000 copies & it was because of the demand of the existence of which such a request was proof that you consented to the publication of the volume by us.

I am glad to say that the publication of the volume was justified. We have already disposed of the first 1000 copies & are reprinting.

The sales of all the books during the past year have been very satisfactory as you will see from the accounts which will reach you on the first of October.

With kind regards, I am,

Yours very truly,
Frederick Macmillan.

Miss Pater

CLARA PATER to FREDERICK MACMILLAN, 23 September 1901
MS.: British Library. Printed in *TBB*.

6 Canning Place W. | Sept. 23 1901

Dear Mr. Macmillan,

Thank you for returning the original copy of 'Essays from The Guardian' & also for the new edition. We are very glad to hear that you think we did well in having them published. No, it was not Mr. Gosse. It was a publisher at Oxford, whose name I forget, who asked permission to bring them out, urging that there was a great demand for them.

We are glad that the general sale of the books during the past year has been good & are anxious to see the accounts.

With kind regards

Yours very truly
Clara A. Pater.

1903

FREDERICK MACMILLAN to CLARA PATER, 18 March [1903]
MS.: British Library. Printed in *TBB*.

March 18 3

Dear Miss Pater,

I have been told (though I am not at liberty to mention my informant's name) that you have been approached by some one[1] who has asked your permission to print some letters of your brother's & to publish a biography of him. I don't know whether the information is accurate, but in case it is I think it as well to warn you to be exceedingly careful now or at any time about giving any such permission. There are many inferior book makers about, on the look out for material & it would be [distressing] to you & your brother's friends if by any [misadventure] you were led into giving any kind of sanction to a book that might turn out very unsatisfactory. If any application of the kind is made to you I would advise you to consult Mr. Shadwell or some one like him before acceding to it.

I am,

Yours very truly,
Frederick Macmillan.

Miss Pater

[1] Very likely Thomas Wright (see Biographical Register).

CLARA PATER to THOMAS WRIGHT,[1] 23 March 1903
MS.: Wright MSS. 1878-1907, Lilly Library, Indiana University. Printed in *TBB*.

6 Canning Place | Kensington W. | March 23. 1903

Dear Sir,

In case you should have obtained any letters of the late Mr. Walter Pater, I write to say that my sister & I cannot give you permission to publish them. The copyright of letters legally belongs to the writer and his representatives so that any such letters cannot be published without our consent.

We hope too that you quite understand that we do not in any way authorize the publication of the Biography of our brother which you spoke of writing, and that our names are not to be mentioned.[2]

Believe me

> Yours faithfully
> Clara Pater.

¹ Thomas Wright (1859–1936), schoolmaster, historian, and biographer (see Biographical Register).
² See Thomas Wright, *The Life of Walter Pater*, 2 vols (London: Everett, 1907).

FREDERICK MACMILLAN to CLARA PATER, 11 May 1903
MS.: British Library. Printed in *TBB*.

Miss Pater, | 6 Canning Place, W.

> May 11th. 1903

Dear Miss Pater,

We think there is no reason whatever why you should refuse Mr. Daniel's request¹ for permission to print the essay on *Aesthetic Poetry*.

I am,

> Yours very truly,
> Frederick Macmillan.

¹ Pater revised his essay 'Poems by William Morris', which appeared in the *Westminster Review*, 90 (Oct. 1868), 300–12, and retitled it as 'Aesthetic Poetry' in the first edition of *Appreciations: With an Essay on Style* (1889), 213–27. In his memorial volume, *The Daniel Press* (Oxford: Daniel Press, 1921), Falconer Madan notes that Daniel never printed 'Aesthetic Poetry'. See *CW* vi.

HESTER PATER to CHARLES SHADWELL, 12 May [1903]
MS.: British Library. Printed in Hagiwara.

> 6 Canning Place | May 12

Dear Mr. Shadwell,

We wrote to Mr. Macmillan if he had any objection to Mr. Daniel printing 'Aesthetic Poetry'.¹ He has no objection—so will you kindly tell Mr. Daniel that we shall be pleased for him to print it in his charming style. Thank you for the trouble you took about 'Marcus Aurelius'.

> Yours very sincerely
> Hester Pater.

¹ Daniel did not publish an edition of the essay.

FREDERICK MACMILLAN to CLARA PATER, 11 June 1903
MS.: British Library. Printed in *TBB*.

Miss Pater, | 6 Canning Place, W.

June 11th. 1903

Dear Miss Pater,

If Mrs. Robert Ottley[1] will kindly send us the manuscript of her book when it is ready, it shall have our careful attention.
I am,

Yours very truly,
Frederick Macmillan.

[1] May Ottley (1872–1939), teacher and author, was a close friend of Clara and Hester Pater (see Biographical Register).

GEORGE MACMILLAN to CLARA PATER, 31 July 1903
MS.: British Library. Printed in *TBB*.

Miss Pater. | 6 Canning Place, | Kensington, W.

31st July 1903

Dear Miss Pater,

We have received the enclosed letter[1] of which one passage, which I have marked with a red pencil, concerns you. We have given the printer permission to reproduce as tracts the two writings by F. D. Maurice[2] to which he refers, but before dealing with his similar request in regard to a chapter in 'Marius the Epicurean' we should be glad to have your views on the subject. We do not think it could hurt the book, but you may nevertheless see some objection and we should of course be guided by your wishes in the matter. Please return Mr. Newman's[3] letter.
I am,

Yours very truly,
George A. Macmillan.

[1] The enclosure is missing.
[2] The religious controversies connected with Frederick Denison Maurice (1805–72), theologian, played a significant part in the development of Macmillan and Co. During the period 1858–9 Pater championed the writings of Maurice, and called himself a Christian socialist (Wright, 1: 167–8). See Charles Morgan, *The House of Macmillan*, 34–7.
[3] Unidentified.

CHARLES SHADWELL to THOMAS WRIGHT, 26 August 1903
MS.: Thomas Wright's Scrapbook, Brasenose College archives. Printed in Seiler, *Walter Pater: A Life Remembered*.

26 August 1903

Dear Sir,

Dr. Shadwell presents his compliments to Mr. Thomas Wright. Since Dr. Shadwell last wrote, he has had an opportunity of consulting the family of Mr. Walter Pater, and he learns that they are not inclined to supply information for such a biography as Mr. Wright proposes to undertake. Under these circumstances Dr. Shadwell regrets that he is unable to give Mr. Wright the assistance he desires.

Yours truly,
C. L. Shadwell.

1904

HESTER PATER to THOMAS WRIGHT, 31 January [1904]
MS.: Wright MSS., 1878–1907, Lilly Library, Indiana University. Envelope: Thomas Wright. Esq., | Cooper School, | Olney, | Bucks. Postmark: LEW[ES] Z45PM JA 29 04. Printed in Seiler, *Walter Pater: A Life Remembered*.

6 Canning Place | Jan. 31st.

Dear Sir,

In answer to your letter, I am afraid we cannot help you. We have never wished to have the Life of our brother written. Most Biographies are so unsatisfactory and full of trivial and incorrect details.

My brother's life was very uneventful—his inner life is best known from his books. He was very reticent even with those nearest to him and wrote few letters. As to the house at Weston Underwood it was long ago the house of his grandfather and great-grandfather.

Yours truly
Hester Pater.

MAURICE MACMILLAN to CLARA PATER, 12 February 1904
MS.: British Library. Printed in *TBB*.

Miss Pater. | 6 Canning Place, | Kensington, W.

12th February 1904

Dear Miss Pater,

In my brother's absence I have opened your letter, and have much pleasure in sending you a copy of *Marius*.

I am,

Yours very truly,
Maurice Macmillan.

CLARA PATER to THOMAS WRIGHT, 25 February 1904
MS.: Wright MSS. 1878–1907, Lilly Library, Indiana University. Printed in Seiler, *Walter Pater: A Life Remembered*.

6 Canning Place W. | Feb. 25. 1904

Dear Sir,

My sister & I are still of the same mind as when we saw you,[1] with regard to the Life of Mr. Walter Pater. We do not wish any Biography to be written, unless we should write one ourselves. But of course we cannot prevent your doing so, if you wish to.

In that case we should like, if you are willing, to see the M.S.S. before publication.

We shall not be at home the first week in March.

I am

Yours truly
Clara A. Pater.

---

[1] Wright visited the Pater sisters in London in March 1903 so that he could outline the biography he had planned and seek their support, but they rejected his proposal, saying that they did not want a biography of their brother to be written, and forbade him to quote from unpublished letters. Wright's account of his awkward dealings with the Pater sisters, which he recorded in *Thomas Wright of Olney: An Autobiography* (London: Herbert Jenkins, 1936), 92–5, should be compared with that given in the hostile letters he received from Hester and Clara Pater. The correspondence in question starts with the letter to Thomas Wright, 23 Mar. 1903.

CLARA PATER to THOMAS WRIGHT, 28 February 1904
MS.: Wright MSS. 1878–1907, Lilly Library, Indiana University. Printed in Seiler, *Walter Pater: A Life Remembered*.

6 Canning Place | Kensington | Feb. 28 1904

Dear Sir,

I can only repeat that we do not wish any Biography of Mr. Walter Pater to be written, & are quite sure he would himself have disliked it above measure. We cannot supply you with any information, or ask others to do so.

This note must close the correspondence.

Yours truly
C. A. Pater.

HESTER PATER to THOMAS WRIGHT, 5 March 1904
MS.: Wright MSS. 1878–1907, Lilly Library, Indiana University. Printed in Seiler, *Walter Pater: A Life Remembered*.

6 Canning Place | Kensington | 5 March 1904

Dear Sir,

I am writing to call your attention to a point with regard to the writing of Biographies, which I think has escaped your notice. When near relations do not wish a life written, as a matter of good feeling the idea is always abandoned.

Others besides yourself have applied for leave to write Mr. Pater's life, and as soon as they knew we did not wish it, have immediately given it up. I think that when this is pointed out to you, you will see it in the same light.

I am

Yours truly
H. M. Pater.

HESTER PATER to THOMAS WRIGHT, 10 March [1904]
MS.: Wright MSS. 1878-1907, Lilly Library, Indiana University. Printed in Seiler, *Walter Pater: A Life Remembered.*

6 Canning Place | March 10th.

Dear Sir,

 We must beg to remind you not to mention myself or my sister in the work you are preparing either in genealogical tables or in any way whatever.

Yours faithfully
H. M. Pater.

1905

HESTER PATER to VIOLET PAGET,[1] 10 July [1905]
MS.: Colby College. Printed in *LWP.*

6 Canning Place | July 10th.

My dear Violet,

 Many thanks for the letters and for your own kind and interesting letter. One of them Mr. Benson was very glad to have seen.[2] I think he has written to you about it. Walter's letters are so rare—only a stray one here and there to be found. We shall be in London till the end of this month. On the 1st. of August we go to St. Margaret's-at-Cliffe near Dover where we have taken a cottage for a month[;] perhaps you could come and see us there, it is a lovely place. If not we shall hope to see you here. Clara sends love.

Yours affect[ionate]ly
H. M Pater.

[1] Violet Paget (see Biographical Register).
[2] Probably letter to Paget, 22 July [1883], a portion of which is quoted by Benson, 89-90.

1906

CLARA PATER to THOMAS WRIGHT, 12 June 1906
MS.: Wright MSS. 1878-1907, Lilly Library, Indiana University. Envelope: Mr. Thomas Wright | 20 Upper Road | Tooting | S.W. Postmark: [KENS]INGTON JU 12 06 W. Printed in Seiler, *Walter Pater: A Life Remembered.*

6 Canning Place W. | June 12 1906

Dear Sir,

Thank you for your kind offer of your book. But as it has been written entirely against our wishes, we must decline acceptance of it.

Yours truly
C. A. Pater.

CHARLES SHADWELL to THOMAS WRIGHT, 27 August 1906
MS.: Thomas Wright's *Scrap-Book*, Brasenose College. Printed in Seiler, *Walter Pater: A Life Remembered*.

27 August 1906

Dear Sir,

I am obliged to you for your letter. I shall read your account of Mr. Pater, which you kindly offered to send me, with great interest. I have no knowledge of any such newspaper paragraphs as you refer to: in any case, I should pay no attention to them.

Yours truly,
C. L. Shadwell.

1907

FREDERICK MACMILLAN to CLARA PATER, 21 March [1907]
MS.: British Library. Printed in *TBB*.

March 21 07

Dear Miss Pater,

We had a visit this morning from a young American lady (Miss Ethel Randall,[1] 5 Mecklenburg Square) who came with an introduction from D. Furnivall.[2] She wishes to take the degree of Doctor of Philosophy at the University of Chicago & intends to offer as a thesis an Essay on the Art Teaching of Mr. Pater.

Miss Randall intends to print & publish her Essay & she also has the idea of compiling a Bibliography of Mr. Pater's writings. In addition to this she would like to have permission to reprint some sixteen Reviews[3] of Books which she says exist but which have never been collected. It was this last matter that she came to see us about.

I, of course, told Miss Randall that the question as to which of Mr. Pater's fugitive writings should be reprinted had been carefully considered by you & Mr. Shadwell, and that it did not seem to me at all probable that you would give permission to any other person to reprint articles which you excluded from the Edition of your brother's writings over which you had control. Miss Randall, however, was very anxious that the matter should be laid before you & I promised that I would write to you about it. If you will kindly instruct me as to your wishes I will communicate with Miss Randall. I should imagine that the best plan would be to say that if it is ever decided to reprint any more articles it will be done under Mr. Shadwell's Editorship & in your Edition.

I am,

Yours very truly,
Frederick Macmillan.

---

[1] Ethel Claire Randall attended the University of Chicago, 1900–10. There is no record of her PhD thesis, possibly the very first work of scholarship devoted to the life and work of Pater.

[2] Pater may have read a paper on *Love's Labour's Lost* before the New Shakspere Society, 13 Apr. 1875, an early version of the essay published in *Macmillan's Magazine*, 53 (Dec. 1885), 89–91, and reprinted in *Appreciations* (1889), where it is dated 1878 (see *CW* vi). Frederick James Furnivall (1825–1910), philologist, textual scholar, and editor (see letter to Furnivall, 18 May [1875?]), who founded not only the New Shakspere Society (1873) but the Early English Text Society (1864), may have been impressed, for in May 1875 he asked Pater to edit a play, possibly *Romeo and Juliet*. No such edition was ever published by Pater.

[3] See letters to Hester Pater, 25 Feb. 1901, and Clara Pater, 21 Mar. [1907].

HESTER PATER to VIOLET PAGET, [September 1907]
MS.: Colby College.

6 Canning Place | Kensington

My dear Violet,

I must write to tell you how grieved I was to see the notice of the death of your dear brother[1] and to say how much we empathize with you dear Violet. We have only just come back to London after being away four months. Clara has been ill with a bad attack of neuritis.[2] I hope she is getting a little better now but it is slow.

With love from us both
Always most affectionately

Yours
H. M. Pater

---

[1] Eugene Lee-Hamilton (see Biographical Register) died on 9 Sept. 1907.

[2] Neuritis is a general term for inflammation of a nerve or the general inflammation of the peripheral nervous system.

1908

FREDERICK MACMILLAN to CLARA PATER, 8 January [1908]
MS.: British Library. Printed in *TBB*.

Miss Pater | 3 Radnor Cliff | Folkstone

Jan. 8 08

Dear Miss Pater,

I enclose a cheque for the sum which is due to you in the course of the present month: £419.19.8.

I am very sorry to hear that you have been ill: you are certainly wise to escape from London where it is horribly cold and terribly dark. I think it is the darkness of the winters in London that gets on one's nerves. My wife[1] is in Rome where she says the weather is delightful. She is going to the Riviera at the end of this month. I hope to join her there in February.

With kind regards, I am,

Yours sincerely,
Frederick Macmillan.

[1] Frederick Macmillan worked in New York 1871–6, where he met and married (15 Apr. 1874) Georgina Elizabeth Warrin of Newtown, Long Island.

1910

CLARA PATER to FREDERICK MACMILLAN, 11 January 1910
MS.: British Library. Printed in *TBB*.

6 Canning Place | Jan. 11 1910

Dear Sir Frederick,

I want to present a copy of 'Essays from The Guardian' to a friend, if you would kindly order one to be sent to me.

With kind regards

Yours sincerely,
C. A. Pater.

MACMILLAN AND CO. to CLARA PATER, 12 January 1910
MS.: British Library. Printed in *TBB*.

Miss C. A. Pater, | 6 Canning Place, | Kensington Gate, W.

January 12. 1910

Dear Madam,

In the absence of Sir Frederick Macmillan in the United States, we write to acknowledge receipt of your letter of yesterday addressed to him, and to say that we have much pleasure in sending you a copy of *Essays from 'The Guardian'* by this post.

We are,

Yours faithfully,
Macmillan and Co.

FREDERICK MACMILLAN to CLARA PATER, 2 February [1910]
MS.: British Library. Printed in *TBB*.

Feb. 2 10

Dear Miss Pater,

It has been suggested to us by several large booksellers that it would be a good thing to publish a new & uniform edition[1] of your brother's books in an attractive form at 7/6 per volume. It would not be a serious undertaking as we could print from the existing stereotype plates which are in very good condition & I think that the [fillip] which the publication of such a set would probably give to the sale would have a satisfactory effect on the next annual statement of accounts. The question arises just now because the stock of 'Studies in the Renaissance' is low and it will have to be reprinted in some form within the next few weeks. If you approve of my proposal, we shall publish that book in the new edition about Easter & continue to bring out a book per month until the set is complete.

We must not forget that the copyright of 'The Renaissance' will expire in five years and a year or two before that takes place it will be advisable to bring out a changed edition of the whole series so as to get as much as possible from the books before they fall into the public domain, but there is no necessity to take that step yet, & in the meantime we can, I hope, make something considerable for you & ourselves out of the proposed 7/6 edition.

My wife & I have just come back from America where we went to spend Christmas. We enjoyed our holiday, but are very glad to be back again. With kind regards,

I am,

> Yours very truly,
> Frederick Macmillan.

Miss Pater

¹ A reference to the Library Edition, 1,250 sets of which were issued late in 1910.

HESTER PATER to FREDERICK MACMILLAN, 3 February 1910
MS.: British Library. Printed in Hagiwara and in *TBB*.

> 6 Canning Place | Feb 3rd 1910

Dear Sir Frederick,

We think your proposal of a 7/6 Edition of my brother's books a very good one and the need of the reprint of the 'Studies in the Renaissance' seems a very good opportunity to make the change. We are glad that you think it will be a monetary success.

We should have called on Lady Macmillan in the summer but my sister has been very ill for some months and has had to undergo a very serious operation in a Nursing Home this Autumn so my time has been fully occupied.

With kind regards,

> Yours truly
> H. M. Pater.

HESTER PATER to FREDERICK MACMILLAN, 15 September [1910]
MS.: British Library. Printed in Hagiwara and in *TBB*.

> 17 Elm's Avenue | Eastbourne. | Sept. 15th

Dear Sir Frederick,

Will you kindly forward the next books to Miss Strong[1] [at] 39 Kensington Square, as I am staying here for a month. I suppose you have heard that I have lost my darling sister[2] this August and it has left me a very desolate creature. The expenses in consequence have been very great. I should be glad to know if the new edition is selling well. And would you kindly tell me how long the copyright will last.

Yours sincerely,
Hester M. Pater.

[1] Unidentified.
[2] Clara Pater (see Biographical Register) died on 9 Aug. 1910. Her estate was valued at £50 1s 8d.

FREDERICK MACMILLAN to HESTER PATER, 16 September 1910
MS.: British Library. Printed in *TBB*.

Miss Pater, | 17 Elm's Avenue, | Eastbourne

September 16th 1910

Dear Miss Pater,

I was very sorry indeed to see the announcement[1] of your sad loss in August. I did not write to you yourself at the time, as I knew my wife was doing so.

I am glad to say that the profits on the sales of the books this year will be slightly larger than the last, as you will see from the accounts[2] which I send herewith. If it will be any convenience, we shall be glad to send you a cheque for £100 now, although, as you know, the money is strictly speaking not payable till January next. If I hear from you that you would like the cheque, a cheque shall go immediately.

It is impossible to say what the results of future years' sales will be, but I hope that the decrease will not be large for at any rate some time to come. Unfortunately, the copyright in *Studies in the Renaissance*, which is one of the most important of the books, expires in 1915. There is some hope, however, that the new Copyright Bill[3] which the government has prepared, and which is to be brought into parliament next session, may become law. If it does it will be very greatly to your advantage, as by that Bill copyright will last for fifty years from the date of the death of the author.

I am,

Yours very sincerely,
Frederick Macmillan.

[1] A reference to the death of Clara Pater, 9 Aug. 1910.
[2] The enclosure is missing.
[3] In Great Britain, the first Copyright Act was passed in 1709. It duly recognized 'property' in books, and gave authors copyright for fourteen years, with an additional fourteen years if they were still living. At the time, publishers believed that the books would then become their property. The courts, however, construed the Act to mean that, when the term of copyright expired, the books became anybody's. The Copyright Act of 1842 extended

authors' copyright to seven years after death or forty-two years from the date of publication, whichever was longer. As popular writers soon realized, this Act had no effect in the United States, where unscrupulous publishers circulated thousands of their books without any profit for the writers. Authors such as Charles Dickens crossed the Atlantic to arrange contracts for so-called 'exclusive rights', but publishers in New York, Philadelphia, and Boston continued to 'pirate' whatever English books they thought would sell. Agitation for an international Copyright Act resulted in the Berne Convention of 1886, ratified by a number of governments, but ignored by the United States. In 1891 an Act of Congress provided for mutual copyright arrangements with various countries, including Great Britain. The Copyright Act of 1911 increased the period of copyright to the life of authors and fifty years after their death. According to this Act, after twenty-five years following death, anyone could produce a work for sale after he gave notice to the holder of the copyright and made a payment of 20 per cent of the published price. It also required the delivery of copies of all publications to certain libraries, including the British Museum and the Bodleian Library.

1911

HESTER PATER to FREDERICK MACMILLAN, 9 January [1911]
MS.: British Library. Printed in Hagiwara and in *TBB*.

6 Canning Place | Kensington | Jan 9th

Dear Sir Frederick,

If it would not be inconvenient could you send me the cheque for the book money within the next four days, as I am going away about the middle of the week, and don't know how long I may be away.

With kind regards

Yours sincerely
Hester M. Pater.

FREDERICK MACMILLAN to HESTER PATER, 10 January 1911
MS.: British Library. Printed in *TBB*.

Miss Pater, | 6 Canning Place, | Kensington, W.

January 10th 1911

Dear Miss Pater,

In reply to your note, I have the pleasure of enclosing a cheque for £378.13.6, which is due to you this month.

I am

Yours very truly,
Frederick Macmillan.

FREDERICK MACMILLAN to HESTER PATER, 4 July 1911
MS.: British Library. Printed in *TBB*.

Miss Pater, | 6 Canning Place, | Kensington, W.

July 4th 1911.

Dear Miss Pater,

We are publishing a series of shilling editions[1] of well-known books, with the idea of meeting the demand for cheap copyright literature which seems to be growing, and it has been suggested that *Studies in the Renaissance* would make a very valuable and saleable addition to this series. I am writing therefore to ask whether you will agree to having this done. I do not think that if the 'Renaissance' is the only one of your brother's books which is issued at 1/–, the publication would be likely to have a serious effect on the sale of the more expensive edition, and, indeed, it might possibly have the result of stimulating the desire to read his books among a public who are at present ignorant of them. At the same time we should not like to make this experiment without your full knowledge and concurrence. If you agree, we can publish the shilling edition either on the present basis of half-profits or, if you prefer, on a royalty of ten per cent of the published price. If the proposal meets with your approval, the new edition will be published, with several other volumes of our Shilling Library, during the coming autumn.

I am,

Yours very truly,
Frederick Macmillan.

[1] A shilling edition of *The Renaissance* appeared in 1912.

FREDERICK MACMILLAN to HESTER PATER, 10 August 1911
MS.: British Library. Printed in *TBB*.

Miss Pater, | 6 Canning Place, | Kensington, W.

August 10th 1911.

Dear Miss Pater,

I wrote to you on July 4th to say that we are thinking of including *Studies in the Renaissance* in a series of cheap copyright books which we are putting on the market to meet the demand for such things, but, as I have had no reply, I am afraid that my letter may have miscarried, although in that case it is rather strange that it has not come back to us through the post. However, I now write again to ask if you have any objection to this proposal, and, if not, whether you would prefer that the book should be published on the present half-profits basis or on a ten per cent royalty. My reason for troubling you is that, if the book is to be issued, I wish to get it announced in our Autumn List.

I am

Yours very truly,
Frederick Macmillan.

FREDERICK MACMILLAN to HESTER PATER, 5 October 1911
MS.: British Library. Printed in *TBB*.

Miss Pater, | c/o Miss Strong, | 39 Kensington Square, W.

October 5th 1911.

Dear Miss Pater,

I am sending you the accounts[1] for the sales of your brother's books for the year ending June 30th last. We sent them first to Canning Place, but they came back with a note to say that you had left, and we have got the present address from Canon Ottley.[2] I shall be glad to know if it is permanent, or if not, where you would like your letters sent.

You will be glad to see that the result of the publication of the uniform seven-and-sixpenny edition has been very satisfactory.

The fact of your having moved away from Canning Place probably accounts for my not having had a reply to two letters I wrote during the summer with reference to a proposed shilling edition of *Studies in the Renaissance*. We are issuing a certain number of well-known books at this very low price, and have reason to think that a large sale might be obtained for a shilling edition of 'The Renaissance'. At all events we should like to try it, but do not wish to do so without letting you know, and therefore the thing has been held over. If you do approve, we shall bring out the shilling very shortly. I do not think it would have any bad effect on the sale of the seven-and-sixpenny book, but if we found that it did, we could easily withdraw it from sale.

Believe me,

Yours very truly,
Frederick Macmillan.

[1] The enclosure is missing.
[2] Revd Robert Lawrence Ottley (1856–1933), theologian. See Biographical Register for Mary Kay (May) Ottley and letters to Armour, 24 Mar. [1887], and Clara Pater, 11 June 1903.

HESTER PATER to FREDERICK MACMILLAN, 6 October 1911
MS.: British Library. Printed in *TBB*.

October 6th 1911

Dear Sir Frederick,

I was very glad to hear that the sale of the new edition of the Books has been so very satisfactory. It has relieved my mind of a great deal of trouble and worry. Since I left Canning Place at midsummer I have had no settled address or would have written to you. I have been wandering about in town, and country, looking for a small house but they seem very difficult to find. The London houses are doleful little places, and those in the country too remote and lonely for me.

I very much approve of bringing out a shilling edition of 'The Renaissance'. I think it would be very successful. Till I telegram you of a settled address will you please send letters to Miss Strong, 39 Kensington Square, and she will send them on.

Believe me,

Yours very truly,
Hester M. Pater.

1912

MACMILLAN AND CO. to HESTER PATER, 31 January 1912
MS.: British Library. Printed in *TBB*.

Miss Pater, | 51 Earl's Court Road, | W.

January 31st. 1912

Dear Madam,

An American firm of publishers proposes to introduce into Great Britain a work which they have already issued in the United States entitled 'The Stoddard Library'[1] comprised in twelve volumes, and made up of extracts from the works of various writers, among which is Mr. Walter Pater's story of 'Cupid and Psyche',[2] and an excerpt from 'The Renaissance'.

We have been applied to and have given permission for the use of these extracts, as we do not think that their appearance in a work of this nature, which is only to be sold in sets at a high price, will have any injurious effects upon the sale of Mr. Pater's books. As, however, the proprietors

have made us a payment for the right to use these extracts, we beg to enclose for acceptance a cheque for £9.10.0, representing your share in it.
Yours faithfully,

for Macmillan and Co. Ltd.,
Maurice Macmillan. | Director.

---

[1] John Lawson Stoddard (1850–1931), an American traveller, lecturer, and editor, created several multi-volume works, including *The Stoddard Library: A Thousand Hours of Entertainment with the World's Great Writers*, ed. John L. Stoddard, 12 vols (Chicago and Boston: G. L. Shuman, 1910).

[2] An extract from *Marius the Epicurean*, referred to as 'Cupid and Psyche' in the index, appeared in *The Stoddard Library*, 1: 100–18, and the extract from *The Renaissance* appeared in 9: 328–47.

HESTER PATER to GEORGE MACMILLAN, 4 February [1912]
MS.: British Library. Printed in *TBB*.

51 Earl's Court Road, | Feb. 4th

Dear Mr. Macmillan,

Thanks for the cheque for the extracts for The Stoddard Library. I think it might be an advertisement for my brother's books and so help the sale rather than the reverse.

Yours truly,
Hester M. Pater.

FREDERICK MACMILLAN to HESTER PATER, 28 February 1912
MS.: British Library. Printed in *TBB*.

Miss Pater, | 51 Earl's Court Road, | W.

February 28th 1912.

Dear Miss Pater,

We have lately arranged to undertake the joint publication, with Mr. Philip Lee Warner,[1] a series of books printed in a special type called the 'Riccardi' fount, which was designed for him some years ago by Mr. Herbert Horne.[2] These editions are limited in number, and are never reprinted; they are in fact rather bibliographic toys than books. We should like if possible to bring out in this type a special edition of *Marius the Epicurean*; it would be in two volumes sold at 12s 6d each, and would be limited to a thousand copies. I write to ask if you are willing to license us to print this edition in return for an outright payment of £250? If so, we should like to make such an agreement. I need not say that the existence of this edition could not in any way damage the sale of the ordinary seven-and-sixpenny edition.

With kind regards, I am,

Yours very truly,
Frederick Macmillan.

---

[1] Philip Henry Lee-Warner (1877–1925), a publisher, in 1905 joined Chatto & Windus as a partner. In 1909 the publishing firm incorporated the Medici Society (founded by Lee-Warner and Eustace Gurney in 1908); Lee-Warner served as the managing director and publisher for the Society until 1921.

[2] Herbert Horne (see Biographical Register and letter to Horne, 25 Oct. [1886]) designed three significant typefaces: Montallegro, Florence, and Riccardi. The Riccardi, based on fonts by Antonio Miscomini and cut in 1909, was used in the 'Riccardi Press' edition published by the Medici Society.

HESTER PATER to FREDERICK MACMILLAN, 29 February 1912
MS.: British Library. Postcard addressed to Sir Frederick Macmillan & Co., St. Martin's Street | W. C. Postmarked: Kensington W. | 5:00 p.m., | 29 February 12. Printed in *TBB*.

51 Earl's Court Road | Kensington

I am sending three more fragments[1] for you to see that I could not find yesterday.

H. P.

---

[1] These fragments may have been the papers C. L. Shadwell refers to in the 'Preface' to *Greek Studies*: 'The papers on Greek sculpture are all that remain of a series which, if Mr. Pater had lived, would, probably, have grown into a still more important work. Such a work would have included one or more essays on Phidias and the Parthenon, of which only a fragment, though an important fragment, can be found amongst his papers; and it was to have been prefaced by an Introduction to Greek Studies, only a page or two of which was ever written' (London: Macmillan, 1895), 3. Apparently, Pater was working on the first fragment, 'The School of Phidias', during the last months of his life. He may have intended it as a sequel to 'The Age of Athletic Prizemen', published in the *Contemporary Review*, 65 (Feb. 1894), 242–56, and reprinted in *Greek Studies* (1895); see *CW* viii. The manuscript was in the possession of May Ottley (see Biographical Register) as late as 1936, because in his *Essai sur Walter Pater* (Paris: Libraire Picart, 1936), Lucien Catton states that she allowed him to examine the remaining Pater manuscripts, including 'The School of Phidias' (51–2). Its whereabouts today are unknown. The other fragments, 'Introduction to Greek Studies' and 'The Parthenon', are among the Pater papers at Harvard University. See *CW* x.

FREDERICK MACMILLAN to HESTER PATER, 1 March 1912
MS.: British Library. Printed in *TBB*.

Miss Pater, | 51 Earl's Court Road, | W.

March 1st 1912.

Dear Miss Pater,

I have received the packet containing three more Fragments, and hope to write to you within a few days making some suggestion as to utilising them. It certainly seems a pity from every point of view that they should not be put into print.

I am,

Yours very truly,
Frederick Macmillan.

FREDERICK MACMILLAN to HESTER PATER, 5 March 1912
MS.: British Library. Printed in *TBB*.

Miss Pater, | 51 Earl's Court Road, | Kensington, W.

March 5th 1912.

Dear Miss Pater,

I am much obliged to you for your letter accepting our proposal for the 'Riccardi' edition of *Marius the Epicurean*.

With regard to the 'Fragments' which you left with me the other day, it seems to me the best way of turning them into money would be to get them, in the first instance at all events, published in a good periodical. My feeling is that 'The English Review' would be the most likely to pay a good price for them, and if I have your permission I will at once communicate with Mr. Austin Harrison,[1] the Editor of the Review, and see what offer I can get. You will of course understand that in this matter I shall be acting for you, and not in any sense for my firm; that is to say, anything that is paid for their serial publication will go to you without deduction.

I am,

Yours very truly,
Frederick Macmillan.

---

[1] Austin Frederic Harrison (1873–1928), journalist and editor, was tutored by George Gissing (1857–1903), then a struggling young novelist. He went to Harrow, 1887–90, and

attended the universities of Lausanne, Marburg, and Berlin, where he studied languages, by way of preparing for the Foreign Office examination. After failing this, he found his vocation in journalism. In Berlin, 1898–1905, he worked for *The Times* and then the *Manchester Guardian*, assisting William Thomas Stead (1849–1912), editor of the *Pall Mall Gazette*, 1883–9, and pioneer of investigative journalism, in covering the Hague Peace Conference (1899). In London, Harrison worked as a freelance journalist before serving as political editor of the Sunday *Observer* and later as literary editor and drama critic of the *Daily Mail*. Sir Alfred Mond installed him as editor of the *English Review*, 1909–23, a literary and political monthly. Harrison opened the review to female contributors and to Continental writers. In 1921, Harrison helped to establish PEN International, the world-wide association of writers that promoted intellectual co-operation. After 1923, he concentrated on writing, including a biography of his father, *Frederic Harrison: Thoughts and memories* (London: William Heinemann, 1926).

HESTER PATER to FREDERICK MACMILLAN, [6] March [1912][1]
MS.: British Library. Printed in *TBB*.

51 Earl's Court Road | Kensington | March

Dear Sir Frederick,

Thank you for your kind offer of sending the 'Fragments'[2] to the 'English Review' for me, but I really did not think as much of the money they bring as that they were too interesting to be lost, and that the people who care for the 'Books' generally would be very glad to see them. Do you really think they are finished, and complete, enough as Fragments to be published? If so I should be very glad to have them appear in the 'English Review'. I cannot bear to print anything he might perhaps have not liked to be printed.

With kind regards,

Yours very truly,
H. M. Pater.

[1] So dated on the basis of the letter's position in the Macmillan Letter Book.
[2] See letters to Frederick Macmillan, 29 Feb. [1912] and 19 Mar. [1912], in which Hester Pater agrees not to publish the 'Fragments'.

FREDERICK MACMILLAN to HESTER PATER, 7 March 1912
MS.: British Library. Printed in *TBB*.

Miss Pater, | 51 Earl's Court Road, | Kensington, W.

March 7th 1912.

Dear Miss Pater,

I think that perhaps before sending the 'Fragments' to the Editor of 'The English Review' the matter had better have a little more consideration. I propose to ask the advice of a literary friend[1] on whose judgment

I rely a good deal, and will let you know what he thinks about it. It certainly would be a pity to print anything which your brother would not have liked to appear over his name.

I am,

Yours very truly,
Frederick Macmillan.

[1] Not identified.

FREDERICK MACMILLAN to HESTER PATER, 8 March 1912
MS.: British Library. Printed in *TBB*.

Miss Pater, | 51 Earl's Court Road, | Kensington, W.

March 8th 1912.

Dear Miss Pater,

I put the 'Fragments' which you gave me the other day into the hands of a man whose judgment in such matters we think particularly good. I told him that there was an idea of publishing them, and asked him to let me know how the question struck him. I think I cannot do better than send you a copy of his report.[1] I certainly should not like to advise you to publish the 'Fragments', though of course if you are determined to do so we should like to have them out with our imprint. I feel however that the decision as to whether they should be published at all, or not, should be taken by you and not by us.

I am,

Yours very truly,
Frederick Macmillan.

[1] The report is missing.

HESTER PATER to FREDERICK MACMILLAN, 19 March [1912]
MS.: British Library. Printed in Hagiwara and in *TBB*.

51 Earl's Court Road | Kensington. | March 19th

Dear Sir Frederick,

Thank you so much for the trouble you have taken about the 'Fragments'. I shall most certainly take your advice and that contained in the letter you forwarded to me, and *not* publish them.

Yours very truly,
Hester M. Pater.

FREDERICK MACMILLAN to HESTER PATER, 21 March 1912
MS.: British Library. Printed in *TBB*.

Miss Pater, | 51 Earl's Court Road, | Kensington, | London W.

March 21st 1912.

Dear Miss Pater,

I feel that you are quite right in your decision as to the publication of the 'Fragments'. I return them herewith.

Yours very truly,
Frederick Macmillan.

1913

HESTER PATER to FREDERICK MACMILLAN, 27 January [1913]
MS.: British Library. On a post card. Postmarked 27.1.13. Printed in *TBB*.

38 Pembroke Square | Kensington | Jan 27th

Dear Sir Frederick,

In case you are sending me a cheque, can you send it [to] me tomorrow, as I am going away for a little time on Thursday.

Yours sincerely
H. M. Pater.

FREDERICK MACMILLAN to HESTER PATER, 26 May 1913
MS.: British Library. Printed in *TBB*.

Miss Pater, | 38 Pembroke Square, | Kensington, W.

May 26th 1913.

Dear Miss Pater,

You will remember that some time ago we arranged with you for the publication by the Medici Society of a so-called 'Riccardi' edition of *Marius the Epicurean*,[1] for which you were to receive a lump sum of £250. This book will be ready to-morrow, and two presentation copies will be sent to you. In the meantime I have the pleasure to enclose a cheque for £250.

I remain,

Yours very truly,
Frederick Macmillan.

¹ A critic for the *Classical Review*, 28 (Feb. 1914), 24, acknowledged that the printing of this text was a 'real success': the Medici type was 'thoroughly legible, and restful to the eye'.

HESTER PATER to FREDERICK MACMILLAN, 30 May [1913]
MS.: British Library. Printed in *TBB*.

38 Pembroke Square | Kensington | May 30th

Dear Sir Frederick,

Thanks for the cheque, and the two copies of Marius, which I received on Wednesday.

With kind regards,

Yours very truly
H. M. Pater.

HESTER PATER to [GEORGE] MACMILLAN, 26 July [1913]
MS.: British Library. Printed in *TBB*.

38 Pembroke Square | Kensington | July 26

Dear Mr. Macmillan,

I received this note¹ yesterday. I don't know the name of the publisher of the shilling booklets. I suppose the copyright is only the copyright of the photograph. Please tell me if I should give them permission for the use of the photograph.

Yours sincerely
H. M. Pater.

¹ The enclosure is missing.

GEORGE MACMILLAN to HESTER PATER, 28 July 1913
MS.: British Library. Printed in *TBB*.

Miss Pater, | 38 Pembroke Square, | Kensington, W.

28th July 1913.

Dear Miss Pater,

There is no reason why you should not let Messrs. Elliott & Fry[1] give permission to use the photograph of your brother in the little Calendar from his writings which we have allowed Mr. Palmer[2] to print. Indeed it is we who referred him to Elliott & Fry as the copyright of the portrait is theirs. It shows good feeling on their part that they should consult you in the matter.

I am,

Yours sincerely,
George A. Macmillan.

---

[1] See letter to Pater, 15 Nov. [1887], n. 2.
[2] *The Pater Calendar: A Quotation from the Works of Walter Horatio Pater, for every Day of the Year*, selected by J. M. Kennedy (London: Frank Palmer, 1913) was published in Oct. 1913. The creator of the calendar, J[ohn]. M[cFarland]. Kennedy (1886–1918), writer and translator, also published *English Literature: 1880–1905* (London: Stephen Swift, 1912), which features a chapter on Pater (28–58).

1914

HESTER PATER to FREDERICK MACMILLAN, 6 October [1914]
MS.: British Library. Postcard. Printed in *TBB*.

38 Pembroke Square | Oct. 6th

Dear Sir Frederick,

Thank you for sending me the account of the books. I am very glad to find that they are still selling well.

With kind regards,

Yours sincerely,
H. M. Pater.

FREDERICK MACMILLAN to HESTER PATER, 9 November 1914
MS.: British Library. Printed in *TBB*.

Miss Pater, | 38 Pembroke Square, | Kensington, W.

November 9th 1914.

Dear Miss Pater,

I return Messrs. Jarrold's letter.[1] I do not see what you are to gain by having *A Child in the House* published in their 'Miniature' Classics, and would advise you not to give them permission to do so.

I am,

Yours very truly,
Frederick Macmillan.

[1] The Jarrold printing and publishing firm dates from 1823, when John Jarrold (1773–1823) opened a business in Norwich, where for the first while he and his four sons concentrated on such activities as printing, publishing, and selling stationery. In 1847 the firm opened a London office, where large numbers of educational books were produced. One of their best-known books was Anna Sewell's *Black Beauty* (1877). William Thomas Jarrold (1866–1937) and his brother Thomas Herbert Jarrold (1868–1936) acted as directors for the periods 1888–1937 and 1890–1936 respectively. William and Herbert formed a public limited company in 1902. 'The Miniature Classics', edited by E. G. Goodchild, were published in 1914 by Jarrold and Sons. This series included *The Deserted Village* by Oliver Goldsmith, *The Rime of the Ancient Mariner* by S. T. Coleridge, *The Sensitive Plant* by Percy Bysshe Shelley, *Pippa Passes* and *A Blot on the Scutcheon* by Robert Browning, and *Maud* by Alfred, Lord Tennyson. (These volumes were thread-sewn in sixteen-page sections.) There is no evidence that 'A Child in the House' appeared in this series.

1917

FREDERICK MACMILLAN to HESTER PATER, 7 July 1917
MS.: British Library. Printed in *TBB*.

Miss Pater, | 38 Pembroke Square, | W. 8.

July 7th 1917

Dear Miss Pater,

The compiler of the Calendar[1] which was published by Mr. Palmer did apply to us some time ago for permission to make everyday quotations from the works of Walter Pater. It seemed to us that it could not do the books any harm, and we therefore gave him the permission required.

With kind regards, I am,

> Yours very truly,
> Frederick Macmillan.

[1] See letter to Hester Pater, 28 July 1913.

1919

HESTER PATER to EDMUND GOSSE, 22 September [1919]
MS.: Brotherton Collection, University of Leeds.

> 38 Pembroke Square | Kensington | Sept 22nd.

Dear Mr. Gosse,

I wish to add my name as an old friend, and that of dear Walter to the many letters of recognition you have already received.[1]

With sincere congratulations

> Yours very sincerely
> Hester M. Pater.

[1] Gosse celebrated his seventieth birthday with his family on 21 Sept. 1919. The celebration in Wales included the reading of a letter penned by friends and admirers promising him a bust of himself executed by Sir William Goscombe John (1860–1952), the acclaimed sculptor, medallist, and lithographer; it was unveiled at the Royal Academy in 1920. The following day *The Times* printed this letter, which featured the signatures of 200 eminent men and women, including Arnold Bennett, Max Beerbohm, Sidney Colvin, Louise Imogen Guiney, G. Bernard Shaw, Arthur Symons, and T. Humphry Ward (see *The Times*, 22 Sept. 1919, 13). Evidently Hester read the letter in *The Times* and immediately contacted Gosse.

APPENDIX A

Further Letters by Walter Pater

In this Appendix, I list letters that Walter Pater is known to have written but are no longer extant. For each entry, I give the name of the correspondent, the date (if possible), the source (abbreviated as 'Ref.:'), and whatever is known of the letter's contents. If this information is given elsewhere in this volume, however, I supply only the cross-reference. Letters are arranged in chronological order, as far as I can determine. I do not include the letters (1858–62) that, according to Thomas Wright, Pater wrote to J. R. McQueen, who had been Pater's closest friend at the King's School, Canterbury. In his *Life of Walter Pater* (1907), Wright claims that he had seen, used, and briefly cited these letters, but no other evidence has survived (see Wright, 1: 162, 178–9, 181–4). Four letters are included here from Arthur Symons and two from Thomas Wright.

WALTER PATER to JOHN PENDERGAST, 9 June 1864
    Ref.: Letter of 5 June 1864, n. 2.
    Subject: Pater acknowledges the receipt of £30.

WALTER PATER to JOHN PENDERGAST, 1 August 1864
    Ref.: Letter of 5 June 1864, n. 4. See *Sotheran's Price Current of Literature*, no. 827, item 1289.
    Subject: Pater asks for a further sum of £40.

WALTER PATER to ALEXANDER MACMILLAN, [*c*.27 October 1872]
    Ref.: Letter of George Lillie Craik (see Biographical Register) to Pater, 28 October 1872 (Letter Book XXI).
    Subject: Pater discusses the essay that was withdrawn from his volume of Renaissance studies.

WALTER PATER to JOHN ADDINGTON SYMONDS, [summer 1875]
    Ref.: Letter of Symonds to H. F. Brown, 23 October [1875], in *Letters and Papers of John Addington Symonds*, ed. H. F. Brown (London: John Murray, 1923), 73.
    Subject: Pater praises *Renaissance in Italy: The Age of Despots* (1875) by Symonds. Pater reviewed this book in the *Academy*, 31 July 1887, 105–6. He also praises Symonds's poem on the 'Corpse of Julia', based on an incident recounted in ch. 1 of *The Age of the Despots* and given special attention in Pater's review.

WALTER PATER to CHARLES HENRY JEENS, mid-February [1877]
    Ref.: Pater's letter dated 6 March [1877] to Alexander Macmillan.
    Subject: Pater asks Jeens about the vignette that would be included in the second edition of his Renaissance studies.

WALTER PATER to CHARLES HENRY JEENS, [*c*.24 February 1877]
Ref.: Letters from Alexander Macmillan, 1 February 1877, and to Alexander Macmillan, 24 February 1877.
Subject: Pater inquires about the size of the vignette the latter was preparing for the second edition of *The Renaissance*.

WALTER PATER to MONCURE D. CONWAY,[1] [early January] 1878
Ref.: *Report of a General Conference of Liberal Thinkers* (London: Trübner, 1878), 9.
Subject: Pater expresses an interest in a conference at South Place Chapel.[2]

WALTER PATER to JULIA CONSTANCE FLETCHER, [January 1878]
Ref.: Letter to Alexander Macmillan, 31 January [1878].
Subject: Presumably Pater congratulates Fletcher on the publication of her novel, *Mirage* (1877).

WALTER PATER to MESSRS. R. CLAY, SONS AND TAYLOR, 12 May [1878]
Ref.: Letter to George Grove, 12 May [1878].
Subject: Pater inquires about the proofs of 'The Child in the House'.

WALTER PATER to GEORGE GROVE, [*c*.1 September 1878]
Ref.: Letter of Grove to Pater, 2 September 1878.
Subject: Pater announces that he is working on another essay.

WALTER PATER to FANNY HERTZ, 15 April [1879?]
Ref.: *American Book-Prices Current*, 15 (1954), 600.
Subject: Pater declines an invitation to a dinner party. In a letter dated 18 January [1879] (MS.: Harvard) to his mother, Henry James describes a Sunday evening *conversazione* at the Hertz residence in Harley Street, at which Pater was present. No other evidence of Pater's association with them has been found.

---

[1] Moncure Daniel Conway (1832–1907), an American clergyman and prolific writer, made a name for himself as a Methodist and then a Unitarian minister with an anti-slavery agenda. He moved to London in 1863 to garner support for the North in the American Civil War. The following year he became the minister of South Place Chapel, located at 11 South Place, Finsbury, London (founded in 1793 as a Universalist church by Elhanan Winchester; it continues today as the South Place Ethical Society). Conway encouraged women to preach at South Place Chapel, among them Annie Besant. His work included journalism, book sales, and agency fees (he represented Mark Twain's interests in Great Britain).

[2] At a general meeting on 27 January 1878, Conway discussed plans to organize 'A General Conference of Liberal Thinkers' to examine 'matters pertaining to the religious needs of our time, and the method of meeting them'. At this meeting he announced: 'From Oxford . . . I have letters indicating interest in our movement, from Professors [A. H.] Sayce, [H. D.] Rolleston, [Walter] Pater, &c.' About 400 men and women from various parts of the country attended his conference held at South Place Chapel on 13 and 14 June 1878; participants talked about the 'scientific study of religious phenomena' and 'the emancipation of mankind from the spirit of superstition'. We cannot confirm that Pater attended the conference. See Moncure D. Conway, 'A Discourse at South Place Chapel, London', *Open Court*, 21 November 1895, 4711–15, rptd in *Autobiography: Memories and Experiences* (Boston: Houghton, Mifflin, 1904), 2: 387–94.

WALTER PATER to ARTHUR SYMONS, [April 1887]
  Ref.: Letter of Symons to Dykes Campbell, 26 April 1887, Brit. Lib. Add. MS. 49522.
  Subject: Pater acknowledges a presentation copy of Symons's edition of *Philip Massinger* (1887), an edition of five plays of Massinger in the 'Mermaid' series, published by Henry Vizetelly (1820–94).

WALTER PATER to SELWYN IMAGE, 18 January [1888]
  Ref.: Letter to Herbert Horne, 18 January [1888].
  Subject: Pater invites Image to dinner on 28 January [1888].

WALTER PATER to ARTHUR GALTON, 17 July [1888]
  Ref.: Letter to Herbert Horne, 17 July [1888].
  Subject: Pater invites Galton to a dinner party on 27 July [1888].

WALTER PATER to ARTHUR SYMONS, [*c.* 10 November 1888]
  Ref.: Letter of Symons to Dykes Campbell, 19 November 1888, Brit. Lib. Add. MS. 49522.
  Subject: Pater asks Symons 'for a duplicate copy of proofs [of *Days and Nights*]' to be kept by him.

WALTER PATER to AN UNKNOWN CORRESPONDENT, 23 July 1889
  Ref.: *Autograph Prices Current*, 1 (1916), 124.
  Subject: No information is given in the source.

WALTER PATER to ARTHUR SYMONS, [14 December 1889]
  Ref.: Letter of Symons to Dykes Campbell, dated [21 December 1889], Brit. Lib. Add. MS. 49523.
  Subject: Pater sends Symons a copy of the *Athenaeum* review of *Appreciations* (see letter [22] November 1889), 'with W. P.'s kind regards'.

ARTHUR SYMONS to WALTER PATER, 10 February [1890]
  Ref.: Pater's letter to Symons, dated 22 February [1890].
  Subject: Symons invites Pater to meet Edith Holman Hunt, the wife of Pre-Raphaelite painter William Holman Hunt.

ARTHUR SYMONS to WALTER PATER, 15 April 1890
  Ref.: Beckson and Munro, eds, *Arthur Symons: Selected Letters*, 65.
  Subject: Arthur Symons conveys an offer to translate *Imaginary Portraits* (1887).

ARTHUR SYMONS to WALTER PATER, early May 1890
  Ref.: Letter of Arthur Symons to George Macmillan, 10 May 1890, in Beckson and Munro, eds, *Arthur Symons: Selected Letters*, 66.
  Subject: Charles Victor Marius Morice (1860–1919), French poet and critic, was an inspiring leader and energetic promoter of the Symbolist movement. He writes to Pater offering to translate *Imaginary Portraits* (1887). He published *La littérature de tout à l'heur*e (Paris, 1889), a manifesto of the Symbolist movement, and with Paul Gauguin wrote *Noa Noa: The Tahiti Journal of Paul Gauguin* (1901), an account of

the painter's experiences in Tahiti. Morice, who was Auguste Rodin's secretary in 1908, introduced Symons to Paul Verlaine, among others.

WALTER PATER to OSCAR WILDE, [summer–autumn 1890]
Ref.: *The Trials of Oscar Wilde*, ed. H. Montgomery Hyde (London: William Hodge, 1948), 124, 128, 157, 229–30.
Subject: Pater writes Wilde 'several letters about *The Picture of Dorian Gray*' in consequence of which Wilde 'modified one passage'.

WALTER PATER to GEORGE MACMILLAN, [*c.*11 November 1890]
Ref.: Implied in a letter Macmillan wrote to Pater, 12 November [1890] (Letter Book LIX).
Subject: Pater has sent proofs for the second edition of *Imaginary Portraits* to the printers.

WALTER PATER to FREDERICK MACMILLAN, [*c.*7 December 1890]
Ref.: Implied in letter of Macmillan to Pater, 8 December [1890] (Letter Book LX).
Subject: Pater has sent back 'for press' proofs for the American edition of *Marius*.

WALTER PATER to FREDERICK MACMILLAN, [*c.*7 January 1892]
Ref.: Implied in letter of Macmillan to Pater, 8 January 1892 (Letter Book LXIII).
Subject: Pater proposes that the third edition of *Marius* (1892) 'return to the original form' and suggests an appointment the following week to discuss the idea with Macmillan.

WALTER PATER to FREDERICK MACMILLAN, [*c.*1 May 1892]
Ref.: Implied in letter of Macmillan to Pater, 2 May 1892 (Letter Book LXIV).
Subject: Pater proposes 2,000 copies for the third edition of *Marius*.

WALTER PATER to PERCY WILLIAM BUNTING, 23 October [1892]
Ref.: Letter to William Canton, 23 October [1892].
Subject: Pater accepts Bunting's proposal to print a paper on Plato.

WALTER PATER to HENRY JOHN COCKAYNE CUST, [October? 1892]
Ref.: J. W. Robertson, *The Life and Death of a Newspaper* (London: Methuen, 1952), 370.
Subject: Pater regrets his inability to write a review for the *Pall Mall Gazette*, of which Cust (see letter to *Pall Mall Gazette*, 14 November 1892, n. 1) had just become editor.

WALTER PATER to HENRY JOHN COCKAYNE CUST, [late December 1892?]
Ref.: Letter to *Pall Mall Gazette*, 14 November 1892.
Subject: 'Pater will do a Dante article'. The article proposed may be a review of Shadwell's edition of the *Purgatory* (1892) or an essay on Dante and medieval art, of which an incomplete draft can be found among the Harvard Pater MSS. No evidence in *The Pall Mall Gazette* has been found suggesting that Pater contributed a paper on Dante.

APPENDIX A: FURTHER LETTERS BY WALTER PATER 389

WALTER PATER to WILLIAM CANTON, [February 1893]
   Ref.: *American Book-Prices Current*, 40 (1935), 400.
   Subject: Pater presents a copy of *Plato and Platonism* to Canton [whose name is misread in the source as 'Cantor'].

WALTER PATER to GEORGE MACMILLAN, [*c.*11 June 1893]
   Ref.: Implied in a letter of Macmillan to Pater, 12 June 1889 (Letter Book LXVIII).
   Subject: Pater accepts Macmillan's proposal that he act as publisher's reader (at £2.2s.0d.) for a MS dealing with Plato's theory of education in *The Republic*, by A[rnold]. Guyot Cameron (1864–1947), American scholar and journalist.

WALTER PATER to the SECRETARY of the LONDON LIBRARY, 13 July [1893]
   Ref.: Letter to Gosse, 13 July [1893].
   Subject: Pater writes to decline the invitation to join the Library Committee.

WALTER PATER to FREDERICK MACMILLAN, [*c.*29 October 1893]
   Ref.: Letter of George Macmillan to Pater, dated 30 October 1893 (Letter Book LXX).
   Subject: Pater requests copies of the fourth edition of *The Renaissance* (1893).

ARTHUR SYMONS to WALTER PATER, [January 1894]
   Ref.: Letter of Pater to Symons, 17 January [1894].
   Subject: Symons invites Pater to contribute to the first number of *The Yellow Book*.

WALTER PATER to ARTHUR SYMONS, [June 1894?]
   Ref.: *American Book-Prices Current*, 48 (1942), 299.
   Subject: The letter, a correspondence card, was inserted into a copy of the Daniel Press edition of *An Imaginary Portrait: The Child in the House*; it may be a note presenting the book to Symons. The source gives no indication.

THOMAS WRIGHT to HESTER PATER, [early March 1904]
   Ref.: Thomas Wright, *Thomas Wright of Olney: An Autobiography* (London: Herbert Jenkins, 1936), 92–5.
   Subject: As a matter of courtesy, Wright arranges to call on the Pater sisters with the manuscript of *The Life of Walter Pater* (1907).

THOMAS WRIGHT to C. L. SHADWELL, [August 1906]
   Ref.: Shadwell's letter to Wright, dated 27 August 1906.
   Subject: Wright sends Shadwell details of his biography of Pater and asks the latter for his assistance.

APPENDIX B

Index of Correspondents

The following lists the recipients of Pater's letters, and those of Clara and Hester Pater, included in this volume.

Adams, Robert Dudley 175
Ainslie, Douglas 194, 198, 211, 249, 270, 272, 274–5, 310
Allen, Mr 270
Armour, George Allison 229–30
Bainton, George 199, 258
Barnes, Mr 124
Barnett, John Francis 132
Barrington, Emilie Isabel 233, 266–7
Benson, Arthur Christopher 294–5
Berenson, Bernard 208
Boulton, Howard Edward 188, 202
Bourget, Paul 150, 155–6
Browne, [Charles Gordon?] 59
Browning, Oscar 82–3, 104–8, 119–20, 124
Bunting, Percy William 278, 280, 298, 388
Bury, Mr 242
Butler, Alfred Joshua 130, 335, 339–40
Campbell, Lewis 326–7
Canton, William 281–4, 286, 290–2, 295–9, 313–16, 327–8, 388–9
Chapman, John 36–7, 60, 62, 73
Clark, Messrs R. and R. 203–4, 235
Clark, William Robinson 118
Colles, William Morris 330–1
Congreve, Fr 343–4
Conway, Moncure Daniel 386
Cotton, James Sutherland 249
Cradock, Edward Hartopp 61, 133–4
Cust, Henry J. C. 306, 388
Daniel, Charles Henry Olive 125–7
Daniel, Emily Crabb 320–1, 325, 328
Dilke, Lady (Emilia Francis Strong Pattison Dilke) 179–80, 277
Dyer, Louis 275
Ellerton, Francis George 119

Ernst, Carl Wilhelm 177–8
Escott, Thomas Sweet 123
Eyre, Edward Vincent 310–12
Field, Michael 236–7, 256, 263, 291–2, 305, 341, 345
Fitch, William Clyde 261, 279
Fletcher, Julia Constance 137–8, 386
Furley, G. 49–50
Furnivall, Frederick James 81–2
Galton, Arthur 232, 387
Gardner, Isabella Stewart 171, 180–1
Gosse, Edmund 64, 87, 96, 98–9, 102, 128–9, 167, 182, 187, 193, 218, 301–3, 305, 308–10, 312–13, 341–3, 384
Grant Duff, Sir Mountstuart 83, 172, 195, 214, 226, 252, 267–8, 290
Gray, John Miller 109–10, 131, 166–7
Green, Charlotte Symonds 38–9, 188–9
Grissell, Hartwell de la Garde 99
Grove, George 105–7, 109, 116, 386
Harris, Frank 271–2
Hertz, Fanny 386
Hopkins, Gerard Manley 120
Horne, Herbert 182–3, 194–5, 198, 200–1, 207, 211–12, 216, 219, 223–4, 228, 231–2, 239, 250–1, 293
Image, Selwyn 387
Jebb, Richard Claverhouse 130–1
Jeens, Charles Henry 385–6
Johnson, Lionel 253–4, 307
Knowles, James Thomas 319–20, 323, 326
Lane, John 40, 322–4
Lathbury, Bertha Penrose 245
Le Gallienne, Richard 300, 304
MacColl, Dugald Sutherland 137, 144, 174
MacColl, Norman 213
Mackail, John William 145–6
Macmillan, Alexander 65–7, 69–72, 77, 85–6, 89–96, 101, 103, 110–11, 113–15, 117, 120–1, 156–8, 170–2, 385
Macmillan, Frederick 286, 336–7, 349–51, 354, 356–7, 367, 369–71, 374, 376, 378–82, 388–9
Macmillan, George 288–9, 331, 375, 381, 388–9
Madan, Falconer 146–7, 201, 260, 320
[Marzials, Franck Thomas] 232
Matheson, Percy Ewing 166
Melvill, Harry Edward 214–15
Molesworth, Mary Cicely 273
Moore, George 196–7, 209–10

APPENDIX B: INDEX OF CORRESPONDENTS 393

Morley, John 63, 79
Moulton, Ellen Louise Chandler 237–9, 243, 254–5, 260, 273
Nattali, Benjamin 238
Nevill, Lady Dorothy 274
Nicholson, Edward W. B. 142, 169
Nicoll, Henry James 134
Noel, Roden 75
Paget, Violet (Vernon Lee) 134–6, 140–2, 145, 147–9, 152–4, 160, 364, 366
Pall Mall Gazette 183–4, 299–300
Pater, Clara 332–3, 355–60, 362, 365–8
Pater, Hester 333–4, 336–8, 340, 344–54, 370–5, 377–80, 382–4, 389
Pater, Frederic Loudon 192
Pater, Walter Horatio 66–9, 71–2, 74, 76–9, 84–5, 87–93, 95–7, 103, 110, 112,
    114–17, 121–2, 154, 157–63, 165–6, 170, 172–4, 190–1, 202, 206–7, 210, 219,
    225, 234, 241–3, 248, 253, 255, 257, 259, 262–5, 267, 279–80, 283, 287–9,
    292, 296, 299, 301–2, 307, 309, 314
Patmore, Coventry 261–2
Pendergast, John 34, 51–2, 54–7, 59, 385
Peto, Harold Ainsworth 185–6, 190
Raffalovich, Marc André 151, 154–5, 159, 181, 186
Raffalovich, Marie 155
R. Clay, Sons and Taylor, Messrs 386
Robertson, Graham Walford 285, 310
Rolleston, Humphry Davy 269–70
Rothenstein, William 315–16, 318, 321–2
Rowley, Charles 88
Sadler, Michael Ernest 284–5
Saintsbury, George 84
Sayle, Charles Edward 167–8
Scott, [William Bell?] 64–5, 136–7, 197–8
Secretary of the London Library 389
Shadwell, Charles Lancelot 58, 342, 359, 389
Sharp, William 138–40, 143, 151–2, 163–4, 178, 193, 203, 216, 229, 245–7
Sieveking, Albert Forbes 173
Squire, William Barclay 220–1
Stillman, Marie 233–4
Swinburne, Algernon Charles 74
Symonds, John Addington 385
Symons, Arthur 185, 191, 196–7, 205–6, 213–14, 217–18, 220, 222–4, 227, 230–1,
    234–5, 240, 243–5, 252, 254, 264–5, 269, 271, 318–19, 328–9, 387, 389
Thursfield, James Richard 125, 304
Tichener, Edward Bradford 207–8, 212
Trower, Helen 179
Unknown 79, 118, 131, 189, 194, 200, 221, 226–8, 232, 244, 258–9, 276, 293, 387

Urquhart, Francis Fortescue 276–7
Verschoyle, John Stuart 225–6, 228, 240, 247
Waddington, Samuel 246
Ward, Mary Arnold 160–1, 168–9, 176, 209, 283
Ward, T. Humphry 146
Warren, Thomas Herbert 329, 338–9
Watkins, Philip Morgan 324–5
Waugh, Arthur 312
Wedmore, Frederick 162, 266, 317
White, Miss 257
Wightwick, Thomas Norman 50–1, 53
Wilde, Oscar 97–8, 100–2, 104, 108–9, 215, 251, 256, 388
Wilkinson, Jonas Niel Lyte 265–6
Withers, William Stanley 178–9
Woods, Margaret Louisa 277–8
Woodward, Mrs 347–8
Wright, Thomas 358–9, 361–5

APPENDIX C
Sources of MS. Letters

Academy 307
Amaranth and Asphodel 130
Amherst College 279
Art of Authorship, The 199
Autograph Prices Current 218
Bates College 38, 119, 167–8, 188–9, 194, 198, 211, 233, 249, 266–7, 270, 273–5, 310, 327–8, 330–1
Berenson, Bilbioteca (Florence) 208, Villa I Tatti 208
Blackfriars Priory, Oxford 151, 159, 181, 186
Bodleian Libraries 51–2, 55, 120, 146–7, 169, 201, 260, 277–8, 320, 341–4, 347–8
Bonhams Catalogue 259
Boston College 261–2
Boston Public Library 270
Brasenose College, Oxford 34, 40, 55–9, 61, 63, 83, 125, 132–4, 162, 185–6, 188, 193–4, 203–6, 214–15, 217–18, 235, 238, 244–6, 252–4, 266, 276–7, 281–6, 290–2, 295–9, 304, 309, 313–15, 317, 323–5, 361, 365
British Columbia, University of 136–7
British Library 66–72, 74, 76–7, 84–99, 101, 103, 105–7, 109–117, 120–3, 128–9, 154, 156–63, 165–6, 170–4, 179–80, 190–1, 202, 206–7, 210, 219, 225, 241–4, 248, 253, 255, 257, 259, 262–5, 267, 277, 279–80, 283, 286–9, 292, 296, 299, 301–2, 307, 309, 312–14, 331–40, 344–60, 362, 365–84
Browning, Oscar 82–3
California at Los Angeles, University of 100–2, 104, 108–9, 130–1, 192, 225–6, 228, 240, 247, 251, 256, 258
Chicago, University of 278, 280, 298
Christie's Catalogue 75, 154–5, 257, 306
Church and Parish Chronicle 310–11
Colby College 135–6, 145, 147–9, 152–4, 160, 364, 366
Columbia University 177–8
Cornell University 207–8, 212
Critic 312
Delaware, University of 182–3, 194–8, 200–1, 207, 211–12, 216, 219, 223–4, 228, 231, 239, 250–1, 276, 293–5, 328–9
Early Life of and Letters of John Morley 79
Eisner, Steven J. 213

Elton, Leonard S. 174
Fels Library, Paris 150, 155–6
Field, Michael, Journal of 234–5
Fitch, Clyde, and His Letters 261
Folger Shakespeare Library, Washington DC 224
Francis Edwards Catalogue 222–3
Gardner Museum (Isabella Stewart), Boston 180–1, 190
Glasgow, University of 137, 144
Glass, Sam S. 213–14
Glauber, Cynthia Rich 258
Gonzaga University 59
Gosse, Edmund, The Library of 305
Grant, Sheila Sokolov 172, 195, 214, 226, 267–8, 290
Grolier Club 229–30
Hart-Davis, Sir Rupert 173
Harvard University 209–10, 230–1, 264–5, 269, 310, 315–16, 318, 321–2, 386
Huntington Library, California 81–2, 125–7, 285
Indiana University 326–7, 358–9, 361–5
Ishikawa, Daichi 80, 99
John Miller Gray 109–10, 131–2, 166–7
Kansas, University of 118, 191
King's College, Cambridge 104–8, 119–20, 124
King's School, Canterbury 49–51, 53, 137–8, 242
Kopnicki, Ronald J. 221
Leeds, University of 64, 87, 96, 102, 167, 182, 218, 301–3, 308–10, 342–3, 384
Lhombreaud, Roger A. 185, 196–7, 222, 227, 230, 271, 318–19
Library of Congress, Washington DC 237–9, 243, 254–5, 260, 273
Macmillan, 1843–1943, The House of 65–6
Magdalen College, Oxford 329, 338–9
Maggs Bros. *Catalogue* 64–5, 134, 142, 166, 187, 249
Manchester Central Library 88, 178–9
Michigan, University of 60, 254
Monsman, Gerald C. 232, 252
Moorman, Mary 160–1, 168–9, 209
Morgan Library & Museum, New York 197, 202, 217, 220, 322
New York Public Library, Berg Collection 140–1
New York University 62, 300, 304
New Zealand, National Library of 175
Northwestern University 131, 233–4, 272, 319–20, 323, 326
O'Gorman, Francis 124
Pall Mall Gazette 183–4, 299–300
Pall Mall Magazine 196
Princeton University 215, 227, 315–16
private 145–6

Realm 216
Saintsbury, George, *A History of English Prose Rhythm* 84
Seeney, Michael 200, 269–70
Sharp, Noel F. 245–7
Sharp, William [Chair of English Literature] 229
Sharp, William (Fiona Macleod) by Elizabeth A. Sharp 138–40, 143, 151–2, 163–4, 178, 203
Smith College, Northampton, Mass. 232
Smythe, Colin 243
Sotheby, Wilkinson & Hodge Catalogue 179
Sotheran's Price Current of Literature 54, 385
Study of Walter Pater, A 234–5
Texas, University of 97–8, 236–7, 256, 265–6, 271–2, 275, 291–2, 305, 341, 345
Tucker, Paul 279
Ward, Mrs. Humphry, The Life of 283
Willis, Irene Cooper 32
Wong, Alex 189
Worcester College, Oxford 320–1, 325, 328
Wordsworth, The Life of Bishop John 77–8
Wright, Samuel 244
Yale University 36, 73
York University 240

BIBLIOGRAPHY

Walter Pater's Manuscripts and Papers

Brasenose College Archives, University of Oxford, PP1 B2/1.
Pater Collection, Houghton Library, Harvard University, bMS Eng 1150.

Other Archives

Oscar Browning Letters, King's College Archives, Cambridge, OB/1/1248/A.
Michael Field Papers, British Library, Brit Lib Add MS 46777.
Edmund Gosse, 'The Book of Gosse', Cambridge University Library, MS. Add. 7034.
Edmund Gosse Collection, Cambridge University Library, MS. Add. 7020, 7021.
Macmillan Archives, Brit Lib Add MSS 54786–56035 (including the Macmillan Letter Books, 55030–55542, containing the Pater–Macmillan correspondence).
Mark Pattison Papers, Bodleian Library, Oxford, MS. Pattison 130.
Arthur Symons Papers, British Library, Brit. Lib. Add. MS. 49522.

Published Sources

Abbott, Evelyn, and Lewis Campbell, *The Life and Letters of Benjamin Jowett*, 2 vols (London: John Murray, 1897).
Adams, James Eli, *Dandies and Desert Saints: Styles of Victorian Masculinity* (Ithaca, N.Y.: Cornell University Press, 1995).
Adams, James Eli, 'Gentleman, Dandy, Priest: Manliness and Social Authority in Pater's Aestheticism', *English Literary History*, 59.2 (Summer 1992), 441–66.
Agnew, Lois, 'Vernon Lee and the Victorian Aesthetic: "Feminine Souls" and Shifting Sites of Contest', *Nineteenth-Century Prose*, 26.2 (1999), 127–42.
Ainslie, Douglas, *Adventures Social and Literary* (London: T. Fisher Unwin, 1922).
Ainslie, Douglas, *Escarlamonde and Other Poems* (London: George Bell & Sons, 1893).
Aldington, Richard, ed., 'Introduction', *Walter Pater: Selected Works* (London: William Heinemann, 1948), 1–27.
Alighieri, Dante, *Dante's Divine Comedy: The Inferno, a Literal Prose Translation*, by John Aitken Carlyle (London: Chapman and Hall, 1847).
Alighieri, Dante, *The Divine Comedy of Dante Alighieri*, trans. Henry Wadsworth Longfellow, 3 vols (London: Routledge, 1867).
Alighieri, Dante, *The New Life of Dante Alighieri*, trans. Charles Eliot Norton (Boston: Ticknor and Fields, 1867).
Alighieri, Dante, *The Poems of the Vita Nuova and Convito*, trans. C. Lyell (London: C. F. Molini, 1842).

Alighieri, Dante, *The Vision: or Hell, Purgatory, and Paradise of Dante Alighieri*, trans. H. F. Cary, 3 vols (London: Taylor and Hessey, 1819).
Allen, Grant, 'Decay of Criticism', *Fortnightly Review*, ns 37 (March 1882), 339–51.
Allen, Grant, 'The New Hedonism', *Fortnightly Review*, ns 55 (March 1894), 377–92.
Allott, Kenneth, 'Pater and Arnold', *Essays in Criticism*, 2 (April 1952), 219–21.
[Althaus, T. F.], 'Recollections of Mark Pattison', *Temple Bar*, 73 (January 1885), 31–49.
Altholz, Josef L., 'A Tale of Two Controversies: Darwinism and the Debate over *Essays and Reviews*', *Church History*, 63.1 (March 1994), 50–9.
Altick, Richard, *The English Common Reader: A Social History of the Mass Reading Public, 1800–1900* (Chicago: University of Chicago Press, 1967).
Andrews, Kit, 'The Figure of Watteau in Walter Pater's "Prince of Court Painters" and Michael Field's *Sight and Song*', *English Literature in Transition*, 53.4 (2010), 451–84.
Andrews, Kit, 'Walter Pater as Oxford Hegelian: *Plato and Platonism* and T. H. Green's *Prolegomena to Ethics*', *Journal of the History of Ideas*, 72.3 (July 2011), 437–59.
Annan, Noel, *The Dons: Mentors, Eccentrics, and Geniuses* (London: Harper-Collins, 1999).
Anstruther, Ian, *Oscar Browning: A Biography* (London: John Murray, 1983).
Appleman, Philip, '1859 and the Idea of Crisis: General Introduction', in *1859: Entering an Age of Crisis*, ed. Philip Appleman, William A. Madden, and Michael Wolff (Bloomington: Indiana University Press, 1959), 13–28.
Arnold, Ethel M., 'Social Life in Oxford', *Harper's New Monthly Magazine*, 82 (July 1890), 246–56.
Arnold, Matthew, *The Complete Prose Works of Matthew Arnold*, ed. R. H. Super, 11 vols (Ann Arbor: University of Michigan Press, 1960–77).
Ashton, Rosemary, *142 Strand: A Radical Address in Victorian London* (London: Chatto & Windus, 2006).
Atkinson, G. T., 'Oscar Wilde at Oxford', *Cornhill Magazine*, 66 (May 1929), 559–64.
Austin, Alfred, *Savonarola: A Tragedy* (London: Macmillan, 1881).
[Austin, Alfred], 'University Culture and its Results', *Temple Bar*, 36 (1872), 124–34.
Bacon, Francis, *Novum Organum* [1620], in *The Collected Works of Francis Bacon*, vol. 4, ed. James Spedding, Robert Leslie Ellis, and Douglas Denon Heath (London: Longmans, 1857–74).
Bailey, John, *John Bailey 1864–1931: Letters and Diaries*, ed. by his wife (London: John Murray, 1935).
Bainton, George, *The Art of Authorship: Literary Reminiscences, Methods of Work, and Advice to Young Beginners, Personally Contributed to by Leading Authors of the Day* (London: J. Clarke, 1890).
Ball, Douglas, *Victorian Publishers' Bindings* (London: Library Association, 1985).
Bann, Stephen, ed., *The Reception of Walter Pater in Europe* (London: Thoemmes Continuum, 2004).

Barber, Giles, 'Rossetti, Ricketts, and Some English Publishers' Bindings of the Nineties', *Library*, 25 (March 1990), 314–30.
Barolsky, Paul, *Walter Pater's Renaissance* (University Park: Pennsylvania State University Press, 1987).
Barrington, Emilie Isabel, *The Reality of the Spiritual Life* (Edinburgh: David Douglas, 1889).
Barrington, Emilie Isabel, *A Retrospect and Other Articles* (London: Osgood, McIlvaine, 1896).
[Barry, William Francis], 'Latter-Day Pagans', *Quarterly Review*, 182 (July 1895), 31–58.
[Barry, William Francis], 'Neo-Paganism', *Quarterly Review*, 172 (April 1891), 273–304.
Bassett, Sharon, et al., 'Dating the Pater Manuscripts in the Harvard Library', *Pater Newsletter*, 25 (Fall 1990), 2–8.
Batchelor, John, *Lady Trevelyan and the Pre-Raphaelite Brotherhood* (London: Chatto & Windus, 2006).
Baudelaire, Charles, *Écrits sur l'art*, ed. Francis Moulinat (Paris: Librairie Générale Française, 1999).
Baudelaire, Charles, *Les fleurs du mal* [1857], 5th edn (Paris: Michel Lévy, 1876).
Baudelaire, Charles, 'The Painter of Modern Life' [1863], *The Painter of Modern Life and Other Essays*, trans. and ed. Jonathan Mayne (London: Phaidon Press, 1964), 1–41.
Becker-Leckrone, Megan, 'Pater's Critical Spirit', in *Transparencies of Desire*, ed. Laurel Brake, Lesley Higgins, and Carolyn Williams (Greensboro, N.C.: ELT Press, 2002), 286–97.
Beckson, Karl, *Arthur Symons: A Life* (Oxford: Clarendon Press, 1987).
Beckson, Karl, et al., *Arthur Symons: A Bibliography* (Greensboro, N.C.: ELT Press, 1990).
Benson, A. C., 'Oscar Browning', in *Memories and Friends* (London: John Murray, 1924), 128–46.
Benson, A. C., *Walter Pater* (London: Macmillan, 1906).
Berenson, Bernard, *The Venetian Painters of the Renaissance* (New York and London: G. P. Putnam's Sons, 1894).
Bischoff, S.J., Anthony, *St. Aloysius: The First Eighty Years, 1875–1955* (Oxford: Oxford University Press, 1955).
Bizzotto, Elisa, 'Dis-Continuous Relations', *Rivista di Studi Vittoriani*, 19.20 (2015), 53–68.
Bizzotto, Elisa, 'The Imaginary Portrait: Pater's Contribution to a Literary Genre', in *Transparencies of Desire*, ed. Laurel Brake, Lesley Higgins, and Carolyn Williams (Greensboro, N.C.: ELT Press, 2002), 213–23.
Blake-Hill, Philip V., 'The Macmillan Archive', *British Museum Quarterly*, 36 (Autumn 1972), 74–80.
Bloom, Harold, 'The Crystal Man', in *Selected Writings of Walter Pater* (New York: New American Library, 1974), vii–xxxi.
Bourget, Paul, 'As Others See Us', *Oxford Magazine*, 24 October 1883, 320–1.

Bourget, Paul, *Essais de psychologie contemporaine* (Paris: Alphonse Lemerre, 1883).
Bourget, Paul, *Études et portraits* (Paris: Alphonse Lemerre, 1906).
Bourget, Paul, *L'irréparable* (Paris: Alphonse Lemerre, 1884).
Bowers, Fredson, 'Bibliography and the University', *University of Pennsylvania Library Chronicle*, 15 (1949), 37–51.
Bowra, C. M., 'Walter Pater', *Sewanee Review*, 57 (Summer 1949), 378–400. Rptd in *Inspiration and Poetry* (London: Macmillan, 1955), 199–219.
Brake, Laurel, 'After *Studies*: Walter Pater's Cancelled Book, or *Dionysus* and Gay Discourse in the 1870s', in *Beauty and the Beast*, ed. P. Liebregts and Wim Tigges (Amsterdam: Rodopi, 1996), 115–26.
Brake, Laurel, 'Better Together: The Paters and *Ink Work*', *Life Writing*, 14.2 (2017), 257–65.
Brake, Laurel, 'A Commentary on "Arezzo": An Unpublished Manuscript by Walter Pater', *Review of English Studies*, ns 27 (August 1976), 266–76.
Brake, Laurel, 'The Discourses of Journalism: "Arnold and Pater" Again—and Wilde', in *Pater in the 1990s*, ed. Laurel Brake and Ian Small (Greensboro, N.C.: ELT Press, 1991), 43–61.
Brake, Laurel, 'Judas and the Widow: Thomas Wright and A. C. Benson as Biographers of Walter Pater', *Prose Studies*, 4 (1981), 39–54.
Brake, Laurel, 'Michael Field in Their Time and Ours', *Tulsa Studies in Women's Literature*, 29.1 (Spring 2010), 159–79.
Brake, Laurel, 'Pater the Journalist: *Essays from The Guardian*', *English Literature in Transition*, 56.4 (2013), 483–96.
Brake, Laurel, *Print in Transition: Studies in Media and Book History* (London: Palgrave, 2001).
Brake Laurel, *Subjugated Knowledges: Journalism, Gender and Literature in the Nineteenth Century* (New York: New York University Press, 1994).
Brake, Laurel, 'Vernon Lee and the Pater Circle', in *Vernon Lee: Decadence, Ethics, Aesthetics*, ed. Catherine Maxwell and Patricia Pulham (Basingstoke: Palgrave Macmillan, 2006), 40–57.
Brake, Laurel, *Walter Pater* (Plymouth: Northcote House, 1994).
Brake, Laurel, and Anne Humphreys, 'Critical Theory and Periodical Research', *Victorian Periodicals Newsletter*, 22.3 (1989), 1–17.
Brake, Laurel, and Ian Small, eds, *Pater in the 1990s* (Greensboro, N.C.: ELT Press, 1991).
Brake, Laurel, Lesley Higgins, and Carolyn Williams, eds, *Transparencies of Desire* (Greensboro, N.C.: ELT Press, 2002).
Bristow, Joseph, '"A Complex Multiform Creature": Wilde's Sexual Identities', in *The Cambridge Companion to Oscar Wilde*, ed. Peter Raby (Cambridge: Cambridge University Press, 1997), 195–217.
Bristow, Joseph, *Effeminate England: Homoerotic Writing after 1885* (Buckingham: Open University Press, 1995).
Bristow, Joseph, ed., *Wilde Discoveries: Traditions, Histories, Archives* (Toronto: University of Toronto Press, 2013).

Brittain, Vera, *The Women at Oxford: A Fragment of History* (New York: Macmillan, 1960).
Brock, M. G., and M. C. Curthoys, eds, *The History of the University of Oxford*, 8 vols (Oxford: Clarendon Press, 1997–2000).
Browning, Oscar, *Goethe: His Life and Writings* (London: Swan Sonnenschein, 1892).
Browning, Oscar, *Memories of Sixty Years at Eton, Cambridge, and Elsewhere* (London: Bodley Head, 1910).
Browning, Oscar, 'Recollections', *Cam*, 14 February 1906, 4–5.
Browning, Robert, *Parleyings with Certain People of Importance in their Day* (London: Smith & Elder, 1887).
Bruder, Anne, 'Constructing Artist and Critic between J. M. Whistler and Oscar Wilde: "In the Best Days of Art there were no Art-Critics"', *English Literature in Transition*, 47.2 (2004), 161–80.
Bruford, W. H., *The German Tradition of Self-Cultivation: 'Bildung' from Humboldt to Thomas Mann* (Cambridge: Cambridge University Press, 1975).
Bruford, W. H., 'Goethe, Walter Pater, and "the Aesthetic Consciousness"', in *Festschrift for E. W. Herd*, ed. August Obermayer (Dunedin: University of Otago Press, 1980), 44–54.
Buchan, John, 'Nine Brasenose Worthies', *Brasenose Quatercentenary Monographs*, 2 vols (Oxford: Clarendon Press, 1909), vol. 2, part 2, 3–30.
Bullen, J. B., 'The Historiography of *Studies in the History of the Renaissance*', in *Pater in the 1990s*, ed. Laurel Brake and Ian Small (Greensboro, N.C.: ELT Press, 1991), 155–67.
Bullen, J. B., *The Myth of the Renaissance in Nineteenth-Century Writing* (Oxford: Clarendon Press, 1994).
Burstein, Janet, 'Victorian Mythography and the Progress of the Intellect', *Victorian Studies*, 18.3 (March 1975), 309–24.
Bury, Richard de, *The Philobiblon of Richard de Bury*, ed. Andrew Fleming West (New York: Grolier Club, 1889).
[Bussell, F. W.], 'Walter Pater', *Oxford Magazine*, 17 October 1894, 7–8.
Butler, Alfred Joshua, *Amaranth and Asphodel: Poems from the Greek Anthology* (Oxford: Basil Blackwell, 1922).
Butler, Alfred Joshua, *Amaranth and Asphodel: Songs from the Greek Anthology* (London: Kegan Paul, 1881).
Caine, T. Hall, *Recollections of Dante Gabriel Rossetti* (London: Elliott Stock, 1882).
Campbell, Kate, 'W. E. Gladstone, W. T. Stead, Matthew Arnold, and a New Journalism: Cultural Politics in the 1880s', *Victorian Periodicals Review*, 36.1 (Spring 2003), 20–40.
Canton, William, *The Invisible Playmate: A Story of the Unseen* (London: Isbister, 1894).
Canton, William, *A Lost Epic and Other Poems* (Edinburgh and London: William Blackwell and Sons, 1887).
Canton, William, 'New Corn from Old Fields', *Good Words*, 33 (August 1892), 545–49.

Canton, William, *The Poems of William Canton*, ed. Guy D. Canton (London: G. G. Harrap, 1927).
Capes, William W., 'Sermon on the New "Humanitarian Culture"', *Oxford Undergraduates' Journal*, 27 (November 1873), 98–9.
Card, Tim, *Eton Renewed: A History from 1860 to the Present Day* (London: John Murray, 1994).
Carlyle, Thomas, 'Death of Goethe', *New Monthly Magazine*, 34.138 (June 1832), 507–12.
Carlyle, Thomas, 'Goethe', *Foreign Review*, 2 (July 1828), 80–127.
Carlyle, Thomas, 'Goethe's Helena', *Foreign Review*, 1 (April 1828), 429–68.
Carlyle, Thomas, *The Life of Friedrich Schiller* (London: Taylor and Hessey, 1825).
Carlyle, Thomas, *Sartor Resartus* (London: Chapman and Hall, 1838).
Carrier, David, 'Baudelaire, Pater, and the Origins of Modernism', *Comparative Criticism*, 17 (1995), 109–21.
Carrier, David, 'Walter Pater's "Winckelmann"', *Journal of Aesthetic Education*, 35.1 (2001), 99–109.
Carroll, Lewis, *see* Dodgson, Charles.
Cary, Richard, 'Vernon Lee's Vignettes of Literary Acquaintances', *Colby Library Quarterly*, 9.3 (September 1970), 179–99.
Catton, Lucien, *Essai sur Walter Pater* (Paris: Libraire Picart, 1936).
Cecil, David, 'Walter Pater', in *The Fine Art of Reading, and Other Studies* (London: Constable, 1957), 203–21.
Chambers, David, and Martyn Oud, *The Daniel Press in Frome* (Bath: Old School Press, 2011).
Chandler, Edmund, *Pater on Style* (Copenhagen: Rosenkilde and Bagger, 1958).
Chapman, Alfred K., 'Thomas Bird Mosher', *Colby Library Quarterly*, 4 (February 1959), 229–44.
Charteris, Evan, *The Life and Letters of Sir Edmund Gosse* (London: William Heinemann, 1931).
Cheeke, Stephen, 'Pateresque: The Person, the Prose Style', *Cambridge Quarterly*, 46.3 (September 2017), 251–69.
Child, Ruth C., *The Aesthetic of Walter Pater* (New York: Macmillan, 1940).
'Civil Lists Pensions' [for Hester Pater and Clara Pater], *The Times*, 12 July 1895, 4.
Clarendon, Edward Hyde, *History of the Rebellion and Civil Wars in England* (Oxford: at the Theatre, 1704).
Clark, William Robinson, *Savonarola: His Life and Times* (London: Society for Promoting Christian Knowledge, 1878).
Clements, Elicia, and Lesley Higgins, eds, *Victorian Aesthetic Conditions: Pater across the Arts* (Basingstoke: Palgrave Macmillan, 2010).
Clements, Patricia, *Baudelaire and the English Tradition* (Princeton: Princeton University Press, 1985).
Clements, Patricia, '"Strange Flowers": Some Notes on the Baudelaire of Swinburne and Pater', *Modern Language Review*, 76 (January 1981), 20–30.
Coates, John, 'Controversial Aspects of Pater's Style', *Papers on Language and Literature*, 40.4 (Fall 2004), 384–411.

Coates, John, 'Pater's Apologia: "The Child in the House"', *Essays in Criticism*, 54.2 (April 2004), 144–64.

Cockshut, A. O., *Truth to Life: The Art of Biography in the Nineteenth Century* (London: Collins, 1974).

Cohen, Morton, N., 'Lewis Carroll and the House of Macmillan', *Browning Institute Studies*, 7 (1979), 31–70.

Cohen, Morton N., and Anita Gandolfo, eds, *Lewis Carroll and the House of Macmillan* (Cambridge: Cambridge University Press, 1964).

Cohen, Rachel, 'The Very Bad Review' [Edmund William Gosse and John Churton Collins], *New Yorker*, 6 October 2003, 52–67.

Colby, Vineta, *Vernon Lee: A Literary Biography* (Charlottesville: University of Virginia Press, 2003).

[Collins, John Churton], 'English Literature at the Universities', *Quarterly Review*, 163 (October 1886), 289–309.

Collins, L. C., *Life and Memoirs of John Churton Collins* (London: The Bodley Head, 1912).

Colvin, Sidney, *Children in Italian and English Design* (London: Seeley, Jackson, and Halliday, 1872).

Colvin, Sidney, 'English Painters and Painting in 1867', *Fortnightly Review*, ns 2 (October 1867), 464–76.

Colvin, Sidney, 'English Painters of the Present Day. IV. Simeon Solomon', *Portfolio*, 1 (March 1870), 33–5.

Colvin, Sidney, *Memoirs and Notes of Persons and Places: 1852–1912* (London: E. Arnold, 1921).

Colvin, Sidney, 'A Note on Simeon Solomon', *Westminster Review*, ns 35 (April 1869), 595–6.

Comparato, Frank E., *Books for the Millions: A History of the Men whose Methods and Machines Packaged the Printed Word* (Harrisburg, Penn.: Stackpole, 1971).

Conlon, John J., 'Three Letters of Walter Pater', *Notes and Queries*, ns 22.3 (August 1973), 317–18.

Conlon, John J., *Walter Pater and the French Tradition* (Lewisburg, Oh.: Bucknell University Press, 1982).

Conroy, Carolyn, '"He hath Mingled with the Ungodly": The Life of Simeon Solomon after 1873, with a Survey of the Extant Works' (Diss.., University of York, 2009).

'The Corridors of Time: A Retrospect', *Clarendonian*, 1 (January 1920), 105–07.

Coste, Bénédicte, 'Two Unpublished Letters from Walter Pater to Paul Bourget', *Pater Newsletter*, 61/62 (Spring/Fall 2012), 4–20.

C[otton], J. S., 'Walter Pater', *Academy*, 11 August 1894, 102.

Court, Franklin E., *Walter Pater: An Annotated Bibliography of Writings about Him* (De Kalb: Northern Illinois University Press, 1980).

Courthope, W. J., 'Wordsworth and Gray', *Quarterly Review*, 141 (January 1876), 104–36.

Crawford, Robert, 'Pater's Renaissance, Andrew Lang, and Anthropological Romanticism', *English Literary History*, 53.4 (Winter 1986), 849–79.

Creighton, Louise, *The Life and Letters of Mandell Creighton*, 2 vols (London: Longmans, Green, 1904).
Crinkley, Richmond, *Walter Pater: Humanist* (Lexington: University of Kentucky Press, 1970).
Croft-Cooke, Rupert, *Feasting with Panthers: A New Consideration of Some Late Victorian Writers* (London: Holt, Rinehart and Winston, 1967).
Crook, J. Mordaunt, *Brasenose: The Biography of an Oxford College* (Oxford: Oxford University Press, 2008).
Cruise, Colin, ed., *Love Revealed: Simeon Solomon and the Pre-Raphaelites* (London and New York: Merrel, 2005).
Curtius, Ernst, *The History of Greece*, trans. Adolphus William Ward, 5 vols (London: R. Bentley, 1868–73).
Daley, Kenneth, 'Pater's Books and the *Collected Works* Digital Archive', *Pater Newsletter*, 61/62 (Spring/Fall 2012), 43–56.
Daley, Kenneth, *The Rescue of Romanticism: Walter Pater and John Ruskin* (Athens, Ohio: Ohio University Press, 2001).
Daniel, Charles Henry, *The Garland of Rachel* (Oxford: H. Daniel, 1881).
'Daniel Macmillan', *The Times*, 5 September 1882, 3.
Darwin, Charles, *On the Origin of Species* (London: John Murray, 1859).
d'Aurevilly, J. A. Barbey, *Of Dandyism and of George Brummell*, trans. Douglas Ainslie (London: J. M. Dent, 1897).
Davis, Michael, 'The Sexual Position of Walter Pater', *Pater Newsletter*, 52 (Spring 2007), 45–51.
'Death of Mr. Macmillan', *The Times*, 27 January 1896, 10.
'Death of Mr. Swinburne', *The Times*, 12 April 1909, 12.
'Death of Mr. Whistler', *The Times*, 18 July 1903, 12.
'Death of the Rector of Lincoln', *The Times*, 31 July 1894, 6.
DeLaura, David, *Hebrew and Hellene in Victorian England: Newman, Arnold, and Pater* (Austin: University of Texas Press, 1969).
DeLaura, David, 'Reading Inman rereading Pater Reading: A Review Essay', *Pater Newsletter*, 26 (Spring 1991), 2–9.
Dellamora, Richard, 'The Androgynous Body in Pater's "Winckelmann"', *Browning Institute Studies*, 11 (1983), 51–68.
Dellamora, Richard, *Masculine Desire: The Sexual Politics of Victorian Aestheticism* (Chapel Hill: University of North Carolina Press, 1990).
Denney, Colleen, *At the Temple of Art: The Grosvenor Gallery, 1877–1890* (Cranbury, N.J.: Associated University Presses, 2000).
d'Hangest, Germain, *Walter Pater. L'homme et l'oeuvre*, 2 vols (Paris: Didier, 1961).
Dilke, Sir Charles W., 'Memoir', in Emilia Dilke, *The Book of the Spiritual Life* (London: John Murray, 1905), 1–128.
Dilke, Lady Emilia, *The Book of the Spiritual Life*, by the late Lady Dilke, with a Memoir of the Author by the Rt. Hon. Sir Charles W. Dilke (London: John Murray, 1905).
Dodgson, Charles Lutwidge, *Alice's Adventures in Wonderland* (London: Macmillan, 1865).

Dodgson, Charles Lutwidge, *Through the Looking Glass* (London: Macmillan, 1871).
Donoghue, Denis, 'The Man Who Suffers, the Mind that Creates', *New York Times Book Review*, 11 March 1984, 31–3.
Donoghue, Denis, *Walter Pater: Lover of Strange Souls* (New York: Alfred A. Knopf, 1995).
Donoghue, Emma, *We are Michael Field* (London: Bell, 1998).
Doughty, Oswald, *A Victorian Romantic: Dante Gabriel Rossetti* (London: Oxford University Press, 1960).
Douglas, Lord Alfred, *Autobiography* (London: Martin Secker, 1929).
Douglas, Lord Alfred, *Oscar Wilde and Myself* (New York: Duffield, 1914).
Douglas, Lord Alfred, 'Pater and Dorian Gray', *The Times Literary Supplement*, 12 August 1939, 479.
Dowling, Linda, 'The Aesthete and the Eighteenth-Century', *Victorian Studies*, 20.4 (Summer 1977), 357–77.
Dowling, Linda, *Hellenism and Homosexuality in Victorian Oxford* (Ithaca, NY: Cornell University Press, 1994).
Dowling, Linda, *Language and Decadence in the Victorian Fin de Siècle* (Princeton, N.J.: Princeton University Press, 1986).
Dowling, Linda, 'Ruskin's Pied Beauty and the Constitution of a "Homosexual" Code', *Victorian Newsletter*, 75 (Spring 1989), 1–8.
Dowling, Linda, 'Walter Pater and Archaeology: The Reconciliation with Earth', *Victorian Studies*, 31 (Winter 1988), 209–31.
'Dr. C. L. Shadwell', Obituary, *The Times*, 14 February 1919, 10.
Duclaux, Mary [née Robinson], 'Souvenirs de Walter Pater', *Revue de Paris*, 15 January 1925, 339–58.
Dyer, Louis, *Studies of the Gods in Greece at Certain Sanctuaries Recently Excavated* (London: Macmillan, 1891).
Eastham, Andrew, *Aesthetic Afterlives: Irony, Literary Modernity, and the Ends of Beauty* (London: Continuum, 2011).
Edel, Leon, *Henry James: A Life* (New York: Harper and Row, 1985).
Edwards, D. L., *A History of the King's School, Canterbury* (London: Faber, 1957).
Eliot, T. S., 'Arnold and Pater', *The Bookman*, 72 (September 1930), 1–7. Rptd in *Selected Essays* (London: Faber, 1951), 431–43.
Eliot, T. S., 'The Place of Pater', rptd in *The Eighteen-Eighties*, ed. Walter de la Mare (Cambridge: Cambridge University Press, 1930), 93–106.
Ellegard, Alvar, *Darwin and the General Reader* (Chicago: University of Chicago, 1958).
Ellis, Ieuan Pryce, '*Essays and Reviews* Reconsidered', *Theology*, 74 (1871), 394–404.
Ellmann, Richard, 'James among the Aesthetes', in *Henry James and Homo-Erotic Desire*, ed. John R. Bradley (London: Macmillan, 1999), 25–44.
Ellmann, Richard, 'Oscar at Oxford', *New York Review of Books*, 29 March 1984, 23–8.
Ellmann, Richard, *Oscar Wilde* (New York: Alfred A. Knopf, 1988).
Embury, J. W., 'Fifty Years Ago', *Clarendonian*, 1 (July 1919), 66–8.
Engel, A. J., *From Clergyman to Don: The Rise of the Academic Profession in Nineteenth-Century Oxford* (Oxford: Clarendon Press, 1983).

Escott, T. H. S., *Club Makers and Club Members* (London: T. Fisher Unwin, 1914).
Escott, T. H. S., *England: Its People, Polity, and Pursuits*, 2 vols (London: Cassell, Peter, 1879).
Escott, T. H. S., *Masters of English Journalism: A Study of Personal Forces* (London: T. Fisher Unwin, 1911).
Escott, T. H. S., 'Some Oxford Memories of the Prae-Aesthetic Age', *National Review*, 24 (October 1895), 232–44.
Escott, T. H. S., 'Walter Pater and Other Memories', *Bookman's Journal and Print Collector*, 10 (July 1924), 109–11.
Esdaile, Arundell, 'The New Hellenism', *Fortnightly Review*, ns 88 (1910), 707–22.
Essays and Reviews, ed. [Henry Bristow Wilson] (London: John W. Parker and Son, 1860).
Evangelista, Stefano, *British Aestheticism and Ancient Greece: Hellenism, Reception, Gods in Exile* (London: Palgrave Macmillan, 2009).
Evangelista, Stefano, 'The German Roots of British Aestheticism: Pater's "Winckelmann", Goethe's Winckelmann, and Pater's Goethe', in *Anglo-German Affinities and Antipathies*, ed. Rüdiger Görner (Munich: Ludicium, 2004), 57–70.
Evangelista, Stefano, '"Life in the Whole": Goethe and English Aestheticism', *Publications of the English Goethe Society*, 82.3 (December 2013), 180–92.
Evangelista, Stefano, '"Outward Nature and the Moods of Men": Romantic Mythology in Pater's Essays on Dionysus and Demeter', in *Transparencies of Desire*, ed. Laurel Brake, Lesley Higgins, and Carolyn Williams (Greensboro, N.C.: ELT Press, 2002), 107–18.
Evangelista, Stefano, 'Platonic Dons, Adolescent Bodies: Benjamin Jowett, John Addington Symonds, Walter Pater', in *Children and Sexuality*, ed. G. Rousseau (London: Palgrave Macmillan, 2007), 206–35.
Evangelista, Stefano, 'A Revolting Mistake: Walter Pater's Iconography of Dionysus', *Victorian Review*, 34.2 (Fall 2008), 200–18.
Evangelista, Stefano, 'Walter Pater: The Queer Reception', *Pater Newsletter*, 52 (Spring 2007), 17–24.
Evangelista, Stefano, 'Walter Pater Unmasked: Impressionistic Criticism and the Gender of Aesthetic Writing', *Literature Compass*, 1.1 (2004), 1–4.
Evangelista, Stefano, and Katherine Harloe, 'Pater's "Winckelmann"', in *Pater the Classicist: Classical Scholarship, Reception, and Aestheticism*, ed. Charles Martindale, Stefano Evangelista, and Elizabeth Prettejohn (Oxford: Oxford University Press, 2017), 63–80.
Evans, Lawrence, 'Walter Pater', in *Victorian Prose: A Guide to Research*, ed. David DeLaura (New York: Modern Language Association, 1973), 321–59.
Faber, Geoffrey, *Jowett: A Portrait with Background* (London: Faber & Faber, 1957).
Farnell, Lewis Richard, *An Oxonian Looks Back* (London: M. Hopkinson, 1934).
Farrar, Frederic William, 'The Voice of History', in *The Silence and the Voices of God, with other Sermons* (London: Macmillan, 1874), 51–68.
Fichte, J. G., *On the Nature of the Scholar* (London: J. Chapman, 1845).

Field, Michael, *Binary Star: Leaves from the Journal and Letters of Michael Field, 1846–1914*, ed. Ivor C. Treby (Bury St Edmunds, Suffolk: De Blackland Press, 2006).
Field, Michael, *Long Ago* (London: George Bell and Sons, 1889).
Field, Michael, 'Original Verse: Walter Pater', *Academy*, 11 August 1894, 102.
Field, Michael, *Sight and Song* (London: Elkin Mathews and John Lane, 1892).
Field, Michael, *Stephania: A Trialogue* (London: Elkin Mathews and John Lane, 1893).
Field, Michael, *The Tragic Mary* (London: George Bell and Sons, 1890).
Field, Michael, *Works and Days: From the Journal of Michael Field*, ed. T. and D. C. Sturge Moore (London: John Murray, 1933).
Fitch, William Clyde, *Clyde Fitch and His Letters*, ed. Montrose J. Moses and Virginia Gerson (Boston: Little, Brown, 1924).
Fitch, William Clyde, *The Knighting of the Twins, and Ten Other Tales* (Boston: Roberts Brothers, 1891).
Flaubert, Gustave, *Trois contes* (Paris: G. Charpentier, 1877).
Fletcher, Constance Julia, *A Nile Novel* (London: Macmillan, 1876).
Fletcher, Ian, 'The 1890s: A Lost Decade', *Victorian Studies*, 4 (June 1961), 345–54.
Fletcher, Ian, 'The Art of the High Wire: Pater in Letters' [with Donald Gordon], *The Times Literary Supplement*, 26 February 1971, 229–31.
Fletcher, Ian, 'Herbert Horne: The Earlier Phase', *English Miscellany*, 21 (1959), 117–57.
Fletcher, Ian, *Rediscovering Herbert Horne: Poet, Architect, Typographer, Art Historian* (Greensboro, N.C.: ELT Press, 1990).
Fletcher, Ian, *Swinburne* (Harlow, Essex: Longmans Green, 1973).
Fletcher, Ian, *Walter Pater* (London: Longmans Group, 1959; revised, 1971).
Fletcher, Ian, 'In the Way of an Introduction: *Marius* Past and Present', *English Literature in Transition*, 27.1 (1984), 5–10.
Fletcher, Ian, *W. B. Yeats: And His Contemporaries* (Brighton: Harvester, 1987).
Foldy, Michael S., *The Trials of Oscar Wilde: Deviance, Morality, and Late-Victorian Society* (New Haven: Yale University Press, 1997).
Ford, Julia Ellsworth, *Simeon Solomon: An Appreciation* (New York: Frederic Fairchild Sherman, 1907).
Foster, Joseph, *The Register of Admissions to Gray's Inn, 1521–1889: Together with the Register of Marriages in Gray's Inn Chapel, 1695–1754* (London: Hansard Publishing Union, 1889).
Francis, Mark, 'The Origin of *Essays and Reviews*: An Interpretation of Mark Pattison in the 1850s', *Historical Journal*, 17.4 (1974), 797–811.
Franklin, Colin, *Poets of the Daniel Press* (Cambridge: Rampant Lions Press, 1988).
Franklin, Colin, *The Private Presses* (London: Studio Vista, 1969).
Fraser, Hilary, *The Victorians and Renaissance Italy* (Oxford: Blackwell, 1992).
Frazer, Adrian, *George Moore, 1852–1933* (New Haven: Yale University Press, 2000).

Fredeman, William E., 'The Bibliographical Significance of a Publisher's Archive', *Studies in Bibliography*, 23 (1970), 183–91.

Fredeman, William E., 'The Letters of Pictor Ignotus: William Bell Scott's Correspondence with Alice Boyd, 1859–1884', *Bulletin of the John Rylands Library*, 58.1 (1975), 66–111.

F. [Freeman, J. E.], 'In Pater's Rooms', *Speaker*, 26 August 1899, 207–08.

Friedman, Arthur, 'Principles of Historical Annotation in Critical Editions of Modern Texts', *English Institute Annual* (New York: Columbia University Press, 1942), 115–28.

Fyffe, C. A., 'Study and Opinion in Oxford', *Macmillan's Magazine*, 21 (December 1869), 184–92.

Gagel, Amanda, 'Letters as Critical Texts', *Scholarly Editing*, 36 (2015), www.scholarlyediting.org/2015/essays/essay.gagel.html.

Gagel, Amanda, 'Selected Letters of Vernon Lee, 1856–1935', 2 vols (Diss., Boston University, 2008).

Gagnier, Regenia, *Idylls of the Marketplace: Oscar Wilde and the Victorian Public* (Stanford, CA: Stanford University Press, 1986).

Galton, Francis, 'Composite Portraits', *Journal of the Anthropological Institute*, 1 (1879), 132–48.

Gautier, Léon, *La chanson de Roland*, 2 vols (Tours: Alfred Mame et fils, 1872).

Gautier, Théophile, *Les beaux-arts en Europe* (Paris: Michel Lévy, 1855).

Gautier, Théophile, *Mademoiselle de Maupin* [1835], trans. Helen Constantine (London: Penguin, 2005).

Gissing, Alfred C., *William Holman Hunt: A Biography* (London: Duckworth, 1936).

Gladstone, William E., '*Robert Elsmere* and the Battle of Belief', *The Nineteenth Century*, 23 (May 1888), 766–88.

Glaister, Geoffrey Ashall, *Glossary of the Book* (London: George Allen and Unwin, 1960).

Goethe, J. W. von, *Poetry and Truth {Dichtung und Wahrheit}* (1811–33), trans. John Oxenford (London: Henry G. Bohn, 1848).

Goethe, J. W. von, *Wilhelm Meister's Apprenticeship {Wilhelm Meisters Lehrjahre}* (1795–96), trans. Thomas Carlyle (Edinburgh: Oliver & Boyd, 1824).

Goethe, J. W. von, *Winckelmann and His Century {Winckelmann und sein Jahrhundert in Briefen und Aufsätzen}* (1805), trans. and ed. Hugh Barr Nisbet in *German Aesthetic and Literary Criticism: Winckelmann, Lessing, Hamann, Herder, Schiller, Goethe* (Cambridge: Cambridge University Press, 1985), 236–58.

Goldhill, Simon, *Who Needs Greek? Contests in the Cultural History of Hellenism* (Cambridge: Cambridge University Press, 2002).

Goldman, Lawrence, 'Oxford and the Idea of a University in Nineteenth-Century Britain', *Oxford Review of Education*, 30.4 (December 2004), 575–92.

Goldring, Douglas, *The Last Pre-Raphaelite: A Record of the Life and Writing of Ford Madox Ford* (London: Macdonald, 1948).

Gopnik, Adam, 'The Invention of Oscar Wilde', *New Yorker*, 18 May 1998, 76–82, 84–6, 88.

Gosse, Edmund, *Ernest Renan: In Memoriam* (London: Macmillan, 1893).
Gosse, Edmund, *Father and Son: A Study of Two Temperaments* (London: William Heinemann, 1907).
Gosse, Edmund, *French Profiles* (New York: Dodd, Mead, 1905).
Gosse, Edmund, *From Shakespeare to Pope: An Inquiry into the Causes and Phenomena of the Rise of Classical Poetry in England* (Cambridge: Cambridge University Press, 1885).
Gosse, Edmund, *Gray* (London: Macmillan, 1882).
Gosse, Edmund, *The Library of Edmund Gosse*, ed. E. H. M. Cox (London: Dulau, 1924).
Gosse, Edmund, *The Life of Algernon Charles Swinburne* (London: Macmillan, 1917).
Gosse, Edmund, *Life of William Congreve* (London: Walter Scott, 1888).
Gosse, Edmund, 'Lord Arthur Russell', *Proceedings of the Royal Geographical Society*, 14 (May 1892), 328–41.
Gosse, Edmund, *Madrigals, Songs and Sonnets* (London: Longmans, Green, 1870).
Gosse, Edmund, *Notes from a Diary, 1851–1972*, 14 vols (London: John Murray, 1897–1905).
Gosse, Edmund, 'A Plea for Certain Exotic Forms of Verse', *Cornhill Magazine*, 26 (July 1877), 53–71.
Gosse, Edmund, *Questions at Issue* (London: William Heinemann, 1893).
Gosse, Edmund, *The Secret of Narcisse: A Romance* (London: William Heinemann, 1892).
Gosse, Edmund, *TransAtlantic Dialogue: Selected American Correspondence of Edmund Gosse*, ed. Paul F. Mattheisen and Michael Millgate (Austin: University of Texas Press, 1965).
Gosse, Edmund, *The Unknown Lover: A Drama for Private Acting* (London: Chatto & Windus, 1878).
Gosse, Edmund, 'Walter Pater: A Portrait', *Contemporary Review*, 66 (December 1894), 795–810. Rptd in *Critical Kit-Kats* (London: William Heinemann, 1896), 241–71.
Graham, John William, *The Destruction of Daylight: A Study in the Smoke Problem* (London: George Allen, 1907).
Grant Duff, Mountstuart, *Studies in European Politics* (London: Edmonston and Douglas, 1886).
Graves, Charles L., *Life and Letters of Alexander Macmillan* (London: Macmillan, 1910).
Gray, John, *The Poems of John Gray*, ed. Ian Fletcher (Greensboro, N.C.: ELT Press, 1988).
Gray, John Miller, 'David Scott: R.S.A.', *Blackwood's Edinburgh Magazine*, 130 (November 1881), 589–611.
Gray, John Miller, *John Miller Gray: Memorial and Remains*, ed. J. Balfour Paul and W. R. Macdonald, 2 vols (Edinburgh: David Douglas, 1895).
Gray, Thomas, *The Works of Thomas Gray in Prose and Verse*, ed. Edmund Gosse, 4 vols (London: Macmillan, 1884).

Green, John Richard, *A Short History of the English People* (London: Macmillan, 1874).
Green, V. H. H., *Oxford Common Room: A Study of Lincoln College and Mark Pattison* (London: Edward Arnold, 1957).
Greenslet, Ferris, *Walter Pater* (New York: McClure, Phillips, 1903).
Greg, W. W., 'The Rationale of Copy-Text', *Studies in Bibliography*, 3 (1950–1), 19–36.
Grieve, Alastair, 'Rossetti's Applied Art Designs (2): Book-Bindings', *Burlington Magazine*, 115 (February 1973), 79–84.
Grissell, Hartwell de la Garde, *Ritual Inaccuracies; Or, Errors Commonly Made in the Celebration of the Holy Eucharist* (London: J. Masters, 1865).
Gross, John, *The Rise and the Fall of the Man of Letters* (London: Penguin Books, 1969).
Grosskurth, Phyllis, *Havelock Ellis: A Biography* (London: Allan Lane, 1980).
Grosskurth, Phyllis, *John Addington Symonds: A Biography* (London: Longmans, Green, 1964).
Grosskurth, Phyllis, 'Swinburne and Symonds: An Uneasy Literary Relationship', *Review of English Studies*, ns 14.55 (August 1963), 257–68.
Grote, George, *History of Greece*, 12 vols (London: John Murray, 1846–56).
Grove, George, *Dictionary of Music and Musicians*, 4 vols (London: Macmillan, 1879–90).
Guiney, Louise, *Goose-Quill Papers* (Boston: Roberts Brothers, 1885).
Guiney, Louise, *Songs at the Start* (Boston: Cupples, Upham, 1884).
Gunn, Peter, *Vernon Lee: Violet Paget, 1856–1935* (Oxford: Oxford University Press, 1964).
Gurney, Emelia Russell, *Dante's Pilgrim's Progress* (London: Elliot Stock, 1893).
Gurr, A. J., '*Macmillan's Magazine*', *Review of English Literature*, 6 (January 1965), 39–55.
Hagiwara, Hiroko, *Walter Pater and his Circle*, intro. by Tatsuhiko Arakawa (Tokyo: Yushodoh, 1984).
Haight, Gordon S., *George Eliot & John Chapman: With Chapman's Diaries* (New Haven: Yale University Press, 1940).
Halsband, Robert, 'Editing the Letters of Letter-Writers', *Studies in Bibliography*, 11 (1958), 25–37.
Harland, Henry, *Grandison Mather; Or an Account of the Fortunes of Mr. and Mrs. Thomas Gardiner* (New York: Cassell, 1889).
Harland, Henry, *Mea Culpa: A Woman's Last Word* (New York: J. W. Lovell, 1891).
Harland, Henry, *Two Voices* (New York: Cassell, 1890).
Harris, R. J., 'Emilia Francis Strong: Portraits of a Lady', *Nineteenth-Century Fiction*, 8.2 (September 1953), 81–98.
Harris, Frank, 'A Modern Idyll', *Fortnightly Review*, ns 55 (June 1891), 985–1008.
Harris, Frank, *Oscar Wilde: His Life and Confessions* (New York: Covici Friede, 1930).
Harris, Frank, 'Walter Pater', *Academy*, 28 October 1911, 530–1.
Harris, Frank, 'Walter Pater', *Contemporary Portraits*, 2nd series (New York: privately printed, 1919), 203–26.

Harris, Frank, 'Walter Pater: The Pagan', *John Bull*, 8 September 1906, 329–30.
Harris, Wendell, 'Ruskin and Pater—Hebrew and Hellene—Explore the Renaissance', *Clio*, 17.2 (1988), 173–85.
Harrison, Frederick, 'Neo-Christianity', *Westminster Review*, 18 (October 1860), 293–332.
Harrison, Frederick, 'Thoughts by the Way. II. The Aesthete', *Pall Mall Gazette*, 3 May 1882, 4.
Harrison, John Smith, 'Pater, Heine, and the Old Gods of Greece', *PMLA*, 39 (September 1924), 655–86.
Harvard Guide to American History, The, ed. Oscar Handlin et al. (Cambridge, Mass.: Belknap Press, 1974).
Hatch, Ethel, 'Walter Horatio Pater', *Brazen Nose*, 13 (1964), 254.
Hegel, G. W. F., *Aesthetics: Lectures on Fine Art {Vorlesungen über die Ästhetik}* [1835–8], trans. T. M. Knox (Oxford: Clarendon, 1975).
Hegel, G. W. F., *Phenomenology of Mind {Phänomenologie des Geistes}* [1807], trans. J. B. Bailliee (London: Swan Sonnenschein, 1910).
Herrick, Robert, *Hesperides: Poems by Robert Herrick*, ed. Herbert Horne (London: Walter Scott, 1887).
Hext, Kate, 'Recent Scholarship on Walter Pater: "Antithetical Scholar of Understanding's End"', *Literature Compass*, 5.2 (2008), 407–23.
Hext, Kate, *Walter Pater: Individualism and Aesthetic Philosophy* (Edinburgh: Edinburgh University Press, 2013).
Higgins, Lesley, 'But Who is She? Forms of Subjectivity in Walter Pater's Writings', *Nineteenth-Century Prose*, 24.2 (1997), 37–65.
Higgins, Lesley, 'Hopkins and "The Jowler"', *Texas Studies in Literature and Language*, 31 (Spring 1989), 143–67.
Higgins, Lesley, 'Living Effectively: Charlotte Green and Walter Pater', *Studies in Walter Pater and Aestheticism*, 2 (Autumn 2016): 57–70.
Higgins, Lesley. 'Pater and the "Laws" of Victorian Iconography', *Journal of Pre-Raphaelite Studies*, ns 19 (Fall 2010), 66–82.
Higgins, Lesley, and David Latham, 'Privileging the Later Pater: The Choice of Copy-Text for *The Collected Works*', in *Testing New Opinions and Courting New Impressions: New Perspectives on Walter Pater*, ed. Anne-Florence Gillard-Estrada, Martine Lambert-Charbonnier, and Charlotte Ribeyrol (New York: Routledge, 2018), 37–50.
Hinchcliffe, Tanis, *North Oxford* (New Haven: Yale University Press, 1992).
Hinchliff, Peter, *Benjamin Jowett and the Christian Religion* (Oxford: Clarendon Press, 1987).
Hirsch, Jr., E. D., *Validity in Interpretation* (New Haven: Yale University Press, 1967).
Hirst, Francis Wrigley, *Early Life and Letters of John Morley*, 2 vols (London: Macmillan, 1927).
Holland, Vyvyan, *Son of Oscar Wilde* (London: Penguin Books, 1954).
Hopkins, Gerard Manley, *Correspondence 1852–1881*, ed. R. K. R. Thornton and Catherine Phillips, *The Collected Works of Gerard Manley Hopkins*, vol. 1 (Oxford: Oxford University Press, 2013).

Hopkins, Gerard Manley, *Oxford Essays and Notes*, ed. Lesley Higgins, *The Collected Works of Gerard Manley Hopkins*, vol. 4 (Oxford: Oxford University Press, 2006).

Horne, Herbert P., 'William Bell Scott', *Century Guild Hobby Horse*, ns 6 (January 1891), 16–27.

Horne, Philip, ed., *Henry James: A Life in Letters* (New York: Penguin, 1999).

Hough, Graham, *The Last Romantics* (London: Methuen, 1947).

Hughes, Gillian, 'Editing the Letters of a Scottish Author', *Studies in Scottish Literature*, 39.1 (2013), 31–7.

Hughes, Thomas, *Memoir of Daniel Macmillan* (London: Macmillan, 1883).

Hughes, Thomas, *Tom Brown's School Days* (London: Macmillan, 1857).

Hume, David, *A Treatise of Human Nature* [1738–40], in *Philosophical Works*, vol. 1 (Edinburgh: A. Black and W. Tait, 1826).

Huysmans, Joris-Karl, *Against Nature*, trans. Robert Baldick (Harmondsworth: Penguin, 1959).

Hyde, H. Montgomery, *The Cleveland Street Scandal* (New York: Coward, McGann and Geoghegan, 1976).

Hyde, H. Montgomery, *Lord Alfred Douglas: A Biography* (London: Methuen, 1984).

Hyde, H. Montgomery, *Oscar Wilde: A Biography* (London: Eyre Methuen, 1976).

Hyde, H. Montgomery, *The Trials of Oscar Wilde* (New York: Dover, 1962).

Inman, Billie Andrew, '"Dorian Gray" and the Theme of Subservience in Pater's Works of the 1890s', *Comparative Criticism*, 17 (1995), 85–107.

Inman, Billie Andrew, 'Estrangement and Connection: Walter Pater, Benjamin Jowett, and William M. Hardinge', in *Pater in the 1990s*, ed. Laurel Brake and Ian Small (Greensboro, N.C.: ELT Press, 1991), 1–20.

Inman, Billie Andrew, 'The Intellectual Context of Walter Pater's "Conclusion"', in *Walter Pater: An Imaginative Sense of Fact*, ed. Philip Dodd (London: Frank Cass, 1981), 12–30.

Inman, Billie Andrew, 'Pater's Appeal to His Readers: A Study of Two of Pater's Prose Styles', *Texas Studies in Literature and Language*, 14.4 (Winter 1973), 643–65.

Inman, Billie Andrew, 'Pater's Conception of the Renaissance: From Sources to Personal Ideal', *Victorian Newsletter*, 47 (Spring 1975), 19–24.

Inman, Billie Andrew, 'Pater's Letters at Pierpont Library', *English Literature in Transition*, 34.4 (1991), 410–12.

Inman, Billie Andrew, '"Sebastian van Storck": Pater's Exploration into Nihilism', *Nineteenth-Century Fiction*, 30.4 (March 1976), 457–76.

Inman, Billie Andrew, 'Tracing the Pater Legacy'; and 'Tracing the Pater Legacy, Part 2', *Pater Newsletter*, 11 (Spring 1983), 3; and 32 (Winter 1995), 3–8.

Inman, Billie Andrew, *Walter Pater and His Reading, 1874–1877: With a Bibliography of His Library Borrowings, 1878–1894* (New York: Garland, 1990).

Inman, Billie Andrew, *Walter Pater's Reading: A Bibliography of his Library Borrowings and Literary References, 1858–1873* (New York: Garland, 1981).

Inman, Billie Andrew, 'The Younger and the Older Pater: Some Textual Differences', *Pater Newsletter*, 38 (Spring 1999), 7–14.

'In Memoriam. Mark Pattison', *Academy*, 9 August 1884, 92–4.

International Library Company, *The International Library of Famous Literature, selections from the world's great writers, ancient, mediaeval, and modern, with biographical and explanatory notes and critical essays by many eminent writers*, ed. Richard Garnett et al., 20 vols (London: The Standard, 1899).

Iser, Wolfgang, *Walter Pater: The Aesthetic Moment*, trans. David Henry Wilson (Cambridge: Cambridge University Press, 1987).

Israel, Kali, *Names and Stories: Emilia Dilke and Victorian Culture* (New York: Oxford University Press, 1999).

Jackson, Thomas Graham, *Modern Gothic Architecture* (London: H. S. King, 1873).

Jackson, William Walrond, *Ingram Bywater: The Memoir of an Oxford Scholar, 1840–1914* (Oxford: Clarendon Press, 1917).

Jacobi, Charles R., *On the Making and Issuing of Books* (London: Elkin Mathews, 1891).

James, Elizabeth, 'The Macmillan Archive at the British Library', *Publishing History*, 32 (1992), 57–68.

James, Henry, *The Europeans: A Sketch* (London: Macmillan, 1878).

James, Henry, *Letters*, ed. Leon Edel, 4 vols (London: Macmillan, 1974–84).

James, Henry, 'Théophile Gautier', *North American Review*, 116 (April 1873), 310–29.

Jenkyns, Richard, *The Victorians and Ancient Greece* (Oxford: Basil Blackwell, 1980).

Johnson, Lionel, *The Collected Poems of Lionel Johnson*, ed. Ian Fletcher, 2nd edn (New York: Garland, 1982).

Johnson, Lionel, *The Complete Poems of Lionel Johnson*, ed. Ian Fletcher (London: Unicorn Press, 1953).

Johnson, Lionel, 'For a Little Clan', *Academy*, 23 October 1900, 314.

Johnson, Lionel, 'A Friend', *Spirit Lamp*, 4 (May 1893), 18–19.

Johnson, Lionel, 'A Note, upon Certain Qualities in the Writings of Mr. Pater: As Illustrated by his Recent Book', *Century Guild Hobby Horse*, 6 (January 1890), 36–40.

Johnson, Lionel, 'The Work of Mr. Pater', *Fortnightly Review*, ns 62 (September 1894), 352–67.

Jones, H. S., *Intellect and Character in Victorian England: Mark Pattison and the Invention of the Don* (Cambridge: Cambridge University Press, 2007).

Jopling, Louise, *Twenty Years of My Life* (London: John Lane, 1925).

Jordan-Smith, Paul, *For the Love of Books: The Adventures of an Impecunious Collector* (London: Oxford University Press, 1934).

Jowett, Benjamin, *College Sermons*, ed. E. H. Fremantle (London: J. Murray, 1896).

Jowett, Benjamin, *The Epistles of St. Paul to the Thessalonians, Galatians, Romans, with critical notes and dissertations*, 2 vols (London: John Murray, 1855).

Jowett, Benjamin, *Letters of Benjamin Jowett*, ed. Evelyn Abbott and Lewis Campbell (London: J. Murray, 1899).

Jowett, Benjamin, ed., *The Dialogues of Plato*, trans. into English with Analyses and Intros, 4 vols (Oxford: Clarendon, 1871).

Kaiser, Matthew, 'Pater's Mouth', *Victorian Literature and Culture*, 39 (2011), 47–64.

Kearney, Anthony, 'Settling Scores: Edmund Gosse on Mallock and Pater', *Pater Newsletter*, 63 (Spring 2013), 67–71.

Keble, John, *The Christian Year* (Oxford: J. Parker, 1827).

Kennedy, J. M., ed., *The Pater Calendar: A Quotation from the Works of Walter Horatio Pater, for Every Day of the Year* (London: Frank Palmer, 1913).

Kerlinger, F., *Foundations of Behavioural Research*, 2nd edn (New York: Holt, Rinehart, and Winston, 1973).

Kermode, Frank, *Romantic Image* (London: Routledge and Kegan Paul, 1957).

King, A., and A. F. Stuart, *The House of Warne* (London: Frederick Warne, 1965).

Kingsley, Charles, *Alton Locke, Tailor and Poet*, 2 vols (London: Chapman and Hall, 1850).

Knight, William, *Memoir of John Nichol* (Glasgow: James MacLehose, 1896).

Knoepflmacher, U. C., 'Pater's Religion of Sanity: *Plato and Platonism* as a Document of Victorian Unbelief', *Victorian Studies*, 6.2 (December 1962), 151–68.

Knoepflmacher, U. C., *Religious Humanism and the Victorian Novel: George Eliot, Walter Pater, and Samuel Butler* (Princeton, N.J.: Princeton University Press, 1965).

'Lady Dilke', *The Times*, 25 October 1904, 4.

Landor, Walter Savage, *Imaginary Conversations of Literary Men and Statesmen*, 5 vols (London: Taylor and Hessey, 1824–9).

Landow, George P., 'Walter Pater to Charles Rowley', *Notes and Queries*, ns 22.10 (October 1975), 44.

Lang, Andrew, 'Literary Chronicle', *Cosmopolis*, 1 (January 1896), 70–87.

Lang, Andrew, *Oxford*, rev. edn (London: Seeley, 1906).

Latham, David, '"Shadows Hot from Hell": Swinburne's Poethics', *Journal of Pre-Raphaelite Studies*, ns 18 (Spring 2009), 5–15.

Latham, David, 'A "World of Its Own Creation": Pre-Raphaelite Poetry and the New Paradigm for Art', *Journal of Pre-Raphaelite Studies*, ns 25 (Spring 2016), 5–27.

Lechmere, W. L., 'Oxford, 1863–1867', *Oxford and Cambridge Review*, 19 (1912), 78–118.

Lee-Hamilton, Eugene, *Apollo and Marsyas, and Other Poems* (London: Elliott Stock, 1884).

Lee-Hamilton, Eugene, *The New Medusa, and Other Poems* (London: Elliott Stock, 1882).

Lee, Vernon, *see* Paget, Violet.

Le Gallienne, Richard, 'On Re-Reading Walter Pater', *North American Review*, 195 (February 1912), 214–24.

Le Gallienne, Richard, *The Romantic '90s* (London: Putnam, 1925).

Lemerre, Alphonse, ed., *Le tombeau de Théophile Gautier* (Paris: A. Lemerre, 1873).
Levey, Michael, *The Case of Walter Pater* (London: Thames and Hudson, 1978).
Lewes, George Henry, *The Life of Goethe* (London: Smith, Elder, 1864).
Lhombreaud, Roger, *Arthur Symons: A Critical Biography* (London: Unicorn Press, 1963).
'Lionel Johnson', *Athenaeum*, 18 October 1902, 521.
'Literary Gossip', *Athenaeum*, 11 August 1894, 196.
Locke, John, *Essay Concerning Human Understanding* (Oxford: Oxford University Press, 1975).
Loesberg, Jonathan, *Aestheticism and Deconstruction: Pater, Derrida, and de Man* (Princeton, N.J.: Princeton University Press, 1991).
London University, *Chair of English Literature: Testimonials in Favour of Mr. William Sharp* (London: University of London Press, 1889).
Lucas, Francis, *Sketches of Rural Life and Other Poems* (London: Macmillan, 1889).
Lynch, Hannah, 'A. Mary F. Robinson', *Fortnightly Review*, ns 71 (February 1902), 260–76.
Lyons, Sara, *Algernon Swinburne and Walter Pater: Victorian Aestheticism, Doubt, and Secularism* (London: Legenda, 2015).
MacColl, D. S., 'A Batch of Memories. XII. Walter Pater', *Week-End Review*, 4 (December 1931), 759–60.
MacColl, D. S., 'Victorians at Oxford', *Times Literary Supplement*, 8 December 1945, 583.
MacColl, D. S., 'Walter Pater: A Correction', *Week-End Review*, 4 (December 1931), 796.
Mackail, J. W., *The Life of William Morris*, 2 vols (London: Longmans, Green, 1899).
Mackail, J. W., H. C. Beeching, and J. B. B. Nichols, eds, *Love in Idleness: A Volume of Poems* (London: Kegan Paul, Trench, 1883).
Mackarness, John Fielder, *A Charge Delivered in the Diocese of Oxford* (Oxford and London: J. P. Parker, 1875).
Macmillan and Co., *A Bibliographical Catalogue of Macmillan and Co.'s Publications from 1843 to 1889* (London: Macmillan, 1891).
Macmillan, Frederick, *The Net Book Agreement 1899* (Glasgow: Robert McLehose, 1924).
Macmillan, George A., *Letters of Alexander Macmillan* (London: Macmillan, 1908).
Macmillan, Malcolm, *Selected Letters of Malcolm Macmillan* (London: privately printed, 1893).
Mackmurdo, Arthur Heygate, *Wren's City Churches* (Orpington, Kent: G. Allen, 1883).
Madan, Falconer, *The Daniel Press: Memorials of C. H. O. Daniel, with a Bibliography of the Press, 1845–1919* (Oxford: Daniel Press, 1921).
Madan, Falconer, 'Notes on Brasenose Cricket', *Brasenose College Quatercentenary Monographs*, 2 vols (Oxford: Clarendon Press, 1909), vol. 2, pt. 2, 83–4.

Madan, Falconer, *Oxford Outside the Guide Books* (Oxford: Basil Blackwood, 1923).
Mallet, Charles Edward, *A History of the University of Oxford*, 3 vols (London: Methuen, 1924–7).
Mallock, William Hurrell, *Memoirs of Life and Literature* (London: Chapman and Hall, 1920).
Mallock, William Hurrell, *The New Republic; Or, Culture, Faith, and Philosophy in an English Country House*, 2 vols (London: Chatto and Windus, 1877). Rptd with an Intro by John Lucas (Leicester: Leicester University Press, 1975).
Mansfield, Elizabeth, 'Articulating Authority: Emilia Dilke's Early Essays and Reviews', *Victorian Periodicals Review*, 31 (Spring 1998), 75–86.
Manson, Edward, 'Recollections of Walter Pater', *Oxford Magazine*, 7 November 1906, 60–1.
Marshall, Alan, *Changing the Word: The Printing Industry in Transition* (London: Comedia Publishing Group, 1983).
Marshall, Arthur, *The Oxford Undergraduate of Twenty Years Ago* (London: R. Washbourne, 1874).
Martin, Robert K., 'Parody and Homage: The Presence of Pater in *Dorian Gray*', *Victorian Newsletter*, 63 (Spring 1983), 15–18.
Martindale, Charles, Stefano Evangelista, and Elizabeth Prettejohn, eds, *Pater the Classicist: Classical Scholarship, Reception, and Aestheticism* (Oxford: Oxford University Press, 2017).
Mason, Stuart Wilde [pseud. Christopher Sclater Millard], ed., *Bibliography of Oscar Wilde* (London: T. Werner Laurie, 1914).
Maxwell, Catherine, 'Pater and the Pre-Raphaelites', *Pater Newsletter*, 63 (Spring 2013), 77–90.
Maxwell, Catherine, and Patricia Pulham, eds, *Vernon Lee: Decadence, Ethics, Aesthetics* (Basingstoke: Palgrave Macmillan, 2006).
McGann, Jerome, *The Textual Condition* (Princeton, N.J.: Princeton University Press, 1991).
McGrath, F. C., *The Sensible Spirit: Walter Pater and the Modernist Paradigm* (Tampa: University of South Florida Press, 1986).
McKenna, Neil, *The Secret Life of Oscar Wilde* (New York: Basic Books, 2005).
Meisel, Perry, *The Absent Father: Virginia Woolf and Walter Pater* (New Haven: Yale University Press, 1980).
Men and Women of the Time: A Dictionary of Contemporaries, ed. George Washington Moon (London: George Routledge, 1891).
Metcalf, Priscilla, *James Knowles: Victorian Editor and Architect* (Oxford: Clarendon Press, 1980).
Meyers, Terry L., 'On Drink and Faith: Swinburne and John Nichol at Oxford', *Review of English Studies*, 55 (June 2004), 392–424.
'Michael Field', *The Times*, 28 September 1914, 10.
Michaelson, Alexander [Marc André Raffalovich], 'Walter Pater: In Memoriam', *Blackfriars*, 9 (August 1928), 463–71.
Michelet, Jules, *La Renaissance* (Paris: Chamerot Librairie-Éditeur, 1855).

Middleton, Bernard, *A History of English Craft Bookbinding Techniques* (London: Hafner Publishing, 1963).
Mill, J. S., *Autobiography*, intro. Harold J. Laski (London: Oxford University Press, 1969).
Mill, J. S., *On Liberty* (London: John W. Parker and Sons, 1859).
Miller, Andrew H., and James Eli Adams, eds, *Sexualities in Victorian Britain* (Bloomington: Indiana University Press, 1996).
Milton, John, *Milton's Poetical Works*, ed. David Masson (London: Macmillan, 1877).
'Miss E. E. Cooper', *The Times*, 15 December 1913, 10.
Mitchell, F. L., 'Walter Pater: A Study in Temperament', *Bookman's Journal and Print Collector*, 3 March 1920, 367.
Monsman, Gerald, 'Editing *Gaston de Latour*', in *Pater in the 1990s*, ed. Laurel Brake and Ian Small (Greensboro, N.C.: ELT Press, 1991), 21–32.
Monsman, Gerald, '*Gaston de Latour* and Pater's Art of Autobiography', *Nineteenth-Century Fiction*, 33 (March 1979), 33–41.
Monsman, Gerald, 'Old Mortality at Oxford', *Studies in Philology*, 67 (July 1970), 359–89.
Monsman, Gerald, 'Pater and his Younger Contemporaries', *Victorian Newsletter*, 48 (Fall 1975), 1–9.
Monsman, Gerald, 'Pater's Aesthetic Hero', *University of Toronto Quarterly*, 40 (Winter 1971), 136–51.
Monsman, Gerald, 'Pater's "Child in the House" and the Renovation of the Self', *Texas Studies in Literature and Language*, 28.3 (Fall 1985), 281–95.
Monsman, Gerald, *Pater's Portraits: Mythic Patterns in the Fiction of Walter Pater* (Baltimore: Johns Hopkins Press, 1967).
Monsman, Gerald, 'The Platonic Eros of Walter Pater and Oscar Wilde: "Love's Reflected Image" in the 1890s', *English Literature in Transition*, 45.1 (2002), 26–45.
Monsman, Gerald, 'On Reading Pater', in *Walter Pater: An Imaginative Sense of Fact* (London: Frank Cass, 1981), 1–11.
Monsman, Gerald, 'Two Pater Letters to George Bainton', *Pater Newsletter*, 63 (Spring 2013), 73–5.
Monsman, Gerald, *Walter Pater* (Boston: Twayne, 1977).
Monsman, Gerald, *Walter Pater's Art of Autobiography* (New Haven: Yale University Press, 1980).
Montgomery Hyde, H., *Oscar Wilde: A Biography* (London: Methuen, 1976).
Moore, George, *Avowals* (London: privately printed, 1919).
Moore, George, 'Avowals. VI. Walter Pater', *Pall Mall Magazine*, 33 (August 1904), 527–33.
Moore, George, *Confessions of a Young Man* (London: William Heinemann, 1888).
Moore, George, *A Mere Accident* (London: Vizetelly, 1887).
Moore, George, *Modern Painting* (London: Walter Scott, 1893).
Moore, Rayburn S., *The Correspondence of Henry James and the House of Macmillan, 1877–1914* (Baton Rouge: Louisiana State University Press, 1993).

Moran, James, *Clays of Bungay*, rev. edn (Bungay, Suffolk: Richard Clay, 1984).
Moran, Maureen, 'Walter Pater's House Beautiful and the Psychology of Self-Culture', *English Literature in Transition*, 50.3 (2007), 291–312.
Morgan, Charles, *The House of Macmillan: 1843–1943* (London: Macmillan, 1943).
Morgan, Thaïs, 'Reimagining Masculinity in Victorian Criticism: Swinburne and Pater', *Victorian Studies*, 36 (Spring 1993), 315–32.
Morison, Samuel Eliot, 'The Editing and Printing of Manuscripts', *Harvard Guide to American History*, ed. Oscar Handlin et al. (Cambridge, Mass.: Belknap Press, 1954), 95–104.
Morley, John, 'Mr. Pater's Essays', *Fortnightly Review*, ns 19 (April 1873), 469–77.
Morley, John, 'Reply to "Z." ', *Examiner*, 10 April 1873, 410.
Morris, William, *The Ideal Book* (London: Transactions of the Bibliographic Society, 1893). Rptd (London: L. C. C. Central School of Arts and Crafts, 1957).
Moulton, Louise Chandler, *In the Garden of Dreams: Lyrics and Sonnets* (Boston: Roberts Brothers, 1889).
'Mr. Arthur Symons', *The Times*, 25 January 1945, 7.
'Mr. Charles Henry Jeens', *Athenaeum*, 1 November 1879, 66–8.
'Mr. George Moore', *The Times*, 23 January 1933, 14.
'Mr. Humphry Ward', *The Times*, 19 May 1926, 21.
'Mr. Louis Dyer', *The Times*, 21 July 1908, 12.
'Mr. Oscar Browning', *The Times*, 8 October 1923, 17.
'Mr. Richard Le Gallienne', *The Times*, 16 September 1947, 6.
'Mr. Walter Pater', *The Times*, 31 July 1894, 10.
'Mr. Walter Pater', *Saturday Review*, 4 August 1894, 118–19.
'Mr. William Sharp', *The Times*, 15 December 1905, 6.
'Mrs. Humphry Ward.' *The Times*, 25 March 1920, 20.
Müller, K. O., *The History and Antiquity of the Doric Race*, trans. Henry Tufnell and George Cornewall Lewis, 2 vols (Oxford: Oxford University Press, 1830).
Mumby, Frank Arthur, and Ian Norrie, *Publishing and Bookselling* (London: Cape, 1974).
Nehamas, Alexander, *The Art of Living: Socratic Reflections from Plato to Foucault* (Berkeley: University of California Press, 1998).
Nelson, James G., 'The Bodley Head and the Daniel Press', *Papers of the Bibliographical Society of America*, 77.1 (1983), 35–44.
Nelson, James G., *The Early Nineties: A View from the Bodley Head* (Cambridge, Mass.: Harvard University Press, 1971).
Nettleship, Henry, *Lectures and Essays on Subjects Concerned with Latin Literature and Scholarship* (Oxford: Clarendon Press, 1885).
Newton, Charles Thomas, *Essays on Art and Archaeology* (London: Macmillan, 1886).
Nicholson, Edward Williams Byron, *Lord Jim: A Poem* (Oxford: privately printed, 1882).
Nietzsche, Friedrich, *The Birth of Tragedy*, trans. Walter Kaufmann (New York: Vintage, 1967).

Nietzsche, Friedrich, *Twilight of the Idols, or How to Philosophize with a Hammer*, trans. Richard Polt (Cambridge: Hackett Publishing, 1997).
Noel, Roden, *Essays upon Poetry and Poets* (London: Kegan Paul, Trench, 1886).
Noel, Roden, *The House of Ravenburg* (London: Daldy, Isbister, 1877).
Noel, Roden, *Life of Byron* (London: Walter Scott, 1890).
Noel, Roden, *A Little Child's Monument* (London: C. K. Paul, 1881).
Noel, Roden, *The Red Flag and Other Poems* (London: Strahan, 1872).
Noel, Roden, 'A Note on Walter Pater: By One who knew Him', *The Bookman*, 6 (September 1894), 173–5.
Nowell-Smith, Simon, ed., *Letters to Macmillan* (London: Macmillan, 1967).
'Obituary: Simeon Solomon', *The Times*, 19 August 1905, 5.
O'Faoláin, Seán, 'Pater and Moore', *Mercury*, 34 (August 1936), 330–38.
O'Gorman, Francis, 'Walter Pater and Oscar Browning: The "Last" Meeting', *Journal of Pre-Raphaelite Studies*, ns 20 (Fall 2011), 73–6.
Olmert, Michael, *The Smithsonian Book of Books* (Washington, DC: Smithsonian Books, 1992).
Østermark-Johansen, Lene, 'The Daniel Press Edition of Walter Pater's Last Book', *Journal of Pre-Raphaelite Studies*, ns 25 (Fall 2016), 73–86.
Østermark-Johansen, Lene, '"Don't forget your promise to come soon": Seven Unpublished Letters from Walter Pater to Oscar Browning', *Pater Newsletter*, 59.60 (Fall/Spring 2011), 17–31.
Østermark-Johansen, Lene, 'Pater and the "Painterly" Imaginary Portraits', *English Literature in Transition*, 56.3 (2013), 343–54.
Østermark-Johansen, Lene, *Walter Pater and the Language of Sculpture* (Farnham: Ashgate, 2011).
O'Sullivan, Vincent, *Aspects of Wilde* (London: Constable, 1936).
Owen, John, *The Sceptics of the French Renaissance* (London: Swan Sonnenschein, 1893).
Owen, John, 'The Oxford Conference on Secondary Education', *Oxford University Extension Gazette*, November 1893, 17–18.
P., 'Reputations Reconsidered. II. Walter Pater', *Academy*, 1 January 1897, 13–14.
Paget, Violet, 'Apollo the Fiddler: A Chapter in Artistic Anachronism', *Fraser's Magazine*, ns 26 (July 1882), 52–67.
Paget, Violet, *Baldwin: Being Dialogues on Views and Aspirations* (London: T. Fisher Unwin, 1886).
Paget, Violet, *Belcaro: Being Essays on Sundry Aesthetical Question* (London: W. Satchell, 1887).
Paget, Violet, 'Dionysus in the Euganean Hills: W. H. Pater in Memoriam', *Contemporary Review*, 120 (September 1921), 346–53.
Paget, Violet, *Euphorion: Being Studies of the Antique and Medieval in the Renaissance*, 2 vols (London: T. Fisher Unwin, 1884).
Paget, Violet, 'The Handling of Words: A Page of Walter Pater', *Life and Letters*, 9 (1933), 287–310.
Paget, Violet, *Hauntings and Other Fantastic Tales*, ed. Catherine Maxwell and Patricia Pulham (Peterborough, Ont.: Broadview, 2006).

Paget, Violet, *Juvenilia: Being a Second Series of Essays on Sundry Aesthetical Questions*, 2 vols (London: T. Fisher Unwin, 1887).
Paget, Violet, *Miss Brown: A Novel*, 3 vols (Edinburgh: W. Blackwood, 1884).
Paget, Violet, *Ottilie: An Eighteenth-Century Idyll* (London: T. Fisher Unwin, 1883).
Paget, Violet, 'The Portrait Art of the Renaissance', *Cornhill Magazine*, 47 (May 1886), 564–81. Rptd in *Euphorion* (1884).
Paget, Violet, *Renaissance Fancies and Studies: Being a Sequel to Euphorion* (London: Smith, Elder, 1895).
Paget, Violet, 'The Responsibilities of Unbelief', *Contemporary Review*, 43 (May 1883), 685–710. Rptd in *Baldwin* (1886).
Paget, Violet, *Vernon Lee's Letters*, ed. Irene Cooper Willis (London: privately printed, 1937).
Palgrave, Francis Turner, *Golden Treasury of English Songs and Lyrics* (London: Macmillan, 1861).
Pater, Walter, 'The Aesthetic Life', Houghton Library bMS 1150 (7).
Pater, Walter, 'The Age of Athletic Prizemen: A Chapter in Greek Art', *Contemporary Review*, 65 (February 1894), 242–56.
Pater, Walter, 'Amiel's Journal: The Journal Intime of Henri-Frédéric Amiel', *The Guardian*, 17 March 1886, 406–7.
Pater, Walter, *Appreciations: With an Essay on Style* (London: Macmillan, 1889).
Pater, Walter, 'Arezzo', Houghton Library bMS 1150 (24).
Pater, Walter, 'Aucassin et Nicolette', in *Studies in the History of the Renaissance* (1873), 1–17; revised as 'Two Early French Stories', in *The Renaissance: Studies in Art and Poetry* (1877; 1888; 1893).
Pater, Walter, 'The Bacchanals of Euripides', *Macmillan's Magazine*, 60 (May 1889), 63–72; revised in *The Bacchae of Euripides*, ed. Robert Yelverton Tyrrell (London: Macmillan, 1892).
Pater, Walter, 'The Beginnings of Greek Sculpture. I. The Heroic Age of Greek Art', *Fortnightly Review*, ns 33 (February 1880), 190–207.
Pater, Walter, 'The Beginnings of Greek Sculpture. II. The Age of Graven Images', *Fortnightly Review*, ns 33 (March 1880), 422–34.
Pater, Walter, 'The Character of the Humourist: Charles Lamb', *Fortnightly Review*, ns 30 (October 1878), 466–74.
Pater, Walter, *Classical Studies*, ed. Matthew Potolsky, *The Collected Works of Walter Pater*, vol. viii (Oxford: Oxford University Press, 2020).
[Pater, Walter], 'Coleridge's Writings', *Westminster Review*, 75 (January 1866), 106–32.
Pater, Walter, *Collected Works* [Edition de Luxe], 8 vols (London: Macmillan, 1900–01).
Pater, Walter, 'Corot and French Landscape Painting', Houghton Library bMS Eng 1150 (25).
Pater, Walter, 'Correspondence de Gustave Flaubert', *Athenaeum*, 3 August 1889, 155–6.

Pater, Walter, *Die Renaissance. Studien in Kunst und Poesie*, trans. Wilhelm Schölermann (Leipzig: Eugene Diederichs, 1902).
Pater, Walter, 'English Literature', Houghton Library bMS Eng 1150 (13).
Pater, Walter, *Essays from 'The Guardian'*, ed. Edmund Gosse (London: Macmillan, 1901). Rptd in *Collected Works* (London: Macmillan, 1910).
Pater, Walter, 'Evil in Greek Art', Houghton Library bMS Eng 1150 (15).
Pater, Walter, 'A Fragment on Sandro Botticelli', *Fortnightly Review*, ns 8 (August 1870), 155–60.
Pater, Walter, *Gaston de Latour: An Unfinished Romance*, ed. Charles L. Shadwell (London: Macmillan, 1896).
Pater, Walter, *Gaston de Latour*, ed. Gerald Monsman, *The Collected Works of Walter Pater*, vol. iv (Oxford: Oxford University Press, 2019).
Pater, Walter, 'Giordano Bruno. Paris: 1586', *Fortnightly Review*, ns 46 (August 1889), 234–44.
Pater, Walter, *Greek Studies: A Series of Essays*, ed. C. L. Shadwell (London: Macmillan, 1895).
Pater, Walter, 'Gustave Flaubert', Houghton Library bMS Eng 1150 (29).
Pater, Walter, 'The History of Philosophy', Houghton Library bMS Eng 1150 (3).
Pater, Walter, *An Imaginary Portrait: The Child in the House* (Oxford: H. Daniel, 1894).
Pater, Walter, 'Imaginary Portraits. 1. The Child in the House', *Macmillan's Magazine*, 38 (August 1878), 313–21.
Pater, Walter, 'Imaginary Portraits. 2. An English Poet', *Fortnightly Review*, ns 129 (April 1931), 433–48.
Pater, Walter, *Imaginary Portraits* (London: Macmillan, 1887).
Pater, Walter, *Imaginary Portraits*, ed. Lene Østermark-Johansen, *The Collected Works of Walter Pater*, vol. iii (Oxford: Oxford University Press, 2019).
Pater, Walter, 'Introduction', *The Purgatory of Dante Alighieri*, trans. Charles Lancelot Shadwell (London: Macmillan, 1892), xiii–xxviii.
Pater, Walter, 'Introduction to Greek Studies', Houghton Library bMS Eng 1150 (6).
Pater, Walter, 'Lacedaemon', *Contemporary Review*, 61 (June 1892), 791–808.
Pater, Walter, *Letters of Walter Pater*, ed. Lawrence Evans (Oxford: Clarendon Press, 1970).
Pater, Walter, 'The Life and Letters of Gustave Flaubert', *Pall Mall Gazette*, 25 August 1888, 1–2.
Pater, Walter, 'M. Lemaître's Serenus, and Other Tales', *Macmillan's Magazine*, 52 (November 1887), 71–80.
Pater, Walter, 'The Marbles of Aegina', *Fortnightly Review*, ns 33 (April 1880), 540–8.
Pater, Walter, *Marius the Epicurean: His Sensations and Ideas* (London: Macmillan, 1885).
Pater, Walter, *Marius the Epicurean: His Sensations and Ideas*, ed. Ian Small (Oxford: Oxford University Press, 1985).

Pater, Walter, *Miscellaneous Studies: A Series of Essays*, ed. C. L. Shadwell (London: Macmillan, 1895).
Pater, Walter, 'Moral Philosophy', Houghton Library bMS Eng 1150 (17).
Pater, Walter, *New Library Edition of the Works of Walter Pater*, 10 vols (London: Macmillan, 1910).
Pater, Walter, 'Notes on Leonardo da Vinci', *Fortnightly Review*, ns 12 (November 1869), 494–508.
Pater, Walter, 'Notre Dame de Troyes', Houghton Library bMS 1150 (20).
Pater, Walter, 'A Novel by Mr. Oscar Wilde', *The Bookman*, 1 (November 1891), 59–60.
Pater, Walter, 'On Love's Labour's Lost', *Macmillan's Magazine*, 53 (December 1885), 89–91.
Pater, Walter, 'On Wordsworth', *Fortnightly Review*, ns 21 (April 1874), 455–65.
Pater, Walter, 'Pascal', *Contemporary Review*, 47 (February 1895), 168–81.
Pater, Walter, 'Pico della Mirandola', *Fortnightly Review*, ns 16 (October 1871), 377–86.
Pater, Walter, *Plato and Platonism: A Series of Lectures* (London: Macmillan, 1893).
[Pater, Walter], 'Poems by William Morris', *Westminster Review*, 90 (October 1868), 300–12.
Pater, Walter, 'The Poetry of Michelangelo', *Fortnightly Review*, ns 16 (November 1871), 559–70.
Pater, Walter, 'Raphael', *Fortnightly Review*, ns 68 (October 1892), 458–69.
Pater, Walter, *The Renaissance*, ed. Lawrence Evans (Chicago: Academy Books, 1977).
Pater, Walter, *The Renaissance: Studies in Art and Poetry* (London: Macmillan, 1873).
Pater, Walter, *The Renaissance: Studies in Art and Poetry*, shilling edn (London: Macmillan, 1912).
Pater, Walter, *The Renaissance: Studies in Art and Poetry*, ed. Kenneth Clark (London: Collins, 1961).
Pater, Walter, *The Renaissance: Studies in Art and Poetry*, ed. Donald L. Hill (Berkeley: University of California Press, 1980).
Pater, Walter, [unsigned] review of *Love in Idleness* (1883), *Oxford Magazine*, 7 March 1883, 144–5.
Pater, Walter, 'Romanticism', *Macmillan's Magazine*, 35 (November 1876), 64–70.
Pater, Walter, 'Samuel Taylor Coleridge', in *The English Poets: Selections with Critical Introductions by Various Writers and a General Introduction by Matthew Arnold*, ed. T. Humphry Ward, 4 vols (London: Macmillan, 1880), 4: 102–14.
Pater, Walter, 'The School of Giorgione', *Fortnightly Review*, ns 28 (October 1877), 526–38.
Pater, Walter, *Sketches and Reviews* (New York: Boni and Liveright, 1919).
Pater, Walter, 'Some Great Churches of France. I. Notre-Dame d'Amiens', *The Nineteenth Century*, 35 (March 1894), 481–8.
Pater, Walter, 'Some Great Churches of France. II. Vézelay', *The Nineteenth Century*, 35 (June 1894), 963–70.
Pater, Walter, 'The Study of Dionysus. I. The Spiritual Form of Fire and Dew', *Fortnightly Review*, ns 26 (December 1876), 752–72.

Pater, Walter, *Uncollected Essays* (Portland, Maine: Thomas B. Mosher, 1903).
Pater, Walter, 'Vernon Lee's "Juvenilia"', *Pall Mall Gazette*, 5 August 1887, 5.
[Pater, Walter], 'Winckelmann', *Westminster Review*, 87 (January 1867), 80–110.
Pater, Walter, 'The Writings of Cardinal Newman', Houghton Library bMS Eng 1150 (12).
Patmore, Coventry, *The Angel in the House: The Betrothal* (London: John W. Parker, 1854).
Patmore, Coventry, *Principle of Art, etc.* (London: George Bell, 1889).
Patmore, Coventry, *Religio Poetae, etc.* (London: George Bell, 1893).
Patmore, Derek, *The Life and Times of Coventry Patmore* (London: Constable, 1949).
Pattison, Emily, 'French Châteaux of the Renaissance (1460–1547)', *Contemporary Review*, 30 (September 1877), 579–97.
Pattison, Emily, *The Renaissance of Art in France*, 2 vols (London: C. Kegan Paul, 1979).
Pattison, Emily, *The Shrine of Death and Other Stories* (London: George Routledge, 1886).
Pattison, Emily, *The Shrine of Love and Other Stories* (London: George Routledge, 1891).
Pattison, Mark, *Essays*, ed. Henry Nettleship (Oxford: Clarendon, 1889).
Pattison, Mark, *Isaac Casaubon, 1559–1614* (London: Longmans, Green, 1875).
Pattison, Mark, *Memoirs* (London. Macmillan, 1885).
Pattison, Mark, 'Philosophy at Oxford', *Mind*, 1.1 (1876), 82–97.
Pennell, Elizabeth, and Joseph Pennell, *The Life of James McNeill Whistler*, 2 vols (London: Heinemann, 1908).
Percival, John, *A Memoir of Canon Capes* (Hereford: Wilson and Phillips, 1916).
Peterson, William S., and Sylvia Holton Peterson, *The Daniel Press & The Garland of Rachel* (New Castle, D.E.: Oak Knoll Press, 2016).
Pfeiffer, Franz, ed., *Theologia Germanica: Which setteth forth many fair lineaments of divine truth, and saith very lofty and lovely things touching a perfect life*, trans. Susanna Winkworth, with a preface by Charles Kingsley (London: Macmillan, 1874).
Pick, John, 'Divergent Disciples of Walter Pater', *Thought*, 23 (March 1948), 114–28.
'The Poetry Professorship at Oxford', *Saturday Review*, 2 June 1877, 669–70.
Potts, Alex, *Flesh and the Ideal: Winckelmann and the Origins of Art History* (New Haven: Yale University Press, 1994).
Preston, Harriet Waters, 'Vernon Lee', *Atlantic Monthly*, 55 (February 1885), 219–27.
Prettejohn, Elizabeth, *After the Pre-Raphaelites: Art and Aestheticism in Victorian England* (New Brunswick, N.J.: Rutgers University Press, 1999).
Prettejohn, Elizabeth, *Art for Art's Sake: Aestheticism in Victorian Painting* (New Haven: Yale University Press, 2007).
Prettejohn, Elizabeth, 'Solomon, Swinburne, Sappho', *Victorian Review*, 34 (Fall 2008), 103–28.
Price, Bonamy, 'Oxford', *Fraser's Magazine*, 78 (November 1868), 545–66.

Pritchard, H. Baden, 'Messrs. Elliott & Fry', *The Photographic Studios of Europe* (London: Piper & Carter, 1882), 42–5.
Pulham, Patricia, and Catherine Maxwell, eds, *Vernon Lee: Decadence, Ethics, Aesthetics* (Basingstoke: Palgrave Macmillan, 2006).
Pullar, Philippa, *Frank Harris: A Biography* (New York: Simon and Shuster, 1976).
Quilter, Harry, 'The New Renaissance; or, the Gospel of Intensity', *Contemporary Review*, 42 (September 1880), 391–400.
R., R., 'A Note on Simeon Solomon', *Westminster Gazette*, 24 August 1905, 1–2.
Rabbe, Félix, *Shelley. Sa: sa vie et ses oeuvres* (Paris: Nouvelle Libraire Parisienne, 1887).
Raffalovich, Marc André, *Cyril and Lionel* (London: Kegan Paul, 1884).
Rajan, Gita, '*Écriture Fféminine* as Autobiography in Walter Pater' (Diss., University of Arizona, 1990).
Reade, Brian, ed., *Sexual Heretics* (London: Routledge and Kegan Paul, 1970).
Reichel, Oswald J., *Instructions in the Way of Life: An Attempt to Reply to Some Practical and Theological Questions* (London: J. Masters, 1881).
Rhymers' Club, *The Book of the Rhymers' Club* (London: Elkin Mathews, 1892).
Rhymers' Club, *The Second Book of the Rhymers' Club* (London: Elkin Mathews and John Lane, 1894).
Richards, Bernard. 'A Possible Identification of a Pater Acquaintance', *Pater Newsletter*, 6 (Autumn 1980), 2–3.
Richards, Bernard, 'Walter Pater at Oxford', *Brasenose College: The Pater Society*, ed. Gregory McGrath, 2nd edn (Brasenose College: The Pater Society, 1988), 1–14.
Ricketts, Charles, *Michael Field*, ed. Paul Delaney (Edinburgh: Tragara Press, 1976).
Ricks, Christopher, 'Arnold, Pater, and Misquotation', *Times Literary Supplement*, 25 November 1977, 1383–5.
Ritchie, Anne Thackeray, *Chapters from Some Memoirs* (London: Macmillan, 1894).
Robertson, Walford Graham, *Time Was: The Reminiscences of W. Graham Robertson* (London: Hamish Hamilton, 1931).
Robinson, A. Mary F., *The Crowned Hippolytus*, trans. from Euripides, with new poems (London: C. Kegan Paul, 1881).
Robinson, A. Mary F., *A Handful of Honeysuckle* (London: C. Kegan Paul, 1878).
Robinson, A. Mary F., 'Souvenirs sur Walter Pater', *La Revue de Paris*, 15 January 1925, 339–58.
Rogers, James E. Thorold, *Education in Oxford: Its Method, Its Aids, and Its Rewards* (London: Smith, Elder, 1861).
Rogers, James E. Thorold, 'Oxford Professors and Oxford Tutors', *Contemporary Review*, 56 (December 1889), 926–36.
Rolleston, George, *Forms of Animal Life* (Oxford: Clarendon Press, 1870).
Rooksby, Rikky, *A. C. Swinburne: A Poet's Life* (Aldershot: Scolar Press, 1997).
Ross, Robert, 'Mr. Benson's Pater', *Academy*, 21 July 1906, 61–2.
Ross, Robert, *Masques and Phases* (London: Arthur L. Humphreys, 1909).
Rossetti, Dante Gabriel, *The Collected Works of Dante Gabriel Rossetti*, ed. William Michael Rossetti, 2 vols (London: Ellis and Scrutton, 1886).

Rossetti, Dante Gabriel, *The Correspondence of Dante Gabriel Rossetti*, ed. William E. Fredeman et al., 10 vols (Cambridge: D. S. Brewer, 2002–15).
Rossetti, Dante Gabriel, *Poems* (London: F. S. Ellis, 1870).
Rossetti, Maria Francesca, *A Shadow of Dante: Being an Essay towards Studying Himself, His World, and His Pilgrimage* (London: Rivington, 1871).
Rothenstein, William, *Contemporaries: Portrait Drawings* (London: Faber and Faber, 1937).
Rothenstein, William, *English Portraits: A Series of Lithographed Drawings* (London: G. Richards, 1898).
Rothenstein, William, *Men and Memories: Recollections of William Rothenstein, 1872–1900*, 2 vols (London: Faber and Faber, 1931).
Rothenstein, William, *Oxford Characters: A Series of Lithographs* (London: Bodley Head, 1893–5).
Rothenstein, William, *Twelve Portraits* (London: Faber and Faber, 1929).
Rowley, Charles, *Fifty Years of Ancoats* (Manchester: privately printed, 1899).
Rowley, Charles, *Fifty Years of Work without Wages* (London: Hodder and Stoughton, 1911).
Ruskin, John, *The Works of John Ruskin*, ed. E. T. Cook and Alexander Wedderburn, 39 vols (London: George Allen, 1903–12).
Saintsbury, George, *A History of Criticism and Literary Taste*, 3 vols (London: William Blackwood, 1902–4).
Saintsbury, George, *A History of English Prose Rhythm* (London: Macmillan, 1912).
Saintsbury, George, *A History of Nineteenth-Century Literature, 1780–1895* (London: Macmillan, 1896).
Saintsbury, George, *A Short History of English Literature* (London: Macmillan, 1898).
Saintsbury, George, *A Short History of French Literature* (Oxford: Clarendon Press, 1882).
Saintsbury, George, *Specimens of English Prose Style: From Malory to Macaulay* (London: Kegan Paul, Trench, 1885).
Saintsbury, George, 'Walter Pater', *The Bookman*, 30 (August 1906), 165–70.
Samuels, Ernest, *Bernard Berenson: The Making of a Connoisseur* (Cambridge, Mass.: Belknap Press, 1979).
Sanderson, Michael, ed., *The Universities in the Nineteenth Century* (London: Routledge & Kegan Paul, 1975).
Sarrazin, Gabriel, *Poètes modernes de l'Angleterre* (Paris: Paul Ollendorff, 1885).
Sarrazin, Gabriel, *La renaissance de la poésie anglaise, 1798–1889* (Paris: Perrin, 1889).
Saunders, Max, *Self-Impression: Life-Writing, Autobiografication, and the Forms of Modern Literature* (Oxford: Oxford University Press, 2010).
S[aunders], T[homas]. B[ailey]., 'Mr. Walter Pater', *Athenaeum*, 4 August 1894, 161–2.

Savoy, Eric, 'Embarrassments: Figure in the Closet', *Henry James Review*, 20.3 (1999), 227–36.

Savoy, Eric, 'Hypocrite Lecteur: Walter Pater, Henry James, and Homotextual Politics', *Dalhousie Review*, 72.1 (1992), 12–36.

Sayce, A. H., *Reminiscences* (London: Macmillan, 1923).

Sayle, Charles Edward, *Annals of Cambridge University, 1278–1900* (Cambridge: Cambridge Library, 1916).

Sayle, Charles Edward, *Bertha: A Story of Love* (London: Kegan Paul, Trench, 1885).

Sayle, Charles Edward, *In Praise of Music* (London: Elliott Stock, 1897).

Sayle, Charles Edward, *Wiclif: An Historical Drama* (Oxford: James Thornton, 1887).

Schiller, Friedrich, *On the Aesthetic Education of Man* (New Haven: Yale University Press, 1954).

Schnaase, Karl Julius Ferdinand, *Geschichte der bildenden Künste*, 7 vols, ed. W. Lubke (Dusseldorf: J. Buddeus, 1843–64).

Scott, J. W. Robertson, *The Life and Death of a Newspaper* (London: Methuen, 1952).

Scott, William Bell, *Autobiographical Notes*, ed. W. Minto, 2 vols (London: James R. Osgood, McIlvaine, 1892).

Sedgwick, Eve Kosofsky, *Between Men: English Literature and Male Homosexual Desire* (New York: Columbia University Press, 1985).

Seiler, Robert M., 'Editing Walter Pater', *Prose Studies*, 41 (May 1981), 78–80.

Seiler, Robert M., 'Walter Pater Studies: 1970–1980', *Prose Studies*, 41 (May 1981), 84–95.

Seiler, Robert M., ed., *The Book Beautiful: Walter Pater and the House of Macmillan* (London: Athlone Press, 1999).

Seiler, Robert M., ed., *Walter Pater: The Critical Heritage* (London: Routledge and Kegan Paul, 1980).

Seiler, Robert M., ed., *Walter Pater: A Life Remembered* (Calgary: University of Calgary Press, 1987).

Sewell, Brocard, *Footnote to the Nineties: A Memoir of John Gray and André Raffalovich* (London: Cecil and Amelia Woolf, 1968).

Shadwell, C. L., and H. E. Salter, *Oriel College Records* (Oxford: Clarendon Press, 1926).

Shairp, John Campbell, 'English Poets and Oxford Critics', *Quarterly Review*, 153 (1882), 431–63.

Shakespeare, William, *The Works of William Shakespeare*, ed. Henry Irving and Frank A. Marshall, 8 vols (London: Blackie, 1889).

Sharp, William, *Dante Gabriel Rossetti: A Record and a Study* (London: Macmillan, 1882).

Sharp, William, *Earth's Voices, Transcripts from Nature, Sospitra, and Other Poems* (London: Elliott Stock, 1884).

Sharp, William, *The Human Inheritance, The New Hope, Motherhood* (London: Elliott Stock, 1882).

Sharp, William, *Life of Percy Bysshe Shelley* (London: Walter Scott, 1887).
Sharp, William, *Papers Critical and Reminiscences, by William Sharp*, ed. Mrs. William Sharp (London: William Heinemann, 1912).
Sharp, William, *Romantic Ballads and Poems of Phantasy* (London: Walter Scott, 1888).
Sharp, William, 'Some Personal Reminiscences of Walter Pater', *Atlantic Monthly*, 74 (December 1894), 801–14.
Sharp, William, *William Sharp (Fiona Macleod): A Memoir*, ed. Elizabeth A. Sharp (London: William Heinemann, 1910).
Sherard, Robert Harborough, *The Real Oscar Wilde* (London: T. Warner Laurie, 1916).
Shorthouse, Joseph Henry, *John Inglesant: A Romance* (Birmingham: Cornish Brothers, 1880). Rpt, 2 vols (London: Macmillan, 1881).
Shrimpton, Nicholas, 'Pater and the "Aesthetic Sect"', *Comparative Criticism*, 17 (1995), 61–84.
Shrimpton, Nicholas, 'Ruskin and the Aesthetes', *Ruskin and the Dawn of the Modern*, ed. Dinah Birch (Oxford: Oxford University Press, 1999), 131–51.
Shuter, William F., 'The Arrested Narrative of "Emerald Uthwart"', *Nineteenth-Century Literature*, 45 (June 1990), 1–25.
Shuter, William F., 'Dating the Harvard Manuscripts', *Pater Newsletter*, 24 (Spring 1990), 10–11.
Shuter, William F., 'History as Palingenesis in Pater and Hegel', *PMLA*, 86 (1971), 411–21.
Shuter, William F., 'The "Outing" of Walter Pater', *Nineteenth-Century Literature*, 48 (March 1994), 480–506.
Shuter, William F., 'Pater as Don', *Prose Studies*, 11 (May 1988), 41–60.
Shuter, William F., 'Pater, Douglas, and the Impact of "Greats"', *English Literature in Transition*, 46.3 (2003), 250–78.
Shuter, William F., 'Pater on Plato: "Subjective" or "Sound"?', *Prose Studies*, 5 (1982), 215–28.
Shuter, William F., 'Pater's Reshuffled Text', *Nineteenth-Century Literature*, 43 (March 1989), 500–25.
Shuter, William F., *Rereading Walter Pater* (Cambridge: Cambridge University Press, 1997).
Shuter, William F., 'Walter Pater: Origins and Issues', *Psyart*, 1 January 2004. Online.
Shuter, William F., 'What is Early and What is Late in Pater's Work? The Evidence of a Reshuffled Text', *Nineteenth-Century Prose*, 24.2 (Fall 1997), 78–87.
Sidebotham, J. S., *Memorials of the King's School, Canterbury* (Canterbury: n.p., 1865).
Sieveking, Albert Forbes, *In Praise of Gardens: A Prose Cento, Collected and in Part Englished* (London: Elliott Stock, 1885).
Sieveking, Albert Forbes, *Gardens Ancient and Modern: An Epitome of the Literature of the Garden-Art* (London: J. M. Dent, 1899).
Sieveking, Albert Forbes, *The Sentiment of the Sword: A Country-House Dialogue* (London: Horace Cox, 1911).

Sismondi, J. C. L. Simonde de, *Histoire des républiques italiennes du moyen âge*, 16 vols (Paris: H. Nicolle, 1809–18).
Small, Ian, ed., *The Aesthetes: A Sourcebook* (London: Routledge & Kegan Paul, 1979).
Small, Ian, *Conditions for Criticism: Authority, Knowledge, and Literature in the Late Nineteenth Century* (Oxford: Clarendon Press, 1991).
Small, Ian, 'The Editor as Annotator as Ideal Reader', in *The Theory and Practice of Text-Editing*, ed. Ian Small and Marcus Nash (Cambridge: Cambridge University Press, 1991), 186–209.
Small, Ian, 'The Vocabulary of Pater's Criticism and the Psychology of Aesthetics', *British Journal of Aesthetics*, 18.1 (1978), 81–7.
Small, Ian, and Marcus Walsh, eds, *The Theory and Practice of Text-Editing: Essays in Honour of James T. Boulton* (Cambridge: Cambridge University Press, 1991).
'Sir Edmund Gosse', *The Times*, 17 May 1928, 18.
'Sir Frederick Macmillan', *The Times*, 2 June 1936, 14.
'Sir W. Rothenstein', *The Times*, 15 February 1945, 7.
Smith, Esther Marian Greenwell, *Mrs. Humphry Ward* (Boston: Twayne, 1980).
Smith, Gordon W., 'Letters from Paul Bourget to Vernon Lee', *Colby Library Quarterly*, 3 (August 1954), 236–44.
[Smith, Logan Pearsall], 'On Re-Reading Pater', *Times Literary Supplement*, 3 February 1927, 65.
Smith, W. C., *Olrig Grange* (Glasgow: MacLehose, 1872).
Snodgrass, Chris, 'Arthur Symons', *Encyclopedia of British Humorists: Geoffrey Chaucer to John Cleese*, ed. Steven H. Gale (New York: Routledge, 1996), 1092–102.
Sparling, H. Halliday, *The Kelmscott Press and William Morris, Master-craftsman* (London: Macmillan, 1924).
Stead, W. T., 'The Future of Journalism', *Contemporary Review*, 50 (November 1886), 663–79.
Stephen, Leslie, 'Art and Morality', *Cornhill Magazine*, 32 (July 1875), 91–101.
Stetz, Margaret D., and Mark Samuels Lasner, *England in the 1880s: Old Guard and Avant-Garde* (Charlottesville: University of Virginia Press, 1989).
Stevens, Michael E., and Steven B. Burg, *Editing Historical Documents: A Handbook of Practice* (Walnut Creek, Calif.: AltaMira Press, 1997).
Stone, Donald D., 'Goethe and the Victorians', *Carlyle Annual*, 13 (1992/93), 17–34.
Stoddard, John L., ed., *The Stoddard Library: A Thousand Hours of Entertainment with the World's Great Writers*, 12 vols (Chicago and Boston: G. L. Shuman, 1910).
Strachey, Lytton, *Eminent Victorians* (London: Chatto & Windus, 1918).
Sturgis, Matthew, *Oscar: A Life* (London: Head of Zeus, 2018).
Super, R. H., 'Arnold's Oxford Lectures on Poetry', *Modern Language Notes*, 70 (1955), 581–4.
Super, R. H., 'Vivacity and the Philistines', *Studies in English Literature*, 6 (1966), 629–37.
Surtees, Virginia, *Lindsay Coutts, 1824–1913* (London: Michael Russell, 1993).

Sussman, Herbert, *Victorian Masculinities: Manhood and Masculine Poetics in Early Victorian Literature and Art* (Cambridge: Cambridge University Press, 1995).
Sutcliffe, Peter, *The Oxford University Press: An Informal History* (Oxford: Clarendon Press, 1978).
Sutherland, John, *Mrs. Humphry Ward: Eminent Victorian, Pre-Eminent Edwardian* (Oxford: Oxford University Press, 1991).
Swinburne, Algernon Charles, *Essays and Studies* (London: Chatto & Windus, 1875).
Swinburne, Algernon Charles, 'Mr. Whistler's Lecture on Art', *Fortnightly Review*, ns 43 (June 1888), 745–51.
Swinburne, Algernon Charles, 'Notes on Designs of the Old Masters at Florence', *Fortnightly Review*, ns 10 (July 1868), 16–40.
Swinburne, Algernon Charles, *Poems and Ballads*, 2nd series (London: Chatto & Windus, 1878).
Swinburne, Algernon Charles, 'Simeon Solomon: Notes on his *Vision of Love* and Other Studies', *Dark Blue*, 1 (July 1871), 568–71.
Swinburne, Algernon Charles, '1. Sonnet (with a copy of *Mademoiselle de Maupin*)'; 2. 'Memorial Verses on the Death of Théophile Gautier', *Fortnightly Review*, ns 13 (January 1873), 68–73.
Swinburne, Algernon Charles, *The Swinburne Letters*, ed. Cecil Y. Lang, 6 vols (New Haven: Yale University Press, 1959–62).
Swinburne, Algernon Charles, 'Victor Hugo. L'année terrible', *Fortnightly Review*, ns 12 (September 1872), 243–67.
Symonds, John Addington, *Letters of John Addington Symonds*, ed. Herbert Schueller and Robert Peters, 3 vols (Detroit: Wayne State University Press, 1967–9).
Symonds, John Addington, *Letters and Papers of John Addington Symonds*, ed. Horatio F. Brown (London: John Murray, 1923).
Symonds, John Addington, *The Memoirs of John Addington Symonds*, ed. Phyllis Grosskurth (London: Hutchinson, 1984).
Symonds, John Addington, *The Renaissance in Italy*, 7 vols (London: Smith, Elder, 1875–86).
Symonds, John Addington, *Studies of the Greek Poets* (London: Smith, Elder, 1873).
Symons, A. J. A., 'Wilde at Oxford', *Horizon*, 3 (April 1941), 253–64, 336–58.
Symons, Arthur, *Arthur Symons: Selected Letters, 1880–1935*, ed. Karl Beckson and John M. Munro (Iowa City: University of Iowa Press, 1989).
Symons, Arthur, *Days and Nights* (London: Macmillan, 1889).
Symons, Arthur, 'The Decadent Movement in Literature', *Harper's New Monthly Magazine*, 87 (November 1893), 858–69.
Symons, Arthur, *An Introduction to the Study of Browning* (London: Cassell, 1886).
Symons, Arthur, *Spiritual Adventures* (London: Archibald Constable, 1905).
Symons, Arthur, *Studies in Seven Arts* (London: Archibald Constable, 1906).
Symons, Arthur, *A Study of Walter Pater* (London: C. J. Sawyer, 1932).
Symons, Arthur, 'Walter Pater', *Monthly Review*, 24 (September 1906), 14–24.

Symons, Arthur, 'Walter Pater: Some Characteristics', *Savoy*, 3 (December 1896), 33–41. Rptd in *Studies in Prose and Verse* (London: J. M. Dent, 1904), 64–76.

Talfourd, Thomas Noon, *Letters of Charles Lamb, with a Sketch of His Life* (London: Edward Moxon, 1837).

Tanselle, G. Thomas, 'The Editing of Historical Documents', *Studies in Bibliography*, 31 (1978), 1–56.

Tanselle, G. Thomas, 'The Editorial Problem of Final Authorial Intention', *Studies in Bibliography*, 29 (1976), 167–211.

Tanselle, G. Thomas, 'Some Principles for Editorial Apparatus', *Studies in Bibliography*, 25 (1972), 41–88.

Tanselle, G. Thomas, 'Textual Criticism and Deconstruction', *Studies in Bibliography*, 43 (1990), 1–33.

Tanselle, G. Thomas, *Textual Criticism and Scholarly Editing* (Charlottesville: Bibliographical Society of the University of Virginia, 1990).

Taylor, John Russell, *The Art Nouveau Book in Britain* (London: Methuen, 1966).

Tebbel, John, *A History of Book Publishing in the United States*, 3 vols (New York: R. R. Bowker, 1972–8).

Thogartin, Clyde, *The National Daily Press of France* (Birmingham, AL: Summa, 1998).

Thursfield, James R., and George S. Clarke, *The Navy and the Nation: Naval Warfare and Imperial Defence* (London: J. Murray, 1897).

Thwaite, Ann, *Edmund Gosse: A Literary Landscape* (Oxford: Oxford University Press, 1985).

Tildesley, Matthew Brinton, '*The Century Guild Hobby Horse* and Oscar Wilde: A Study of British Little Magazines, 1884–1897' (Diss., Durham University, 2007).

Titchener, E. B., 'Walter Horatio Pater', *Book Reviews*, 2 (October 1894), 201–05.

Trevelyan, Janet Penrose, *The Life of Mrs. Humphry Ward* (London: Constable, 1923).

Tucker, Paul, 'An Unpublished Letter of Walter Pater', *Pater Newsletter*, 64 (Fall 2013), 49–66.

Turner, Frank M., *The Greek Heritage in Victorian Britain* (New Haven: Yale University Press, 1981).

Tyler, E. B., *Primitive Culture* (London: John Murray, 1871).

Tyrwhitt, R. St John, 'The Greek Spirit in Modern Literature', *Contemporary Review*, 29 (March 1877), 552–66.

Unwin, Stanley, *The Truth about Publishing* (London: George Allen and Unwin, 1926).

Updike, D. B., *Printing Types: Their History, Form, and Use*, 2 vols (Cambridge, Mass.: Harvard University Press, 1961).

Vadillo, Ana Parejo, 'Walter Pater and Michael Field: The Correspondence, with Other Unpublished Manuscript Materials', *Pater Newsletter*, 65 (Spring 2014), 27–85.

VanArsdel, Rosemary T., 'Macmillan and Company', in *British Literary Publishing Houses, 1820–1880*, ed. Patricia J. Anderson and Jonathan Rose (Detroit: Gale Research, 1991), 178–95.

Vernon, Peter, 'Walter Pater to Thomas Escott: A New Letter', *Notes and Queries*, ns 30 (August 1983), 311.
Verschoyle, John, 'In the Forests of Navarre and Aragon', *Fortnightly Review*, ns 46 (October 1889), 516–37.
Vicinus, Martha, *Intimate Friends: Women Who Loved Women, 1778–1928* (Chicago: University of Chicago Press, 2004).
Vilain, Jean-François and Philip R. Bishop, *Thomas Bird Mosher and the Art of the Book* (Philadelphia, Penn.: F. A. Davis, 1992).
Vogeler, Martha Salmon, 'The Religious Meaning of *Marius the Epicurean*', *Nineteenth Century Fiction*, 19 (December 1964), 287–99.
Waddington, Samuel, *A Century of Sonnets* (London: George Bell, 1889).
Waddington, Samuel, *Chapters of my Life: An Autobiography* (London: Chapman and Hall, 1909).
'Walter Pater', *Illustrated London News*, 4 August 1894, 135.
'Walter Pater', *Nation*, 23 August 1894, 137–8.
'Walter Pater', *New York Times*, 1 August 1894, 5.
'Walter Pater: By an Undergraduate', *Pall Mall Gazette*, 2 August 1894, 3.
Ward, Anthony, *Walter Pater: The Idea in Nature* (London: MacGibbon and Kee, 1966).
Ward, Mrs Humphry, *The History of David Grieve*, 3 vols (London: Smith, Elder, 1892).
Ward, Mrs Humphry, *Miss Bretherton* (London: Macmillan, 1884).
Ward, Mrs. Humphry, *Robert Elsmere*, 3 vols (London: Smith, Elder, 1888).
Ward, Mrs. Humphry, *A Writer's Recollections*, 2 vols (London: W. Collins Sons, 1918).
Ward, T. Humphry, 'Reminiscences: Brasenose, 1864–72', *Brasenose College Quatercentenary Monographs*, 2 vols (Oxford: Clarendon Press, 1909), vol. 2, part 2, 71–8.
Ward, W. R., *Victorian Oxford* (London: Frank Cass, 1965).
Warner, Oliver, *A Century of Writers, 1855–1955* (London: Chatto & Windus, 1955).
Warren, Thomas Herbert, *The Death of Virgil: A Dramatic Narrative* (Oxford: B. H. Blackwood; London: John Murray, 1907).
Warren, Thomas Herbert, *Epigrams of Art, Life, and Nature* (Liverpool: Gilbert G. Walmsley, 1884).
Warren, Thomas Herbert, *Lachrymae Musarum and Other Poems* (London: Macmillan, 1893).
Warren, Thomas Herbert, *The Prince's Quest and Other Poems* (London: C. Kegan Paul, 1880).
Warren, Thomas Herbert, *By Severn Sea, and Other Poems* (Oxford: H. Daniel, 1897).
Warren, Thomas Herbert, *Wordsworth's Grave, and Other Poems* (London: T. F. Unwin, 1890).
Watry, Maureen, *The Vale Press: Charles Ricketts, a Publisher in Earnest* (London: The British Library/Oak Knoll Press, 2004).

Watson, Edward William, *Life of Bishop John Wordsworth* (London: Longmans, Green, 1915).
Waugh, Arthur, 'London Letter', *Critic*, 1 September 1894, 145–6.
[Waugh, Arthur], 'Walter Pater', *Critic*, 11 August 1894, 93–4.
Wedmore, Frederick, *Four Masters of Etching* (London: Fine Art Society, 1883).
Wedmore, Frederick, *Memories* (London: Methuen, 1912).
Wedmore, Frederick, *Pastorals of France* (London: Richard Bentley, 1877).
Wedmore, Frederick, *Pastorals of France [and] Renunciations* (London: Elkin Mathews and John Lane, 1893).
Wedmore, Frederick, *Turner and Ruskin: An Exposition of the Works of Turner from the Writings of Ruskin* (London: George Allen, 1900).
Wedmore, Frederick, *Whistler's Etchings: A Study and a Catalogue* (London: A. W. Thibaudeau, 1886).
Weintraub, Stanley, *Whistler: A Biography* (New York: Weybright and Talley, 1974).
Whistler, James Abbott McNeill, *The Gentle Art of Making Enemies* (London: William Heinemann, 1892).
Whiting, Lilian, *Louise Chandler Moulton: Poet and Friend* (Boston: Little, Brown, 1910).
Wilde, Oscar, *The Complete Letters of Oscar Wilde*, ed. Merlin Holland and Rupert Hart-Davis (London: Fourth Estate, 2000).
Wilde, Oscar, 'The Grosvenor Gallery', *Dublin University Magazine*, 90 (July 1877), 118–26.
Wilde, Oscar, *The Happy Prince and Other Tales* (London: David Nutt, 1888).
Wilde, Oscar, 'Magdalen Walks', *Irish Monthly*, 6 (April 1878), 211.
Wilde, Oscar, 'The Picture of Dorian Gray', *Lippincott's Monthly Magazine*, 46 (July 1890), 3–100.
Wilde, Oscar, *The Picture of Dorian Gray* (London: Ward, Lock, 1891).
Wilde, Oscar, *The Picture of Dorian Gray: The 1890 and 1891 Texts*, ed. Joseph Bristow, in *The Complete Works of Oscar Wilde*, vol. 3 (Oxford: Oxford University Press, 2005).
Wilde, Oscar, *Selected Letters of Oscar Wilde*, ed. Rupert Hart-Davis (Oxford: Oxford University Press, 1979).
Williams, Carolyn, *Transfigured World: Walter Pater's Aesthetic Historicism* (Ithaca, N.Y.: Cornell University Press, 1989).
Williford, Daniel Patrick, 'The Aesthetic Book of Decadent Literature, 1870–1914' (Diss., University of California, Los Angeles, 2015).
Winckelmann, Johann Joachim, *History of Ancient Art among the Greeks* [1764], trans. G. Henry Lodge (London: John Chapman, 1850).
Wollheim, Richard, *On Art and Mind: Essays and Lectures* (London: Allen Lane, 1973).
Wollheim, Richard, 'Walter Pater: From Philosophy to Art', *Comparative Criticism*, 17 (1995), 21–40.
Wood, Antony à, *Life of Lovelace* (Oxford: Daniel Press, 1896).
Woodruff, C. E., and H. J. Cape, *Schola Regia Cantuariensis: A History of Canterbury School* (London: Hughes, 1908).

Woods, Margaret L., *Esther Vanhomrigh* (London: John Murray, 1891).
Woods, Margaret L., 'Oxford in the Seventies', *Fortnightly Review*, ns 150 (1941), 276–82.
Woolf, Virginia, 'Slater's Pins have no Points', *Forum*, 78 (January 1928), 58–63.
Wordsworth, John, *Fragments and Specimens of Early Latin, with Introduction and Notes* (Oxford: James Parker, 1874).
Wordsworth, John, *The Gospel according to St. Matthew, from the German MS* (Oxford: Clarendon Press, 1883).
Wordsworth, John, *University Sermons on Gospel Subjects* (Oxford: James Parker, 1878).
Wortham, H. E., *Oscar Browning* (London: Constable, 1927).
Wright, Samuel, *A Bibliography of the Writings of Walter H. Pater* (New York: Garland, 1975).
Wright, Samuel, *An Informative Index to the Writings of Walter H. Pater* (West Cornwall, CT: Locust Hill Press, 1987).
Wright, Samuel, 'Richard Charles Jackson', *Antigonish Review*, 1 (Winter 1971), 81–91.
Wright, Thomas, 'The Difficult Art of Prose', *Oxonian Review*, 16 May 2011.
Wright, Thomas, *The Life of Walter Pater*, 2 vols (London: Everett, 1907).
Wright, Thomas, *Thomas Wright of Olney: An Autobiography* (London: Herbert Jenkins, 1936).
Yeats, William Butler, *Autobiographies* (London: Macmillan, 1955).
Yeats, William Butler, *Essays and Introductions* (London: Macmillan, 1974).
Yeats, William Butler, *Memoirs: Autobiography and Journal*, ed. Denis Donoghue (New York: Macmillan, 1972).
Yeats, William Butler, ed., *The Oxford Book of Modern Verse, 1892–1935* (Oxford: Clarendon Press, 1936).
Z., 'Modern Cyrenaicism', *Examiner*, 12 April 1873, 381–2.
Zorn, Christa, *Vernon Lee: Aesthetics, History, and the Victorian Female Intellectual* (Athens: Ohio University Press, 2003).

INDEX

WHP indicates Walter Horatio Pater

Abbott, Evelyn 327
Academy xliv, xlvi, l, lxv, 13, 14, 92, 110, 112, 128, 166, 249, 250, 300, 307
   WHP's contribution to xxviii, xli, 20, 82
Académie Gleyre xlvii
Académie Julian 315
Adams, Robert Dudley 175
   The Song of the Stars and other Poems 175
Aeschylus lxiv
Aesthetic movement lvii, 1, 13, 98
Ainslie, Grant Duff Douglas xxxvii, 19, 24, 25, 172, 173, 181, 194, 198, 211, 249, 270, 272, 274, 275, 310
   Adventures Social and Literary xxxvii
   Escarlamonde and Other Poems 274, 275
   Oxford University Dramatic Society (OUDS) xxxvii
Aldington, Richard 16, 31
Alighieri, Dante xxxiv, lxiii, 119, 120, 121, 122, 189, 286, 287, 299, 306
Allen, Mr. 270
Alleyne, Leonora Blanche 73
Altholz, Joseph L. 28
American Academy of Arts and Sciences, The 239
Amiel, Henri-Frédéric xxx
   Amiel's Journal xxx, xxxi, 176
Anderson, Mary 172
Anderson, Melville B. 258
Andrews, Emily Augusta 262
Andrews, Kit 29
Anstruther-Thomson, Clementina (Kit) xxxv, lviii, 29
Apollo xxx, xxxv, 141, 160, 295, 302, 314
Architectural Review lii
Aristotle xl, li, 113, 145
   Nicomachean Ethics xl, 113
   Politics li
Armour, George Allison 229, 230, 320, 373
Arnold, Matthew xxv, xxvi, xxvii, xliv, xlv, lii, liii, lv, lvi, lxvi, 5, 13, 17, 22, 23, 29, 175, 182, 274
   WHP attends Arnold's lectures xxvii, 5
   Essays in Criticism 13
   The Strayed Reveller, and Other Poems xxv
Arnold, Thomas lxvi

Arts and Crafts movement xlix, 183, 195
Ashmolean Museum 108, 129
Association for Promoting Higher Education for Women, Oxford lix
Athenaeum xliii, 14, 92, 93, 112, 163, 165, 182, 202, 213, 248, 249, 252, 299, 313
   WHP's contribution to xxxii, xxxiii, 20, 213, 228
Athens xxxvii, liv, 221
Atlantic Monthly 30, 140
Aurelius, Marcus 15, 31, 132, 313, 348, 359
Austin, Alfred 184, 300
Authors' Syndicate 331

Bacchus lxiv, 216
Bacon, Francis 4, 5
   Novum Organum 5
Bagehot, Walter 233
Bailey, John Cann 119
Bainton, Revd George 199, 258
   The Art of Authorship 199, 258
Ballad Society 81
Balliol College, Oxford xxvii, xxviii, xlv, xlvi, xlvii, xlviii, l, li, liv, lv, lxi, lxiv, lxv, 8, 22, 59, 61, 73, 79, 96, 105, 145, 188, 189, 275, 276, 324, 326, 327, 329
Bampton Lectures lii, 79
Bann, Stephen 30, 345
Barbey d'Aurevilly, Jules 173
   WHP's reading of 173
Barnett, John Francis 132
Barrington, Emilie Isabel 33, 233, 266–7
Bartoli, Daniel 189
Bartolozzi, Francesco 94
Batchelor, John 65
Baudelaire, Charles xxvi, xxvii, xxxviii, lxviii, 68, 74
   Les fleurs du mal xxvi, xxxviii, 74
Beardsley, Aubrey xxxv, 2, 322
Beckson, Karl 191, 355
Beeching, Henry Charles xxx, 144, 146
Beethoven, Ludwig van xlvii, 116
Belgravia xxxix, lv

Bellay, Joachim du 65, 66, 73, 203
Bennett, Arnold 331, 384
Benson, Arthur Christopher xxiii,
    xxxv, xxxvii–xxxviii, xlv, lx,
    lxiii, 13, 18, 24, 28, 30, 31, 32,
    49, 176, 275, 294, 295, 302, 308,
    329, 364
  biography of his father, Revd E. W.
    Benson xxxvii
  Le cahier jaune: Poems 294
  From a College Window xxxvii
  The Upton Letters xxxvii
  Walter Pater xxiii, lx, lxiii, 28, 29, 30, 31,
    32, 49, 61, 168, 176, 274, 275,
    296, 302, 329, 364
Benson, Revd E. W. xxxvii
Berenson, Bernard xlix, 180, 208
Berkeley, George 9
Berlin, Germany xlviii, 94, 378
Bernard, Claude 181
Bernhardt, Sarah 285
Bible 1, 6
Birkbeck Literary and Scientific
    Institution 293
Birmingham University xli
Bischoff, S.J., Anthony 99
Bizzotto, Elisa iv, 30
Blackfriars lxii
Blackwood's Edinburgh Magazine 132
Blake, William xlii, lxvi, lxix, 136, 137, 183,
    285
Boardman, Elizabeth xv
Bodleian Library, Oxford xvi, xvii, liv,
    142, 146, 169, 198, 252, 260,
    305, 342, 371
Bodley Head Press xxxii, 300, 322, 323
Book of Common Prayer 25
Bookman, The 84
  WHP's contribution to xxxiv, lxviii, 20
Booksellers' Provident Institution liii
Boston Herald lvii
Botticelli, Sandro xxviii, 134, 142, 336
Boulton, Howard Edward 188, 202
Bourget, Paul Charles xxxviii, 24, 150,
    155–6
  Cruelle énigme xxxviii
  Essais de psycholgie contemporaine
    xxxviii, 150
  L'irréparable 156
  Études et portraits 150
  'Sensations d'Oxford' xxxviii
Bowes, George Brimley xxxviii
Bowes, Robert xxxviii, liii
Boyd, Alice 64, 198

Bradley, Katharine Harris xxxiii, xliii–xliv,
    26, 234, 236, 237, 256, 263,
    291, 305
  see also 'Michael Field'
Brake, Laurel 30, 31, 32, 66, 115, 294,
    295, 308
Brasenose College, Oxford xv, xvii, xxvii,
    xxviii, xxx, xxxi, xxxvi, xxxix, xl,
    lii, liv, lxiv, lxvii, 9, 10, 13, 21,
    23, 25, 34, 40, 44, 54, 56, 60, 61,
    65, 66, 67, 69, 70, 72, 73, 76, 77,
    78, 79, 83, 84, 85, 88, 99, 106,
    107, 118, 119, 120, 121, 123,
    124, 128, 129, 130, 131, 133, 143,
    144, 147, 152, 162, 172, 175, 177,
    178, 179, 185, 188, 194, 203,
    207, 208, 209, 212, 214, 216, 221,
    222, 227, 228, 229, 232, 233, 235,
    243, 244, 245, 246, 247, 252, 257,
    258, 259, 261, 264, 265, 266,
    269, 274, 276, 277, 278, 286, 287,
    288, 290, 291, 292, 294, 295,
    296, 297, 298, 299, 300, 301, 304,
    307, 308, 313, 314, 315, 316, 319,
    323, 324, 325, 326, 335
Brett, George Edward xxxix, liii, 262
Brett, George Platt xxxix, 262
Bridges, Robert xlii, xlviii, xlix, 126
Bright, John xlv
Brimley, Caroline liii
British Library xv, xvii, 325
British Museum xv, xli, 25, 108, 221, 262,
    371
Brooks, James 195
Brown, Ford Madox xlv, lxiii, 65, 87,
    88, 234
  The Last of England 87
  Work 87
Brown, Horatio Forbes 75
Browne, Charles Gordon 59, 220
Browne, Henry Llewelyn 59
Browning, Oscar xxviii, xxxix, 19, 23, 25,
    82, 83, 104, 105, 106, 107, 119,
    124, 232, 252
  Goethe: His Life and Writings xxxix
  Historical Studies xxxix
  *A History of the Modern World,
    1815–1910* xxxix
  *An Introduction to the History of
    Educational Theories* xxxix
  Life of George Eliot xxxix
  *Memories of Sixty Years at Eton,
    Cambridge, and Elsewhere* 124
  Modern France: 1814–1879 124

INDEX

Browning, Robert xliii, xlvi, lviii, lxi, lxiii, lxv, 9, 15, 103, 152, 167, 182, 185, 189, 199, 225, 229, 383
  'Andrea del Sarto' 9
  'Fra Lippo Lippi' 9
Browning Society lxv, 81
Bruford, W. H. 29
Bruno, Giordano 16, 178, 240, 244
Bryce, James xli
Bullen, J. B. 30
Bunting, Percy William 17, 20, 278, 280, 281, 297, 298, 314, 316
Burckhardt, Jacob xliii
Burg, Steven B. 45
Burges, William xlii
Burke, Edmund lvii
Burne-Jones, Edward xlvi, lxiv, lxviii
Bussell, Frederick William xxxi, xxxvi, xxxix–xl, 19, 26, 270, 306, 313, 314, 318, 321, 322, 323, 324, 330, 335
  Augustine's City of God xl
  The Future of Ethics xxxix
  The School of Plato xxxix
Butler, Alfred Joshua xxx, 128, 129, 130, 131, 335, 339, 340
Buxton College, Derbyshire lxix
Byles, Marianne 262
Byron, Lord George Gordon 22
Bywater, Ingram xxvi, xxxviii, xl, xli, xlvi, l, lxi, 4, 6, 19, 28, 29, 107, 125, 150

Caine, T. Hall 206
Caird, Edward 125, 324
Calderón de la Barca, Pedro 213
Cam xxxix
Cambridge xvi, xvii, xxxvii, xxxviii, xxxix, xli, xliv, xlv, l, lii, liii, liv, lxviii, 4, 49, 75, 81, 84, 104, 106, 131, 167, 168, 182, 184, 193, 194, 213, 230, 269, 278, 294, 299, 331, 339
Cambridge University Day Training College xxxix, 82
Cameron, Arnold Guyot 307, 309
Cameron, Julia Margaret 234
Campbell, James Dykes 191, 214, 217, 218, 220, 223, 227, 231, 235, 244, 252
Campbell, Lewis 29, 326–7
Campo Santo, the 119
Canterbury xvi, xxv, xxxvii, lv, lviii, lx, 3, 49, 50, 51, 52, 156, 177, 184, 276, 294, 297
Canton, William 20, 24, 133, 280, 281, 282, 283–4, 286, 290, 291, 292, 295, 296–7, 298, 313, 314–15, 316, 327–8
  The Invisible Playmate 281, 292, 328
  A Lost Epic, and Other Poems 282, 296
Cape, H. J. 49
Capes, William Wolfe xxvi, 4, 176
Carlyle, Thomas lv, 7, 29, 64
Carr, J. Comyns 97
Carroll, Lewis (pseud.), *see* Dodgson, Charles Lutwidge
Carte, D'Oyly lxviii
Catholicism xxv, xliv, xlviii, l, 99, 149, 249, 262, 276, 311
Century Guild of Artists xlix, 195
Century Guild Hobby Horse xliv, xlix, 183, 201, 219, 223, 231, 250, 253
  WHP's proposed contribution 201 n.2
Century Magazine xlv
Cervantes (Saavedra), Miguel de 213
Chandler, Edmund 171
  Pater on Style 171
Chapman, John xxi, xl–xli, 20, 36, 60, 62, 66, 73
Charteris, Evan 308
Chatto and Windus 376
Chaucer, Geoffrey lxvii, 81
Chaucer Society 81
Christ Church College, Oxford li, lii, lviii, lxii, 105, 108, 126, 265, 285
Christ Church Meadows 25
Christian Socialist Movement 5, 81, 360
Church of England xliv, l, li, 28, 79, 99, 118, 315, 325
Civil List Pension xlv, lx, 234
Clare College, Cambridge xliv
Clarendon Press xlii, 70, 71, 112, 113, 116
Clark, Kenneth 68
Clark, R. & R. 171, 202, 203, 235, 241, 242, 253
Clark, Robert 171
Clark, William Robinson 118
Clarke, Thomas Chatfield 195
Classical Review 327, 381
Clay, Richard 109
Clay and Sons 109
Clifton College, Bristol 120
Clough, Arthur Hugh 169, 246
Coates, John 32
Cockerell, Charles Robert 108
Coleridge, Samuel Taylor xxvii, 10, 139, 140, 178, 216, 225, 276, 383
Colles, William Morris 330–1
Collins, John Churton xli, 182, 184, 308

Colvin, Sidney xxviii, xli–xlii, 19, 62, 76, 82, 107, 120, 123, 126, 384
  Children in Italian and English Design xxviii, xli
  Memories and Notes of Persons and Places, 1852–1912 xlii
  A Selection from Occasional Writings on Fine Art xli
Combe, Thomas 70, 71
Comber, Eleanor Pater 192
Comte, Auguste xliii
Congreve, William 218
Conington, John 166
Constable, Archibald 109, 171
Contemporary Review xxxiv, xxxv, xxxvi, xlv
  WHP's contribution to xxxiv, xxxv, xxxvi, xlv
Cooper, Edith Emma xxxiii, xliii–xliv, 234, 237, 256, 266, 291, 305, 345
  see also 'Michael Field'
Cornhill Magazine xxvii, xli, xlv, lxii, 31, 99, 142, 147
copyright 71, 241, 296, 301, 302, 334, 344, 358, 368, 369, 370–1, 372, 381, 382
Copyright Act of 1709 370
Copyright Act of 1842 370
Copyright Act of 1911 liii, 371
Copyright Association (1872) 331
Corpus Christi College, Oxford 125, 165, 311
Cotton, James Sutherland xxxv, 249, 310
Courbet, Gustave lxvii
Cowper School, Olney lxvii
Cradock, Revd Edward Hartopp 61, 120, 133
Craik, George Lillie xlii, liii, 66, 68
Crane, Walter 336
Crawford, Robert 73
Crayon, The 234
Creighton, Revd Mandell 19, 84, 125, 145
Creighton, Louise 84, 145
Critic 312
Croce, Benedetto xxxvii
Crook, J. Mordaunt 61, 134
Crystal Palace Company xxv, xxxii, xlvii
Cuddesden, Oxford lii
Cust, Henry John Cockayne 299

Daily Chronicle xxxv, l
Daily Telegraph 312
Daley, Kenneth xv, 30

Daniel, (Charles) Henry Olive xxxv, xlii, lxvii, 19, 125–6, 126–7, 300, 321, 328, 329, 342, 359
Daniel, Emily Crabb Olive xlii, lxvii, 35, 320–1, 328
Daniel Press xxxv, xlii, 109, 126
  The Garland of Rachel xlii, 126
  An Imaginary Portrait: The Child in the House xxxv, xlii, 328
  Odes, Songs, and Lyrics of John Keats xlii
  Songs of Innocence xlii
Dante Alighieri lxiii, 119, 120, 121, 122, 146, 178, 189, 299
  Convito 120, 121
  Inferno 121
  Purgatorio lxiii, 286
  WHP proposes an article on 306
Darmesteter, James 129
Darwin, Charles xxvi, 6, 28, 207
  On the Origin of Species xxvi, 6, 28
da Vinci, Leonardo xxviii, xxxiv, 15, 21, 66, 92, 95, 203, 238, 285
Davos Platz, Switzerland lxv
Davy, Sir Humphry 269
Debussy, Claude xxxviii
decadence xii, xxxviii, lxiv, lxv
  decadent authors xxxviii, lxiv, lxv
  see also Gautier, Théophile; Symons, Arthur; Swinburne, A. C.; Wilde, Oscar; the *Yellow Book*
DeLaura, David J. 29, 31
della Robbia, Luca 12, 15, 65, 66
del Sarto, Andrea 9
Dent, Joseph Malaby 109
Dial 258
Dibdin, Mary Winnifred xl
Dickens, Charles lxix, 232, 293, 371
Dilke, Sir Charles Wentworth xliii, 179, 180
Dilke, Lady Emilia Francis Strong Pattison xl, xlii–xliii, lxi, 19, 85, 98, 172, 179–80, 277, 291
  The Book of the Spiritual Life 179, 180
  The Renaissance of Art in France xliii
  The Shrine of Death and Other Stories 180, 277
  reviews *Imaginary Portraits* xliii
  reviews *Studies in the History of the Renaissance* xliii
Dionysus 14, 92, 111, 114, 117, 177, 275, 333

INDEX

Disraeli, Benjamin xlv
Dobson, Austin xlii, 126, 246
Dodgson, Charles Lutwidge ('Lewis Carroll') xlii, liii, 121, 126
   Alice's Adventures in Wonderland 126
   Through the Looking Glass 126
Dodgson, Edward Spencer 120, 121
Dombrain, Henry xxvi, lv
Donoghue, Denis xv, 28, 31
Doughty, Oswald 88
Douglas, Lord Alfred l, lxviii
Dowling, Linda 29, 108
Dowson, Ernest l, 168, 316
Dramatic Review xxxvii
du Bellay, Joachim, *see* Bellay
Dublin, Ireland xlix, liv, lxviii, 288
Du Maurier, George 98
Durand, John 234
Dyer, Louis xxxiv, 96, 97, 275
   The Greek Question and Answer 275
   Studies of the Gods in Greece at Certain Sanctuaries Recently Excavated xxxiv, 275

Earle, John 107, 126
École Impériale et Spéciale de Dessin lxvii
Economist 245
Edinburgh, Scotland xvi, xlvi, lxi, lxiii, 84, 171, 235, 253
Edinburgh Courant xlvi, 110, 166
Edinburgh Review 97
Edinburgh, University of xvi, 84, 171
Edwards, Georgina xv, xvii, 335
Eliot, George (pseud. for Mary Ann Evans) xl, xli, 18
Eliot, T. S. lxvi
Ellegard, Alvar 28
Ellerton, Revd Francis George 119
Ellerton, Revd John 119
Elliott & Fry 202, 245, 258, 337, 382
Ellis, Havelock xxxii, 214
Ellis, Robinson xl
Eells, Emily 345
Emison, Patricia 136
empiricism 7, 9, 10, 11
Engel, A. J. 28, 407
English Men of Letters series xxxviii, lvi, lxvii, 129, 137
Enfield Grammar School xxv, 3
Epps, Ellen (Nellie) xxix, xlv
Ernst, Carl Wilhelm 177–8
   The Constitutional History of Boston: An Essay 178

Essays and Reviews 1, lxi, 6, 7, 28
Escott, Thomas Hay Sweet 123, 176
Eton College xxviii
Euripides 111
   Bacchae 288, 289, 292
Evangelista, Stefano 28, 29, 30, 32
Evans, Lawrence xv, xxiii, xxxvi, 2, 18, 25, 26, 31, 32, 33, 35, 45, 63, 66, 82, 131, 164, 185, 229, 235
Evening News xlviii, 226
Evergreen Circle lxiii
examinations xli, 4, 5, 49, 59, 78, 79, 86, 87, 184, 339, 378
Examiner 79
Exeter College, Oxford xl
Eyre, Revd Edward Vincent 310–11, 312

Faber, Geoffrey 29
Fabre, Ferdinand xxxiii, 273
   WHP recommends novel by 273
Faithfull, Emily 233
Fell type xlii, 325
see also typesetting
Feuerbach, Ludwig xl
   The Essence of Christianity xl
Field, Michael (pseud. of Katharine Bradley and Edith Emma Cooper) xxxii, xxxiii, xxxiv, xliii–xliv, 19, 24, 26, 32, 181, 231, 234, 236–7, 256, 263, 266, 267, 271, 282, 291, 305, 341, 345
   Long Ago xxxii, xliii, 234, 236
   Sight and Song xxxiv, 305
   Stephania: A Trialogue 305
   The Tragic Mary xxxiii, 256, 263
   Works and Days: From the Journal of Michael Field xliv, 266, 267
FitzGerald, Edward xxxvii, lxix
Fitch, William Clyde xxxiii, 32, 261, 271, 279
   The Knighting of the Twins, and Ten Other Tales 279
Fitzwilliam Museum, Cambridge xli
Flaubert, Gustave xxvi, xxix, xxxi, xxxviii, 21, 224, 228
   Madame Bovary xxvi
   Trois contes xxix, 100
Fletcher, Ian xv, 1, 23, 27, 31, 32, 307
Fletcher, Julia Constance (pseud. 'George Fleming') 103, 109, 137–8
   A Nile Novel 103
Florence, Italy xvii, xlix, li, lviii, 118, 141, 145, 147, 208, 239, 275
Ford, Onslow 308
Foreign Review 29

Fortnightly Review xxviii, xxix, xxx, xxxii, xxxiii, xxxiv, xxxvi, xli, xlviii, l, lvi, lvii, lviii, 10, 12, 13, 14, 16, 20, 24, 63, 68, 73, 74, 75, 79, 82, 84, 91, 92, 111, 116, 123, 134, 162, 177, 178, 188, 201, 221, 222, 226, 228, 240, 244, 247, 265, 266, 272, 285
Fraser, Hilary 30
Fraser's Magazine 140, 141
Friedman, Arthur 45
Frome, Somerset xlii
Froude, James Anthony xl, 274
Fry, Clarence Edmund 202
Fry, Roger xlix
Furley, George 49, 50
Furley, William Henry 49, 50
Furnivall, Frederick James 81, 82, 184, 365, 366

Gagel, Amanda 45
Galpin, Charles Alexander 333
Galpin, H. F. 333
Galton, Revd Arthur Howard xliv, 25, 32, 168, 216, 219, 231, 232, 253, 254, 307
  Acer in Hostem xliv
  The Character and Times of Thomas Cromwell xliv
  Studies of Five Living Poets xliv
  Two Essays upon Matthew Arnold, with Some Letters to the Author xliv
Gardner, E. Bensley 71
Gardner, Isabella Stewart xvii, 180, 181
Gardner, John Lowell 181
Gautier, Théophile xii, 22, 24, 68, 74, 82
  WHP's recommendation of xii
  Mademoiselle de Maupin 22, 74
  Swinburne's verses on 74
Geddes, Patrick lxiii
George, Ernest 186
Gerson, Virginia 261, 279
Gibbon, Edward 31
Gilbert (William Schwenck) and (Arthur) Sullivan xxix, lxviii, 98
  Patience xxix, lxviii, 98
Gilchrist, H. H. 183
Giorgione (da Castlefranco) 14, 66, 111, 139, 140, 177, 221
Gissing, George 331, 377
Gladstone, William Ewart lvi, lvii, 184, 278
Glasgow lii, lxiii, 71, 72, 324, 330, 346
Glasgow Herald 247, 281, 324

Glasgow, University of xvi, xxxv, xxxv, xlii, 72, 131, 324, 327, 346
Glasgow Weekly Herald 281
Godley, Alfred Denis 189
Goethe, Johann Wolfgang von 7, 8, 9, 11, 148
  Poetry and Truth 8, 29
  The Sorrows of Young Werther 8
  Wilhelm Meister's Apprenticeship 7, 8
  Wilhelm Meister's Travels 7
Goldsmith, Oliver lvii, 383
  The Deserted Village 383
  Vicar of Wakefield lvii
Goncourt, Edmond and Jules de lxvi
Goodchild, E. G. 383
Good Words 281, 292, 295, 296, 297, 298, 299, 313, 314
  WHP's proposed contribution 281, 292, 295, 296, 297, 298, 299, 313
Goscombe, Sir William 384
Gosse, Edmund W. xiv, xxviii, xxix, xxx, xxxii, xxxiv, xxxv, xxxvi, xxxviii, xli, xlii, xliv–xlv, lvii, lx, lxi, 1, 13, 18, 19, 24, 25, 28, 30, 31, 56, 64, 65, 82, 87, 96, 98, 99, 102, 126, 128, 129, 130, 131, 145, 167, 168, 181, 182, 184, 187, 188, 193, 218, 230, 232, 245, 246, 260, 263, 273, 274, 301–2, 303, 305, 308, 309, 310–13, 316, 318, 330–1, 335, 341–2, 343, 349, 357, 384
  edits WHP's 'Pascal' xxxvi, xlv, 342
  Father and Son xliv
  French Profiles 273
  From Shakespeare to Pope xxx, 167, 182, 308
  Life of Congreve xxxii, 218
  memorial article on WHP xlv
  On Viol and Flute xxxiv
  prepares *Essays from 'The Guardian'* xiv, xxxvi, xlv
  reviews *Plato and Platonism* 305
  Questions at Issue 308
  The Secret of Narcisse: A Romance xxxiv, 302, 303
  The Unknown Lover: A Drama for Private Acting 102
Gosse, Philip Henry xlv
Gothic architecture 63, 105, 133, 195, 311
Government School of Design, Newcastle-upon-Tyne 64
Graham, John William 207

INDEX

Grant Duff, Mountstuart Elphinstone xxviii, xxxii, xxxiii, xxxiv, xlv–xlvi, 19, 25, 83, 172, 181, 195, 214, 226, 239, 245, 252, 267, 268, 290
  Ernest Renan: In Memoriam xlv
  Notes from a Diary, 1851–1972 xlv, 83, 181, 195, 239, 268
  Studies in European Politics xlv
Graves, Charles L. 89, 97, 170
Gray, John Henry lxi
Gray, John Miller xxix, xlvi, 24, 109–10, 131–2, 166, 167, 169, 181, 256, 263
  David Scott, R.S.A., and his Works xlvi
  reviews *Marius* xlvi, 166
Gray, Thomas 129, 230
Green, Charlotte Symonds xxi, xxxv, xlvi–xlvii, lxv, lxvii, 11, 38, 63, 188, 189, 330
Green, John Richard xxix, xl, xlvi, 89, 188
  A Short History of the English People 89
  Stray Studies from England and Italy xxix, 89, 90
Green, Thomas Hill xxx, xl, xlvi, xlvii, lxv, lxvi, lxvii, 11, 29, 63
Greenough, Richard Saltonstall 238, 239
Grissell, Hartwell de la Garde xlix, 99
  Ritual Inaccuracies 99
Grosvenor Gallery, London xlv, 97, 98, 234
Grove, Sir George xlvii, 15, 20, 105–6, 107, 109, 110, 116, 140, 157
  Dictionary of Music and Musicians xlvii, 116
  and *Macmillan's Magazine* xlvii, 15, 20, 105, 106, 107, 109, 157
Guardian, The xiv, xxxi, xxxii, xxxiii, xxxiv, xxxvi, xlv, lxvi, 20, 84, 169, 184, 196, 209, 214, 343, 345, 346, 349, 350, 354, 355, 356, 357, 367, 368
  WHP's contributions to xiv, xxxi, xxxii, xxxiii, xxxiv, xxxvi, xlv, lxvii, 20, 84, 169, 184, 196, 214, 245, 343, 345, 346, 349, 350, 354, 355, 356, 357, 367, 368
Guggenheim, Julius Nicholas Franz 101, 102
Guiney, Louise Imogen 260, 384
  Goose-Quill Papers 260
  Songs at the Start 260

Hagiwara, Hiroko xxiii, 2
Hague, The xxxvii, 378
Hall, Edward Pickard 71
Hallé, Charles Edward 97

Halsband, Robert 45
Hamilton, Walter Kerr lii
d'Hangest, Germain 31, 32
Hardinge, William Money xxviii, xlvii, 22, 23, 308
Hardy, Thomas xxxi, liii, 171, 199, 221, 224, 310
  WHP lunches with xxxv, 310
Harland, Henry 318
  Grandison Mather 318
  Mea Culpa 319
  The Yellow Book 319
  Two Voices 319
Harloe, Katherine 30
Harper's New Monthly Magazine xxxv, 315
  WHP's contribution to xxxv, 315
Harris, James Frank Thomas xlviii, lii, 226, 271, 272, 316
  The Bomb xlviii
  Contemporary Portraits xlviii
  'A Modern Idyll' 271, 272
  My Life and Loves xlviii
Harris, Wendell 30
Harrison, Austin Frederic lvi, 377, 378
Hartopp, Sir Edmund Cradock 61
Hartopp, Edward Cradock 61, 119, 120, 133
Hearth and Home lvii
Hegel, Georg Wilhelm Friedrich l, 9, 94
  The Phenomenology of Spirit 9
Heidelberg, Germany xxvi, xlviii, li, lix, 7, 51, 52, 94
Heinemann, William 312, 316
Hellenism 5, 7
Henley, William Ernest 103
Heraclitus xl, 4, 17
Herodotus 189
Herder, Johann Gottfried von 176
Herrick, Robert 198
  WHP reads Horne's edition of 198
Hertford College, Oxford 118, 119, 329
Hext, Kate 9, 28, 29, 30
Hiatt, Charles 221
Higgins, Lesley xviii, 29, 30, 31, 32, 108
Hill, Donald L. xxiii, 30, 68, 118
Hill, Emma 234
Hill, Octavia 233
Hinchcliffe, Tanis 30, 63
Hirst, F. W. 79
Hobbes, Thomas 9
Hobby Horse: see Century Guild Hobby Horse
Hogge, Helen Julia 238
Holdsworth, Annie E. li

Hollyer, Frederick 271, 353
Holmes, Sr., Oliver Wendell lvii, 300
Holywell Cemetery, Oxford xxxvi, lx
Homer 73, 111
homosexuality xlvii, l, lxi, 31, 196
Hooker, Richard 3
Hopkins, S.J., Gerard Manley xxvii, xxviii, xxix, xxxiii, xlviii–xlix, lii, lxiv, 9, 19, 25, 99, 120, 262
   'The Wreck of the Deutschland' xlviii
Horace 189
Horne, Herbert Percy xxxii, xliv, xlix, lxiv, 19, 25, 35, 182–3, 188, 194, 195, 198, 200, 201, 207, 208, 211, 212, 214, 216, 219, 221, 223, 224, 228, 231, 232, 239, 240, 250, 251, 254, 258, 263, 293, 307, 316, 375, 376
   Alessandro Filipepi, commonly called Sandro Botticelli, Painter of Florence xlix
   edits *Hesperides: Poems by Robert Herrick* 198
   edits *Nero and Other Plays* 213, 214
Houghton, Esther Rhoads 226
Hueffer, Francis 233, 234
Hughes, Gillian 45
Hughes, Thomas liii, 81, 86
Hugo, Victor Marie xxviii, 232
Humboldt, Wilhelm von 6
Hume, David 9
Hunt, Marion Edith 254
Hunt, William Holman xxv, lxiii, 70, 254
   The Light of the World 70
Huxley, Thomas Henry xl, 23, 28, 184, 199, 300
Huysmans, Joris Karl lxvi

Iliad, see Homer
Illustrated London News 293
Image, Selwyn xliv, xlix, 183, 195, 200, 201, 305, 316
Imperial War Museum, London 173
Impressionism lii, lvi, 29, 162
Independent Theatre 272
Inman, Billie Andrew xv, 10, 28, 29, 30, 32, 45, 52, 66, 133, 188, 197, 217, 220, 221, 308
   Walter Pater's Reading, 1858–73 29, 45, 66
   Walter Pater and His Reading, 1874–1877 32
International Exhibition, London 88
Irvine, Ayrshire lii

Isabella Stewart Gardner Museum, Boston xvii, 181

Jackson, Richard C. lxix, 31
Jackson, Thomas Graham 133, 134
Jackson, William Walrond 28, 29, 125
Jackson's Oxford Journal 242
James, Henry xxxiii, xxxviii, xlv, liii, lviii, lxi, 18, 103, 113, 156, 160, 180, 199, 285
   The Europeans (WHP reads) 113
Jarrold, John 383
Jarrold, Thomas Herbert Curteis 383
Jarrold, William Thomas Fisher 383
Jarrold and Sons Ltd 383
Jeens, Charles Henry 86, 87, 89, 90, 91, 93, 95
Jesus College, Oxford 59, 125
Johnson, Lionel Pigot xxxiii, xliv, xlix–l, 19, 24, 26, 125, 168, 208, 253, 260, 307, 322
   The Art of Thomas Hardy l
   Ireland, with Other Poems l
   memorial article on WHP l
   reviews *Appreciations* xxxiii, 250, 253, 254
Jones, Inigo 182
   WHP reads Horne's essay on 182, 183
Jopling, Louise 98
Journal of Hellenic Studies 109
Jowett, Benjamin xxvi, xxxv, xl, xlv, xlvi, xlvii, xlviii, l–li, lii, lv, lxv, 4, 5, 8, 9, 13, 22, 23, 28, 32, 59, 79, 142, 145, 199, 308, 326, 327, 329
   Dialogues of Plato li, 145
Joyce, James 21

Keats, John 20, 216, 225
Keble, John xxviii, li, 3
   Sermons for the Christian Year xxviii
Keble College, Oxford 70
Kelmscott Press xxxiv
Kemp-Welch, Wilhelmina Louise 291
Kemp-Welch, William 291
King's College, Cambridge xvi, xxxvii, xxxix, 105, 118
King's College, London lix, 49, 123
King's School, Canterbury xvi, xxv, xxvi, lv, lvii, lvii, lviii, lxix, 3, 49, 50, 51, 52, 53, 132, 177, 276, 294
King's School Feast Society 49
Kingsley, Charles liii, 5, 81, 86, 170
Kipling, Rudyard 103, 293, 299, 349

Knowles, James Thomas 20, 174, 319, 320, 323, 326
Knopff, Georges 225
Kopnicki, Ronald J. 221

Lady Margaret Hall, Oxford lix, lxvi
Lamb, Charles xxix, 14, 21, 111, 177, 201, 349, 350
Landor, Walter Savage 15, 225
Lane, John xxi, xxxii, xxxv, 40, 291, 300, 315, 316, 317, 319, 321, 322, 323, 324
Lang, Andrew xlii, 19, 73, 199
Lang, Cecil 45
Lasner, Mark Samuels xv, xvi
Latham, David xviii, 32
Lathbury, Bertha Penrose 245
Lathbury, Daniel Conner 245
Leader lvi
Lectures for Women Committee, Oxford lix, lxvi
'Lee, Vernon', *see* Violet Paget
Lee-Hamilton, Jacob Eugene xxx, li, lviii
  Apollo and Marsyas, and Other Poems xxx
  The New Medusa, and Other Poems li
Lee-Warner, Philip Henry 376
Le Gallienne, Richard Thomas xxxiv, 18, 24, 300, 304, 322
  The Book-Bills of Narcissus xxxiv, 300
  reviews *Plato and Platonism* 18, 304
Leighton, Frederic xliii, 98, 233, 271
Legros, Alphonse lxviii
Lemaître, Jules xxxiii, 274
  WHP's admiration for 274
Leonardo, *see* da Vinci, Leonardo
Lepelletier, Edmond Adolphe 264
Levey, Michael 27, 31, 32, 192, 330
Lewes, George Henry xl
Lhombreaud, Roger A. 185
Liddon, Revd Henry Parry xlviii, li–lii, 54, 99
Lincoln College, Oxford xliii, lii, lv, lvi, lx, lxi, 21, 23, 137, 165
Lincoln's Inn, London lxii, 6, 81, 213, 249, 278
Lindsay, Lady Blanche 97
Lindsay, Sir Coutts 97
Lippincott's Monthly Magazine xxxiii, 256
Lister, Harriet 61
Literae Humaniores xxvii, 4
Literature Compass 29
Lock, Ward 109
Locke, John 9
London Institute xxxiv, xlviii, 142, 259, 265, 266, 267, 329

London Society for the Extension of University Teaching (Education) xli
London University lii
Longfellow, Henry Wadsworth lvii
Lorrain, Claude xliii
Louvre Museum, Paris 90, 92, 93, 142
Lovelace, Richard 320, 321
  WHP considers writing on 321
Lowell Institute, Boston 182, 275
Lloyd, Constance lxi, lxviii, 325
Lucas, Francis 253
Lucas, Margaret Helen liv
Lucian 221
Ludlow, John Malcom 81
Lunatic Asylum, Fareham lx
Lunatic Asylum, Stafford lx

MacColl, Dugald Sutherland lii, 18, 25, 31, 137, 144, 146, 174
  Confessions of a Keeper and Other Papers lii
  Nineteenth Century Art lii
MacColl, Norman 213
Mackail, John William 144, 145, 146, 166
  reviews *Marius* 146
Mackmurdo, Arthur Heygate xlix, 183, 194, 195, 201
MacLehose, James 72, 346
MacLehose, Norman 72
MacLehose, Robert 72, 346
Macmillan, Alexander xxxviii, xxxix, xlii, lii, liii, 11, 12, 14, 17, 65, 66, 67, 68, 69, 70–1, 72, 73, 74, 76, 77, 84, 85, 86, 87, 89, 90, 91, 92–3, 93–4, 95–6, 101, 103, 110–11, 112, 113, 114, 115, 117, 120–1, 138, 154, 156–7, 158, 159–60, 161, 163, 164, 165, 168, 170–1, 204, 218, 262, 275
Macmillan and Co. xxix, xxxvi, xxxviii, xxxix, xlii, lii–liii, liv, lvi, lxvii, lxix, 2, 11, 12, 16, 17, 20, 24, 66, 68, 76, 86, 89, 103, 113, 129, 164, 170, 171, 172, 207, 217, 227, 235, 241, 245, 262, 275, 286, 302, 304, 305, 315, 333, 348, 368
Macmillan, Barclay, and Macmillan liii
Macmillan, Daniel xxxviii, lii, liii, liv, 70, 72, 248
Macmillan, Frederick Orridge liii, 172, 173, 174, 190, 191, 202, 207, 210, 219, 241, 242, 243, 257, 259, 262, 263, 264, 267, 279, 280, 283, 286,

Macmillan, Frederick Orridge (*Cont.*)
287, 295, 296, 299, 301, 302, 334, 336, 336–7, 337, 338, 340, 344–5, 346, 349, 349–50, 350, 350–1, 351, 352, 353, 354, 355, 356, 356–7, 357, 358–9, 359, 360, 365–6, 367, 368–9, 368–9, 370, 371, 372, 372–3, 373, 374, 374–5, 375–6, 376, 377, 378–9, 379, 380–1, 381, 382, 383, 383–4
Macmillan, George Augustin xxxviii, liii–liv, lxix, 103, 121, 157, 217, 218, 225, 231, 253, 255, 265, 275, 288–9, 292, 301, 307, 309, 314, 331, 332, 346, 360, 375, 381, 382
Macmillan, Harold liii
Macmillan Letter Books 164
Macmillan, Malcolm Kingsley liv, 101, 275
  Dragonet the Jester liv
Macmillan, Margaret Anne 96, 275
Macmillan, Maurice Crawford liv, 248, 347, 362, 375
  First Latin Grammar liv
Macmillan's Magazine xxix, xxxi, xxxii, xxxiii, xxxiv, xlvii, liii, lvi, lxvii, 15, 16, 20, 81, 84, 105, 106,109, 110, 111, 140, 154, 157, 162, 168, 169, 174, 177, 178, 191, 224, 261, 274, 281, 32, 366
  WHP's contributions to xxix, xxxi, xxxii, xxxiii, 15, 16, 81, 105, 106, 109, 110, 111, 140, 157, 162, 168, 169, 174, 177, 178, 224, 261, 274, 281, 325, 366
Madan, Falconer liv–lv, lviii, 23, 146, 147, 201, 238, 260, 320, 325, 359
  The Daniel Press liv, 325, 359
  A Handbook of the Literature of C. L. Dodgson lv
  Oxford outside the Guide-Books lv
Maeterlinck, Maurice lxvi
Magdalen College, Oxford xv, xxix, lxv, lxviii, 189, 329, 339
Magdalene College, Cambridge xxxvii, 294
Magrath, John Richard 107, 108
Mahaffy, John Pentland liv
Maine, Sir Henry lxvii
Mallarmé, Stéphane xxxv, lxvi
Mallock, William Hurrell xxix, xlvii, lv, 23, 308
  Memoirs of Life and Literature lv
  The New Republic xxix, lv, 23
Manchester Guardian 378
Mandeville, Bernard de 189

Marquess of Queensberry xxxvi, lxviii
Martineau, James xl
Marvell, Andrew 286
Marzials, Frank Thomas 232
Masson, David 84, 113
Matheson, Percy Ewing 166
Mathews, Charles Elkin xxxii, 317, 319, 322
Maugham, Somerset 331
Maurice, Frederick Denison 5, 6, 81, 360
  Theological Essays 6
McKenna, Neil 261
McMaster, Kenneth Hovil 314, 315
McQueen, John Rainier xxvi, xxvii, lv–lvi, lxix, 54
Melvill, Henry Edward 214–15
Meredith, George xlviii, 199, 229
Mérimée, Prosper xxxiv, xlviii, lxvi, 82, 142, 259, 265, 266, 329
  WHP lectures on xxxiv, xlviii, lxvi, 82, 259, 265, 266, 329
Merton College, Oxford 73, 84, 126
Metropolitan Museum of Art, New York City 180, 233
Michelangelo di Lodovico Buonarroti 143
Michelet, Jules 10, 176
Middendorf, John H. 45
Mill, John Stuart xxvi, lvi, 4, 6, 10
  On Liberty xxvi, 6
Millais, John Everett xxv
Milton, John 113, 136, 137
Mind 208
Mirandola, Pico della xxviii, 66, 119, 424
Molesworth, Mary Cicely 273
Mommsen, Theodor 31
Monkhouse, Cosmo 246
Monsman, Gerald xi, xv, xvi, 31, 79, 258
Montaigne, Michel de 21, 29
Monthly Review 302
Moore, Albert 285
Moore, George xxxi, xxxv, lvi, 19, 21, 24, 26, 32, 43, 156, 196, 197, 209, 210
  Avowals 32, 196, 210
  Confessions of a Young Man xxxi, lvi, 24, 197, 209, 210
  WHP's reading of lvi, 197, 209
  Esther Waters xxxv, lvi
  Flowers of Passion lvi
  A Mere Accident 156, 196
  A Modern Lover lvi
  Modern Painting xxxv, lvi
  Pagan Poems lvi
Morelli, Giovanni 208
Morgan, Charles 66, 360

INDEX

Morison, Samuel Eliot 45
Morley, Henry 229
Morley, John, 1st Viscount Morley of
    Blackburn lvi–lvii, 20, 63, 79,
    92, 123, 129, 154, 156, 157
  reviews *Studies in the History of the
    Renaissance* lvii, 79
Moroni, Giovanni Battista 302
Morris and Co. xlix
Morris, William xxvii, xxxiv, xlix, lxiii,
    lxiv, 18, 66, 146, 195, 216, 285,
    312, 330, 331
  The Earthly Paradise xxvii
Mosher, Thomas B. xxxvi, 355
Moulton, Louise Chandler lvii, 19, 32,
    199, 237, 238, 239, 243, 254–5,
    260, 272, 273
  *In the Garden of Dreams: Lyrics and
    Sonnets* 255
  This, That, and the Other lvii
  reviews *Appreciations* 255
Moulton, William lvii
Müller, F. Max 107, 184, 300
Mulock, Dinah Maria xlii
  John Halifax, Gentleman xlii
Musi, Agostino de' 136
Myers, Frederic William 184
Myra's Journal lvii

Nation 97, 275, 325
National Club xxxv, xxxviii, 295, 310
Nattali, Benjamin 238, 242
Nehamas, Alexander 29
Net Book Agreement of 1890 liii
Nettleship, Henry 165, 166
Nettleship, Richard Lewis xlvii
Nevill, Lady Dorothy Walpole 274
Nevill, Reginald Henry 274
New (later the Savile) Club xxviii
New College, Oxford xliv, xlix, 79, 105,
    120, 167, 168, 201, 254, 312
Newdigate Prize xlvii, lii, lv, 109, 312
New Gallery 234
Newman, John Henry xxv, xlviii, lx, 17, 31,
    99, 199, 224, 256, 360
Newman, William Lambert lxvii
New Monthly Magazine 29
New Review xxxiv, 18, 20, 265, 276,
    295, 305
  WHP's contributions to xxxiv, 20, 265,
    276, 295
New Shakespere Society 81, 366
Newton, Sir Charles Thomas 108
New York Tribune lvii

Nichols, John Bowyer Buchanan 144, 146
Nicholson, Edward Williams Byron liv,
    142, 147, 168, 169
  Jim Lord: A Poem 142
Nicoll, Henry James 134
Niebuhr, B. G. 31
Nietzsche, Friedrich Wilhelm 29
Nightingale, Florence xlvii, li
Nineteenth Century xxxiii, xxxv, 20, 174,
    267, 319, 323
  WHP's contributions to xxxiii, xxxv,
    319, 323
Noel, Roden 75
  Beatrice, and Other Poems 75
  Essays upon Poets and Poetry 75
  A Little Child's Monument 75
  The Red Flag, and Other Poems 75
North, Catherine lxv
Norton, Charles Eliot 122, 208

Oates, J. C. T. 168
Obermayer, August 29
Odyssey, see Homer
Old Mortality Society xxvii, lxii, lxiv, lxv,
    58, 59, 79
Old Testament lxiii, 6
Opera Comique theatre 98
Oriel College, Oxford xxv, li, lx, lxii,
    58, 79
Orridge, Frances liii
Østermark-Johansen, Lene xv, 30, 108,
    228, 325
Ottley, Constance Mary lviii
Ottley, Mary Kay (May) xvii, lvii–lviii, lx,
    15, 100, 133, 230, 260, 373, 376
  Beauty of Figure lvii
  A Modern Boetia lvii
Ottley, Revd Robert L. lvii, 373
Oxford English Dictionary xxx, xl
Oxford Magazine xxx, xxxi, xl, lii, 20, 144
  WHP's contributions to xxx, xxxi,
    20, 144
Oxford Movement xlviii, 3
Oxford Proctorship xxviii
Oxford Undergraduate's Journal 102
Oxford Union Library 64
Oxford University Catholic Society xlix
Oxford University Gazette 265, 268
Oxford University Newman Society 99
Oxford University Press xvii, xl, 71, 81,
    108, 113

paganism xiii, lxiii, 11
Pageant 1

INDEX

Paget, Violet ('Vernon Lee') xxx, xxxii,
  xxxv, xlvii, li, lviii–lix, 15, 19, 20,
  24, 25, 26, 31, 32, 129, 135, 136,
  140–1, 145, 147–8, 149, 152–3,
  154, 156, 160, 181, 199, 272, 275,
  310, 364, 366
  WHP's influence on her fiction lix
  Baldwin: Being Dialogues on Views and Aspirations 147, 149
  Beauty and Ugliness and Other Studies in Psychological Aesthetics lviii
  Belcaro xxx, 135, 136
  Euphorion: Being Studies of the Antique and the Mediaeval in the Renaissance xxx, lix, 147, 148, 152, 153
  The Golden Keys and Other Essays on the Genius Loci lviii
  The Handling of Words and Other Studies in Literary Psychology lviii
  Juvenilia: Being a Second Series of Essays on Sundry Aesthetical Questions xxxii, lix, 142
  Limbo and Other Essays lviii
  Miss Brown: A Novel xxx, lviii, 160
  Music and its Lovers lviii
  Ottilie: An Eighteenth-Century Idyll 147
  Studies of the Eighteenth Century in Italy lviii
Palgrave, Francis Turner liii
Pall Mall Gazette xxxi, xxxii, xxxiii, xli,
  xlii, lvi, lix, lxii, 20, 31, 65, 91,
  92, 93, 182, 183–4, 228, 230, 299,
  306, 324, 378
  WHP's contributions to xxxi, xxxii,
    xxxiii, lix, lxii, 20, 31, 183, 184,
    228, 230
Pall Mall Magazine 196, 210, 331
Paris Commune (1871) 264
Parmenides 17
Pascal, Blaise 21, 329, 341, 342
Pater, Anne xxvi, 52
Pater, Ann Nash 192
Pater, Clara Ann xvii, xxv, xxvi, xxxi,
  xxxvi, xxxviii, xlv, xlvi, xlvii, liii,
  lvii, lix, lx, lxiii, lxvi, lxvii, lxix,
  2, 3, 11, 15, 19, 27, 31, 52, 55, 84,
  94, 100, 147, 148, 150, 192, 253,
  322, 330, 331, 332, 333, 334, 335,
  338–9, 339, 342, 343, 343–4,
  347–8, 350–1, 351, 354, 355, 356,
  356–7, 357, 358, 358–9, 359, 360,
  362, 363, 364–5, 365–6, 367, 368,
  368–9, 370, 373
Pater, Foster lix
Pater, Frederic Loudon 57, 192
Pater, Hester Elizabeth ('Aunt Bessie')
  xxvi, xxvii, 52, 55
Pater, Hester Maria xvii, xxv, xxvi, xxxi,
  xxxvi, xxxviii, xlv, xlvii, liii, lviii,
  lix–lx, lxiii, lxvii, lxix, 2, 11, 19,
  27, 31, 52, 129, 145, 150, 154,
  192, 200, 225, 264, 291, 296,
  322, 333, 334, 336–7, 337, 338,
  339, 340, 341–2, 342, 343,
  344–5, 345, 346, 347, 348, 349,
  349–50, 350, 351, 352, 353, 354,
  359, 360, 361, 362, 363, 364,
  366, 369–70, 370, 371, 372,
  372–3, 373, 374, 375, 375–6,
  376, 377, 378, 378–9, 379, 380,
  380–1, 382, 383, 383–4
Pater, John Thompson 52
Pater, Joseph 57, 192
Pater, Maria Hill 52
Pater, Richard Glode 192
Pater, Walter
  biographical references:
  attends the King's School, Canterbury
    (1853–8) xxv, xxvi, lv, lxix, 3, 49,
    50, 51, 52, 53, 132, 177, 276
  desires to take holy orders 54
  studies classics at Queen's College,
    Oxford (1858–62) xxvi, xxvii, xl,
    3, 4, 6, 9, 49, 50, 51, 52, 53, 59,
    176, 276, 327
  experiences religious doubt lv, 7
  Fellow of Brasenose College (1864) 152,
    177, 229
  Lecturer of Brasenose College
    (1867) 13, 61
  teaching xxix, xxxiv, xxxiv, 119, 284,
    285, 329, 331
  holidays in:
    Heidelberg, 1858–62 xxvi, lix, 7, 51, 52
    Italy, 1865 xxvii, lxii
    France, 1877 xxix, 98
    Rome, 1882–3 xxx, 15, 135, 139, 141,
      143, 145
    France, 1887 xxxii, 196, 197
    Italy, 1882 135, 139, 141, 147, 148
    Switzerland, 1888 xxxii, 218, 331
    Italy, 1890 263, 264
    Italy, 1891 xxxiv
    France, 1893 xxxv, 313
  receives honorary degree (1894) xxxv,
    324, 330
  University Extension teaching 284,
    285, 331
  projected works:
    trilogy of works of fiction 16, 177, 179

INDEX

second series of Imaginary
  Portraits 281, 295, 302
series on 'Some Great Churches in
  France' xxxv, 319, 320, 323
works:
  *An Imaginary Portrait: The Child in
    the House* xiii, xxxv, xlii, 15, 106,
    325, 328, 329
  *Appreciations: With an Essay on
    Style* xiii, xxiii, xxxiii, xliv, lx,
    lxiii, lxviii, 17, 81, 111, 140, 146,
    171, 192, 201, 222, 224, 235, 241,
    243, 244, 245, 246, 247, 248, 249,
    250, 253, 255, 256, 257, 258, 259,
    262, 263, 276, 293, 359, 366
    reviews of xxxiii, lxiii, lxviii, 17,
      244, 246, 247, 249, 250, 253, 255,
      256, 293
    'Aesthetic Poetry' (*see also* 'Poems
      by William Morris') xxxiii, 17,
      263, 342, 359
    'Charles Lamb' (originally 'The
      Character of the Humourist:
      Charles Lamb') xxix, 111, 201
    'Coleridge' 140
    'Coleridge's Writings' 140
    'Dante Gabriel Rossetti' 146
    'Love's Labour's Lost' 81, 366
    'Measure for Measure' (originally
      'A Fragment on *Measure for
      Measure*') xxviii, 14, 82, 111,
      134, 177
    'Postscript' (originally
      'Romanticism') 111
    'Shakespeare's English Kings' 224
    'Style' xliv, 222, 235
    'Wordsworth'
  Classical Studies
    'The Age of Athletic Prizemen'
      xxxv, 276, 297, 315, 316, 376
    'Art Notes in North Italy' xxxiv, 265
    'The Bacchanals of Euripides'
      xxxiii, 111, 288, 289, 333
    'The Beginnings of Greek
      Sculpture' xxx, 116, 177
    'The Marbles of Aegina'
      xxx, 116, 177
    'The Myth of Demeter and
      Persephone' xxix, 14, 92, 111, 134
    'A Study of Dionysus' xxix, lxiv,
      14, 92
  'Diaphaneitè' xxvii, xxxvi, lxii
  Essays from 'The Guardian' xiv, xxxvi,
    xlv, 345, 346, 349, 354, 355, 356,
    357, 367, 368

'Ferdinand Fabre' (review of Fabre's
  Norine) xxxiii
Gaston de Latour xiv, xxiii, xxxii,
  xxxvi, lx, lxiii, 5, 16, 31, 176, 178,
  244, 263, 281, 344, 349
  'A Clerk in Orders' 176
  'Gaudioso, the Second' 265
  'The Lower Pantheism' (originally
    'Giordano Bruno') 244
  'Our Lady's Church' 176
  'Shadow of Events' lx
Greek Studies xiv, xxxvi, lxiii, 14, 159,
  202, 216, 289, 297, 333, 334, 337,
  342, 344, 352, 353, 376
  reviews of 216, 342
Imaginary Portraits xiii, xxiii, xxix,
  xxxi, xxxiv, xxxvi, xliii, lviii, lxiii,
  lxviii, 15, 16, 17, 30, 106, 109,
  131, 140, 162, 171, 190, 193, 194,
  197, 201, 243, 257, 265, 274, 275,
  276, 281, 295, 325, 344, 349
  reviews of xliii, lxviii, 197, 201
  'Apollo in Picardy' xxxv, 295,
    302, 314
  'The Child in the House' xiii, xxix,
    xxxv, xlii, xlvi, xlvii, 8, 15, 16,
    106, 109, 110, 116, 140, 178, 261,
    294, 325, 328, 329
  'Emerald Uthwart' xxxiv, 276, 294,
    295, 302
  'An English Poet' xxxvi, 132
  'Hippolytus Veiled' xxxiii, 224,
    295, 302, 325, 333, 334
  'A Prince of Court Painters' xxxi,
    162, 292
'Introduction' (to Shadwell's
  Purgatory) xxxiv, 286, 287
Letters of Walter Pater, ed. Lawrence
  Evans xxiii, xxxvi, 2, 31, 32
Marius the Epicurean xiii, xxx, xxxi,
  xlvi, lxiii, lxvii, lxix, 5, 8, 15, 16,
  31, 89, 132, 140, 142, 146, 149,
  150, 151, 153, 154, 157, 161, 163,
  164, 165, 166, 167, 168, 169, 170,
  171, 172, 173, 174, 175, 177, 179,
  180, 181, 194, 195, 210, 221, 241,
  262, 263, 267, 275, 276, 279, 280,
  281, 283, 287, 290, 300, 342, 348,
  360, 362, 375, 377, 380, 381
  second edition xxxi, 89, 132, 158,
    170, 172, 173, 174, 177, 279
  third edition xxxiv, 132, 171,
    279, 287
  reviews of lxiii, lxvii, 140, 146, 164,
    166, 169, 175

Pater, Walter (*Cont.*)
   Miscellaneous Studies xiv, xxxvi, lxiii, 295, 342, 344
   'Notre-Dame d'Amiens' xxxv, 319
   'A Novel by Mr. Oscar Wilde' (review of *The Picture of Dorian Gray*) xxxiv, lxviii
   'Pascal' xxxvi, xlv, 329, 341, 342
   Plato and Platonism xii, xiii, xxiii, xxxiv, xxxv, 1, 17, 28, 29, 125, 268, 278, 280, 281, 290, 295, 296, 302, 304, 305, 327
     reviews of 125, 304, 305, 327
     'The Doctrine of Plato' 295, 298
     'The Genius of Plato' xxxiv, 133, 278, 280, 281
     'Lacedaemon' xxxiv, 290, 291
     'Plato and the Doctrine of Motion' (originally 'A Chapter on Plato') xxxiv, 280
     'Plato and the Doctrine of Music' 280
     'Plato and the Doctrine of Rest' 280
   'Poems by William Morris' (see also *Appreciations*, 'Aesthetic Poetry') xii, xxviii, 10, 11, 30, 62, 66, 140, 359
   'Prosper Mérimée' xxxiv, xlviii, lxvi, 259, 265, 266, 329
   'Raphael' xxxiv, lxvi, 26, 285
   The Renaissance (first edn *Studies in the History of the Renaissance*) xi, xii, xiii, xiv, xxviii, xxxiv, xxix, xxxii, 5, 10, 11, 12, 13, 14, 15, 21, 28, 29, 30, 32, 60, 63, 65, 66, 68, 69, 79, 85, 95, 96, 103, 111, 113, 118, 119, 177, 202, 203, 204, 285
     second edition xi, xxix, 14, 85, 89, 93, 111, 112, 134
     third edition xxxii, xliii, 17, 66, 68, 73, 169, 171, 202
     fourth edition xxxv
     reviews of xli–ii, lvii, lxv, 13, 79
     'Conclusion' xi, xii, xxix, xxxii, 13, 14, 15, 28, 30, 32, 66, 79, 85, 202, 204
     'Joachim du Bellay' 65, 66, 203
     'Luca della Robbia' 12, 15, 65, 66
     'Leonardo da Vinci' xxviii, xxxiv, 15, 21, 66, 203, 285
     'Pico della Mirandola' xxviii, 66, 119
     'The Poetry of Michelangelo' xxviii, 63, 66
     'Preface' xii, 5, 13, 65, 66, 68, 69, 95, 204
     'Sandro Botticelli' xxviii, 66
     'The School of Giorgione' xiv, xxix, 14, 66, 68, 96, 111, 113, 177, 203, 204
     'Two Early French Stories' (originally 'Aucassin and Nicolette') 85
     'Winckelmann' xi, xiii, xxvii, 10, 11, 12, 15, 28, 29, 30, 60, 65, 103, 118
   Review of Colvin's *Children in Italian and English Design* xxviii, xli
   Review of Fabre's *Toussaint Galabru* xxxiii, 273
   Review of Lemaître's *Sérénus* xxxii, 274
   Review of *Love in Idleness* xxx, 144, 145, 146
   Review of Symonds's *Age of the Despots* xxviii, 385
   Review of Symons's *Days and Nights* xxxiii, lxv, 230
   'Robert Elsmere' (review of Ward's *Robert Elsmere*) xxxii, lxvii, 29, 169, 176, 209, 214
   Sketches and Reviews xxxvi, 355
   Studies in the History of the Renaissance, see *The Renaissance*
   Uncollected Essays xxxvi, 334, 355
   The Works of Walter Pater, Edition de Luxe xxxvi, 349, 350, 352, 353, 354, 355
   unpublished manuscripts
     'The Aesthetic Life' 226, 228, 247
     'Arezzo' 66
     ['Rubens'] 329, 330, 331
     'Thistle' 178
     'Tibalt the Albigense' 275
     'Vézelay' xxxv, 319, 323
Pater, William Grange 52
Pater, William Thompson 52, 57, 192
Patmore, Coventry xlv, 261–2
   The Angel in the House 262
   Principles in Art 262
   WHP's reading of 261
   Religio Poetae 262
Paton, William Roger 124
Patrick, Arthur W. 32, 253

Pattison, E. F. S., *see* Dilke, Lady
Pattison, Mark xxx, xxxviii, xl, xliii, lv,
    lx–lxi, lxvi, 4, 19, 21, 28, 36, 87,
    107, 136, 137, 150, 166, 278
  contributes to *Essays and Reviews* xliii, lxi
  Memoirs lxi, 166
Paul, C. Kegan 128, 224
Pausanias 116
Payne, John Burnell lxix
Pembroke College, Cambridge 230, 278
Pembroke College, Oxford lviii
Pendergast, John xxi, 34, 51, 52, 54, 55, 57, 59
Penny Illustrated Paper 293
Percival, Francis William 246
Percival, Revd John 120
Persius 123
Peto, Harold Ainsworth 185–6, 190
Photographic Society of London 271
Pignatel, Jeanne Barbe Emma liii
Pillian, Henry 270
Pilot 245
Plato xii, xiii, l, li, 7, 17, 18, 125, 145, 208,
    212, 268, 280, 281, 297, 298, 301,
    304, 305, 326, 327
  Phaedrus lv
  Republic lii, lv, 5, 329
  see also Pater, works, *Plato and Platonism*
Poe, Edgar Allan 232
Pope Leo XIII 99
Powell, Frederick York xxxv, 316
Poynter, Edward 98
Pre-Raphaelites xxv, 12
  see also Brown, Ford Madox; Burne-
    Jones, Edward; Hunt, William
    Holman; Morris, William;
    Rossetti, Christina; Rossetti,
    Dante Gabriel; Rossetti, William
    Michael; Solomon, Simeon;
    Swinburne, A. C.
Prettejohn, Elizabeth 30
Price, Bonamy 245
Pritchard, H. Baden 202
Publishers' Association liii
Pullar, Philippa 226
Punch 98
Pusey, Revd Edward Bouverie xlviii, li, lii
Pythagoras 17

Quarterly Review 182, 184
Queen's College, Oxford xxvi, xxvii, xl, 3,
    4, 6, 9, 49, 50, 51, 52, 53, 59, 107,
    108, 120, 176, 249, 276, 327
Quinet, Edgar 10, 176

Rabbe, Félix 203
Raffalovich, Madame Marie 155, 181
Raffalovich, Marc André xxxiii, lxi–lxii,
    19, 24, 25, 151, 154–5, 159, 181,
    186, 261
  It is Thyself xxxiii
  Uranism and Unisexuality lxii
  A Willing Exile lxi
Raimondi, Marcantonio 136
Ralston, R. S. 182
Randall, Ethel Claire 365, 366
Raphael (Raffaello Santi) lxvi, 26,
    136, 285
Ray, Martin 221
Read, Herbert 27
Reichel, Revd Oswald J. 59
Renan, Ernest xxxviii, 133, 181
Reveue de Paris, La xxvi, 129
Rhodes Foundation 97
Rhymers' Club l, lxvi
  The Book of the Rhymers' Club 300
  The Second Book of the Rhymers' Club 300
Rhys, Ernest 198
Richards, Bernard xv, 119
Richardson, George 346
Ricketts, Charles xliv
Ritchie, Anne Thackeray lxii, 83, 188, 189
Ritchie, David George 166
River Cherwell 63
River Thames 268
Robertson, Eric Sutherland 203, 218
Robertson, Walford Graham 285, 310
  Pinkie and the Fairies 285
  Time Was 285, 310
Robinson, Alfred 105
Robinson, Agnes Mary Francis (also Mary
    Darmesteter, Mary Duclaux) lvi,
    lvii, lix, 19, 126, 128, 129
  A Handful of Honeysuckle 129
Robinson, Frances Mabel lix, 128
Robinson, George T. 128
Rolleston, George 269
Rolleston, Humphry Davy 269, 386
Ronsard, Pierre de 73
Rossetti, Christina xxvii, liii, 122, 199
Rossetti, Dante Gabriel xxv, xxviii, xxx,
    xxxvii, lxiii, lxiv, lxvii, 12, 18, 24,
    65, 88, 121, 122, 139, 140 143,
    146, 156, 178, 205, 206, 216, 225,
    234, 256, 266, 267
Rossetti, Maria Francesca 122
Rossetti, William Michael xxv, 122, 229
Rothenstein, William v, xxi, xxxv, xxxvi,
    315, 316, 318, 321, 322, 324

Rothenstein, William (*Cont.*)
  Contemporaries 316
  Men and Memories 318, 321
  drawing of WHP: *Oxford Characters* v, xxi, xxxv, xxxvi, 322
Rousseau, Jean-Jacques lvii
Routledge, George 109, 336
Rowley, Charles 88
  Fifty Years of Ancoats 88
  Fifty Years of Work without Wages 88
Royal Academy xxviii, lxiv, 22, 94, 97, 384
Royal Academy of Music 132
Royal Academy Schools lxiii
Royal College of Art 285, 316
Royal Geographical Society xlv
Royal Historical Society xlv
Royal Institute of British Architects 174, 186
Royal Manchester (now Royal Northern) College of Music 179
Rubens, Peter Paul 329, 330, 331
Rugby School 120
Ruskin, John xxviii, xxix, xxxi, xli, xlix, lii, lxviii, 5, 11, 12, 23, 64, 65, 68, 88, 108, 115, 134, 140, 162, 195, 285
  Modern Painters 12, 134
Ruskin School of Drawing 195, 201
Russell, Bertrand 208
Russell, Lord Arthur Edward John xxxiii, 290

Sadler, Michael Ernest 168, 284, 285, 329
St Hugh of Avalon 296, 297, 313
Sainte-Beauve, Charles Augustin 15, 273
Saintsbury, George Edward Bateman xxx, 84
  Specimens of English Prose Style from Malory to Macaulay xxx, 84
  A History of Criticism and Literary Taste 84
  A Short History of English Literature 84
  A Short History of French Literature 84
Salisbury Cathedral 126
Sappho xliii, 234, 236
Sargent, John Singer xxxviii, 156, 180, 285
Sarrazin, Gabriel lvii, 225
Saturday Review xlv, xlviii, xlix, lii, lvi, 93, 165, 286
Savonarola, Girolamo 118
Savoy 1, 316
Savoy Theatre 98
Sayle, Charles Edward 167, 168
  Bertha: A Story of Love 167
  Early English Printed Books in the University Library, Cambridge, 1475–1640 168
  Wiclif: An Historical Drama 168

Sayce, Revd Archibald Henry liv, 107, 270
Schiller, Friedrich von 7, 10
Schnaase, Karl Julius Ferdinand 94
Schölermann, Wilhelm 164
Schreiner, Olive lvii
Scott, David 131, 132
  WHP reads Gray's article on 131–2
Scott, George Gilbert 105, 133
Scott, William Bell xlv, xlvi, lxiii, 24, 64–5, 87, 132, 136, 137, 197–8
  Autobiographical Notes 65
Scottish National Portrait Gallery xlvi, 167, 169
Scotto, Robert M. 31
Scribner's Magazine xxxiii, 224, 230, 231
  WHP's contribution to xxxiii, 224, 230, 231
Sedding, John Dando 311, 312
Seiler, Robert M.
  The Book Beautiful: Walter Pater and the House of Macmillan xxiii, 2, 21, 30
  Walter Pater: A Life Remembered 2, 31, 32, 49, 308, 361
  Walter Pater: The Critical Heritage 30
Shadwell, Charles Lancelot xiv, xxvii, xxxvi, l, lx, lxii–lxiii, 16, 19, 58, 224, 286, 287, 289, 297, 299, 325, 333, 339, 341, 342, 355, 356, 358, 359, 361, 365, 366, 376
  Registrum Orielense, 1500–1900 lxii
  trans. *The Purgatory of Dante Alighieri* lxiii, 287
Shakespeare, William xlviii, 13, 17, 81, 82, 210
  Hamlet 210
  Henry VIII 220, 252
  Love's Labour's Lost 14, 81, 82, 111, 366
  Macbeth 220, 224
  Measure for Measure xxviii, 14, 82, 111, 134, 177
  Twelfth Night xxxvii, 155
Sharp, Elizabeth Amelia xxxi, lxiii, 113, 138, 140, 163, 164, 178, 193, 229
Sharp, William (pseud. 'Fiona Macleod') xxx, xxxi, lvii, lxiii, 1, 19, 20, 24, 25, 26, 30, 32, 113, 129, 132, 138, 139, 140, 151–2, 154, 163–4, 178, 193, 203, 216, 218, 229, 232, 245–6, 247
  Dante Gabriel Rossetti: A Record and a Study xxx, lxiii, 24, 140, 143
  WHP's reading of 143

INDEX

Earth's Voices: Transcripts from Nature, Sospitra, and Other Poems lxiii, 151, 152
The Human Inheritance, The New Hope, Motherhood lxiii
   WHP's reading of lxiii
Life of Percy Bysshe Shelley 203
   WHP's reading of 203
memorial article on WHP 30, 32, 129, 138
Pagan Review lxiii
Romantic Ballads and Poems of Phantasy xxxii, 216
Sonnets of this Century xxxi, 178
   reviews *Marius* lxiii, 140, 164
   reviews *Appreciations* lxiii, 245, 246, 247
   reviews *Greek Studies* 216
Shaw, George Bernard xlviii, 171, 299, 384
Shaw, Victor 28
Shelley Memorial 23
Shelley, Percy Bysshe lxiii, 23, 203, 225, 308, 383
Shelley Society 81
Sherard, Robert Harborough 102
Sheridan, Richard Brinsley 155
   The Rivals 155
Shields, Frederic 88
Shorter, Clement King 244, 293
Shorthouse, Joseph Henry 170
   John Inglesant: A Romance 170
Shuter, William F. xv, 28, 31, 208
Sidgwick, Henry xxxvii
Sidgwick, Mary xxxvii
Sidmouth, Devon lix, 59
Sieveking, Albert Forbes 173
   Gardens Ancient and Modern 173
   In Praise of Gardens 173
   The Sentiment of the Sword 173
Slade Professorship xxviii, xxx, xli, 5, 23, 201, 285
Small, Ian xv, 30, 31, 32, 45
Smart, Christopher 189
Smith, Alys Pearsall 208
Smith, Henry John xxviii, xlvi, 83
Smith, Logan Pearsall 208
Smith, Sarah 224
Society for the Protection of Ancient Buildings 195
Society of Authors 331
Society of Gentlemen Educated at Canterbury School 49, 50
Socrates lv, 29
Solomon, Simeon xxviii, xli, lxiii–lxiv, lxv, 2, 19, 65, 222, 239, 271
   Bacchus lxiv

The Bride, The Bridegroom, and Friend of the Bridegroom lxiv
Chanting the Gospel lxiv
Isaac Offered lxiv
Love in Autumn lxiv
Somerset House, London 293
Somerville College, Oxford xlvii, lvii, lix, lxvi, 3, 120, 339
Sotheby, Charlotte Cornish xl
South Kensington School of Art xliii, 285 n.1
Speaker l, 251, 256
Spectator l, lii, 18, 162
Spencer, Herbert xl, lvi
Spirit Lamp 307
Squire, William Barclay 220, 221
Stacey, John 71
Standard 123, 162, 331
Stanley, Arthur Penrhyn l, 5
St Aloysius's Church, Oxford xxix, 99, 120
St Bartholomew's Hospital, London 269
St Edmund Hall, Oxford lii
St Anne's College, Oxford xlvii
St George's Hospital, London 269
St Giles's Workhouse lxiv
St James's Gazette xlv
St Mary's Church, Oxford 324
St Paul's School, London liv
Star 18, 244, 293, 300, 304
Stead, William Thomas lxix, 378
Stendhal (Marie-Henri Beyle) 150
Stephen, James Fitzjames 82
Stephen, Leslie lvi, lxii, 82, 83, 199, 313
Stephen, Virginia (Virginia Woolf) lix, lxii
Stevens, Michael E. 45
Stevenson, Robert Louis xxxi, xlv, 293
Stillman, Marie Spartali 98, 233, 234
Stoddard, John Lawson 375
Stoddard's Library 374, 375
Stoicism 31
Stone, Donald D. 29
Stonehill, C. A. and H. W. 289
Stonyhurst College, Lancashire xlix
Straus, David Friedrich xl
   The Life of Jesus, Critically Examined xl
Surtees, Virginia 97
Sussman, Herbert 29
Sutcliffe, Peter 113
Swift, Jonathan 278
Swinburne, Algernon Charles xii, xxvii, xlv, lvi, lvii, lxiii, lxiv–lxv, 2, 9, 18, 19, 24, 65, 74, 75, 182, 225
   Atalanta in Calydon lxiv
   Poems and Ballads xxvii, lxiv, 74

Swinburne, Algernon Charles (*Cont.*)
  William Blake: A Critical Essay lxv, 74–5
  Songs before Sunrise lxv
Symonds, John Addington xxxv, xxviii,
    xlvi, lxv, 9, 18, 75, 126, 129, 162,
    199, 208, 221
  Animi Figura lxv
  A Problem in Greek Ethics lxv
  A Problem in Modern Ethics lxv
  The Renaissance in Italy lxv, xxviii
  Studies of the Greek Poets lxv
Symons, Arthur William xxxii, xxxiii, l, lxi,
    lxv–lxvi, 1, 19, 24, 25, 26, 32, 185,
    191, 196–7, 205–6, 213, 214,
    217–18, 220, 221, 222, 223, 224,
    227, 230–1, 232, 234, 235, 236, 240,
    243, 244, 245, 249, 252, 275, 345
  Days and Nights xxxiii, lxv, 24, 205–6,
    217, 218, 223, 227, 230, 231, 232
    WHP reads proofs 206, 220, 222, 254,
      264, 269, 271, 272, 275, 302, 316,
      318, 325, 328, 345, 353, 355, 384
  'The Decadent Movement in
    Literature' lxvi
  An Introduction to the Study of Browning
    xxxii, lxv, 185, 252
  Philip Massinger 191
  A Study of Walter Pater lxvi, 185, 269, 275
  *The Symbolist Movement in
    Literature* lxvi
  reviews *Imaginary Portraits* 197

Tacitus, Publius Cornelius 189
Taine, Hippolyte xxxviii, lxi, 199
Tait, Revd Archibald Campbell lv, 54
Talfourd, Thomas Noon 201
Tanselle, G. Thomas 45
Tate Gallery lii
Taylor, Harriet 6
Taylor Institution, Oxford xxxiv, 108, 176,
    259, 265, 329
Taylor, Jeremy 260
Taylor, Tom 97
Teachers' Training Syndicate, Cambridge 124
Tebbel, John A. 262
Tennyson, Lord Alfred xxxv, xlii, liii, lxii,
    132, 133, 182, 199, 225, 295, 299,
    300, 312, 313, 349, 350, 383
Terry, Ellen 155, 285
Thackeray, William Makepeace xxvii, lxii
Theocritus 73
Thucydides li
Thursfield, James Richard 18, 125, 304
Time 164, 165, 196, 197

Times, The xlv, lxvi, lxvii, 18, 22, 32, 65,
    97, 115, 125, 182, 189, 295, 304,
    308, 316, 325, 378, 384
Titchener, Edward Bradford 207–8, 212
  Experimental Psychology 208
Toynbee Hall, London xxxiv, 266
Tree, Herbert Beerbohm 285
Trevelyan, Lady Pauline 64
Trevelyan, Sir Walter 64
Trinity College, Cambridge xli, xlv, 75,
    131, 182, 299
Trinity College, Dublin liv, lxviii, 288
Trinity College, Oxford xxvii, 54, 99, 120,
    142, 249, 278, 285, 327
Trower, Helen 179
Turgenev, Ivan xxxviii
typesetting xlii, 62, 66, 68, 70, 111, 114, 115,
    117, 170, 171, 191, 227, 283, 325,
    349, 350, 354, 368, 375, 376, 381
Tyrrell, Robert Yelverton 288
  edits *The Bacchae of Euripides* 288,
    289, 292

Universal Exhibition, Paris, 1867 88
Universities Tests Act, 1871 xxviii,
    28, 78
University Extension, Oxford 120, 284,
    285, 329, 331
University of Cambridge Act, 1856 4
University College, Dublin xlix
University College, London 174, 229,
University College, Oxford 23, 105, 215,
    285, 308
University of Oxford Act, 1854 4
University of Oxford Press (OUP) xvii,
    xxiii, xl, 71, 81, 108, 113
University of St Andrews 327
University Museum, Oxford 28, 83
Urquhart, Francis Fortescue 276, 277, 291

Vassall, Oliver Rodie 99
Verlaine, Paul xxxv, lxvi, 264, 315, 316
  WHP unable to attend lecture 315
Verschoyle, Revd John Stuart 226, 228,
    240, 247
Victoria, Queen xxxvii, 75, 173
Vigers, George xlix
Virgil (Publius Maro) 146
Voltaire (François-Marie Arouet) lvii
Von Herkomer, Hubert 23

Waddington, Samuel 246
  A Century of Sonnets 246
Wadham College, Oxford 133

INDEX

Walker, Pierre G. 45
Ward, Mary Arnold xxx, xxxii, xxxiv, lii,
    lviii, lxi, lxvi–lxvii, 11, 19, 22, 28,
    31, 63, 103, 125, 160–1, 162,
    168–9, 170, 172, 176, 209, 278,
    283, 331
  Miss Bretherton xxx, lxvi, 161
    WHP's reading of 161
  contributions to *A Dictionary of Christian
    Biography* lxvi
  The History of David Grieve xxxiv,
    lxvi–lxvii, 283
    WHP's reading of 283
  Marcella lxvii
  Robert Elsmere xxxii, lxvi, 29, 209
    WHP's reading of xxxii, lxvii, 29, 209
  translation of *Amiel's Journal* xxx, 176
    WHP's reading of 176
  A Writer's Recollections lxvii
  reviews *Marius* lxvii, 169
Ward, Thomas Humphry xlvi, lviii, lxi,
    lxvii, 11, 21, 31, 63, 107, 125,
    126, 137, 140, 146, 147, 162, 384
  edits *The English Poets* lxvii
  edits *Selections from the English
    Poets* lxvii, 140, 146
Ward, William Reginald 28
Ward, William Welsford 97, 109
Warne, Frederick 336
Warne and Co. 336
Warren, Thomas Herbert 32, 329, 338–9
Warrin, Georgina Elizabeth liii, 367
Watkins, Philip Morgan 32, 324–5
  Rules for Latin Prose 325
Watson, John William 249
  reviews *Appreciations* 249
Watteau, Jean-Antoine 162, 292
Watts, George Frederic 98, 233, 266–7, 271
Watts-Dunton, Theodore lxiii
Waugh, Arthur 312
Wedmore, Frederick xxix, xlvi, 162, 168,
    266, 317
  The Four Masters of Etching 162
  Pastorals of France xxix, 162, 317
  Turner and Ruskin 162
  Whistler's Etching 162
Week-End Review 31
Weimar 8
Welby-Gregory, Emmeline Mary
    Elizabeth 299
Wells, Herbert George 299
Westminster Review xxvii, xxviii, xl, xli,
    xliii, 10, 12, 20, 24, 60, 62, 65, 73,
    78, 134, 140, 276, 359

WHP's contribution to xxvii, xxviii, 10,
    12, 60, 62, 65, 73, 78, 134, 140,
    176, 359
Wharton, Edith li
Whistler, James Abbott McNeill xxix, xxx,
    lvii, lxvii–lxvii, 2, 18, 98, 110,
    115, 162, 285
  *Arrangement in Grey and Black, No. 1:
    Portrait of the Artist's
    Mother* lxvii
  The Gentle Art of Making Enemies lxviii
  *Nocturne in Black and Gold: The Falling
    Rocket* xxix, lxvii–lxviii
  *Symphony in White, No. 1: The White
    Girl* lxvii
  Ten O'Clock Lecture xxx
Whitla, William 28
Whitman, Walt 44, 225
Wightwick, Thomas Norman 50, 51, 53
Wilde, Oscar xvii, xxix, xxxv, xxxvi, xxxvii,
    xxxviii, l, liii, lvii, lx, lxi, lxviii, 2,
    18, 19, 22, 24, 25, 26, 30, 31, 33,
    97, 98, 100, 101, 102, 103, 104,
    107, 108, 109, 156, 183, 201, 208,
    215, 251, 256, 261, 265, 274, 278,
    285, 300, 307, 322, 325
  Ballad of Reading Gaol lxviii
  De Profundis lxviii
  The Happy Prince and Other Tales
    xxxii, 215
    WHP's reading of 215
  The Importance of Being Earnest lxviii
  Lady Windemere's Fan lxviii
  The Picture of Dorian Gray xxxiii, xxxiv,
    lxviii, 256
  'Ravenna' 109
  reviews *Appreciations* lxviii, 256
  reviews *Imaginary Portraits* lxviii
Wilkinson, Jonas Niel Lyte 259, 265
Wilkinson, William 63
Williams, Carolyn xv, 31
Willis, Irene Cooper xxiii, 32
Wilson, Henry 312
Winckelmann, Johann Joachim xi, xiii, 8,
    10, 11, 12, 15, 21, 65
Winkworth, Susanna 86
Withers, William Stanley 178–9
Wollheim, Richard 29
Wolvercote, Oxford 70
Women's Anti-Suffrage Association lxvii
Woodruff, C. E. 49
Woods, Margaret Louisa 277–8
  Esther Vanhomrigh 277
    WHP's reading of 277–8

Woods, Margaret Louisa (*Cont.*)
  A Village Tragedy 278
  Wilde Justice 278
Woods, Revd Henry George 278
Woodward, Mrs 347–8
Worcester College, Oxford xvi, xxxv, xlii, 129, 321, 325, 328
Wordsworth, Revd John 13, 23, 79
  Fragments and Specimens of Early Latin 79
  The Gospel according to St. Matthew, from the St. Germain MS. 79
Wordsworth, William xxxiv, xlii, 13, 14, 18, 66, 79, 111, 133, 134, 177, 225, 257, 266
Working Men's College, London 81
Wortham, Hugh Evelyn 82, 83
Wright, Samuel xv, 133, 221, 325

Wright, Thomas (biographer of WHP) xxiii, xxxviii, xlv, lv, lvi, lx, lxiii, lxix, 2, 18, 27, 28, 29, 30, 32, 49, 52, 126, 308, 355, 358–9, 361, 362, 363, 364–5
  The Life of Walter Pater xxiii, lxix, 27, 49, 359
  Thomas Wright of Olney: An Autobiography 362

Yeats, William Butler l, lxvi, 260
Yellow Book xxxv, 300, 316, 318, 319, 322
  proposed WHP contribution to 318
Yogananda, Paramahansa xxxvii

Zacharias, Greg W. 45
Zola, Émile lvi, 264